Defining
the
Horrific

Defining the Horrific

READINGS ON GENOCIDE AND HOLOCAUST IN THE TWENTIETH CENTURY

William L. Hewitt

West Chester University

PEARSON

Prentice Hall

Upper Saddle River, New Jersey 07458

Library of Congress Cataloging-in-Publication Data

Defining the horrific: readings on genocide and Holocaust in the 20th century/[edited by]
    William Hewitt.
        p. cm.
    Includes bibliographical references.
    ISBN 0-13-110084-X
    1. Genocide–History–20th century.   2. Holocaust, Jewish (1939-1945)
    3. Crimes against humanity–History–20th century.   4. World politics–20th century.
    5. Totalitarianism–History–20th century. I. Hewitt, William

    HV6322.7.D43 2004
    364.15'1'0904—dc21

                                                    2003052829

Editorial Director: Charlyce Jones Owen
Senior Acquisitions Editor: Charles Cavaliere
Associate Editor: Emsal Hasan
Executive Marketing Manager: Heather Shelstad
Production Liaison: Louise Rothman
Manufacturing Manager: Nick Sklitsis
Manufacturing Buyer: Tricia Kenny
Cover Design: Bruce Kenselaar
Production Supervision and Composition: Preparé Inc.
Printer/Binder: RR Donnelley – Harrisonburg
Cover Printer: Phoenix Color Corp.

Credits and acknowledgments borrowed from other sources and reproduced in this textbook with permission appear on appropriate page within text.

Pearson Prentice Hall™ is a trademark of Pearson Education, Inc.
Pearson® is a registered trademark of Pearson plc
Prentice Hall® is a registered trademark of Pearson Education, Inc.

Pearson Education LTD.
Pearson Education Singapore, Pte. Ltd
Pearson Education, Canada, Ltd
Pearson Education–Japan
Pearson Education Australia PTY, Limited
Pearson Education North Asia Ltd
Pearson Educación de Mexico, S.A. de C.V.
Pearson Education Malaysia, Pte. Ltd

10 9 8 7 6 5 4 3 2 1
ISBN 0-13-110084-X

Contents

Preface

Horrific Crimes

Genocide is the most horrific crime inflicted on one group of people by another. Destroying or conspiring to destroy a classification of people because of their national, ethnic, or religious identity constitutes the crime of genocide. Yet since the Polish legal scholar Raphael Lemkin coined the word to describe Nazi Germany's attempted annihilation of the Jewish people and the Romani, the definition and application of the word proved problematic.

Part of the problem lies in the broadness of Lemkin's definition, and the consequent all-too-frequent application of the term. The Introduction to this study provides more than one definition of the term, and parses their meanings.

The first chapter looks at America's history with Native Americans and debates the use of terms such as *Holocaust* and *genocide* in characterizing that history. Chapter Two looks at early twentieth century imperialism and the attempt to eliminate the Hereros and other African peoples. The Armenian genocide, presented in Chapter Three, arguably often called the first genocide of the twentieth century, also remained for various reasons relatively obscure until recently. The Ukrainian man-made famine ranks as genocide counted in the millions. Possibly the most familiar genocidal event of the twentieth century is the Holocaust, discussed in Chapter Five. In 1997, Iris Chang focused attention on the Japanese during the 1930s in her book, *The Rape of Nanking: The Forgotten Holocaust of World War II*, the subject of Chapter Six. In the next chapter, the editor offers a controversial and provocative examination of the American conduct of World War II.

Social scientists chronicle at least sixteen genocides perpetrated or attempted by nations after Raphael Lemkin coined the term at the end of World War II. In an eerie parallel to the Soviet Ukrainian famine, the Chinese communists under Mao Tse-tung engineered a famine that claimed thirty million people. Chapter Nine selectively looks at Rwanda, Sudan, and Angola, but one could also include Biafra, Chad, Ethiopia, and many others. Similarly in Latin America, Argentina and Guatemala could be augmented by Paraguay, Brazil, and others.

Some analysts of genocide put Cambodia in a special category all its own, since the slaughter killed a larger proportion of the population—approximately one half—than any other mass murder. Chapter Twelve, Indonesia and Bangladesh, and the following chapter on Bosnia, offer additional case studies of counties ripped apart by genocide.

The chapter on the Middle East will undoubtedly anger some readers. America's bifurcated relations with the parties involved, added to the high voltage of religion and politics, produces intensely emotional reactions to allegations and perpetration of genocide. Less controversial, but also politically charged by George W. Bush's characterization of an "Axis of Evil," including Iran and Iraq, is North Korea, another example of man-made famine claiming millions of victims.

The Conclusion asks the reader to reconsider the application of the term genocide, and consider ways to study and prevent it. One thing that is clear after surveying these events is that most Americans only vaguely, if at all, understand the horrific carnage that characterized the history of the twentieth century.

An American sense of mission, superiority, and moral certitude, what Robert N. Bellah termed collectively as *Habits of the Heart*, grounded in the past and ourselves, resists change. A few critics—including Ward Churchill and Edward Said, among others—offer alternative viewpoints. Like a visiting team trying to shout instructions in a stadium filled with fans for the other team, their voices are not heard.

Limited by space, this book is an attempt to shout signals to Americans, over the din in the arena; to see the twentieth-century world differently. At the same time, there is a limit to the human appetite for human misery—deportation, torture, and murder. Reading a conventional history of the twentieth century, at the same time, will help the reader keep a perspective for these accounts of horror. The disquieting realization is that the horrific intrudes into the other narrative all too frequently, or the author obfuscates or minimizes these events, for one motive or another.

The concept for this book arose from a need for a comprehensive, chronological arrangement of provocative materials for discussion and writing prompts in teaching a course on genocide. My students' interests and discussions steered me to consider a wide range of twentieth-century events in an inquisitive atmosphere of open inquiry. I would like to express my thanks to the following people for their help in preparing this volume: Roger W. Arthur; Jonathan Cohen; Kimberly Fleischer; Mark T. Flores; C. Patrick Mundy; Asaf Romirowsky; Meri Sellers; Steven J. Silva; Wesley Spahr; Kathleen Stank; Jennifer Stewart; and Lotta Stone. Many of these students are pursuing graduate degrees related to Holocaust/genocide studies.

Rodney Vosburgh collaborated on the early research phase of collecting material. The chairperson of my department, Richard Webster, encouraged me at various stages in the preparation of the manuscript, and the assistant chair of the department, Thomas Heston, "kept out of the way," as he put it.

My thanks to the reviewers of this book for their helpful comments: Charles Cross, Edinboro University of Pennsylvania; William Cooney, Briarcliff College; and Severin Hochberg, United States Holocaust Museum.

I would also like to thank the staff at Prentice Hall for their patient assistance, and especially Editor Charles Cavaliere for keeping me on track and giving me valuable assistance. I dedicate this volume to my friend and mentor, Roger L. Williams, who will be appalled at the arguments in some of these readings.

About the Author

William Hewitt, professor of history at West Chester University in West Chester, Pennsylvania, received his Ph.D. from the University of Wyoming in 1984. Professor Hewitt helped conceive and institutionalize West Chester University's new graduate Holocaust/Genocide Studies program. He has taught courses on genocide for several years. His research specialties include genocide, Native American history, the American West, race, and sexuality. He has published numerous journal articles, written four documentary videos under the direction of Gary Nash, and most recently a historical novel for young adults.

List of Maps

Defining
the
Horrific

Introduction

DEFINING THE HORRIFIC

In a tragic irony, the twentieth century witnessed great advances in science, technology, mass media, and government organization, generally celebrated as "progress," while at the same time, that century's ledger is crowded with gruesome statistics of genocide. Beginning with the 10 million Africans killed in King Leopold's Congo, the death numbers often required decimals of millions to be recorded. The Turkish massacre of the Armenians claimed 1.5 million; Stalin's purges and famine killed an estimated 20 million people—and the millions kept accumulating with each new twentieth-century atrocity.

The "Rape of Nanking" and World War II atrocities necessitated a new lexicon of terror and death. New terms for mass murder included "the Holocaust," "genocide," "the Killing Fields" and "autogenocide," "the Dirty War, and "disappeared," among other descriptors universally applied to specific events and mass murder. The new terminology, however, failed to foster better understanding of these events. While the legacy of the Nuremberg and Tokyo trials and other tribunals and truth commissions attempted to bring the perpetrators to account, the side of the ledger sheet totting up moral accounting failed miserably to match the crimes.

Diane F. Orentlicher offers a starting point for defining "Genocide" in the first reading in this Introduction. Next, Scott Straus takes on the task of working through the changing nuances of defining genocide in "Contested Meanings and Conflicting Imperatives: A Conceptual Analysis of Genocide." Some instances of mass death need another designation, according to political scientist R. J. Rummel in "When and Why to Use the Term Democide for 'Genocide.'" Finally, Deborah Harris in "Defining Genocide: Defining History?" provides a starting point for debating the application of terms and definitions to specific examples of genocide.

As readers encounter and analyze each piece included here, they should question where they stand in relation to the collective and comparative history of the *worst that human beings can do.* Is it possible to fully understand genocide? Can genocide be prevented? What should be done with the perpetrators of genocide? How should these events be studied and remembered?

Genocide

Diane F. Orentlicher

Invoked with a frequency, familiarity, and reverence rarely associated with instruments of law, the 1948 Convention on the Prevention and Punishment of the Crime of Genocide has come to embody the conscience of humanity.

Its moral force is surely ironic. For the record of the Genocide Convention since its adoption has been notable above all for States' nearly wholesale failure to enforce its terms.

Although the treaty envisages (but does not require) the creation of an international court to punish genocide, forty-five years passed before the first international criminal tribunal was established. Its jurisdiction was limited to crimes, including genocide, committed in the former Yugoslavia since 1991. A similar, more circumscribed, tribunal was created for Rwanda one year later. It was not until September 2, 1998—a half-century after the United Nations General Assembly adopted the Genocide Convention—that the first verdict interpreting the convention was rendered by an international tribunal following a trial (one other defendant had previously pleaded guilty to genocide). On that day the Rwanda Tribunal found Jean-Paul Akayesu guilty on nine counts for his role in the 1994 Rwandan genocide.

Nor did any State bring a case under the Genocide Convention to the World Court until 1993, and this was scarcely a milestone in international enforcement efforts. The case was brought by a State that had endured genocidal crimes—Bosnia-Herzegovina—against a State allegedly responsible—the former Yugoslavia—and not by other States determined to enforce the law of universal conscience on behalf of desperate victims beyond their borders.

To the contrary, when those same crimes were being committed—and gruesomely portrayed in the daily media—legal experts in the U.S. government were asked, in the words of a former State Department lawyer, "to perform legal gymnastics to avoid calling this genocide." And as Rwandan Hutus slaughtered hundreds of thousands of Tutsis, the Clinton administration instructed its spokespeople not to describe what was happening as genocide lest this "inflame public calls for action," according to the *New York Times*. Instead, the State Department and National Security Council reportedly drafted guidelines instructing government spokespeople to say that "acts of genocide may have occurred" in *Rwanda*.

Five decades of nonenforcement have left the Genocide Convention's core terms shrouded in considerable ambiguity, making it that much easier for recalcitrant politicians to equivocate. (Such equivocations nonetheless fly in the face of the convention, which requires States' parties not only to punish genocide—a measure that does demand legal certainty—but also to prevent and repress the crime—action that by its nature must not await the certain knowledge that genocide has occurred.)

The definition of genocide set forth in the Genocide Convention is authoritative and has been incorporated verbatim in the statutes of the Yugoslavia and Rwanda tribunals as well as that of a permanent International Criminal Court (ICC) that will be created after sixty states have ratified the statute adopted in Rome in July 1998. After affirming that genocide is a crime under international law whether committed in time of peace or war, the 1948 convention defines genocide as

---

Diane F. Orentlicher, "Genocide," Roy Gutman and David Rieff, eds. from Crimes of War: What the Public Should Know (New York: W. W. Norton & Company), 1999, 153–157. Reprinted with permission.

"any of the following acts committed with intent to destroy, in whole or in part, a national, ethnical, racial or religious group, as such: killing members of the group; causing serious bodily or mental harm to members of the group; deliberately inflicting on the group conditions of life calculated to bring about its physical destruction in whole or in part; imposing measures intended to prevent births within the group; forcibly transferring children of the group to another group."

In the 1948 convention, then, the crime of genocide has both a physical element—comprising certain enumerated acts, such as killing members of a racial group—and a mental element—those acts must have been committed with the intent to destroy, in whole or in part, a national, ethnic, racial, or religious group "as such." In its verdict in the Akayesu case, the Rwanda Tribunal found that the systematic rape of Tutsi women in Taba Province constituted the genocidal act of "causing serious bodily or mental harm to members of the [targeted] group."

In addition to the crime of genocide itself, the 1948 convention provides that the following acts shall be punishable: conspiracy to commit genocide, direct and public incitement to commit genocide, attempt to commit genocide, and complicity in genocide.

What was left out of the convention is as important as what was included. Although earlier drafts of the convention listed political groups among those covered by the intent requirement, this category was omitted during final drafting stages. Too many governments, it seemed, would be vulnerable to the charge of genocide if deliberate destruction of political groups fell within the crime's compass.

Also excluded was the concept of cultural genocide—destroying a group through forcible assimilation into the dominant culture. The drafting history makes clear that the 1948 convention was meant to cover physical destruction of a people; the sole echo of efforts to include the notion of cultural extermination is the convention's reference to forcibly transferring children of a targeted group to another group.

In this and other respects the conventional definition of genocide is narrower than the conception of Polish scholar Raphael Lemkin, who first proposed at an international conference in 1933 that a treaty be created to make attacks on national, religious, and ethnic groups an international crime. Lemkin, who served in the U.S. War Department, fashioned the term genocide from the Greek word genos, meaning race or tribe, and the Latin term for killing, cide. (In his 1944 book, *Axis Rule in Occupied Europe*, Lemkin noted that the same idea could also come from the term ethnocide, consisting of the Greek word 'ethnos'—nation—and the Latin word 'cide.'")

Although Lemkin's conception included the physical extermination of targeted groups, this was, in his view, only the most extreme technique of genocide:

> By "genocide" we mean the destruction of an ethnic group … Generally speaking, genocide does not necessarily mean the immediate destruction of a nation, except when accomplished by mass killings of all members of a nation. It is intended rather to signify a coordinated plan of different actions aiming at the destruction of essential foundations of the life of national groups, with the aim of annihilating the groups themselves. The objectives of such a plan would be disintegration of the political and social institutions, of culture, language, national feelings, religion, and the economic existence of national groups, and the destruction of the personal security, liberty, health, dignity, and even the lives of the individuals belonging to such groups …
>
> Genocide has two phases: one, destruction of the national pattern of the oppressed group; the other, the imposition of the national pattern of the oppressor. This imposition, in turn, may be made upon the oppressed population which is allowed to remain, or upon the territory alone, after removal of the population and colonization of the area by the oppressor's own nationals.

Four years would pass before Lemkin's crime was recognized in an international treaty, but the legal foundation was laid during the 1945 Nuremberg and other postwar prosecutions.

Although the Nuremberg Charter did not use the term genocide, its definition of *crimes against humanity* overlapped significantly with Lemkin's conception of genocide. The term genocide was used in the indictment against major war criminals tried at Nuremberg, who were accused of having "conducted deliberate and systematic genocide, viz., the extermination of racial and national groups, against the civilian populations of certain occupied territories in order to destroy particular races and classes of people and national, racial or religious groups." Nuremberg prosecutors also invoked the term in their closing arguments, and it also appeared in the judgments of several U.S. military tribunals operating in Nuremberg.

Shortly after the trial of major war criminals at Nuremberg, the UN General Assembly adopted a resolution affirming that genocide is a "crime under international law." In its preamble, the 1946 resolution termed genocide "a denial of the right of existence of entire human groups, as homicide is the denial of the right to live of individual human beings."

The comparatively narrow terms of the 1948 convention—in particular, its exclusion of political groups and its restrictive intent requirement—have enabled political leaders to raise doubts about whether probable genocides satisfy the convention's stringent criteria. Did the authors of the Anfal campaigns of 1988, in which at least fifty thousand Iraqi Kurds are estimated to have been massacred, intend to kill Kurds "as such" or, in the words of one leading scholar, was their aim to eliminate "the Kurdish movement as a political problem?" Did Serb perpetrators of *ethnic cleansing* in Bosnia intend to destroy Muslims and Croats "as such," or did they "merely" seek to establish homogeneous Serb control over coveted territory?

As these questions suggest, a key source of ambiguity is the meaning of the 1948 convention's intent requirement. Although the

drafting history is somewhat ambiguous, I believe that it is a mistake to treat the convention's use of the term intent as though it were synonymous with motive. That Serb perpetrators of ethnic cleansing may have slaughtered Muslims so that they could obtain control over territory does not negate their intent to destroy Muslims "as such" in order to achieve their ultimate goal.

The Genocide Convention imposes a general duty on States' parties "to prevent and to punish" genocide. Those charged with genocide are to be tried either in the State where the crime occurred or "by such international penal tribunal as may have jurisdiction with respect to those Contracting Parties which shall have accepted its jurisdiction." Although the convention does not mention a third possibility—prosecution in a third State—it is now well established that any State can assert jurisdiction over crimes of genocide, wherever the crimes occurred and whatever the nationality of the perpetrators and victims.

In addition to individual criminal responsibility for genocide, the convention also establishes State responsibility—that is, international legal responsibility of the State itself for breaching its obligations under the convention. Parties to the convention can bring a case before the International Court of Justice alleging that another State party is responsible for genocide. As noted above, the first case of this sort was brought against Yugoslavia by Bosnia-Herzegovina in 1993 and is still pending.

Article 8 of the convention contemplates measures not only to punish genocide, but also to stop it in its tracks: "Any Contracting Party may call upon the competent organs of the United Nations to take such action under the Charter of the United Nations as they consider appropriate for the prevention and suppression of acts of genocide or any of the other acts enumerated in article 3." States that are parties to the convention could, for example, seek Security Council authorization to use military force to stop genocide being committed in another country.

Finally, although treaties themselves are binding only on States that are parties to the treaties, in a 1951 advisory opinion the International Court of Justice observed that the principles underlying the Genocide Convention are part of customary international law, which binds all states.

GENOCIDE IN HISTORY

Although Lemkin implied that Nazi crimes were fundamentally different from any previously committed, Hitler's "Final Solution" was not the first campaign of extermination that would meet Lemkin's definition of genocide. The systematic extermination of Armenians by the Young Turks beginning in April 1915 was the first genocide in this century. Emboldened by the world's acquiescence in the slaughter of Armenians— over 1 million are estimated to have been put to death—Hitler is famously reported to have reassured doubters in his ranks by asking, "Who after all is today speaking of the Armenians?"

Among more recent episodes of wholesale slaughter, at least some scholars have concluded that the Turkish massacre of Kurds in the district of Dersim in 1937–1938, the massacre of Hutus by Tutsi perpetrators in Burundi in 1972, the Khmer Rouge campaign of extermination in the mid-1970s, and the 1988 Anfal campaign against Iraqi Kurds meet the legal definition of genocide.

Among these cases, perhaps none better illustrates the complexities of the 1948 convention's definition of genocide than the case of Cambodia. In view of the magnitude of the carnage there—1.5 million out of Cambodia's 7 million citizens are believed to have died as a result of Khmer Rouge policies—there has been a keen desire to affix the term genocide to their crimes. Since, however, both the perpetrators and the majority of victims were

Khmer, reaching this conclusion has required agile legal reasoning. Some scholars have invoked the concept of autogenocide, arguing that it is possible to satisfy the 1948 convention's definition even when the perpetrators sought to kill a substantial portion of their own ethnic/national group. Others, more conservatively, have conceded that the vast majority of victims were killed for reasons that may be broadly termed political, but note that certain minority groups, such as the Muslim Cham and Khmer Buddhists, were specially targeted for destruction and argue that at least the crimes against these groups were genocidal.

While some campaigns of extermination more clearly qualify as genocide than others— the Holocaust and the 1994 Rwandan genocide are instances—the truth is that plausible arguments can be raised with respect to most cases of possible genocide. In the absence of judicial resolution or political resolve, virtually any case of genocide can be questioned. The first defendant tried before the Rwanda Tribunal argued, for example, that the massacres in Rwanda were politically motivated, a gruesome manner of waging civil war. In response the tribunal concluded that, "alongside the conflict … genocide was committed in Rwanda in 1994 against the Tutsi as a group." That the execution of this genocide "was probably facilitated by the conflict" did not negate the fact that genocide occurred.

The dearth of precedents enforcing the convention—a grim testament to the international community's failure of will—has for decades left experts able to do little more than argue knowledgeably about whether well-known candidates for the label "genocide" meet the legal definition. The ambiguities built into the Genocide Convention can finally be resolved only when States are willing to acknowledge forthrightly that genocide has occurred and to enforce the law of conscience.

QUESTIONS TO CONSIDER

1. What are the physical and mental elements of a definition of genocide?

2. Describe the two phases of genocide.

3. Why is the designation "genocide" so easily questioned?

Contested Meanings and Conflicting Imperatives: A Conceptual Analysis of Genocide

Scott Straus,

Department of Political Science,
University of California at Berkeley

INTRODUCTION

What is a genocide? That question is as essential for comparative analysis as it is difficult to answer. To investigate common causes among similar cases—a presumptive goal of comparison—researchers must decide what cases belong together. However, despite an abundance of excellent scholarship on definitions, genocide remains a deeply contested concept. Scholars are more likely to disagree than to agree about genocide's core attributes and, by extension, about a universe of genocide cases. While disagreement is healthy, profound conceptual differences limit the theoretical scope of cross-regional and cross-historical study. If developing explanations through comparison is indeed the research goal, conceptual analysis of genocide remains an imperative.

This article primarily reviews prominent definitions and sub-types of genocide.

It develops five core conceptual axes around which existing definitions differ; these axes then become the basis for a typology of definitions (Table 1.1). The article reviews the existing field of sub-types and summarizes this field in a typology (Table 1.2). Both typologies are intended to be aids for other researchers. Furthermore, the article also evaluates each conceptual dimension in detail, proposes a syncretic, etymologically driven definition, and reduces the number of sub-types to two (from a field of 21). These proposals undoubtedly will not be the last word on what defines genocide or on what the major kinds of genocide are. But they might advance conceptual discussion by highlighting important definitional and theoretical concerns. Finally, the article comments generally about conflicting imperatives in the concept of genocide and suggests avenues for further conceptual research.

From Scott Straus, "Contested Meanings and Conflicting Imperatives: A Conceptual Analysis of Genocide," *Journal of Genocide Research* 3(3) (2001): 349–375. Reprinted with permission of Taylor & Francis, Ltd. Website http://www.tandf.co.uk/journals

CONFLICTING IMPERATIVES

As must be clear to anyone who has followed the issue, the label "genocide" is pinned on a huge range of phenomena. During a 12-month period at the University of California–Berkeley, for example, cutbacks in an ethnic studies department, incarceration rates of African Americans, and even George W. Bush's election all were termed "genocide" on campus posters and fliers. In recent publications, "genocide" was used to characterize events in Amazonia, Burma, Chechnya, Chile, China, the Democratic Republic of Congo, East Timor, Guatemala, Kosovo, Iraq, Sri Lanka, the Sudan, and the United States—in addition to hundreds of references to the Jewish Holocaust, to the Armenian slaughter of 1915, to the Khmer Rouge in Cambodia, and to recent events in Bosnia and Rwanda. At the same time, some argue that genocide should only refer to the Holocaust.

"Genocide" is applied so discrepantly, to such heterogeneous phenomena, because the concept embodies several conflicting imperatives and has a strong European prototype. The concept initially referred to Nazi campaigns of mass violence, especially the extermination campaign against Europe's Jewish population. Although prior to the war Western states had committed large-scale atrocities in their colonies and against slaves, the scale of Nazi violence against Europeans in Europe and the idea of intentional human extermination shocked the modern West. Because of this context, the concept that emerged not only characterized a particular type of violence but also had an ineluctable and powerful moral connotation: it was synonymous with the apex of human evil. Not long thereafter, the 1948 United Nations Convention on the Prevention and Punishment of the Crime of Genocide legally bound signatories to stop genocide, thus imbuing the concept with additional legal and political dimensions. Calling an event "geno-cide" now had a codified juridical meaning and potentially significant consequences for states that used the term.

From its inception, then, genocide has been an empirical, moral, legal, and political concept. To one person, "genocide" means evil and demands preventive or punitive action by a government; to another, "genocide" carries a circumscribed juridical meaning, while to still others it designates a specific type of mass violence. These wide-ranging and powerful dimensions—and the relatively small number of terms that connote unspeakable atrocity—ironically have made "genocide" an attractive concept. But these multiple dimensions also have made for a conceptual muddle.

For comparative social research, this muddle is a problem. Concepts determine case selection, which in turn shapes causal inference. Without agreeing on what genocide is, scholars cannot develop plausible comparative explanations of the phenomenon they study. A theory that explains the Nazi and Armenian cases will be quite different from a theory that explains sanctions against Iraq, Augusto Pinochet's rule in Chile, and anthropology's impact on the Yanomami. Even a theory that explains recent events in Rwanda and Bosnia, to take another example, will have quite different emphases from a theory that explains recent events in the Democratic Republic of Congo and Chechnya.

Scholars often retain each of genocide's powerful conceptual dimensions. Studying genocide is then part condemnation, part prevention, and part research. But these goals are not necessarily compatible. When "genocide" is used in order to excoriate, the term refers to evil: genocide cases would be horrible events. When "genocide" is used in a court of law, the term refers to a crime: genocide cases would be individual acts of transgression. When "genocide" is used at the United Nations, the term refers to an event that must be stopped: genocide cases would be ones where member states are willing to intervene. In this article, "genocide" refers to a distinct phenomenon. The goal is comparative social research; the emphasis is on specifying a concept that helps scholars identify what makes genocide different from other types of mass violence.

CONCEPTUAL ORIGINS AND CORE DIMENSIONS

In 1944, the jurist Raphael Lemkin invented the word "genocide." Lemkin argued that Nazi policy was distinctive for targeting populations, not just armies and states. Nazi practice was also distinctive, Lemkin claimed, for promoting group destruction, not just group domination. Lemkin argued that these dimensions warranted a new concept. Combining the Greek word "genos" ("race, stock, family") with the Latin "cide" ("killing"), Lemkin settled on "genocide" to refer to the "destruction of a nation or of an ethnic group." Lemkin elaborated by calling genocide "a coordinated plan of different actions aiming at the destruction of essential foundations of the life of national groups, with the *aim of annihilating the groups completely*" (emphasis added). The Nazi genocide had different manifestations, he argued. Jews were to be "destroyed completely" while supposedly "non-Germanic" groups were to have their "national foundations" destroyed.

The core idea in Lemkin's concept of genocide can thus be described as intentional group annihilation. "Intentional" refers to Lemkin's claim that genocide is a "coordinated" and "previously prepared" "plan" with the "aim" of group annihilation. The emphasis on groups is self-evident. However, "annihilation" is arguably both the key notion and the most ambiguous term. According to the *Oxford English Dictionary*, annihilation means "the action or process of reducing to nothing; or of blotting out of existence." But this definition is not specific enough. What, in fact, does reducing to nothing mean? What counts as existence? These are difficult ontological and scientific questions that will not be resolved here.

Instead, the article holds that annihilation has three necessary conditions. First, annihilation must have a mode; there must be a way in which destruction is carried out. Second, annihilation must have a subject—an actor, someone or something that annihilates. And third, annihilation must have a direct object—an acted upon, something or someone that is annihilated, a victim. For an analysis of genocide, these three dimensions correspond to three fundamental research questions. First, how is annihilation carried out? Are mass murder, cultural repression, and starvation all modes of genocide? Second, who annihilates? Is genocide an act of state, a private act, an act of non-governmental organizations, or all of the above? Third, who or what is annihilated? Is genocide a campaign against a class, an invented group, a social collectivity, or only against ethnic and national groups? What, in fact, constitutes a group?

Lemkin had answers to these questions. Regarding the mode of annihilation—what he called "techniques of genocide"—Lemkin argued that destruction of vital political, social, cultural, and economic institutions, birth rate reduction, starvation, endangerment of health, mass killing, religious persecution, and moral debasement would all be modes of genocide. Therefore, he argued, Jews *and* Slavs faced genocide during World War II. If Lemkin had defined genocide as taking the form only of mass killing, the term probably would not have applied to Slavs. For Lemkin, then, the mode of violence was a crucial dimension for determining cases of genocide.

Regarding the agent of annihilation, Lemkin contended that genocide is a "coordinated plan" of government. Since Lemkin analyzed Nazi policy, this point is unambiguous in his essay, but this dimension became central for later genocide scholars. The basic question is whether the state is the definitive agent of genocide. Regarding the victim of annihilation, Lemkin argued that genocide is practiced against "ethnic" and "national" groups—communities that the actor committing genocide considered to have a "blood" or "biological" basis. If Lemkin had chosen different criteria for deciding what groups were targets of genocide—say groups constituted by sexual preference—his cases of genocide might have included the Nazi campaign against homosexuals.

Following Lemkin, this paper proposes that five dimensions serve as the basis for comparing different definitions of genocide: (1) whether intentional group annihilation is a definition's core idea; (2) how intent is conceptualized; (3) how the mode of annihilation is defined; (4) how the agent of annihilation is defined; and (5) how the victim of annihilation is defined. These dimensions are central to most definitions of genocide; they highlight the domains where authors tend to disagree; and they correspond to fundamental questions for comparative analysis. When pairing cases, scholars are likely to ask how much weight to give to intention, to the mode of violence, to the agent of violence, and to the type of victim. The answers to these questions determine case selection and hence theories about genocide's causes.

REVIEW OF SOME PROMINENT DEFINITIONS

Despite widespread dissatisfaction with the UN Convention, the document is a benchmark for genocide scholars and an important place to begin a review of definitions. The Convention defines genocide as "acts committed with intent to destroy, in whole or in part, a national, ethnical [sic], racial, or religious group, as such." Turning to the criteria established above, the Convention (1) does not posit intentional group annihilation as the core idea (because genocide can mean partial group destruction as opposed to group annihilation); (2) conceptualizes intention as "intent"; (3) identifies the modes of destruction as "killing members of the group," "causing serious bodily or mental harm to members of the group," "deliberately inflicting on the group conditions of life

calculated to bring about its physical destruction in whole or in part," "imposing measures intended to prevent births within the group," and "forcibly transferring children of the group to another group"; (4) does not specify the agent of destruction; and (5) identifies "national, ethnical, racial or religious" groups as potential victims.

Since 1948, a recurring criticism of the UN definition is that it excludes "political" groups from the possible victims of genocide. "Political" here generally refers to groups that have a real or purported class basis, political party affiliation, or regime loyalty. This category was excluded, at least in part, because the Soviet Union rejected the idea that genocide could be committed against social classes. The UN definition also is criticized for being too broad. A campaign against "part" of a group that causes "serious bodily or mental harm to members" would include a huge range of cases. This lack of specificity has contributed to the Convention's unenforceability. To date, no signatory to the Convention has intervened to stop a genocide.

In one of the first comprehensive reworkings of the concept, Dutch legal scholar Pieter Drost proposed a more inclusive definition. Drost defined genocide as "the deliberate destruction of physical life of individual human beings by reason of their membership of any human collectivity as such." Drost's definition (1) does not specify intentional group annihilation as the core idea (destruction here refers to individuals, not to groups); (2) conceptualizes intent as "deliberate"; (3) identifies the mode of destruction as "destruction of physical life," which is interpretable as "killing"; (4) does not specify an agent of destruction; and (5) identifies the victim group as any "human collectivity." The last is Drost's most durable contribution, as later genocide scholars have adopted the term "collectivity." The term broadly defines the victim group, thus including "political" groups among the potential targets of genocide.

Genocide scholar Israel Charny also has emphasized the need for an inclusive definition. Charny argues that genocide is a "generic" term that should include "all known types of mass murder and mass death that are brought about at the hands of man." Definitions, he contends, should not let terrible events "fall by the theoretical wayside." Charny thus defines "genocide" as the "mass killing of substantial numbers of human beings, when not in the course of military action against the military forces of an avowed enemy, under conditions of the essential defenselessness and helplessness of the victims." Charny's definition (1) does not specify intentional group annihilation as the core idea (neither group nor annihilation are part of the definition); (2) does not specify intent; (3) names "mass killing" as the mode of destruction; (4) does not identify a particular agent of destruction; and (5) defines the victim group as "defenseless" and "helpless" people. Charny's definition suggests that genocide is any mass murder of non-combatants; however, he labels the 1989 Tiananmen Square a "genocidal massacre" and the bombing of Hiroshima and Nagasaki a "war crime against humanity."

Leo Kuper pioneered the comparative study of genocide; however, Kuper was not always clear on definitional questions. Although dissatisfied with the exclusion of "political" groups and with the ambiguities of "in part" destruction in the Convention, Kuper argued that the UN definition should be maintained as useful. Nonetheless, for his comparative investigation, Kuper defined genocide as a "crime against a collectivity, taking the form of massive slaughter, and carried out with explicit intent." The latter definition (1) does not specify intentional group annihilation as the core idea (genocide here is a *crime* against a group, not group annihilation); (2) cites "explicit intent"; (3) identifies the mode of destruction as "massive slaughter"; (4) does not specify the agent of destruction; and (5) defines the victim group as a "collectivity."

Historian Frank Chalk and sociologist Kurt Jonassohn also have been in the forefront in the comparative study of genocide. Chalk and Jonassohn define genocide as "a form of one-sided mass killing in which a state or other authority intends to destroy a group, as that group and membership in it are defined by the perpetrator." This definition (1) specifies intentional group annihilation as the core idea; (2) uses the verb "intend"; (3) defines the mode of destruction as "one-sided mass killing"; (4) identifies the actor as "the state or other authority"; and (5) sees the victims as any "group as that group and membership in it are defined by the perpetrator." The authors' formulation of a perpetrator-defined victim group avoids endorsing the problematic concepts of race or ethnicity, a point that will be discussed in detail in the next section.

Sociologist Helen Fein, too, has been in the forefront of the comparative study of genocide and of establishing a precise definition. Fein defines genocide as "sustained purposeful action by a perpetrator to physically destroy a collectivity directly or indirectly, through interdiction of the biological and social reproduction of group members, sustained regardless of the surrender or lack of threat offered by the victim." Fein (1) specifies intentional group annihilation as the core idea; (2) uses the phrase "sustained purposeful action" to indicate intent; (3) defines the mode of violence as direct physical destruction or the interdiction of biological and social reproduction; (4) does not name an agent of genocide; and (5) associates the victim group with any collectivity. Fein's attention to reproduction in the definition is an important contribution that will be discussed in the next section.

The conceptual analysis followed here can be applied to other definitions of genocide. This article references other important contributions by Yehuda Bauer, Levon Chorbajian, Barbara Harff and Ted Gurr, Irving Louis Horowitz, Henry Huttenbach, Steven Katz, Robert Melson, and Ervin Staub. Table 1.1 summarizes the information generated from the definitions analyzed here as well as these other definitions.

TABLE 1.1 Definitions

Author	Intentional group annihilation as core idea	Formulation of intent	Mode of annihilation	Agent of annihilation	Target of annihilation	Definition
Raphael Lemkin (1944)	Yes	"Coordinated plan"	Killing; institutional destruction; starvation; religious persecution	State	"Nation"; "ethnic group"	"Destruction of a nation or of an ethnic group."
UN Definition (1948)	No	"Intent"	Killing; harm; destructive conditions; birth prevention; forcible child transference	Unspecified	"National, ethnical, racial, or religious" group	Acts committed with intent to destroy, in whole or in part, a national, ethnical, racial, or religious, group as such."
Pieter Drost (1959)	No	"Deliberate destruction"	Killing	Unspecified	"Human collectivity"	"Deliberate destruction of physical life of individual human beings by reason of their membership of any human collectivity as such."
Leo Kuper (1981)	No	"Explicit intent"	Mass killing	Unspecified	"Collectivity"	"Crime against a collectivity, taking the form of massive slaughter, and carried out with explicit intent."
Israel Charny (1994)	No	None	Mass killing	Unspecified	"Defenseless," "helpless" human beings	"Mass killing of substantial numbers of human beings, when not in the course of

Continued

11

TABLE 1.1 *Continued*

Author	Intentional group annihilation as core idea	Formulation of intent	Mode of annihilation	Agent of annihilation	Target of annihilation	Definition
						military action against the military forces of an avowed enemy, under conditions of the essential defenselessness and helplessness of victims."
Frank Chalk, Kurt Jonassohn (1990)	Yes	"Intend"	Mass killing	State or "other authority"	"Group, as that group and membership in it are defined by the perpetrator"	"A form of one-sided mass killing in which a state or other authority intends to destroy a group, as that group and membership in it are defined by the perpetrator."
Helen Fein (1990)	Yes	"Sustained purposeful action"	Physical destruction; interdiction of biological and social reproduction	Unspecified	"Collectivity"	"Sustained purposeful action by a perpetrator to physically destroy a collectivity directly or indirectly, through interdiction of the biological and social reproduction of group members, sustained regardless of the surrender or lack of threat offered by the victim.'

Continued

TABLE 1.1 *Continued*

Author	Intentional group annihilation as core idea	Formulation of intent	Mode of annihilation	Agent of annihilation	Target of annihilation	Definition
Yehuda Bauer (1999)	Yes	"Purposeful attempt"	Mass murder*	Unspecified	"Ethnicity"; "nation"	"A purposeful attempt to eliminate an ethnicity or a nation, accompanied by the murder of large numbers of the targeted group."
Levon Chorbajian (1999)	Unclear: "large numbers of deaths"	"Premeditated"	"Death"; "great cruelty"	"Authoritarian state"	"Targeted populations"	"Initiated by authoritarian states, premeditated, involving great cruelty, and bringing about large numbers of deaths in absolute terms and deaths as a percentage of target populations."
Barbara Harff and Ted Gurr (1988)	No	"Promotion and execution"	Killing	"State or its agents"	"Group" defined by "communal characteristics, i.e., ethnicity, religion, or nationality"	"The promotion and execution of policies by a state or its agents which result in the deaths of a substantial portion of a group."

Continued

TABLE 1.1 *Continued*

Author	Intentional group annihilation as core idea	Formulation of intent	Mode of annihilation	Agent of annihilation	Target of annihilation	Definition
Irving Louis Horowitz (1997)	No	"Systematic destruction"	Unspecified	State	"Innocent people"	"Structural and systematic destruction of innocent people by a state bureaucratic apparatus."
Henry Huttenbach (1988)	Yes	Intent is secondary to fate of group	Physical destruction	Unspecified	"Specific group"	"Destruction of a specific group within a given national or even international population."
Steven Katz (1994)	Yes	"Actualization of intent"	"Whatever means"	Unspecified	"National, ethnic, racial, religious, political, social, gender, or economic group as these groups are defined by the perpetrator"	"Actualization of the intent, however successfully carried out, to murder in its totality any national, ethnic, racial, religious, political, social, gender, or economic group, as these groups are defined by the perpetrator, by whatever means."

Continued

TABLE 1.1 *Continued*

Author	Intentional group annihilation as core idea	Formulation of intent	Mode of annihilation	Agent of annihilation	Target of annihilation	Definition
Robert Melson (1992)	No	"Intent"	Unspecified	State	"Social collectivity or category, usually a communal group, class, or a political faction."	"A public policy mainly carried out by the state whose intent is the destruction in whole or in part of a social collectivity or category, usually a communal group, class, or a political faction."
Ervin Staub (1989)	Yes	"Intention"	Killing; destructive conditions	Unspecified	"Racial, ethnic, religious, cultural, or political group"	"An attempt to exterminate a racial, ethnic, religious, cultural, or political group, either directly through murder or indirectly by creating the conditions that lead to the group's destruction."

*Bauer's 1984 definition lists four additional modes of genocide.

15

TOWARD A SYNCRETIC DEFINITION OF GENOCIDE

For Lemkin, the distinguishing feature of geno-cide was intentional group annihilation, and this core should be maintained. Genocide is not just mass violence, but rather a specific type of mass violence, namely, an attempt to destroy a group. Genocide can be further distinguished from other terms that are sometimes considered syn-onymous, such as atrocity, civil war, deportation, disease-related death, ethnic discrimination, eth-nic cleansing, ethnocide, human rights abuse, lynching, mass expulsion, mass murder, mas-sacre, pogrom, riot, slavery, starvation, terror-ism, and war crimes. Each of these phenomena may coincide with genocide in particular cases, but by itself none of them amounts to genocide.

Nonetheless, intentional group annihi-lation is conceptually insufficient because the words "intentional," "group," and "annihila-tion" all are contested. Regarding intent, some scholars argue that intention is secondary to the empirical question of group destruction. However, most include some notion of inten-tionality in their definition. The words "intent," "intention," or "intends" are included in defi-nitions proposed by the UN, Kuper, Chalk and Jonassohn, Katz, Melson, and Staub. Lemkin formulates intent as a "coordinated plan"; Drost uses "deliberate action"; Horowitz cites "sys-tematic destruction"; Fein employs "sustained purposeful action"; and Chorbajian uses the word "premeditated."

Scholarly concern with intent reflects a crucial question for labeling events "genocide": namely, whether group annihilation is the pri-mary objective or overall design of a campaign of violence. But the term "intent" arguably has two limitations for social research. First, "intent" usually refers to individuals and to the contents of their thought, reflecting a legal concern with individual criminality. "Intent" does not char-acterize actions by regimes or states. Second, intent may be difficult to demonstrate where

no proof of thought exists. An annihilation cam-paign might be evident, even though intent is never publicly declared or recorded. Given these concerns, a preferable term to designate genocide's specificity might be "organized" as in "organized group annihilation" or "organized attempt to annihilate a group." Organization implies that annihilation is a killing campaign's objective, but the term focuses attention at an aggregate regime or institutional level rather than at an individual level. Thought need not be demonstrated; rather, the research question is whether annihilatioan was planned, coordi-nated, systematic, patterned, and, above all, car-ried out.

With regard to annihilation, a first ques-tion is whether a particular mode of violence constitutes genocide. Lemkin and Fein argue that genocide has several modes, including killing, starvation, and the destruction of in-stitutions necessary for a group's social and bi-ological reproduction. The UN definition identifies additional modes, including the forcible transference of children from one group to another. In 1998, the United Nations International Criminal Tribunal for Rwanda determined rape was a mode of genocide. By contrast, Charny, Kuper, and Chalk and Jonas-sohn, among others, name killing as the mode of genocide.

How can scholars adjudicate between these methods of violence? Killing is arguably distinguishable from other modes of violence and might be considered the definitive mode of genocide. Ending life is an irreversible, di-rect, immediate, and unambiguous mode of an-nihilation. By contrast, cultural destruction does not necessarily bring about elimination. Even if publicly outlawed, language, custom, and arts can survive in private. Starvation also is not a de-finitive mode of genocide. Starvation that kills would be a mode of annihilation, but starvation that is designed to bring a group into submis-sion would not be. Acts that prevent a group's bi-ological reproduction are more difficult to classify. On the one hand, mass sterilization could amount to a group's *future* annihilation. On the other hand, this mode allows an element of chance by not annihilating the group at once. Therefore, one can distinguish a direct mode of annihilation, which is physical destruction, and an indirect one, prevention of a group's reproduction—a distinction already present in Fein's and Staub's definitions.

Who annihilates is another fundamental question. Some researchers specify the state or an "other authority" as the agent in genocide, whereas others do not specify a particular actor. Lemkin, Chalk and Jonassohn, Chorbajian, Harff and Gurr, Horowitz, and Melson are among the former; the UN definition, Drost, Kuper, Charny, Fein, Bauer, Huttenbach, Katz, and Staub are among the latter. A state-directed campaign of annihilation would be importantly different from group annihilation carried out by most non-state actors. A state campaign involves ideology, law, and institutions. How state officials decide on annihilation, how they convince a population to commit genocide, and which institutional configurations permit genocide are crucial questions. State involvement, in short, significantly shapes the character and causes of annihilation.

But is the state a necessary attribute in the definition of genocide? It is hard to imagine a modern annihilation campaign that could occur without state involvement. Systematic annihilation requires coordinated planning and massive resources, which would most likely emanate from a state. However, no *prima facie* reason exists for why the state must be the agent committing genocide. If non-state actors mobilized to eliminate a population, then that campaign should be considered genocide. Nonetheless, distinguishing between state-sponsored and non-state-sponsored genocide in some cases will be valuable for comparative study.

Who is annihilated in a genocide is the most complicated question. Genocide is distinctive for commission against those not engaged in combat. Charny, Chalk and Jonassohn, Fein, Horowitz, and Harff and Gurr explicitly make this point. They aim to distinguish genocide from a codified act of war. The empirical problem here is that genocide, including the Holocaust, often is committed during a war. States committing genocide justify campaigns of violence against non-combatants as legitimate wartime behavior, especially when combating a guerrilla army with grassroots support. Here again, remembering that the core idea in genocide is organized group annihilation is useful. Strategies of war that destroy an entire group are genocide.

But what kind of group is annihilated during a genocide? Lemkin defined genocide as acts committed against "ethnic" or "national" groups—against groups with a purported "genos." This formulation was crucial for him. He believed that the Nazis committed genocide, at least in part, because of their preoccupation with biology. Bauer similarly argues that genocide "means the murder of an ethnicity." "Genocide" can be distinguished from "political mass murder," he argues, because racial and ethnic groups have an "avenue of escape." This is a sensible, etymologically driven formulation, and it suggests that a group's extermination—the ending of its biological existence—is a better formulation than annihilation.

However, the problem with restricting genocide to "racial" or "ethnic" groups is that these groups do not, in fact, have a biological basis. They are not natural, pre-political groups. Racial groups, if they exist at all, are not genetically homogenous. Ethnic identity and ethnic group membership are fluid, shifting, and malleable, not immutable. In short, where applied to large social groups, "genos" is a fiction. Perhaps more importantly, during a genocide, the agent of violence, not the victim, defines group membership. Genocide is not carried out against a group bounded by essential internal properties. Rather, genocide is carried out against a group that the perpetrator believes has essential properties. Thus, a "class" group is potentially a victim of genocide—as long as that group is constituted as a "people."

Wary of excluding particular groups, Drost, Kuper, Chalk and Jonassohn, Charny, Fein, Huttenbach, and Melson employ the non-specific term "collectivity" or "group" to characterize the potential victims of genocide. Staub includes "political group" in his definition, while Katz lists several potential victim groups. By claiming that genocide is carried out against a "group as … defined by the perpetrator," Chalk and Jonassohn importantly recognize that the agent of violence defines group boundaries, while not treating race or ethnicity as objective categories.

However, Chalk and Jonassohn's formulation might be considered too general because it applies to any group. Genocide is arguably more specific. As a campaign of annihilation, genocide is an attempt to wipe out a present *and* future threat. As such, genocide is not just an attempt to destroy a group's living members, but also to destroy their purported reproductive capacity. Biology is therefore crucial. The belief in a group's biological foundation gives rise to the idea that defeating a group, especially a group construed as a long-standing enemy, is accomplished only through annihilating its "genos." Differently stated, only when a group is seen to have biological immutability, hereditary qualities, and therefore the possibility of reproduction does the idea of genocide arise. A necessary condition of genocide may be, then, that the victim group is considered an organic unit—a natural, reproducing, essentially unified collectivity, however fictive such a belief might be. In analyzing genocide against groups not commonly thought to have a biological foundation, the task is to demonstrate an organic logic in the perpetrator's conception of the group.

For establishing a working definition of genocide, I would suggest that Chalk and Jonassohn's formulation be modified to annihila-tion of a "group that a perpetrator constitutes as an organic collectivity." Organic collectivity indicates that a group is seen as a natural, interconnected unit with reproductive capacity and biological qualities. When a perpetrator claims a group has a genetic, kinship, or racial basis, that group is being constituted as an organic collectivity. The proposed modification eschews treating race and ethnicity as pre-political, fixed entities; the modification can include groups defined by political, economic, or other non-racial and non-ethnic criteria, as long as these groups are constituted as organic collectivities; and it focuses attention on the genocidal agent. Most importantly, the modification returns the concept of genocide to its etymological roots—namely, the destruction of a "genos."

Three final points are pertinent to defining the victim group. The first concerns territorial boundaries: the concept of annihilation depends on specifying a group within bounded space. For example, if all group members in a village were killed while group members outside the village were spared, would that be genocide? Probably not: genocide is annihilation of an end group under a perpetrator's territorial control. But organized group destruction also could occur outside a perpetrator's territorial control; indeed, genocide has occurred during the course of territorial invasion or expansion. This suggests that territory matters but is not constitutive. Genocide can occur either within a territory under a perpetrator's control or outside it, but, again, genocide's distinctive feature is commission against an entire group.

A related question is whether genocide should occur within a particular time frame. In this domain, genocide might be considered a continuous phenomenon, like a war or a revolution. Analysts should be able to identify a beginning and end to a series of interrelated events that together constitute organized group annihilation. The period of time need not have a limit or maximum. This point is implicit, and need not be specified in the definition.

A final question is whether genocide should have a numerical threshold. Genocide is committed against a collectivity and therefore occurs on a mass scale. But what constitutes "mass"? Chary, Bauer, Chorbajian, and Harff and Gurr, respectively, claim that genocide involves the killing of "substantial numbers," "large numbers," a "large … percentage," and "a substantial portion" of a group's population. These are useful ways of operationalizing group annihilation, but, as with the question of time, need not be specified in the definition.

Based on the above review, "genocide" might be redefined as an organized attempt to annihilate a group that a perpetrator constitutes as an organic collectivity. This definition can be expanded to meet research agendas. For example, an indirect genocide would be an organized attempt to prevent the reproduction of a group that a perpetrator constitutes as an organic collectivity. Another variation would be a state-directed, organized attempt to annihilate a group that a perpetrator constitutes as an organic collectivity. Researchers also can refer to genocides that occur within a perpetrator's territorial control or to those outside that control.

This definition emphasizes that systematic mass murder is genocide when violence is directed at an entire group and when that group is purported to have a biological foundation. By contrast, politicide might be considered a campaign to physically destroy members of a political party or every "educated" individual. The key difference between these phenomena is that genocide would entail killing members of the group as well as their families—destroying the group by destroying its purported reproductive capacity. Empirically, cases of mass murder are likely to be mixed; in other words, cases might have politicidal and genocidal elements. To distinguish

between the two phenomena, researchers might determine empirically which mode of violence is primary.

Given the territorial dimension discussed here, deportation and genocide are quite related phenomena. In both cases, the perpetrator's overall objective may be to create a group-free territory. However, the act of attempting to annihilate the group (genocide) and the act of expelling the group (deportation) are different enough that distinguishing between them is important. As with the example of politicide, deportation may include acts of killing while genocide may include acts of expulsion. Again, researchers might label cases after making an empirical assessment about which mode of violence is primary.

SUB-TYPES OF GENOCIDE

Another domain of broad conceptual disagreement is sub-type classification. To date, genocide scholars have proposed at least 21 different kinds of genocide. Among the scholars under review, Kuper, Charny, Chalk and Jonassohn, Harff and Gurr, and Fein have put forward sub-types, as has Roger Smith. Harff and Gurr also have created four sub-types of politicide; Charny has proposed the categories of "war crimes against humanity" and "genocidal massacre"; and Kuper has proposed the category of "mass murder of political groups."

In distinguishing sub-types, genocide scholars tend to employ three bases for classification: (1) type of victim group; (2) historical and social context; and (3) perpetrator objective. Table 1.2 summarizes these classification criteria as well as the different sub-types and the corresponding cases.

How can these sub-types and classification criteria be evaluated? One place to start is consistency of classification. Sub-types are bound up with theory; they indicate a kernel of explanation about why a genocide happened.

TABLE 1.2 Sub-types

Author	Sub-types	Included cases[†]	Classification criteria
Leo Kuper (1984)	• "Genocide against indigenous people" • "Genocide following upon decolonization of a two-tier structure of domination" • "Genocide in the process of struggle for power by ethnic, racial, or religious groups" • "Genocide against hostage or scapegoat groups" • "Mass murder of political groups"	• During colonization of the Americas, Australia, and Africa; in Paraguay and Brazil in the twentieth century • Rwanda (1962–1963); Burundi (1972) • Pakistan-Bangladesh (1971) • Turks against Armenians; Nazi Germany against Jews and Gypsies; Yugoslav Croat against Serbs (WWII) • Stalinist USSR against Kulaks and "national groups"; Indonesia (1965), Cambodia; Uganda under Idi Amin; Argentina; Chile; El Salvador	Historical and social context; type of victim group
Israel Charny (1994)	• "Genocidal massacre" • "Intentional genocide" • "Genocide in the course of colonization or consolidation of power" • "Genocide in the course of aggressive war" • "War crimes against humanity" • "Genocide as a result of ecological destruction and abuse"	• Sri Lanka; Tiananmen Square • Armenians; Nazi Germany against Jews, Gypsies, and homosexuals; Indonesia; Iraq against Kurds • Paraguay; Cambodia; Stalinist USSR • Nazi Germany and Japan (WWII); Iraq • Nagasaki; Hiroshima; and Dresden • Germany against Herero • Hole in the ozone layer; water poisoning; air pollution; nuclear pollution	Historical and social context; perpetrator objective
Frank Chalk, Kurt Jonassohn (1990)	• "To eliminate a real or potential threat" • "To spread terror among real or potential enemies" • "To acquire wealth" • "To implement a belief, a theory, or an ideology"	• Numerous wars in antiquity (including possible cases of Hittites; Carthage; Anasazi Indians; Hurons). Twentieth century cases include Burundi; Pakistan; Indonesia • Assyria; Athens against Melos; Genghis Khan, Shaka Zulu, USSR in Ukraine, Ethiopia • US against Pequots and tribes in Virginia; Germany against Herero • "Transitional cases" include Cathars and Knights Templar in France; witches in Europe; Christians in Roman Empire, etc.; twentieth century cases include Armenians; USSR; Nazi Germany against Jews, Gypsies; Cambodia	Perpetrator objective

Continued

TABLE 1.2 *Continued*

Author	Sub-types	Included cases†	Classification criteria
Helen Fein (1990)	• "Ideological" • "Retributive" • "Developmental" • "Despotic"	• Armenians; Nazi Germany; Cambodia • Burundi; Rwanda; Sudan; Ethiopia; East Timor; Tibet; Afghanistan; Guatemala; Indonesia; etc. • Paraguay; Brazil • USSR; Equatorial Guinea; Uganda	Perpetrator objective
Barbara Harff, Ted Gurr (1988)	• "Hegemonial genocides" • "Xenophobic genocides" • "Retributive politicides" • "Repressive politicides" • "Revolutionary politicides" • "Repressive/hegemonial politicides" • "Mixed"	• National groups in USSR, Tibet • Paraguay; Nigeria (1966), Burma (1978) • Algeria (1962); Rwanda (1963–1964); Chile (1973–1976) • Repatriated nationals and Ukrainians in USSR; China against Taiwanese nationalists (1947); Madagascar (1947–1948); Angola (1961–1962); etc. • China (1950–1951, 1966–1975); N. Vietnam (1953–1954); Zaire (1964–1965); Ethiopia (1974–1979); Cambodia, Afghanistan (1978–) • Malaysia (1948–1956); Pakistan (1958–1974), Iraq (1959–1975), etc. • Laos (1963–1965); Indonesia (1965–1966); Uganda (1979–1986); Iran (1981–); Ethiopia (1984–1985)	Perpetrator objective
Roger Smith (1987)	• "Retributive" • "Institutional" • "Utilitarian" • "Monopolistic" • "Ideological"	• Genghis Khan • Ancient warfare; crusades; Timur Lek • Colonial conquests against indigenous people • Pakistan; Burundi; Nigeria • Cities in Ancient Israel; Albigensians; Cambodia	Perpetrator objective

†Unless otherwise indicated, dates are included where there might be some doubt as to which time period is being referenced; in some cases, dates are not included because authors do not specify the historical period to which they are referring. "Etc." in the Chalk/Jonassohn, Fein, and Harff/Gurr rows indicates that these authors cite more cases than are reproduced here (for space reasons). For the complete list, see the original texts.

Finding a consistent basis for differentiation is thus important for building logically consistent theory, and therein lies a weakness in Kuper's and Charny's schemes. Kuper labels sub-types according to the social and historical context ("genocide following upon decolonization") *and* according to victim group type ("genocide against indigenous groups"). Charny distinguishes sub-types on the basis of social and historical context ("genocide as a result of consolidation of power") and perpetrator objective ("intentional genocide").

But which of the three classificatory criteria is best? This question can be answered by turning to the Rwanda and Cambodia cases. Using the classificatory criteria above, in Rwanda (1) the victim group was "ethnic"; (2) the context was civil war; and (3) the primary perpetrator objective was total military defeat. By contrast, in Cambodia, (1) the victim group was "political"; (2) the context was Communist revolution; and (3) the primary perpetrator objective was "ideological." This breakdown shows that the second and third sub-type criteria are quite similar. If the context is civil war, the objective will be military defeat. If the context is revolution, the objective will likely be ideological, and so on. The question then becomes whether the victim group or the perpetrator objective/context should characterize sub-types.

Different scholars are likely to answer this question differently, but focusing on the genocidal actor seems promising for mainly two reasons. First, explanations about what causes genocide are likely to center on the agent committing the genocide. Second, as discussed above, victim groups do not necessarily have internal properties; their boundaries and membership are malleable; and, during a genocide, their boundaries and membership are dependent on a perpetrator's decision. Thus, the perpetrator's objective is more significant than the type of victim. However, this still leaves at least

fourteen perpetrator-centered sub-types. How can they be assessed?

Ideology is the basis of several sub-types, including "ideological" genocide, "intentional" genocide, and genocide "to implement a belief, an ideology, or a theory." The problem here is twofold. First, ideology is a broad concept with different meanings to different scholars. Second, ideology and belief are likely to play central roles in every case of extraordinary violence. "Ideological genocide" therefore will often overlap with other sub-type categories. For example, the Rwandan genocide would likely fall into the categories "to eliminate a real or potential threat" or "retributive genocide." Cambodia, by contrast, is categorized as an "ideological genocide" or a genocide "to implement a belief, an ideology, or a theory." But this distinction does not hold up. Regarding Rwanda, although the massacres were indeed to eliminate real and potential threats and to respond to invasion, the genocidal regime also promoted an ideology and a belief—Hutu nationalism. Although the Khmer Rouge's practices were nominally based on Communism, some massacres were carried out to eliminate real and imaginary threats to the revolution and, retributively, to eliminate real and imagined dissent or invasions.

Similar criticisms apply to other sub-types. Regarding the sub-type "to eliminate a real or potential enemy," since genocide is defined here as group annihilation and since most groups targeted for annihilation will be considered enemies, this sub-type effectively restates the definition. Regarding retribution, much political violence is predicated on a perception of pre-existing injustice or violation, such as an assassination, exploitation, rebel invasion, or hidden oppression. Whether the violation is real or fantasized, campaigns of violence often have an element of retribution. Other sub-types have different weaknesses. "Monopolistic genocide," for example, is evocative of a group seizing power for itself.

However, this notion elides potential cohabitation or collaboration with groups other than the one targeted for genocide; it also elides potential divisions within the genocidal actor's group. "Institutional genocide" refers to routinized (rather than intentional or premeditated) group destruction, especially during ancient warfare. However, this category disappears if the idea of intention or premeditation is removed from the definition of genocide.

This brief discussion is not meant to be exhaustive, but rather to demonstrate that subtype classification is necessarily tied to empirical assessment, theoretical explanation, and definition. As long as authors disagree in their evaluation of evidence, in their analyses, and in their understanding of what genocide is, sub-types are likely to remain idiosyncratic. For my work, I see a broad and important difference between genocides carried out during territorial invasion or annexation and genocides carried out within societies. Thus, I would propose only two sub-types of genocide. The first is colonial genocide. This type of genocide is directly linked to colonization and generally is carried out against prior inhabitants, or "indigenous" groups. This category draws on and includes Kuper's sub-type of "against indigenous populations," Charity's sub-type of "in the course of colonization," Chalk and Jonassohn's sub-type of "to acquire wealth," Fein's sub-type of "developmental," and Smith's sub-type of "utilitarian."

The second sub-type I propose is revolutionary genocide. This type of genocide is directly linked to the planned and sustained internal transformation of a society. In these cases, genocide is a method of violence to bring about the desired radical change. The category partly draws on and incorporates the various "ideology" sub-types as well as Harff and Gurr's "hegemonial" genocide and "revolutionary" politicide sub-types. The category also is indebted to Melson's theoretical analysis.

CONCLUSION

Throughout this article, I have argued that, despite inherent ambiguities, "genocide" is a useful social scientific concept that refers to a specific, even exceptional, phenomenon. In establishing a definition for comparative analysis, I have sought to center the definition on the genocidal actor, to retain genocide's etymological meaning as destruction of a genos, however fictive, and to synthesize the strengths of various pre-existing definitions. The result is a restrictive definition to which relatively few cases in the twentieth century would correspond. This definition excludes numerous cases of organized mass violence, which together amount to a death toll even greater than that of genocide cases.

To avoid ranking atrocities while maintaining specificity, a crucial next step is to develop an extensive conceptual vocabulary for mass violence. If "genocide" is to remain one concept among several, researchers might acknowledge that genocide is not necessarily morally worse than another type of mass murder. Equally, researchers might uncouple genocide's empirical dimension from its legal and political dimensions.

A vocabulary of violence can move in two directions. The first direction would specify an umbrella concept that refers to a generic phenomenon of which genocide is one instance. Genocide might be considered a sub-set of "democide," mass crime, mass death, mass violence, political violence, or conflict. This point recognizes that genocide is ultimately a middle-range phenomenon that shares key aspects with other forms of violence, but is, nonetheless, importantly different and quite specific. A second direction would be to develop a range of concepts that refer to other types of mass violence (assuming "mass violence" is the umbrella notion). Some concepts already in use include ethnocide, massacre, "partial genocide," pogrom, politicide, and deportation.

However, given the frequency with which violence characterizes politics, research is in need of a fuller spectrum.

QUESTIONS TO CONSIDER

1. According to the author, why is the term "genocide" applied so arbitrarily?
2. What is the core of Raphael Lemkin's invention of the word "genocide"?
3. According to the author, what are the three necessary conditions for genocide?
4. What is the recurring criticism of the UN definition of genocide?
5. How does Israel Charny's definition of genocide make it more inclusive?
6. Discuss the scholarly problem with intent.
7. Who is annihilated in a genocide is the most complicated question. Why?
8. State the definition of genocide arrived at by the author after reviewing the various problems in defining the term.
9. How is ideological genocide distinguished from other forms of genocide?

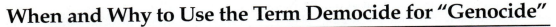

When and Why to Use the Term Democide for "Genocide"

R. J. Rummel,

Professor Emeritus, University of Hawaii

It is impossible to dissociate language from science or science from language, because every natural [or social] science always involves three things: the sequence of phenomena on which the science is based; the abstract concepts which call these phenomena to mind; and the words in which the concepts are expressed.

Antoine Laurent Lavoisier, 1789

The field of "genocide" studies is growing rapidly, research is diversifying, and our knowledge of individual "genocides" is multiplying and deepening (I will soon make clear why I use the quotation marks). Many related institutes are now at work on "genocide" and a variety of web sites have been constructed. There are very good people at work on one form of "genocide" or another and there soon should be the methods and works to justify "genocide" as an independent, academic discipline. Still, comparative works on "genocides" are rare and usually follow the cafeteria approach, unsystematically picking and choosing among "genocides" according to the interest of the writers. But I have no doubt that this will change in the next decade or so.

I look forward to the time when all this work can be connected by a web ring: a reciprocal linking of Internet web sites presenting the major research for those involved in the field, as well as for practitioners, students, and the general public. Given the state of "genocide"

From R. J. Rummel, "When and Why to Use the Term Democide for 'Genocide,'" *Idea: A Journal of Social Issues* 6(1). Reprinted with permission.

research two decades ago, the field of "genocide" studies has undergone revolutionary growth and such a web ring is now overdue. (I am not writing about cross-linking sites per se, but about interlinking sites containing full research results, reports, and books.)

But with such a fast growth the field must now undergo integration and rationalization. And this is hampered by multiple and confusing uses of the term genocide. To call all government murder genocide is to leave us without a concept for the killing of people because of their indelible group membership. To call attempts to destroy a culture without killing its members genocide is also to leave us without a clear concept for killing people because of their group membership. I believe it best to limit the term to such killing, but if we do we must also recognize that genocide so understood is a small percentage (even considering the Holocaust) of those murdered by government for other reasons (about 38,000,000 of the total near 170,000,000 murdered 1900–1987, as detailed in my *Death By Government* and *Statistics of Democide*). To avoid this confusion in my own work and to be clear about what I was analyzing, I invented the term democide. This then fills the void created by necessarily limiting genocide to killing by virtue of group membership. What do we call murder by quota, then? Democide. What about killing political opponents? Democide (or politicide as a type of democide). And the Holocaust? Genocide (as another type of democide).

What are the differences and similarities between democide and genocide? As defined, elaborated, and qualified in Chapter 2 of *Death By Government*, democide is any murder by government—by officials acting under the authority of government. That is, they act according to explicit or implicit government policy or with the implicit or explicit approval of the highest officials. Such was the burying alive of Chinese civilians by Japanese soldiers, the shooting of hostages by German soldiers, the starving to death of Ukrainians by communist cadre, or the burning alive of Japanese civilians purposely firebombed from the air by American airmen.

Genocide, however, is a confused and confusing concept. It may or may not include government murder, refer to wholly or partially eliminating some group, or involve psychological damage. If it includes government murder, it may mean all such murder or just some. Boiling all this down, genocide can have three different meanings.

One meaning is that defined by international treaty, the Convention on the Prevention and Punishment of the Crime of Genocide. This makes genocide a punishable crime under international law, and defines it as:

> any of the following acts committed with intent to destroy, in whole or in part, a national, ethnical, racial or religious group, as such:
>
> a. Killing members of the group;
> b. Causing serious bodily or mental harm to members of the group;
> c. Deliberately inflicting on the group conditions of life calculated to bring about its physical destruction in whole or in part;
> d. Imposing measures intended to prevent births within the group;
> e. Forcibly transferring children of the group to another group.

Note that only the first clause includes outright killing, while the other clauses cover nonkilling ways of eliminating a group. I will call this definition of genocide the *legal meaning*, since it is now part of international law.

Regardless of this definition and doubtlessly influenced by the Holocaust, ordinary usage and that by students of genocide have tended to wholly equate it with the *murder and only the murder* by government of people due to their national, ethnical, racial or religious (or, what is called *indelible*) group membership. This way of viewing genocide has become so ingrained that it seems utterly false to say, for example, that the United States committed genocide against ethnic Hawaiians by forcing their children to study English and behave according to American norms and values. Yet, in the legal view of genocide, this is arguably true. The equating of genocide with the killing of people because of their indelible group membership I will label the *common meaning* of genocide.

In some usage and especially among some students of genocide, the concept has been redefined to fill a void. What about government murdering people for other reasons than their indelible group membership? What about government organized death squads eliminating communist sympathizers, assassinating political opponents, or cleansing the population of antirevolutionaries? What about simply fulfilling a government death quota (as in the Soviet Union under Stalin)? None of such murders are genocide according the legal and common meanings. Therefore, some students of genocide have stretched its meaning to include all government murder, whether or not because of group membership. This may be aptly named the *generalized* meaning of genocide.

As obvious, the problem with the generalized meaning of genocide is that to fill one void it creates another. For if genocide refers to all government murder, what are we to call the murder of people because of their group membership? It is precisely because of this conceptual problem that I created the concept of democide.

We now have three meanings of genocide: legal, common, and generalized. How do these relate to democide? Let me try to make this clear through Venn Diagrams. Figure 1.1 shows two circles, one containing all cases of democide, the other all cases of genocide. Outside of the two circles are all other forms of behavior that is neither democide nor genocide. Now, for the legal meaning of genocide, only part of the circle of genocide will overlap that of democide, as shown in the figure. This is because the legal meaning includes nonkilling, while democide includes only killing. The overlap portion of the circles comprise those cases of democide that are the genocidal murder of people in order to eradicate their group in whole or part. That part of the democide circle

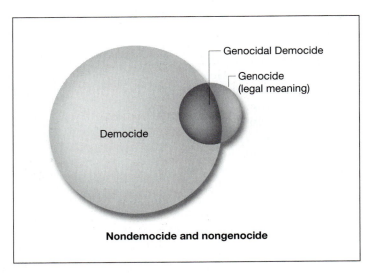

FIGURE 1.1 The Relationship Between Democide and the Legal Meaning of Genocide

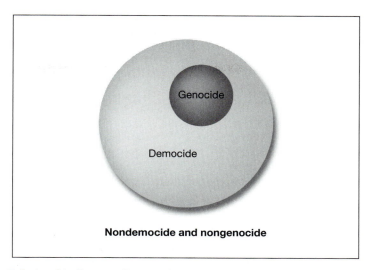

FIGURE 1.2 The Relationship Between Democide and the Common Meaning of Genocide

outside of the overlap contains those murdered for other reasons.

Figure 1.2 shows the circle of genocide in its common meaning. Here the genocide circle is a smaller one inside the democide circle. That is, in this meaning genocide is a kind of democide, but there are other types of democide as well, such as politicide or the bombing of civilians (see Table 2.1 of *Death By Government*).

Now referring to Figure 1.3 for the generalized meaning of genocide, the genocide and democide circles are the same: democide is genocide and genocide is democide. One of the concepts is then redundant against the other. But then, as I so often point out, what do we call the murder of people because they are, say, Moslems, Jews, or Armenians? This surely is a kind of murder that must be discriminated and understood.

The progress of our knowledge of government murder depends fundamentally on the clarity and significance of our concepts. Especially, these concepts should refer to real world behavior and events that can be clearly and similarly discriminated regardless of the observers and their prejudices. For if any area of social study is laden with predispositions and biases, it surely has to do with the who, why, when, and how of government murder. (The meaning of "government" and "murder" are themselves concepts that require clarification, as I tried to do in aforementioned Chapter 2.)

For these reasons I believe that both genocide in its common meaning and democide as I have defined it have an important role in understanding government murder. The legal view of genocide, however, is too complex and subsumes behavior too different in kind, such as government murder, government induced psychological damage, government attempting to eliminate a group in whole or in part (what empirical meaning can we give to "in part"?), or government removing children from a group (removing what percentage constitutes genocide?), and so on.

In the case of democide, the vast majority of government killing is manifestly murder—the intent to commit murder is inherent in the act itself. For example, soldiers lining up civilians against a wall and shooting them to death without a fair trial is manifestly government

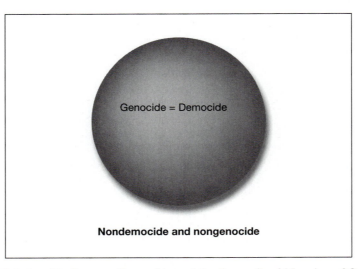

FIGURE 1.3 The Relationship Between Democide and the Generalized Meaning of Genocide

murder. And in its common meaning, most cases of genocide can be equally discriminated, as in the Holocaust or of the Armenian genocide in Turkey during 1915–1916.

In sum, *genocide should ordinarily be understood as the government murder of people because of their indelible group membership (let the international lawyers struggle with the legal meaning) and democide as any murder by government, including this form of genocide.*

Besides this conceptual issue, the field of democide studies, to now use this term in place of "genocide," is also retarded by a lack of concern with research methods and quantitative analysis. A few, such as Helen Fein in her *Accounting for Genocide* (1979), have done quantitative research, but if hypotheses and theories about democide or genocide are to be tested and such research accumulated, then methodology and quantitative techniques must be in the field's toolbox. This is not to say that historical scholarship, case studies, and sociological

analysis are to be ignored. No. These are essential, and I have done many myself. I am only saying that we must add to them—complement them—if well-rounded research on democide is to be accomplished. Even simple statistics can be most helpful and qualitatively important. Just consider the monumental significance of just two numbers: the 170,000,000 people probably murdered by government compared to the near 38,000,000 combat dead in all foreign and domestic wars over the same period.

In any case, let's first clean up this conceptual problem that so bedevils this field so extraordinarily crucial to the lives and welfare of our fellow human beings.

QUESTIONS TO CONSIDER

1. According to R. J. Rummel, what are the three permutations of genocide?
2. What is the distinction between genocide and democide?

Defining Genocide: Defining History?

Deborah Harris,

Melbourne University

INTRODUCTION

A heated debate on the most appropriate definition of genocide exists within the field of genocide studies. In books, journal articles, reviews and electronic sources scholars contest the relative merits of the United Nations definition versus alternative definitions, the importance of particular facets of the crime to understanding its fundamental nature, and which of the multitude of atrocities in the last century can truly be called genocide. This dialogue reflects the complex and difficult nature of the subject matter. Scholars examining genocide are attempting to comprehend the most heinous and extreme of crimes, and one that the perpetrators have often gone to great lengths to mask. An appropriate definition of genocide is a crucial tool through which to understand and interpret both specific instances of genocide and the phenomenon more generally. Yet no definition is without shortcomings or consequences. The definition of genocide has the power to influence how the history of genocide is written, and even which parts of that history are written. Furthermore, such discourse influences our response to contemporary issues surrounding genocide. This article will examine the strengths and weaknesses of various approaches to understanding genocide, and the impact of these approaches on the resulting scholarship.

DEFINING GENOCIDE

The term "genocide" was coined in 1944, by Polish Jewish scholar Raphael Lemkin, who combined the Greek *genos* (race, tribe) with the Latin *cide* (killing) to describe the horror of the Jewish experience in Hitler's Germany. In 1946, it was largely as a result of Lemkin's determined lobbying that the issue of the prevention and punishment of genocide was first addressed at the United Nations. After discussion in the General Assembly, on 11 December 1946, resolution 96-I was passed, declaring genocide to be a crime under international law, and requesting the Economic and Social Council of the UN to draw up a draft Convention. Lemkin's position as a consultant on the first draft of the Convention had considerable influence upon the proposed definition of "genocide." Many of his ideas, elucidated earlier in his seminal work *Axis Rule in Occupied Europe*, found strong expression in the draft. These included the concepts of cultural genocide as the destruction of the essential foundations of life of the group, biological genocide as the prevention of births within a group, and his focus upon racial and ethnic groups as those most in need of protection. This draft was then submitted to the Economic and Social Council, where, in extensive debate, almost every point was contested. The final wording of the definition of "genocide" and the provisions of the Convention were achieved through debate and compromise among the member states, which is strongly reflected in the document.

On 9 December 1948, the *Convention on the Prevention and the Punishment of the Crime of Genocide* was adopted by the General Assembly. The crime of genocide was defined as:

From Deborah Harris, "Defining Genocide: Defining History?" *Eras* (2001): 1–16. Reprinted with permission.

any of the following acts committed with intent to destroy, in whole or in part, a national, ethnical, racial or religious group, as such:

a. Killing members of the group;
b. Causing serious bodily or mental harm to members of the group;
c. Deliberately inflicting on the group conditions of life calculated to bring about its physical destruction in whole or in part;
d. Imposing measures intended to prevent births within the group;
e. Forcibly transferring children of the group to another group.

Genocide, conspiracy to commit genocide, direct and public incitement to commit genocide, attempt to commit genocide and complicity in genocide were all declared punishable. Contracting Parties, nations ratifying the Convention, acknowledged genocide as a crime under international law, "which they undertake to prevent and to punish." The Convention came into effect in 1951, after being ratified by the minimum of twenty nations, and it remains in effect and unmodified.

The *Genocide Convention* has provided scholars examining genocide with an internationally recognised definition with which to engage. However, as a definition designed to enable international action to address the crime, it is essentially legal in nature. It quickly became apparent that it was ill-suited for historical scholarship. Nevertheless, many genocide scholars have chosen to work with the UN definition of genocide, despite its legal construction. Those who use this definition do not deny these shortcomings, but point to its stance as an internationally recognised definition of this odious crime. This is the definition nations acknowledge when they ratify the *Genocide Convention,* and as such is of enormous significance. If nation states choose to address the problem of genocide at any level, they will almost certainly use the UN definition.

There are, however, distinct disadvantages to using this definition. Its narrowness has meant that a number of atrocities do not "qualify" as

genocide. In particular, political groups and social classes are not included under the Convention: political groups due to the opposition of Russia and the Eastern Bloc, and social classes due to the opposition of Western European democracies. Atrocities experienced by these groups must therefore be canvassed under titles such as "Related Atrocities" or excluded from analysis altogether. And indeed, the definition is so narrow that in 1986 the *Wall Street Journal* was able to point out that no genocide since the Holocaust had yet "qualified" under the UN criteria. The requirement that genocidal acts must be "committed with intent" also poses great difficulties, as intent is very difficult to prove conclusively.

A significant number of scholars investigating genocide have proposed and/or use an alternative definition to that provided by the UN. Alternative definitions have focused on one or a combination of elements that the author/s consider most fundamental to the nature of genocide. These have included the intent of the perpetrator, the type of acts that may be considered genocidal, the nature of the victim groups, and the role of the State as perpetrator. There are many such definitions in use. A good example is that formulated by Chalk and Jonassohn in *The History and Sociology of Genocide.* According to these authors, who focus primarily on perpetrator intent and the nature of the victim group, genocide is "A form of one-sided mass killing in which a state or other authority intends to destroy a group, as that group and membership in it are defined by the perpetrator." Scholars like Chalk and Jonassohn defend their use of an alternative definition on the grounds that the shortcomings of the UN definition make it untenable for historical scholarship. The use of an alternative definition overcomes these difficulties, and allows the historian to define the phenomenon of genocide more clearly and accurately.

However, such an approach is not without its own disadvantages. A plethora of alternative definitions of genocide now exist. While many are complementary, there are important differences and even contradictions between them, further complicated by distinctions drawn by some scholars between concepts such as "biological" and "cultural" genocide. Furthermore, a number of scholars have attempted to clarify the topic with more detailed typologies of genocide, which have been even more variable.

A third alternative has been to avoid the term altogether. Scholars have employed terms such as "democide," "state-sponsored mass murder," "ethnocide," "ethnic cleansing" and "politicide" to describe events otherwise referred to as genocide. Many of these terms have been utilised in situations where a label of genocide is contentious, for example in describing the persecution of a political group. While this is a valid option, it is one that only a minority of scholars have preferred. Those who have preferred this option must address many of the issues faced by scholars using an alternative definition of genocide, and are often left with a term that is not as readily understood.

The result is a scholarship that has focused a great deal of energy on the issue of defining genocide. Arguably, this has limited the scope of the scholarship. What is certain, however, is the impact of a chosen definition on the resulting analysis. For scholars examining genocide, whether historians, sociologists, psychologists or anthropologists, the definition employed serves as the filter through which events are understood and interpreted. For example, a definition that only recognises particular acts as "genocidal" may result in a history that focuses upon these events to the exclusion of others. In an area of investigation as complex as genocide studies, the definition of "genocide" can be crucial to our understanding and analysis of events.

The choice of the most appropriate definition also has wider ramifications. As the British sociologist Anthony Giddens has argued, "theorising in social science is not about an environment which is indifferent to it, but one whose character is open to change in respect of that theorising." That is, our understanding of past events can have contemporary consequences. In an area of study where those events are as extreme and as terrible as genocide, the scholar must be particularly mindful of such ramifications. For example, a determination of a past event as "genocide" or otherwise may influence survivors' claims for compensation, or the efforts of the international community to punish perpetrators. Perhaps even more significantly, attempts to prevent future occurrences of genocide rest upon our current understanding of the crime. A definition of genocide that provides a broader understanding may lead to more effective preventative measures.

Such consequences of genocide scholarship must be given serious attention. Two case studies, an examination of the Killing Fields of Cambodia and the experiences of Indigenous Australians in the last two centuries, highlight these potential consequences, and just how significant they can be. The pivotal role of the definition of genocide in our understanding of these histories, and our contemporary response to them, is readily apparent.

DEFINING HISTORY: THE CAMBODIAN GENOCIDE

On 17 April 1975 the Khmer Rouge gained control of Cambodia. Under Pol Pot, the Cambodian people were subjected to probably the most radical political, social and economic revolution ever. The Cambodian people knew only of *Angkar*, the "organisation," as the power behind the sudden transformation of their nation. Cities were evacuated, and the whole populace was forced to labour for *Angkar*, planting, tending and harvesting rice, constructing dams and irrigation channels, and clearing land for cultivation. There were no wages, and *Angkar* distributed food, usually inadequate quantities of rice. Schools and hospitals were closed, medical care became almost non-existent, the nation's currency and markets were abolished, and religion and cultural practices were suppressed. Numerous groups were targeted for persecution, and often treated as "enemies" to be eliminated. These included former urban dwellers, the Vietnamese and Chinese minorities, the Cham Muslim people, former government/military officials and the educated classes. Between April 1976 and January 1979, when the Vietnamese invasion of Cambodia ended the genocide, an estimated 1.5 million Cambodians out of a population of 8 million died. Major causes of death included execution, starvation, exhaustion and lack of medical care.

Historians have been instrumental in the task of investigating the atrocities that occurred in Cambodia under the Pol Pot regime. The role of the definition of genocide in influencing this history has been significant. Historians using the UN definition of genocide have gone to great lengths to classify the atrocities of the Pol Pot regime between 1975 and 1979. The provisions of the UN definition, and its limitation of victim groups to "national, ethnic, racial or religious" have meant that not all victims of the Khmer Rouge can be considered victims of genocide. However, researchers working in the period following the atrocities were able to gather evidence that several groups targeted by the Khmer Rouge did meet the criteria of the UN definition. These included minority Cham Muslims, Christians, Buddhist monks, and the Vietnamese and Chinese minorities. Arguably, Cambodians from the Khmer Rouge defined "Eastern Zone" of Cambodia may also be considered victims of genocide. Historians, most notably Ben Kiernan and Gregory Stanton, worked to gather evidence not only that these groups were particularly targeted by the Pol Pot regime, but also to prove beyond a reasonable doubt the genocidal intent of the Khmer Rouge. Such history is invaluable. Beyond documenting the period, this history serves to publicly declare the Killing Fields of Cambodia as genocide, placing pressure on the UN and nations that have ratified the *Genocide Convention*

to respond accordingly. Such careful determinations of genocide make it ever more difficult for governments concerned with political expediency to brush aside the atrocities.

However, there are other consequences of writing history using the UN definition of genocide, which must also be considered. The way we perceive the genocide in Cambodia is clearly influenced by the UN definition. As some victims of the atrocities are included as victims of genocide and others are excluded, does that imply that there is a qualitative difference in their experiences? Is it appropriate to accept, for example, that those victims of the atrocities targeted because they were from an educated class were subject to a different phenomenon from those targeted because they were Buddhist monks? Such questions are crucial to developing a fuller understanding of the genocide. Also important to consider in developing a comprehensive understanding of events are the perceptions of the Khmer Rouge perpetrators of the genocide. Did the Khmer Rouge perceive targeting ethnic and religious groups as qualitatively distinct from targeting social classes? Equally, the perspective of the victims must be considered. It is unlikely that Cambodians perceived these different groups targeted by the Khmer Rouge as subject to different persecutory campaigns. Memoirs from survivors certainly do not make such a differentiation. Are we then imposing a Western, even Orientalist interpretation upon these events? Indeed, one could suggest that the entire attempt to understand the atrocities of the Khmer Rouge through a categorisation according to Western labels is of little relevance to Cambodians.

Using the UN definition of genocide also influences not only how, but which parts of this history are written. The quest to establish minorities within Cambodia as victims of genocide, has perhaps led to an inordinate focus on the particular experiences of these groups. Considerably more research appears to have been conducted into those groups whose experiences may "qualify" as genocidal. This has resulted in a body of scholarship which has not focused sufficiently on the experiences of all of Cambodian society. Furthermore, a number of scholars have charged that authors such as Kiernan, in their efforts to declare the Cambodian experience "genocide," have focused on the racial nature of the killing to the exclusion of the influence of class, education, or political beliefs. This may result in a skewed understanding of the reasons victims were targeted under the Pol Pot regime.

The alternative approach to writing the history of the Cambodian genocide is to use a different definition of the word "genocide." Serge Thion, in an article entitled "Genocide as a Political Commodity," argues strongly that this would lead to a more accurate conception of the genocide. Thion argues that "generally speaking, people were persecuted under the DK [Democratic Kampuchea] regime because of what they believed, or were supposed by security organs to believe, and because of family links with those suspected of harbouring wrong beliefs or thoughts detrimental to the state." Furthermore, he reminds us that the greatest part of the human losses must be ascribed to the *economic* policy of the Khmer Rouge. According to Thion, the use of the UN definition of genocide in describing the atrocities in Cambodia leads to a particularly partisan, political interpretation of events, and one with which the Cambodians themselves would not identify. An alternative approach would allow a more inclusive history of the Killing Fields of Cambodia to be written. Victims of the Khmer Rouge were targeted for a number of reasons, and each of these reasons, and their combination, must be explored fully. A definition of genocide that facilitates such exploration will lead to a better understanding of events than one that restricts it.

Nevertheless, there may be some negative consequences to divorcing the history of the Cambodian atrocities from the UN legal definition of genocide. Since the time of the Killing Fields, efforts to bring the Khmer Rouge

leadership to justice have been slow and inadequate. In this time, historical scholarship on the atrocities has been a strong source of pressure calling for the punishment of the crime of genocide under the *Genocide Convention*. Removing this pressure would not only decrease the focus on an appropriate response to this heinous crime, but may also influence the perception of public pressure in responding to future genocides.

DEFINING HISTORY: INDIGENOUS–SETTLER RELATIONS IN AUSTRALIA

The definition of genocide has also been of great significance to the discussion around the Stolen Generations in Australia in recent times. The "Stolen Generations" is a term that refers to the victims of Australia's former policy of forcibly removing Aboriginal children from their families and communities. This was a systematic policy of State, Territory and Federal governments, with the aim of assimilating Aboriginal children into Anglo-Australian culture. Children, at a very young age, were routinely removed from their parents, and placed in institutions, or fostered or adopted into white families. Parents were disallowed contact with their children, and in most cases had no legal recourse. This policy spanned 150 years of Australia's history, and was pursued until the late 1960s. The proportion of Aboriginal children subjected to removal is estimated at between one in three and one in ten. The consequences of this policy to Indigenous Australians have included broken families, loss of language, culture and connection to traditional lands, fractured communities and a negative impact on physical and mental health. The term "Stolen Generations," first used by Australian historian Peter Read, reflects not only the forcible nature of the removal, but some of the anguish that resulted from this policy.

In 1997, *Bringing Them Home: Report of the National Inquiry into the Separation of Aboriginal and Torres Strait Islander Children from their Families*, examined the issue of genocide and the Stolen Generations. Using the UN definition of genocide, the report concluded that the events under question did, in fact, constitute genocide. In light of this conclusion, it is perhaps surprising that "genocide" is a word used rarely, and only very recently, in describing the history of Indigenous Australian and non–Indigenous Australian relations. As Colin Tatz describes so aptly, "Almost all historians of the Aboriginal experience—black and white—avoid it. They write about pacifying, killing, cleansing, excluding, exterminating, starving, poisoning, shooting, beheading, sterilising, exiling, removing—but avoid genocide." Perhaps one explanation for the reluctance to use the term "genocide" in describing Indigenous–Settler relations can be traced back to the nature of the UN definition. In this legal definition, genocide is described as one or more of a number of acts. This effectively equates the act of "Killing members of the group" with "Forcibly transferring children of the group to another group," an equation which invites direct comparison of events as disparate as the experiences of the Stolen Generations with those of the Jews in Nazi Germany. Few historians are comfortable with this type of analysis.

However it is understandable that even historians who give little import to such concerns may hesitate to use the word "genocide" in describing the experiences of the Stolen Generations. It is extraordinary to suggest that while the experiences of the Stolen Generations are considered genocide under the UN definition, the decimation of ninety per cent of Indigenous Australians between 1788 and 1900, may not "qualify." As Tony Barta elucidates in "Relations of Genocide: Land and Lives in the Colonisation of Australia," "It [the term genocide] has succeeded in devaluing all other concepts of less planned destruction, even if the effects are the same. To be *really* terrible, an ordeal inflicted on a people now has to be 'genocidal.'" Barta believes "If they [historians] have

not spoken of genocide—the word appears very rarely—it is for reasons of definition which have made the concept inadequate in a case crying out for its use." One can understand the historian's reluctance to use the term "genocide" in describing the experience of the Stolen Generations if in doing so there may be an implicit devaluation of the earlier decimation of the Indigenous Australian population.

Nevertheless, the historian must consider the ramifications of excluding the term "genocide" from such discourse. Such an omission may serve to devalue the experiences of the Stolen Generations, particularly given the conclusions presented in *Bringing Them Home*. Admittedly, thus far there have been fairly negative political consequences to this classification of the Stolen Generations. The political response has been to reject and discount this conclusion, and use this polemic to avoid seriously considering a plethora of related historical and Indigenous issues. Indeed, the role of this political response in influencing the use or omission of the term "genocide" from discussion surrounding the Stolen Generations can be a powerful force itself. However, as the political discussion on this issue continues, and particularly as it encompasses issues of a possible treaty and reparations, it may become a far more useful category for conceptualising the history of the Stolen Generations. Historians working in this area must consider not only immediate but more long term consequences of their history.

A small number of scholars have chosen to use the term "genocide" in their discussion of Settler–Indigenous relations in Australia. Colin Tatz has analysed the Indigenous Australian experience in light of the UN definition of genocide. He believes Australia may be guilty of multiple acts of genocide:

> Australia is guilty of at least three ... acts of genocide: first, the essentially private genocide, the physical killing committed by settlers and rogue police officers in the nineteenth century, while the state, in the form of the colonial authorities,

stood silently by (for the most part); second, the twentieth century official state policy and practice of forcibly transferring children from one group to another with the express intention that *they cease being Aboriginal*; third, the twentieth century attempts to achieve the biological disappearance of those deemed "half-caste" Aborigines.

Tatz highlights that not only genocide, but also "complicity in genocide," is punishable under the Articles of the *Genocide Convention*— a provision almost invariably overlooked. Furthermore, he also explores a very interesting issue surrounding the definitional problems associated with the requirement of "intent to destroy, in whole or in part" in the UN definition. The definition does not rule out, either implicitly or explicitly, intent with *bona fides*, good faith, "for their own good." It may therefore be possible to conclude that the ultimate purpose of the crime is irrelevant, as long as intentional destruction of a protected group takes place.

There is also a recognisable trend towards using an alternative definition of genocide when using this term to describe Settler–Indigenous relations. Tony Barta argues strongly for a different definition of genocide to that provided by the UN. Barta believes that it would be more useful to develop a conception of genocide which focuses upon relations of destruction, and without the current emphasis on the policies and intentions which brought it in to being. Alison Palmer argues that nineteenth century Queensland witnessed a distinctive form of genocide between 1840 and 1897. While she believes "The structure and resources of the Queensland government were so limited during this period that any plan to systematically annihilate the Aborigines would have failed," this does not prevent her from referring to the events in Colonial Queensland as a case of genocide. However, intent to destroy a group is required by the UN definition for an atrocity to be considered genocide. Palmer justifies her choice of terminology with the contention that it is only through

examining colonial genocides, atrocities which mostly do not fit the narrow UN definition, that we can develop a richer definition of genocide and a clearer understanding of genocides more generally.

Clearly, there are very significant potential consequences associated with the choice of terminology by the scholar in the field of Settler–Indigenous relations. The use of the UN definition of genocide has the advantage of keeping the issue firmly on the Australian political agenda. However, an alternative definition of genocide, without the restrictions of the UN definition, may lead to a more comprehensive history of the Indigenous experience of dispossession, murder and removal in the last two centuries.

CONCLUSION

Defining genocide has been a contentious task for historians. The ongoing and often passionate debate surrounding the most appropriate definition is a reflection of its power to influence and shape the resulting scholarship. Indeed, we have seen how differing conceptions of genocide have led historians of both the Cambodian and Australian genocides to focus on very different facets and interpretations of events. While some of these have been complementary, for others the interpretation differs so widely as to be highly conflicting. In light of these findings, the important question to be considered is "Which definition leads to better history?" That is, which definition most facilitates a fuller recording of events, and a broader understanding of the meaning of these events?

I believe the answer lies in a more inclusive definition of genocide. Few would argue with the proposition that genocide is a complex, extreme event. Yet most definitions are relatively narrow, asserting a small number of descriptors as fundamental for an atrocity to be "genocide," and then insisting that all such criteria must be met for the event to "qualify." This focus diverts the scholar's attention from developing a comprehensive examination of genocide. In addition, events that appear to be of a similar nature, but do not meet these rigorous criteria, are excluded from our understanding of genocide. A more inclusive definition would encourage more comprehensive explorations of genocidal events, as scholars seek to discover the range of mechanisms involved in particular occurrences. Furthermore, the inclusion of atrocities not currently reckoned as genocide would increase our understanding of the phenomenon more generally, leading to a richer concept of genocide.

A more inclusive conception might accept only one or two criteria as essential for a definition of genocide, such as a targeted victim group and some type of genocidal process. Other facets of the crime, such as perpetrator intent, the role of the State and so forth could be recognised as likely to play a role, but not essential. As noted earlier, Chalk and Jonassohn's definition of genocide, as "a form of one-sided mass killing in which a state or other authority intends to destroy a group, as that group and membership in it are defined by the perpetrator" is a good example of an alternative conception of genocide. However, it requires that perpetrator intent be provable. A broader definition might read "A form of one-sided mass killing in which a state and/or other authority/ies target a specific victim group, as that group and membership in it are defined by the perpetrator." This would allow the inclusion of atrocities in which perpetrator intent is problematic, or in which perpetrators only partially fulfilled their genocidal aims. It would also encompass instances where the organisation of genocidal acts was decentralised. Such a definition would include, for example, colonial settlers killing Indigenous inhabitants, while colonial authorities ignored or were complicit in the killings. Israel Charny, a noted Holocaust schol-

ar, extends this argument still further. Charny believes that all mass killing should be regarded as genocide, with cases being classified in different subgroups according to their characteristics.

The definition proposed above limits our understanding of genocide to instances of mass killing. However, there are other types of destruction of a group that may also be considered genocide. Indeed, the UN definition acknowledges that causing serious harm to members of a group, imposing measures intended to prevent births within a group and forcible transfer of children of a group to another group may all be considered genocidal acts. To encompass acts such as these, where clearly the aim is one of destroying a victim group but where mass killing may not be involved, I believe a broader definition is required. I suggest the following definition may be most appropriate. "Genocide is a one-sided attempt by a state or other authority/ies to destroy a specific victim group, as that group and membership in it are defined by the perpetrator." I believe the goal of the destruction of a victim group lies at the core of our understanding of genocide; the means of destruction, whether they be mass killing or forced assimilation, are designed to meet this goal. Therefore I believe that a definition that focuses upon this fundamental aspect of genocide, and does not preclude from consideration any atrocities in which this aspect is present, will lead to the most comprehensive understanding of genocide.

We have also seen the influence that genocide scholarship can have on contemporary events, and how significant that impact can be. I believe that the responsible historian must always be mindful of these potential consequences. While the *Genocide Convention* remains in effect, there is a strong argument for considering atrocities also in light of the UN definition of genocide. Only thus can the perpetrators of genocide be held responsible for their actions under international law. An examination of an event utilising both the UN definition and a more inclusive definition may be ideal in this circumstance, resulting in a comprehensive history and ensuring there will not be negative contemporary consequences.

Ultimately, however, I believe that a more inclusive definition of genocide will result in a scholarship with the most positive future rami- fications. Scholars, activists and even governments that address the question of preventing genocide rely on a comprehensive understanding of the nature of the crime to do so; historians and other scholars provide the bulk of this information. An historical scholarship that can provide a comprehensive, balanced understanding of the crime of genocide will provide the basis upon which the most effective preventative measures can be implemented.

MAKING CONNECTIONS

1. According to Deborah Harris, what are the "distinct disadvantages" to using the UN definition of genocide?

2. How is Chalk and Jonassohn's definition different from the UN definition?

3. In the case study of Cambodia, how does defining genocide influence how history is written?

4. What are the "Stolen Generations" in Australia?

5. Why is the term "genocide" not applied in the Stolen Generations discussion, according to Tony Barta?

✔ RECOMMENDED RESOURCES

Andreopoulos, George J., ed. *Genocide: Conceptual and Historical Dimensions.* Philadelphia: University of Pennsylvania Press, 1994.

Chalk, Frank, and Kurt Jonassohn. *The History and Sociology of Genocide: Analyses and Case Studies.* New Haven, CT: Yale University Press, 1990.

Charny, Israel W., ed. *Encyclopedia of Genocide*, Vol. 1 and Vol. 2, Santa Barbara, CA:ABC–CLIO, 1999.

Dorst, Pieter N. *The Crime of State: Penal Protection for Fundamental Freedoms of Persons and Peoples,* Bk. 1, *International Governmental Crimes Against Individual Human Rights*, Bk. 2, *Genocide: United Nations Legislation on International Criminal Law* Leyden, MA: A. W. Sythoff-Leyden, 1959.

Fein, Helen. *Genocide: A Sociological Perspective.* London: Sage, 1993.

Horowitz, Irving Louis. *Taking Lives: Genocide and State Power.* 4th ed., exp. Piscataway, NJ: Transaction Publishers, 1997.

Kressel, Neil J. *Mass Hate: The Global Rise of Genocide and Terror.* Boulder, CO: Westview Press, 2002.

Kuper, Leo. *The Prevention of Genocide.* New Haven, CT: Yale University Press, 1985.

Mills, Nicolaus, and Kira Brunner, eds. *The New Killing Fields: Massacre and the Politics of Intervention.* New York: Basic Books, 2002.

Power, Samantha. *A Problem From Hell: America and the Age of Genocide.* New York: Basic Books, 2002.

Totten, Samuel, William Parsons, and Israel Charny, eds. *Century of Genocide: Eyewitness Accounts and Critical Views.* New York: Garland Publishing, Inc., 1997.

Wallimann, Isidor, and Michael N. Dobkowski, eds. *Etiology and Case Studies of Mass Death.* New York: Syracuse University Press, 1987.

CHAPTER 1

CLOSE TO HOME: NATIVE AMERICAN GENOCIDE

In any field of study, there are major differences of opinion among scholars about a wide range of issues. One of the most contentious issues among historians is the application of the term "genocide." For instance, could the murders of large numbers of black slaves taken forcibly from Africa to the New World and the dehumanizing conditions imposed on them thereafter, be classified as genocide or not? As Israel W. Charny points out in his introduction to the *Encyclopedia of Genocide*, "There are many scholars who want to have pure definitions of genocide. For example, one scholar writes that '*torching villages, killing men, and even wiping out communities are often done without the intent to eliminate an entire people,*' and therefore, for this scholar these events may be called *mass murder, massacre,* or *slaughter, human rights abuses, annihilation, pogroms*—or anything but *genocide.*"

Refusing to acknowledge genocide may be deliberate, as it is in many specific instances, such as the American reluctance to apply the "g-word" to its history with Native Americans. A spate of recent scholarship, however, with titles such as *Stolen Continents: The "New World" Through Indian Eyes*, by Ronald Wright; *The Invasion of America: Indians, Colonialism, and the Cant of Conquest*, by Francis Jennings; *American Indian Holocaust and Survival: A Population History Since 1492*, by Russell Thornton; and *American Holocaust: Columbus and the Conquest of the New World*, by David E. Stannard, indicate a sympathetic scholarly shift toward labeling Indian/White history a "holocaust" or "genocide."

Chapter One examines a more familiar subject for Americans, and one closer to home—the treatment of indigenous peoples by invading Europeans. The application of the terms "genocide" and "holocaust" to this part of America's history generates exciting debate among historians. In the reading "The Pequot War Reconsidered," Steven Katz, professor of Near Eastern Studies (Judaica) at Cornell University, analyzes the intent of the English settlers to exterminate the Pequots in that conflict.

The reading "Nits Make Lice," by Ward Churchill, concludes this chapter. The author is an enrolled Keetoowah Cherokee and professor of American Indian Studies with the Department of Ethics at the University of Colorado/Boulder. Churchill elaborates on the subsequent genocidal intent of Americans in his book, *A Little Matter of Genocide: Holocaust and Denial in the Americas 1492 to the Present*. The reading included here is an excerpt from that book.

The Pequot War Reconsidered

Steven T. Katz,
Cornell University

It is well known that in the 1970s and 1980s traditional scholarly analyses and judgments of the motives and events surrounding the Pequot War of 1637 came to be revised. In place of the view that the English were simply protecting themselves by preemptively attacking the Pequots, the revisionists argued that the Europeans used earlier, limited threats against them as cause to bring mass destruction on the Pequots. That assault is then taken to be a harbinger, a symbol of a larger, premeditated exterminatory intent that characterized the invasion of the New World. While there is surely room for a more penetrating critical reconstruction of the meaning of America's conquest and settlement than has yet appeared, one must be cautious in allowing legitimate moral outrage at the treatment of the Indians to substitute for a careful sorting of the evidence about the Pequot War. If we examine the facts closely and try to analyze them within their particular historical context, our judgments of the wrongs done the Native Americans will be more nuanced, balanced, and discriminating than radicalizing polemics allow and thus ultimately will better serve our efforts to understand the processes and consequences of colonization.

I

My first cautionary comment regarding the war is that it should not be viewed in strictly racial or ethnic terms of Red vs. White. I do not dispute that the colonists viewed the Indians through racial stereotypes, or that those stereo-types affected their behavior, but the particular circumstances of the Pequot War certainly seem to argue against the charge that it was a universal offensive against "Indianness" per se. The most telling of these circumstances is the presence of rival Indian groups on the side of the colonists. The crucial role of the Narragansetts, first in rejecting Pequot overtures to join a pan-Indian front against the English and then, in October 1636, in allying with the English against the Pequot, is but the earliest and most prominent case of European–Indian collaboration in the conflict. Following this alliance, the Mohegans, the Massachusetts and River Tribes, and later the Mohawks all sided with the British. Although the reasons for these alliances have been disputed for three centuries, seventeenth-century evidence—for example, the "Remonstrance of New Netherland," John Winthrop's *History of New England,* and John De Forest's *History of the Indians*—is clear that at least intermittent hostility between the Pequots and the Narragansetts and their tributaries preceded the war.

Once we are able to hold our charges of racism in reserve, we can attend to the specifics of the war. Our distance from the events obviously blurs our vision. Many facts about the war have been contested, including the particular causes for the outbreak of hostilities; however, there can be no doubt that both sides had cause to feel aggrieved. From the perspective of most Indians, exceptions notwithstanding, the very presence of the European was an act of aggression. Filling in the outlines of this generalized aggression was an already considerable

The New England Quarterly V. 64, no. 2 June 1991 for "Pequot War Reconsidered" by Steven T. Katz. Copyright held by *The New England Quarterly.* Reproduced by permission of the publisher and the author.

and well-documented body of particular crimes committed by unscrupulous individuals like John Oldham, whose murder in 1636 set in motion the events that led to the war. Oldham was not, moreover, the only Englishman the Pequots or their tributaries had murdered. In 1634 they had killed two English captains, including the notorious and disreputable John Stone, who had kidnapped and held several Indians for ransom, and in the next two years they had killed at least six more colonists. Alternatively, the English leadership was disturbed that the Pequots had taken no action against the guilty among them and disheartened that the Pequots had abrogated the terms of the treaty they had signed. Fears increased when Jonathan Brewster, a Plymouth trader, passed word that Uncas, sachem of the Mohegans, had reported that

> the Pequents have some mistrust, that the English will shortly come against them (which I take is by indiscreet speeches of some of your people here to the Natives) and therefore out of desperate madnesse doe threaten shortly to sett upon both Indians [Mohegans] and English, joyntly.

Uncas may well have fabricated the rumor, but the colonists were certainly in a frame of mind to take it seriously. Their numbers were small, and news of the Virginia uprising of 1622, with its 350 casualties, had still not faded from memory. What the Puritans sought was a stratagem that would put an end to unpredictable, deadly annoyances as well as forestall any larger, more significant Indian military action like that suggested by Uncas's report. However one estimates the "good faith" or lack thereof of the Massachusetts leadership, efforts were made to negotiate, but these efforts failed, or at least were perceived to have failed. The colonists then chose as their best course of action a retaliatory raid, intended both to punish and to warn, on the Indians of Block Island, who were specifically charged with Oldham's murder.

The Pequots were involved, according to William Hubbard, because the murderers had "fled presently to the Pequods, by whom they were sheltered, and so became also guilty themselves of his blood."

Ninety Englishmen participated in the raid commanded by John Endecott. John Winthrop noted that Endecott was ordered

> to put to death the men of Block Island, but to spare the women and children, and to bring them away, and to take possession of the Island; and from thence to go to the Pequods to demand the murderers of Capt. Stone and other English, and one thousand fathom of wampom for damages, etc., and some of their children as hostages.

None of the mainland Pequot at Pequot Harbor were to be harmed if they capitulated to his demands. In the event, the raid on Block Island turned into an extensive assault, and the Indian settlement there was looted and burned. However, although property was destroyed and several Indians were wounded, "the Naymen killed not a man, save that one Kichomiquim, an Indian Sachem of the Bay, killed a Pequot." The fact that only one Indian was killed seems to confirm John Winthrop's belief that the colonists "went not to make war upon [the Pequots] but to do justice." Not all colonists defined "justice" as Winthrop did, however, for the Endecott raid on the Harbor Indians was condemned by the colonial leaders of Plymouth, Connecticut, and Fort Saybrook.

In response to Endecott's assaults, the Pequots plagued the settlers with a series of raids, ambushes, and annoyances. On 23 April, Wethersfield, Connecticut, was attacked. Nine were killed, including a woman and child, and two additional young women were captured. A number of other raids claimed the lives of thirty Europeans, or five percent of all the settlers in Connecticut. In addition to these offensive actions, the Pequot set about developing alliances, particularly with the Narragansett, to galvanize support for a war to destroy European settlement in their territory, if not in New England entirely. Many colonists who learned of the plan for a broad effort against them, which was frustrated only at the last minute through the intervention of Roger Williams, rightly felt, given their demographic vulnerability, that their very survival was threatened. Even Francis Jennings, the most severe critic of Puritan behavior, acknowledges that "Had these [Pequot] proposals [for alliance with the Narragansetts] been accepted by the Narragansetts, there would have without a doubt arisen a genuine Indian menace ... Whether the colonies could long have maintained themselves under such conditions is open to serious question."

The Pequot War was the organized reaction of the colonists of Connecticut and Massachusetts to these intimidating events. In choosing to make war, they were choosing to put an end to threats to their existence as individuals and as a community. They did not decide to fight out of some a priori lust for Indian blood based on some metaphysical doctrine of Indian inferiority, however much they may have held that view, or some desire for further, even complete, control over Indian territory, much as they coveted such land. They fought, initially, a defensive war. They may well have provoked events, as even Winthrop tacitly acknowledged, by their over-reactive raid on Block Island, but, in the early stages of the conflict, they did not intend to enter into a full-scale war with the Pequot until the Pequot raised the stakes with their response to the events at Block Island and Pequot Harbor. Of course the Indians cannot be blamed for so replying, for they too saw themselves as acting legitimately in self-defense, both narrowly and more generally in defense of traditional Indian rights to their own native lands. In effect, both sides acted to defend what they perceived as rightly theirs. In this context, if either side can be said to have harbored larger geo-political ambitions, it was the Pequot, though defeat would certainly bury those desires.

The major action of the war was an attack by 70 Connecticut and 90 Massachusetts colonists along with 60 Mohegans, plus some scattered Narragansett and Eastern Niantics, against the Pequot Fort at Mystic, which held an Indian population of between 400 and 700, including women and children. The colonists and their Indian allies surprised the Pequots and burned their fort to the ground. During the battle two English soldiers were killed and about 20 were wounded, while almost half the Indians allied with them were killed or wounded; almost all the Pequots were killed.

Richard Drinnon, in his *Facing West: The Metaphysics of Indian Hating and Empire Building* (1980), has argued that the unusual violence of the operation signals the colonists' "genocidal intentions." In evaluating the behavior of the English in this particular instance, however, it should be recognized that the tactics employed were neither so unconventional nor so novel that they can be taken to mark a turning point in Puritan-Indian relations, nor were they so distinctive as to indicate a transformation in Puritan awareness of the otherness of their adversaries. Given the relative strength of the enemy, the inexperience of the colonial forces, and the crucial fact that Sassacus, chief of the Pequot, and his warriors were camped only five miles from Mystic Fort and were sure to arrive soon, as in fact they did, one need not resort to dramatic theories of genocidal intentionality to explain the actions of the English. The simple, irrefutable fact is that had the battle been prolonged, Sassacus would have had time to reach Mystic and deflect the English attack.

II

Although he does not use the term *genocide* per se, it is clear from the rhetorical thrust of his argument and his use of phrases like "deliberate massacre" that Francis Jennings is an insistent advocate of the genocidal thesis. Given the force of his prose, the popularity of his work, and its long-standing influence, it is useful to deconstruct Jennings's argument to evaluate the legitimacy of the heinous charge leveled against the English colonists.

Jennings attributes to Capt. John Mason, the expedition's leader, an overt, *ab initio* desire to massacre the Indians. "Mason proposed," he writes,

> to avoid attacking Pequot warriors, which would have overtaxed his unseasoned, unreliable troops. Battle, as such, was not his purpose. Battle is only one of the ways to destroy an enemy's will to fight. Massacre can accomplish the same end with less risk, and Mason had determined that massacre would be his objective.

Ignoring all other reports of Mason's intentions and actions, Jennings bases his conclusions on Mason's own terse account of the event. Jennings cites Mason's reasons for his strategy, with special reference to his concluding "'and also some other [reasons],'" which he says "'I shall forebear to trouble you with.'" Even Jennings labels this comment cryptic, but he still does not forebear using it as unambiguous evidence of a hidden, premeditated plan to massacre all the Indians at Fort Mystic.

Jennings also refers to Mason's discussion with his colleagues Lt. Lion Gardiner and Capt. John Underhill as well as with the expedition's Chaplain Stone. He takes Mason's request that the chaplain "'commend our Condition to the Lord, that night, to direct how in what manner we should demean our selves'" to be a covert reference to the existence of a plan to massacre the Indians the next day. But on the eve of such a battle, especially given Puritan sensibilities, such a request is neither surprising nor, given the text before us, indicative of any special intent; to read it as an implicit confession of genocidal desire, Jennings has to over-interpret the brief original source dramatically.

Jennings charges that "all the secondary accounts of the Pequot conquest squeamishly evade confessing the deliberateness of Mason's strategy, and some falsify to conceal it." What Jennings adduces as confirmation of both the premeditated plot to massacre and the later conscious suppression of that fact emerges in the course of a curious argument, which I quote in full.

> Mason's own narrative is the best authority on this point. The Massachusetts Puritans' William Hubbard brazened out his own misquotation by telling his readers to "take it as it was delivered in writing by that valiant, faithful, and prudent Commander Capt. Mason." With this emphatic claim to authority he quoted Mason as saying, "We had resolved a while not to have burned it [the village], but being we could not come at them, I resolved to set it on fire." Despite Hubbard's assurance, these were not Mason's words. His manuscript said bluntly, "we had formerly concluded to destroy them by the Sword and save the Plunder."

Jennings's conclusion does not follow logically from the texts he cites nor from his juxtaposition of them. They neither suggest premeditation to massacre nor falsification of the record; instead, Hubbard's paraphrase of Mason's words accords perfectly with his stated intent to plunder the settlement. Jennings himself recognizes that such economic motives were central to the Block Island raid, as well as other actions by the English. Burning Fort Mystic would, of course, severely limit its economic potential; the sword was a less efficient tool of human destruction but would preserve goods of value to the English. In fact, Mason's vow to "destroy" the Pequots "by the Sword" is a phrase not at all unusual to the language of military conflict and in that context such comments almost always signal not the annihilation of the enemy but the disruption of its capacity to fight. This understanding of Mason's comment is supported by the Puritans' further prosecution of the war.

Jennings continues to press home his point in his increasingly confused and confusing reconstruction of events. I quote:

> The rest of Mason's manuscript revealed what sort of inhabitants had been occupying the Mystic River village and proved conclusively that mere victory over them was not enough to satisfy Mason's purpose. After telling how the attack was launched at dawn of May 26, and how entrance to the village was forced, the account continued thus:

> At length William Heydon espying the Breach in the Wigwam, supposing some English might be there, entred; but in his Entrance fell over a dead Indian; but speedily recovering himself, the Indians some fled, others crept under their Beds: the Captain [Mason] going out of the Wigwam saw many Indians in the Lane or Street; he making towards them, they fled, were pursued to the End of the Lane, where they were met by Edward Pattison, Thomas Barber, with some others; where seven of them were Slain, as they said. The Captain facing about, Marched a slow Pace up the Lane he came down, perceiving himself very much out of Breath; and coming to the other End near the Place where he first entred, saw two Soldiers standing close to the Pallizado with their Swords pointed to the Ground: The Captain told them that We should never kill them after that manner: The Captain also said, WE MUST BURN THEM: and immediately stepping into the Wigwam where he had been before, brought out a Fire Brand, and putting it into the Matts with which they were covered, set the Wigwams on Fire.

From this sparse, unsophisticated description, Jennings concludes that "It is terribly clear ... that the village, stockaded though it was, had few warriors at home when the attack took place." Mason himself, however, asserts that just the day before the English attack, 150 braves had reinforced the Indian garrison holding the fort, but Jennings cavalierly dismisses this claim in a marvelous display of selective reading. The reasons he musters for denying Mason's express testimony on such a vital matter are offered both in Jennings's text and in a dizzying footnote. The burden of the main argument is that insofar as Mason's account portrays

Indians fleeing and creeping under their beds for protection, those so described could only have been "women, children, and feeble old men," who had no other recourse but to resort to such cowardly stratagems. Surely 150 warriors—and the Pequots had already well demonstrated "their willingness to fight to the death"—would not have "suddenly and uncharacteristically turned craven." At the end of this convoluted denial of part—and only part, indeed the most straightforward and factual part—of Mason's account is Jennings's assumption that Mason marched on Fort Mystic because he had received advance intelligence from Narragansett allies that "there were no 'reinforcements.'" Destroying the "wretches" would be easily accomplished.

But the original narratives of the battle suggest a very different reading. Mason indicates that he found his first plan unworkable, that only after the attack had begun did he realize how costly it might prove for the English; only then, in self-protection, did he make the decision to burn rather than to plunder the settlement. This analysis of events is confirmed by Underhill's record of the battle, which also has the virtue of emphasizing the bravery of the Indians involved. "Most courageously," he writes, "these Pequots behaved themselves." Only when the battle grew too intense did the British, out of necessity, torch the fort. Even then, Underhill states, "many courageous fellows were unwilling to come out and fought most desperately through the palisadoes ... and so perished valiantly. Mercy did they deserve for their valor, could we have had opportunity to bestow it." Jennings does not cite Underhill's crucial and disarming testimony; instead, he engages in some more verbal sleight of hand, carefully choosing the texts he wishes to manipulate.

In a footnote he replays his charge against Mason. Leaving out only the citations, I quote in full:

…Underhill and Hubbard omitted the reinforcements assertion. Winthrop assigned as Pequot casualties "two chief sachems, and one hundred and fifty fighting men, and about one hundred and fifty old men, women, and children." … Mason's and Winthrop's "reinforcements" thus became Winthrop's total of warrior casualties. Even if this is true, it means that Mason planned the attack before those warriors arrived, but the likelihood of its truth is remote. No matter how these wriggly texts are viewed, they testify to Mason's deliberate purpose of massacring noncombatants. He had advance information of the Pequot dispositions.

First, it should be recognized that because Underhill and Hubbard do not mention the 150 Indian reinforcements, Jennings uses their silence as confirmation of the dishonesty of Mason's account. But arguments from silence "say" very little, and extreme caution should be exercised in employing them, especially in the face of explicit testimony to the contrary. Jennings next uses Winthrop's narrative, which supports Mason's claim about reinforcements, to diminish that claim by impugning Winthrop's veracity. But such doublethink will not do, for if Winthrop is unreliable, the truth of his account "remote," he cannot serve to discredit Mason; if he is reliable, his depiction of events cannot be taken lightly. Then, out of this morass of conflicting facts and conclusions, Jennings draws the non sequitur that Mason was intent on massacring noncombatant Pequots; in fact, all contemporary accounts simply state that noncombatants were massacred, not that there was any premeditated plan to do so. It appears that Jennings would have us believe that his highly ambiguous, contradictory reconstruction of the facts proposed 340 years after the event and premised on a dubious dialectical analysis of silence, a great deal of hermeneutical confusion, and a series of non sequiturs is to be given precedence over the description of circumstances provided by several contemporary and first-person accounts in our possession. Assuredly, the Connecticut militiamen acted reprehensibly and with unnecessary severity against noncombatants that spring day in 1637, but they did not do so for the reasons, nor in the manner, advanced in Jennings's moving, but untrue, retelling of the tale.

III

Following the destruction of Mystic Fort, the colonists and their Indian allies pursued the surviving Pequots. In the first major encounter of this subsequent stage in the conflict, approximately 200 Indians were captured, of whom 22 or 24 were adult males; these braves were executed. The remaining women and children, almost 80 percent of the total captured, were parceled up about evenly, as was common Indian practice, among the victorious Indian allies and the colonists of Massachusetts Bay. A second and larger engagement took place on 14 July near modern Southport, Connecticut, where Sassacus and the majority of the remaining Pequots, numbering several hundred, were surrounded. In the ensuing battle, women, children, and old men, again a majority of the Pequots present, were allowed to seek sanctuary while about 80 warriors fought to their death. In the final phase of the war, various Indian tribes in the area, vying for English friendship and seeking to settle old tribal debts, hunted down and murdered Pequot braves while dispersing their womenfolk and children. Sassacus was killed, and in early August the Mohawks sent his head to the British in Hartford.

Alden Vaughan describes the aftermath of these events:

> Toward the end of 1637 the few remaining sachems begged for an end to the war, promising vassalage in return for their lives. A peace convention was arranged for the following September. With the Treaty of Hartford, signed on September 21, 1638, the Pequots ceased to exist as an independent polity.

The treaty arrangement as well as the previous pattern of killing all adult males suggests that the anti-Pequot forces, both Indian and European, were determined to eliminate the Pequot threat once and for all. The 180 Pequots captured in the assault on Sassacus were parceled out among the victors: 80 to the Narragansett, 80 to the Mohegans, and 20 to the Eastern Niantics. The survivors were now no longer to be known as Pequots or to reside in their tribal lands, and the Pequot River was renamed the Thames and the Pequot village, New London. These treaty stipulations, which required the extinction of Pequot identity and the assignment of Pequot survivors to other tribes, and some to slavery, suggest an overt, unambiguous form of *cultural* genocide, here employed in the name of military security. However, the dispersement of the remaining communal members—the elderly, the women, and the children, almost certainly a majority of the tribe as a whole—directly contradicts the imputation of any intent to commit *physical* genocide, as some revisionists insist.

A more constrained reading of events would not deny that the Puritans, as their postwar writings reflect, were conscious that they had acted with great, perhaps even excessive, destructive force. Almost certainly composed as responses to English and Indian critics, these after-the-fact appraisals should not, however, be misconstrued as evidence of either genocidal intent prior to the event or even of genocidal behavior during and after the war. Rather, given the Puritan mentality, saturated as it was with concerns to detect God's providential design in temporal matters, these post-hoc accountings, even were we to call them rationalizations, were attempts to satisfy the Puritans' own internal axiological demand that their taking of lives on such a large scale, and in such a bloody way, was justified. Puritans had to know, and they wanted their critics to know, that what they had done was

sanctioned by heaven. This concern for ethical legitimation should not be mistaken as evidence that the Puritans, however aware they were *after the event* of the contentious nature of the massacre they had wrought, looked upon this happening as signaling some fundamental re-orientation in their relationship either to their New World surroundings in general or with their New England Indian neighbors in particular. Neither Edward Johnson's approval of the Puritan preachers' exhortation to "execute vengeance upon the heathen," nor William Bradford's description of the burning of the inhabitants at Fort Mystic as a "sweet sacrifice" to the Lord, nor Underhill's appeal to scriptural precedent that in conquering a grossly evil people, such as the Pequot, "women and children must perish with their parents" are proof to the contrary. Indeed, they are exactly the sort of theological pronouncements one would expect within the Puritan conceptual environment, fed as it was by recycled scriptural paradigms.

In general, the English did not relish their victory in an unseemly way. John Mason, for example, "refused to publish his accounts of his exploits, deeming them too immodest and likely to detract from the glory ascribed to God in those events." Captain Underhill, by contrast, did publish his version of the tale, but as Richard Slotkin has written, "Captain Underhill was a man clearly out of step with the Massachusetts way and one proscribed and exiled by the Puritan community." Underhill's "enthusiasms," in fact, were repeatedly met with censure rather than emulation. Mason, by contrast, the modest, self-effacing, God-extolling leader, was considered a worthy model in early American literature.

When the actions of the Puritans are placed in their appropriate context, when they are deconstructed as part and parcel of the historical reality of the seventeenth century, the accusations of genocide leveled against them are recognized to be exaggerations. However excessive the force wielded by the colonists, they had already seen—and would continue to see—their own die at the hands of the Indians. The Virginia Indian uprisings of 1622 have already been mentioned. In April 1644, a second uprising took the lives of approximately 500 whites, and in 1675, 300 more colonists were killed. The bloody events of King Philip's War (1675–76) would certainly have intensified the fears that had long plagued those living at the edge of the frontier. Much Indian violence was, of course, a response to English greed, but for those charged with protecting the members of expanding English communities, the violence had to be stopped at all costs. In the New World—an environment so uncertain, so hostile—the colonists' need to limit threats to their survival was intense. Their responses could be excessive, but their fears were not unfounded.

From our point of view, it is easy to sympathize with the Pequots and to condemn the colonists' actions, but the scope of our condemnation must be measured against the facts. After the Treaty of Hartford was signed, Pequots were not physically harmed. Indeed, in 1640 the Connecticut leadership "declared their dislike of such as would have the Indians rooted out," that is, murdered. Before the Pequots capitulated, many of their tribe had died, but the number killed probably totaled less than half the entire tribe. Sherburne Cook's estimate is even lower: "If the initial population [of Pequots] was 3,000 and 750 killed, the battle loss was twenty-five percent of the tribe."

While many Pequots were absorbed by other tribes—it is estimated that Uncas's Mohegan tribe, for example, received hundreds—evidence clearly indicates that soon after the conclusion of the war, the Pequot began to regroup as a tribe. By 1650 four special towns were created to accommodate them, each

ruled by a Pequot governor, and in 1667 Connecticut established permanent reservations for the tribe, which by 1675 numbered approximately 1,500–2,000 members. That year, no more than two generations after the Pequot War had ended, the Pequots allied with the colonists to fight King Philip's War. As recently as the 1960s, Pequots were still listed as a separate group residing in Connecticut. Such factors suggest that while the British could certainly have been less thorough, less severe, less deadly in prosecuting their campaign against the Pequots, the campaign they actually did carry out, for all its vehemence, was not, either in intent or execution, genocidal.

This revision of the revisionists is not meant to deny the larger truth that the conquest of the New World entailed the greatest demographic tragedy in history. The wrongs done to the Native Americans, the suffering they experienced, the manifest evil involved in the colonial enterprise is in no way to be deflected or minimized. However, this sorry tale of despoliation and depopulation needs to be chronicled aright, with an appropriate sense of the actuality of seventeenth-century colonial existence. False, if morally impassioned, judgments cannot substitute for carefully nuanced and discriminating appraisals. Thus, while it is appropriate to censure the excesses, the unnecessary carnage, of the Pequot War, to interpret these events through the radicalizing polemic of accusations of genocide is to rewrite history to satisfy our own moral outrage.

QUESTIONS TO CONSIDER

1. How did colonists view Native Americans?
2. What was the motive of the colonists?
3. Justify Francis Jennings's genocidal thesis.
4. Why does Katz conclude that accusations of genocide in this case "are recognized to be exaggerations"?

"Nits Make Lice"

THE EXTERMINATION OF NORTH AMERICAN INDIANS, 1607–1996

Ward Churchill (Keetoowah Cherokee),
University of Colorado/Boulder

"Kill and scalp all, little and big ...
Nits make lice."
—Colonel John M. Chivington
Instruction to his troops at
Sand Creek, Colorado

From the time Juan Ponce de León arrived in North America in 1513, searching for gold and a mythical fountain of youth in what the Spanish called *La Florída* (or *Pascua Florída*), until the turn of the twentieth century, up to 99 percent of the continent's indigenous population was eradicated. As of 1900, the U.S. Bureau of the Census reported barely over 237,000 native people surviving within the country's claimed boundaries, and the Smithsonian Institution reported less than a third of a million for all of North America, including Greenland. Although the literature of the day confidently predicted, whether with purported sadness or with open jubilation, that North American Indians would be completely extinct within a generation, two at the most, the true magnitude of the underlying demographic catastrophe has always been officially denied in both the United States and Canada.

The primary means by which this obfuscation was achieved has been through a systematic and deliberate falsification or suppression of data concerning the size of the pre-invasion aboriginal population. By minimizing estimates as to how many people there were to begin with, the extent of native population reduction was made to seem far less severe than it had actually been. Concomitantly, by making it seem that the continental indigenous population had been extraordinarily sparse, such demographic manipulations fostered the impression that much North American territory consisted of *terra nullius*, vacant land, unoccupied and thus open for the taking by any "hardy pioneer" wishing to invest the time, labor, and privation which came with "settling" it.

In this manner, orthodox historians and their cohorts in cinema and popular literature have been able to present the process of Euroamerican "nation-building" north of the Río Grande as something rather noble, not always entirely fair or devoid of conflict, but basically well intended and ultimately in the best interests of all concerned. In this carefully sanitized version of events, the relatively few indigenous people who were here at the outset did indeed die back to a marked degree, but this "tragedy" was something "unfortunate," "unintended," "inadvertent," and "altogether unavoidable." ...

YEA RATS AND MICE OR SWARMS OF LICE

The record of the English colonists who "settled" the already long- and well-settled area which became "New England" is, if anything,

From Ward Churchill, *A Little Matter of Genocide: Holocaust and Denial in the Americas, 1492 to the Present* (San Francisco: City Lights Books, 1997), 129–30, 169–74, 218–45. Reprinted with permission.

worse than that of their colleagues further south. Things got off to a rocky start in 1602, when an exploratory probe of the area around Cape Cod resulted in hostilities with local Wampanoags (Pokanokets), which caused a hasty departure of the explorers. In 1603 the English returned and attempted to erect a fortification, but were again routed, this time by a group of Nausets. In 1605, George Waymouth, sailing for the Plymouth Company, landed along the Kennebec River, kidnapped five Eastern Abenaki, and returned to England. Two years later, George Popham and Raleigh Gilbert, a pair of former pirates turned Plymouth Company stockholders, returned to the Kennebec with 120 men to establish what they called the Sagadohoc Colony. They built a fort, but shortly ran afoul of the Skidwarre and Tahanedo bands of Abenaki and, by 1608, this beachhead was also abandoned.

The primary difficulty encountered by all of these ventures was that there were far too many indigenous people in the immediate area—estimates run as high as 90,000 in 1600—for them to simply impose themselves. This problem was rectified in 1614 by Captain John Smith, of Jamestown fame, who suddenly materialized on the coastline with a company of Plymouth Company voyagers, shot seven Indians in three quick skirmishes, and abducted 27 Patuxet Wampanoags and Nausets to sell as slaves in the West Indies on the way home. Mysteriously—the Indians had had close contact with Europeans for years without getting sick—epidemics broke out in the immediate aftermath of Smith's expedition.

> Between 1616 and 1618, a devastating "virgin soil epidemic" … raged through New England. Fully 90 percent of the Wampanoag died of an unidentified European disease, as did a comparable number of Massachusetts and nearly as many Pawtucket and Eastern Abenaki. Dozens of known coastal villages along Massachusetts Bay were entirely abandoned … [This vastly] improved English chances of establishing a colony successfully in what was now an underpopulated area.

Hence, by the time the "Pilgrims" showed up in 1620, complete with an ample inventory of weapons and a professional soldier, Myles Standish, to oversee their use, there was plenty of "vacant land" for them to select as the site of what was to be England's first durable colony in the north. The Wampanoags, who had been regionally ascendant—and upon whose land the English settled like another plague—were so decimated that the balance of power among the Indians had shifted abruptly to the Narragansetts. They were more or less content, so long as the colonists did not seriously incur upon their territory, a matter which would not become an explosive issue for another half-century.

Under these conditions, there was only minor military scuffling for the next seventeen years as the newcomers consolidated the Plymouth Plantation, as they called it, and imported another thousand constituents. The Massachusetts Bay Colony, founded in 1629, added another 4,000 English. The Indians, for their part, were preoccupied not only with trying to define their relationship to the invaders but with sorting things out among themselves, given the radical alteration of their respective demographics only a decade before. A very intricate web of diplomacy developed, as all sides maneuvered for an advantageous position, a situation further complicated when a new smallpox epidemic ripped through the native communities in 1633.

There is some indication that the disease was deliberately induced by the English with the aim of reducing the power of the 30,000-strong Narragansetts, who were as inclined to align themselves with the New Amsterdam Dutch as with either Plymouth or Massachusetts Bay. As it turned out, the main effect of the disease was to kill about 10,000 of the estimated 13,000 Pequots by 1635. The English devoted substantial diplomatic energy to isolating what was left of the victims from any possibility of defensive alliance other than with their Western Niantic tributaries. With this accomplished by 1637—in fact, the Narragansetts and Mohegans were enlisted as English allies against the Pequots—the leadership of both Plymouth and Massachusetts collaborated with that of the unofficial colony of Connecticut to fabricate a pretext, and then set out on a war of extermination.

Massachusetts mounted a column of ninety men under Captain John Endicott and dispatched it to heavily populated Block Island. The group's orders were to kill every adult male residing there and capture as many women and children as possible since "they would fetch a tidy sum in the West Indies slave markets." The plan failed when Endicott attempted to engage the Pequots, European-style, in open combat. Instead, the Indians used a meeting on the matter as a delaying tactic while they evacuated their noncombatants. In the end, the Pequots, who seem to have wanted to avoid the war which was being forced upon them, simply melted away into the woods, leaving the frustrated English with no way to vent themselves other than by burning homes and fields.

On the mainland, Captain John Mason was much more crafty. Having augmented his own mixed Massachusetts-Connecticut force of ninety men with about eighty Mohegans under Uncas, their principle leader, and nearly 500 Narragansetts led by Miantonomi, he set out to attack a lesser Pequot "fort" on the Mystic River. Taking a circuitous route which allowed them to bypass the truly fortified Pequot River town of Sassacus, named for the principal Pequot leader, and also the defensive cordon the Indians had thrown up to prevent exactly what it was he meant to do, Mason launched his assault in the predawn of May 26. His men were instructed to take no prisoners at all, and it is apparent that they counted on the "savages" who accompanied them to join in the slaughter with gusto. When they realized what was afoot, however, both the Narragansetts and Mohegans refused to participate.

Thus left to his own devices, Mason ordered his militiamen to set fire to the entire town, burning alive as many as 900 "women, children and helpless old men." Those who tried to escape the blaze were cut down with swords and axes. As Plymouth Governor William Bradford later described the scene, paraphrasing Mason's own exultant account:

> It was a fearful sight to see them thus frying in the fire and the streams of blood quenching the same, and horrible was the stink and scent thereof; but the victory seemed a sweet sacrifice, and they gave the praise thereof to God, who had wrought so wonderfully for them, thus to enclose their enemies in their hands and give them so speedy a victory over so proud and insulting an enemy.

There were five known survivors, all of whom managed to hide themselves among Uncas' Mohegans, their traditional enemies, who, along with the Narragansetts, were already denouncing the needlessness of the slaughter. Arriving too late—the English and their Indian "allies" had already left—the Pequot fighters were "astonished and demoralized." About 200 attempted to surrender themselves to the Narragansetts, but most of these were discovered and killed by colonists. Another fifty or so, led by Sassacus, tried to find refuge among the Mohawks, but, at the request of the English, were put to death. For more than a year, the militias of the three participating colonies scoured the woods, killing Pequots whenever and wherever they found them. Before it was over, at least two-thirds—probably more—of all Pequots alive at the beginning of the "war" were dead. Those who survived were mostly absorbed by the Mohegans. The Western Niantics were for all practical purposes totally eradicated.

> The Pequots were "rooted out" as a tribe. Winthrop put the body count [for Mystic alone] at between eight and nine hundred. In 1832 one observer counted only "about forty souls, in all, or perhaps a few more or less" living in the

township of Groton; in the 1960s the official figure was twenty-one Pequots in all of Connecticut. And there would have been no living members of that tribe had the colonizers had their way. They sought, as Mason said, "to cut off the Remembrance of them from the Earth." After the war, the General Assembly of Connecticut declared the name extinct. No survivors should be called Pequots. The Pequot River became the Thames, and the village known as Pequot became New London.

The message was not lost on the remaining indigenous peoples of the region; "New England" was meant to become exactly that: a vast area utterly depopulated of its native inhabitants, occupied exclusively by the English. Shaken by this realization, and by what he'd witnessed at Mystic, Miantonomi underwent a profound change. No longer devoted to advancing Narragansett interests at the expense of other Indians, he was something of a pioneer, becoming one of the first major figures in North American native history to try and weld together a general alliance of indigenous nations to contain—and possibly expel—the invading Europeans.

The colonists' attentions were subsumed for a while by internal bickering—mainly a squabble over who would gain the territorial spoils of eradicating the Pequots—and with the taking of New Netherlands from the Dutch, but they eventually got around to dealing with the "threat" presented by this precursor of Tecumseh. Miantonomi, by this point having engineered a compact with the powerful Mohawks to the west, was captured and held in a Connecticut jail for several months. Eventually, he was executed as one by-product of a May 1643 meeting in New Haven at which the New England colonies proclaimed themselves unified against both Dutch and Indians. Thereafter, any attempt by native people to foster a counterbalancing unity among themselves was termed a "conspiracy" and "provocation" to war.

Connecticut was finally chartered as a royal colony in 1662. Rhode Island followed a year later, and, in 1664, the Dutch holding of New Netherlands became the English colony of New York (it was retaken by the Dutch a bit later and had to be "reconquered" in 1674). Working out the relationships presented by these developments—and raiding the French communities of Acadia—again commanded the bulk of English attention for a full decade. By 1675, however, with more than 50,000 colonists in the general area, New England felt itself strong enough to achieve a "final solution" to its "Indian problem." This took the form of an all-out campaign to obliterate the Narragansetts, Wampanoags, and several smaller peoples such as the Nausets and Nipmucks in what was called "King Philip's War." …

MANIFEST DESTINY

By 1840, with the exception of a handful of tiny Iroquois reservations in upstate New York and the remaining Seminoles in the Florida Everglades, the eastern third of what would become the continental United States had been cleared of its indigenous population. The idea that America west of the Mississippi was ever seriously intended to be the exclusive domain of the continent's native peoples was belied—even before their removal was achieved—by the creation of the territories of Missouri (1816), Arkansas (1819) and Iowa (1838). In 1837, Anglo invaders in Texas fought a war of secession from Mexico, creating a temporary republic which became a state in December 1845. Six months later, on June 15, 1846, the United States acquired the Oregon Territory (present-day Oregon, Washington, and Idaho) from Great Britain. Two years after that, in 1848, the northern half of Mexico—California, Arizona, Nevada, Utah, New Mexico, and southern Colorado—was taken by force.

Thomas Jefferson had made the [1803] Louisiana Purchase in large part to acquire seemingly endless space into which white settlement, always moving west, could push the Indian. Andrew Jackson's policy of removal was also a matter of pushing tribes westward. Neither Jefferson, Jackson, nor the other presidents who contemplated or enacted removal considered the possibility that white settlement of the American West might someday proceed from the west as the United States rapidly evolved into a continental nation.

Native North Americans were now caught in a vise from which there was truly no escape. As Maine Senator Lot Morrill would put it to Congress in 1867, "As population has approached the Indian we have removed him beyond population. But population now encounters him from both sides of the continent, and there is no place on the continent to which he can be removed beyond the progress of population." As pronouncements of Angloamerica's "Manifest Destiny" to enjoy limitless expansion intensified, so too did calls for the outright eradication of Indians, or at least large numbers of them, *wherever* they might be encountered.

Aside from the Mandans and other Missouri Valley peoples exterminated by smallpox in 1837, the first victims of this change were the natives—especially Apaches—of western Texas, New Mexico, and Arizona. By the 1880s, not only a number of Apachean bands but other peoples—the Tonkawas, for instance, and the Karankaras—had been totally liquidated, the various Anglo governments involved having depended largely on "free enterprise" rather than troops to accomplish their exterminatory policies. In this, they drew upon their own heritage as well as the example offered by the Mexican regime they'd displaced.

[They offered] generous bounties for Apache scalps. "Backyard barbering" became a gruesome industry ... which became so lucrative that its practicioners did not limit themselves to Apache warrior scalps ... Scalp hunters would storm whole villages and kill every man, woman and

child. A special examination committee had to be established to certify the authenticity of the scalps, but it soon became evident to the bounty hunters that there was no way to distinguish between the scalps of friendly Indians and those of hostiles. So the harvest of death widened ... [T]he examination committee was incapable not only of distinguishing friendly scalps from hostile, but could not tell the difference between Indian hair and Mexican. Remote Mexican villages ... now fell victim to bounty hunters.

A Colorado militia unit mounted a campaign against the Jicarillas in 1854, and the army fought actual wars against the Mescaleros, Chiricahuas, and other western Apache peoples in 1872–73, 1877–80 (the "Victorio Campaign") and 1881–86 (the "Geronimo Campaign"), each of them extraordinarily brutal. But it was the process of "private citizen actions," occurring under state sanction over a sustained period, which ultimately did the job. By 1890, the Apaches had been reduced to less than ten percent of their original number. More or less the same was true of the other peoples of southern Arizona—the Pimas, Maricopas, and Tohono O'odams (Papagos).

In California and Oregon things got under way a bit later but followed much the same course. Consider a May 1852 "incident," when a peaceful "ranchería of 148 Indians, including women and children, was attacked, and nearly the whole number destroyed," by a mob of whites led by the sheriff of Weaverville, California:

Of the 150 Indians that constituted the ranchería, only 2 or 3 escaped, and those were supposed to be dangerously wounded; so that probably not one ... now remains alive. Men, women and children all shared the same fate—none were spared except one woman and two children, who were brought back as prisoners.

Or, to take another example, there was a "horrible massacre of 200 Indians in Humboldt County," California, in January 1860:

The attack was made at night, when [the Indians] were in their little settlements or villages at some sort of merrymaking. The men were known to be absent … Under these circumstances, bands of white men, armed with hatchets—small bands, but sufficiently numerous for the purpose—fell on the women and children, and deliberately slaughtered them, one and all. Simultaneous attacks were made on different rancherías or encampments … Regularly organized bodies of armed men attacked the settlements of friendly Indians [and] murdered them in like manner.

That the genocidal implications of these slaughters—just two of several hundred comparable atrocities perpetrated during the period—were well understood is readily evident in editorial commentary: "The perpetrators seem to have acted with a deliberate design to exterminate the Indian race." Such butchery was not "official" policy only in the most technical sense. The massacres were well reported in the local press, and the "vigilantes" who carried them out were paid bounties by the government for the scalps of their victims. Although the military was quite aware of what was being done, as its commanders' own dispatches make clear, no effort was made to intervene or punish the offenders. Indeed, the process of extermination was often carried out under color of—if not direct participation by—"martial authority."

When the army did take to the field, it was to eliminate whatever capacity the peoples of California had to defend themselves. Thus, in the socalled "Mariposa War" in northern California, troops were used in 1851 to "subdue and disarm" the Miwoks, Tularenos, and Yokuts, who, consequently defenseless, were quickly annihilated by local whites. Much the same pattern prevailed in southern California, where separate campaigns were mounted against the Yumas, Mohaves, Cocopas, and Cahuillas. The final mop-up operation in California was in the north, where in 1872 the army engaged in an especially ugly campaign against the last fifty-or-so Modocs, a peaceful people whose

main "offense" was to refuse removal to Oregon. Small wonder the bulk of all indigenous peoples in California were declared extinct before the end of the nineteenth century—more followed in the twentieth—while the remainder were "pushed into the rocks."

In the Oregon Territory, where "settlers loudly demanded" that the army "annihilate" the region's native peoples, several campaigns for such purposes were undertaken. The first of these, a short 1848 offensive against the Cayuses, set the stage. In 1855, the "Rogue River War" left the the Takelama and Tutuni so decimated that the handful of survivors were lumped together under the heading "Siletz Indians" and confined to a tiny parcel of land near the present-day city of Newport. The same year, an arbitrary declaration by Governor Isaac Stevens that opened the entire territory to white settlement resulted in the so-called "Yakima War," waged not only against the Yakimas, but the Walla Wallas, Umatillas, Palouses, and the remains of the Cayuses as well.

This was followed, in 1857, by the "Coeur d'Alene War," which pitted that people and allied Spokanes, along with a combination of Yakima, Palouse, Umatilla, and Cayuse "recalcitrants," against "a superior force … each man having been issued brand-new long-range rifles." In the aftermath, the leaders of the Indians were executed for the "crime" of having resisted dispossession of their homelands. Thoroughly "dispirited, the tribes of the Columbia Basin waged no more war, but resignedly marched to the reservations prescribed by Governor Stevens' treaties, which the Senate hurriedly ratified on March 8, 1859."

For the next two decades, the army conducted a series of mop-up operations throughout eastern Oregon and most of what is now Idaho, beginning with the "Snake War" of 1866–68, in which the Yahuskin and Walpapi bands of Northern Paiutes were all but obliterated. In 1877, there was the famous and devastating pursuit of the Nez Percé—about a third of whom were killed—driven from their ancestral territory and frantically trying to reach sanctuary in Canada. The Bannocks, as well as remnants of the Cayuses and Northern Paiutes, were mauled in an 1878 campaign. Finally, in 1879, regional warfare died out after troops were dispatched to pacify the "Sheepeaters," a small group of Bannock and Shoshoni holdouts whose name derived from their willingness to subsist almost entirely on mountain sheep rather than surrender their way of life.

THE WAY WEST

For a time it appeared that the indigenous population might actually be left with a vast expanse of the continental interior—the "Great American Desert" consisting of the plains region as well as most of the present states of Utah and Nevada—in which to maintain themselves. Since the land at issue was deemed to be without value to whites, it was considered an ideal dumping ground for peoples displaced from more useful locales. At the outset, all that was required of those native to the region was that they admit such transplants along the fringes of their territories, engage in some limited amount of trade with whites, and allow safe passage to columns of Euroamerican migrants making their way from the East to California and Oregon.

In theory, the overall framework for this was constructed in 1851 through a series of treaties negotiated at Fort Laramie—just west of the Black Hills, in present-day Wyoming—with a number of nations, including the Lakotas, Cheyennes, Arapahos, Crows, Shoshonis, Comanches, Kiowas, and Kiowa Apaches. In the Fort Laramie treaties, the United States formally acknowledged every square inch of the Great Plains as being the sovereign territory of one or another of these counterpart nations and pledged itself to prevent the establishment of permanent communities of its citizens within

their domains. Early encounters with these peoples (whom Colonel George Armstrong Custer would later describe as being "the best light cavalry in the world") had convinced the United States that to do otherwise would not be worth the cost of taking a more bellicose stance.

Things more or less worked out for a time, although there were ominous precursors of what would follow. By the late 1850s, however, gold had been discovered in the Rocky Mountains, leading large numbers of white prospectors and other speculators to establish illegal mining camps in the western reaches of Cheyenne/Arapaho territory, at places like Denver. Not only did the government not attempt to uphold its treaty commitments to the Cheyennes and Arapahos by preventing this, it engineered a completely fraudulent "supplanting treaty" in 1861, by which the unknowing Indians supposedly ceded more than 90 percent of their central plains homelands. When the Cheyennes refused to acknowledge the validity of this travesty they were declared to be "aggressors," and military preparations for their outright extermination commenced.

Gold, silver, and other minerals were also discovered in the mountains of western Montana at about the same time. One result was that a new wagon route, the "Bozeman Trail" was cut diagonally through the heart of prime Lakota hunting territory in Wyoming, another direct violation of the 1851 treaty. Since the influx of traffic greatly disrupted the buffalo herds upon which they depended for subsistence, the Indians had little alternative but to respond militarily to this invasion, and the army quickly began building a string of forts along the route in order to secure it. Although eradication was not at that time considered a viable option with regard to the Lakotas, who were much more populous than the Cheyennes, it was believed they might be "chastised" into acquiescence.

Meanwhile, on the southern plains, Texas cattle interests had begun what was to become a concerted effort to breach the "Co-manche Wall," which had prevented all but the most transient white penetration of the Llano Estacado—the "Staked Plains" or "Texas Panhandle" region—for generations. A special unit, the Texas Rangers, had been assembled to deal with the "menace" presented by Co-manche, Kiowa, and Kiowa Apache defense of their treaty-guaranteed homelands. However, the Comanches and their allies proved more than a match for such adversaries. By the late 1850s, Texans were demanding with increasing shrillness that regular troops be used to clear these indigenous nations from their homelands, preferably by annihilation.

In all probability the federal government would have accommodated local extermina-tionist sentiments on at least one of these three fronts during the early 1860s, had its ability to do so not been dissolved by the start of the Civil War in 1861. From then until the war between the states ended in 1865, both the regular army and most militia units, both North and South, were completely tied up in fighting one an-other. Indian fighting in the West was thus con-signed mainly to happenstance or to ad hoc units formed by the territories after official troop levies had been met. This slowed but by no means halted the process of obliterating the peoples of the plains. Indeed, it is fair to say that the pattern by which it would proceed was well established by 1864, catalyzed not by events in the region itself, but by examples set else-where, in Minnesota and Utah, by regiments of volunteers.

In 1862, the final "Woodlands" conflict—with the Santee Dakotas in Minnesota—was provoked by the United States through the sim-ple expedient of cutting off the Indians' food supply while white settlers illegally overran their remaining landbase. When the starving San-tees erupted in a desperate "revolt," they were immediately targeted for total elimination under the premise, voiced by Governor Alexan-der Ramsey, that "the Sioux Indians must be

exterminated or driven from the state." Gen-eral Henry H. Sibley—called the "Long Trad-er" by the Santees because of his practice of cheating them in commercial relations—then led several thousand militia troops against the Indians, quickly killing more than a quarter of their fighting men and as many as a thou-sand noncombatants.

When the bedraggled survivors surren-dered—a scalp bounty was proclaimed against all who did not—they were herded into cattle pens at Mankato. The roughly 600 men among the 2,000 captives were chained together, subjected to summary court mar-tial (without benefit of defense counsel), and 303 of them condemned to death. On De-cember 26, thirty-nine of them were hanged in the largest mass execution in U.S. histo-ry, and the remainder imprisoned, all for the "crime" of having tried to feed their starving families.

> Sibley [also] decided to keep the remaining 1,700 Santees—mostly women and children—as pris-oners, although they were accused of no crime other than having been born Indian. He ordered them transferred overland to Fort Snelling, and along the way they too were assaulted by angry white citizens. Many were stoned and clubbed; a child was snatched from its mother's arms and beaten to death.

The killing continued. On July 3, 1863, when Lit-tle Crow, the principal Santee leader, attempted to return to his people from asylum in Canada, he was ambushed and shot to death. His mur-derers were paid a $25 bounty for his scalp, plus a $500 bonus, given the identity of their prize. Little Crow's scalp and skull were then placed on public display for the edification of the gentle souls of St. Paul. Six months later, Minnesota vi-olated Canadian neutrality in order to bring two other Santee leaders, Shakopee and Medicine Bottle, back into U.S. jurisdiction, where they were promptly hanged. Those Santees who es-caped the scalping knives were deported en masse, and their remaining lands in Minnesota were impounded as a "reparation" for expenses incurred by the state in annihilating them.

> Crow Creek on the Missouri River was the site chosen for the Santee reservation. The soil was barren, rainfall scanty, wild game scarce, and the alkaline water unfit for drinking. Soon the surrounding hills were covered with graves; of the 1,300 Santees brought there in 1863, less than a thousand survived their first winter.

Meanwhile, far to the west, in Utah, Colonel Patrick E. Connor took to the field at the head of about a thousand California volunteer cavalrymen. His target was the Shoshonis, who had grown increasingly "restive" over Salt Lake City and other Mormon communities recently—and quite illegally—established on their lands. On January 27, 1863, about a third of this force slammed into a sizable village in southern Idaho, along the Bear River. Of the approximately 700 Indians living there as many as 500 were slaughtered with all the savagery customary to such assaults.

> Soldiers reported … that Indians who were so incapacitated they could not move "were killed by being hit in the head with an axe" … [A] soldier found a dead woman clutching a little infant still alive. The soldier "in mercy to the babe, killed it" … [Numerous women] "were killed because they would not submit quietly to being ravaged, and other squaws were ravaged in the agony of death."

After systematically mutilating the dead, Connor's men loaded their own fourteen casualties of the "battle" aboard sleds and returned to their base camp. Many of them then returned to civilian life in northern California, where they immediately resumed the relentless slaughter of the indigenous population in that region. For their part, the Mormons celebrated the colonel's frankly genocidal "victory"—Connor was soon promoted in recognition of his "achievement"—as "an intervention of the Almighty," a sentiment the Puritan Fathers of Plymouth Colony would have expressed neither differently nor better.

NITS MAKE LICE

In 1864, inspired by the success of Sibley's and Connor's butchery, the government of Colorado Territory, whose two regiments of volunteer troops were fully committed to fighting Confederates further east, mustered in a whole new unit—the Third Colorado Volunteer Cavalry Regiment—exclusively for the purpose of killing Cheyennes, Arapahos and any other native people they might encounter over a 100-day period. This was done in a climate which was exterminationist in the extreme: "Of twenty-seven stories concerned directly or indirectly with Indians [published in the Denver press during 1863], ten overtly favored 'extermination' of Indians." By mid-1864, the paper's rhetorical advocacy of genocide—mostly written by its publisher, William N. Byers—had, if anything, escalated.

> Eastern humanitarians who believe in the superiority of the Indian race will raise a terrible howl over this policy [of extermination], but it is no time to split hairs nor stand upon delicate compunctions of conscience. Self preservation demands decisive action, and the only way to secure it is [through a] few months of active extermination against the red devils.

On the day this was written, the publisher was joined by Colorado Governor John Evans who, after announcing—on the basis of no discernible evidence—that the Cheyennes had "declared war on the United States," pronounced his judgment that "Any man who kills a hostile Indian is a patriot!" A day later, the governor clarified his stance, publishing a proclamation in the *News* in which he claimed "the evidence [was] now conclusive" that most Indians on the Plains were "hostile," calling upon area whites to "organize [themselves] to pursue, kill and destroy" Cheyennes and Arapahos wherever they might be found. As the Colorado Third was being formed, Byers chimed in again, inquiring of his readers: "Shall we not go for them, their lodges, squaws and all?"

The answer was shortly announced by Colonel John Milton Chivington, a former Methodist minister with political ambitions, who commanded the unit. "My intention is to kill all Indians I may come across," he explained. The colonel elsewhere elaborated that this included everyone from the most elderly and infirm to newborn infants, the latter for no reason other than that they would one day grow up to become adult Cheyennes. "Nits make lice," Chivington asserted, echoing H. L. Hall, a rather notorious mass-murderer of Indians in northern California. "I long to be wading in gore," Chivington put … it on another occasion. Such statements quickly became rallying cries for his troops and were enthusiastically embraced by the Colorado citizenry at large.

The problem for Chivington was that his men came across almost no Indians to kill. Aside from an incident on October 10, when forty men led by Captain David Nichols managed to surprise a small Cheyenne hunting camp near Buffalo Springs and slaughter everyone in it—six men, three women, and a fourteen-year-old boy—the only "savages" the colonel and his volunteers had seen by the time the troops' hundred-day enlistments had begun to run out were a group of "peace chiefs"—notably the Cheyennes' Black Kettle and White Antelope, and Left Hand (Niwot), an Arapaho—escorted by Major Edward Wynkoop of the First Colorado into Camp Weld, near Denver, in mid-September. Under Wynkoop's watchful eye, these Indians had been allowed to place themselves and their people—about 750 in all—under the protection of the military. In exchange for official recognition of their noncombatant status, they were required to surrender their weapons and accept de facto internment under Wynkoop's supervision at a specified site along Sand Creek, near Fort Lyon in the 1861 reservation area.

By early November, Chivington's fearless "Indian fighters" had become a laughingstock, derisively referred to by Coloradans as the "Bloodless Third." At some point mid-month—prompted by a visit by Connor—both the embarrassed officers and their men agreed to serve beyond the expiration of their terms of service in order to make a full-scale assault upon the peace chiefs' immobilized and defenseless village. Moving under cover of a blizzard, the regiment suddenly appeared at Fort Lyon on November 27, and to preserve the secrecy of their arrival—Chivington was determined to preserve the "element of surprise" against his unarmed and woefully outnumbered opponents—"threw a cordon of pickets around the post with orders that no one would be allowed to leave, under penalty of death."

At 8 p.m. that night, the colonel led about 900 soldiers out of the fort and headed for the village, about thirty miles away. He instructed his troops to "use any means under God's heaven to kill [the] Indians" and to be sure to "kill and scalp all, little and big." The volunteers struck at dawn, despite the fact that both American and white flags were flown over the sleeping encampment. When 75-year-old White Antelope, hands open to show he bore no weapons, attempted to halt the attacking cavalrymen, he was unceremoniously shot to death. A soldier who was visiting the village at the time also tried to head off the attackers. Although waving another white flag of surrender, he too was fired upon.

> The Indians fled in all directions, but the main body of them moved up the creek bed, which alone offered some protection from the soldiers' bullets. They fled headlong until they came to a place above the camp where the banks of the river were cut back by breaks. Here, the Indians frantically began digging in the loose sand with their hands to make holes in which to hide. The larger percent of these were women and children … .

As the scene was later described by Robert Bent, the mixed-blood son of a local trader and a Cheyenne woman who had guided the attackers from Fort Lyon to the village:

I saw five squaws under a bank for shelter. When the troops came up to them they ran out and showed their persons, to let the soldiers know they were squaws and begged for mercy, but the soldiers shot them all ... There were some thirty or forty squaws collected in a hole for protection; they sent out a little girl about six years old with a white flag on a stick; she had not proceeded but a few steps when she was shot and killed. All the squaws in the hole were afterwards killed ... The squaws offered no resistance. Every one I saw dead was scalped. I saw one squaw cut open with an unborn child, as I thought, lying by her side ... I saw quite a number of infants in arms killed with their mothers.

Other soldiers were running down Indians who had fled in different directions, killing some as far as five or six miles from the village. By then, mutilation of the dead and dying had begun in earnest, and the few prisoners taken were being summarily executed. As a lieutenant in the New Mexico Volunteers who'd ridden along "to gain experience," would later testify:

Of from five to six hundred souls [who were killed], the majority of which were women and children ... I did not see a body of man, woman, or child but was scalped, and in many instances their bodies were mutilated in a most horrible manner—men, women, and children's privates cut out, &c; I heard one man say that he had cut out a woman's private parts and had them for exhibition on a stick; I heard another man say he had cut off the fingers of an Indian to get the rings on the hand ... I also heard of numerous instances in which men had cut out the private parts of females and stretched them over the saddle bows and wore them over hats while riding in the ranks ... I heard one man say that he had cut a squaw's heart out, and he had it stuck up on a stick.

Or, to quote from the testimony of John Smith, a frontiersman who served as a scout:

All manner of depredations were inflicted on their persons. They were scalped, their brains knocked out; the men used their knives, ripped open women, clubbed little children, knocked them in the head with their guns, beat their brains out, mutilated their bodies in every sense of the word ... worse mutilated than any I ever saw before ... [C]hildren two or three months old; all lying there, from sucking infants up to warriors.

In the aftermath of the massacre the Cheyenne Dog Soldiers, joined by several hundred Lakotas, finally gave Colorado a genuine dose of the "war" its officials had been prattling on about. Denver was virtually sealed off from the east for some months, and it soon became apparent that, however proficient they might be in slaughtering the helpless, outfits like Chivington's "Bloody Third"—as the *News* now proudly dubbed the "bold sojer boys"—couldn't begin to cope with the response they'd provoked. Infuriated that regular army troops would be required to resolve the situation, the federal government convened three separate investigations of Sand Creek—one each by the House, Senate, and War Department—all of them concluding that a hideous crime had been committed, and that Chivington, Evans, and other whites were entirely responsible.

Armed with these conclusions, and promising reparations (which were never paid), federal negotiators attempted unsuccessfully to effect an accommodation with the Dog Soldiers through the Treaty of the Little Arkansas during the fall of 1865. Another effort was made via the 1867 Treaty of Medicine Lodge, following a spectacularly unsuccessful military campaign headed up by General Winfield Scott Hancock. This was followed, a year later, with an offensive commanded by General Phil Sheridan, a leading proponent of "total war." Pursuing a strategy which combined winter campaigning—to catch the Indians in camp, during the period of their least mobility—with wholesale massacre, Sheridan was at last able to drive the Cheyennes virtually out of existence.

If [a winter campaign] results in the utter annihilation of these Indians ... I will say nothing and do nothing to restrain our troops from doing what they may deem proper on the spot, and will allow no vague general charges of cruelty and inhumanity to tie their hands.

The primary instrument of the general's campaign was the newly formed Seventh Cavalry Regiment, commanded by Lt. Colonel George Armstrong Custer. On November 27, 1868, almost four years to the day after Sand Creek, Custer's men attacked an unsuspecting winter encampment on the big bend of the Washita River, in western Oklahoma. The village was again that of Black Kettle, who'd survived Sand Creek and was still vainly seeking to avoid conflict while securing some kind of sanctuary for native noncombatants. Of the 103 people killed in Custer's dawn assault, "93 were women, old men, and children—as well as Black Kettle, who had been cut down with his wife as they were riding double on a pony in a desperate attempt to forestall the attack."

The Washita Massacre took the heart out of most of the remaining Cheyennes in the south. Although a group of Dog Soldiers made their way to the Powder River Country of Montana to merge with their Northern Cheyenne cousins, the bulk of the survivors surrendered to the army at Fort Sill during the spring and summer of 1869. Thus confined, and with many of their remaining leaders sent to prison at Fort Marion, Florida, a few years later—a policy which led to the Sappa Creek Massacre in 1875—they had declined to near-extinction by the early twentieth century.

The "Conquest of the Southern Plains" was not yet complete, however. Sheridan's campaign in particular had embroiled the Comanches, Kiowas, and Kiowa Apaches. Although these peoples accepted an uneasy "peace" for about three years after the Cheyenne decimation, the army's unofficial policy of fostering the extermination of their traditional "commissary," the buffalo, forced an all-out counteroffensive against white hunters operating in their territory in 1874. Although early victories were won at places like Adobe Walls, none was decisive, and a campaign headed by General Nelson A. Miles was soon mounted to subdue them once and for all.

Miles brought in the Fourth Cavalry, under Colonel Ranald Mackenzie, fresh from a "limited invasion" of Mexico to "punish" a group of long-suffering Kickapoos who had found sanctuary there. Another practitioner of total war, Mackenzie conducted a brutal winter campaign inaugurated by a September 28, 1874, surprise attack on the main body of Comanches and Kiowas, who had withdrawn to what had always been an inaccessible joint refuge in the Palo Duro Canyon, far out on the Llano Estacado. Although few Indians were killed—the various bands quickly scattered when the assault began—the soldiers were able to capture and kill almost all their horses, and to destroy virtually everything else they possessed. Starving, freezing, and harried relentlessly by Mackenzie's patrols during the coldest months, the fragments of each people shortly began to surrender.

By May 25, 1875, the "hard core"—a small group of Kiowas led by Satank, and Quannah Parker's Quahadi Comanches—had laid down their arms. With that, all military resistance by the plains nations south of the Dakota Territory finally ceased. Thereafter, like the Arapahos and Cheyennes (a small number of whom, led by Grey Beard, had joined in the "Buffalo War"), both the Kiowas and Comanches, as well as their Kiowa Apache allies, were stripped of what little land remained to them, rendered absolutely dependent upon their conquerors for subsistence, and rapidly declined to nadir population (by 1900 the Kiowas, for example, who numbered more than 6,000 in 1800, had fewer than 1,300 survivors; there were less than 500 Kiowa Apaches by that point, and the Comanches were reduced by about 90 percent, overall).

DEATH SONG

The northern plains proved a more difficult proposition for the United States. In the summer of 1866, Red Cloud (Mahpiya Luta), a preeminent Oglala political leader, was able to bring all seven bands of his people together, along with the Northern Cheyennes and Arapahos, as well as some refugee Santees, and lay siege to Fort Phil Kearny, most northerly of the posts thus far completed along the Bozeman Trail. With more than 3,000 warriors, the Indians constituted a formidable opponent for the army, especially since the bulk of its available resources were tied up in Kansas and Colorado, trying to contain the indigenous response to Sand Creek.

The situation was greatly exacerbated on December 21, when a unit under Captain William J. Fetterman was annihilated near Fort Kearny. As the months dragged on it became apparent that the Indians were becoming steadily stronger. Unable to muster anything approaching the number of troops needed to defeat Red Cloud's alliance, and in constant danger of suffering even more catastrophic losses in its undermanned Wyoming garrisons, the army began sending out peace feelers during the late summer of 1867. Red Cloud's response was that he would not be interested in negotiating until all U.S. forces had been withdrawn from Lakota territory and the Bozeman Trail posts destroyed. After procrastinating for several months, the army complied with these terms and Red Cloud finally agreed to a treaty, signed at Fort Laramie in November 1868.

This new instrument reaffirmed much of what had been established by its 1851 predecessor with respect to the Lakotas and allied Cheyennes and Arapahos. It defined their territory as extending from the east bank of the Missouri River westward to the Big Horn Mountains, and southward from the upper Missouri to the North Platte River (an area, centering on the Black Hills, totaling about 5 percent of the 48 states). Under the 1868 treaty, the army could not build forts in Indian Country and was required to patrol the borders to prevent U.S. nationals from trespassing therein. No portion of the treaty territory could be sold or otherwise alienated without the express written consent of at least three-quarters of all adult male Lakotas.

The treaty was actually honored to a large extent for several years while the army concentrated on winning its "Buffalo War" on the southern plains. With the end of that conflict in sight by 1874, however, things began to change in the north. During the summer of that year, Custer's Seventh Cavalry was ordered to make a "reconnaissance in force" into the Black Hills for purposes of assessing potential mineral wealth there. Although it is dubious whether anything was actually found, Custer, writing under a pseudonym, reported in the Eastern press that he'd discovered "gold at the grassroots." In short order, whites were pouring into Paha Sapa—as the Lakotas called this, their most sacred area—and the army was doing nothing to fulfill its treaty obligation to prevent their coming.

Indeed, after a follow-up expedition in 1875 (during which gold *was* found), the United States demanded that the Lakotas sell the entire region. When the Indians refused, it was announced in Washington that they'd "declared war on America," and a huge three-pronged invasion of their territory—the so-called "Centennial Campaign"—was set in motion during the spring of 1876. Although the offensive itself fared rather poorly—some 1,200 Lakotas and Cheyennes led by Crazy Horse (Tesunke Witko) defeated a 1,500-man column under General George Crook at the Rosebud Creek on June 17, and Custer's regiment, overconfident and expecting to perpetrate another Washita-style massacre, was shredded in the valley of the Little Big Horn on the 25th—the writing was on the wall.

As early as 1867, General of the Army William Tecumseh Sherman had opined that, "We must act with vindictive earnestness against the [Lakotas], even to their extermination, men, women and children." During the winter of 1876–77, Ranald Mackenzie was brought to Wyoming to duplicate his success against the Comanches and Kiowas a year earlier. Beginning in mid-October, the colonel's command, as well as forces under Generals Crook and Miles, scoured the Powder River Country, attacking each village they came across. Mackenzie's November 25 assault on the camp of Dull Knife, a noted Cheyenne leader, was indicative:

> It was the month of the Deer Rutting Moon, and very cold, with deep snow in the shaded places and ice-crusted snow in the open places. Mackenzie had brought his troops up to attacking positions during the night, and struck the Cheyennes at first daylight ... They caught the Cheyennes in their lodges, killing many of them as they came ... awake. Others ran out naked into the biting cold, the warriors trying to fight off ... the onrushing soldiers long enough for their women and children to escape ... Some of the best warriors of the Northern Cheyennes sacrificed their lives in those first furious moments of fighting; one of them was Dull Knife's oldest son. Dull Knife and Little Wolf [another prominent leader] finally managed to form a rear guard along the upper ledges of a canyon, but their scanty supply of ammunition was soon exhausted. Little Wolf was shot seven times before he and Dull Knife broke away to join their women and children in full flight toward the Bighorns. Behind them Mackenzie was burning their lodges, and after that was done he herded their captured ponies against the canyon wall and ordered his men to shoot them down ... .

More than a hundred Cheyennes, two-thirds of them women, children, and elders, had been killed before the survivors managed to get away. Their ordeal, however, was just beginning.

> During the first night of flight, twelve infants and several old people froze to death. The next night,

the men killed some of the ponies, disemboweled them, and thrust small children inside to keep them from freezing ... For three days they tramped across the frozen snow, their bare feet leaving a trail of blood, [before reaching Crazy Horse's Oglala encampment on the Box Elder Creek].

On January 8, Miles's troops located and attacked this village as well, and so the whole process was repeated. And so it went, month after month. By the end of April 1877, even Crazy Horse's people had surrendered, and the last "Sioux recalcitrants"—a handful of Hunkpapas led by Sitting Bull (Tatanka Yatanka) and Gall (Pizi)—had fled to sanctuary in Canada. In short order, disarmed, dismounted, and dispirited, the Northern Cheyennes were deported to the reservation of their southern cousins in Oklahoma. In the fall, Crazy Horse was assassinated, and rations to the captive Lakotas were suspended until a scattering of leaders finally agreed to sign a document allegedly transferring ownership of the Black Hills to the United States.

In September 1878, about half the remaining Northern Cheyennes, horrified at the attrition they were suffering under the conditions imposed upon them in Oklahoma, broke out of their confinement and attempted to return to their Powder River homeland. Led by Dull Knife and Little Wolf, they were stalked by more than 15,000 troops as they struggled northward, and the initial body of "renegades" was again ground down to about half its size. Finally, in utter exhaustion, Dull Knife's group of some 150 people—composed, as usual, almost exclusively of women, children, and old men—gave themselves up at Camp Robinson, Nebraska. Confined to an unheated guardhouse in the dead of winter, without rations, the prisoners were informed they would be shipped back to the south. At that point, more desperate than ever, they tried to escape again on the night of January 9, 1879.

[The] soldiers began overtaking scattered bands of women and children, killing many of them before they could surrender … When the morning came, the soldiers herded 65 Cheyenne prisoners, 23 of them wounded, back into [Camp] Robinson … . Only 38 of those who had escaped were still alive and free; 32 were together, moving north through the hills and pursued by four companies of cavalry and a battery of mountain artillery … For several days the cavalrymen followed the 32 Cheyennes, until at last they were trapped in a deep buffalo wallow. Charging to the edge of the wallow, the cavalrymen emptied their carbines into it … . Only nine Cheyennes survived.

By this point, fewer than 500 Northern Cheyennes—less than 10 percent of their original number—remained alive. Although the Lakotas never came this close to outright extermination, they experienced considerable population losses during the early reservation years. By the late 1880s, nearly 90 percent of their treaty territory had been taken from them, their sociopolitical and spiritual life had been abolished under penalty of law, and they were being deliberately starved. One response to these circumstances was an increasingly widespread adoption of the Ghost Dance—a belief that if certain rituals were performed with sufficient devotion, the whites would disappear, while the buffalo and other dead relatives would be reborn, making life as it had once been.

While it is obvious that this forlorn practice presented absolutely no threat to the United States or its citizens, the army seized upon it as an opportunity to simultaneously break the last traces of native resistance, and to extract another measure of revenge for the humiliations it had experienced at the hands of the Lakotas in 1868 and 1876. More than 3,000 troops were fielded to put down the Ghost Dance "insurrection," Sitting Bull—who had returned from Canada in 1881—was murdered on December 15, 1890, and the reconstituted Seventh Cavalry captured a terrified group of about 350 Minneconjous, led by Big Foot, on the Wounded Knee Creek on December 28. On the morning of the 29th, the troops proceeded to massacre their unarmed prisoners, using both rifles and Hotchkiss guns carefully placed on surrounding hills for the purpose.

[All] witnesses agree that from the moment it opened fire, [the Seventh] ceased to be a military unit and became a mass of infuriated men intent on butchery. Women and children attempted to escape by running up a dry ravine, but were pursued and slaughtered—there is no other word—by hundreds of maddened soldiers, while shells from the Hotchkiss guns, which had been moved to allow them to sweep the ravine, continued to burst among them. The line of bodies afterward was found to extend more than two miles from the camp—and they were all women and children. A few survivors eventually found shelter in brushy gullies here and there, and their pursuers had scouts call out that women and children could come out of hiding because they had nothing to fear … Some small boys crept out and were surrounded by soldiers who then butchered them. Nothing Indian that lived was safe.

The dead—more than 300 in all—were buried in a mass grave on New Year's Day 1891, while editorialists like L. Frank Baum of the *Aberdeen Saturday Pioneer* (who would later attain fame as the gentle author of the *Wizard of Oz*) called for the army to "finish the job" by exterminating *all* remaining Indians. "The nobility of the Redskin is extinguished … . The Whites, by law of conquest, by justice of civilization, are masters of the American continent, and the best safety of the frontier settlements will be secured by the total annihilation of the few remaining Indians. Why not annihilation? Their glory has fled, their spirit broken, their manhood effaced; better that they should die than live the miserable wretches that they are." Thus ended the "Indian Wars."

QUESTIONS TO CONSIDER

1. According to Churchill, how have historians portrayed "nation building"?

2. Is the Colonel John M. Chivington quote "Kill and scalp all, little and big ... Nits make lice," used by Churchill to sum up the colonial attitudes toward Native Americans appropriate? Why or why not?

3. Were the proponents of Manifest Destiny deliberately genocidal?

4. Was the Minnesota uprising genocidal?

5. Was the Sand Creek event a genocide?

MAKING CONNECTIONS

1. Describe the parallels between the Australian aboriginal experience and the American treatment of indigenous peoples.

2. Explain why Australians and Americans are loath to use the "g-word."

✔ RECOMMENDED RESOURCES

Churchill, Ward. *A Little Matter of Genocide: Holocaust and Denial in the Americas 1492 to the Present*. San Francisco: City Lights Books, 1997.

Drinnon, Richard. *Facing West: The Metaphysics of Indian-Hating and Empire Building*. New York: New American Library, 1980.

Jennings, Francis. *The Invasion of America: Indians, Colonialism, and the Cant of Conquest*. New York: W. W. Norton, 1976.

Stannard, David. *American Holocaust: Columbus and the Conquest of the New World*. New York: Oxford University Press, 1992.

Thornton, Russell. *American Indian Holocaust and Survival: A Population History Since 1492*. Norman, OK: University of Oklahoma Press, 1987.

Wright, Ronald. *Stolen Continents: The "New World" Through Indian Eyes Since 1492*. Boston: Houghton Mifflin Company, 1992.

CHAPTER 2

WHAT IS YOURS IS MINE:
COLONIALISM

Broadly speaking, there were two colonial experiences: the one by the colonizers, and the one by the colonized. The colonizers displaced the indigenous inhabitants, sometimes violently, or inadvertently through the introduction of diseases. Some indigenous peoples tried unsuccessfully to drive the foreigners out of their lands, while others accepted imperial rule.

James O. Gump, chair of the Department of History at the University of San Diego, introduces some of the issues in studying specific instances of genocide by comparing the Sioux and the Zulu at the end of the nineteenth century. He compares the 1876 Sioux and Cheyenne defeat of Custer's command with the 1879 annihilation of a British force by Zulu warriors, at Isandhlwana in South Africa. Both defeats of regular army forces by tribesmen, regarded as undisciplined savages, stunned American and England. In the aftermath, indigenous peoples succumbed to the domination of the imperial powers involved.

European imperialism surged at the beginning of the twentieth century. European states such as Great Britain, France, Germany, and Belgium divided Africa and Asia among themselves. This "New Imperialism," driven by the industrial revolution, sought raw materials, markets, and control of strategic passages such as the Strait of Gibraltar and the Suez Canal. The advocates of imperialism used nationalist and racial arguments to garner public support for empire building. Many Europeans, including missionaries, sought to uphold their duty, defined by the British writer Rudyard Kipling as "The White Man's Burden," to take civilization to "heathen savages" of foreign lands. Before 1870, Europeans controlled little of Africa, but by 1914 nearly all of Africa fell under European dominance. White people ruled millions of black people, often cruelly.

The twentieth century opened with the European powers engaged in genocidal campaigns against some of the last surviving tribal peoples in the world. The German conquest of Southwest Africa was one of the most brutal, especially following the revolt of the Hereros in 1904. General Lothar von Trotha, the commander sent to put down the uprising, made his aims clear from the start: "It was and remains my policy to apply force by unmitigated terrorism and even cruelty. I shall destroy the rebellious tribes by shedding rivers of blood." The Germans could not accomplish this completely, even with their technological superiority. After the defeat of the Hereros at the Battle of Waterberg, von Trotha cut off their escape route in order to kill women and children. The German army continued to push them into the desert and then sealed off the whole area for a year. In 1904, at the beginning of the revolt, there were over 80,000 Hereros. By the end of the first decade, there were fewer than 15,000 left alive. Similarly, genocide eliminated people in other parts of the globe. In Paraguay, the Aché Indians were almost annihilated. In Brazil, an ongoing push of settlers into the Amazon Forest killed tens of thousands of Indians. The first of the deliberate, ideologically motivated twentieth-century genocides occurred in World War I in the Turkish Empire.

Adam Hochschild, who teaches writing at the Graduate School of Journalism at the University of California at Berkeley, recounts in his book, *King Leopold's Ghost*, the acquisition of the Congo by King Leopold of Belgium, who made it his personal fiefdom. In 1902, writer Joseph Conrad recounted a similar story in *The Heart of Darkness*, describing the methods of Kurtz, a European ivory trader who locally implemented imperialism. "The Tribe Germany Wants to Forget" looks at the reparation problems in the aftermath of genocide in Africa. Finally, Anne Applebaum describes the evolution of concentration camps in the twentieth century in her review of the book *Le Siècle des Camps*, entitled "A History of Horror."

The Dust Rose Like Smoke:
The Subjugation of the Zulu and the Sioux

James O. Gump,
University of San Diego

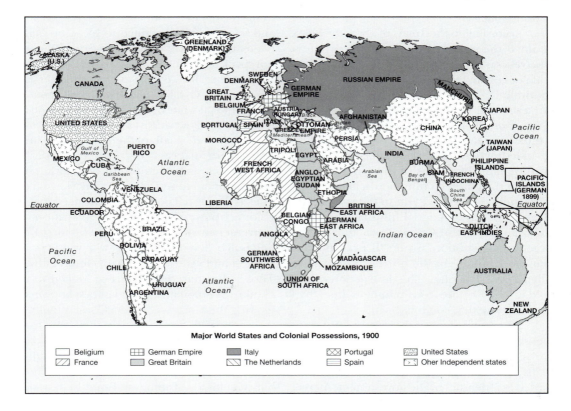

Major World States and Colonial Possessions, 1900

The 1870s marked a decisive turning point for the Sioux and Zulu. Both peoples, plagued with internal economic woes and destabilized by endemic political factionalism, had become barriers to an advancing white frontier. The Great Sioux Reservation and unceded territory blocked the exploitation of the Black Hills, hindered the development of the Northern Pacific Railroad, and foiled the Indian Bureau's schemes to concentrate and civilize the Lakotas. Zululand, one of the last independent African states in southern Africa, posed an obstacle to Britain's confederation plans in the region, bottled up labor supplies for the mining industries, and harnessed spacious tracts of land fancied by Natalian sugar farmers. In these circumstances, the intercultural bonds forged in the 1860s began to unravel. Formerly sympathetic white administrators, responding to political expediencies in the 1870s, came to view total war against the Zulu and Sioux as an inescapable necessity. Obsessed with manufacturing a *casus belli*, these agents of empire paved the roads to the Little Bighorn and Isandhlwana.

According to the Treaty of 1868, the Sioux retained the right to live outside government reservations as long as a sufficient number of buffaloes existed to justify the hunt. Some herds continued to roam the northern central plains throughout the 1870s, but their ranks were thinning. Under siege by professional buffalo hunters, the North American bison population faced extinction. "Hide hunters" who arrived on the plains by means of the Union Pacific Railroad slaughtered entire herds, killing up to three million beasts per year in the early 1870s. Pleased by this carnage, Philip H. Sheridan, commander of the Great Plains during the Grant administration, wrote, "If I could learn that every buffalo in the northern herd were killed I would be glad. The destruction of this herd would do more to keep Indians quiet than anything else that could happen."[1]

The diminution of their most important subsistence resource forced thousands of Tetons into government agencies during the early 1870s. Some camped permanently and were regarded as "friendly" by the government. A great many others, however, oscillated between the unceded territory and the camps. General D. S. Stanley referred to the latter as "violent and troublesome fellows" who spent half their time at the agencies "and the other half at the hostile camps." Stanley alleged that these "hostiles" would "abuse the agents, threaten their lives, kill their cattle at night, and do anything they can to oppose the civilizing movement, but eat all the provisions they can get."[2]

The competing attractions of security and freedom polarized Sioux politics, galvanizing new leadership. The government continued to court Red Cloud and Spotted Tail, each of whom collaborated to gain the greatest possible advantage for his followers.[3] For example, both leaders held out for government agencies outside the Great Sioux Reservation, ones closer to their traditional hunting territories. After years of haggling, the government relented in 1873, establishing the Red Cloud and Spotted Tail agencies in northwestern Nebraska.[4] But even though Red Cloud and Spotted Tail continued to speak on behalf of great numbers of Oglalas and Brulés, they did not speak for all the Lakota people. New leaders such as the Hunkpapa Sitting Bull and Crazy Horse of the Oglalas, who advocated armed resistance to all whites, began to attract many followers to the Powder River country.

In the aftermath of the 1868 treaty, Sitting Bull in particular came to personify the spirit of uncompromising, ethnocentric hostility to white encroachment found among many Sioux at the time. A deeply religious man, convinced that his visionary powers derived from a harmonious convergence with universal spiritual forces, Sitting Bull believed that contact with whites would weaken and eventually destroy Teton culture. Those who shared his concern looked to the Hunkpapa holy man as their last best hope in defending the Sioux way of life. Consequently, by the early 1870s Sioux recalcitrants came to regard Sitting Bull as head chief of all the Lakotas.[5]

Sitting Bull's obstinacy spawned a fair number of detractors, but his compassion gained him a multitude of admirers. Fanny Kelly, a white captive who spent the better part of five months living with Sitting Bull and his family, described the Hunkpapa leader as "a true nobleman, and great man. He was uniformly gentle, and kind to his wife and children and courteous and considerate in his intercourse w. others." During Kelly's captivity in 1864, the Sioux experienced disastrous food shortages. Sitting Bull "and his wife," Kelly reported, "often suffered w. hunger to supply me w. food."[6] The interpreter Frank Grouard said the "name Sitting Bull was a 'tipi word' for all that was generous and great. The bucks admired him, the squaws respected him highly, and the children loved him."[7]

But many Sitting Bull enthusiasts admired him for his unqualified hatred of white civilization, Fanny Kelly notwithstanding. Mrs. C. Weldon, a missionary to the kunkpapas, reported that Sitting Bull "distrusted the innovations sought to be forced upon the Indians … white civilization," with its hypocrisy and avarice, "did not impress him," she said. "He never signed a treaty to sell any portion of his people's inheritance, and he refused to acknowledge the right of other Indians to sell his undivided share of the tribal lands."[8] In the words of Evan Connell, Sitting Bull "was about as consistent and inflexible as a man could be."[9]

The swelling ranks of Sitting Bull enthusiasts gravely concerned military authorities. In the winter of 1873–74, for example, Sioux dissidents from the north entered Red Cloud and Spotted Tail agencies, plundered stores, and killed several whites, including a Lieutenant Levi Robinson. In response, General Sherman ordered up cavalry and infantry from Fort Laramie under the command of Colonel John E. Smith to quell the unrest. By the time the troops arrived, however, following a harrowing winter trek, the crisis had passed. Nevertheless, Smith established a military post near Red Cloud Agency in case of future trouble. He named it Fort Robinson, in honor of the fallen lieutenant.[10]

In response to the Sioux provocation at the agencies, Sherman wrote Sheridan in March 1874 that many people "even [Interior Secretary Columbus] Delano, would be happy if the troops should kill a goodly proportion of those Sioux, but they want to keep the record to prove that they didn't do it. We can afford to be frank and honest," Sherman continued, "for sooner or later these Sioux have to be wiped out or made to stay just where they are put."[11] Sherman's vow came true sooner rather than later, hastened along by events at the periphery of empire.

Like the Sioux, the Zulu faced a severe subsistence crisis during the 1870s. Analogous to the diminishing buffalo population in the Great Plains, the Zulu kingdom was plagued by cattle shortages. Several factors underlay the problem. First, new diseases such as lung sickness, introduced by white traders from Natal, ravaged Zululand herds between the late 1850s and early 1870s. Second, pasture degeneration, a product of severe over-grazing during the reigns of Dingane and Mpande, an indirect precipitant of pre-Shakan state formation, contributed to the depletion of stock.

Compounding ecological degradation, the Zulu population had increased significantly during the early years of Mpande's rule. By the early 1870s it stood at 300,000, a threefold increase since 1840. Finally, drought, a periodic bane to Zululand farmers, returned with a vengeance during the 1860s and 1870s, with 1878–79 representing an especially dry season.[12]

Since cattle were used for patronage and paying fines, diminished livestock reserves also affected the power of the Zulu monarch.[13] But Cetshwayo, who became king at Mpande's death in 1872, faced even more troubling issues of authority. Namely, the king had to combat the persistent decentralizing forces in his kingdom, especially the problem of divided loyalties among some of his more powerful white advisers and territorial chiefs. The most notable examples, John Dunn and Hamu, both defected to the British side at the outset of the Anglo-Zulu War.

John Dunn, born in Natal and orphaned at an early age by his English parents, took up transport riding and hunting in his teens. He first visited the Zulu kingdom in 1853, and in 1856 joined forces with Mbuyazi during his struggle with Cetshwayo's Usuthu. Regardless, Cetshwayo befriended Dunn, viewing the white man's bilingualism a useful skill in Zulu relations with Natal. The future king invited Dunn to settle in Zululand in 1858 and granted him a substantial territory in the south of the kingdom. From this base, Dunn amassed considerable wealth and power by the 1870s. While serving as Cetshwayo's major adviser to the white colonies, Dunn married forty northern Nguni women, accumulated over three thousand head of cattle, hired a private army of 250 African hunters, and recruited Tsonga laborers for Natal at an annual salary of three hundred pounds. Dunn also imported the lion's share of the twenty thousand antiquated, muzzle-loading firearms that reportedly entered Zululand during the 1870s. Yet Dunn's extensive ties to the colonial world rendered his loyalty suspect. Indeed, Dunn joined the British soon after Isandhlwana and profited by Cetshwayo's demise.[14]

Even more troubling for Cetshwayo was the disposition of his elder brother, Hamu. Unlike Dunn, Hamu supported Usuthu in 1856, and since that time had built up a strong personal following in northwestern Zululand. In addition, Hamu developed extensive trading interests outside the Zulu kingdom through the advice of Herbert Nunn, a white trader whom the Zulu chief allowed to reside in his northwestern district. Abutting the Transvaal in the Blood River frontier, Hamu's northwestern boundary with the Boers had been a source of contention for years. During the 1870s Hamu grew increasingly critical of Cetshwayo's handling of the border controversy, with tensions exploding at the *umkhosi* in 1878. At this first-fruits festival, Hamu's Thulwana regiment assaulted Ngobomakhosi, Cetshwayo's favorite *ibutho*, leaving scores dead. Hamu's wider loyalties with the colonial world, combined with a festering sibling rivalry, led him to negotiate with the British for postwar concessions on the eve of the Anglo-Zulu War itself.[15]

Similar schisms emerged among the southern Nguni-speaking Xhosa in the 1850s. Following a half century of military subjugation, expropriation, missionary enterprise, and commercial temptation, the Xhosa lost over 100,000 cattle to a lung sickness epidemic that struck in 1854. This devastating epidemic, combined with the experience of defeat, resulted in Xhosa prophecies predicting that the dead would rise and the British driven into the sea if only the Xhosa people killed the rest of their cattle. The

majority of Xhosa complied. By the end of 1857 they had destroyed 400,000 head of cattle, and in the ensuing famine, over 40,000 Xhosa died of starvation. The Xhosa cattle-killing experience divided the people into two parties, the "soft" believers and the "hard" unbelievers. The majority "soft" faction regarded itself as the loyal defender of the traditional Xhosa values of mutual aid and communal solidarity. The "hard" party, composed principally of men like Hamu who benefited from the economic and social opportunities of the colonial presence, considered the killing senseless.[16]

To combat the centrifugal forces in his kingdom, as well as to cement his alliance with Natal in order to gain diplomatic advantage in the Transvaal–Zululand border dispute, Cetshwayo invited Theophilus Shepstone to the king's "coronation" in 1873. What seemed like prudent diplomacy at the time later proved to be a major miscalculation. Shepstone possessed an agenda quite distinct from Cetshwayo's, one that placed Zulu interests in a most precarious position.

Shepstone, the son of a Methodist missionary, was raised on the eastern Cape frontier. Before taking up the post of Natal's secretary for native affairs in 1853, a position he would hold for the next twenty-two years, Shepstone served as an agent for the African refugees of the Shakan wars and diplomatic agent for the African peoples of Natal. Shepstone's experience with dispossessed Africans fashioned a paternalistic temperament, as well as a conviction that he retained an intimate understanding of the "native mind." As secretary for native affairs, Shepstone believed that Africans should be governed separately and not allowed to settle permanently in "white" areas. He also felt that "divide and rule" represented an effective means of preventing a "native combination" that might challenge white supremacy. As he said, "tribal distinctions that obtain among [Africans] are highly useful in managing them in detail."[17]

In effect, Shepstone exercised an early form of indirect rule—Nguni chiefs enjoyed semi-independence in their respective territories under the paternal guidance of Natalian officials. Such stable African communities could be taxed, serving two significant functions. First, tax revenues paid the costs of colonial administration, saving the European taxpayer unnecessary expense; and second, taxes nudged the African from subsistence production into the colonial economy, a necessary preliminary for the indigene's civilizational "uplift." Shepstone possessed supreme confidence that his system of African administration assured all Natalians peace, prosperity, and racial harmony.[18]

African leaders who deviated from Shepstone's paternalistic utopia found themselves at risk. In 1873, for example, the Hlubi leader Langalibalele, whose people had been "located" in the Drakensberg foothills following their departure from Zululand to Natal in 1848, ran afoul of the Shepstonian system. His offense was failing to see to it that all the guns in his reserve were registered. In theory, all Africans possessing guns in South African colonies were required to register them with colonial magistrates. By the early 1870s a number of Langalibalele's young men had purchased guns while away working at the diamond mines, raising fears among Natalian authorities of a conspiratorial "combination." When Langalibalele failed to appear before the court in Pietermaritzburg after repeated summons, Shepstone and Lieutenant Governor Benjamin Pine planned, organized, and accompanied a punitive mission.[19]

On October 29, 1873, sixty-five hundred troopers invaded the Hlubi reserve. Although Langalibalele had escaped into Basutoland, the British force attacked the location, killing two hundred resisters. Eventually the Hlubi chief was captured and, in early 1874, tried before a court that included Shepstone and Pine. Denied defense counsel, Langalibalele was banished from his location for life and conveyed to

Robben Island, outside Cape Town, in August 1874. In addition, Natal confiscated the live stock and expropriated the lands of the chief's subjects. Shepstone later characterized his own motives in the Langalibalele affair as originating from an "ardent love of justice."[20]

As a colonial agent Shepstone was motivated by a number of concerns, perhaps none more important than his grandiose vision of British imperial expansion. For years, Shepstone had dreamed of using the Blood River territory under dispute between the Zulu and Boers as part of a "safety valve" for "surplus" and potentially volatile Africans in Natal, as a passage for migrant laborers from the north, and most importantly, as a road for British expansion up to the Zambesi frontier.[21] That ultimately this safety valve "will also be occupied by Europeans cannot be doubted," Shepstone argued,

> but if the land can be acquired, and put to the purpose I have suggested, the present tension in Natal will be relieved, and time be gained to admit of the introduction of a larger population of white colonists. ... But it will be a mistake to suppose that the relief afforded by this measure would be but temporary or that the difficulty it is proposed to abate could ever again reach its present dimensions; because the outlet being to the North, the abatement admits of permanent extension towards a climate unsuited to Europeans but not so to natives.[22]

For these reasons, Shepstone regarded the "coronation" as an opportunity to gain special political leverage in the Zulu kingdom, using the occasion to cast a decisive shadow over Zulu sovereignty.

In fact, the so-called coronation of September 1, 1873 was a farce. Shepstone later argued that he installed Cetshwayo as king, when in reality the Zulu had held a separate ceremony a month before Shepstone's celebrated "installation."[23] Moreover, Shepstone promulgated certain laws restricting the implementation of capital punishment within the Zulu kingdom, and he argued that these regulations had been accepted as binding by Cetshwayo himself. Later in the 1870s Shepstone and High Commissioner Bartle Frere would cite violations of these laws as a pretext for declaring war on the Zulu kingdom. In truth, the laws were worded ambiguously and could be interpreted as restricting the activities of Cetshwayo's territorial chiefs rather than the king.[24] Cetshwayo found it extraordinary that he had supposedly accepted laws from Natal whose "breaking" might serve as an excuse for war. As he said in 1876, "I do not agree to give my people over to be governed by laws sent to me by [Natal] … Mr. Shepstone … deceived the white men, saying I had agreed to his laws."[25]

Nonetheless, the "coronation" is significant in that it marks the first, albeit farcical, attempt by the British to subject the Zulu to imperial overrule in the 1870s. Britain's attempt to combine its South African territories into a white-dominated confederation during the remainder of the 1870s made future overtures toward the Zulu much more deadly serious.

As in South Africa, the activities of "men on the spot" played a considerable role in bringing on war with the Sioux. Sherman's brusque sentiments toward nonreservation Sioux remained consistent throughout the 1860s and 1870s. As he wrote in 1873, the Sioux "must be made to know that when the Government commands they must obey, and until that state of mind is reached, through persuasion or fear, we can not hope for peace."[26] But after Sherman moved his headquarters from Washington to St. Louis in May 1874, the result of a dispute with Secretary of War William Belknap, the general distanced himself from the decision-making loop. As far as the Sioux were concerned, two other individuals played more significant roles in enforcing Grant's peace policy: Lieutenant Colonel George Custer, the Seventh Cavalry commander, and Major General Philip Sheridan, commander of the Division of the Missouri.

Custer, the "Boy General" of Civil War fame, regarded himself an expert on the sub-

ject of the Great Plains, especially when it came to understanding the "Indian problem." In an essay written in 1868 entitled "The Red Man," Custer judged the Sioux and other Indians as noble savages yet doomed to extinction. In sententious prose, Custer argued that Indians "once stood in their native strength and beauty, stamped with the proud majesty of free born men, whose souls never knew fear or whose eyes never quailed beneath the fierce glance of man. But … now," he wrote, "they are like withered leaves of their own native forest, scattered in every direction by the fury of the tempest." Custer predicted that the Indian was perched "on the verge of extinction, standing on his last foothold, clutching his bloodstained rifle, resolved to die amidst the horrors of slaughter." Soon, Custer concluded, the Indian would "be talked of as a noble race who once existed but have now passed away."[27]

In the same year as his "Red Man" essay, Custer sought to fulfill his dire predictions at Black Kettle's Cheyenne village on the Washita River, in present-day Oklahoma. Black Kettle, a consistent peace advocate, had been victimized by Colonel John M. Chivington's volunteers at Sand Creek, Colorado, four years earlier. The chief's encampment now lay within range of Sheridan's winter campaign in the southern plains. Sheridan's orders to Custer were simple and direct: "To proceed south, in the direction of the Antelope hills, thence towards the Washita River, the supposed winter seat of the hostile tribes; to destroy their villages and ponies; to kill or hang all warriors, and bring back all women and children."[28]

As dawn broke on November 27, Custer divided his command and prepared for an attack. He had yet to ascertain the size of the village or the nature of the surrounding terrain, an omission for which he was later criticized. Nevertheless, to the accompaniment of his regimental band's rendition of "Garry Owen," Custer led the charge across the river into the village. For the startled inhabitants, the ensuing melee was deadly—Black Kettle, his wife, and nearly three hundred villagers, including many women and children, perished in the onslaught. And as per Sheridan's instructions, Custer ordered the Cheyenne pony herd slaughtered as well.[29]

"We have cleaned Black Kettle and his band out so thoroughly that they can neither fight, dress, sleep, eat or ride without sponging upon their friends," Custer boasted in a letter to Sheridan the day following the Washita battle. Although Washita established Custer's reputation as the preeminent plains Indian fighter of the era, it nevertheless served to tarnish his image as well. Specifically, Custer deserted a missing unit under the command of Major Joel Elliot at Washita, only to find the mutilated remains of Elliot and his men some ten days later. The episode strained Custer's relations with a number of his fellow officers and men, including his Little Bighorn cohort, Frederick Benteen.[30] In addition, Custer, whose wife, Libbie, remained in Monroe, Michigan, in 1868, may have taken on a teenage mistress named Monahsetah from the Cheyenne captives at Washita. According to Cheyenne oral tradition, Monahsetah bore a child fathered by the "Boy General."[31]

Custer, tainted victor at Washita, played a central role in two major provocations leading directly to the outbreak of the U.S.-Sioux War of 1876–77: the Yellowstone expedition of 1873 and, the following year, the reconnaissance of the Black Hills. The Yellowstone expedition occurred in conjunction with the proposed extension of the Northern Pacific Railroad, which had proceeded from Minnesota to the Missouri River between 1870 and 1872. In 1873 the Northern Pacific proposed to advance up the Yellowstone Valley, arguably part of the unceded territory from the 1868 treaty. As far as the Sioux were concerned, the northern boundary of this "unceded" cession was irrelevant. The advance of the railroad promised to bring hunters, soldiers, and immigrants, guaranteeing the destruction of the last great buffalo herd on the plains. For Sitting Bull's people, the only alternative was war. In stark contrast to the Lakota view, Custer, like his superiors Sherman and Sheridan, regarded railway development as the supreme pacifier:

> The experience of the past, particularly that of recent years, has shown too that no one measure so quickly and effectually frees a country from the horrors and devastations of Indian wars and Indian depredations generally as the building and successful operation of a railroad through the region overrun … So earnest is my belief in the civilizing and peace-giving influence of railroads [that their extension] through an Indian country … would for ever after have preserved peace with the vast number of tribes infesting the [plains].[32]

Custer, who represented mainstream thinking on the "Indian question" by the 1870s, reflects the contradictory impulses in the formulation of United States Indian policy. In the words of the historian Richard Slotkin, "the makers of the Indian policy wanted both to subjugate the Indians—which implied making war—and to establish a regime characterized by peace; they wanted to protect Indian rights, while at the same time extinguishing Indian title to the land to facilitate the building of railroads."[33]

The army provided munificent escorts for each Northern Pacific survey. In 1873, for example, fifteen hundred soldiers, including ten troops of the Seventh Cavalry under Custer's command, accompanied the surveyors. Looking to "subdue and intimidate" any hostile Sioux, Custer engaged Lakota warriors on two occasions in early August. In the first engagement, near the mouth of the Tongue River, Custer ordered his cavalry to charge about three hundred Sioux combatants. He later exulted that "despite their superiority in numbers [the Sioux] cowardly prepared for flight." One week later, on the Yellowstone, Custer's troops encountered around five hundred Teton warriors, who, despite giving significant resistance, once again broke and fled. Custer believed the Sioux coalition to have been organized by Sitting Bull. The Hunkpapa leader, Custer concluded, had for once "been taught a lesson he will not soon forget."

Custer's confidence as an Indian fighter without equal carried over into an even riskier venture the following year: a survey of the Black Hills. The Black Hills expedition of 1874, like the Washita campaign, was conceived by General Sheridan. "Little Phil" Sheridan, whom Sherman compared to a "persevering terrier dog," sympathized with the plight of the Sioux but did not allow sentimentality to dictate military policy. "I have the interest of the Indian at heart as much as anyone," he wrote in 1872, "but many years of experiences have taught me that to civilize and Christianize the wild Indian it is not only necessary to put him on Reservations but it is also necessary to exercise some strong authority over him." More explicitly, Sheridan wrote Adjutant General E. D. Townsend in 1869 that the

> Indian is a lazy, idle vagabond; he never labors, and has no profession except that of arms, to which he is raised from a child; a scalp is constantly dangled before his eyes, and the highest honor he can aspire to is, to possess one taken by himself. It is not to be wondered at, therefore, if he aims for this honor when he grows up; especially in there is no punishment to follow the barbarous act. The Government has always been very liberal to Indians, especially whenever they have settled on reservations; the lands allotted to them have been of the very best character, making them perhaps by far the richest communities in the country.

As for nonreservation Tetons, Sheridan saw "no other way to save the lives and property of our people, than to punish [the Sioux] until peace becomes a desirable object." Toward this end, Sheridan obtained permission from the Interior Department in 1873 to conduct a reconnaissance of the Black Hills for the stated purpose of establishing a major fort. This region, part of the Great Sioux Reservation guaranteed to the Sioux in the Treaty of 1868, was the most sacred of Lakota territories.

Sheridan appointed Custer to lead the expedition. Custer's coterie in the summer of 1874 included two companies of infantry, several reporters to immortalize the adventure, and two miners Custer hired at his own expense to scout the region for gold. The miners found what Custer later reported as "paying quantities" of the precious metal, precipitating an invasion of the region by thousands of gold seekers in 1874 and 1875. Sheridan ordered his officers to deter the influx if possible, but added that "should Congress open up the country to settlement by extinguishing the treaty rights of the Indians, [I] will give cordial support to the settlement of the Black Hills." Even before the expedition Custer had expressed a preference for the occupation of the region by white farmers and stockmen. Prior to his departure, Custer wrote General Terry that "the country to be visited is so new and believed to be so interesting that it will be a pity not to improve to the fullest extent the opportunity to determine all that is possible of its character, scientific and otherwise." Should the Sioux resist this effort, Custer recommended "a sound drubbing."

In his report on the Black Hills expedition, Custer offered lavish descriptions of the terrain and its resources. For example, on one occasion he ascended Harney Peak and was struck by the contrast between "the bright, green verdure of these lovely parks with the sunburned and dried yellow herbage to be seen in the outer plains." Custer compared the soil to that of a rich garden, sprouting hundreds of acres of delicious raspberries. "Nowhere in the States have I tasted cultivated raspberries of equal flavor to those growing here," he wrote. Custer's enthusiasm for the agricultural potential of the Black Hills validated the claims of contemporary railroad brochures that spoke of "parks" and "Edenic verdure" to promote the agrarian development of the West.

Custer's expedition to the Black Hills, which did much to advertise the mineral and agricultural potential of the region, precipitated the crisis that resulted in his own demise.

Outraged by white trespassers, Sioux recalcitrants attacked miners, settlers, and emigrants throughout 1875. The acting interior secretary, B. R. Cowan, pointed out emphatically to the governor of Dakota Territory that the Treaty of 1868 guaranteed no one but the Sioux were "permitted to *pass over, settle upon, or reside*" in the Black Hills. "The only power to alter this provision," Cowan pointed out, "is that which made the treaty and then it must be done with the consent of the Indians." General Terry, in contrast to Sheridan and Custer, strongly upheld Cowan's position: "I submit that it is of the greatest importance that any attempt to defy the law and to trample on the rights secured to the Sioux by the Treaty of 1868 should be met in the most rigorous manner *at the very outset.*"

At first, the government sought to quell the unrest by purchasing the Black Hills from the Sioux. A commission headed by Senator William B. Allison traveled to Red Cloud Agency in September 1875 and parleyed with Red Cloud, Spotted Tail, and several other Lakota chiefs. The negotiations went nowhere—the government offered six million dollars, but Red Cloud insisted on six hundred times that amount to take care of "seven generations ahead." Insulted by what he regarded as penurious commissioners, the Oglala chief opted to watch an Arapaho sun dance rather than attend the final meeting.

Unable to halt white trespassers and unsuccessful in purchasing the Black Hills outright, the government then turned to the final solution to the Sioux "problem." In a meeting in Washington on November 3, 1875, President Grant, Secretary of War Belknap, Interior Secretary Chandler, Commissioner of Indian Affairs Edward Smith, and generals Sheridan and Crook decided to stop the army's Black Hills anti-miner campaign and to punish nonreservation Sioux. Six days after the Washington conference, Indian Bureau Inspector Erwin C. Watkins filed an angry report replete with Frereian echoes that met with the full approval of Watkins's superiors. Watkins argued that the Sioux held United States troops "in contempt, and, surrounded by their native mountains, relying on their knowledge of the country and powers of endurance, they laugh at the futile efforts that have thus far been made to subjugate them." The Sioux, Watkins continued, were "lofty and independent in their attitude and language to Government officials, as well as the whites generally," and furthermore, he pointed out, they "claim to be the sovereign rulers of the land." Watkins then proceeded to issue his draconian recommendation:

> In my judgment, one thousand men, under the command of an experienced officer, sent into their country in the winter, when the Indians are nearly always in camp, and at which season of the year they are most helpless, would be amply sufficient for their capture or punishment. The Government has done everything that can be done, peacefully to get control of these Indians, or to induce them to respect its authority. Every effort has been made, but all to no purpose. They are still as wild and untamable, as uncivilized and savage, as when Lewis and Clark first passed through their country … The true policy, in my judgment, is to send troops against them in the winter—the sooner the better—and whip them into subjection.

Heretofore, the policy of Interior had been to protect Indian title, negotiate with indigenous mediators, and keep the military at bay. In November 1875, however, the agency reversed nearly three decades of tradition. Interior Secretary Zacharia Chandler, "a blustering ex-Senator and Michigan political hack," literally handed the disposition of Sioux affairs to General Sheridan. The general issued an ultimatum to nonreservation Sioux to report to their agencies by January 31, 1876, or face military reprisals. Sheridan, who believed the Sioux would regard the ultimatum as "a good joke," worried that "unless they are caught before early spring they cannot be caught at all."

The irony of Sheridan's concern expressed itself poignantly on the afternoon of June 25, 1876. In the end, however, the general's troops prevailed. The Americans believed in the destiny of white settlement and capitalist expansion, demanded its indigenous foe to comply, and precipitated crises at the periphery of empire that ensured a military showdown. That Custer and Sheridan bear significant responsibility for the war against the Sioux seems clear; but their actions make sense only in relation to the broader policy objectives formulated by bureaucrats in Washington. As will be seen, similar circumstances prevailed in the events leading to the outbreak of the Anglo-Zulu War.

The conflict against the Zulu kingdom arose in the context of Britain's attempt to unite its South African possessions into a white-dominated confederation during the 1870s. Confederation became the orthodoxy of Lord Carnarvon, colonial secretary from 1874 to 1878. The fastidious Carnarvon, nicknamed "Twitters" by Disraeli, viewed confederation as a logical extension of Britain's strategic and economic interests in the region. As he wrote to Bartle Frere in 1876, the British "must be prepared to apply a sort of Munro [sic] doctrine to much of Africa." "But the most immediately urgent reason for general union," Carnarvon reasoned in the same year, "is the formidable character of the native question, and the importance of a uniform, wise and stern policy in dealing with it."

The Zulu kingdom, wedged between Natal and the Transvaal, represented the heart of the so-called native question. In the broadest sense, the Colonial Office regarded a strong, independent Zulu kingdom as a dangerous example for other Africans in the region, who might wish likewise to achieve equality with whites. The very existence of an independent Zululand fueled conspiracy theories among colonial officials throughout the 1870s of a Zulu-led "native combination" to rid the region of Europeans. Sir Garnet Wolseley put the issue bluntly in 1875: "[I do] not believe it to be possible for the two races to live together on perfect terms; one or the other must be the predominant power in the State, and if the very small minority of white men is to be that power, the great native majority must be taught not only to confide in its justice, but to realise and acknowledge its superiority." In addition to their concern over Zululand's independent existence, the British anguished over two other problems. First, the ongoing conflict between the Zulu kingdom and the Transvaal over disputed territory in the Blood River frontier posed a security threat for the region. Second, an independent Zululand bottled up potential laborers for white farmers and harnessed vast tracts of fertile farmland, coveted by Transvaal Boers and Natalian sugar planters.

Carnarvon selected apostles who shared his imperial vision and seemed likely to execute the confederation scheme successfully, especially with regard to the "native question." In 1876 he dispatched Theophilus Shepstone to the Transvaal with vague instructions authorizing the native secretary to annex the Boer republic to the British Crown. Shepstone had consistently backed Cetshwayo's position in the Zulu-Boer boundary dispute since the "coronation" of 1873. In that year Shepstone wrote that Cetshwayo was "a man of considerable ability, much force of character," dignified, frank, and sagacious. Shepstone thought Cetshwayo to be not "very war-like," yet nonetheless "proud of the military traditions of his family, especially the policy and deeds of his uncle and predecessor, Chaka."

In 1877 political expedience dictated a shift in Shepstone's thinking. Having annexed the Transvaal on behalf of Great Britain in April, Shepstone, the newly appointed administrator there, openly supported Boer claims in the boundary dispute. To justify his switch, Shepstone claimed to have found new evidence favorable to the Boers. Since he failed to ever reveal the location of such evidence, a more likely explanation for Shepstone's policy adjustment related to his expansionist goals. Mocking Shepstone's change of heart, John Sanderson wrote in the *Fortnightly Review* that "it is—as the Zulus have not been slow to observe—at least remarkable that it is only since Sir T. Shepstone became Administrator of the Transvaal country, that he has become convinced of the justice of the Transvaal claims." Cetshwayo likened Shepstone to a woman with twins— "he has given one the breast, and now he gives it to the other." Arguably, however, by annexing the disputed territory to the Transvaal, now a British dependency, Shepstone could proceed to carry out his grand vision of a "safety valve" and road to the north.

At a meeting with Zulu notables on the western boundary of the Blood River on October 18, 1877, Shepstone tried to rationalize his change of heart in soothing, paternalistic rhetoric. Unconvinced, the Zulu delegation berated Shepstone and accused the former secretary of betraying them. "Their bearing was haughty," Shepstone wrote of the Zulu leaders, "and it seemed difficult for them to treat me with the respect that they had usually paid me." It was evident, Shepstone concluded, "that our meeting was not to be a very cordial or pleasant one."

Spurned at the Blood River encounter, Shepstone's memoranda to the Colonial Office assumed a decided bellicosity. For example, he informed Carnarvon in December 1877 "that if hostilities should occur with Cetshwayo, which I shall endeavor by all means in my power to avoid, … nothing short of the complete breaking up of the Zulu power will afford any guarantee of quiet in the future." Perhaps Shepstone revealed his hand even more clearly in a memorandum dispatched to Carnarvon a fortnight later: "Had Cetshwayo's thirty thousand warriors been in time changed to labourers working for wages, Zululand would have been a prosperous peaceful country instead of what it now is, a source of perpetual danger to itself and its neighbours."

In June 1878 the bishop of Natal, John William Colenso, told F. W. Chesson, secretary of the Aborigines Protection Society, that "I have lost all faith in [Shepstone's] sense of justice & truthfulness." Colenso, who had once been a close friend of Sir Theophilus, believed that Shepstone would "never forget or forgive the rebuff he got from the Zulus at the Blood River" and might now engage in "crafty underscheming." Colenso expressed fear "that some-

thing will be done to provoke a war with [Cetshwayo], a war which would be most unjustifiable and wicked."

Colenso, bishop of Natal between 1852 and his death in 1883, established Bishopstowe, near Pietermaritzburg, and founded the mission Ekukhunyeni. The bishop spent his career in South Africa defending free religious inquiry against the theological obscurantism of the Anglican Church hierarchy and, throughout the last decade of his life, championing the rights of Africans in Natal and Zululand. For his "heretical" pursuits the settler community ostracized him, and colonial officials branded Colenso a "meddler." Colenso, as Jeff Guy puts it, was not "a twentieth-century liberal who somehow wandered into the wrong century." He was a product of his times—Colenso, much like the "humanitarian" Indian commissioner Nathaniel Taylor, assumed the superiority of his culture and believed it his duty to subordinate Africans to his world vision. Appropriately, Africans knew him as the paternalist Sobantu, "the father of the people." A courageous and principled man, Colenso was nonetheless unable to see that injustice was the essence of imperialism. Thus, when Bishop Colenso witnessed British officials maneuvering for a showdown with the Zulu kingdom in the late 1870s, he was pushed to the limits of his faith. That Britain initiated such unjustifiable aggression "negated the basic principles upon which his political, moral and religious existence was founded."

As Colenso surmised, Shepstone had been prejudiced by the Blood River encounter. Furthermore, Shepstone's opinions carried significant weight with Carnarvon as well as with the colonial secretary's second major missionary for confederation, Bartle Frere. Frere arrived in Cape Town in March 1877 as Britain's new high commissioner to South Africa. As a former president of the Royal Geographical Society and fervent evangelical Christian, Frere lobbied enthusiastically in the 1870s for the extension of British civilization to the Zambesi and beyond. Frere's previous administrative experience in India instilled a commanding self-confidence and convinced him that "a native and comparatively uncivilised power [could] co-exist alongside a European power, and … be gradually raised by it to a higher civilisation." Frere believed, however, that "it is undoubtedly necessary that the two powers should settle from the first which is to be the superior, and which is to be subordinate." Following such logic, Frere's task in South Africa became clear. In his mind, a defensible, self-governing white dominion could exist only if all potential black resistance was eliminated. He perceived the Zulu kingdom, revitalized under Cetshwayo and seemingly as powerful as ever, as the principal African obstacle. Therefore, the Zulu must be subjugated.

Frere grounded his bellicosity on a number of considerations. First, he believed that subjugation would bear significant economic fruits. He wrote that the Zulu were not "the wolf-like savages one might suppose from their mode of attack." Indeed, he posited, "the Zulu military organization is an excrescence quite alien to the natural habit of the people." Their training "develops every animal power and instinct," he argued, "till they become parts of a frightfully efficient man-slaying war-machine." If Cetshwayo's "iron rule" could be completely broken down, Frere reasoned, the Zulu might be transformed into a menial labor force: "They belong to the same race which furnishes the good-humoured volatile labourers and servants who abound in Natal, men very capable of being moulded in the ways of civilization and, when not actually trained to manslaughter, not naturally blood-thirsty, nor incurably barbarous."

In addition, Frere believed Cetshwayo was working behind the scenes to promote a black "combination" to rid Natal of all Europeans, a view shared and inspired by Shepstone. "I need not observe that in this Colony the existence of a very great mass of natives within it, who are often supposed to be under very imperfect con-

trol," Frere wrote in September 1878 to Michael Hicks Beach, Lord Carnarvon's replacement as colonial secretary, "and to be liable to follow the lead of their former fellow subjects across the border, has been always regarded as a cause for anxiety." Although "the Colonial natives are said to be, at present, unusually quiet and free from excitement," Frere warned, "I have heard this variously accounted for, sometimes as an evidence of their complicity with the warlike intentions of the Zulu nation." In a similar vein, Frere wrote R. W. Herbert in the same year "that Shepstone and others of experience in the country, were right as to the existence of a wish among the great chiefs to make this war a general and simultaneous rising of Kaffirdom against white civilization."

Furthermore, Frere as well as Shepstone made extensive use of missionary reports from Zululand, especially those of the Anglican Robert Robertson, to justify aggression toward Cetshwayo. Robertson, who enjoyed little success in attracting African converts, had grown frustrated and embittered by the late 1870s. A notorious drunk, and vulnerable to the sexual attractions of young women on his station, Robertson blamed his personal misery on Cetshwayo and those "thousands of wild Zulus" who had only "learned the name of the Evil one" from the white man. By late 1877 Robertson lamented that as tragic as a conflict with the Zulu might be, "there are worse things than war sometimes."

Frere had reached similar conclusions. Working feverishly during 1878 to lay the groundwork for confederation, Frere prepared the Colonial Office for war against the Zulu kingdom. In September, for example, he wrote that "the preservation of peace in Natal depends simply on the sufferance of the Zulu Chief, that while he professes a desire for peace every act is indicative of an intention to bring about war, and that this intention is shared … by the majority of his people." In manufacturing a *casus belli*, Frere exaggerated the significance of various incidents, including the exodus of missionaries from Zululand in mid-1878. Frere informed the colonial secretary that virtually every missionary had been "terrified out of the country." Although Cetshwayo disliked most Christian missionaries, he had never persecuted them. According to Colonel Anthony Durnford, the mission stations in Zululand had converted only a handful of Africans, "as the king considers that the moment a man becomes a Christian he is *no use*. Indeed he is right in his own point of view, as the few *supposed* Christians are an idle useless lot." In all likelihood, the missionaries decided to quit Zululand on the advice of Shepstone, who warned them of an impending "political crisis."

Alarmed at the unremitting enmity toward the Zulu reflected in Frere's memoranda to the Colonial Office during the latter months of 1878, Michael Hicks Beach, the new colonial secretary, cautioned Frere to avoid an expensive and unnecessary colonial conflict. The somber Hicks Beach, known to his political enemies as "Black Michael," advised Frere in October "that by the exercise of prudence, and by meeting the Zulus in a spirit of forebearance and reasonable compromise, it will be possible to avert the very serious evil of a war with Cetshwayo." In November Hicks Beach added that with mounting problems in Eastern Europe and Afghanistan, "we cannot now have a Zulu war." But a certain fatalism regarding hostilities with Zululand had overtaken the Colonial Office by late 1878. For example, in October Hicks Beach asked the Foreign Office to seek Portuguese consent to land British troops at Delagoa Bay in case of war. The government's failure to restrain Frere prompted Sir William Harcourt, during parliamentary debate, to portray an imaginary letter from Hicks Beach to the High Commissioner:

My dear Sir Bartle Frere,
    I cannot think you are right. Indeed I think you are very wrong but after all, I feel you know a great deal better than I do. I hope you won't do what you're going to do; but if you do I hope it will turn out well.

On December 10, 1878, the day before Frere's commissioners delivered to a Zulu delegation an ultimatum sure to bring war, the high commissioner wrote Hicks Beach that "after the most anxious consideration I can arrive at no other conclusion than that it is impossible to evade the necessity for now settling this Zulu question thoroughly and finally." In fashioning the ultimatum, Frere dismissed a boundary commissioners' report submitted in July 1878 that awarded the bulk of the disputed Blood River territory to the Zulu kingdom. Shortly after the ultimatum lapsed and British forces invaded in January, Frere expressed puzzlement to the colonial secretary over the Zulu's "innate tendency to suspicion of the motives and acts of everyone. It is, perhaps," Frere speculated, "to a great extent the result of their present system of government."

Alternatively, the Zulu had grown cynical by Shepstone's duplicity, Frere's manufactured *casus belli*, and the Colonial Office's acquiescence. As in the United States, "men on the spot" engineered a crisis at the periphery of empire that made war inevitable. Their decisions, despite the handwringing one might find at the metropolis, complemented the broader policy objectives of imperial expansion. The carnage at Isandhlwana and Rorke's Drift, as well as the Little Bighorn, was the immediate price for this unglamorous adventure in empire building. The Zulu and Sioux people sustained the long-range costs.

QUESTIONS TO CONSIDER

1. Could the letter Sherman wrote to Sheridan in March 1874 be construed as genocidal policy by the U.S. government?

2. How was Zulu reliance on cattle analogous to Native American reliance on bison?

3. Were Custer's actions at the Washita River genocidal?

4. Did Bartle Frere have genocidal intent with regard to the Zulu?

5. What is the nexus between empire building and genocide?

King Leopold's "Heart of Darkness"

Adam Hochschild,

University of California at Berkley

In 1885, King Leopold II of Belgium gained a vast area in central Africa as his personal possession. His greed and the system of forced labor he imposed there prompted the first human rights movement of the 20th century.

Five years after most European nations and the United States had granted colonial status to King Leopold's "Congo Free State," a young merchant seaman traveled up the Congo River in a steamboat. Joseph Conrad was one of the first outsiders to witness and later write about the horrors committed by Leopold's regime in its greedy pursuit of Congo ivory and wild rubber.

In 1902, Conrad published his novel *The Heart of Darkness*. In this fictional story, a man much like himself travels up a river into a rain forest where he meets a European ivory trader named Kurtz. The methods Kurtz uses to force the native people to bring him the ivory elephant tusks are symbolized by his guns and a ring of poles around his house. On top of each pole is a human head.

Conrad attempted to show that the "heart of darkness" lay deep within the Europeans who exploited the land and people of the Congo. But the full story of the Congo Free State not only involves the evil acts committed there, but also the campaign to expose them to world public opinion.

EXPLORING THE CONGO

Ten years before Columbus reached America, the Portuguese entered the mouth of Africa's Congo, one of the great rivers of the world. At first, good relations developed between the Portuguese and the several million inhabitants of the Kingdom of the Congo. The Portuguese didn't want to conquer or colonize the Congo. They only hoped to trade and to introduce Christianity.

The Kingdom of the Congo was a strong unified state known for its advanced working of copper and iron. The Congo king welcomed Portuguese traders, artisans, and missionaries.

Slavery was a part of the Congo culture. Most slaves were war captives, criminals, or debtors who could eventually earn back their freedom. But Congo clan chiefs and African Muslim slave traders from upriver were happy to sell their slaves to the Portuguese and other Europeans who transported them to America. This slave trading gradually depopulated and weakened the once-powerful Kingdom of the Congo.

In the mid-1800s, European maps marked central Africa as "unexplored." It remained one of the few areas of the vast continent not colonized by a European imperial power. But in 1871, journalist Henry M. Stanley electrified Europe when he found adventurer David Livingstone who had disappeared years earlier on an African expedition. Stanley then became determined to fully explore the interior of Africa.

Financed by New York and London newspapers, Stanley left the east coast of Africa in 1874 to lead a massive expedition. Battling native peoples and mutinies among his own men, he reached the headwaters of the Congo River. He then navigated down the Congo for a thousand miles before encountering a 200-mile stretch of rapids. He finally arrived at the Atlantic Ocean in 1877, having traveled 7,000 miles across Africa. He announced that the

From "King Leopold's 'Heart of Darkness,'" *The Bill of Rights in Action* 16(2) (2000): 1–4. By Permission of Constitutional Rights Foundation, 610 South Kingsley Drive, Los Angeles, CA 90005.

Congo "is and will be the grand highway of commerce to west central Africa."

LEOPOLD II GETS HIS COLONY

Leopold II, the king of the Belgians, enthusiastically followed press accounts of Stanley's travels. Leopold was frustrated that tiny Belgium possessed no colonies. As a constitutional monarch, he held little power at home. But he yearned to rule a rich colonial empire.

Leopold invited Stanley to Belgium and persuaded the now famous explorer to return to the Congo acting as the king's personal agent. Leopold instructed Stanley, under the guise of doing scientific explorations and combating slavery, to secretly establish monopoly control over the rich Congo ivory trade. To do this, Stanley had to get local clan chiefs to sign treaties turning over their lands and the labor of their people to Leopold.

Over the next five years, Stanley signed more than 450 treaties with Congo chiefs. Clearly, they had no idea what they were signing in exchange for the cloth, trinkets, alcohol, and other cheap goods Stanley gave them. After Leopold sent agents to lobby Congress, the United States became the first nation to recognize his claim to the Congo.

In 1884–85, a conference held in Berlin, Germany, decided the colonial status of central Africa. Suspicious of each other's ambitions in the region, the European powers and the United States agreed to grant Leopold possession of the Congo River basin. This encompassed nearly a million square miles, an area 80 times larger than Belgium. Of course, the people of the Congo took no part in the Berlin Conference and were unaware that their lives were about to tragically change.

"THE HEART OF DARKNESS"

On May 29, 1885, King Leopold's agents proclaimed him "sovereign" (supreme authority) of the "Congo Free State." In reality, it was neither free nor a state, but the personal possession of Leopold to do with as he pleased. The delegates to the Berlin Conference assumed that all nations would trade freely in Leopold's colony. "Sovereign" Leopold, however, had other ideas.

Leopold, who never visited the Congo, issued decrees from Belgium. He required the native people to trade only with his state agents or with his "concessions" (private companies that paid him 50 percent of their profits). The natives hunted elephants for their ivory tusks and gathered sap from wild rubber vines growing in the rain forest. This involved the hard labor of many men who were often away from their families for long periods.

Leopold and the concessions gave bonuses to their agents for paying native workers little for the ivory and rubber. When the Congo people finally refused to continue working under these conditions, Leopold had to develop a new system of labor. By 1890, Leopold's regime and the concessions were paying Congo chiefs to supply "volunteer" workers. The Congo Free State also purchased or forcibly took slaves from Muslim slave traders to work as laborers or soldiers.

In the early 1890s, Leopold's private African army, the Force Publique (Public Force), drove the powerful Muslim slave traders out of the Congo. While Leopold portrayed this as a great humanitarian act, his real purpose was to gain control of the upper Congo River and to acquire more workers.

Up to this point, Leopold's Congo enterprises had not made a profit. But his fortunes changed in the mid-1890s. A world rubber boom suddenly started, following the invention of the inflatable tire. Leopold and his licensed concessions now needed even more workers to go deeper into the forest in search of wild rubber.

Leopold decided to "tax" his Congo subjects by requiring local chiefs to supply men to collect rubber. Leopold's agents held the wives and children of these men as hostages until they returned with their quota of rubber.

The Congo people rebelled by ambushing army units, fleeing their villages to hide in the wilderness, and setting the rubber vine forests on fire. But Leopold's Force Publique crushed the rebellion. By 1905, the Force Publique had grown to a fearsome but poorly disciplined army of 16,000 African mercenary soldiers led by some 350 European officers. They burned villages, cut off the heads of uncooperative chiefs, and slaughtered the women and children of men refusing to collect rubber.

Force Publique officers sent their soldiers into the forest to find and kill rebels hiding there. To prove they had succeeded, soldiers were ordered to cut off and bring back the right hand of every rebel they killed. Often, however, soldiers cut off the hands of living persons, even children, to satisfy the quota set by their officers. This terror campaign succeeded in getting workers back to collecting rubber. As a result, Leopold's profits soared.

"A SECRET SOCIETY OF MURDERERS"

Edmund Dene Morel was a young British shipping clerk. Periodically, his company sent him to the Belgian port of Antwerp to supervise the loading and unloading of ships. In the late 1890s, Morel made a horrifying discovery. He noticed that while the Congo Free State exported tons of raw rubber to Belgium, little was shipped back except guns and bullets. He guessed rightly that the many natives needed to collect the rubber were forced to do so at gunpoint. "I had stumbled upon a secret society of murderers with a king for a [partner]," he later wrote.

After reading reports written by missionaries about Congo atrocities, Morel quit his shipping job in 1901 and began a campaign to expose Leopold's Congo regime. Morel worked as a newspaper reporter, made speeches, and wrote books and pamphlets condemning the mistreatment of the Congo people. His relentless activity caused the British government

to send diplomat Roger Casement to the Congo Free State to investigate conditions there. Casement uncovered widespread evidence of hostage-taking, floggings, mutilation, forced labor, and outright murder.

Following the publication of his report in 1904, Casement joined Morel in organizing the Congo Reform Association, which resulted in the first major human rights movement of the 20th century. To expose Leopold's bloody Congo enterprise, Morel used photographs and slide shows picturing children whose hands had been cut off. Morel also expanded his movement to the United States where he met with President Theodore Roosevelt and enlisted the support of Booker T. Washington and Mark Twain.

Leopold struck back with a massive propaganda effort, which included lobbying both the British Parliament and U.S. Congress. But Morel's pleas for human rights in the Congo turned public opinion against the Belgian king.

Under pressure from Britain and the United States, Leopold turned over ownership of the Congo Free State to the Belgian government in 1908. But he demanded and received a huge cash payment and other benefits from Belgium for "his great sacrifices made for the Congo." Again, the Congo people had no say in their fate.

The Belgian government eliminated the worst abuses against the native people of the Congo. But the land along with its rubber and mineral resources remained firmly under European control. Belgium did little to improve the well-being of the people or to involve them in administering the colony.

Rich in copper, diamonds, oil, uranium, and other minerals, the Congo became an independent nation in 1960. In 1965, however, army leader Joseph Mobutu seized power. Like Leopold, Mobutu used his dictatorial powers to funnel the wealth of the Congo into his own pockets. Although Mobutu was finally overthrown in 1997, the future of self-rule in today's Democratic Republic of the Congo still remains uncertain.

King Leopold's Congo Free State was an economic, environmental, cultural, and human disaster for the Congo people. Historians estimate that 8–10 million persons perished from the violence, forced labor, and starvation caused by Leopold's lust for power and profits. When he died in 1909 at age 74, much of the world despised him. American poet Vachel Lindsay wrote this epitaph:

> Listen to the yell of Leopold's ghost
> Burning in Hell for his hand-maimed host,
>   Hear how the demons chuckle and yell
>   Cutting his hands off, down in Hell.

QUESTIONS TO CONSIDER

1. Describe the system of labor put into place by Leopold to gather ivory and wild rubber. Was this a form of slavery?
2. How did Edmund Morel almost single-handedly convince the world that something terrible was happening in King Leopold's Congo Free State?
3. What was "the heart of darkness"?

The Tribe Germany Wants to Forget

Regina Jere-Malanda,

New African, Associate Editor

According to reparation watchers, Germany has paid over DM90 billion to Israel since 1949 in voluntary reparations essentially in atonement for the gas chambers of Auschwitz. Yet the same Germany does not want to hear the name, Herero. It is a little known tribe in Namibia which was nearly wiped off the face of the earth by German colonial forces in the early 1900s. Historians say the first seeds of the Nazi holocaust were sown in Hereroland after the Germans had annihilated over 80% of the Hereros in a brutal attempt to take their land. As Namibia celebrates 10 years of independence this month, descendants of the Herero victims, after reading *New African's* reprint of Lord Anthony Gifford's legal basis for reparations, are going to court to seek justice and reparations from Germany. But, as Regina Jere-Malanda reports here, Germany is not at all happy with the Herero action.

The great general of the German troops, sends this letter to the Herero people. Hereros are no longer German subjects … . All the Hereros must leave the land. If the people do not want this, then I will force them to do it with the great guns. Any Herero found within the German borders with or without a gun, with or without cattle, will be shot. I shall no longer receive any women or children; I will drive them back to their people—otherwise I shall order shots to be fired at them … . No male prisoner will be taken. I will shoot them. This is my decision for the Herero people.
Signed:
The Great General of the Mighty Kaiser, Lt-Gen Lothar von Trotha.
2nd October, 1904.

The powerful, great German Kaiser wants to grant clemency to those of the Hottentot [Nama] people who surrender themselves voluntarily. They will be presented with life. Only those who at the beginning of the rebellion have committed murder against whites or have commanded that

From "The Tribe Germany Wants to Forget," *New African* (2000): 1–7. Reprinted with Permission.

whites be murdered, have by law forfeited their lives. This I declare publicly and state further that of the few who have not been defeated, it will fare with them, just as it fared with the Hereros, who in their blindness also believed that they could make successful war against the powerful German Kaiser and the great German people.

I ask you, where are the Hereros today, where are their chiefs? Samuel Maherero, who at one time styled himself the ruler of thousands of children, has, hunted like a wild animal, fled across the English border. He has become as poor as the poorest field Herero and now owns nothing. Just so has it fared with the other Herero people, most of whom have lost their lives—some having died of hunger and thirst in the Sandfeld, some having been killed by German Reiters, some having been murdered by the Owambos.

No harm will befall the Hottentot people as soon as they voluntarily appear and turn over their weapons. You should come with a white cloth on a stick along with your entire household and nothing will happen to you. You will be given work and receive food until after the conclusion of the war when the great German Kaiser will present new rules governing the affairs of the protectorate. He who after this chooses not to make an application for mercy must emigrate, because where he allows himself to be seen in the German area, he will be shot until all are exterminated.

For the surrender of the murderous culprits, whether dead or alive, I offer the following rewards: for Hendrik Witboi, 5,000 marks; Sturmann, 3,000 marks; Cornelius 3,000 marks; and all the remaining guilty leaders, 1,000 marks. Signed:

Lt-Gen Lothar von Trotha,
22 April 1905.

With these words, Germany's Lt-Gen von Trotha and his forces completed the savage extermination of almost the entire Herero tribe of Namibia (then called German South West Africa), leaving in its wake labour camps, sex slaves and wounds that have refused to heal.

Most historians now agree that the annihilation of the Hereros is actually "the first genocide of the 20th century." It is also now becoming increasingly clear that this merciless German undertaking in Namibia, sowed the first seeds from which Adolf Hitler plucked ideas for his racial experiments against the Jews in the Nazi holocaust that came 40 years later.

Indeed, as Namibia celebrates 10 years of independence this month, this ugly blot in the country's troubled past would not just go away. Attempts by Germany to cajole everyone, including President Sam Nujoma's government in Namibia, into believing that this is a better-forgotten issue, have just not worked.

The descendants of the Herero survivors of this little known holocaust, are today reviving the issue with aroused vigour, demanding from the German government not only an apology for the atrocities that culminated in the 1904 butchery of their ancestors, but reparations as well.

They say if Germany can pay DM90bn to Israel in voluntary reparations in 50 years for the gas chambers in Auschwitz alone, and is still paying billions more to the Jewish people for the other crimes committed against the Jews and other slave labourers, it is only fair that the Hereros get a just recompense.

Elsewhere in Europe and America, banks, governments and others are owning up to their Nazi past, and are paying reparations or making restitution to the Jewish people.

Japan recently apologised for its brutal colonial rule in Korea and paid reparations to the "comfort women" (sex slaves) used by the Japanese troops in World War II.

But this atonement has so far passed the Hereros by.

THE HISTORY

Although Germany joined the European colonial plunder of Africa quite late, it effected in record time one of the worst landmarks on the continent. The German presence in Africa began, effectively, in 1884 when it colonised Togo, Cameroon, Namibia and Tanzania. In Namibia, the German presence had actually started in the 1870s with the arrival of a handful of German missionaries.

But in January 1894, following the discovery of diamonds in Namibia, the German leader, Otto von Bismarck, sent Major Theodor Leutwein as his representative in the territory. Luetwein was "a professional officer with a classical education and a background in law, but had no experience in colonial matters and knew nothing about Africa."

Apparently, Bismarck sent him to Africa because he was a "level-headed and judicious man." However, it wasn't long before Leutwein showed his true colours.

First, he played the two main tribes in the country (the Herero and Nama) against each other, using the time-tested divide-and-rule tactics so loved by all the European colonialists. At one time the Herero even allied themselves with the Germans against the Nama (also known as Hottentots). This ploy paid Leutwein handsome dividends.

But soon both tribes realised what the man was really up to—they were losing their best land and cattle to the handful of German settlers in the territory.

Leutwein had, by this time, been carried away by the profits of his exploits in land grabbing. He started to arrange for more Germans to come in. But to do this he needed more land. And the best land, at the time, still belonged to the Herero.

So Leutwein decided to play tough. Ignoring the simmering discontent among the Herero against his betrayal and land grabbing antics, he went ahead and brought in boatloads of Germans. They, in turn, came along with guns, arrogance and coarse racism. And this is where the problems really started.

The Germans began to slowly push the Herero from their traditional land—at first, through persuasion and bribery. But by 1900, the Germans were going all out to grab Herero land with brazen insolence. Nothing, and no one, was there to restrain them.

By January 1904, the Herero had had enough! With barely any land and cattle left

for them, their chief Samuel Maherero led an armed rebellion. The target: the now ubiquitous German military post. At least, 123 Germans were killed at the beginning of the Herero uprising.

The Herero, like the Nama tribe, intensely disliked the Germans taking their land, and eroding their centuries-old rights to common pastures and water resources. Both tribes also resented the Germans introducing foreign laws and taxes.

When the Herero revolt started, the Nama chief Hendrik Witbooi even felt compelled to draw Leutwein's attention to the injustice being perpetrated by the Germans. He wrote to Leutwein thus:

> The German himself … is just what he described the other nations … he makes no requests according to truth and justice and asks no permission of a chief. He introduces laws into the land [which] are entirely impossible, untenable, unbelievable, unbearable, unmerciful and unfeeling.
>
> He punishes our people [in] Windhoek and has already beaten people to death for debt. It is not just and right to beat people to death for that. He flogs people in a shameful and cruel manner. We stupid and unintelligent people, for so he thinks us to be, we have never yet punished a human being in such a cruel and improper way. For, he stretches people on their backs and flogs them on the stomach and even between the legs, be they male or female. So, Your Honour can understand that no one can survive such a punishment.

What happened next is the dirty, brutal secret that the German government and strangely, also the Namibian government, want buried.

Back home in Berlin, the Herero uprising was very badly received by "the Mighty Kaiser," Wilhelm II. He chastised Leutwein for being "too soft," and so relieved him of his military command and made him the governor of the territory.

In Leutwein's place as commander-in-chief, the "Mighty Kaiser" sent a hard man called Lt-Gen Lothar von Trotha. He was an experienced, "extremely resolute" soldier, renowned for his brutal involvement in the suppression of the Chinese Boxer Rebellion in 1900 in which the Chinese had risen up against what they saw as European/American attempts "to destroy traditional Chinese culture."

Trotha was also involved in the bloody suppression of African resistance to German colonial rule in German East Africa (today's Burundi, Rwanda and Tanzania).

So Trotha knew a thing or two about being brutal to Africans. In Namibia, he actually threw all caution to the wind. He disregarded commands and refused to take advice from his superiors in Berlin. He had a mission—not to quell the Herero uprising but to annihilate the tribe altogether and set an example to others intending to challenge the German occupation.

Trotha quickly came up with a battle plan that was simple but well calculated. It achieved the intended result in the quickest possible time.

With 10,000 heavily armed German men ready to obey his every word, Trotha began to shepherd the Herero north into the sandy Waterberg region. Here they were surrounded and attacked from three fronts—leaving only one possible escape route: into the Omaheke Desert (now called the Kalahari Desert). With nowhere else to run, and German guns pointing directly at them, the Herero had no choice but take to the desert.

Even then, Trotha would not leave them alone. He offered huge rewards to his men to pursue the fleeing, thirsty, hungry and unarmed Hereros deep into the desert. The Kalahari, thus, became the killing fields where the "first genocide of the 20th century" happened.

The German brutality didn't end there. They killed more Hereros by poisoning the few water holes in the desert, and forcing fathers and mothers perishing from thirst to share breast milk with their dying babies.

To complete the slaughter, Trotha erected guard posts along the 150-mile border of the Kalahari. Any Herero who tried to escape was mercilessly bayoneted to death.

THE SURRENDER

Emaciated, diseased and left with no other choice, the Herero surrendered by September 1904. Chief Maherero had managed to flee into neighbouring Bechuanaland (now Botswana). By then over 80% of the Herero had been killed! But Trotha rejected their pleas of surrender. Instead, he issued the Vernichtunsfehl or extermination order: "…Within the German borders, every Herero, whether armed or unarmed, with or without cattle … will be shot. I shall not accept anymore, men, women or children …"

This dashed any hopes for mercy. The Herero men who tried to surrender were shot at sight, while the women and children were forced back into the desert.

To seal his mercilessness, Trotha wrote in his diary: "To accept women and children, most of whom are ill, is a serious danger to the [German] troops. And to feed them is an impossibility. I find it appropriate that the nation perishes instead of infecting our soldiers."

As expected, international condemnation of Trotha's carnage fell on deaf ears in Berlin. By the time a reluctant Kaiser Wilhelm II brought himself to condemn and withdraw Trotha's extermination order, the damage had already been done.

The few surviving Hereros were finally rounded up, forbidden to own land or keep cattle and became a reservoir of slave labour for the German settlers.

They were sent into labour camps where they were overworked and died of hunger and diseases such as typhoid and smallpox in scenes reminiscent of the Nazi concentration camps of the 1940s.

As their men died in the camps, thousands of Herero women were turned into sex slaves by the Germans. By now, less than 15,000 of an estimated 80,000 Herero population remained.

Not only did the Herero men in the labour camps suffer death, slavery and hunger,

Hitler's theories of racial purity of his Aryan race can be traced to these camps. It was here that the German geneticist, Eugene Fischer first came to do his racial medical experiments. He used the Herero and mulattos (the offspring of the German settlers and Herero women) as guinea pigs.

Fischer believed that there were genetic dangers arising from race mixing, and he came to the Namibian camps to find out how and why. A book he wrote about his findings, *The Principles of Human Heredity and Race Hygiene,* became one of Hitler's favourites. Fischer's warped racial ideas, thus, provided Hitler with a kind of scientific legitimacy to justify his Nazi terror.

Fischer later become chancellor of the University of Berlin, where he taught medicine to Nazi physicians. One of his prominent students was Josef Mengele, the notorious doctor who did weird genetic experiments on Jewish children at Auschwitz.

ZERO RESPONSE

The Herero ordeal would be incomplete without mentioning that, soon after their defeat and extermination by the Germans, their tribal rivals, the Nama (Hottentots) led by Chief Hendrik Witboi, tried to mount a similar revolt against the Germans. But it was a short, sharp, shock for the Nama. The Germans routed them. Here, Trotha's hard-heartedness was again crudely exposed.

Today, the Jewish survivors of the Nazi holocaust are rightly being compensated and drawing worldwide support for their suffering. But for the Herero, despite their heart-rending ordeal, they have been denied a seat on the compensation bandwagon. The German government, despite acknowledging the country's dark past in Namibia, has flatly refused to apologise and compensate the Herero.

Visiting Namibia in 1998, the German president, Roman Herzog, acknowledged that

the Herero massacre was "a dark chapter in our bilateral relations." Yet he refused to apologise, saying "too much time has passed for a formal apology to the Hereros to make sense."

The nearest President Herzog came to an apology was to admit that Trotha "acted incorrectly" and that the killing of the Herero was "a burden on the conscience of every German." These were appeasing words all right, but they did not go far enough.

As a result, the Herero have recently sharpened the campaign for a proper apology and compensation from the German government. On 16 January this year, Professor Mburumba Kerina, a prominent Herero campaigner and secretary general of the Chief Hosea Kutako Foundation (the leading group highlighting the Herero plight), wrote to the British lawyer, Lord Anthony Gifford QC, asking him to take on their case.

Lord Gifford is an activist par excellence who has campaigned on behalf of oppressed people in many parts of Africa, including Mozambique, Angola and South Africa. He fully supports Africa's claim to reparations for the slave trade, and in 1993 published a detailed paper outlining the legal basis to this claim. *New African* printed the full version of his paper in our December 1999 and January 2000 issues.

Lord Gifford confirmed to *New African* that he had been asked by the Herero people to represent them, but said he had written back to them for further instructions.

In the letter to Lord Gifford, made available to *New African,* Prof Kerina wrote: "The Chief Hosea Kutako Foundation of the Herero Nation in Namibia has been mandated to explore the possibility of meeting with leaders and representatives of the German government to discuss reparations … . Unfortunately our efforts have ended in zero response."

Indeed, for years, the Herero leaders have pleaded with the German government to lend them an ear. In March 1999, the German foreign ministry wrote to Prof Kerina in response to numerous requests from the Herero for a meeting to discuss the issue. Signed by Dr. Ludger Volmer, an official in the German foreign ministry, the letter said: "I very much regret to have to inform you that direct reparations to the Herero are not possible due to legal constraints. Rest however assured that the Federal Government would further, intensively, support your country and especially the Herero nation within the framework of its financial means."

The letter continued: "We are aware of our moral and especially our historical obligation towards Namibia and the Hereros. Therefore, the Federal Republic maintains a comprehensive and unusually intensive developmental co-operation with Namibia. Your country obtains the highest per capita financial development contributions of all recipient states from Germany. However, our developmental commitment must extend to all regions of Namibia. The Federal government strives to include more strongly, the Herero nation in the bilateral development co-operation in accordance with agreements with the Namibia government."

Prof Kerina, who has a German grandparent, has made it categorically clear that the Herero do not want cash. Their compensation request is very modest, he says. "All we want is a mini-Marshall plan," he has told the Germans.

But it appears that the Germans are dragging their feet over the Herero issue because of the land "problem" at the heart of the whole affair. What will happen to the 25,000 or so rich German settlers still occupying Herero land, if Germany apologises and makes restitution to the Hereros? Both the settlers and Germany fear that this might lead to the loss of land, and the thought terrifies them!

Professor Lora Wildenthal of the Massachusetts Institute of Technology even betters this argument: "There is fear that a payoff would invite multitudes of similar claims for colonial-era crimes. I do not think any colonial power will go anywhere near this," she told the U.S. paper, *Salt Lake Tribune*, in an interview.

To this day, German ranchers in Namibia who insist that there was no genocide in the country, still own millions of acres seized from the Herero over 90 years ago. In the meantime, it is not only the Herero, but also half of Namibia's 1.8 million population live on crowded, impoverished land.

The current paramount chief of the Hereros, Chief Kuima Riruako, is quite conciliatory on the land issue: "We want reparations to buy land and give it to people who need it ... We do not want to seize it the way they are doing it in Zimbabwe."

This time last year, Chief Riruako was talking about taking the Herero case to the International Court of Justice in The Hague (The Netherlands). "On the threshold of the new millennium," Chief Riruako said at the time, "the Hereros have decided to take Germany to the International Court of Justice for a decision regarding reparations. We also warn the Namibian government not to stand in our way as we explore this avenue to justice."

The relationship between the Herero and President Nujoma's government is quite frosty. The government is dominated by people from the Ovambo tribe. President Nujoma is an Ovambo himself. The Ovambos were lucky not to be touched by the Germans during their rule of terror. The Ovambos, again, happened to lead the liberation struggle in Namibia that led to independence in 1990 from South Africa.

But the majority of the Herero, it so happens, belongs to the opposition and are viewed as rivals by Nujoma's government. In addition, the government receives millions of deustche marks in aid each year from the German government (about $400m in direct aid since 1990). As a result, the Nujoma government does not want to rock the boat.

But Prof Kerina, who is a member of parliament himself, says the Herero will not be pushed around any longer. Not by Germany. Nor the Namibian government.

QUESTIONS TO CONSIDER

3. Describe the reparations issues raised in the Herero case.

1. Why are the Herero reviving the issue of German atrocities that culminated in the 1904 genocide?
2. Were General von Trotha's actions genocidal?

A History of Horror

A REVIEW OF *LE SIÈCLE DES CAMPS*

Joel Kotek and Pierre Rigoulot

Le Siècle des Camps
JC Lattes, 805 pages.

Contrary to what might be expected, the first recorded use of the expression "concentration camps" did not occur in either Germany or Russia. Nor, even, was the term originally English, as many also mistakenly believe. In fact, as far as it is possible to ascertain, the first person to speak of concentration camps or, more precisely, to speak of a policy of "*reconcentración*"—was Arsenio Martinez Campos, then the commander of the Spanish garrison in Cuba. The year was 1895, and Martinez Campos was fending off the latest in what seemed to be a never-ending series of local insurgencies. Looking for a permanent end to the Cuban independence struggle, he proposed, in a confidential letter to the Spanish government, to "reconcentrate" the civilian inhabitants of the rural districts into camps. Although he conceded that the policy might lead to "misery and famine," it would also, he explained, deprive the insurgents of food, shelter and support, thereby bringing the war to a more rapid conclusion.

Martinez Campos didn't manage to carry out the policy, but his successor did. Over the following two years, from 1896 to 1898, General Valeriano Weyler y Nicolau forcibly removed many thousands of Cuban peasants from their homes. As

predicted, "misery and famine" ensued. Theoretically, the camps were meant to consist of suitably built dwellings, on fertile land, near sources of water. In practice, the Cuban peasants were thrown into "old shacks, abandoned houses, improvised shelters," wherever it happened to be convenient to throw them. Food was distributed irregularly. Typhus and dysentery spread rapidly. Young girls prostituted themselves for a bit of bread. As many as 200,000 *reconcentrados* may have died.

Indeed, one contemporary Cuban historian has described these first, Cuban camps as a "holocaust of gigantic proportions." Given the connotations of the word "holocaust," this is an inappropriate description. Nevertheless, there is a curious and rather surprising chain of connections between these first Cuban concentration camps, and the Nazi concentration camps which came into existence less than four decades later.

In fact, both the term and the idea spread and evolved rather quickly. By 1900, a mere two years after the Cuban camps were closed, the Spanish term *reconcentración* had already been translated into English and was used to describe a similar British project, initiated for similar reasons, during the Boer War in South

From Anne Applebaum, "A History of Horror," *The New York Review of Books* (October 18, 2001): 40–43. Reprinted by permission of the author.

Africa. Just as the Spanish had grown frustrated with the guerrilla tactics of the Cubans, so too had the British been flummoxed by the Boer soldiers' ability to live off their civilian sympathizers. These civilian sympathizers were duly "concentrated" into camps, in order to deprive Boer combatants of shelter and support. Once again, misery and famine, as well as sickness and hardship, were the result. To contemporaries, the connection between the South African camps and the Cuban camps was clear: at the time, the British were both praised and attacked for adapting "General Weyler's methods" to the Transvaal.

Four years later, the same policy was again adopted, again in a colonial setting, although a slightly different one. This time, the colonizers were not Spanish or English but German. As not everybody remembers, the Germans briefly had African colonies: one of them was Deutsche Sud-West Afrika, now Namibia. The territory was populated by the Herero, a tribe whose presence the Germans resented; not only did their numbers hamper white settlement, but their presence violated the ethnic purity of the new "German" state. At first, the colonial policy was simply to slaughter the Herero. To some of the German colonists, this seemed inefficient. Following the British example in neighboring South Africa, the Herero were duly driven into concentration camps. But the Herero were not merely starved. They also died of exhaustion, carrying out forced labour on behalf of the German colony. At the beginning of 1905, there had been 14,000 Herero in captivity. By the end of that year, half were dead.

Because of the Herero, the word *Konzentrationslager* first appeared in German, in 1905. It was also in these African camps that the first German medical experiments were conducted on human beings. Two of Joseph Mengele's teachers, Theodor Mollison and Eugen Fischer, carried out research on the Herero, the latter in an attempt to prove his

theories about the superiority of the white race. Nor was he alone in his beliefs. In 1912, a bestselling German book, *German Thought in the World*, claimed that nothing "can convince reasonable people the preservation of a tribe of South African kaffirs is more important for the future of humanity than the expansion of the great European nations and the white race in general," and that "it is only when the indigenous peoples have learned to produce something of value in the service of the superior race … that they can be said to have a moral right to exist."

The resemblance to the racist language of the Holocaust is clear enough; there was, in addition, one further strange coincidence. The first imperial commissioner of Deutsche Sud-West Afrika was one Dr. Heinrich Goering, the father of Hermann, who set up the first Nazi camps in 1933. The authors of *Le Siècle des Camps* ask, "*Ceci explique peut-être cela?*"—can the one, perhaps, help to explain the other? The corrupting experience of colonialism—which both reinforced the myth of white racial superiority and legitimized the use of violence against other races may, perhaps, have helped pave the way for the totalitarianism of the twentieth century.

It isn't that simple, of course: the German camps cannot be "explained" by South African or Cuban camps, any more than the Soviet camps can be "explained" by the fact that the term *kontslager* also first appeared in Russian as a translation from the English, probably thanks to Trotsky's familiarity with the history of the Boer War. Nevertheless, these are points worth exploring. Shelves full of books have already been written, arguing that Nazi camps can be wholly explained by German anti-Semitism, or by German intellectual history, or by the Prussian legacy. Likewise, the Soviet camps have been attributed to the particular nature of Bolshevik revolutionary theory, to the personality of Lenin, to the tsarist legacy. Yet although different nations made very different use of camps, and although concentration camps developed in very particular national contexts for particular reasons, the phenomenon of the concentration camp also has a multi-national history. Perhaps it is time to explore how methods of repression—like methods of warfare—were transmitted across borders and across cultures.

That, at any rate, is the argument of *Le Siècle des Camps*, the first attempt at a history of the twentieth-century concentration camp. But it is an argument that the book's authors make very carefully. Writing it, they have taken into account the controversy over the views of the German historian Ernst Nolte, who has argued, to put it succinctly, that the crimes of Hitler can be "explained" by the fact that the Soviet Union built its concentration camps at an earlier date. They also appear to want to avoid some of the fuss caused by the *Livre Noir de Communism*, the *Black Book of Communism*—a similarly cross-cultural, similarly lengthy, and similarly French attempt to tally the harm done by communist regimes, from Lenin to Mao to Kim Il Sen. (Pierre Rigoulot, one of the two co-authors of *Le Siècle des Camps*, was also a contributor to the *Black Book*.) Upon publication, the *Black Book* set off a storm of controversy across France, in part because its editor pointedly noted, in his introduction, that more people had been killed in more different ways by communist regimes than had ever been killed by Hitler. To some, this again seemed an attempt to reduce the significance of the Holocaust.

In their introduction to *Le Siècle des Camps*, Rigoulot and Joel Kotek, his coauthor, announce they intend to avoid the essentially sterile "who was worse, Hitler or Stalin" argument (along with the "who was worse, Stalin or Mao, China or Cambodia, authoritarian Latin America or totalitarian Europe" arguments). Nor do they want to equate the British in South Africa with the Communists in China with the Nazis in Auschwitz, or to agree that the American de-

tention camps built for Japanese-Americans during the Second World War can, simply because they were camps, rightly be described as "the American Gulag," as they often are. Nevertheless, they argue that comparisons will, in the end, help us to see the horror of the most terrifying camps more clearly, to understand where it came from and why it happened:

> To say that Treblinka is "unique" is to presume that one has compared it with other camps and that one has come to the conclusion that it is radically different. The comparative study of the phenomenon of the concentration camp is not only legitimate, but necessary, if one wants to extricate the specific traits of each particular case.

In the end, their research is illuminating because the global phenomenon is one to which we haven't given much thought. Because of the horror that the term "concentration camp" evokes, there is a natural desire not to analyze it: "it was a nightmare," we say, and sweep the subject away. Because of the desire not to lump together separate crimes which took place in different circumstances and at different times, we tend not to worry about global definitions. But do we really know what, exactly, we mean by the term "concentration camp"—or why we use it the way that we do? Perhaps it is easier to start by defining what it is that a concentration camp is not, and that is how Rigoulot and Kotek begin. A concentration camp is not, for example, a prisoner of war camp or a refugee camp, although at times both have resembled concentration camps; one thinks, for example, of the conditions in which Soviet prisoners of war were held in Nazi Germany, or the conditions in which some displaced persons lived in Europe after the Second World War.

Nor is a concentration camp the same thing as an ordinary prison, or even an ordinary criminal prison camp, although the line between prisons and concentration camps is not always easy to draw either. Generally speaking, criminals are condemned by a judicial system that addresses individual guilt, whereas people are sent to concentration camps by police and armed forces carrying out political orders. Again, this distinction also sometimes breaks down. In the case of the Soviet Union, there was a judicial system set up to condemn large numbers of "enemies of the state" to concentration camps. That system was perfunctory—"trials" rarely took longer than a few minutes—but it did exist, helping to legitimate the camps in the eyes of those who designed them. So did the fact that Soviet political prisoners, criminal prisoners, and even captured war criminals were frequently kept together in the same camps and jails.

A system of concentration camps is not quite a system for mass murder either. Although these definitions also blur, most concentration camps—including the majority of the Nazi camps, were not organized merely to eliminate people, even if that was the practical result of forced hard labour, desperately poor hygiene, and starvation rations. The authors point out, as have others, that the Nazis did not consider their death camps—that is, camps where prisoners arrived and were immediately executed—to be part of the same system as their concentration camps. There were four such camps—Belzec, Chelmno, Sobibor and Treblinka. In addition, Majdanek and Auschwitz served both as concentration camps and as death camps. These six camps were sometimes called *Vernichtungslager*, extermination camps, rather than concentration camps.

It should be evident, moreover, that camps are not necessary to carry out mass murder: many regimes, in many places, over many centuries, have found methods of murdering large numbers of people without resorting to camps at all. While Rigoulot and Kotek's decision to focus their book only on camps certainly makes sense, it also creates some imbalances. For example, they include a brief mention of the South Vietnamese government's resettlement policy, which concentrat-ed civilians into "strategic villages," in order to damage communist guerrillas. A cruel policy, to be sure but not crueler than the Soviet government's bombardment of Afghanistan, which is thought to have killed a million people. That policy was also intended to reduce support for guerrillas, but doesn't fit into the scheme of this book.

Still, as we compare concentration camps to other forms of incarceration, a definition slowly emerges. Rigoulot and Kotek conclude that when we speak of concentration camps, we generally mean camps for people who have been imprisoned not for what they have done, but for who they are. Concentration camps are not built for individuals, but rather for a particular type of noncriminal, civilian prisoner, the member of an "enemy" group, or at any rate of a category of people who, for reasons of their race or their presumed politics, are judged to be dangerous or extraneous to the society. In his first recorded use of the term *kontslager* in August, 1918—he appears to have picked it up from Trotsky—Lenin called not for the "guilty" to be condemned to camps, but for the mass imprisonment of "unreliable elements." It is no coincidence that concentration camps reappeared in Europe in the past decade during the Bosnian war, which was a war about establishing ethnic purity in certain parts of former Yugoslavia.

Beyond their pursuit of a particular type of prisoner, the camps described in *Le Siècle des Camps* cannot to be said to have had much in common. Some, like the detention camps set up for Japanese-Americans during World War II, were genuinely intended solely to isolate people who were seen, without individual evidence, as potentially disloyal. Others were designed to make full use of cheap inmate labour: at its height, the Soviet camp system was a vital part of the Soviet economy, as prisoners were used in every industry imaginable. Still others have been intended to "re-educate" prisoners of doubtful loyalty, sometimes by demanding self-accusation and false confession as well as by administering harsh treatment. Generally speaking, democratic regimes have used concentration camps as temporary measures, during wartime. Totalitarian regimes deploy them as a permanent and intrinsic part of the system: by definition, totalitarian regimes are those which establish a social ideal, and then seek to eliminate or re-educate everyone who doesn't fit into it.

Rigoulot and Kotek grapple with these differences in part through an exploration of what was unique about daily life within each one of the camp complexes, using what secondary sources are available. These accounts are very uneven, which is perhaps to be expected: not all of the camps created in the past hundred-odd years have been studied with the same thoroughness. Nor is documentation always available. The Nazi camps are described in hundreds of memoirs, archival documents, and a secondary literature which continues to expand. We know of the contemporary camps of North Korea only through descriptions of the very occasional defector. Nevertheless, the authors sometimes appear not to be aware of publications from recently opened Soviet archives; they speculate, for example, about the possible existence of "special regime camps"—i.e., camps with particularly brutal regimes—for political prisoners, when in fact the existence of such camps has been amply documented.

The authors also classify camps into four rather crude categories: those designed merely to isolate (Cuba, South Africa), those designed to profit from forced labor (Soviet, early Nazi, Chinese and other Asian camps), those designed to first humiliate and then eliminate prisoners (later Nazi camps) and finally the six *Vernichtunslager*, which were actually not "camps," at all, but killing factories. The authors admit that some of the distinctions between categories are hard to draw. Nevertheless, both the somewhat over-lengthy individual histories and the categories do serve a function.

They are, simply, a device which enables Rigoulot and Kotek to discuss the global phenomenon of the concentration camp without having to say that all concentration camps, or all totalitarian regimes, were everywhere exactly the same, or that the existence of horrific crimes in one country lessens the guilt of those who carried out horrific crimes in another.

When the camps are considered from a global perspective, patterns emerge. It is striking, for example, how many of the camp systems began spontaneously. Goering himself, at the time of his Nuremburg trial, remarked that the first Nazi camps had come about simply because, from one day to the next, "we found ourselves with several thousand prisoners on our hands." The same was true in the Soviet Union, where prisoners from 1918 onwards were often placed as an emergency measure in old monasteries and churches. Even as late as 1943, the Italian camps for Jews that had begun to appear in 1939, under the direct influence of Hitler—were still located in "schools, villas, convents, castles." During the Greek civil war, camps were hurriedly set up on islands, where inmates lived in ripped tents or simply slept under the stars.

It is also striking how often they emerged in the context of war, revolution, and wider violence. Along with arguing that the legacy of imperialism has been overlooked as an influence in the prehistory of twentieth-century totalitarianism, Kotek and Rigoulot also underline the brutalizing influence of twentieth-century warfare, particularly as practiced during World War I in Europe. New weapons and new inventions (barbed wire among them) made it suddenly easier to terrorize more people more rapidly. World War I also spawned its own camps: vast internment camps, in Alsace-Lorraine, for "suspect" civilians, and enormous prisoner of war camps farther east as well. The hellish experience of the trenches might also have helped, in Germany and Russia, to produce the disregard for human life which was a fundamental component of totalitarianism.

But for a mass system of camps to expand, and to persist over a long time as they did in Nazi Germany, in the Soviet Union, and in China—something else besides the immediate and spontaneous need to incarcerate many prisoners, to treat them as cattle or as cargo, had to be present. Ideology is one word for it, but it might also be more precisely said that there had to be a rhetoric of dehumanization, of depersonalization. As has been described many times, the Nazi dehumanization of the Jews preceded the actual creation of the camps: before the Jews were actually rounded up and deported, they were deprived of the right to work as civil servants, as lawyers, as judges; they were forbidden to marry Aryans, forbidden to attend Aryan schools, forbidden to slaughter animals according to Kosher law; they were forced to wear gold stars of David, subjected to beatings and humiliation on the street.

Within the camps, the process deepened, grew more extreme. Gitta Sereny, in her long interview with Franz Stangl, the commander of Treblinka, at one point focused on this issue. She asked him why camp inmates, before being killed, were also beaten, humiliated, deprived of their clothing. Stangl answered, "To condition those who actually had to carry out the policies. To make it possible for them to do what they did."

In his hugely influential *The Order of Terror: The Concentration Camp*, the German sociologist Wolfgang Sofsky has also shown how the dehumanization of prisoners in the Nazi camps was methodically built into every aspect of camp life, from the torn, identical clothing, to the deprivation of privacy, to the heavy regulation (there were strict rules for making beds) to the constant expectation of death.

Nor, perhaps, is it wholly coincidental that, in the Soviet case, attitudes to prisoners underwent a profound transformation precisely at the time that the camp system began to expand … From the late 1930s, Stalin began pub-

licly to refer to Enemies of the People using what one historian has called "biological-hygienic terms." He denounced them as vermin, as pollution, as filth which had to be "subjected to ongoing purification," as "poisonous weeds."

Prisoners were at the same time "excommunicated" from Soviet life, were not allowed to refer to one another as "comrade," and could no longer earn the title of "Stakhanovite" or "shock-worker," no matter how well they behaved or how hard they worked. So powerfully did this exclusion from Soviet society affect prisoners brought up in it, writes Jacques Rossi, that as late as the 1940s, he witnessed,

> A brigade that had just completed an eleven and a half hour shift agree to stay and work the next shift only because the chief engineer said to the prisoners: "I ask that you do this, comrades."

Those Asian societies which set up mass camp systems, and mass systems of repression, were no exception. In China, the Cultural Revolution demonized the "blacks" as opposed to the "Reds." In Cambodia, venom was poured upon the "75ers," who were expelled from the cities in 1975. In North Korea, the authorities speak of the "unreformables," who are like "harmful weeds which must be uprooted."

Whether this sort of language was transmitted across borders, with one set of revolutionaries picking it up from others (and it is worth noting how often the "weeds" metaphor has been used)—or whether the need to dehumanize outsider groups is somehow intrinsic to human nature is a matter for philosophers to decide. But it is clear that methods of organizing camps could be and were exported. Leaving aside the probably unresolvable question of how much Hitler actually knew about Stalin's camps, we can say without a doubt that the Chinese knew a great deal about them. At the height of Sino-Soviet collaboration in the early 1950s, Soviet "experts" helped set up several Chinese camps, and organized forced labor brigades at a coal mine near Fushun.

In post-war Eastern Europe, communist camps were often not merely set up with Soviet advice, but were actually organised and run, in the early days, by the Red Army and the Soviet secret police. Certainly this was the case in East Germany—where some camps were located right inside the recently evacuated Nazi camps, including Sachsenhausen and Buchenwald. In Romania, which also set up a large system of Soviet-style forced labor, the secret police were operating under direct orders from their Soviet counterparts.

Nothing, of course, prevented other cultures from re-designing the Soviet model to suit their own needs. After Stalin's death, even the camps in the East European puppet states began to vary widely. Although the Czechs slowly disbanded their camps, the Bulgarian communists maintained several hard labour camps well into the 1970s, long after the mass system of Soviet camps had been disbanded. The Chinese camps *laogai* still exist, of course, although they no longer resemble the Stalinist camps they were set up to emulate. Although the Stalinist camps did maintain "cultural-educational" departments, and although their commanders paid lip service to the idea of re-education, they had nothing like the rigid re-educational system which the Chinese camps now have, a system in which prisoners' atonement, and ritual abasement before the Party—another form of depersonalization—seems to have a far higher importance to the authorities than the goods that the prisoners manage to produce. The idea of the concentration camp, then, was general enough to export; but the specific details of what the camps were used for, how they ultimately developed, how rigid or disorganized they became, how cruel or liberal they remained—all of this depended on the particular country, on the culture, on the regime.

In the end, any exploration of the general subject of camps invariably leads back to a discussion of what was different about each one, and what was unique about the regimes which designed them. Which doesn't mean that comparisons will stop: in fact, as we now begin to look back on the history of the twentieth century as a whole, the subject will be hard to avoid. Indeed, in their conclusion, the authors of *Le Siècle des Camps* note that the "globalization" of the history of camps may have already begun. Two former victims of Asian camps, Pramoedya Ananta Toer of Indonesia and Harry Wu of China, have visited the sites of Nazi camps. I was present at a seminar in Krakow where Nazi, Soviet and North Korean camps were all discussed. One of the most interesting recent books about what the French call "le phénomène concentrationnaire," Tzvetan Todorov's *Facing the Extreme*, examines the experiences of prisoners in both the Nazi and Soviet systems, exploring the question of whether it was possible for them to maintain any sort of morality in the inhuman world of the camps.

Nor is globalization entirely new. It was Hannah Arendt, after all, who called for the writing of a history of the concentration camp, "from their beginnings in the imperialist countries, passing by their utilization as a temporary measure in wartime, arriving at their institutionalization as a permanent organ of government in regimes of terror." Kotek and Rigoulot humbly admit that this book is merely the beginning of a response to her proposal. One hopes there will be others.

QUESTIONS TO CONSIDER

1. Describe the lineage of *reconcentración* from Cuba to Germany.
2. When are concentration camps not a government's implementation of genocidal methods?
3. What made the camps in Nazi Germany, the Soviet Union, and China different in nature?
4. What do the authors of *Le Siècle des Camps* mean by a "globalization" of the history of concentration camps?

MAKING CONNECTIONS

1. Does what happened in the Congo classify as genocide?

2. Are American Indian reservations concentration camps?

✔ RECOMMENDED RESOURCES

August, Thomas G. *The Selling of the Empire: British and French Imperialist Propaganda, 1890–1940.* Westport, CT: Greenwood Press, 1985.

Blackburn, Julia. *The White Men: The First Response of Aboriginal Peoples to the White Man.* New York: HarperCollins, 1979.

Cocker, Mark. *Rivers of Blood, Rivers of Gold: Europe's Conquest of Indigenous Peoples.* New York: Grove Press, 1998.

Conrad, Joseph. *Heart of Darkness: An Authoritative Text, Backgrounds and Sources, Criticism* (Norton Critical Editions). New York: W. W. Norton & Company, 1988.

Fieldhouse, D. K. *The Colonial Empires: A Comparative Survey from the Eighteenth Century.* 2d ed. London: McMillan, 1982.

Lindqvist, Sven. *Exterminate All the Brutes.* Translated by Joan Tate. New York: The New Press, 1992.

CHAPTER 3

THE ALMOST FORGOTTEN GENOCIDE: ARMENIA

The Armenian genocide wiped a people, and almost three thousand years of material and spiritual culture, from the Turkish landscape. This first deliberate and ideologically motivated genocide occurred during World War I. The antipathy between the Turks and the Armenians erupted in massacres of over 100,000 Armenians in 1895 to 1896. Killing on a smaller scale continued for the following two decades. The entry of Turkey into the First World War in 1914 and the start of fighting with Russia changed the situation. Turkish authorities feared that the Christian Armenians in the eastern provinces might side with the Russians. The Turks saw the Armenians as traitors and proceeded to disarm Armenian soldiers. Turkish authorities then arrested and deported the Armenian intelligentsia. The next stage involved killing Armenian men as the Turks managed deportation of the rest of the Armenian community to the Syrian Desert. The death toll is reliably estimated at 1.5 million.

In the wake of these horrific acts and the creation of the Turkish Republic from the crumbled Ottoman Empire in 1923, the new government created its history glorifying the republic and vilifying the empire. Thus the empire's sultan for its last quarter century, Abdulhamid II, pales in comparison to the exalted founder of the republic, Mustafa Kemal Ataturk. In forging a unified Turkish state, Ataturk masterfully led the Muslims to see the Armenian Christians generally as traitors, and the Armenians see the Turks as oppressors.

Generations of descendants of the survivors sought international recognition of the 1915 genocide. Turkey, at the same time, continued to ignore the genocide. The Armenian genocide, and the continuing denial of it, provides illuminating case studies for the comparative examination of genocide. The event provides an early example of the elements of genocide, and shows that the perpetrators of the future learn from the perpetrators of the past. Its denial offers lessons for understanding, as well as combating, new instances of persecution and denial.

Rouben Adalian offers an overview of events and the denial in "The Armenian Genocide: Contest and Legacy." Richard G. Hovannisian, professor of Armenian and Near Eastern History and associate director of the Near Eastern Center at the University of California at Los Angeles, addresses the aftermath in "The Armenian Genocide and Patterns of Denial." Historian Robert Melson is a professor of political science and co-director of the Jewish Studies Program at Purdue University, won the 1993 International PIOOM award from Leiden University for the best book on human rights for his work, *Revolution and*

Genocide: On the Origins of the Armenian Genocide and the Holocaust. His speech to the House of Representatives, "The United States Training on and Commemoration of the Armenian Genocide Resolution," offers suggestions for looking at this event and other instances of genocide.

The Armenian Genocide: Context and Legacy

Rouben Adalian,

Johns Hopkins University

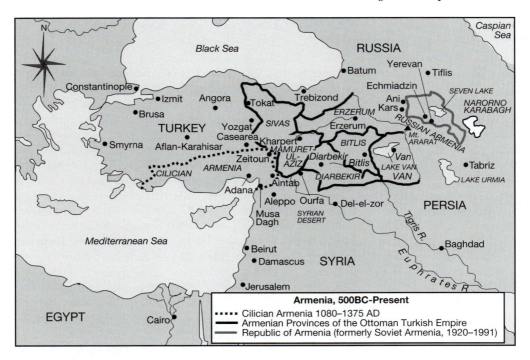

Armenia, 500BC-Present

·········· Cilician Armenia 1080–1375 AD
▬▬▬▬ Armenian Provinces of the Ottoman Turkish Empire
▬▬▬▬ Republic of Armenia (formerly Soviet Armenia, 1920–1991)

Between 1915 and 1918 the Ottoman Empire, ruled by Muslim Turks, carried out a policy to eliminate its Christian Armenian minority. This genocide was preceded by a series of massacres in 1894–1896 and in 1909, and was followed by another series of massacres beginning in 1920. By 1922 Armenians had been eradicated from their historic homeland.

There are at least two ways of looking at the Armenian experience in the final days of the Ottoman Empire. Some scholars regard the series of wholesale killings from the 1890s to the 1920s as evidence of a continuity in the deteriorating status of the Armenians in the Ottoman Empire. They maintain that, once initiated, the policy of exposing the Armenians

From Rouben Adalian, "The Armenian Genocide: Context and Legacy," *Social Education: The Official Journal of the National Council for the Social Studies* (February 1991) 99–104. Reprinted by permission of NCSS.

to physical harm acquired its own momentum. Victimization escalated because it was not countermanded by prevailing outside pressure or attenuated by internal improvement and reconciliation. They argue that the process of alienation was embedded in the inequalities of the Ottoman system of government and that the massacres prepared the Ottoman society for genocide.

Other scholars point out that the brutalization of disaffected elements by despotic regimes is a practice seen across the world. The repressive measures these governments use have the limited function of controlling social change and maintaining the system. In this frame of reference, genocide is viewed as a radical policy because it reaches for a profound alteration of the very nature of the state and society. These scholars emphasize the decisive character of the Armenian genocide and differentiate between the periodic exploitation and occasional terrorization of the Armenians and the finality of the deliberate policy to exterminate them and eliminate them from their homeland.

Like all empires, the Ottoman Empire was a multinational state. At one time it stretched from the gates of Vienna in the north to Mecca in the south. From the sixteenth century to its collapse following World War I, the Ottoman Empire included areas of historic Armenia. By the early part of the twentieth century, it was a much shrunken state confined mostly to the Middle East. Yet its rulers still governed over a heterogeneous society and maintained institutions that favored the Muslims, particularly those of Turkish background, and subordinated Christians and Jews as second-class citizens subject to a range of discriminatory laws and regulations imposed both by the state and its official religion, Islam.

The failure of the Ottoman system to prevent the further decline of the empire led to the overthrow of the government in 1908 by a group of reformists known as the Young Turks. Formally organized as the Committee of Union and Progress, the Young Turks decided to Turkify the multiethnic Ottoman society in order to preserve the Ottoman state from further disintegration and to obstruct the national aspirations of the various minorities. Resistance to this measure convinced them that the Christians, and especially the Armenians, could not be assimilated. When World War I broke out in 1914, the Young Turks saw it as an opportunity to rid the country of its Armenian population. They also envisioned the simultaneous conquest of an empire in the east, incorporating Turkish-speaking peoples in Iran, Russia, and Central Asia.

The defeat of the Ottomans in World War I and the discrediting of the Committee of Union and Progress led to the rise of the Turkish Nationalists. Their objective was to found a new and independent Turkish state. The Nationalists distanced themselves from the Ottoman government and rejected virtually all its policies, with the exception of the policy toward the Armenians.

This essay focuses on three aspects of the Armenian genocide that have broader applicability to any study of genocide: (1) distinction between massacres and genocide; (2) use of technology in facilitating mass murder; and (3) the legacy of genocide.

DISTINGUISHING BETWEEN THE MASSACRES AND THE GENOCIDE

From 1894 to 1896, Sultan Abdul-Hamid II carried out a series of massacres of the Armenian population of the Ottoman Empire. The worst of the massacres occurred in 1895, resulting in the death of thousands of civilians (estimates run from 100,000 to 300,000) and leaving tens of thousands destitute. Most of those killed were men. In many towns, the central marketplace and other Armenian-owned businesses were destroyed, usually by conflagration. The killings were done during the day and were witnessed by the general public.

This kind of organized and systematic brutalization of the Armenian population pointed to the coordinating hand of the central authorities. Widespread violence erupted in towns and cities hundreds of miles apart over a matter of weeks in a country devoid of mass media. At a time when the sultan ruled absolutely, the evidence strongly implicated the head of state.

Intent of Massacres

The massacres were meant to undermine the growth of Armenian nationalism by frightening the Armenians with the terrible consequences of dissent. The furor of the state was directed at the behavior and the aspirations of the Armenians. The sultan was alarmed by the increasing activity of Armenian political groups and wanted to curb their growth before they gained any more influence by spreading ideas about civil rights and autonomy. Abdul-Hamid took no account, however, of the real variation in Armenian political outlook, which ranged from reformism and constitutionalism to separatism. He hoped to wipe away the Armenians' increasing sense of national awareness. He also continued to exclude the Armenians, as he did most of his other subjects, from having a role in their own government, whether individually or communally. The sultan, however did not contemplate depriving the Armenians of their existence as a people. Although there are similarities between Abdui-Hamid's policies and the measures taken by the Young Turks against the Armenians, there are also major distinctions.

The 1915 Measures

The measures implemented in 1915 affected the entire Armenian population: men, women, and children. They included massacres and deportations. As under the sultan, they targeted the able-bodied men for annihilation. The thousands of Armenian men conscripted into the Ottoman army were eliminated first. The rest of the adult population was then placed under arrest, taken out of town, and killed in remote locations.

The treatment of women was quite different. … Countless Armenian women lost their lives in transit. Before their tragic deaths, many suffered unspeakable cruelties, most often in the form of sexual abuse. Many girls and younger women were seized from their families and taken as slave-brides.

During the time of the sultan, Armenians were often given the choice of converting to Islam in order to save themselves from massacre. However, during the genocide years, this choice was usually not available. Few were given the opportunity to accept Islam as a way of avoiding deportations. Most Armenians were deported. Some lives were spared during deportation by random selection of involuntary conversion through abduction, enslavement, or the adoption of kidnapped and orphaned children.

The Cover of War

A second distinguishing feature of the genocide was the killing of the Armenians in places out of sight of the general population. The deportations made resistance or escape difficult. Most important, the removal of Armenians from their native towns was a necessary condition of maintaining as much secrecy about the genocide as possible. The Allies had warned the Ottoman government about taking arbitrary measures against the Christian minorities. The transfer of the Armenian population, therefore, was, in appearance, a more justifiable response in a time of war.

When the Ottomans entered World War I, they confined journalists to Istanbul, and since the main communications system, the telegraph, was under government control, news from the interior was censored. Nonetheless, the deportations made news as soon as they occurred, but news of the massacres was delayed because they were done in desolate regions away from places of habitation. Basically, this provided cover for the ultimate objective of destroying the Armenian population. Inevitably the massacres followed the deportations.

State of Confiscation of Armenian Goods and Property

A third feature of the genocide was the state confiscation of Armenian goods and property. Apart from the killing, the massacres of 1895 and 1909 involved the looting and burning of Armenian neighborhoods and businesses. The objective was to strike at the financial strength of the Armenian community which controlled a significant part of the Ottoman commerce. In 1915 the objective of the Young Turks was to plunder and confiscate all Armenian means of sustenance, thereby increasing the probability of extinction.

Unlike the looting associated with the massacres under Sultan Abdul-Hamid II, the assault against the Armenians in 1915 was marked by comparatively little property damage. Thus, the genocide effortlessly transferred the goods and assets—homes, farms, bank accounts, buildings, land, and personal wealth—of the Armenians to the Turks. Since the Young Turk Party controlled the government, the seizure of the property of the Armenians by the state placed local party chiefs in powerful positions as financial brokers. This measure escalated the incentive for government officials to proceed thoroughly with the deportation of the Armenians.

The Young Turks did not rely as much on mob violence as the sultan had. They implemented the genocide as another military operation during wartime. The agencies of government were put to use, and where they did not exist, they were created. The Young Turk Party functionaries issued the instructions. The army and local gendarmerie carried out the deportations. An agency was organized to impound the properties of the Armenians and to redistribute the goods. "Butcher battalions" of convicts released from prisons were organized into killer units. The Young Turks tapped into the full capacity of the state to organize operations against all 2 million Armenian inhabitants of the Ottoman Empire, and did it swiftly and effectively.

THE USE OF TECHNOLOGY FOR MASS KILLINGS

The Armenian genocide occurred at a time when the Ottoman Empire was undergoing a process of modernization. Apart from the new weapons of war, the telegraph and the railroad were being put to expanded use. Introduced in the second half of the nineteenth century, the networks of transport and communication reached the areas of heavy Armenian concentration by the early part of the twentieth century. Whereas the telephone system was largely confined to the capital city of Istanbul, telegraph lines extended throughout the empire. The rail system connected many of the largest towns in the Ottoman Empire, but it was less extensive than the rail networks in the European countries.

The Telegraph

Coordination of the massacres during the reign of Abdul-Hamid II, and of the deportations under the Young Turks, was made possible by the telegraph. Of all the instruments of the state government, the telegraph dramatically increased the power of key decision-makers over the rest of the population. The telegraph system allowed for the kind of centralization that heretofore was impossible.

During the 1895 massacres, the telegraph in the Ottoman Empire was a government service. It was managed by a separate ministry. Therefore, all the communicating during the massacres was done by the Ottoman government. During the genocide of 1915, the telegraph was controlled by the Minister of Interior, Talat, who was in charge of the government agencies that implemented the genocide. Talat began his government career as a telegrapher, and he had a telegraph machine installed in his office so that he could personally send messages across the Ottoman Empire. This gave Talat immediate connection, literally and technologically, with the enforcement of mass death. His ability to use the telegraph gave him unsurpassed access to subordinates and allowed him to circumvent other government officials and agencies in Istanbul. For the most part a telegram from Talat was sufficient authorization to proceed with the decimation of the Armenians.

Modern states rely on their bureaucracies in order to handle the paperwork involved in carrying out a policy affecting vast portions of their population. The same applies to the policy of genocide. The more modernized the state, the greater the mountain of paper generated. If not destroyed, a monumental record is left behind. In the case of the Armenians, it might be said that their genocide was carried out not so much bureaucratically as much as telegraphically, thus minimizing the record keeping and leaving behind a great deal of confusion about the degree of individual responsibility.

The Trains

To expedite the transfer of Armenians living in proximity of the railways, orders were issued instructing regional authorities to transport Armenian deportees by train. Instructions were explicit to the point of ordering the Armenians to be packed to the maximum capacity in the cattle cars which were used for their transport. The determination of the government to complete this task is demonstrated by the deportation of the Armenians in European Turkey who were ferried across the Sea of Marmara to Anatolia and then placed on trains for transport to Syria.

The removal of Armenians from Anatolia and historic Armenia was carried out mostly through forced caravan marches or by the use of trains. Although a large portion of the Armenians survived the horrific conditions of the packed cattle cars, they were not able to endure the Syrian desert where they were to die of hunger and thirst. In contrast, the majority of the Armenians in the caravans never reached the killing centers in the Syrian desert; many were murdered by raiding groups of bandits or died from exposure to the scorching days and cold nights. Most of those who were able to endure the "death marches" could not survive the starvation, exhaustion, or the epidemics that spread death in the concentration camps of the Syrian desert.

LEGACY OF THE ARMENIAN GENOCIDE

All too often the discussion of genocide centers on the numbers killed and fails to consider the wider implications of uprooting entire populations. Genocides are cataclysmic for those who survive because they carry the memory of suffering and the realization of the unmitigated disaster of genocide. Genocides often produce results and create conditions that make it impossible to recover anything tangible from the society that was destroyed, let alone permit the subsequent repair of that society. From this standpoint, it can be argued that the ultimate objective of genocide is a permanent alteration of the course of a people's history.

Losing a Heritage

In a single year, 1915, the Armenians were robbed of their 3000-year-old heritage. The desecration of churches, the burning of libraries, the ruination of towns and villages—all erased an ancient civilization. With the disappearance of the Armenians from their homeland, most of the symbols of their culture—schools, monasteries, artistic monuments, historical sites—were destroyed by the Ottoman government. The Armenians saved only that which formed part of their collective memory. Their language, their songs, their poetry, and now their tragic destiny, remained as part of their culture.

The Scattering of a People

Beyond the terrible loss of life (1,500,000), and the severing of the connection between the Armenian people and their historic homeland, the Armenian genocide also resulted in the dispersion of the survivors. Disallowed from resettling in their former homes, as well as stateless and penniless, Armenians moved to any country that afforded refuge. Within a matter of a few decades Armenians were dispersed to every continent on the globe. The largest Armenian community is now found in the United States.

By the expulsion of the Armenians from those areas of the Ottoman Empire that eventually came to constitute the modern state of Turkey, the reconfiguration of Armenia took a paradoxical course. Whereas the genocide resulted in the death of Armenian society in the former Ottoman Empire, the flight of many Armenians across the border into Russian territory resulted in compressing part of the surviving Armenian population into the smaller section of historic Armenia ruled by the Russians. Out of that region was created the present country of Armenia, the smallest of the republics of the USSR.

The contrast on the two sides of that frontier spotlights the chilling record of genocide. Three and half million Armenians live in Soviet Armenia. Not an Armenian can be found on the Turkish side of the border.

The Absence of Justice and Protection in the Postwar Period

During the genocide, the leaders of the world were preoccupied with World War I. Some Armenians were rescued, some leaders decried what was happening, but the overall response was too little too late.

After the war, ample documentation of the genocide was made available and became the source of debate during postwar negotiations by the Allied Powers. It was during these negotiations for a peace treaty that the Western leaders had an opportunity to develop humanitarian policies and strategies that could have protected the Armenians from further persecution. Instead of creating conditions for the prevention of additional massacres, the Allies retreated to positions that only validated the success of ideological racialism. The failure at this juncture was catastrophic. Its consequences persist to this day.

With the defeat of their most important ally, Germany, the Ottomans signed an armistice, ending their fight with the Allies. The Committee of Union and Progress resigned from the government and in an effort to evade all culpability soon disbanded as a political organization. Although many of the Young Turk leaders, including Talat, had fled the country, the new Ottoman government in Istanbul tried them in absentia for organizing and carrying out the deportations and massacres. A verdict of guilty was handed down for virtually all of them, but the sentencing could not be carried out.

The Istanbul government was weak and was compromised by the fact that the the capital was under Allied occupation. Soon it lost the competence to govern the provinces, and finally capitulated in 1922 to the forces of Nationalist Turks who had formed a separate government based in Ankara. As for the sentences of the court against the Young Turk leaders, they were annulled. The criminals went free.

The postwar Ottoman government's policies toward the Armenians were largely benign. They desisted from further direct victimization, but rendered no assistance to the surviving Armenians to ease recovery from the consequences of their dislocation. Many Armenians returned to their former homes only to find them stripped of all furnishings, wrecked, or inhabited by new occupants. Their return also created resentment and new tensions between the Armenians, filled with anger at their mistreatment, and the Turks, who, because of their own great losses during the war, believed they had a right to keep the former properties of the Armenians. In the absence of the Ottoman government's intervention to assist the Armenians, this new hostility contributed to increasing popular support for the Nationalist movement.

RISE OF THE TURKISH NATIONALISTS

The armistice signed between the Allies and the Ottomans did not result in the surrender of Turkish arms. On the contrary, it only encouraged the drive for Turkish independence from Allied interference. Organized in 1919 under the leadership of an army officer, named Mustafa Kemal, the Turkish Nationalist movement rejected the authority of the central government in Istanbul and sought to create an exclusively Turkish nation-state.

As the Kemalist armies brought more and more territory under their control, they also began to drive out the surviving remnants of the Armenian population. The Nationalist Turks did not resort to deportation as much as to measures designed to precipitate flight. In a number of towns with large concentrations of Armenian refugees, massacres again took a toll in the thousands. With the spread of news that the Nationalist forces were resorting to massacre, Armenians selected two courses of action. In a few places some decided to resist, only to be annihilated. Most chose to abandon their homes once again, and this time for good.

The massacres staged by the Nationalist forces so soon after the genocide underscored the extreme vulnerability of the Armenians. Allied troops stationed in the Middle East did not attempt to save lives. Even if the Turkish Nationalist forces could not have been stopped militarily, the failure to intervene signified the abandonment of the Armenians by the rest of the world.

Silence and Denial

For the Allies, their failure to protect the Armenians had been a major embarrassment, one worth forgetting. For the Turks, their secure resumption of sovereignty over Anatolia precluded any responsibility toward the Armenians in the form of reparations. All the preconditions were created for the cover-up of the Armenian genocide. The readiness of people on the whole to believe the position of legitimate governments meant that the suggestion that a genocide had occurred in the far reaches of Asia Minor would be made the object of historical revisionism and, soon enough, complete denial.

For almost fifty years, the Armenians virtually vanished from the consciousness of the world. Russian Armenia was Sovietized and made inaccessible. Diaspora Armenians were resigned to their fate. The silence of the world and the denials of the Turkish government only added to their ordeals.

The insecurities of life in diaspora further undermined the confidence of Armenians in their ability to hang on to some form of national existence. Constant dispersion, the threat of complete assimilation, and the humiliation of such total defeat and degradation contributed to their insecurities.

The abuse of their memory by denial was probably the most agonizing of their many tribulations. Memory, after all, was the last stronghold of the Armenian identity. The violation of this "sacred memory," as all survivors of the genocidal devastation come to enshrine the experience of traumatic death, has reverberated through Armenian society.

The persecution and later the abandonment of the Armenians left deep psychological scars among the survivors and their families. Sixty years after the genocide, a rage still simmered in the Armenian communities. Unexpectedly it exploded in a wave of terrorism. Clandestine Armenian groups, formed in the mid-1970s, sustained a campaign of political assassinations for a period of about ten years. They were responsible for killing at least two dozen Turkish diplomats.

Citing the Armenian genocide and Turkey's refusal to admit guilt as their justification, the terrorists were momentarily successful in obtaining publicity for their cause. They were unsuccessful in gaining broad-based support among Armenians or in wrenching any sort of admission from Turkey. Rather, the government of Turkey only increased the vehemence of its denial policy and embarked on a long-range plan to print and distribute a stream of publications questioning or disputing the occurrence of a genocide and distorting much of Armenian history.

Seeking International Understanding for the Armenian Cause

During these years of great turmoil other Armenians sought a more reasonable course for obtaining international understanding of their cause for remembrance. In the United States, commemorative resolutions were introduced in the House of Representatives, and in the Senate as recently as February 1990. These resolutions hoped to obtain formal U.S. acknowledgment of the Armenian genocide. But,

the intervening decades had seen a close alliance develop between the United States and Turkey. The State Department opposed passage of these resolutions. The Turkish government imposed sanctions on U.S. businesses and military installations in Turkey. In the final analysis the resolutions failed to muster the votes necessary for adoption.

Terrence Des Pres observed: "When modern states make way for geopolitical power plays, they are not above removing everything—nations, cultures, homelands—in their path. Great powers regularly demolish other peoples' claims to dignity and place, and sometimes, as we know, the outcome is genocide." These words are important in establishing the context in which peoples, Armenians and others, seek congressional resolutions, and perform other commemorative acts. It is part of the continuing struggle to reclaim dignity. The reluctance of governments to recognize past crimes points to the basic lack of motivation in the international community to confront the consequences of genocide.

Conclusion

It is helpful to distinguish between the attitudes and policies of the Ottoman imperial government, the Young Turks, and the Nationalist movement. The Ottoman government, based on the principle of sectarian inequality, tapped into the forces of class antagonism and promoted the superiority of the dominant group over a disaffected minority. It made rudimentary use of technology in the implementation of its more lethal policies.

The Young Turks, based on proto-totalitarianism and chauvinism, justified their policies on ideological grounds. They marshaled the organizational and technological resources of the state to inflict death and trauma with sudden impact. When the Young Turks deported the Armenians from Anatolia and Armenia to Syria, the result was more than simply transferring part of the population from one area of the Ottoman Empire to another. The policy of exclusion placed Armenians outside the protection of the law. Yet, strangely, because they were still technically in the Ottoman Empire, there was the possibility of repatriation for the survivors given a change in government.

The Nationalists tapped the popular forces of Turkish society to fill the vacuum of power after World War I. Their policy vis-à-vis the Armenians was formulated on the basis of racial exclusivity. They made the decision that even the remaining Armenians were undesirable. Many unsuspecting Armenians returned home at the conclusion of the war in 1918. They had nowhere else to go. With the expulsion from Nationalist Turkey, an impenetrable political boundary finally descended between the Armenians and their former homes. The possibility of return was canceled.

Genocide contains the portents of the kind of destruction that can erase past and present. For the Armenian population of the former Ottoman Empire, it meant the loss of homeland and heritage, and a dispersion to the four corners of the earth. It also meant bearing the stigma of the statelessness.

At a time when global issues dominate the political agenda of most nations, the Armenian genocide underlines the grave risks of overlooking the problems of small peoples. We cannot ignore the cumulative effect of allowing state after state to resort to the brutal resolution of disagreements with their ethnic minorities. That the world chose to forget the Armenian genocide is also evidence of a serious defect in the system of nation-states which needs to be rectified. In this respect, the continued effort to cover up the Armenian genocide may hold the most important lesson of all. With the passage of time, memory fades. Because of a campaign of denial, distortion, and cover-up, the seeds of doubt are planted, and the meaning of the past is questioned and its lessons for the present are lost.

QUESTIONS TO CONSIDER

1. Describe the two ways of looking at the Armenian experience in the final days of the Ottoman Empire, according to Rouben Adalian.
2. What is the distinction between genocide and massacre?
3. How did technology facilitate mass murder?
4. Describe the short-term and long-term consequences for the Armenian people.
5. Characterize the Turkish state's position regarding the genocide.

The Armenian Genocide and Patterns of Denial

Richard G. Hovannisian,
University of California/Los Angeles

The admission of genocidal operations by the perpetrator government or its immediate successor is rare in modern times, unlike the boastful inscriptions of ancient tyrants. The post-World War II admission and acceptance of guilt by the West German government stand out in stark contrast with all other cases in the twentieth century. But even in Germany, which made itself answerable for the guilt of the Nazi regime and engaged in various compensatory acts, thousands of implicated individuals claimed innocence or ignorance in the face of the incriminating evidence. Still, the postwar German governments, whether of free will, through coercion, or a combination of the two, extended reparations to the survivors, the families of the victims, and the state of Israel. Discussion of the moral and political implications of the Holocaust has now found a place in the educational curricula, literature, mass-media productions, and the scholarly forums of Germany.

No similarities exist in the Turkish response to the Armenian genocide. There has been neither candid admission nor willing investigation, neither reparation nor rehabilitation. On the contrary, state-sponsored attempts to suppress discussion of the Armenian genocide have reached unprecedented proportions. Presumably, the underlying cause for the Turkish attitude is political, for there still exists an aggrieved party, however disorganized and scattered, that demands some form of compensation. While many of the aggrieved would be satisfied with a simple Turkish admission of wrongdoing and the granting of dignity to the hundreds of thousands of victims by an end to efforts to erase the historical record, there are others who insist upon financial and even territorial restitution, thus adding to Turkish anxieties and attempts to obscure the past.

This political dimension at once raises the point that fundamental differences exist between the Armenian experience in World War I and the Jewish experience in World War II. Although comparative studies rightly draw parallels between the two tragedies, they cannot lose sight of the fact that the Armenians were still living in their historical homelands, had passed through cultural and political movements to the formulation of programs of

social, economic, and administrative reforms in the Ottoman Empire, and were perceived as an obstacle to the realization of the designs espoused by some members of the ruling Turkish Union and Progress party. This observation in no way diminishes responsibility for the genocide or mitigates its effects. In fact, to question whether or not genocide occurred only serves to cloud the issue. Rather, a more appropriate direction of investigation lies in the study of the causes for the genocide, its implementation and dimensions, its consequences, and its relevance today.

At the time of the deportations and massacres beginning in 1915, there was virtually universal condemnation of the act and of its perpetrators. The accounts of eyewitnesses and officials of many nationalities as well as the testimony of the survivors themselves were too detailed and corroborative to doubt the systematic nature of the operation. Being born into the targeted group was in and of itself sufficient to mark an individual for elimination. United States Ambassador Henry Morgenthau testified that the deportations to the Syrian and Mesopotamian deserts were unquestionably meant to annihilate the Armenian population:

> The Central Government now announced its intention of gathering the two million or more Armenians living in the several sections of the empire and transporting them to this desolate and inhospitable region. Had they undertaken such a deportation in good faith it would have represented the height of cruelty and injustice. As a matter of fact, the Turks never had the slightest idea of reestablishing the Armenians in this new country. They knew that the great majority would never reach their destination and that those who did would either die of thirst and starvation, or be murdered by the wild Mohammedan desert tribes. The real purpose of the deportations was robbery and destruction; it really represented a new method of massacre. When the Turkish authorities gave the orders for these deportations, they were merely giving the death warrant to a whole race; they understood this well, and, in their conversations with me, they made no particular attempt to conceal the fact.

The large corpus of evidence of genocide notwithstanding, the mechanism of denial and rationalization was put in motion as soon as the deportations began. Since then, that mechanism has moved through several major phases. During and immediately after World War I, with the evidence too fresh for total denial, the emphasis was placed on rationalization. Turkish publications and official declarations pointed to Armenian disloyalty, exploitation, and imminent general rebellion at a time when the fatherland was struggling for survival in a war on several fronts. The next phase, beginning with the international abandonment of the Armenian Question and the founding of the Republic of Turkey in 1923, was characterized by downplaying of the unpleasant past and concentration on a new image, that of a new Turkey, in which minorities enjoyed cultural and religious freedom. Apparently convinced that the Armenian problem would evaporate in time, the Turkish government under Mustafa Kemal and his successors tried to deal with Armenian matters as quietly and expeditiously as possible through diplomatic channels with countries having active Armenian communities.

But in 1965 the worldwide Armenian commemorations of the fiftieth anniversary of the genocide and the increasingly demonstrative and militant stance taken by many second- and third-generation Armenians of the dispersion ushered in a new phase in Turkish strategy. While continuing to capitalize upon the geopolitical, military, and economic importance of their country in efforts to pressure foreign governments to disregard Armenian manifestations, Turkish leaders also authorized an active campaign of counterpropaganda. The resulting books and brochures were usually sent out from Ankara in the month of April, to detract from the annual Armenian commemorative programs marking the onset of the 1915 massacres, and were addressed primarily to policymakers and opinion makers abroad, to members of legislatures and state and local governments, and to libraries, scholars, and teachers.

Only in the most recent phase, brought on by intensified Armenian violence against Turkish officials, has the strategy been directed toward public opinion in general. In newspaper advertisements, brochures and newsletters, and other popular literature, the heavily financed campaign aims at linking Armenian activism with an international conspiracy associated with the Soviet Union and the Palestine Liberation Organization. Giving special attention to Jewish leaders and Jewish opinion, the strategy attempts to dissociate the Jewish experience from the Armenian one and to drive a broad wedge between the two peoples by expressing profound sympathy for the victims and survivors of the "true" Holocaust, while characterizing the Armenian "genocide" as a hoax and "the greatest lie of the century." Enlisting the services of Turkish academics and some non-Turkish writers, the architects of this strategy appeal to a Western sense of fair play in insisting that the "other side" of a grossly misrepresented situation be taken into consideration and that the Armenian movement be exposed historically as a treacherous but abortive national rebellion and currently as a scheme to subvert Turkey and alienate it from its allies. That the repeated denials and refutations have achieved a degree of success is evidenced by the recent use by some Western reporters and commentators of qualifiers such as "alleged" and "asserted" in reference to the genocide.

The transformation of a historic genocidal operation into a controversial issue causes anger and frustration among some, and leads others to ask if there might not be credibility in the Turkish assertions. This development may also serve as a warning of things to come. While several anti-Semitic groups have challenged the truth of the Holocaust, they have by and large been discredited, and the world remains strongly aware of the decimation of European Jewry. Yet, I would suggest that given conditions similar to those affecting the Armenians, the Holocaust, too, would be challenged, not only by prejudiced extremists and guilty governments but also by well-intentioned individuals who believe that in a relativist world there are always two sides to a story. To be more specific, let us ask how the Holocaust might be regarded under the following ten conditions, which approximate the Armenian situation. What if

1. the Jewish survivors of the Holocaust, left largely to their own devices, had scattered the world over as refugees;

2. the survivors, having no sovereign government to represent them, had to struggle for years merely to ensure the physical and economic survival of their families, with their limited community resources concentrated on the establishment of a new network of schools and temples to preserve the national-religious heritage as well as possible in diverse lands and circumstances;

3. no independent Jewish nation-state had been created, and the Allied victors, despairing of assisting the survivors, abandoned the Jewish question;

4. the Jewish communities were deprived of the leadership, inspiration, and impetus provided by a Jewish nation-state;

5. in the absence of such a state, few resources were allocated for the founding of research institutes and other bodies for the gathering and analyses of materials relating to the Holocaust;

6. Jewish survivors and expatriates were too few and lacked sufficient political and financial influence to affect their host governments or succeed in having the Holocaust dealt with in the media and in educational programs;

7. the survivors, nearly all with vivid memories and indelible details of the genocide, gradually passed from the scene, and their children and grandchildren found it increasingly difficult to recount with preciseness the experiences of the survivors or to challenge deniers with firsthand eyewitness accounts;

8. the German government, defying the harsh terms initially imposed by the Allies, succeeded in writing a new peace settlement that did not necessitate some form of compensation to the survivors or even a formal acknowledgment of the genocidal operation;

9. the strategic geopolitical, military, and economic value assigned to Germany in international relations was sufficiently compelling to incline foreign governments to disregard Jewish claims against Germany and even to participate in the cover-up;

10. a new generation of foreign students, scholars, and officials interested in German affairs espoused the goal of showing Germany in a new light as a progressive, democratic state and of revising its much maligned image and unfair stereotypes, such as an oversimplified picture of a victimizing Germany and a victimized Jewry.

It is likely that in these circumstances the Jewish people today would be facing the same general indifference and even annoyance that surround Armenians in their efforts to keep their case before world opinion, raising for them the question whether truth and justice can ever prevail in the absence of sheer political and military power.

With this broad overview of the problem, a look at the shifting character of the denials may prove instructive. In the first phase, during World War I, the Turkish authorities initially tried to hide the enactment of the deportations and massacres, but once the operations had gotten well under way, they shifted the blame for Armenian troubles to the Armenians themselves. In response to the discomfort of Turkey's wartime allies, the attempted intercession of neutral states, and the threatening behavior of the Entente powers who gave notice that they would hold all members of the Turkish government personally responsible, the Young Turk rulers issued several publications incriminating the Armenians. With a selective compilation of hostile editorials from Armenian newspapers abroad, copies of seditious correspondence between members of Armenian revolutionary societies, and photographs of Armenian bands and arms caches (many of them actually from the period of Sultan Abdul-Hamid II), the Turkish leaders attempted to convince the world of Armenian treachery. Going even further, Ambassador to Washington Ahmed Rustem Bey insisted that a government could not sacrifice its preservation to sentiments of humanity, especially because the laws of humanity were suspended in time of war. After the Russian imperial armies and Armenian volunteer units from Transcaucasia had occupied most of the eastern provinces of Van, Bitlis, Erzerum, and Trebizond in 1916, Turkish publications focused on the oppression of the Turkish and Kurdish population in the region, in an effort to show that the supposed Armenian lambs were quite capable of becoming merciless wolves.

The Turkish wartime publications were roundly refuted in the West, and it seethed that with the Ottoman defeat in late 1918 the Allied Powers would now fulfill their pledges to punish Turkey and its leaders and to rehabilitate the Armenian survivors. At this time various Turkish groups and political figures who had opposed the Young Turk dictatorship surfaced with the goal of deflecting blame away from the Turkish people and holding Turkish losses to a minimum. Acting under names such as the National Congress (Milli Congre) of Turkey, they reiterated the charge that many Armenians had been subverted by Russian and revolutionary propaganda and had turned against their government by assisting the armies of the Allies and creating grave security problems. The Armenian deportations, therefore, could be justified by the "exigencies of war," but the same did not hold true for the "policy of extermination and robbery" enacted by the Young Turk leaders, who ranked "among the greatest criminals of humanity."

Justice demanded that the Turkish people not be punished for the "criminal aberration" of an "unnatural government," which caused as much torment to Muslims as to Armenians. Similar arguments were made by Grand Vizier Damad Ferid Pasha as he pleaded the Turkish case before the Paris Peace Conference in mid-1919. Admitting that terrible crimes had been committed, he shifted the blame to the Germans and Young Turk dictators and reminded the Allies of Armenian excesses as well. Armenians and Turks had lived together peaceably for centuries, and there was no validity in the view that the Armenians were victims of innate Turkish racial or religious intolerance.

Of the postwar Turkish writers, United States-educated journalist Ahmed Emin [Yalman] was perhaps the most candid in admitting that genocidal acts had occurred. Ascribing these to an unfortunate past, Emin's intent was to play upon the new, progressive image of Turkey in the 1930s. Without discarding the standard rationalizations about the Armenian threat to state security in time of war, he nonetheless wrote, in a relativist manner, that the action against the Armenians "was not commensurate with military necessity" and added "a sad chapter to the horrible practices generally resorted to among Near Eastern peoples as a means of crushing revolts and securing unity." Noting that the deportees, whom he identified as being mostly women and children, were subjected to the harshness of climate and geography and to the primitiveness of facilities, he continued:

> In addition, as the event proved, the sufferings of the deported were by no means confined to those which were unavoidable in view of strict military necessity of the existing general conditions. In the first place, the time allowed for leaving a town or village and for selling out all movable goods was extremely short, being limited in some cases to a day or two. Second, the

deported were not only left unprotected from attacks which were sure to come from marauders, but the "special organization" created with the help of the two influential members of the Committee of Union and Progress was in some cases directly instrumental in bringing about attacks and massacres. Third, the area chosen as the home of the deported was in part a desert incapable of supporting the existence of a large mass of people who reached it from a cold mountain climate after endless hardships. The deportations taken as a whole, were meant to be only a temporary military measure. But for certain influential Turkish politicians they meant the extermination of the Armenian minority in Turkey with the idea of bringing about racial homogeneity in Asia Minor.

Emin added that in 1917, because of the intensity of enemy propaganda and the pressure of those in government who opposed the greatly extended scope of the deportations, an official commission of inquiry looked into the reported violations, but "those favoring the deportations being very influential in the Government, the whole thing amounted more to a demonstration rather than a sincere attempt to fix complete responsibility." Those who pushed for "the policy of general extermination," Emin explained, knew that they would be universally condemned and believed that their personal sacrifice for the national cause might be recognized "only in a very distant future." Ironically, the prediction gradually came to pass. The remains of Talaat Pasha have now been returned to a resting place of honor in Turkey, and there has been a general rehabilitation of persons widely regarded as the prime organizers of the genocide.

Not only did the opponents of the Young Turks attempt to lift the heavy onus of the massacres from the Turkish people in the postwar period but members of the Young Turk triumvirate themselves addressed the issue while they were fugitives under the sentence of death. Before his assassination in Berlin in

1921, former Minister of Interior and Grand Vizier Talaat Pasha joined his own Turkish detractors in combining denials, disclaimers, and rationalizations. Insisting that the Ottoman Empire had been forcibly drawn into the war, he repeated the charges against the Armenians, yet still made partial admissions that went further than subsequent Turkish governments and many revisionist historians have been willing to go. The Armenians, he said, were deported from the eastern provinces but not upon a premeditated plan of annihilation. The responsibility for their fate fell foremost upon the Armenians themselves, although it was true that the deportations were not carried out lawfully everywhere and that many innocent people suffered because some officials abused their authority. "I confess it. I confess, also, that the duty of the Government was to prevent these abuses and atrocities, or at least to hunt down and punish their perpetrators severely."

Absolving himself of personal guilt, Talaat claimed that those involved were either common criminals and looters, or simple, uneducated, zealous but sincere Turks who believed that the Armenians should be punished and that they acted for the good of the country. Although it would have been relatively easy to deal with the first group, he explained, the second was strong and numerous and any punitive measures against it would have created great discontent among the masses "who favored their acts." It was not possible to divide the country and create anarchy in Anatolia when internal unity was essential for the war effort. Talaat concluded: "The preventive measures were taken in every country during the war, but, while the regrettable results were passed over in silence in the other countries, the echo of our acts was heard the world over, because everybody's eyes were upon us."

Young Turk triumvirate member Ahmed Jemal Pasha was away from the capital during most of the war. He commanded the Ottoman army in Syria at the time of the deportations and remains the most controversial of the triumvirate as regards his attitude toward the Armenians. Deploring the breakdown of the traditional symbiotic relationship between Turks and Armenians and the subversion of the Armenians by alien influences, he indirectly admitted that the Armenian male population had been eliminated by claiming that he had managed to save as many as 150,000 widows and orphans, who made up the deportation caravans. He insisted that the decisions for the deportations had been made without his participation and that he had taken every possible measure to ensure that the type of violence reported in areas such as Kharput and Diarbekir would not occur in territories under his jurisdiction. Jemal stated that when orders for deportation had been extended to include the Armenians of Adana and Aleppo, he had opposed the decision not only on humanitarian grounds but because of the terrible consequences it would have upon the economic, especially agricultural, situation. The deportation operations, however, were in the hands of the civilian authorities, and Jemal, obliged to yield, managed to save thousands from certain death. "Just as I had nothing to do with the aforementioned negotiations about the deportations of the Armenians, I am equally innocent of ordering any massacres; I have even prevented them and caused all possible help to be given to all emigrants at the time of the deportations." He added that "the crimes perpetrated during the deportations of 1915 justly roused the deepest horror, but those committed by the Armenians during their rising against the Turks and Kurds do not in any way fall short of them in cruelty and treachery." Unfortunately, the government's response to the Armenian Question had opened the way to crimes committed by the Kurdish and Turkish populations, and one

could not but wonder whether some other solution to the Armenian problem might have been found.

The postwar writings of both the Young Turks and their opponents, therefore, include partial admissions of wrongdoing and even oblique references to wholesale massacres and adherents of extermination. These are mixed with charges of Armenian treachery and disclaimers of personal and collective responsibility for the Armenian tragedy.

The triumphal conclusion of Mustafa Kemal's "War of Independence" and the establishment of the Republic of Turkey in 1923 began a new phase in the official Turkish attitude toward the Armenian problem. Having taken arms against the Armenians, destroying their hopes of a reconstituted homeland, annexing the Russian Armenian districts of Kars and Ardahan, and expelling thousands of survivors who had repatriated to Cilicia under French and English auspices, Mustafa Kemal nonetheless disassociated himself from the wartime massacres. His successful defiance of the Allies culminated in the treaties of Lausanne in which the former victors in war had to acknowledge the new frontiers of Turkey, which wiped away plans for an Armenian independent state or for even a small Armenian national home under Turkish sovereignty. The Lausanne treaties in 1923 marked the international abandonment of the Armenian cause. Although anti-Turkish sentiment was still too strong in the United States to allow for ratification of the treaty, diplomatic relations were resumed in 1927 and rapid strides were made in normalizing relations and developing economic and cultural bonds. United States educational and missionary groups that had previously called for the repatriation and protection of the Armenian survivors now joined economic interests in fostering the rapprochement through various friendship societies and investment schemes. Mustafa Kemal was viewed as a great reformer who moved forcefully to secularize and modernize his country, and American missionaries made their peace with the Turkish government in the hope of propagating an "unnamed Christianity" through educational and humanitarian endeavors.

Efforts to surmount the stereotype of the "terrible Turk" were facilitated by Turkish reform programs and the general approval of these changes in the West. In the United States, the Department of State took steps to enhance the rapprochement and managed to push forward, despite the annoying but now waning pro-Armenian manifestations and reminders of unrequited wrongs. During this period the Turkish authorities tried to play down the unpleasant past. There was little discussion of Armenians in Turkish publications, and the rare references to Armenians in textbooks were found only in brief passages relating to sinister but unsuccessful Armenian and Greek imperialistic designs to encroach upon the integrity of the Turkish homeland. While writers such as Ahmed Emin and noted feminist Halidé Edib appealed for understanding from the Western world and spoke of the sad but not entirely one-sided excesses of the past world war, they essentially shared Halidé Hanum's sentiment that about such things: "It is best not to speak much—the sooner they are forgotten the better."

In its approach to continued though weakened Armenian efforts to keep the Armenian case before world opinion, the Ankara government relied heavily on diplomatic channels in this period. An example of this tactic is the case involving the projected filming in Hollywood of Franz Werfel's celebrated novel, *The Forty Days of Musa Dagh*, the story of the desperate resistance of several Armenian settlements near Antioch during the deportations and the eventual rescue of some 4,000 of the defenders by Allied naval vessels. Plans by Metro-Goldwyn-Mayer studios to begin production in 1934 evoked strong Turkish protests. Requesting intervention by the Department of State, the Turkish ambassador complained that such a film would be "full of arbitrary calumnies and contempt against the Turkish people" and would give "an utterly false conception of Turkey," thereby hindering the course of friendly Turko-American relations. In response to the State Department's active involvement in the issue, the studio offered to alter the script to remove the most objectionable features and then agreed to allow the Turkish embassy to approve the revised script before filming began. The embassy, however, insisted that the story was so political and prejudicial that, regardless of what changes might be made, it could not be acceptable. At the same time, Turkish authorities let it be known that release of the film would lead to a Turkish ban on all U.S. films. To appease the Turks, the State Department wrote to the president of the Motion Pictures Producers and Distributors of America, asking for his assistance in a matter that had taken on "very large proportions in the minds of the officials at Ankara." After more than a year of exchanges, MGM announced that plans to produce the film were being dropped. Ambassador Münir Ertegun, in his letter of appreciation to the Department of State, concluded:

> I have already informed my government of the satisfactory result reached through the kind support of the State Department.
>
> In this connection it is an agreeable duty for me to extend to you my best thanks and hearty appreciation for the efforts you have been so kind to exert in this matter without which the happy conclusion which has created as excellent impression in my country could not possibly have been attained.

An attempt in 1938 to revive the project met with a repetition of Turkish protests and State Department intercession, leaving the film in abeyance for more than four decades until its release in 1982 by a private group of Armenian businessmen. By the beginning of World War II, the Armenian massacres had faded from recent memory in the wake of new international crises, and the Turkish government, no longer acknowledging an Armenian Question, managed to keep the issue suppressed through diplomatic channels.

Turkey's wavering neutrality during World War II and the popular belief that some Turkish leaders admired and favored Adolf Hitler raised hopes among Armenians that the Soviet Union would apply enough pressure to restore the former Russian Armenian districts of Kars and Ardahan to Soviet Armenia. Armenian petitions were addressed to the United Nations in support of such a border rectification, but the Turkish government firmly rejected all bids and used the rapidly developing Cold War to gain strong U.S. support against the Soviet claims, which were soon withdrawn. Nonetheless, the occasional mention of Armenians in international forums brought renewed brief references to Armenians in Turkish publications. The passages were intended for foreign readers in Western nation-states that had recently passed through a world war. Writing about Turkey in the 1950s, the press attaché of the Turkish embassy in Washington asserted that the Armenians had acted as willing agents of a foreign government and therefore had to be subjected to a limited deportation: "Turkish response to Armenian excesses was comparable, I believe, to what might have been the American response, had the German-Americans of Minnesota and Wisconsin revolted on behalf of Hitler during World War II." Fortunately, he continued, almost all the ill-feeling toward Turkey had disappeared and even the "poor starving Armenians" had largely been forgotten.

Efforts to make the Armenian genocide a nonissue had registered impressive gains by 1965, the year marking the fiftieth anniversary of the deportations and massacres. The once

influential and highly vocal Armenophile organizations around the world had virtually disappeared, and Armenian woes seemed to slip into an increasingly remote and nonrelevant past. But then the unexpected occurred. The relatively quiescent Armenian communities, though unable to sustain external interest in their cause, burst forth with unprecedented activity in the half-century year of the Armenian tragedy. The wave of demonstrative commemorations swept across international frontiers, driving the usually reserved Soviet Armenians and the diaspora Armenians alike into the streets. These manifestations received some media coverage, and a new, partially assimilated generation of Armenians in many countries began to express the pain and aspirations of the survivor generation and to place the Armenian Question among other human rights issues. With increasing frequency municipal officials, legislators, governors, prime ministers, and presidents mentioned the Armenian tragedy when speaking about the obligation to remember the lessons of past instances of man's inhumanity to man. Armenian memorials were erected, studies and memoirs relating to the genocide appeared in various languages, and a rising generation took to the streets with placards and chants to remind the Turkish government and the world that the Armenian Question still existed. Then, in 1973, the words *Armenian* and *Turk* captured headlines for a moment when an aged Armenian survivor assassinated two Turkish consular officials in California. Armenian acts of political terrorism increased in subsequent years, focusing media attention not only on the violence but also on its background, the Armenian historical experience, and the Turkish denials of genocide.

The Armenian manifestations that began in 1965 drew the Turkish authorities reluctantly back into the arena. Initially, the Ankara government, together with many Armenians, believed that Armenians were incapable of such violent acts: the last political assassinations by Armenians had taken place in the 1920s and these had been directed against Young Turk fugitives who had been convicted of wartime crimes. Turkish political observers and newspapers now pointed the finger of guilt at the Greek Cypriots and suggested that the terrorists might well be Greeks hiding behind an Armenian mask. Yet, as Armenian demonstrations and sporadic political violence against Turkish diplomats continued, the veil of doubt lifted and the Turkish government found itself face to face with the stubborn Armenian annoyance. Nor were the Turkish government's attempts to rely on diplomatic channels to suppress Armenian endeavors as successful as in the past. Diplomatic pressure to prevent the erection of Armenian memorial monuments in Los Angeles and in Marseilles, for example, failed despite sympathy from some quarters within the United States and French governments.

By the 1970s the Turkish government came to the conclusion that it could no longer simply dismiss or ignore the Armenian problem and formulated a campaign to counteract Armenian propaganda. In this phase of the denial process, pamphlets and brochures sent out from Ankara to foreign countries were mostly reprints of the Turkish publications first issued between 1917 and 1919 and intended to cast blame for Armenian troubles on the Armenians themselves and, after the war, to minimize the Ottoman losses. Evolving from this type of literature by the mid-seventies were new tracts prepared by several Turkish historians and contemporary writers. These materials, which were intended to prove the baselessness of Armenian claims, included nothing new and were riddled with contradiction, misquotation, and distortion. In his essay entitled *Armenian Question*, for example, Enver Zia Karal asserted that, despite their treacherous behavior, the Armenians were protected throughout Anatolia after the war. According to Karal, Major General James G. Harbord, head of an American military mission of inquiry to Asia Minor and Transcaucasia in 1919, admitted to this when he supposedly reported:

> Meanwhile, the Armenian, unarmed at the time of deportations, a brave soldier who served in thousands in the armies of Russia, France and America is still unarmed *and safe* [italics added] in a land where every man but himself need to carry a rifle.

What Harbord actually wrote gives the opposite picture:

> Meanwhile, the Armenian, unarmed at the time of the deportations *and massacres* [italics added], a brave soldier by thousands in the armies of Russia, France, and America during the war, is still unarmed in a land where every man but himself carries a rifle.

Typical of the distortions in this genre of political pamphleteering is the substitution by Karal of the words "and safe" for the words "and massacres." Harbord's real attitude about the genocide is public record:

> Massacres and deportations were organized in the spring of 1915 under definite system, the soldiers going from town to town. The official reports of the Turkish Government show 1,100,000 as having been deported. Young men were first summoned to the government building in each village and then marched out and killed. The women, the old men, and children were, after a few days, deported to what Talaat Pasha called "agricultural colonies," from the high, cool, breeze-swept plateau of Armenia to the malarial flats of the Euphrates and the burning sands of Syria and Arabia ... Mutilation, violation, torture, and death have left their haunting memories in a hundred beautiful Armenian valleys, and the traveler in that region is seldom free from the evidence of this most colossal crime of all the ages.

Sometimes efforts to defame the Armenians entered the realm of the absurd. In a pamphlet sent out from Ankara entitled *Truth about Armenians*, Ahmet Vefa, aside from repeating the standard Turkish allegations, alerted the English-reading public to the existence of correspondence in the Hoover Institution archives at Stanford University, making it known that "the Armenians were not and never could be desirable citizens, that they would always be unscrupulous merchants." Of greater interest is Vefa's contention that when Adolf Hitler asked rhetorically in 1939, "Who after all speaks today of the annihilation of the Armenians," he was making reference not to Turkish excesses against Armenians, but rather to the Armenian destruction of the pre-Armenian Urartuans in the seventh century before Christ.

Unable to make significant headway with this type of literature, Turkish officials encouraged sympathetic foreign scholars to present the "Turkish side" in the West and even afforded limited access to a few relevant archival files. But long before the astounding writings of Stanford J. Shaw in the 1970s, the trend toward revisionism had already influenced a number of scholars involved in Turkish studies. Because the existence of the Republic of Turkey was seen as a good thing, there was a tendency to justify the events that had led up to it and its current boundaries. This disposition is reflected in the writings of Lewis V. Thomas, Richard Robinson, Norman Itzkowitz, and a significant number of younger scholars.

The tenor of the revisionist approach was already set in the 1950s in the works of Professor Thomas, who admitted that the Turks had overreacted to a perceived Armenian threat and who regretted the agony of the Armenians, but who nonetheless explained that the Turks had been driven to desperation. He put forth the following rationalization:

> By 1918, with the definitive excision of the total Armenian Christian population from Anatolia and the Straits area, except for a small and wholly insignificant enclave in Istanbul city, the hitherto largely peaceful process of Turkification and Moslemization had been advanced in one great surge by the use of force. How else can one assess

the final blame except to say that this was a tragic consequence of the impact of western European nationalism upon Anatolia? Had Turkification and Moslemization not been accelerated there by the use of force, there certainly would not today exist a Turkish Republic, a Republic owing its strength and stability in no small measure to the homogeneity of its population, a state which is now a valued associate of the United States.

In the 1970s revisionism reached levels that transcended all previous bounds in the writings of Professor Stanford J. Shaw. Under the guise of scholarly research he not only repeated but also enhanced the worn, unsubstantiated accusations against the Armenians. His treatment of the Armenian Question in *History of the Ottoman Empire and Modern Turkey* includes gross errors and surpasses even the excuses of the Young Turk perpetrators. Setting a theme for subsequent Turkish propaganda, Shaw contests sources showing that there were between 2 and 3 million Armenians in the Ottoman Empire and maintains that there were actually no more than 1,300,000, thereby minimizing the number that could have been deported or killed. Characterizing the Armenians as the invariable aggressors, the victimizers rather than the victims, the privileged rather than the oppressed, and the fabricators of unfounded tales of massacre, he insists that the Young Turk government took all possible measures to ensure the safety of those people who had to be removed from the border districts and to provide them with food, water, and medical attention while en route to suitable new homes in prearranged relocation centers.

> Specific instructions were issued for the army to protect the Armenians against nomadic attacks and to provide them with sufficient food and other supplies to meet their needs during the march and after they were settled. Warnings were sent to the Ottoman military commanders to make certain that neither the Kurds nor any other Muslims used the situation to gain vengeance for the long years of Armenian

terrorism. The Armenians were to be protected and cared for until they returned to their homes after the war. A supplementary law established a special commission to record the properties of some deportees and sell them at auction at fair prices, with the revenues being held in trust until their return. Muslims wishing to occupy abandoned buildings could do so only as renters, with the revenues paid to the trust funds, and with the understanding that they would have to leave when the original owners returned. The deportees and their possessions were to be guarded by the army while in transit as well as in Iraq and Syria, and the government would provide for their return once the crisis was over.

In the face of the voluminous documentary evidence and eyewitness accounts to the contrary, Professor Shaw would have the reader believe that the Armenians were removed only from a few strategic regions, and this with the utmost concern for the safety of their persons and properties.

The counterpart of Stanford Shaw among Turkish writers who have learned the selective use of archival materials to support their denials is Cypriot-born Salahi R. Sonyel. Initiating his refutations early in the 1970s, he subsequently authored several pamphlets with titles such as *Shocking New Documents Which Belie the Armenian Claim that the Ottoman Government Was Responsible for the Armenian Tragic Adventure 60 Years Ago* and *Greco-Armenian Conspiracy Against Turkey Revived*. Denouncing Armenians who "stage demonstrations and publish propaganda material in certain European, American and Middle East capitals," Sonyel complained:

> These hysterical, illogical and sentimental fanatics seem to prefer sensationalism to scholarly research, and, being a party to the case, undoubtedly have an axe to grind, giving absolutely biased accounts of Armenian and Greek deportations and "massacres." ... They prefer to write propaganda accounts, rather than to produce scholarly works based on *facts* and *figures*, which would be more appreciated. But then they

are typical vociferous Greek and Armenian propagandists, some of whom, recent documents prove beyond any doubt, were themselves directly responsible for the misfortune of the Greek and Armenian people.

With the intent of showing that Talaat Pasha and other Young Turk officials, far from planning the elimination of the Armenian people, had taken measures to limit, localize, and ameliorate the deportations, Sonyel published in 1978 a batch of Turkish documents that had been deposited in the British archives. It was established long ago that official correspondence relating to the safety of, and provisions for, the deportees was used to conceal what actually was happening to the Armenians, and this particular group of documents pertaining to the western Anatolian district of Hudavendigar was carefully selected and excerpted. Even so, there is evidence even in these papers that betrays Sonyel's objective, as seen in the following examples:

- **23 July 1915** The Armenians within the province should be transported to the areas previously determined. The Catholics should be excluded from this displacement procedure.
- **25 July 1915** It is decided that the Armenians should be moved to the interior of the country. In view of this, it is requested that necessary measures be taken to prevent the Armenian soldiers in the Workers Battalions within your area from violating the order and that a copy of this message be despatched to the Commanders of the Workers Battalions in your area.
- **29–30 July 1915** The personal property belonging to the Armenian children who later became Moslem, got married or left under the care of reliable persons for training or educational purposes, will be left to the said children, if their legators are dead, their share of the property will be paid to them.
- **[no date]** The families of the military, the Protestants and Catholics who have not yet been displaced from their areas, the artists who are allowed to stay by the local authorities, the workers working in the factories producing the goods required by the people and those working in the railways and stations as well as their families will not be displaced.

- Boys older than 15 years and married women are not considered among the dependents of the head of a family.

The boldness of contemporary writers such as Shaw and Sonyel has been facilitated by the death of most survivors of, and foreign eye-witnesses to, the massacres and is paralleled by renewed militancy within the Turkish government. Determined to prevent the Armenian Question from ever again becoming a topic of international diplomacy, the Ankara government has engaged in strong political lobbying to expunge even passing references to the Armenians. This policy is exemplified by the tactics used in relation to a United Nations subcommission draft report on the prevention and punishment of genocide. In 1973 the special rapporteur of the Subcommission on Prevention of Discrimination and Protection of Minorities wrote in paragraph 30 of the introductory historical section:

> Passing to the modern era, one may note the existence of relatively full documentation dealing with the massacres of Armenians, which have been described as "the first case of genocide in the twentieth century."

The paragraph makes no mention of either the Ottoman Empire or of Turks, yet the Turkish mission to the United Nations and the Turkish government regarded the sentence as menacing and immediately applied pressure on governments and delegations represented on the full Human Rights Commission. Yielding to this pressure the commission adopted a recommendation that historic events preceding recent genocidal acts and the contemporary definition of genocide be omitted from the report. "It was pointed out that there was the dangerous pitfall of confusing the crime of genocide with the eventual consequences which might occur as a result of a given war and making such parallels without taking into account the historical and socio-economic background of the past events." Matters that had been subject "to controversial explanations

and evaluations in different publications" should be avoided. Hence paragraph 30 should be deleted.

When the issue was raised again in 1975, one delegate noted that the tragedy of 1915 was historical fact, "but in a civilized international community, consideration should also be given to the desire of a state not to be defamed on account of its past acts, which had been perpetrated by a previous generation and were probably regretted by the present generation." When the subcommission's rapporteur submitted the revised version of his report in 1978, the historical section began with the Nazi-perpetrated Holocaust. In the words of Leo Kuper, the Armenian genocide "had disappeared down the memory hole." When a few members of the subcommission questioned the deletion, it was now the rapporteur who explained:

> Concern had been expressed that the study of genocide might be diverted from its intended course and lose its essential purpose. Consequently, it had been decided to retain the massacre of the Jews under Nazism, because that case was known to all and no objections had been raised; but other cases had been omitted, because it was impossible to compile an exhaustive list, because it was important to maintain unity in the international community in regard to genocide, and because in many cases to delve into the past might reopen old wounds which were now healing.

When the Turkish measures to erase even the memory of the Armenian victims in a draft report of a United Nations subcommission became known, the story spread swiftly throughout the Armenian communities. Armenian groups around the world now mounted their own campaign, publicly invoking the human rights declarations of several member states of the UN Human Rights Commission. The subsequent lead of the United States in reversing its position during the Carter administration in 1979 was followed by several other countries, resulting in the request to the special rapporteur to take into account the various statements made in and to the commission about the Armenian tragedy. Now, after more than a decade, the matter of whether to mention the Armenians in the introductory historical section of the belabored report is still unresolved.

The most recent phase of denial, advanced in the 1980s by the Turkish military and civil governments, is characterized by efforts to reach the public at large. The decision to allocate substantial financial resources for newspaper advertisements, brochures intended for mass distribution, and various programs and productions enhancing Turkey's image abroad was taken in response to the more frequent acts of Armenian violence and, correspondingly, the more frequent attention given Armenians and Armenian history in newspapers and journals and on television.

One aim of the current phase is to create a broad breach between Jews and Armenians by emphasizing the true horror of the Holocaust and playing up Turkey's ties with Israel, while cautioning against an Armenian scheme to detract from the Holocaust and dishonor the memory of its victims by winning recognition for a mythical genocide fabricated solely for political purposes. This approach has been used in public announcements, in private meetings and written exchanges with Jewish leaders, and in international diplomatic correspondence. All these means have also been employed in repeated efforts to dissuade the United States Holocaust Council from including the Armenian genocide in any of its projected educational and commemorative activities. In this campaign to drive the wedge as deep as possible, Turkish sources link Armenian activism with the Palestine Liberation Organization and Soviet manipulation. "We recognize that Armenian terrorists have confirmed ties with international communist and terrorist organizations. As such they are tools in the hands of those who seek to destabilize the precarious peace of the Middle East and Europe." When a Turkish terrorist attempted to

assassinate Pope John Paul in 1981, Ambassador to the United States Şükrü Elekdağ and other Turkish officials tried in vain to establish an Armenian connection. Prominent Armenians in Turkey have also been pressed into service by having to sign statements attesting to their enjoyment of full human rights, condemning Armenian extremism past and present, and ascribing Armenian unrest abroad to the "Greek intrigue" to defame the Turkish republic and alienate it from its NATO allies.

Although the Turkish rationalizations during and immediately after World War I were rejected by most foreign governments, they did include minor admissions that now seem to have paled before the unqualified contemporary denials. Speaking before the Los Angeles World Affairs Council in November 1981, for example, Ambassador Elekdağ declared: "The accusation that Ottoman Turks, sixty-five years ago, during World War I, perpetrated systematic massacres of the Armenian population in Turkey, to annihilate them and to seize their homeland, is totally baseless."

This argument has been subsequently reiterated by Elekdağ, and elaborated in a booklet published in 1982 entitled *Setting the Record Straight on Armenian Propaganda Against Turkey*. The opening lines read: "In recent years claims have been made by some Armenians in Europe, America, and elsewhere that the Armenians suffered terrible misrule in the Ottoman Empire. Such claims are absurd." Reflecting both the style and the methodology of the extreme revisionist historians, the brochure attempts to show that the Armenians, despite their many privileges, in the nineteenth century became Russian agents and initiated an indiscriminate reign of terror. "Muslims were brutalized as much as possible in order to stimulate reprisals and to bring about cycles of massacre and counter-massacre, which could only be ended by European intervention. Realizing the terrorist intentions, Abdulhamit II and his successors did all they could to prevent Muslim reprisals for the Armenian massacres, and they were largely successful." In this manner the great Armenian pogroms in the 1890s are dismissed and Sultan Abdul-Hamid, previously discredited by many Turkish writers, is portrayed as a patient and tolerant ruler.

As for the events during World War I, there were, the brochure asserts, no generalized massacres, except by Armenians, and certainly no genocide. Perhaps as many as 100,000 Armenians may have died of various causes between 1915 and 1918, but that was not unusual compared with Turkish losses: "There was no genocide committed against the Armenians in the Ottoman Empire before or during World War I. No genocide was planned or ordered by the Ottoman government and no genocide was carried out. Recent scholarly research has discovered that the stories of massacres were in fact largely invented by Armenian nationalist leaders in Paris and London during World War I and spread throughout the world through the British intelligence." Moreover, "the Armenian nationalists have continued to spread their message of hate, relying on repetition of the 'big lie' to secure acceptance of their claims in a Christian world predisposed to accept the claims of Christians whenever they are in conflict with Muslims."

The Turkish publication to "set the record straight" concludes with a denunciation of Armenian oral history programs: "Carefully coached by their Armenian nationalist interviewers, these aged Armenians relate tales of horror which supposedly took place some 66 years ago in such detail as to astonish the imagination, considering that most of them already are aged eighty or more. Subjected to years of Armenian nationalist propaganda as well as the coaching of their interviewers, there is little doubt that their statements are of no use whatever for historical research ..."

The history of the denial of the Armenian genocide has passed through several phases, each somewhat different in emphasis but all characterized by efforts to avoid responsibility and the moral, material, and political conse-

quences of admission. Only under the impact of the defeat of the Ottoman Empire and the flight of the Young Turk leaders were there partial admissions, but this trend was halted by the successful Kemalist defiance of the Allies and the subsequent international abandonment of the Armenian Question. In the absence of external force, neither the perpetrators nor successive Turkish governments have been willing to face the skeleton in their closet. Rather, they have resorted to various forms of avoidance, denial, repudiation, and vilification to keep the door shut. In the meantime, Turkish writers and scholars are still unable to deal honestly with their national past and continue to be drawn, wittingly or unwittingly, into the wheels of rationalization and falsification. Taking advantage of its strategic geopolitical and military importance, the Republic of Turkey has repeatedly impressed on other governments and international bodies that dwelling on a complex but no longer relevant past is unproductive, disruptive, and antagonistic. Yet the problem has persisted, and the tone and tenor of the denials are now more forceful than ever before. The Turkish position severely obstructs investigation of the genocide, its causes, effects, and implications, and the scholarly and humanitarian ends to which such studies should be directed.

As the number of persons who lived through World War I and who have direct knowledge of the events diminishes, the rationalizers and debasers of history become all the more audacious, to the extent of transforming the victims into the victimizers. At the time of the deportations and massacres, no reputable publication would have described the genocide as "alleged." The clouding of the past, however, and the years of Turkish denials, diplomatic and political pressures, and programs of image improvement have had their impact on some publishers, correspondents, scholars, and public officials. In an increasingly skeptical world, the survivors and descendants of the victims have been thrust into a defensive position from which they are required to prove time and again that they have indeed been wronged, individually and collectively. It is not surprising that they should look with envy upon Jewish Holocaust survivors, who do not have to face an unrepentant and uncompromising German government and a high-powered political campaign of denial that a state-organized plan of annihilation was in fact enacted. The Armenians search desperately for morality in politics and ask if there may be any just and practical alternative to the dictum "might makes right."

QUESTIONS TO CONSIDER

1. Did the United States take a position regarding the massacres beginning in 1915?

2. What does the author mean by "the mechanism of denial and nationalization"?

3. What are the points of convergence and divergence between the Armenian genocide and Jewish Holocaust?

4. Characterize the "Young Turks."

5. Describe Turkish–U.S. relations after the establishment of the Republic of Turkey in 1923.

6. Did World War II aid the Armenian cause? Explain your answer.

7. By the 50th anniversary of the massacre, which characterization of the genocide prevailed?

8. How did Turkey influence the American academic community?

9. Give the details of the phase of denial in the 1980s, explaining Turkish–Israeli relations.

The Armenian Genocide

Robert F. Melson,
Purdue University

I. INTRODUCTION

When confronted with mass death and forced deportations, the contemporary world community has often reached for the Holocaust as a paradigmatic case of genocide, in order both to make sense of and to condemn current events. This essay suggests that it is the Armenian Genocide, not the Holocaust, that sets a more accurate precedent for current ethnic disasters, especially those as in the post-communist and Third Worlds, that are the products of nationalism. By the same token the Holocaust is a prototype for genocidal movements that transcend nationalism and are motivated by ideologies that have global scope.

In this century the world has experienced four tidal waves of national and ethnic conflict and genocide in the wake of crumbling states and empires. These waves were punctuated by the First and Second World Wars and by the post-colonial and postcommunist eras. During the First World War and its aftermath, as the Ottoman Empire collapsed it committed genocide against its Armenian minority. In the same period, the disintegration of the German and Austro-Hungarian empires set off *Volkisch*, nationalist and fascist movements that repressed

Reprinted from Robert F. Melson, "Hearing on House Resolution 398, The United States Training on and Commemoration of the Armenian Genocide Resolution" Subcommittee on International Operations and Human Rights (September 14, 2000).

minorities and precipitated the Second World War. In the context of that war, the Nazis attempted to exterminate the Jews and Gypsies and committed partial genocide against other peoples. Following the Second World War, as former European colonial empires, notably Britain and France, withdrew from their possessions, they left behind fragile regimes that lacked legitimacy. Such "Third World" governments frequently ruled over culturally plural societies and tried to impose the hegemony of one ethnic group over the rest. In reaction, minorities rebelled and sought self-determination. This led to ethnic wars and genocide in places like Indonesia, Burundi, Sri Lanka, Nigeria, Pakistan, Ethiopia, Sudan, and Iraq. In the wake of the recent collapse of communist regimes in the Soviet Union and Yugoslavia, we are experiencing the fourth wave of nationalist upsurge, ethnic conflicts, and genocide. Meanwhile, as in contemporary Rwanda, it should be noted, the third wave of post-colonial genocide has not yet spent its force.

The Armenian Genocide and the Holocaust are the quintessential instances of total genocide in the 20th century. In both instances a deliberate attempt was made by the government of the day to destroy in part or in whole an ethno-religious community of ancient provenance that had existed as a segment of the government's own society. In both instances genocide was perpetrated after the fall of an old regime and during the reign of a revolutionary movement that was motivated by an ideology of social, political, and cultural transformation. And in both cases genocides occurred in the midst of world wars. These may be said to account for some of the basic similarities between the two genocides, but there were significant differences as well.

The perpetrators of the Armenian Genocide were motivated by a variant of nationalist ideology, the victims were a territorial ethnic group that had sought autonomy, and the methods of destruction included massacre, forced deportations, and starvation. In con-

trast, the perpetrators of the Holocaust were motivated by racism and anti-Semitism, ideologies of global scope, the victims were not a territorial group and so for the most part they had sought integration and assimilation instead of autonomy, and the death camp was the characteristic method of destruction.

Though in some essential ways the Armenian Genocide and the Holocaust resemble each other, the point of this essay is that contemporary instances of partial genocide such as occurred for instance in a Third World Country like Nigeria in 1966–70 and in post-communist Yugoslavia in 1991–1999, have more in common with the Armenian Genocide than they do with the Holocaust. This stems from the character of the victim groups compared, from the ideology of the perpetrators, and from the methods of destruction. As in Armenia and unlike the Holocaust, in Nigeria and Yugoslavia, the groups singled out were territorial and had sought self-determination, the ideology of the perpetrators was a variant of nationalism, and the method of destruction was forced deportation, starvation, and massacre.

This analysis will start by briefly laying out some essential similarities and differences between the Armenian Genocide and the Holocaust. It will then show how the former bears more of a resemblance to contemporary partial genocides such as have occurred in Nigeria and Yugoslavia than does the Holocaust.

II. SIMILARITIES

The similarities between the course of the Armenian Genocide and the Holocaust may be briefly noted. These include the low social status and rapid ascent of the two minorities in the Ottoman Empire and Imperial Germany respectively; the revolutionary transformations of both empires and the coming to power of revolutionary vanguards like the Committee of Union and Progress (CUP) and the Nazis; the redefinition and recasting of the identities of the majority and minority communities, Turks and Armenians, on the one hand, and Germans and Jews, on the other; and the implementation of genocide following the revolutionary state's engagement in international war.

The Armenian Genocide

In traditional Ottoman society Armenians, like other Christians and Jews, were defined as a *dhimmi* millet, a non-Muslim religious community of the Empire. Their actual treatment by the state varied to some extent with the military fortunes of the empire, with the religious passions of its elites, and with the encroachment upon their land of Muslim refugees from the Balkans and the Caucuses, and of Kurdish pastoralists.

Although by and large *dhimmis* were free to practice their religion, they were considered to be distinctively inferior to Muslims in status. However, in the 19th century the Armenians challenged the traditional hierarchy of Ottoman society, as they became better educated, wealthier, and more urban. In response, despite attempts at reforms, the empire became more represssive, and Armenians, more than any other Christian minority, bore the brunt of persecution.

Throughout the 19th century the Ottoman sultans were caught in the vise between great power pressures on the one hand and the demand for self-determination among their minorities on the other. By the time Abdul Hamid II came to power in 1876, he had set a course of political and social repression and technological modernization. Nevertheless, he could not halt the military and political disintegration of his regime, and he was replaced in 1908 by a political revolution of Young Turks with new and radical ideas of how to address the Ottoman crisis.

In the first instance, the Committee of Union and Progress (CUP), the political organization formed by the Young Turks, attempted radically to transform the regime following liberal and democratic principles that had been embodied in the earlier constitution of 1876. They hoped for the support of the Great Powers for their reforms, but neither the European powers nor the minorities reduced their pressures. On the contrary, they took the opportunity of internal Ottoman disarray and revolutionary transformation to press their demands, and between 1908 and 1912 they succeeded in reducing the size of Ottoman territory by forty percent and its population by twenty percent.

Concluding that their liberal experiment had been a failure, the CUP leaders turned to Pan-Turkism, a xenophobic and chauvinistic brand of nationalism that sought to create a new empire based on Islam and Turkish ethnicity. This new empire, stretching from Anatolia to western China, would exclude minorities or grant them nominal rights unless they became Turks by nationality and Muslim by religion.

This dramatic shift in ideology and identity, from Ottoman pluralism to an integral form of Turkish nationalism, had profound implications for the emergence of modern Turkey. At the same time Pan-Turkism had tragic consequences for Ottoman minorities, most of all for the Armenians. From being once viewed as a constituent millet of the Ottoman regime, they suddenly were stereotyped as an alien nationality. Their situation became especially dangerous because of their territorial concentration in eastern Anatolia on the border with Russia, Turkey's traditional enemy. Thus the Armenians, at one and the same time, were accused of being in league with Russia against Turkey and of claiming Anatolia, the heartland of the projected Pan-Turkic state.

This was the situation even before the First World War. When war broke out, however, the Young Turks led especially by Enver joined the German side in an anti-Russian alliance that would allow the Pan-Turkists to build their state at Russia's expense. It was in this context of revolutionary and ideological transformation and war that the fateful decision to destroy the Armenians was taken.

By February 1915 Armenians serving in the Ottoman army were turned into labor battalions and either worked to death or killed. By April that same year the remaining civilians were deported from eastern Anatolia and Cilicia, in an early form of "ethnic cleansing," toward the deserts near Aleppo. The lines of Armenian deportees were set upon again and again by Turkish and Kurdish villagers who were often incited and led by specially designated killing squads, *Teshkilat-i Makhsusiye*, that had been organized by members of the CUP. Those who escaped massacre were very likely to perish of famine on the way. In this manner, between 1915 and the armistice in 1918, some one million people, out of a population of two million, were killed. Later a half million more Armenians perished as Turkey sought to free herself of foreign occupation and to expel minorities. Thus between 1915 and 1923, approximately three quarters of the Armenian population was destroyed in the Ottoman Empire.

The Holocaust

The Holocaust had similar origins, albeit with significant variations. Jews were a traditional pariah caste in Europe that in the 19th century began to advance in social, economic, cultural, and political spheres. It is in this context that the anti-Semitic movement got its start. Initially it was dedicated to revoke Jewish emancipation and to undermine Jewish progress. Later it spawned an ideology that identified the Jews as a biologically alien tribe that was part of a worldwide conspiracy to control the world. In Imperial Germany, however, anti-Semitic political parties failed to make significant inroads, and on the eve of the Great War, the movement was marginalized and in retreat.

Like the Young Turks, the Nazis came to power after the collapse of an old regime. The German state experienced defeat in the First World War, a failed revolt from the left, inflation, depression, and the collapse of the democratic Weimar Republic. It was this revolutionary interregnum, starting with the fall of Imperial Germany, that enabled the Nazis to come to power.

Led by Hitler, whose charismatic persona and ideology united them, the Nazis were a movement centered on a cult of the fuhrer and racialist anti-Semitism. Once in power the Nazis sought to recast Germany as an "Aryan" nation from which they would eradicate Jews and banish what they called the "Jewish spirit." Between 1933 and 1945 Germans scrambled to prove to themselves and to each other that their lineage had not been "polluted" by the infusion of Jewish "blood" and that their character had not been shaped by Jewish, or even Christian, values.

Indeed, the higher one went in the Nazi hierarchy the "purer" and more brutal one was expected to be. This attempt to recast one's identity in opposition to a mythical "Jew" and his Weltanschauung accounts in part for the growing radicalization of Nazi policy. In order to please Hitler and the Nazi elite, various spheres of the party and state began to compete with each other over Jewish policy and over the mantle of who was most radical on the "Jewish Question."

The Holocaust was implemented in three overlapping stages. Thus between 1933 and 1939 Jews were defined, expropriated, and expelled from Germany. Between 1939 and 1941, as the Germans invaded Poland and set off the Second World War, Jews were concentrated in ghettos near railroad transit centers, especially in Poland and the other occupied countries of eastern Europe. Between 1941 and 1945, as Germany invaded Russia, the seat of the supposed "Jewish World Conspiracy," Jews were first massacred by shooting squads, and later, for the sake of efficiency and secrecy, they were deported to killing centers where they were gassed and cremated.

III. DIFFERENCES

Like their similarities, the differences between the Armenian Genocide and the Holocaust may be plotted along the same dimensions: Jews and Armenians differed in status in the two empires; Nazi racist anti-Semitism differed significantly from the Pan-Turkist nationalism of the Young Turks; and the killing of the Armenians relied mostly on massacre and starvation rather than the death camps.

Like the Armenians in the Ottoman Empire, the Jews were an ethnoreligious community of low status in Christian Europe. Unlike the Armenians, however, who were the subject of contempt for being non-Muslims, the Jews of feudal Europe became a pariah caste stigmatized as "killers of the Son of God." Thus Jews were not only despised in most parts of Europe, they were also hated and feared in a manner that the Armenians in the Ottoman Empire were not.

In the 19th century, to the extent that the state became bureaucratic, society meritocratic, and the economy capitalistic, Armenians and Jews began to advance in status and wealth. Indeed, it has been suggested that Armenian and Jewish progress was viewed as illegitimate and subversive, which precipitated antagonistic reactions both in the Ottoman Empire and in Imperial Germany, respectively.

Here at least two variations may be noted. Whereas Armenians were a territorial group that increasingly made known its demands for greater autonomy and self-administration within the Ottoman system, Jews were geographically dispersed, and thus, with the exception of the Zionists who sought a Jewish state in Palestine, most made no territorial demands on the larger societies in which they lived. Instead, to the extent that they accepted the modern world, most Jews sought assimilation to the culture and integration into the wider society.

The reaction against Jewish progress, assimilation, and attempts at integration became a European-wide movement of anti-Semitism, a form of racism that set up unbridgeable obstacles to Jewish inclusion. According to anti-Semites, like Duhring for example, not even conversion would allow Jews to become the equals of Germans or other Europeans. Already in 1881, he wrote:

> A Jewish question would still exist, even if every Jew were to turn his back on his religion and join one of our major churches. Yes, I maintain that in that case, the struggle between us and the Jews would make itself felt as ever more urgent … It is precisely the baptized Jews who infiltrate furthest, unhindered in all sectors of society and political life.

According to Wilhelm Marr, for example, Jews were not only an alien race, they also constituted an international conspiracy whose aim was the domination of Germany, Europe, indeed the whole world. Thus anti-Semites founded not only a movement that opposed Jewish progress and assimilation, they also formulated a far-reaching ideology that helped them to explain the vacillations and crises of the modern world. It was an ideology that came to rival liberalism and socialism in its mass appeal.

By way of contrast no such ideology of anti-Armenianism developed in the Ottoman Empire. Armenians may have been popularly despised for being *dhimmis*, or *Gavur*, and later under the Young Turks they may have been feared as an alien nation supposedly making claims to Anatolia, the heartland of the newly valued "Turkey." However, even Pan-Turkism left the door open to conversion and assimilation of minorities, something that racism and anti-Semitism explicitly rejected.

Moreover, though the Young Turks may have claimed that the Armenians were in league with their international enemies, especially the Russians, their nationalism never led them to the bizarre excesses which later became Nazi anti-Semitism. There was no equivalent in the Pan-Turkish view of Armenians to the Nazis' hysterical struggle against the "Jewish spirit" which was said to linger in Germany and Europe even after most of the Jews had been murdered.

Finally it should be noted that the death camp, a conception of the Nazi state, was an extraordinary organization, not seen before or since. It was a factory managed by the SS but staffed at all levels by the inmates themselves. Its primary aim was to dehumanize and kill its prisoners after confiscating their property and making use of their labor. Although Jews like Armenians perished in massacres and by starvation, the use of the death camp as a method of extermination differentiated the Holocaust from the Armenian Genocide.

It will readily be seen that partial genocide in Nigeria and other culturally plural societies in the Third World, as well as genocide in post-communist states like Yugoslavia bear closer resemblance to the Armenian Genocide than they do to the Holocaust.

IV. NIGERIA

Genocide has been committed throughout the Third World. Here are a few examples: Indonesia, Burundi, Rwanda, Sudan, East Pakistan, and Iraq. In all of these instances a shaky and hardly legitimate post-colonial state ruling over a culturally plural society attempted to establish the hegemony of a leading ethnic group over other ethnic segments of society. This attempt at domination provoked movements of resistance and self-determination, which the post-colonial state then tried to halt by force, including massacre and partial genocide.

Nigeria gained her independence from Great Britain in 1960. It was organized as a federation of three states, each centering on a major ethnic group. The Northern state was dominated by the Hausa-Fulani, the Western by the Yoruba, and the Eastern by the Ibo. The major ethnic groups jockeyed for power at the federal level, while each had its "minorities"

that felt discriminated against at the state level of the federation.

The post-independence government, dominated by Hausa-Fulani Muslims, was resisted by southern largely non-Muslim groups, especially the Ibos. In 1966, after a failed military coup, the thousands of Ibos were massacred in Northern Nigeria. In 1967, a year after the massacres, the Ibos tried to secede. They called Eastern Nigeria, "Biafra," and fought a war of self-determination until 1970, when their secession collapsed.

During the war over a million Biafrans starved to death as a result of the deliberate Nigerian policy of blockade and disruption of agricultural life. Thus, between 1966 and 1970, a "genocide-in-part" occurred in Nigeria, following the UN definition. It is important, however, to recall that what happened in Biafra differed from the Holocaust and the Armenian Genocide in that the policies of the Nigerian Federal Military Goverment (FGM) did not include extermination of the Ibos.

V. YUGOSLAVIA

A definitive history of the recent and current conflict in former Yugoslavia does not yet exist, but it is possible to render a provisional sketch. The Yugoslav disaster stems from the failure of the communist regime to establish legitimate politial institutions, a viable economy, and a compelling political culture. After Tito's death in 1980, ethnically based nationalist movements started to mobilize and to demand greater autonomy, if not yet self-determination. The process of dissolution and disintegration was drastically accelerated with the rise of Milosevic, who articulated an integral form of Serbian nationalism and irredentism that called for the creation of a Yugoslavia dominated by Serbia, such as had existed after the First World War. This frightened the other nationalities and encouraged intransigent elements.

Milosevic's integral Serbian nationalism in a context of Yugoslav and communist institutional decay and insecurity, helped to sharpen ethnic enmities, to strengthen centrifugal forces throughout the federation and to accelerate the processes of disintegration. Thus on September 27, 1989, the parliament of Slovenia adopted amendments to its constitution giving the republic the right to secede from Yugoslavia. Thousands of Serbs demonstrated in Novi Sad, fearing for their status in an independent Slovenia. On July 3, 1990, the Parliament of Slovenia declared that the laws of the republic took precedence over those of Yugoslavia, on December 22, 1990, Slovenia reported that 95 percent of the voters supported a plebiscite on independence, and on June 25, 1991, Slovenia declared its independence from Yugoslavia.

A similar march of events occurred in Croatia, which also declared its independence on June 25, 1991. The big difference between Slovenia and Croatia, however, was the presence of a large Serbian minority in the latter. Moreover, no sooner was independence declared in Croatia, than the Tudjman regime launched an anti-Serb campaign that would have alarmed the Serbs, even if nationalist elements among them had not been earlier mobilized by Milosevic. Now that their kin were being threatened in Croatia, Milosevic and other Serbian nationalists could call forth the terrible history of the Ustasha genocide of the Second World War to mobilize the Serbs against Croatian independence and in support of Serbian irredenta.

After June 25, 1991, when Slovenia and Croatia declared their independence, thereby creating Serbian minorities, especially in Croatia, the Serb radicals, using the cover of the Yugoslav army, launched an attack whose main intent was to incorporate Serbian populated Croatian territory. To this end Serbian forces not only initiated hostilities but set out on a path of terrorism and massacre in order to drive Croats out of areas that they desired to incorporate into Greater Serbia.

This policy of terrorism and "ethnic cleansing" was set in motion with even greater ferocity against Bosnia when it declared its independence on March 3, 1992. Indeed, in time both Serb and Croat forces descended on Bosnia with the clear intention of carving up and destroying a state that initially had tried to stand aside from ethnic nationalism and had opted for a pluralist society. But both Serb and Croat nationalists were intent on either carving up and destroying Bosnia or making of it a rump state that would in time collapse. To this end, especially the Serbs, led by Karadzic in Bosnia practiced massacre, "ethnic cleansing," and cultural destruction against those they called the "Turks." A few years later the pattern of ethnic cleansing and genocide was repeated in Kosovo. Taken together such policies of destruction on a wide scale are called genocide.

Keeping Nigeria and Yugoslavia in mind, however, it is also important to note the great fear and insecurity that possesses everyone when a government is challenged and a state begins to disintegrate. This great fear, especially in culturally plural societies, leads people to seek the shelter of their families and kin and persuades various groups to band for protection and to view each other as potential enemies.

Indeed, before the culturally plural state like Nigeria or Yugoslavia disintegrates, its politics may revolve about various ethnic issues of group status and the distribution of scarce goods, but once a state crashes, for whatever reasons, ethnic groups begin to fear for their lives, as well they should. Once a political order disintegrates, who can guarantee an ethnic group that its mortal enemies won't come to power and won't destroy it? It is this great fear that has seized all the groups in Yugoslavia, including those Serbs who are the main perpetrators of partial genocide.

VI. THE ARMENIAN AND BIAFRAN GENOCIDES

In both the Nigerian and Bosnian cases we can see some parallels to the Armenian Genocide. A dominant ethnic group in a culturally plural society attempted to establish its hegemony. It was resisted by minorities that attempted some form of autonomy or self-determination. In reaction, the dominant group perpetrated repression and genocide. There are significant differences as well that may be even more instructive, since it is the differences that tell us how genocide varies under different conditions.

The crucial difference between a total domestic genocide as occurred in the Armenian case and a partial one, as occurred in Nigeria, can also be seen by comparing the two. Unlike the Armenians, once Biafra was defeated and the danger of secession passed, the Ibos were not massacred or further expelled from Nigeria. On the contrary, there was a genuine attempt to reintegrate the Ibos population into Nigeria when the war ended.

This difference may be due to two reasons. First, although the Federal Military Government was dominated by Hausa-Fulani elements, it included minorities in its leadership indeed General Gowon; its commander, was a Christian from the north. Thus the FMG never developed an ideology of "Northernization" or "Muslimization" the way the Young Turks relied on Turkification and sought to create an ethnically homogeneous Turkey.

Second, the territorial issue, a crucial element in the Armenian case, was missing. The Ibos of the North were "strangers" and not "sons-of-the-soil," thus they could not make a legitimate claim to Northern territory. Moreover, it is significant that the Ibos had their own area, which, except for its oil, the North did not covet. Once the Ibos were driven from the North back into their space, and the Biafran secession was defeated, the Northern elements in the army and elsewhere had succeeded in their major aims. Further massacre and starvation of the Ibos was unnecessary for ideological, territorial, or any other reasons and the partial genocide ceased.

The Biafran state was never claimed as the "homeland" of the Hausa-Fulani in the manner that Anatolia had been staked out by the Turks. Thus a federal solution to ethnic conflict could be implemented in Nigeria, the way it could not in the Ottoman Empire. The Armenians could not be driven back to "their" lands, since their lands were claimed to be the "heartland" of Turkey. Indeed, it may be suggested that this Turkish claim to Armenian lands was a major reason why the Armenian Genocide, unlike the mass death of Biafra, became total in the manner of the Holocaust.

VII. THE ARMENIAN AND BOSNIAN GENOCIDES

Two major similarities between the Armenian Genocide and the partial genocide that occurred in Bosnia should be apparent. Like the Young Turks, the Serbian, and to some extent the Croat, nationalists aspired to a large state that would include their peoples and exclude other ethnic and national groups. Like the Armenians, the Muslims, an ethnoreligous community making claims to land, was massacred and driven out by Serb and Croat nationalist movements that sought to incorporate their lands and "cleanse" the area of their presence and to destroy their culture.

However, the status of Bosnia as an independent state recognized by the international community marks a significant difference between the situations of Ibos in Nigeria and of Armenians in the Ottoman Empire. Neither Armenians nor Biafrans were widely recognized as members of independent states while their destructions were in process.

Some major similarities and differences in comparison between the Armenian Genocide and the current wave of mass murder, may be the role of the international community. The Armenians were largely abandoned to their fate, in part because the genocide occurred in the midst of a world war. During the cold war, both the Eastern and the Western blocs discouraged movements of self-determination, fearing superpower involvement; and the African states did the same, fearing their own disintegration along ethnic lines. This explains in part, why Ibos like Armenians were also abandoned, except for some humanitarian relief.

In the current period following the Cold War, the international community is giving mixed signals about how it will react to partial genocide. On the one hand it acted forcefully to limit the Iraqi attack on the Kurds; on the other hand, it delayed its intervention in Bosnia and Kosovo, despite the apparent massacres that were perpetrated by the Milosevic regime. It seems that the international community intervened rapidly and with force in Iraq because some member states saw their national interests threatened by Iraqi aggression. Since no such clear interests seemed to lie in Bosnia and Kosovo, intervention was long delayed beyond the time that massacres and even genocide were perpetrated.

VIII. CONCLUSION

The Armenian Genocide is a more accurate archetype than is the Holocaust for current mass murders in the post-colonial "Third World," and in the contemporary postcommunist world. In Nigeria and Yugoslavia, for example, as in the Armenian case, and unlike the Holocaust, minorities were territorial ethnic groups, aiming at some form of autonomy or self-determination while the perpetrators were driven by a variant of nationalism, and the methods of destruction involved massacre and starvation. In the Holocaust the victims were not a territorial group, the ideology was a variant of a global racism and anti-Semitism, not nationalism, and the characteristic method of destruction was the death camp. Thus in being a total genocide rather than a partial destruction the Armenian Genocide was a precursor of the Holocaust. Moreover, because the perpetrators were intent not only in destroying a minority but also in seizing its lands, the Armenian Genocide was a prototype of contemporary nationalist genocides. In both ways the Armenian Genocide set a terrible precedent for our century.

QUESTIONS TO CONSIDER

1. In what ways does Robert Melson see the Armenian genocide and Holocaust resemble each other?

2. Why does Melson believe that "instances of partial genocide" in Nigeria and Yugoslavia have more in common with the Armenian genocide than the Holocaust?

3. How does the Armenian genocide compare with the Biafran genocide?

MAKING CONNECTIONS

1. Discuss the actions of the Turks in relation to British policies in South Africa.

2. Is what the Turks did to the Armenians similar to the United States' policies toward Native Americans?

✔ RECOMMENDED RESOURCES

Hovannisian, Richard G. *The Armenian Genocide in Perspective.* Piscataway, NJ: Transaction Publishers, 1998.

Kuper, Leo. *Genocide: Its Political Use in the Twentieth Century.* New Haven, CT: Yale University Press, 1981.

Melson, Robert. *Revolution and Genocide: On the Origins of the Armenian Genocide and the Holocaust.* Chicago: University of Chicago Press, 1995.

Suny, Ronald G. *Armenia in the Twentieth Century.* Chino, CA: Scholars Press, 1983.

CHAPTER 4

DEATH BY HUNGER: UKRAINE

The death of one man is a tragedy;
The death of a million is a statistic.
—Joseph Stalin

Following the 1921 famine in the midst of the post–World War I civil war, Joseph Stalin induced the New Economic Policy that liberalized agricultural policies.

Thus a man-made famine, sanctioned by Joseph Stalin, devastated the Ukraine—the ethnic Ukranian region of northern Caucasus and the lower Volga River region in 1932 to 1933. Stalin, with the aid of Lazar Kagonovich, sought to destroy the independence of the Ukrainian farmer, *kulaks*, and force them into collectivization. Soviet officials increased the grain quota for the Ukraine by 44 percent, knowing that it would cause hardship. Communist party officials employed the military with People's Commissariat of Internal Affairs (NKVD) secret police units to ferret out hardened grain. They also restricted the movement of peasants in desperate search for food, thus making the Ukraine a vast military preserve. Suspected horders faced deportation or execution. The estimated death toll ranged from 6 to 10 million.

The reversal of liberalization after 1928 coincided with the Soviet's political goal of dekulakization—the liquidation of "rich" peasants and collectivization of agriculture. The Soviet strategy of withholding food targeted the Ukraine.

In 1986, James E. Mace chaired the Commission on the Ukraine Famine. He describes the *Holodomor*, or famine-genocide. Ian Hunter, emeritus in the Faculty of Law at the University of Western Ontario and the first biographer of Malcolm Muggeridge, reveals how *New York Times* reporter Walter Duranty dissembled the truth about the *Holodomor*, cancelling the critical reportage of Malcolm Muggeridge. Finally, Roman Serbyn describes the denial of the *Holodomor*, which makes the aftermath a sordid postscript to the disaster.

The Great Famine-Genocide in Soviet Ukraine (*Holodomor*)

THE NINTH CIRCLE BY OLEXA WOROPAY: EDITOR'S INTRODUCTION

James E. Mace,

Ukrainian Studies Fund, Inc. 1983

Readers in the English-speaking world will find much of what Olexa Woropay says hard to believe. The world he describes with such eloquent simplicity is completely alien to anything they have ever experienced: it is cut from the same cloth as Hitler's death camps, a world gone mad on the blood of human beings sacrificed on the altar of political expediency.

When Americans think of the Soviet Union, they tend to think of Russia and assume that all those who live there are Russians. In fact, about half the inhabitants of the USSR are not Russian at all: they belong to nations as diverse as Armenians in the South, Lithuanians in the North, Muslim Kazakhs and Tatars, and an array of Siberian peoples not unlike our own American Indians. There are over one hundred languages spoken in the Soviet Union, and Russian is only one of them.

According to the 1979 census, over forty million of the Soviet Union's inhabitants were Ukrainians, a Slavic nation like the Russians and Poles as different from them as they are from each other. The Ukrainians have a historical record that extends back to the tenth century when their ruler, Prince (St.) Volodymyr accepted Christianity and brought what was then called Rus' into the ranks of the Christian nations of Europe. They have a rich culture of which they are rightly proud, and the central figure of their literary tradition is the poet Taras Shevchenko, a nineteenth-century bard

Woropay, Olexa. *The Ninth Circle: In Commemoration of the Victims of the Famine of 1933.* Cambridge, Massachusetts, 1983.

who was born a serf and rose to the highest levels of cultured society in the Russian Empire. The reader will learn from Woropay what happened in Shevchenko's native village in 1933.

In 1933 Ukraine and certain neighboring areas were victims of what those who survived remember as the Velyky Holod, the Great Famine or, more precisely, the Great Hunger. It is also often referred to as Shtuchny Holod, the Artificial or Man-Made Hunger, for it was not, like most famines, due to some natural calamity or crop failure. Figures on the Ukrainian harvest were published in the press at the time, and they show that the grain crop was only a little below the precollectivization average; there was certainly no crop failure capable of causing a famine. A few years earlier the Soviet government had collectivized agriculture, forced the farmers to give up their individual farms, pool whatever resources could be taken from them, work the land in common on estates not unlike that on which Shevchenko worked as a serf, and give a far greater share of what they produced to the state. The farmers fought against this, and they also fought for their national culture, which was under attack by the Soviet regime. It was in order to break this resistance that government agents were sent into the countryside and ordered to take away all foodstuffs. As a result, the people starved.

We have far more than Woropay's word for this. For one thing, we have census figures published by the Soviet government, and we have various other official Soviet population studies, which allow us to put the census figures in perspective. According to Soviet Ukrainian figures from the late twenties and early thirties, the number of Ukrainians in the USSR was increasing at well over one percent a year. Yet, the 1939 census—itself somewhat suspect—shows that the number of Ukrainians declined by almost ten percent, over three million people, from what it had been in 1926 when the last published census was taken.

A Polish Communist historian calculated from these figures that there were 9.3 million fewer Ukrainians in 1939 than would have been expected from the population trends of the 1920s. Some of this was due to a lowered birth rate during the famine and some to assimilation at a time when Soviet government was actually attempting to destroy Ukrainian culture, but this still leaves several millions who could only have perished from starvation and famine-related diseases.

There are also thousands of eyewitness accounts like those Woropay presents. The Harvard University Refugee Interview Project conducted interviews with thousands of displaced persons who left the Soviet Union during and shortly after World War II, and the project files contain hundreds of accounts virtually identical with those in this book. Many more survivors published accounts of their experiences in books of testimonies published by Ukrainian groups in the West. They have highly emotional titles like *The Black Deeds of the Kremlin* and *Moscow's Biggest Crime.* After one reads Woropay's book, one might begin to understand how these people became so emotionally and vehemently anti-Communist. For Ukrainians, Communism has come to be just another name for Russian imperialism, one even more oppressive than the tsarist imperialism under which their grandparents lived. There are also quite a number of Western accounts by non-Ukrainians.

Lastly, we have one truly unimpeachable source. Nikita Khrushchev, who ruled the Soviet Union from the mid-fifties until 1964, related the following in his unofficial memoirs, published in the West from tape recordings smuggled out of the USSR after his death:

Mikoyan told me that Comrade Demchenko, who was then First Secretary of the Kiev Regional Committee, once came to see him in Moscow. Here's what Demchenko said: "Anastas Ivanovich, does Comrade Stalin for that matter, does anyone in the Politbureau know what's happening in the Ukraine? Well, if not, I'll give you some idea. A train recently pulled into Kiev loaded with corpses of people who had starved to death. It had picked up corpses all the way from Poltava to Kiev ..."

The fact that Khrushchev was not in Ukraine at the time and can only give the story second-hand does little to undermine its credibility. Khrushchev might have lied about many things, but he had no reason to lie about this. In order to understand why the famine of 1933 occurred, one must go back at least to 1917, perhaps even to 1900 when the first Ukrainian political parties were formed in the Russian Empire. The Ukrainians were at that time almost entirely a nation of peasants, just as the Czechs had been not long before. If one visited Prague in, say, 1800, the language one would hear in the streets and shops would have been German, not Czech. Only later was Prague "Czechized." By the same token, the cities of Ukraine were predominantly Russian-speaking in 1917. Although they were largely Ukrainized in the late 1920s, they were later re-Russified to the point where today Ukrainian is seldom heard in the streets of Kiev. In order to prevent the development of a Ukrainian national movement, the tsarist Russian government made it illegal to write or publish in the Ukrainian language up to 1905. The concessions made in that year were gradually withdrawn to the point that very little could be published legally in Ukrainian by the time the First World War broke out. Ukrainian writers had two choices: either publish legally in Russian and hope to slip something past the censor through the use of Aesopian language, or publish in Ukrainian in Austrian-ruled Western Ukraine (Eastern Galicia) and try to have their work smuggled over the border illegal-

ly. Despite these obstacles, the Ukrainians produced an educated stratum, the intelligentsia, and this group organized political parties, which sought national liberation, social justice for the peasants, and some sort of home rule for Ukraine.

In 1917 the Russian Empire disintegated. The tsar abdicated, the police were slaughtered or went into hiding, and the imperial army began to fall apart. The Russian Provisional Government had little real power, particularly in outlying areas. A Ukrainian national council, the Central Rada, was organized in Kiev. Led by the two largest Ukrainian socialist parties, the Socialist Revolutionaries and Social Democrats, it gradually evolved into an autonomous national government. After the Bolsheviks took power in Petrograd and began an invasion of Ukraine the Rada declared Ukraine independent in January 1918. For years Ukraine was fought over by Ukrainian governments, the Bolsheviks Denikin's Russian Volunteer Army (which sought to turn the clock back to before the revolution), the Poles, and a number of rural warlords known as otamans. Although by 1921 the Bolsheviks were able to defeat their various rivals in the field of battle, large-scale guerrilla warfare continued in the Ukrainian countryside. Ukrainian governments were driven from the country, but the Ukrainian peasantry remained unconquered.

The Bolsheviks decided to concede the peasants the minimum of what they demanded. In 1921 the New Economic Policy was adopted, ending forced requisitions of foodstuffs and allowing farmers to sell their products in a limited free market. In 1923, a series of policies known as indigenization were adopted in non-Russian areas. These policies provided for the recruitment of non-Russians into the Party and state, teaching Russians the local language, and actively supporting the cultural life of the non-Russian peoples. Belorussianization, Tatarization,

Yiddishization, and so forth, proceeded through the rest of the decade.

Since the Ukrainians of all the non-Russian nations were the most numerous and constituted the greatest political threat to Moscow, Ukrainization went much farther than any of its counterparts. Many prominent Ukrainian intellectual and political leaders returned from exile to take advantage of the cultural opportunities afforded by this relatively benevolent policy. A national cultural revival of unprecedented creativity took place in literature, scholarship, and the arts. Even within the Communist Party (Bolshevik) of Ukraine, a strong Ukrainian wing demanded that Ukrainization lead to the end of Russian domination. This group, led by Oleksander Shumsky, Mykola Khvylovy, and Mykhailo Volobuev, was condemned as "nationalistic deviationist," and the Party repudiated their views.

By the end of 1927 Mykola Skrypnyk emerged as Ukraine's political strongman. His official post, Commissar of Education, placed him in charge of the Ukrainization policy and of supervising cultural life in general. By eschewing any hint of anti-Russian sentiment, he was briefly able to achieve much of what Shumsky, Khvylovy, and Volobuev had called for. Under Skrypnyk, Soviet Ukraine evolved more and more in the direction of a national government, defending its prerogatives from Moscow and even demanding it be allowed to defend the national interests of Ukrainians residing in Russia itself.

The regime used the respite provided by the New Economic Policy and Ukrainization to penetrate the Ukrainian countryside in a variety of ways. Committees of Non-Rich Peasants (*komnezams*, KNS), which had earlier seized peasants, crops and held absolute power in the villages, were retained. There was no counterpart to these organizations in Russia. After 1925 they were stripped of political power and turned into voluntary organizations, and during collectivization and the early stages of the famine they played an important role in expropriating those the regime wanted to get rid of, forcing the peasants into collective farms (*kolhosps*), and searching for hidden grain to seize. In this later period, however, they often performed these functions under the leadership of someone sent from the outside to supervise *dekulakization*, collectivization, and the deliveries of grain to the state. Village soviets were also organized, and the countryside was covered by a dense network of secret police collaborators known as the *seksoty*. Because of this penetration of the countryside, the regime was in a far stronger position relative to the peasants than it had been in 1921. Whereas the Bolsheviks had hitherto come to the villages as complete strangers, they now had organized supporters ready to do their bidding and provide information on potential opponents who could be singled out for elimination.

Stalin saw the nationalities question and peasant question as indissolubly linked. In his view, the peasants constituted the social basis of national movements, the reservoir from which such movements drew strength. As he once put it, "The nationality problem is by its essence a peasant problem." Thus, concessions to the peasants meant concessions to the non-Russian nations and vice versa. By the same token, repression in the countryside and repression against those nations were bound to go together. They were two sides of the same coin.

In 1929 Stalin decided to eliminate the *kulaks* (well-to-do peasants, *kurkuls* in Ukrainian) as a class, begin forcing peasants into collective farms, and use what could be taken from the peasants to finance rapid industrialization. This was possible because, although collectivization did nothing to increase crop yields (the current problems of Soviet agriculture are largely attributable to forced collectivization), harvesting was done in common, and the state could supervise the harvest directly and take as much as it wished directly from the threshing room floor. This is precisely what happened, and the idea that the state should take all it required from "first proceeds," that is, the threshing room, became known as the First Commandment of Soviet agriculture.

At the same time as peasants were being forced into collective farms, the first steps were taken to end the indigenization policies. Since Ukraine was the largest stumbling block, these steps took the form of indirect attacks on Skrypnyk and his clients. In 1929 one of his most important subordinates, the ideological watchdog of historians, Matvyi Yavorsky, was attacked for "treating the history of Ukraine as a distinctive process." The political implication of such a charge was quite obvious: if Ukraine did not have its own history, it was not a distinctive country and ought not to be considered as such. This was the beginning of the end of Skrypnyk. At the same time, the Ukrainian Autocephalous Orthodox Church was banned and its priests were executed on a mass scale. In 1930 a show trial was held of an imaginary conspiracy called the Union for the Liberation of Ukraine. At this trial some of Ukraine's most distinguished intellectual and spiritual leaders were convicted of a host of crimes known in the jargon of the day as "wrecking." Among these charges was a most interesting one: linguistic sabotage, which consisted of spelling words in such a way as to make the Ukrainian language closer to Polish than to Russian. Despite the absurdity of this charge, it held particularly ominous political implications for Skrypnyk, who had participated directly in various linguistic discussions of the 1920s. When Skrypnyk was denounced and removed from his post in

1933, one of the major charges leveled against him was that he had advocated the use of the letter G in Ukrainian.

The famine of 1933 succeeded in breaking the Ukrainian peasantry as a political force, completed the destruction of the entire social structure of the Ukrainian nation, and made possible far-reaching political changes. In addition to the fall of Skrypnyk, the Ukrainization policy was ended and a policy of Russification was instituted. The Ukrainian wing of the Communist Party ceased to be an independent policy force and over the next several years what was left of its old cadres was "liquidated" (a singularly inappropriate euphemism since such people did not melt; they were executed), and the Ukrainian intelligentsia was to all intents and purposes destroyed. Ukrainian culture was thus decapitated by the loss of its intellectual and political leaders, pushed out of the cities and back on the farms by a return to Russification, and Soviet spokesmen began to glorify everything Russian, including the tsarist past. At roughly the same time, internal passports were issued to urban dwellers but not to collective farmers. Since farmers could not live in the cities and towns without such documents, this meant legally attaching the agricultural population to the land. The word customarily used to describe such a state of affairs is serfdom.

QUESTIONS TO CONSIDER

1. What was this famine *not*, according to Mace?
2. Census figures verify what?
3. Who was the "one truly unimpeachable source" for verifying the famine?
4. According to Mace, Stalin's attack on the kulaks was the first step in a campaign to do what?
5. What did the famine accomplish for Stalin?

A Tale of Truth and Two Journalists

MALCOLM MUGGERIDGE AND WALTER DURANTY

Ian Hunter,
University of Western Ontario, Emeritus

It is hard to credit that a decade has slipped away since the death of Malcolm Muggeridge on November 14, 1990. The most compellingly readable of journalists, hardly a day goes by that I do not recall one of Muggeridge's insights or marvel afresh at his prophetic vision.

Muggeridge's journalistic integrity was shaped by one searing experience; in 1932 he went to Moscow as correspondent for the *Manchester Guardian.*

Joseph Stalin's twin manias—collectivization of agriculture and dekulakization of peasants—were then at their bloodthirsty zenith, but few Westerners could have guessed it from the sycophantic foreign reporting.

The Dean of the Moscow press corps was Walter Duranty of the *New York Times.* Joseph Alsop would later say of him: "Lying was Duranty's stock in trade."

For two decades Duranty was the most influential foreign correspondent in Russia. His dispatches were regarded as authoritative; indeed Duranty helped to shape U.S. foreign policy.

His biographer, Susan Taylor (*Stalin's Apologist*, Oxford University Press, 1990) has demonstrated that Duranty's reporting was a critical factor in President Roosevelt's decision in 1933 to grant official recognition to the Soviet Union.

Duranty, an unattractive, oversexed little man, with a wooden leg, falsified facts, spread lies and half truths, invented occurrences that never happened, and turned a blind eye to the man-made famine that starved to death more than 14 million people (according to an International Commission of Jurists which examined this tragedy in 1988–90). When snippets of the truth began to leak out, Duranty coined the phrase: "You can't make an omelette without breaking eggs."

This phrase, or a variant thereof, has since proved useful to a rich variety of ideologues who contend that a worthy end justifies base means. Yet when the Pulitzer committee conferred its prize on Duranty (in 1932, at the height of the famine) they cited his "scholarship, profundity, impartiality, sound judgment, and exceptional clarity."

One story that circulated among Moscow correspondents trying to explain Duranty was that he was a necrophiliac; in exchange for favourable reporting, the Soviet authorities may have allowed him unsupervised night access to the city morgues. Whether true or not (and Duranty's biogra-

From Ian Hunter, "A Tale of Truth and Two Journalists: Malcolm Muggeridge and Walter Duranty," *Report Magazine* (March 27, 2000). Reprinted with permission.

pher, Susan Taylor, leaves this question open), certain it is that the regime had some sort of hold on Duranty; they showered benefits on him—a fancy apartment, an automobile, and fresh caviar daily.

Enter Malcolm Muggeridge. In the spring of 1933 Muggeridge did an audacious thing; without permission he set off on a train journey through what had formerly been the breadbasket of the Soviet Union, the Ukraine and North Caucasus. What Muggeridge witnessed, he never forgot.

In a series of articles smuggled out in the diplomatic pouch, he described a man-made famine that had become a holocaust: peasants, millions of them, dying like famished cattle, sometimes within sight of full granaries, guarded by the army and police. "At a railway station early one morning, I saw a line of people with their hands tied behind them, being herded like cattle into trucks at gunpoint—all so silent and mysterious and horrible in the half light, like some macabre ballet."

At a German co-operative farm, an oasis of prosperity in the collectivized wilderness, he saw peasants kneeling down in the snow, begging for a crust of bread. In his Diary, Muggeridge wrote: "Whatever else I may do or think in the future, I must never pretend that I haven't seen this. Ideas will come and go; but this is more than an idea. It is peasants kneeling down in the snow and asking for bread. Something that I have seen and understood."

But few believed him. His dispatches were cut. He was sacked by the *Guardian* and forced to leave Russia. Muggeridge was vilified, slandered and abused, not least in the pages of the *Manchester Guardian*, where sympathy to what was called "the great Soviet experiment" was de rigueur.

Walter Duranty's voice led the chorus of denunciation and denial, although privately Duranty told a British foreign office acquaintance that at least 10 million people had been starved to death—adding, characteristically, "but they're only Russians."

Beatrice Webb (Muggeridge's aunt by marriage) admitted that "In the Soviet Union, people disappear," but she still denounced Muggeridge's famine reports as "base lies." The Very Reverend Hewlett Johnson, Dean of Canterbury, applauded Stalin's "steady purpose and kindly generousity." George Bernard Shaw made a whirlwind tour and pronounced himself fully satisfied that there was ample food for all in the worker's paradise.

If vindication was a long time coming, it cannot have been sweeter than when Duranty's biographer, Susan Taylor, wrote in 1990:

> But for Muggeridge's eyewitness accounts of the famine in the spring of 1933 and his stubborn chronicle of the event, the effects of the crime upon those who suffered might well have remained as hidden from scrutiny as its perpetrators intended.
>
> Little thanks he has received for it over the years, although there is a growing number who realize what a singular act of honest and courage his reportage constituted.

Alas, when these words came to be written, Muggeridge had died. Still, they are worth remembering.

QUESTIONS TO CONSIDER

1. Characterize the nature of Walter Duranty's reporting on the Ukranian famine.

2. How did Malcolm Muggeridge contradict Duranty?

3. What was the contemporary reaction to Muggeridge? Why?

The Last Stand of the Ukrainian Famine-Genocide Deniers

Roman Serbyn,

University of Quebec/Montreal

Concluding his review of Douglas Tottle's book *Fraud, Famine and Fascism*, Wilfred Szczesny writes: "Members of the general public who want to know about the famine, its extent and causes, and about the motives and techniques of those who would make this tragedy into something other than what it was will find Tottle's work invaluable." (*The Ukrainian Canadian*, April 1988, p. 24) In the era of glasnost, Szczesny could have rendered his readers no greater disservice.

For an editor-in-chief of a Ukrainian magazine to invite people to consult Tottle's tract is as appropriate as for a publisher of a Jewish periodical to recommend *The Hoax of the Twentieth Century* by the Holocaust denier A. R. Butz. If in Szczesny's statement quoted above the reader substitutes "Holocaust" for "famine" and "Butz" for "Tottle," the affront to the reader's dignity in both cases will become apparent. Tottle is no more interested in discovering the truth about the forced starvation of Ukrainians than Butz about the gassing of Jews.

Tottle is a self-confessed famine-genocide denier. No longer able to negate the famine as such, Tottle questions its genocidal character. Traditional *famine-denial* has been updated to *famine-genocide denial*, but the essence of the ideological trappings is the same. Today's famine-genocide deniers are the spiritual heirs of the first famine negators, Stalin and those who helped him carry out the most heinous of crimes against the Ukrainian nation or to deny its existence.

With his book Douglas Tottle has become a sort of guru to a strange collection of latter-day famine-genocide deniers. He has inspired militant articles by Jeff Coplon ("In Search of a Soviet Holocaust," *Village Voice*, 12 January, 1988); Wilfred Szczesny ("Fraud, Famine and Fascism," *The Ukrainian Canadian*, April 1988); and Donne Flanagan ("The Ukrainian Famine: Fact or Fiction," *McGill Daily*, 22 November, 1988). How vile and trite is the campaign of the famine-genocide deniers should become clear from the following three examples of how Tottle practices the misdeeds of which he accuses others.

First, let us consider the photographs of the famine. Tottle latches on to them as if they were the main proof of the historicity of the tragedy and the principle argument for its classification as genocide. Tottle does this because he thinks that the photographs form a weak link in the famine-genocide story: break this link and the whole structure will collapse. Well, this is not so. The famine has a solid documentary basis (documents published in the West and in the Soviet Union) of which the photographs form a very minor (and I might add, dispensable) component. There are few photographs from the 1932–33 famine and we could hardly expect otherwise, since the totalitarian regime wanted to keep the famine hidden and took the necessary measures to ensure this.

Many more photographs have come down to us from the earlier Soviet famine of

Roman Serbyn, "The Last Stand of the Ukranian Famine-Genocide Deniers." Reprinted from *The Ukranian Canadian* (February 1989) pages 7–10, 14. Kobzar Publishing Company LTD.

1921–23. Some of these pictures were eventually used in connection with the second famine and this fact provided Tottle with his basic argument against the famine-genocide: photographs depicting a natural famine of 1921–22 in Russia are used as proof of man-made starvation in Ukraine in 1932–33. To make his accusation stick, Tottle resorts to a mixture of irrelevant truths, half-truths and outright lies.

Tottle constantly refers to the Russian famine of 1921–22, but never mentions the contemporaneous famine in Ukraine. Yet most of Tottle's "illustrative" material is taken from Ukraine and not Russia. On page 32, Tottle reproduces three title pages of what he describes as "publications devoted to the Russian famine of 1921–22," even though two of them deal only with Ukraine. One is *Holod na Ukraini*, an excellent documentary by Ivan Herasymovych based on personal observations and containing excerpts from the Soviet Ukrainian press and a number of photographs. Tottle identifies the second text (the reduced reproduction is almost illegible to the naked eye) as "Dr. Fridjof Nansen's International Committee for Russian Relief, *Information No. 22*, Geneva, April 30, 1922," but fails to give the title of the report contained on that page. It reads: "Famine Situation in Ukrania." With the help of a magnifying glass the reader can decipher the following revealing information about the famine conditions in Ukraine, sent by Nansen's representative from Kharkiv on 22 March, 1922:

[N]ot before the 11th of January of this year could the goubernia of Donetz stop their obligatory relief work for the Volga district and begin to take care with all their forces of their own famine problem, at a time when already more than every tenth person in the Donetz was without bread. In the beginning of March this year, you could still see, in the famine-stricken goubernia Nicolaev (Mykolaiv), placards with "Working masses of Nikolaev (sic), to the help of the starving Volga district!" The goubernia of Nicolaev itself had at the same time 700,000 starving people, about half the population. On my way to

Ukrania I sought information in Moscow about the situation from presumably well informed persons. They told me that in Ukrania the situation was very bad, about half a million people starving. In reality the number was more than six times greater.

Further on, the envoy continues:

The whole of the 4 goubernias of Odessa, Nicolaev, Yekaterinioslav [Katerynoslav], and Donetz, as well as the southern parts of Krementchoug, Poltava and Kharkov, are stricken by famine. Of a total population of about 16 million in these goubernias, between four and five millions are now starving, and before the new harvest the number will perhaps have risen to between six and seven millions. Almost the whole population of Ukrania is suffering to a certain extent from lack of food and all the conveniences of life, but the above mentioned millions are literally starving to death.

In a follow-up report, dated 13 April, 1922, and reproduced in the same document, we read:

Five million persons are now without food and probably more than ten thousand die daily of starvation … In a word, the famine has reached such dimensions and such insignificant relief is given, that the starving population loses every hope and dies.

What Nansen's man was describing was the first man-made famine in Ukraine which lasted from 1921 to 1923 (and not 1922) and took 1.5 to 2 million lives. In spite of the drought in its southern provinces, Ukraine had enough grain to feed its population, provided the foodstuffs were kept in the country and not exported. But during these two years Soviet authorities removed enough agricultural produce from Ukraine to feed several times the population which died from hunger. Ukrainian grain was sent to Russia both years to feed the cities and the famished population on the Volga. (A severe famine was also ravaging southern Russia, especially the Volga region.) The second year it was also sold in Western Europe. Aid offered by foreign countries was accepted immediately for the Volga region but let into Ukraine only eight months later.

Since both famines in Ukraine were man-made, it was quite legitimate to use in the film *Harvest of Despair* photographs from the famine of the 1920s along with those of the 1930s. The weakness of the film lies not in these photographs but in the insufficient explanation the film gave of the first famine. This shortcoming has no bearing on the authenticity of the famine-genocide of the 1930s. To suggest the opposite, as Tottle, Coplon, Flannagan and Szczesny do, is to display ignorance or lack of intellectual integrity.

Second, let us see how even the great Ukrainian historian Mykhailo Hrushevsky is made to serve the famine-genocide deniers' propaganda machine. Szczesny writes:

> Tottle cites a number of historians and other writers whose works contradict the claim that the famine was a deliberate act of genocide, including Isaac Mazepa and M. Hrushevsky, both of whom discuss the causes of the famine with no suggestion that it was a deliberate effort to destroy the Ukrainian people.

Taken at face value, Szczesny's contention sounds serious. If Ukraine's foremost historian could analyze the famine and find no deliberate action against the Ukrainian people, then surely his findings carry more weight than the claims of lesser scholars. And yet to anyone the least familiar with contemporary Ukrainian history it sounds incredible that Hrushevsky should have written such things about the famine. What are the facts?

In 1941, Yale University Press published a translation of Michael Hrushevsky's *History of Ukraine*. As the Ukrainian text stopped in 1905, the editor, Professor O. J. Frederiksen of Miami University (Ohio), decided to update it. Two chapters were added. One, entitled "Ukrainian Independence," covered the peri-

od 1914–1918 and was based on Hrushevsky's other writings. The second chapter, "Recent Ukraine," brought the events up to 1940; it was written by the editor from notes provided by Dr. Luke Myshuha and had nothing to do with Hrushevsky.

In the Frederiksen/Myshuha chapter references to the 1932–33 famine are very skimpy, but there are two passages that have some bearing on the subject. Skrypnyk, the Commissar of Education in Soviet Ukraine, is reported as having "committed suicide in 1933 in protest against Soviet policies there, and in particular against the *export of foodstuffs*." It is also claimed that after a year of drought and chaotic agricultural conditions, "during the winter of 1932–33 a great famine, like that of 1921–22, swept across Soviet Ukraine, again costing the lives of *several million* men, women and children." [My emphasis—R.S.] In the next paragraph the reader learns that "Hrushevsky was arrested in 1930 and transferred from Kiev to a town near Moscow; he died on November 26, 1934, at Kislovodsk, in the northern Caucasus."

Now let us see how Tottle reconstructs these references:

> However, *A History of Ukraine* by Mikhail (sic) Hrushevsky—described by the Nationalists themselves as "Ukraine's leading historian"—states: "Again a year of drought coincided with chaotic agricultural conditions; and during the winter of 1932–33 a great famine, like that of 1921–1922, swept across Soviet Ukraine. …" Indeed, nowhere does *History of Ukraine* claim a deliberate, man-made famine against Ukrainians and more space is actually devoted to the famine of 1921–22.

Tottle then adds laconically that Hrushevsky's history was published posthumously in 1941 and that it was updated to 1940 based on notes by Dr. Luke Myshuha. Tottle does not deem it necessary to mention the work of Professor Frederiksen, or to specify when and where Hrushevsky died, although these facts are essential to appreciate the reference to the famine. He does, however, go out of his way to point out that Myshuha was "editor-in-chief of *Svoboda*," and that he had "visited Berlin in 1939, speaking over Nazi radio in Ukrainian," information quite irrelevant to the analysis of the famine, but necessary to make the perfidious famine-Nazi link which I shall discuss further on.

Here again we have a mixture of irrelevant truths, misleading half-truths, and lies. The comments by Myshuha/Frederiksen on the famine are deformed (damaging reference to Skrypnyk's suicide to protest the export of grain while several million starved is left out), and even though Tottle does not actually attribute them to Hrushevsky, he words his statement in such a way as to create that impression. Whether Szczesny was privy to Tottle's ruse or was duped by the insinuation, the result is the same: a lie about Hrushevsky's alleged denial of the famine-genocide.

Third, a few words are in order on the subliminal Nazification of the Ukrainian famine-genocide. If there is one common denominator to all the famine-genocide denial literature, it is the effort to tie the Ukrainian famine to the Nazis and sandwich between them that part of the Ukrainian diaspora which defends the right of the Ukrainian nation to exist as a sovereign state. Genocide deniers would be happiest if they could blame the famine on the Nazis and the "Ukrainian collaborators" as Stalin pinned Katyn on the Germans. But since this can not be done, they try the next best thing: link with Nazis those who speak out about the famine (including famine survivors and descendants of famine victims).

On the cover of Tottle's book one can see a photograph of a woman with an undernourished child, and looming over the photograph a hand with a paintbrush. The brush is about to be dipped into oilpaint profusely pouring out of a tube marked with a swastika. What a disgusting spectacle, and yet how descriptive of the author and the book! Isn't Tottle getting ready to apply Nazi colours to the famine victims?

When one checks the book's table of contents one notices that only one chapter is classified as "famine," the other nine deal with "fraud" and "Fascism." In fact, at least ten times as much space is devoted to the task of making the famine-Fascism connection as is given to the study of the famine. Unabashed, the author admits that he "does not attempt to study the famine in any detailed way." He is more interested in the "Nazi and fascist connections" and the "coverups of wartime collaboration." Both topics, even if they had been objectively treated, are completely irrelevant to the study of the famine and can neither prove nor disprove the existence of the famine or define the nature of the tragedy. (Many of Tottle's attacks on the various segments of the Ukrainian diaspora constitute hate literature and should be dealt with in our courts of law.)

The attempt to hush up serious examination and legitimate condemnation of the famine-genocide, or to dismiss it as Nazi-related propaganda, makes the writings of Tottle and the other famine-genocide deniers particularly repugnant. They have the impudence to desecrate the memory of millions of innocent people deliberately starved to death by criminals who have never even been punished for their diabolical act. Perhaps it was people like the famine-genocide deniers that Oleksandr Dovzhenko had in mind when he made this entry in his diary written on the German front on May 4, 1942:

If all the heroism of the sons of Ukraine in the Fatherland war, all the sacrifices and suffering of (its) people, and all (their) victorious energy after the war, cunning hands and pens of certain clever fellows throw into a common… pot, and on account of Ukrainians, these same hands thrust artificially created Hitlerite Petliurivshchyna and anti-Semitism with all the consequences of slaughterhouses, it would be better for me to die and no longer witness human baseness, bottomless hate, and fathomless eternal lies which entangle us.

In his review of Tottle's book Szczesny writes: "The theory of the big lie is that the bigger the lie and the more often it is repeated, the more it will be believed." Szczesny should have added that in order to render their own lie more credible, the hoaxsters accuse their opponents of the deception they themselves practice, while presenting their own fabrication as a corrective to their opponents' alleged lie. Need we be reminded that the real hoax is not the Holocaust but what Butz has to say about it, and the great fraud is not the famine-genocide but Tottle's treatment of it?

Documents on the famine published recently in the West (M. Carynnyk, et al., *The Foreign Office and the Famine*, Kingston, Ont., 1988, and others), and in the Soviet press (isn't it about time that the "UC" reprinted some of them?) leave no room for doubt that the famine in Ukraine was man-made. As Yuri Shcherbak, the author of a novel on Chornobyl states, "the famine of 1932–33 was in no way a natural disaster. There was no drought, no hurricane as its origin … The Ukrainian harvest of 1932 while not a record one was totally adequate. Yet there was an unusual famine. From the beginning to the end it was organized from the top … Peasants, packed on train rooftops, tried to flee the famished regions. But on the border between Russia and Ukraine… units of border guards were stationed…"

Is it legitimate to call this famine genocide?

Ten years ago few people outside the Ukrainian diaspora would have ventured such an opinion: in the West because of what was thought to be a lack of reliable evidence (diplomatic archives were closed and testimony from "refugees" was viewed with suspicion), and in the Soviet Union because the very subject was taboo. All this has radically changed in the last few years.

Taking advantage of glasnost, Ukrainians began to speak openly about the crime of the "33rd," calling it "man-made famine," "artificial famine," "extermination by starvation

(*holodomor*). Although they use the more familiar traditional expressions, in their minds these terms are synonymous with genocide." What else is the deliberate starvation of millions of people, if not genocide? Occasionally, one even comes across the words "holocaust" and "genocide" as when Wasyl Pakharenko answered those who do not recognize the specificity of the Ukrainian famine. "The uniqueness of our (Ukrainian) tragedy lies in this that in Ukraine, the social-class genocide coincided with the cultural-national (genocide)."

The notion that the famine was genocide is also gaining acceptance in the West. Michael R. Marrus, professor of history at the University of Toronto, and the author of *The Holocaust in History*, in his forward to *The Foreign Office and the Famine* (cited above), comes to the conclusion that the evidence presented by the British documents suggests that there was a genocidal attack upon Ukrainians. Leo Kuper, professor emeritus at the UCLA and author of Genocide, a pioneer work on the subject, writes in his latest work *The Prevention of Genocide* about the "many millions who died in the Soviet man-made (sic) famine of 1932–33." Kuper accepts the argument that "this artificially induced famine was in fact an act of genocide, designed … to undermine the social basis of a Ukrainian national renaissance."

In the light of all the evidence we now possess on the famine, how bleak and ignoble appear the statements of genocide deniers of the Stalin era (unscrupulous journalists like Walter Duranty of the *New York Times*, credulous and dishonest intellectuals like the British writer Bernard Shaw, the French politician Edouard Herriot). It took fifty years to debunk their big lie; how long will it take the defenders of truth to dispose of the big lie promoted by Tottle and his supporters? The challenge is before the Ukrainian community. Will *The Ukrainian Canadian*, for one, have the courage to take it up and make the last stand of the famine-genocide deniers a short one?

QUESTIONS TO CONSIDER

1. What is the analogy Roman Serbyn makes with Douglas Tottle's book? Why?

2. Why does Serbyn criticize Tottle's use of photographic evidence?

3. How does Serbyn answer his own question: "Is it legitimate to call this famine genocide?"

MAKING CONNECTIONS

1. Was the *Holodomor* different in nature from the elimination of the Hereros?

2. Is Ukrainian famine denial similar to the denials of other genocides?

✔ RECOMMENDED RESOURCES

Conquest, Robert. *The Harvest of Sorrow: Soviet Collectivization and the Terror-Famine.* New York: Oxford University Press, 1986.

_____. *Reflections on a Ravaged Century.* New York: W.W. Norton & Company, 2000.

Courtois, Stephanie, et al. *The Black Book of Communism: Crimes, Terror, Repression.* Trans. Jonathan Murphy and Mark Kramer. Cambridge, MA: Harvard University Press, 1999.

Mace, James E. *Communism and the Dilemmas of National Liberation: National Communism in Soviet Ukraine, 1918–1933.* Cambridge, MA: Harvard University Press, 1983.

CHAPTER 5

THE HOLOCAUST

The Holocaust seems almost irrevocably linked to the admonition "Never Again!" If something is to be learned from the Holocaust, arguably, this phrase could sum up its basic lesson. But in the attempt to memorialize and commemorate the loss of millions of people, any lesson to be conveyed may be lost through the commercialization of the Holocaust. According to Tim Cole, in *Selling the Holocaust: From Auschwitz to Schindler: How History Is Bought, Packaged, and Sold*, the meaning of the Holocaust is reduced to ledger sheets and reparations payments, commercial films, and museums obscuring the past via "virtual Holocaust" exhibits. Has the Holocaust become a macabre tableau for the twentieth century?

Another study in the same vein, *The Holocaust Industry: Reflections on the Exploitation of Jewish Suffering*, by Norman Finkelstein, goes so far as to suggest that the tragedy provides the source for a boom in litigation. This is exemplified by

> Edward Fagan, an obscure personal injury lawyer from San Antonio, Texas, who claims to have signed up 31,000 clients in record time. For his role in the Swiss settlement [Jewish wealth in Swiss banks], he submitted to the court a bill for $4 million, or $640 an hour. The pension that Holocaust survivors today receive from the German government is $640 a *year.*

If there is a deeper lesson to be learned from the Holocaust, it may be that hate and murder know no boundaries—there is no pity in systematic death. Thus the magnitude of horror in the Holocaust stands as the genocide by which others are compared. Attempting to understand the event in a limited amount of space proves a daunting task. In this chapter, historian Franklin Bialystok provides a broad perspective with "The Holocaust: An Historical Overview." Saul Friedman in "There Are no Wise Men in Chelm: A Journey of Conscience to Poland, Spring 2002" surveys the vast historical literature on the Holocaust. Some Holocaust studies committed minimization or denial of other victims by omission. Ian Hancock provides some remedy for this by bringing attention to other victims in "*O Baro Porrajmos*—The Romani Holocaust." In an excerpt from *Long Shadows: Truth, Lies and History*, Erna Paris asks her readers to question where they stand as individuals in relation to their own selective and biased histories. The memory of the Holocaust needs the same kind of critical analysis.

The Holocaust: An Historical Overview

Franklin Bialystock

THE RISE OF THE NAZI PARTY

The most pernicious anti-Semitism arose after World War I in the Weimar Republic. Some opponents of the Republic blamed Jews for the ill-fated Socialist coup of 1919, the demilitarization of the state, and the inflammatory cycle of 1922–23. Some disenchanted Germans joined Adolf Hitler's newly created National Socialist party in 1923. Although the Nazis enjoyed popular support in the 1920s, they announced a program of national regeneration based on the anti-Semitic racial theories of the late nineteenth century. With the Great Depression of the early 1930s and the threat of Communist takeover in Germany, President Hindenburg invited Hitler to become Chancellor in January, 1933. Within months, Hitler had total political power in Germany.

Hitler's view of the Jews was a crude adoption of racial anti-Semitic stereotypes. The Jews were depicted as an anti-race, bent on taking over the world. In this incarnation they were both rapacious capitalists who controlled the world's economy and the architects of the anticapitalist Communist conspiracy. According to Nazi ideology, a Jew was defined as a person having one Jewish parent or grandparent who adhered to the Jewish religion. In the illogical ideology of the anti-Semitism, followers of a certain religion also possessed specific biological attributes that made them racially unfit as citizens of the state.

In the months immediately following Hitler's accession, a series of laws and administrative orders were passed which excluded Jews from public life, including the armed forces, the press, banks, and education. Recent Jewish immigrants were deprived of German citizenship. Some Jews, together with German religious and political opponents and homosexuals, were imprisoned in the first concentration camp, Dachau, in 1933. In 1935, anti-Jewish legislation was legalized in the Nuremberg Laws. The Laws denied citizenship to all Jews, outlawed intermarriage, and defined who was Jewish and who was of "mixed blood," by again applying grotesque religious criteria. Anti-Jewish feeling was whipped up in the popular press and the state-controlled radio.

In the spring of 1938, laws were passed which eliminated Jews from the German economy, and required all German Jewish passports to be marked with a "J" (Jude—German for Jew). The height of anti-Jewish action occurred on November 9–10, 1938. Synagogues were burned, Jewish businesses were destroyed, and 36 Jews were killed. Soon after, 30,000 Jews were sent to German concentration camps. This event, called Kristallnacht (the Night of Broken Glass), presaged the tragedy that was to follow.

WORLD WAR II (TO 1942)

After Germany signed a non-aggression pact with the Soviet Union (the Ribbentrop-Molotov agreement) eliminating the danger of a war on two fronts, the Wermacht (German Army) attacked Poland on September 1, 1939. Britain and France declared war on Germany in response to the invasion. Nevertheless, Poland was militarily isolated and was conquered quickly. Western Poland was annexed to Germany; central Poland was under direct German occupation and was termed the General Government; eastern Poland was annexed by the Soviet Union.

Franklin Bialystok, "The Holocaust: An Historical Overview" reprinted by permission of the author. Centre for Jewish Studies at York University.

In the spring of 1940 Germany invaded Denmark and Norway prior to attacking Belgium, the Netherlands, and France. On June 22, France capitulated and was divided into two zones. The northern one was under direct German occupation; the southern one (Vichy France) was unoccupied, but collaborated with Germany. With western and central Europe in its grasp, Germany attacked Britain by air (the Blitz), but was repelled. Turning to the south and east, Germany occupied part of North Africa and invaded the Balkans, Yugoslavia, and Greece.

On June 22, 1941, Germany invaded the Soviet Union (Operation Barbarossa) in violation of the nonaggression pact. By fall, it had conquered much of the territory between the frontier and Moscow. In the winter of 1941–42, the Soviet army stalled the German advance and then defeated them at Stalingrad. This was the major turning point in the War on the eastern front. Meanwhile, Germany's ally, Japan, attacked the American fleet at Pearl Harbor, Hawaii, on December 7, 1941, bringing the United States into the conflict.

In the first two years of the war, Germany succeeded not only in capturing territory, but in imposing a "new order" that reflected Nazi racial ideology. Members of "inferior" races were transferred to Germany as slave laborers, their property expropriated and their military, political, and intellectual elites murdered. Concentration and forced labor camps were constructed and the first steps of the Holocaust were implemented.

GHETTOS

The concentration points for Jewish citizens were called ghettos, a term that originated in 15th century Italy. These ghettos, erected in eastern Europe, were designed for slave labor, systematic persecution, and humiliation and death by starvation and selective murder. Ghettos were established in all major cities and towns. Jews from neighboring villages were rounded up and transported to them.

Ghetto life was brutal and often ended in death. Since wages were meager, the consuming passion was preventing starvation. In "open" ghettos, provisions were smuggled and sold on the black market. The penalty for smuggling was execution. The main cause of death was a variety of epidemic diseases. In 1941, for example, 10 percent of the Warsaw ghetto population died from typhus. Nevertheless, there were heroic attempts at creating a "normal" life. Self-help organizations organized soup kitchens, hospitals, and clothing centers. Clandestine religious services were carried on in defiance of Nazi strictures. Observant Jews followed dietary laws and sent their children to religious schools and academies (called yeshivot). Other Jewish children also went to school. In addition, there were underground cultural institutions including libraries and newspapers.

THE FINAL SOLUTION

Persecutions and ghettoization were the initial stages of the Holocaust. The next stage, the destruction of European Jewry, given the code name "Final Solution" by the Nazi leaders, became German policy in the spring of 1941. With the rapid conquest of much of Europe, there were no moral restraints on the Nazi leaders. Eastern Europe was virtually sealed off from the Allies. Hitler's belief that the Jewish race would have to be destroyed, which he articulated on January 30, 1939, became an integral part of Nazi policy.

With the attack on the Soviet Union on June 22, 1941, two million additional Jews fell under German occupation. Prior to the attack, Heinrich Himmler the head of the SS, ordered that mobile action units, called Einsatzgruppen, were to follow the conquering German army. While the Einsatzgruppen murdered 90 percent of the Jews in German-occupied Soviet

Union, Himmler felt that the "strain" of continual killing was too great for his men. He advocated a more efficient and impersonal form of extermination. He was also under pressure to keep some Jews alive to serve as slave labor for the war machine. Consequently, Nazi administrators, including Heydrich and Adolf Eichmann met at Wannsee, a Berlin suburb on January 20, 1942.

Jews would be forcibly transported from all occupied countries to concentration camps. The camps were designed for forced labor resulting in death or selective murder. Within weeks, trains transporting Jews from all occupied countries were rumbling toward the camps.

from the local population for fear of reprisal. Against all odds, armed Jewish revolts took place in almost every major ghetto, usually after most of the inhabitants had been transported to the camps.

The most famous revolt occurred in the Warsaw ghetto beginning on April 19, 1943. Jewish fighters held out for several weeks. Some were found alive in the rubble six months later. The anniversary of the Warsaw Ghetto Uprising is celebrated by Jewish communities and their non-Jewish compatriots throughout the world. This day is called "Yom HaShoah," literally, the Day of Destruction. It is also the Day of Remembrance for the victims of the Holocaust.

ARMED RESISTANCE

When considering the concentration and murder of European Jewry, the issue of armed resistance is problematic. Several significant factors worked against the possibility of organized resistance. First, was disbelief. Few victims actually comprehended their fate. The Nobel Prize winner Elie Wiesel chronicles disbelief in all the steps to murder, from the towns of Hungary, where Jews were rounded up, to the doors of the gas chamber of Auschwitz. Second was the relative lack of aid by both the local populace, who were themselves brutalized by the occupation, and the Allies. Third was the cohesion of the family and the group in the ghettos and the camps. Resistance or flight meant leaving one's parents and friends. Reprisals were swift and severe. In Dollynov, two Jews escaped from the prison and hid in the ghetto where they could not be found. In reprisal, 1,540 Jews were murdered.

Despite the factors that prevented resistance, thousands of Jews were active in armed opposition. Some were able to escape from the ghettos or flee before the round-ups for transport and join underground movements. These partisans often had to hide their Jewish identity

CONCENTRATION CAMPS

Concentration camps were one of the first features of the totalitarian regime established in Germany in 1933. By 1938 camps had been established in Dachau, Sachsenhausen, Esterwegen, Buchenwald, Ravensbruk (for women), and Mauthausen (in Austria). Initially the camps were for the "reeducation" of political prisoners. Inmates were stripped of all rights and were brutalized physically and mentally. Under the administration of the SS, the camps were widely publicized throughout the Third Reich as a means of instilling fear in the populace. At first, only a tiny percentage of the political prisoners were Jewish. After Kristallnacht in 1938, 30,000 Jews were incarcerated.

While the camps were at first a temporary measure, Himmler persuaded Hitler that they should be administered by the SS. In 1939, there were 25,000 inmates; 1945, there were 715,000 prisoners. Until 1939, aside from political opponents, the camps held clergy critical of the regime, Jehovah's Witnesses, homosexuals, and prisoners of war. During the war the population swelled with civilians from occupied countries who were deemed racially "unfit," especially Poles and Gypsies.

The main purpose of the camps in prewar Germany as instruments of terror changed with the onset of war as the camps became associated with slave labor for the war effort. Larger camps such as Dachau had a whole system of sub-camps which formed an industrial base. Major German corporations such as I. G. Farben, Krupp, Slemens, and Daimler-Benz either built factories within the camp complex or leased slave laborers from the camps. The most chilling example was the Monowitz Camp—one of the three camps at Auschwitz which was a slave labor center for the chemical producer I. G. Farben. Slave laborers were also used for German munitions productions in monstrous underground factories safe from Allied bombing.

Slave labor increasingly became one form of deliberate mass murder. In Mauthausen, almost one hundred thousand inmates died working in the stone quarries. In Auschwitz, up to one-quarter of each work detail died every day. While there was a need for cheap labor to fuel the demands of war, the considerations of the Final Solution for the Jews and the brutal and inhumane treatment of non-Jews was more pervasive.

TRANSIT CAMPS

Concentration camps were the main feature of Nazi dehumanization policies until 1941. With the onset of the Final Solution, plans were made to systematically deport Jews from all parts of Europe that were either directly occupied, or administered collaborators with Germany. Jews were to be sent to the concentration and extermination camps in the east. In western Europe, transit camps were established as collection points for Jewish residents. The first Jews to be deported were those who had migrated to the west in the prewar years from Germany and Poland. As the demand for the destruction of all European Jewry intensified, Jewish nationals were also rounded up.

Near Paris, Drancy was the transit camp for deportations to the east. From March 1942 to July 1944, 80,000 French Jews were sent to their deaths. Twenty-five thousand Belgian Jews were deported from the transit camp of Malines. One hundred thousand Dutch Jews, including Anne Frank and her family, were concentrated at Westerbork and Fught for expulsion to Auschwitz and Sobibor.

Deportations also began in southeastern Europe in 1942. Jews from Greece and Yugoslavia were sent to the camps. In Romania, 185,000 Jews were deported to the provinces of Transnistria and Bessarabia, where they died in slave labor. From May to July, 1944, Budapest was the center for the last major deportations of the Holocaust. Under the command of Adolf Eichmann, 437,000 Hungarian Jews were deported to Auschwitz.

EXTERMINATION CAMPS

From December 1941 to July 1942, six camps were designed specifically as centers for the extermination of European Jewry. Located in occupied Poland they were: Auschwitz-Birkenau in Silesia; Chelmno near Łódź ; Treblinka near Warsaw; Sobibor and Maidanek near Lublin; and Belzec near Lvov. An estimated 200,000 Jews were murdered in Chelmno and Maidanek; 250,000 in Sobibor; 500,000 in Belzec; and 840,000 in Treblinka.

The most widely used method of murder was by gassing the victims. This method was first employed in the euthanasia program. Approximately 100,000 German civilians who were deemed as "unworthy of life" such as people with physical and mental handicaps were killed in the first two years of the war. Despite the protests of the population, another 175,000 were killed before the end of the war. Eventually this program was stopped due to the protests.

In the murder of European Jews, vans filled with carbon monoxide as the agent of death were used in Chelmno, the first extermination camp. In Belzec, Treblinka, and Sobibor, the victims were gassed in sealed buildings. Eventually a more deadly gas, Zyklon B, replaced carbon monoxide.

AUSCHWITZ

The Polish town of Oświęcim in the industrial heartland of Silesia was renamed Auschwitz after the German conquest. In 1940 it became the site for a concentration camp for Poles. Later Soviet prisoners of war and gypsies were interred there. In 1942 it became the main death camp for Jews. By 1943 the original camp had grown into a complex of three camps: Auschwitz One, the main camp and administrative center, had one gas chamber: Auschwitz Two or Birkenau, a much larger camp with four gas chambers: Auschwitz Three, or Monowitz, the slave labor camp controlled by I. G. Farben. The camp was liberated by Soviet troops in January 1945—two months after Himmler ordered the demolition of the gas chambers and crematoria, the evacuation of thousands of inmates to German camps, and the hasty emptying of the warehouses containing the personal effects of the Jews.

Most of the victims on the transports had been deceived into thinking that they were being "resettled in the east." They had no idea of their impending fate. Upon arrival they saw the arch over the entrance at Auschwitz One—"Arbeit Macht Frei"—work makes one free. They were herded out of the trains, dazed, confused, hungry, and clinging to their loved ones who survived the ghettos and the transfers. They stood in lines on the rail platforms waiting to be examined by SS officers. Within seconds they were selected for either immediate death, almost a certainty for children, the elderly, and the sick, or for slave labor. Those who were chosen to die went directly to the gas chambers. Their bodies were burned in adjacent crematoria. The others went through a process of dehumanization. They were separated by gender, relieved of all their possessions including their names, tattooed, hair shaved, and sent to barracks.

Inmates were immediately immersed into a world that they could not comprehend. They had to stand for hours during the appel (roll call), exist on meager rations, contend with the extremes of the climate, and sleep with up to eight others on a three-tiered bunk. Work was designed to extinguish life. The more fortunate inmates were assigned to the warehouses where they could hide provisions. These details worked in "Kanada," the term used by inmates to describe the warehouse containing the victims' possessions. Some inmates, the musselmans, walked in a daze, awaiting imminent death. Others, the sonderkommando or special units, were forced to clean the corpses out of the gas chambers and burn them in the crematoria.

The ultimate manifestation of Nazi racial ideology was created in this camp. Medical experiments were conducted where the prisoners were reduced to the status of laboratory animals. They were supervised by trained doctors, scientists, and academics such as Dr. Josef Mengele, who also headed the selection process on the railway platform.

A Polish historical commission has estimated that of the approximately four million persons who passed through the gates of Auschwitz-Birkenau, perhaps 60,000 were alive at the end of the war. While many victims possessed an indomitable will, survival was dependent upon chance and luck. There was no proscribed method or psychological predisposition that allowed one to survive. At any moment the whim of a guard, an infection that would not heal, or fatigue, could mean death.

Resistance in the camps had its own meaning inside the gates. Individual resistance required daily survival and the attempt at maintaining any shred of personal dignity. On a moral level it might have entailed sharing one's provisions or observing religious practices. Despite the difficulty of armed resistance, Sonderkommandos in Treblinka and Sobibor revolted in 1943. In 1944 the sonderkommandos in Birkenau revolted and destroyed one gas chamber. These revolts were among the very few in all the camps throughout Europe.

THE PROGRESS OF THE WAR 1943–1945

While the first three years of World War II witnessed the ascendancy of the Third Reich over much of the European Continent and North Africa, the second half of the war was marked by the demise of Germany and her Allies. Some of the most significant military turning points occurred in the following order: the defeats at Stalingrad in the Soviet Union and at El Alamein in North Africa; the collapse of Italy; the invasion of Normandy. Meanwhile, Japan was losing decisive battles in the Pacific. By the summer of 1944, Germany was subject to a pincer attack by Britain, the United States, France, the British dominions from the west, and the Soviet Union from the east. As Soviet armies pressed forward, the final stage of the Holocaust was unveiled.

FORCED MARCHES AND LIBERATION

In November 1944, the mass murders at Auschwitz-Birkenau ceased and the camp was evacuated. When the Soviet Army entered two months later, there were only several thousand inmates left. The remainder, together with the prisoners in scores of labor camps in Poland, were sent on forced marches westward toward Germany, in response to Himmler's order. The brutality of the marches rivaled that of the camps. Many prisoners simply dropped dead on the road from starvation and fatigue. Stragglers were shot. The German historian Martin Broszat estimates that one third of the 700,000 inmates of the camps died on the marches. Two hundred thousand of these fatalities were Jews.

The forced marches terminated in concentration camps in Germany. In the winter of 1945, their population swelled to unmanageable numbers. Thousands of inmates died every day of typhus, starvation, and shooting. There was no time to cremate all the bodies in the face of the advancing Allies. The Americans liberated Buchenwald on April 11, Dachau on April 29, and Mauthausen on May 3. British troops, together with Canadian forces, entered Bergen-Belsen on April 15. Soviet troops liberated Thereinstadt on May 9. When the Allied armies opened the camp's gates the world learned conclusively of the last stage of the Holocaust.

While the rotting bodies and walking skeletons provided overwhelming confirmation of the Holocaust, it did not reveal the enormity of the catastrophe. The thousands who died in the German camps in the last months were a fragment of the millions who perished in the ghettos, forests, and extermination camps of eastern Europe. Many victims died even after liberation. At Bergen-Belsen, the British reported that 37,000 died in the three months prior to liberation. Despite the best efforts of Allied doctors, another 14,000 perished.

RETURN AND DISPLACEMENT

Two thirds of the nine million Jews in Europe in 1939 were killed during the Holocaust. Approximately two million survivors were in the Soviet Union away from German occupation. Of these, 200,000 were Polish nationals who were allowed to return to Poland in 1946. Thousands of Jewish survivors returned to their former homes in Poland and other countries. For the majority, the return was a shattering experience. They found that their families had not survived and their former homes had been destroyed or appropriated by their non-Jewish neighbors. Many experienced outright hostility.

Because of the experiences of the returning survivors in their former homes, many sought refuge in displaced persons (D.P.) camps administered by the Allies. In 1946, approximately 300,000 Jews had gathered there. Most wanted to emigrate to Palestine, which was under the British Mandate. Others wanted to move to countries in the Western Hemisphere. With few exceptions, their desires were not granted for two years.

RESPONSE AND RESPONSIBILITY

From 1933 to 1940, the Third Reich conducted a program of discrimination, persecution, and selective murder of German Jewry. From 1941 to the last day of the War, this program had escalated to what the historian Lucy Dawidowicz termed "the war against the Jews," the attempt to murder all Jews in German occupied territory. The question of who was responsible for the Holocaust begins with the Nazi hierarchy, but does not end there. From 1933 to 1945, the Nazis received help from nations, organizations, and individuals who were active collaborators, apathetic accomplices, or mute bystanders.

EUROPE

Broadly speaking, there were five groups of countries in Europe during the war. In each group there are examples of collective and individual collaboration and complicity with the Nazis in the Holocaust, but also of aid to Jews.

The first group consists of countries that were militarily destroyed and occupied by Germany, most notably Poland, the Baltic countries, and western Soviet Union. The brutality suffered by the peoples of this group was unmatched in the rest of Europe. Some six million Poles, half of them Jews, were killed. Sixty percent of the five million Soviet prisoners of war who were captured died in custody. Millions of civilians also perished in the German invasion of the Soviet Union. While these actions severely limited the aid that Soviet and Polish citizens could offer their Jewish neighbors, there were attempts at help. Most civilians, however, were indifferent, and a minority were accomplices in the murder of their countrymen.

The second group of nations consists of those which were occupied, but not destroyed. In the Netherlands, three quarters of Dutch Jews were deported and killed, partly due to the existence of local Nazi collaborators and the SS troops. Nevertheless, many Dutch citizens were active in the attempt at hiding Jews. A smaller proportion of Belgian Jews perished partly because there was little collaboration with the occupying army. Most French Jews were deported. The French citizenry was divided between collaborators, accomplices of the German authorities, and partisans who helped in saving Jews.

The third group of countries consists of conquered nations which were given autonomy. Of these, the regime in Vichy, France, actively aided in the deportations, while Denmark defied German orders to round up its Jews and managed to smuggle them to freedom in neutral Sweden.

The fourth group consists of satellite countries and German allies. The response in this group was mixed. Italy, Germany's major ally, saved most of its Jews by not obeying deportation orders. The Vatican, however, was complicit in the Holocaust by not actively opposing the steps that led to the Final Solution. It did intervene, however, in the deportation of Roman Jews. Some Catholic clergy including the future Pope John XXIII helped to save Jews. Bulgaria was a German satellite that also did not comply with deportation orders so that virtually all Bulgarian Jews were saved. Hungary, however, fell under Nazi sympathizers who helped Eichmann orchestrate the deportations of almost half a million Jews. These deportations occurred despite the heroic efforts of a Swedish diplomat, Raoul Wallenberg. Local Nazi groups assisted the Germans in murdering most of the Jews from Slovakia and Croatia.

The fifth group consists of neutral countries. Switzerland accepted some German Jews prior to the War, but then declared that it was too full for subsequent refugees. Moreover, international organizations situated there, such as the Red Cross, refused to send aid to Jews or to systematically lobby the Allies for help. Spain and Portugal allowed some Jews to pass through on their attempt to find refuge elsewhere. Sweden tried to aid Jews through diplomatic channels.

ALLIES

While responsibility for the Holocaust extended to most European countries, it did not terminate on the continent. Britain and the United States also shouldered some of the responsibility. Prior to the war both countries were reluctant to admit German Jews who wanted to emigrate. Finally, each country took in 50,000 Jews. At the Evian Conference in 1938 they diverted attempts to allow refugees a haven. The United States refused boats full of Jewish refugees, such as the *St. Louis,* to land in its ports. They were forced to return to Germany.

While Britain played a central role in saving civilization from Nazi terror, it was hesitant in responding to pleas to bomb the rail lines to Auschwitz or to allow Jewish refugees to enter Palestine. Its policy in Palestine was steadfast until the end of the Mandate and the creation of the state of Israel in 1948.

The United States officially closed its gates to Jewish immigrants in 1940. In 1943 it maintained this policy at the Bermuda Conference on the refugee situation.

In 1944 it created the War Refugee Board which aided the surviving remnant in Europe, but its immigration policy regarding Jews was not substantially revised until 1948. Several factors account for Allied response to the Holocaust. First, even though Churchill and Roosevelt had conclusive proof of the Final Solution by the end of 1942, they could not truly comprehend the enormity of the catastrophe. Second, prior to the outbreak of war, economic considerations were most prevalent because of the Great Depression. Third, during the war the fate of the Jews was submerged in the global contest. The overriding priority was the military defeat of Germany and its allies. Fourth was the existence of overt and concealed anti-Semitism, especially in the United States, where polls revealed, even after the disclosure of the Holocaust, that the majority of Americans were opposed to the entry of Jewish immigrants.

THE NUREMBERG TRIALS

As the Allies marched through German territory in 1944 and 1945, they liberated the concentration camps. They found letters, diaries, and documents concerned with the plans and practices of the Final Solution. The Nazis had kept careful records of their victims. The Allies felt a need to make the extent of the Nazis' persecutions known to a stunned world. They wanted to prevent the recurrence of another Holocaust by bringing those responsible to trial. For the first time, leaders of a government were brought to an international court of law as symbols of aggressive militarism, of attempted genocide, and of the misuse of power.

In August of 1945, representatives of France, Britain, the USSR, and the USA agreed to an international military tribunal to be held in Nuremberg, Germany, the site of the Nazi mass rallies. Twenty-two (one in absentia) high-ranking Nazi officers were charged with four crimes newly defined: (a) Conspiracy, (b) Crimes against Peace, (c) War Crimes, (d) Crimes against Humanity. Hitler had committed suicide in April 1945. Among those left to be tried were his close aides Hermann Goering, Rudolf Hess, Julius Streicher, Alfred Jodl, and Albert Speer. A common plea of the defense maintained that these were soldiers following orders without choice. Thus a major question raised by the Trials is the extent of personal, moral responsibility during wartime. In the face of overwhelming evidence, the Nazis, once viewed as the enemy, now came to be seen as barbarous throwbacks from civilization. Nineteen defendants were convicted; twelve were sentenced to death; seven were sentenced to imprisonment; three were acquitted. After six years of war, the western world turned to a courtroom to condemn the systematic persecution of human beings.

The Nuremberg Trials can be viewed as a landmark precedent in the struggle for human rights. Winning nations claimed the jurisdiction to dictate how the losing nation should have treated its own subjects. The worldwide press coverage received by the Trials served as a condemnation of totalitarianism. There were (and still are) those who believed in the Nazi cause; to them the Trials established the martyrdom of great leaders by an illegitimate, vengeful victor.

QUESTIONS TO CONSIDER

1. Was the Einsatzgruppen largely responsible for the Holocaust?

2. Does the camp system account for the efficiency of the Final Solution?

3. Were the perpetrators brought to account by the Nuremberg trials?

There Are No Wise Men in Chelm: A Journey of Conscience to Poland, Spring 2002

Dr. Saul S. Friedman,
Youngstown State University

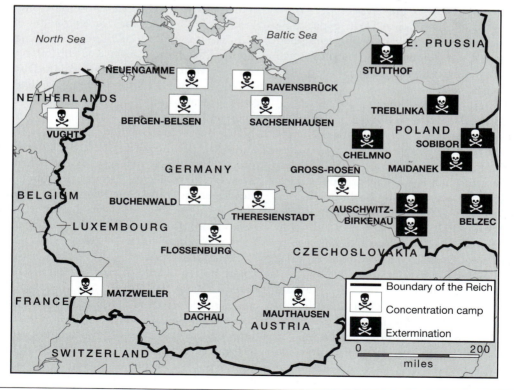

Saul Friedman, "There Are No Wise Men in Chelm: A Journey of Conscience to Poland," Spring 2002. Reprinted by permission of the author.

[2000 years ago, Polybius advised that an essential component of research was autopsy, what he defined as going to the sites where history was made. That was precisely the motivation for a tour that wound through thirteen cities and four concentration camps in Poland in the spring of 2002. Such visitations are not appreciated by people who now reside in locales where massacres were perpetrated. While we encountered many individuals, young and old, who were helpful, and while the Polish government has affirmed its commitment to examination of what transpired in World War II, disinterest and denial pervades that country. The attached article served as the narration for a television documentary broadcast in Ohio in November 2002. It is offered as a personal retrospective and as a criticism of a world that continues to be insensitive toward Jews.]

Once upon a time the Wise Men of Chelm decided to send a spaceship to the sun. When asked if it would burn, they answered, "Not to worry. We'll send it at night." Why expect anything more from foolish elders who counseled their people not to wear shoes in a snowstorm or to turn their hats upside down to keep them dry during a rain shower?

Like other fabled towns (Gotham, England; Mols, Denmark; Schildburg, Germany; Biella, Italy; and Bakka, Iceland), there is a real town of Chelm. Situated 35 miles west of the Bug River, Chelm is one of Poland's oldest cities. By 1931, half of its 30,000 residents were Jews. Invited to Poland by Casimir III, Jews shared the glory of a land that produced freedom fighters like Thadeusz Kosciuszko and Josef Pilsudski, great thinkers like Copernicus and Madame Curie. It was the land of Mickiewicz, Chopin, and Paderewski.

Jews came to Poland as shopkeepers and craftsmen and constructed a new view of Judaism—Hasidism—from the ashes of Cossack massacres. Once upon a time Jews in Chelm lived along the quagmire that was Lubliner Street. Once upon a time characters like Mordecai Bitterfresser, Yossel the Worrier, and Schlemiel the First inspired tales of naivete and *narishkayt*. The shtetl also produced sages

and *mavens*, hard-working tailors and seamstresses, *zaydehs* and *bubbehs*, and children.

On the eve of World War II, there were three million Jews in Poland, comprising 10 percent of the population. Today there may be 6000. There are no Wise Men in Chelm.

In May 2002, eighteen men and women participated in a journey of conscience in Poland. Their number was significant for it represents *chai* (life) in Hebrew. Nine men, nine women; six Jews, twelve Gentiles. They included students from West Chester University (Pennsylvania), Indiana University (Bloomington), Bowling Green, and Youngstown State. Three members of the group were over 60, including one 83-year-old survivor of Nazi concentration camps. Some were drawn by universal lessons of the Holocaust. Some came as a result of a personal commitment—to stand in the place of their fathers. And some came to find people who truly care for their fellow man.

Their journey took them first to Prague, the capital of the Czech Republic that has charmed visitors for 1000 years with its Disney-like castle overlooking the Moldau River and an endless array of outdoor cafes, churches, and architectural styles. Prague's synagogues reflect the history of Jews in Moravia and Bohemia. There is the Altneushul, where the kabbalistic master Judah Loew created the Golem, a mute monster who protected Jews from marauders in the sixteenth century. The Klaus serves as a museum for a Jewish population that once numbered more than 60,000. The radiant Spanish Shul, reflecting Sephardic design, still is used for religious services. And the Pinkas Synagogue lists the name of every Czech Jew murdered in World War II.

Prague served as the administrative headquarters for Reinhard Heydrich who used it as a gateway for transport of Jews to killing fields in the East. Himmler's top aide in the Reichs Main Security Office, Heydrich helped coordinate the *Kristallnacht* pogrom in November 1938. Heydrich directed the creation of the first Jewish councils in Poland. He helped develop *Einsatz* killing squads for the invasion of Russia in 1941. Heydrich received Goering's communique in July 1941, authorizing the Final Solution of the Jewish Question in Europe. He chaired the Wannsee Conference that passed a death sentence upon Jews at Berlin in January 1942.

For months, Heydrich had been advocating the collection of Jews in some secure facility like the township of Terezin 50 miles northwest of Prague. The onetime fortress was already being cleared of Gentiles when Heydrich was assassinated on May 29, 1942. He would not be forgotten. One hundred forty thousand persons passed through the stone barracks of Terezin in the next three years. Fourteen thousand were children. Fewer than 100 returned. Most perished in death camps along the Bug River as part of *Aktion Reinhard*, the extermination scheme designed to honor the man who called himself "the Nazi garbage man of the Jews."

In the spring of 2002, the eight-hour train ride from Prague to Cracow offered little challenge to the group from America. They would soon discover there was little intrigue or romance, only ennui, aboard a European train. Their route paralleled that followed by trains fifty years before—ending in Upper Silesia. But their reception in Cracow was substantially different.

The capital of a united Polish–Lithuanian kingdom till 1596, Cracow is an irresistible city. Of Cracow, the poet Francis Dmochowski once wrote:

> Dear to my heart is every spot of earth
>   on Poland's bosom, where her sons had birth.
> For me, on Cracow's fair surroundings fall
>   a charm, which makes them loveliest of all!
> At every turn, where'er the footstep strays,
>   so many souvenirs arrest the gaze;
>   so many records of the past which tell
>   of Poland's day of glory 'ere she fell.[1]

The core of the city is the three-tiered castle of Sygmunt I, which was constructed atop the Wawel Hill in the sixteenth century. Legend has it that an early hero slew a fire-breathing dragon on the Wawel. The dragon is still here, but the castle shares supremacy with the Cathedral of Saints Stanislaw and Waclaw. Perhaps it was a metaphor for the triumph of King Mieszko over paganism in the tenth century, a paganism that returned in the form of Governor-General Hans Frank and the Nazis who made Cracow the centerpiece of their puppet state in Poland. Remarkably, Cracow was never razed by invading armies. Today, visitors make the uphill hike to enjoy the panorama of the Vistula and to celebrate a thousand years of Christianity.

Buildings endure. Other precious things do not. Just south of the Wawel is the district known as Kazimierz. Jews lived here for 600 years until one night in March 1943. Visitors to Kazimierz are greeted by children playing soccer. They drink to traditional melodies played by *klezmorim* in several Jewish restaurants. They marvel at Jewish artifacts displayed in the Remah Synagogue. And they mourn for the dead at the old Jewish cemetery. The restaurants are "Jewish-style." The musicians are Ukrainians and cannot play *Rozhinkes mit Mandlen*, the most famous Yiddish lullaby. The men who run the souvenir kiosks are Poles, just like the soccer players. The Jewish streets are deserted, the synagogues cold, empty shells.

Once there were 65,000 Jews in Cracow. Today fewer than 500 men and women affirm their Jewish identity. Seek their kinsmen and you will find them in the corners of the synagogues, in the shadows of Oskar Schindler's factory, or in the wind that whips across the neglected memorial at the concentration camp of Plaszow.

Some places need no monuments. Thirty miles west of Cracow is the town of Oświęcim.

---

[1] Paul Sobieski, ed., *Poets and Poetry of Poland*. (Chicago: Knight and Leonard, 1883), p. 185.

Not much distinguishes this drab industrial town from its neighbors. Thirteen years ago there was a controversy over whether to permit the construction of a convent with a giant cross. Two years ago there was another dispute over licensing a discotheque and a retail mall in the area. Currently, historical preservationists debate how far they may go in restoring historical sites in the region.

Once a backwater post for the Austrian army, the town achieved infamy when Himmler created a concentration camp here in April 1940 and called it Auschwitz. Before Russian troops liberated Auschwitz in January 1945, 1.5 million people, including 1.1 million Jews, would perish in its network of forced labor and death camps. The worst was Birkenau. Early in 1942, Adolf Eichmann designated two farmhouses as gas chambers. Ultimately five units were designed to exterminate 10,000 persons per day.

One of those who managed to cheat death in Auschwitz was a wiry young man from Kielce—Abe Honigman. Twenty-two years old when he was deported in 1942, Honigman survived a death march to Sachsenhausen, and slave labor in Hamburg. Abe Honigman returned to Poland in the spring of 2002, accompanied by granddaughters of his friend and fellow survivor Henry Kinast. They listened as a Polish guide explained operations in Auschwitz. Abe offered his own insight as to how people were eliminated with hydrogen cyanide gas. The evidence—luggage culled from deportees all over Europe, mountains of prosthetic limbs, eyeglasses and shoes, girls' dresses, infant pacifiers, tons of human hair—was devastating. Eventually, Abe Honigman located his old building (Block 17) and stood there, defiantly, for a moment. Then he walked away—a free man.

There would be one last stop that day—Birkenau. As the sun began to set, the group would see up close barracks that once held 800 persons, sewers that serviced human seweage. Here as elsewhere, Abe Honigman led the group in traditional Jewish prayers (Kaddish, El Mole Rachamim, and the Twenty-Third Psalm).

Now, empty shells that dot hundreds of acres; then, another planet that offered no hope along the siding of death.

It seemed only fair that after a day as intense as Auschwitz the tour would schedule Zakopane—Poland's winter playground in the Tatra Mountains. This scenic village "at the back of beyond" was boosted as a possible site for the 2004 Winter Olympics. For more than a century, Zakopane has been famed for its invigorating climate and springs.

Recently the townsfolk dedicated an ornate church to honor the recovery of John Paul II from an attempted assassination. The Goral highlanders who inhabit the countryside came here about 500 years ago. An amiable blend of Romanian, Slovak, Polish, and Hungarian mountaineers, they can be fiercely independent as they proved fighting against the Nazis in World War II.

Even Zakopane has its historical dark side. From the moment Professor Tytus Chabulinski extolled the curative powers of Zakopane's spas, Jews were not welcomed in the town. In 1940 Hans Frank declared the region off-limits to Jews. Shortly after, the SS converted a parochial school in Rabka to a training center for death squads. They also operated a forced labor camp that felled some of the timber used in construction of Plaszow, Belzec, and Auschwitz. Between 1939 and 1944, 4,000 Jews of Zakopane were murdered. Only a handful survived among the Schindler Jews. There are no Jews in Zakopane today. No businesses. No synagogues. No memorials.

There is a synagogue in Stary Sacz thirty miles up the road. Once this gateway to Galicia hummed with Hasidic melodies. Jews and Gentiles haggled back and forth on the cobbled stones of the town square. There are a few traces of Jewish life (prayer shawls and *siddurs*) in the town museum and in the padlocked cemetery at nearby Nowy Sacz. Few people brave the high grass to visit broken stones or shrines of the *tsaddikim*. Most of the 25,000 Jews of Stary Sacz and Nowy Sacz were exterminated in Belzec in August 1942.

Nobody liked the next stop: Rzeszow. A drab gray atmosphere evocative of the forty-five-year Soviet occupation hangs over this city of 163,000 people. Its monuments and buildings are artless. The residents of this metropolis that shares a sister relationship with Buffalo, New York, seem beaten and angry. The Polish government supposedly campaigned against racist graffiti in recent years. But in Rzeszow, anti-Semites continue to scrawl or utter insults against Jews and Americans. How ironic, since the first Jews had come to Rzeszow in 1447. By the middle of the eighteenth century, the handiwork of Jews who traded in silver and gold was so renowned that people spoke of "Rzeszower gold."

When the Germans came to Rzeszow on September 10, 1939, Jews constituted one third of the city's population. Fifteen thousand Jews were scaled in a ghetto in January 1942. Six months later, thousands were shipped to death camps along the Bug River. Survivors lived temporarily in a so-called Schmelzer ghetto before the Nazis proclaimed Rzeszow *Judenrein* in February 1944.

Fifteen-year-old Al Friedman left the city in 1912. Ninety years later, two of his children and a granddaughter stood in the same square where he had stood before coming to the hills of Pennsylvania. Finding a Jewish cemetery in Rzeszow was a bit more problematic. The old cemetery on Synagogue Street had been ploughed over, its stones used for a municipal garden.

Finding the cemetery on Dolowa Street proved just as difficult. People seemed unaware of its existence behind stout stone walls. No pretense of maintenance in four foot high grass. And in the midst of desolation, a reminder carved on a memorial to Jews who perished in World War II: *Jude Raus.*

There is a Jewish archival center in Rzeszow, around the corner from a synagogue with a gallows and swastika chalked on its side.

According to the Society of Rzeszower Jews in Israel and America, the last Jew left Rzeszow in 1957. As their *memorbuch* recounts: "The soil of Rzeszow, the town where we and our fathers were born under the Chestnuts… will remain engraved in the memories of the last Rzeszow Jews. But future generations will remember Poland as the country that swallowed their beloved ones, without trace, grave or tombstone." [2]

Most of Rzeszow's Jews perished in Belzec. Those who did not were sent to Sobibor, a death camp near Chelm. Like other *Aktion Reinhard* camps, Sobibor was located in a remote area where few residents were troubled by the process of genocide.

Everything people say about the camp and its environs is true. Beware making the wrong turn that takes you into town and a hostile populace. Go to the opposite side and find the siding where train after train emptied to the sound of Strauss and Offenbach waltzes. The path to the gas chambers is about 500 yards, just as Konnilyn Feig described it: overgrown with weeds and trees, deathly quiet but for the chirping of birds and the incessant assault of sand flies. [3]

Three hundred Jewish girls were gassed in July 1943 to honor a visit from Heinrich Himmler. Three hundred fifty thousand Jews from Poland, Austria, Holland, and France were murdered in Sobibor before Jewish inmates destroyed the camp in October 1943. Just as one aged Jew predicted when he arrived in Sobibor. The old man grabbed a fistful of dirt and taunted an SS man: "You see how I'm scattering this sand grain by grain. That's what will happen to you; this whole great Reich of yours will vanish like flying dust and passing smoke." [4]

There are so many places of pain near Sobibor. Josefow, where a police unit from

---

[2]Manes Fromer, "Five Hundred Years—A Summing Up," in *Rzeszow Jews: Memorial Book* (Tel Aviv: Ahdut Cooperative Press, 1967), p. 12.

[3]Konnilyn Feig, *Hitler's Death Camps* (New York: Holmes and Meier, 1979), pp. 284–85.

[4]Miriam Novitch, *Sobibor: Martyrdom and Revolt* (New York: Holocaust Library, 1980), p. 157.

Hamburg murdered 2000 Jews. The forests of Izbica, the final resting place for many Jews from Terezin, Bitgoraj, and Łuków, where Jewish officials were executed for defying German decrees. Zamość and Nisko, which were to be part of a great Jewish reservation. All of them from the same administrative district—the *Gubernia* of Lublin.

One of Poland's great cities, Lublin was the site of the union between Lithuania and Poland in 1569. In the time of troubles, it staved off the advance of Tatars. Twice in its history, in 1919 and 1944, Lublin served as the temporary capital of Poland. In the winter of 1939–40 the Germans decided to make Lublin capital of unincorporated territories in Poland. What they called the Government General was to serve as a "reservation" for 300,000 local Jews and 650,000 deportees from Austria and Czechoslovakia.

The Nazis revealed what they meant by reservation when they opened the concentration camp of Majdanek on the outskirts of Lublin 1941. Unlike Sobibor and Treblinka, Majdanek was located close by a major city, no more than a few hundred yards from the city limits of Lublin. There was no mistaking the nature of ashes that rained down on the city or the stench from a camp only one-sixth completed when it was overrun by the Soviets.

Unlike Birkenau, many of the barracks are still standing. Some display images of the high command and guards. Other cases contain dolls and toys. One of the first buildings you encounter is marked "disinfection." Pipes protrude from a low ceiling in what once was a functioning gas chamber. The walls are stained a vivid blue, the result of oxidation of hydrogen cyanide gas, proof that Zyklon-B was used to kill inmates.

Another short bus ride and the visitor is at the crematoria. Eighteen thousand Jews were killed in three ditches in November 1943, in what Odilo Globocnik called *Enterfest*, to honor the memory of Reinhard Heydrich. A huge mound of ashes rises like a spaceship over the landscape where 350,000 persons (including 100,000 Slavs) died. And in Lublin, there is also a park dedicated to the memory of that city's Jewish population. It is unkempt, neglected and marked with graffiti.

On March 19, 1946, one of two surviving prisoners of Belzec was beaten to death on the streets of Lublin. 800 Jews were murdered by Polish anti-Semites in the year following the end of World War II. The worst incident occured in Kielce on July 4, 1946. Two thousand Jews were living in one building, awaiting entry permits to Palestine. Using the pretext of ritual murder, a mob, including police and Catholic clergy, killed forty-two Jews. When the massacre ended, Cardinal August Hlond blamed the Jews for the violence.[5]

Before the war, 15,000 Jews lived in Kielce. Abe Honigman had come from Łódź to work and to marry. He and his wife were deported to Auschwitz in 1942. On May 23, 2002, he returned to his home city. With so many changes in housing and streets over the years, Abe could not be faulted for being apprehensive about his last day in Poland. At last Abe found a familiar site—a synagogue that now serves as the center for Kielce's tiny Jewish community. Now he could speak and pray.

That night Abe was saluted in a banquet at the Gromada Hotel. He would be returning to America for the dedication of his wife's tombstone. As he parted the next day, his companions again paid tribute to this indomitable man from Kielce.

By going home early, Abe was spared a visit to the Jsna Goura monastery. Situated on the main road from Cracow to Łódź, the Pauline monastery hosts Poland's most revered icon—the tapestry of the Black Madonna. Visitors swarm to the monastery near Częstochowa

---

[5]Louis Weber, ed., *The Holocaust Chronicle* (Publications International, 2000), pp. 647–49.

for a glimpse of the Byzantine tapestry or treasures donated in its honor. Sometimes tourists are properly informed—of the deeds of Maximilian Kolbe, a priest who was canonized for taking the place of a fellow prisoner sentenced to die in Auschwitz. Sometimes they are not so well informed about what transpired during the Second World War. (According to one Jesuit, "more Poles died in Auschwitz than Jews.")

Legend has it that the Madonna protects the victims of evil, and throughout history Czestochowa has been a bastion against invaders. When the Nazis came to Częstochowa, they found a city accustomed to boycotts, beatings, and insults directed at Jews. There was no miraculous intervention for Częstochowa's Jews sent to Treblinka in September 1942 or 100 families killed in the cemetery at Purim 1943. Survival in Częstochowa depended on employment in labor camps operated by the HASAG works. The Nazis labeled one such camp near the Jasna Goura monastery "Golgotha" and in April 1945 they machine-gunned most of their slave workers.

No one knows how many Jews live in Częstochowa today—or how many identify as Jews in Łódź. Often called Poland's Manchester, Łódź is the second largest city in Poland. Its population swelled to more than a half million at the end of the nineteenth century. Many of its residents were employed in the textile industry. Many of these were Jews. A few, like Julius Kindermann, Gustav Landau Gutentager, and Israel Poznanski made fortunes and erected great mansions. Most Jews, however, lived in squalor near the Baluty ring. By 1939 there were nearly 200,000 Jews in Łódź. Half were totally dependent upon Jewish relief agencies.

When the Nazis overran Poland, they annexed the Polish Corridor and Łódź (which they renamed Litzmannstadt). They also created the first major ghetto here in February 1940. For the next four years, Łódź Jews tried to impress the Germans with their usefulness. Responding to exhortations from *Judenaltester*

Chaim Rumkowski, they reopened factories by jerry-rigging discarded pieces of machinery. To no avail. They starved. Synagogues were burned. And the ghetto was repeatedly thinned.

By July 1944, 140,000 Jews had been sent to Chelmno and Auschwitz. Henry Kinast was one of the few survivors. With the help of another survivor, the Kinast girls found the home of their grandfather and the building that houses the Jewish community council of Łódź.

Łódź redounds with mementos of its Jews, the famous—like pianist Artur Rubinstein—and the common. Buildings that once teemed with Jewish children are still used by the poor. Other tenements are just too ghastly. Guides tell tourists that one synagogue puzzlingly situated in the middle of an apartment complex cannot be visited because it is Saturday (the Jewish Sabbath) and the doors are locked. But, one notes proudly, in the green velt that once was the ghetto there is an impressive statue of Moses. He stands alone, no graffiti marring the base. Unidentified as the Prophet of the Jews, his tablets are blank.

The city of Bialystok lies 200 miles northeast of Łódź along some of Poland's most clogged highways. When the peacemakers at Versailles made over the map of Eastern Europe, they placed Bialystok in the middle of a resurrected Poland. Today it sits virtually on the boundary with Lithuania. A pleasant city accessible to most of Poland's national parks, Bialystok once was the private domain of the Branicki family that built a lesser replica of the palace of Louis XIV at Versailles. Its people are friendly and deeply religious.

During World War II, 60,000 Jews were ghettoized in Bialystok. Just as in Łódź, a Judenrat tried to demonstrate the essential worth of Jews to the German war effort—and failed. *Reichskommissar* Erich Koch deported 16,000 Jews in the fall of 1941. Despite the efforts of Mordecai Tennenbaum and other members of the Jewish Resistance, the Nazis managed to clear the ghetto in August 1943. A plaque commemorates the efforts of the Jewish Fighting Organization in Bialystok. There is no mistaking the significance of another monument that stands in the center of the old Jewish quarter today. The twisted girders once formed the cupola of the great synagogue of Bialystok. When the Nazis arrived on June 26, 1941, they stuffed 1000 Jews into the building and burned them alive.

Fire has a strange appeal in this region of virgin forests, rolling hills, and rye fields. Forty miles back from Bialystok in the district of Łomźa is the village of Jedwabne, sometimes described as nondescript or ugly. Two thousand five hundred persons, all of them Christians, live in Jedwabne, and they resent attention focused on their town. Two years ago, Jan Tomasz Gross published a book which declared, "One day in July 1941, half of the population of a small east European town murdered the other half—some 1600 men, women and children."[6]

There always had been Jews in Jedwabne. Before the war, they accounted for half the town's population. Most shopkeepers were Jews and during the Depression they extended credit to their gentile customers. That idyll ended with the Russian occupation in 1939 when some villagers were tortured to death by the NKVD. Yet no one could have foreseen the rage that transformed the village when the Nazis "liberated" Jedwabne in the summer of 1941.

Encouraged by pogroms in nearby towns, Christians attacked Jews with clubs, axes, and whips. Jewish men were ordered to carry a statue of Lenin to the town square, chanting, "The war is because of us!" Some had their beards ripped away, while others were pelted with rocks. One villager boasted of killing a teenager with a 24-pound stone. Two Jewish blacksmiths were drowned in a pond near Moza Street. The daughter of the town's schoolteacher was beheaded. Elsewhere, the mob cheered as two mothers leaped into the river with their babies and drowned.

Unsated, the villagers drove the rest of Jedwabne's Jews to a barn on the outskirts of town. One young man stood guard with an axe, as more than 1000 Jews were locked in the barn and burned alive. Remnants of the barn door were incorporated in a monument dedicated by the Polish government in July 2001 to the memory of the Jewish victims.

Villagers feign ignorance about the Jewish memorial. When the tour bus driver asked for directions, he was directed out of town. One elderly women stuck her tongue out at the passengers. Finally, a little boy pointed the way—near the well-trimmed Christian cemetery.

The memorial stands near a Jewish cemetery that bears signs of vandalism. The memorial is only a few yards from the town center and Jedwabne's church. The memorial does not specify who perpetrated the massacre.

There are too many monuments in Treblinka. Stones stand at the outer perimeter of the camp. Stones show where the boxcars arrived. Stones in the place where bodies were burned. Stones dedicated to great men like Janusz Korczak, the heroic pediatrician from Warsaw. Stones that commemorate great cities and little towns. Stones that bear no names.

Seven hundred thousand men, women, and children were murdered in Treblinka in little more than a year. All of them were Jews. Most of them were from Warsaw. Of them, the poet Abraham Sutzkever has written:

> You have not vanished. Your emptiness is full.
> Full with your people, as my mother fills my eye.
> Somewhere a synagogue still proudly lifts its head.
> The flames had no power over it, passed it by.

---

[6]Jan Tomas Gross, *Neighbors* (Princeton, NJ: Princeton University Press, 2001).

You are a melody that fine musicians
played generations ago.
The music turned into a street.
Only to the poor and lowly you seem poor
and low.
But those who have vision see how you are
bright.
Their arms are heaped full with your light.

Can the whole measure of 500 years.
Grow less because of our bit of now?
Who says you have vanished? No, you live!
Else how could I walk through you, in the way
I do?

Does not the music live, when the composer
is long lying dead in his place?
I can hear you singing in eternity,
High above time and space.[7]

More than 500,000 Jews were forced into the ghetto of Warsaw during the Second World War, the largest concentration of Jews in Europe. They lived together. They suffered together. And they died together.

Today, vestiges of Russian Communism vie with Western hotels for the soul of Warsaw. The ghetto is an anachronism replaced by apartment complexes, strip malls, chic outlets, and fast-food restaurants. Sections of the ghetto wall remain in place. A stark memorial sprouts inexplicably at a corner that once served as the Umschlagplatz, where boxcars were loaded for Treblinka. The Sienna Street orphanage of Dr. Janusz Korczak still stands—unmarked. Pawiak Prison celebrates the feats of Poles who fought alongside Jews against the Nazis. Markers on the sidewalks extoll the work of Dr. Korczak, the poet Yitzhok Katzenelsen, labor leader Shmul Zygelboim, the historian Emmanuel Ringelblum, and the youthful Zionist Mordecai Anielewicz who directed the ghetto uprising in April/May 1943.

At war's end, the Polish government erected an impressive memorial to those who fought and perished in the ghettos and forests. The current government plans to constuct a Jewish historical museum in the heart of what once was the ghetto. It is a nice idea. But there is still something disturbing about a museum that celebrates a culture that was despised and is now defunct. Most Poles don't care about what happened to Jews in World War II. Seek out people who do care and you may find them at Mila 18, the onetime headquarters of the Jewish Fighting Organization, at the graves of Yitzhok Leibush Peretz, Ludwik Zamenhof, or Rabbi Ber Meisels in the Jewish cemetery of Warsaw.

[Once upon a time there was a great Jewish civilization in Poland. Great sages and philosophers shared the streets of Warsaw, Cracow, and Chelm with the common folk. No more. The tiny, aging Jewish population in Poland offers mute testimony to the triumph of racial bigotry in this land. Like their kinsmen who enjoyed Golden Ages in Pumbeditha, Cordoba, and Salonika, the Jews of Poland will soon be found only among museum displays and the maysim in synagogue attics.]

In May 2002 eighteen Americans came looking for people who cared. They found truth and decency in themselves.

QUESTIONS TO CONSIDER

1. What does the author's journey reveal about the places he visited?

2. What were Judenrats and what did they fail to do?

3. What distinction does Warsaw have during the Nazi era?

---

[7]Abraham Sutzkever, "Jewish Street," *The Golden Peacock: A Treasury of Yiddish Poetry*, J Joseph Leftwich, ed. and trans. (New York: T. Yoseloff, 1961), pp. 450–51.

O Baro Porrajmos—The Romani Holocaust

Ian Hancock,

University of Texas at Austin

The motives invoked to justify the death of the Gypsies were the same as those ordering the murder of the Jews, and the methods employed for the one were identical with those employed for the other.

The greatest tragedy to befall the European Romani population was the attempt to eradicate it as part of the Nazis' plan to have a "Gypsy-free" Europe. Although it wasn't the first governmental plan to exterminate Romanies (German Emperor Karl VI had previously issued such an order in 1721), it was by far the most devastating, ultimately destroying over half of the Romani population in Nazi-occupied Europe. Romanies were the only other population besides the Jews who were targeted for extermination on racial/ethnic grounds in the Final Solution. Note that in Germany, the traditional Romani population calls itself Sinti, while the word *Zigeuner* is the German equivalent of "Gypsy" and should be avoided. In Romani, the Holocaust is referred to as the *Baro Porrajmos*, or "great devouring" of human life. *Porrajmos* is an ugly word, well chosen for the ugliest event in our history. It can also mean "rape," as well as "gaping" as in shock or horror. Some people hesitate to say the word out loud.

When the Nazis came to power in 1933, German laws against Romanies had already been in effect for hundreds of years. The persecution of the Romani people began almost as soon as they first arrived in German-speaking lands because as outsiders, they were, without knowing it, breaking the Hanseatic laws which made it a punishable offence not to have a permanent home or job, and not to be on the taxpayer's register. They were also accused of being spies for the Muslims, whom few Germans had ever met, but about whom they had heard many frightening stories; it was not illegal to murder a Romani and there were sometimes "Gypsy hunts" in which Romanies were tracked down and killed like wild animals. Forests were set on fire, to drive out any Romanies who might have been hiding there.

By the nineteenth century, scholars in Germany and elsewhere in Europe were writing about Romanies and Jews as being inferior beings and "the excrement of humanity"; even Darwin, writing in 1871, singled out our two populations as not being "culturally advanced" like other "territorially settled" peoples. This crystallized into specifically racist attitudes in the writing of Knox, Tetzner, Gobineau and others. By the 1880s, Chancellor von Bismarck reinforced some of the discriminatory laws, stating that Romanies were to be dealt with "especially severely" if apprehended.

In or around 1890, a conference on 'The Gypsy Scum' (*Das Zigeuner-geschmeiß*) was held in Swabia, at which the military was given full authority to keep Romanies on the move. In 1899 the Englishman Houston Chamberlain, who was the composer Richard Wagner's son-in-law, wrote a book called *The Foundations of the Nineteenth Century*, in which he argued for the building of a "newly shaped ... and ... especially deserving Aryan race." It was used to justify the promotion of ideas about German racial superiority and for any oppressive action taken against members of "inferior" populations. In

Ian Hancock, "*O Baro Porrajmos*—The Romani Holocaust," from *We Are the Romani People: Ame Sam e Rromane Dzene* (Hatfield: The University of Hertfordshire, 2002). University of Texas at Austin Reprinted with permission.

that same year, the "Gypsy Information Agency" was set up in Munich under the direction of Alfred Dillmann, which began cataloguing data on all Romanies throughout the German lands. The results of this were published in 1905 in Dillmann's *Zigeuner-Buch*, which laid the foundations for what was to happen to our people in the Holocaust thirty-five years later.

The *Zigeuner-Buch* is nearly 350 pages long, and consists of three parts: first, an introduction stating that Romanies were a "plague" and a "menace" against which the German population had to defend itself using "ruthless punishments," and which warned of the dangers of mixing the Romani and German gene pools. The second part was a register of all known Romanies, giving genealogical details and criminal record if any, and the third part was a collection of photographs of those same people. Dillmann's ideas about "race mixing" later became a central part of the Nuremberg Law in Nazi Germany. In 1920, a psychiatrist, Karl Binding, and a magistrate, Alfred Hoche, published a jointly-authored book called *The Eradication of Lives Undeserving of Life*, using a phrase first coined by Richard Liebich with specific reference to Romanies nearly sixty years earlier. Among the groups that they said were "unworthy of life" were the "incurably mentally ill," and it was to this group that Romanies were considered to belong. Euthanizing such groups received popular support from the author H. G. Wells.

Perceived Romani "criminality" was seen as a transmitted genetic disease, though no account was taken of the centuries of exclusion of the Romanies from German society, which made subsistence theft a necessity for survival. A law incorporating the phrase *lives undeserving of life* was put into effect just four months after Hitler became Chancellor of the Third Reich.

During the 1920s, the legal oppression of Romanies in Germany intensified considerably, despite the official statutes of the Weimar Republic that said that all its citizens were equal. In 1920 they were forbidden to enter parks and public baths; in 1925 a conference on "The Gypsy Question" was held which resulted in the creation of laws requiring unemployed Romanies to be sent to work camps "for reasons of public security," and for all Romanies to be registered with the police. After 1927 everyone, even Romani children, had to carry identification cards bearing their fingerprints and photographs. In 1929, The Central Office for the Fight Against the Gypsies in Germany was established in Munich, and in 1933, just ten days before the Nazis came to power, government officials in Burgenland, Austria, called for the withdrawal of all civil rights from the Romani people.

In September 1935, Romanies became subject to the restrictions of the Nuremberg Law for the Protection of German Blood and Honour, which forbade intermarriage between Germans and "non-Aryans," specifically Jews, Romanies and people of African descent. In 1937, the National Citizenship Law relegated Romanies and Jews to the status of second-class citizens, depriving them of their civil rights. Also in 1937, Heinrich Himmler issued a decree entitled "The Struggle Against the Gypsy Plague," which reiterated that Romanies of mixed blood were the most likely to engage in criminal activity, and which required that all information on Romanies be sent from the regional police departments to the Reich Central Office. In their book published in 1943, the Danish sociologists Erik Bartels and Gudrun Brun echoed this position, evidently unaware that the sterilization of Romanies had already been in effect for a decade:

> The pure gypsies present no great problem, if only we realise that their mentality does not allow of their admittance to the well-ordered general society ... the mixed gypsies cause considerably greater difficulties ... [nothing good has] come from a crossing between a gypsy and a white person ... Germany is at present contemplating the introduction of provisions of sterilization in the case of such families.

Calling a population vermin, or a disease, rather than recognising them as being part of the human family is a technique used to dehumanize it and to distance it from society. Such terms were constantly used to refer to Jews and Romanies in the Third Reich in an effort to desensitize the general population to the increasingly harsh treatment being meted out against them; after all, vermin and diseases need to be eradicated. Disturbingly, this language is still with us—the *Badische Zeitung* for 28 August 1992 carried the headline "A pure disease, these Gypsies!"

Between June 13–18, 1938, "Gypsy Clean-Up Week" (*Zigeuneraufräumungswoche*, also called *Aktion Arbeitschau Reich* and *Bettlerwoche* in the documentation) took place throughout Germany which, like Kristallnacht for the Jewish people that same year, marked the beginning of the end. Also in 1938, the first reference to "The Final Solution of the Gypsy Question" (*die endgültige Lösung der Zigeunerfrage*) appeared in print in a document dated March 24, and again in an order issued by Himmler on December 8 that year. Thus in the *Auschwitz Memorial Book* we find "The final resolution, as formulated by Himmler, in his "Decree for Basic Regulations to Resolve the Gypsy Question as Required by the Nature of Race," of December 8th, 1938, meant that preparations were to begin for the *complete extermination* of the Sinti and Roma" (emphasis added). This was announced to the general public in the *NS-Rechtspiegel* the following 21 February 1939. Also in 1938, Himmler issued his criteria for biological and racial evaluation, which determined that each Romani's family background was to be investigated going back for three generations; the Nazis' racial motive for exterminating Romanies is clear from the fact that they even targeted Romani-*like* people, taking no chances lest the German population be contaminated with Romani blood. Kenrick writes:

> In general, a person with one Jewish grandparent was not affected in the Nazi anti-Jewish legislation, whereas one-eighth "gypsy blood" was con-

sidered strong enough to outweigh seven-eighths of German blood—so dangerous were the Gypsies considered.

This was twice as strict as the criteria determining who was Jewish; had the same also applied to Romanies, nearly 20,000 would have escaped death. On 16 December 1941 Himmler issued the order to have Romanies throughout western Europe deported to Auschwitz-Birkenau for extermination.

In 1939 Johannes Behrendt of the Office of Racial Hygiene issued a brief stating that "[a]ll Gypsies should be treated as hereditarily sick; the only solution is elimination. The aim should therefore be the elimination without hesitation of this defective element in the population." In January 1940 the first mass genocidal action of the Holocaust took place when 250 Romani children from Brno were murdered in Buchenwald, where they were used as guinea-pigs to test the efficacy of the Zyklon-B cyanide gas crystals that were later used in the gas chambers. In June 1940 Hitler ordered the extermination of all Jews, Romanies and communist political functionaries in the entire Soviet Union. Reinhard Heydrich, who was Head of the Reich Main Security Office and the leading organizational architect of the Nazi Final Solution, ordered the Einsatzkommandos to kill all Jews, Romanies and mental patients, although not all of the documentation regarding its complete details, relating to both Jews and Romanies, has so far been found. Müller-Hill writes:

> Heydrich, who had been entrusted with the "final solution of the Jewish question" on 31st July 1941, shortly after the German invasion of the USSR, also included the Gypsies in his "final solution"… The senior SS officer and Chief of Police for the East, Dr. Landgraf, in Riga, informed Rosenberg's Reich Commissioner for the East, Lohse, of the inclusion of the Gypsies in the "final solution." Thereupon, Lohse gave the order, on 24th December 1941, that the Gypsies should be given the same treatment as the Jews.

Burleigh & Wippermann write further that:

> A conference on racial policy organised by Heydrich took place in Berlin on 21st September 1939, which may have decided upon a "Final Solution" of the "Gypsy Question." According to the scant minutes which have survived, four issues were decided: the concentration of Jews in towns; their relocation to Poland; the removal of 30,000 Gypsies to Poland, and the systematic deportation of Jews to German incorporated territories using goods trains. An express letter sent by the Reich Main Security Office on 17th October 1939 to its local agents mentioned that the "Gypsy Question will shortly be regulated throughout the territory of the Reich"… At about this time, Adolf Eichmann made the recommendation that the "Gypsy Question" be solved simultaneously with the "Jewish Question,"… Himmler signed the order dispatching Germany's Sinti and Roma to Auschwitz on 16th December 1942. The "Final Solution" of the "Gypsy Question" had begun.

Himmler's order stated that "all Gypsies are to be deported to the Zigeunerlager at Auschwitz concentration camp, with no regard to their degree of racial impurity." The *Memorial Book* for the Romanies who died at Auschwitz-Birkenau also says:

> The Himmler decree of December 16th 1942 (Auschwitz-Erlaß), according to which the Gypsies should be deported to Auschwitz-Birkenau, had the same meaning for the Gypsies that the conference at Wannsee on January 20th 1942, had for the Jews. This decree, and the bulletin that followed on January 29th 1943, can thus be regarded as a logical consequence of the decision taken at Wannsee. After it had been decided that the fate of the Jews was to end in mass extermination, it was natural for the other group of racially persecuted people, the Gypsies, to become victims of the same policy, which finally even included soldiers in the Wehrmacht.

In a paper delivered in Washington in 1987, at a conference on the fate of the non-Jewish victims of the Holocaust sponsored by the U.S. Holocaust Memorial Council, Dr. Erika Thurner of the Institut für Neuere Geschichte und Zeitgeschichte at the University of Linz stated that:

> Heinrich Himmler's infamous Auschwitz decree of December 16th, 1942, can be seen as the final stage of the final solution of the Gypsy Question. The decree served as the basis for complete extermination. According to the implementation instructions of 1943, all Gypsies, irrespective of their racial mix, were to be assigned to concentration camps. The concentration camp for Gypsy families at Auschwitz-Birkenau was foreseen as their final destination… opposed to the fact that the decision to seek a final solution for the Gypsy Question came at a later date than that of the Jewish Question, the first steps taken to exterminate the Gypsies were initiated prior to this policy decision.

This order appears to have been the result of a direct decision from Hitler himself. Breitman reproduced the statement issued by Security Police Commander Bruno Streckenbach following a policy meeting with Hitler and Heydrich held in Pretsch in June, 1940, *viz.* that "[t]he Führer has ordered the liquidation of all Jews, gypsies (*sic*) and communist political functionaries in the entire area of the Soviet Union." SS Officer Percy Broad, who worked in the political division at Auschwitz and who participated directly in the murders of several thousand prisoners there, wrote in his memoirs twenty-five years later that "… it was the will of the all-powerful Reichsführer to have the Gypsies disappear from the face of the earth." At a party meeting on 14 September 1942 with Joseph Goebbels, Reichsminister of Justice Otto Thierack announced that "with respect to the extermination of antisocial forms of life, Dr. Goebbels is of the opinion that Jews and Gypsies should simply be exterminated."

On 4 August 1944, some 2,900 Romanies were gassed and cremated in a single action at Auschwitz-Birkenau, during what is remembered as *Zigeunernacht*.

Determining the percentage or number of Romanies who died in the Holocaust has not been easy. Bernard Streck noted that "any attempts to express Romani casualties in terms of numbers … cannot be verified by means of lists or card-indexes or camp files; most of the Gypsies died in eastern or southern Europe, shot by execution troops or fascist gang members." Much of the Nazi documentation still remains to be analyzed and, as Streck intimates, many murders were not recorded since they took place in the fields and forests where Romanies were arrested. There are no accurate figures either for the pre-war Romani population in Europe, though the Nazi Party's official census of 1939 estimated it to be about two million, certainly an under-representation. Regarding numbers, König says:

> The count of half a million Sinti and Roma murdered between 1939 and 1945 is too low to be tenable; for example in the Soviet Union many of the Romani dead were listed under non-specific labels such as *Liquidierungsübrigen* [remainder to be liquidated], "hangers-on" and "partisans" … The final number of the dead Sinti and Roma may never be determined. We do not know precisely how many were brought into the concentration camps; not every concentration camp produced statistical material; moreover, Sinti and Roma are often listed under the heading of remainder to be liquidated, and do not appear in the statistics for Gypsies.

In the eastern territories, in Russia especially, Romani deaths were sometimes counted into the records under the heading of Jewish deaths. The *Memorial Book* also discusses the means of killing Romanies:

> Unlike the Jews, the overwhelming majority of whom were murdered in the gas chambers at Birkenau, Belzec, Treblinka and all the other mass extermination camps, the Gypsies outside the Reich were massacred at many places, sometimes only a few at a time, and sometimes by the hundreds. In the *Generalgouvernement* [the eastern territories] alone, 150 sites of Gypsy massacres are known. Research on the Jewish Holocaust can rely on comparison of pre- and post-war census data to help determine the numbers of victims in

the countries concerned. However, this is not possible for the Gypsies, as it was only rarely that they were included in national census data. Therefore it is an impossible task to find the actual number of Gypsy victims in Poland, Yugoslavia, White Ruthenia and the Ukraine, the lands that probably had the greatest numbers of victims.

The 1997 figure reported by Dr. Sybil Milton, the then senior historian at the U.S. Holocaust Memorial Research Institute in Washington, put the number of Romani lives lost by 1945 at "between a half and one and a half million." Significantly, the same figure appeared again in a November 2001 report issued by the International Organization for Migration (the *IOM*), a body designated to locate and compensate surviving Romani Holocaust victims. The brief states that "[r]ecent research indicates that up to 1.5 million Roma perished during the Nazi era." It is certainly a fact that interviews in the past four years by trained Romani personnel who have obtained testimonials at first-hand from claimants throughout central and eastern Europe have already shed startling new light on this issue: the number of Romani survivors is far in excess of anything previously estimated. By extrapolation, and from the same eyewitness accounts documented in recent years, the numbers of Romanies who perished at the hands of the Nazis has also been grossly underestimated. Eventually, these revised figures will find their way into the public record.

Since the end of the Second World War, Germany's record regarding the Romani people has been less than exemplary. Nobody was called to testify in behalf of the Romani victims at the Nuremberg Trials, and no war crimes reparations have ever been paid to Romanies as a people. Today, neo-Nazi activity in many parts of central and Eastern Europe makes the Romanies its prime target of racial violence. Kenrick summarized the situation after 1945 very well:

> In the first years following the end of the Nazi domination of Europe, the Gypsy community was

in disarray. The small [Romani] educational and cultural organizations that had existed before 1939 had been destroyed. The family structure was broken with the death of the older people—the guardians of the traditions. While in the camps, the Gypsies had been unable to keep up their customs—the Romanía—concerning the preparation of food and the washing of clothes. They solved the psychological problems by not speaking about the time in the camps. Only a small number of Gypsies could read or write, so they could not tell their own story. But also they were unwilling to tell their own stories to others, and few others were interested anyway. In the many books written describing the Nazi period and the persecution of the Jews, Gypsies usually appear as a footnote or small section.

We still have a long way to go both with our understanding of the *Porrajmos* and with achieving its proper acknowledgment in the classroom; including a section on the *Porrajmos* must be viewed as essential to any Romani Studies curriculum.

An argument which is sometimes made is that the Romanies simply didn't preoccupy the Nazis; we have even been called an "afterthought" in Nazi policy. This is neither fair nor true, but can probably be accounted for by the fact that our people were far fewer in number, were much more easily identified and disposed of, and had already been the target of discriminatory policy even before Hitler came to power. It required no massive effort on the part of the Nazis to locate and destroy a population which had no one to take its part. Haberer adds to this:

> [Regarding] the persecution of Gypsies, it should be noted that their plight equaled that of the Jews. Their liquidation was part and parcel of the Nazis' agenda to eradicate "worthless life." Wrapped up in the Holocaust *per se*, the genocide of the Roma in the East is still very much an untold story. In some ways, their victimization was practiced even more ruthlessly because they held no "economic value" and were traditionally considered a particular asocial and criminally inclined people [and] more alien in appearance, culture and language.

The United Nations too, did nothing to assist Romanies during or following the Holocaust nor,

sadly, were Romanies mentioned anywhere in the documentation of the U.S. War Refugee Board. Nevertheless, the situation is gradually improving. In Germany itself, the handbook and CD-ROM on Holocaust education prepared for teachers and which was issued by the Press and Information Office of the federal government in 2000 makes clear that

> Recent historical research in the United States and Germany does not support the conventional argument that the Jews were the only victims of Nazi genocide. True, the murder of Jews by the Nazis differed from the Nazis' killing of political prisoners and foreign opponents because it was based on the genetic origin of the victims and not on their behaviour. The Nazi regime applied a consistent and inclusive policy of extermination based on heredity only against three groups of human beings: the handicapped, Jews, and Sinti and Roma ("Gypsies"). The Nazis killed multitudes, including political and religious opponents, members of the resistance, elites of conquered nations, and homosexuals, but always based these murders on the belief, actions and status of those victims. Different criteria applied only to the murder of the handicapped, Jews, and "Gypsies." Members of these groups could not escape their fate by changing their behavior or belief. They were selected because they existed.

QUESTIONS TO CONSIDER

1. What does *Porrajmos* mean? Why are people upset by this particular word?
2. Could the Nazis' policies directed at "non-Aryans" be regarded as a kind of ethnic cleansing?
3. Explain what led up to the Nazis' policy to destroy the European Romani population.
4. Why does there seem to be a reluctance to acknowledge the Nazis' genocidal policy regarding Romanies?
5. Why did they consider "The Final Solution of the Gypsy Question" to be necessary?
6. What has happened to the Romanies who survived the Holocaust in the years since 1945?
7. Do you think that the lack of acknowledgment of the Romanies' plight after the Second World War has any bearing upon their present-day situation?
8. Why is it difficult to estimate the number of Romanies who perished in the *Porrajmos*?

Long Shadows: Truth, Lies and History

Erna Paris

WAR, MEMORY AND IDENTITY

Throughout the long process of constructing a museum to memory (the Holocaust Museum did not officially open until 1993), there were challenges and questions about the meaning of "uniqueness." What about the Gypsies, or Roma-Sinti, as they were more properly called? Were they not a group of people murdered simply because of who they were? What about Turkey's massacre of more than a million Armenians in 1915? This latter attack had preceded the Nazi era and was therefore not integral to the period of the Holocaust per se, but Hitler's decision to eliminate the Jews was explicitly influenced by the indifference of the world to that bloodbath. He had said so openly: "Who today remembers the Armenians?" he retorted when his ministers voiced fears about international opposition.

Not only had the Turkish government never apologized, but it continued to deny that a genocide had occurred. Even in the 1990s, Turkey lobbied to prevent the Armenian story from being included in the museum displays, including threatening consequences should the president of the United States mention the Armenian connection in his planned speech about the Holocaust memorial. (Carter came up with a compromise that headed off trouble.) Ironically, Israel also refused to acknowledge the genocidal nature of the Armenian slaughter: Israel had a strategic relationship with Turkey.

Few reputable historians were about to deny that what had happened to the Armenian community was an act of genocide according to one of the two definitions of the term originally coined by jurist Raphael Lemkin in 1943. Lemkin spoke of "genocide" as the planned annihilation of a people, but he also described it as a progressive process, as a "co-ordinated plan of different actions aiming at the destruction of the essential foundations of the life of national groups, with the aim of annihilating the groups themselves." The Armenian-American community wanted recognition of its history, but some members of council worried that including the Armenian story might open the door to recognizing other tragedies, such as the ravages of Pol Pot in Cambodia, or the massacres of North American Indians. The question was, Who is "in" and who is "out"? Where were the boundaries to be drawn?

According to Edward Linenthal, the Roma-Sinti did not figure in the commission's thinking until the mid-1980s, when persons from that community began to complain that they too had been victims of genocide, and that they should have a seat on the council determining the future shape of the museum. Wiesel and other council members assured the Roma-Sinti representatives that their absence to that point was an oversight and that they would be included. (They were, in 1987, but the delegate was still so angry that he immediately charged the council with "overt racism" for its previous inattention to his community.) Relations did improve over the years, and the council and the museum staff were careful to include the poorly known Roma-Sinti story in the museum narrative.

From Erna Paris, *Long Shadows: Truth, Lies and History* (New York: Bloomsbury, 2002) 333–345. Reprinted with permission.

Polish and Ukrainian Americans also fought for inclusion—in discussions that were exceptionally harrowing for Jewish survivors, who were upset at the prospect of sharing Holocaust memorial space with national groups, some of whose members had collaborated with the Nazis in their destruction. Although Poles and Slavs were marked as *Untermenschen* and destroyed in the millions, and although they might eventually have been designated for all-out genocidal slaughter, no blanket decision was ever taken, possibly because the war ended before things reached that point. All the same, Auschwitz was geographically located in Poland, and it had been the main concentration camp for the occupied Polish territories, the Polish underground and the Polish intelligentsia. Two generations of Poles had memorialized Auschwitz as Catholics, just as generations of Jews memorialized it as Jews. The death camp had emerged as a shared memory space where both groups remembered the past and tried to understand the present. Given this interlocking history, much of it painful, it is not surprising that there were bitter battles on the Holocaust Museum planning committee—in spite of goodwill and general civility.

Some scholars of the Holocaust were uncomfortable with the trans-historical implications of "uniqueness." In his book *The Holocaust in History*, Michael Marrus suggests that it might be more to the point to claim that the Holocaust was unprecedented. "With this we are on more familiar historical terrain [although] to be sure we are speaking in relative terms," he wrote. "No event occurs without antecedents, and few would assert that there were no preceding instances of massacre or anti-Jewish persecution that bear a relationship to the murder of European Jewry. The real question is: How much of a break with the past is this particular event?"

Raul Hilberg was even more direct when we met at his home in Burlington. "For me the Holocaust was a vast, single event, but I am never going to use the word *unique* because I recognize that when one starts breaking it into pieces, which is my trade, one finds completely recognizable, ordinary ingredients that are common to other situations, such as Rwanda or Cambodia and possibly many others I have not examined. In the final analysis, it depends whether we want to emphasize the commonality with other events, or the holistic totality—in which case the Holocaust stands by itself. But I consider the latter perilous. Do we want one Rwanda after the other? You know, when a group of Tutsis sits around and watches a neighbouring village burn, when they say, 'Well, that's them, it's not going to happen to us,' they are repeating the history of the Dutch Jews who, when they heard about the Holocaust in Poland, said, 'This is the Netherlands; it can never happen here.' They are also repeating the words of the Germans in 1096 when they heard what the crusaders were doing in France. It is staggering to draw that line through the centuries and look at the sameness of language. You have to say, 'Wait a minute, what's going on? Should we not look at this? Of course we should.' The alternative is to see the Holocaust as outside of history, as not part of anything. And it is impossible to learn from something that is so apart."

On April 22, 1993, the day the Holocaust Museum finally opened, there were ironies aplenty. Another catastrophe was unfolding in Europe, this time in Bosnia, although Western governments had taken care not to use the *genocide* word, which might compel them to intercede according to the UN Charter, the Geneva Conventions and the Genocide Convention of 1948, all of which had come into being as a result of the Holocaust.

Bill Clinton, by then president of the United States, officiated at the dedication. During the election campaign of 1992, he had solemnly declared that American air power would intervene to end the Bosnian conflict. Nothing happened.

Now, as helpless civilians were again being slaughtered across the sea, the president gravely intoned, "Never again," instantly stripping the pregnant words of their moral meaning. The late Croatian president Franjo Tudjman also was present, he who was party, at that moment, to the ruthless ethnic massacres taking place in Bosnia, he who had cast persistent public doubt on the historical truth of the Holocaust. Back in 1988, Tudjman had written: "The estimated loss of up to six million [Jewish] dead is founded … on exaggerated data in the postwar reckoning of war crimes and on the squaring of accounts with the defeated." (His personal calculations suggested to him that approximately 900,000 Jews might have perished during the Second World War.)

"Tudjman's presence in the midst of survivors is a disgrace," fumed Elie Wiesel, the only person to call attention to the tragedy currently unfolding in Bosnia. "As a Jew I am saying that we must do something to stop the bloodshed in that country," he said to President Clinton before the assembled microphones. "People fight one another and children die. Why? Something, anything, must be done." Clinton was not amused, but he should not have been surprised: Elie Wiesel had written almost identical words about the Holocaust thirty years earlier, in a *Commentary* article on the Eichmann trial. ("Someone should have stopped it. There must have been something they could have done!") And it was Elie Wiesel, the survivor, who had dared to confront Ronald Reagan in 1985 as the president prepared to travel to West Germany to stand beside Chancellor Kohl at the military cemetery of Bitburg, where Waffen-SS soldiers were also buried. No president in postwar America had made the need for a Holocaust museum more transparently clear than Reagan, whose ahistorical understanding of reconciliation involved "putting the past behind him," as he expressed it, without a just appreciation of who was who or what they should be remembered for. It was moral confusion of this

kind that had made a museum to teach the "lessons" of the Holocaust necessary.

Eight years and two presidents later, Wiesel continued on with his prepared text. He said, "We have learned that though the Holocaust was principally a Jewish tragedy, its implications are universal… We have learned that whatever happens to one community, ultimately affects all others."

But had "we" really learned anything at all, I asked myself when I read his words. A museum to the memory of the Holocaust was, and is, a wonderful thing, but if it cannot affect foreign policy at the moment of its dedication, when a new genocide is raging, there are grounds for despair.

"When Sarajevo was surrounded in April 1992, I couldn't work for a week. I said to myself, How the hell can we be building a museum when the same thing is happening over there? We blame people everywhere for not doing anything during the Holocaust and we are just sitting here!" Now director of education, Joan Ringelheim had been on staff at the museum since 1989, starting as head of research. When she arrived on the planning committee, the storyline for the exhibition had already been decided upon: her job was to find the appropriate secondary sources for the designers of each segment. Later on, she produced a section called "Voices from Auschwitz" by editing 130 interviews with survivors and weaving them into a rich quilt of storytelling.

Ringelheim's father lost his entire family in the Holocaust, and she was deeply, personally, involved, but the tension she experienced in April 1992 was too much. "I thought about quitting, but what then?" she says as we talk in her Washington office. "I asked myself, What do I have the power to do?"

In 1996, she was invited to Sarajevo to give a lecture about the U.S. Holocaust Memorial Museum. She tells me she felt unnerved: what could she possibly say to Bosnians who were suffering while she and other Americans were building a museum to an earlier human disaster? While her government dithered and did nothing to help? She went anyway—talked about memory and survival and whether, finally, it does any good to remember when people seem never to learn.

"Does that question still trouble you?" I ask her quietly as we talk together in her Washington office.

"I ask myself that all the time," she replies. "I have only one answer, and it doesn't really bring much comfort, and that is that it is impossible to live without memory; it is the only way we can live. Hannah Arendt once said something about stories. You tell them, you repeat them, because you don't know what the effect will be. Because you don't know whether people learn or not, you have to keep doing it—just in case they do."

She used to be a philosophy teacher, but against the background of her father's survival and the loss of the rest of his family, there was only one thing she wanted to teach: racism and anti-Semitism. "It was also because I grew up in this country in the 1950s and 1960s and saw what happened here with the life-and-death struggle for civil rights. All of it came together in my mind. In 1968, I made up an undergraduate college course called 'Prejudice and Oppression.' We read books on ethics, the philosophy of language, the philosophy of history and the psychology of the prejudiced personality—and I have to say that I have often felt strange working here at the Holocaust Museum when there is not a memorial to slavery in this country. At one time, I hoped that the fact that we exist would push that idea into the forefront. But that hasn't happened."

Her office is filled with the works of Hannah Arendt. "Why is she so important to you?" I ask.

"When I first read Arendt—it was her *New Yorker* piece on Eichmann in Jerusalem in 1963—I was furious at her, like all sorts of other people. But it must have been 1974 or 1975 when a friend said, 'I don't know why you are not rereading her. She is the only twentieth-century philosopher the centre of whose work is the Holocaust.' I had never thought about that. I started reading her, then I began teaching her. I became completely captivated—everything she writes fills the empty space. She is like a mystery writer; I never know quite where she is going. She has a huge richness."

I look at this woman I have just met as at an old friend: I too have been captivated by Arendt's probing explorations of history and prejudice.

Between 1993 and 1999, over eleven million people visited the Holocaust Memorial Museum, including thirty-one thousand school tours. Most were under fifty—born after the war. Although many people initially made special trips to Washington, by the end of the decade the museum was on the itinerary of ordinary tourists who happened to be visiting the capital, the vast majority of whom were non-Jews.

It is hard to imagine anyone entering this powerful place without adequate preparation, for the Holocaust Museum is, without a doubt, one of the most disturbing galleries in the world. It is also one of the most magnificently realized, from its unsettling architecture to the immediacy of the information and emotion it conveys. The architecture is especially remarkable when one considers the conditions under which the architect was working: how, for example, was any professional to design a building meant to represent what Elie Wiesel called the unrepresentable?

After visiting the Auschwitz death camp, James Ingo Freed decided that his design would have to be "expressive of the event," but he was not without reservations. In an interview with *Assemblage* magazine, he acknowledged his problem: "I have to make a building that allows for horror, sadness. I don't know if you can make a building that does this, if you can make an architecture of sensibility." Somehow he succeeded. The result is a self-contained, textured environment of raw materials—brick, steel beams, glass, concrete—and a design that bewilders as we are led into surprising dead-end angles that require us to stop and question where the next step will lead—just as the victims of Nazi terror were disoriented by incoherence and disruption at every turn. The architectural critic Jim Murphy has called Freed's work "the most emotionally powerful architectural event most of us will ever experience."

In the name of memory, the Holocaust Museum is carrying me closer to the awful nature of the experience than most museums would attempt, or desire. ("I've heard people on the street saying, 'I'm going to the Holocaust,'" Joan Ringelheim had complained. "They're *not* going to the Holocaust, they are going to a museum!") A guide offers me a card with the name of a real person of my own sex and information about what happened to her. I am being asked to identify at a vicarious, personal level. I enter a bare steel elevator of a style common in Germany around 1940: it removes me from the everyday world of the main-floor lobby and deposits me in a dimly lit place in front of videos depicting the encounter of American soldiers with Dachau in April 1945. The ceiling here is low and oppressive. It is very quiet. Although there seem to be hundreds of people in this place, there is little noise other than the sounds of shuffling feet as I move through angled, jagged space.

The displays are contextualized with the architecture; the immediacy is startling. To begin with, the "closeness" to the event. At the groundbreaking ceremony on October 16, 1985, the soil of the Washington Mall was ritualistically mixed with soil brought from concentration camps, so the site itself was "sanctified" with an authentic reminder of the dead. Cobblestones from the original Warsaw Ghetto pave a section of the museum floor, and

under a light sits the milk can in which young Emmanuel Ringelblum buried his extraordinary archives of ghetto life (the can was preserved to resemble the way it looked when first excavated from the streets of the city in 1950). Faded, striped concentration-camp uniforms of all sizes, donated by survivors, hang behind a gated prison-like fence.

A bridge connects to another part of the exhibition. Isolated spotlights beam from the ceiling; there is a looming suggestion of watchtowers. This astonishing architect has built a facsimile of a Nazi concentration camp at the heart of America. Then another room, where a cast of the original door of the Łódź ghetto hospital graphically illustrates an accompanying written description: I am informed that on September 1, 1942, all the patients were pulled out through this very door and deported.

An original stained-glass window from the synagogue in Kraków lines part of one wall, near the wrought-iron gate to the old Jewish cemetery in Tarnów, southern Poland. Finally, I stare at one of the carts that carried away the bodies of people who died overnight of disease and starvation at Theresienstadt.

On the floor lie pieces of the railway track that once led into the Treblinka camp near Warsaw, where an estimated 750,000 people were murdered between July 1942 and October 1943. And on these tracks stands a German freight car of the type that was used for human transports. The path of the museum visit leads the visitor into and through the rail car (although it is possible to detour around this experience). I steel myself to enter this symbolically evocative space. Inside is still air and quiet emptiness: open-ended, porous, poised for imaginative understanding. Here, disconnected for a moment, I pause at the heart of the genocidal process: the transport of millions of people from a known world to oblivion.

All these artifacts were collected in Europe by alert museum personnel—located in remote places, dug up or donated by established memory sites such as Auschwitz. Some of the material caused problems for those survivors who subscribed to the idea that the Holocaust is atemporal and holy. From the State Museum at Auschwitz came a mountain of objects, among them toothbrushes, suitcases marked with the names of their owners, shoes (the stylishly strapped women's shoes from the 1940s piled haphazardly with the rest are a startling reminder of the sophisticated life their owners once lived), discarded Zyklon-B cans (another difficult sight) and umbrellas. But Joan Ringelheim had told me that nothing caused more turmoil among staff and council members than nine kilograms of human hair. (Hair shorn from victims was sold to German factories for fifty pfennigs a kilo to make socks for U-boat crews and industrial felt, among other things, and when Auschwitz was liberated by the Russians, they found seven thousand kilos stockpiled for future use.) Some people thought the hair and its uses exposed the utter dehumanization of the victims, but there was concern about the boundaries of acceptable taste, especially about displaying relics from what were once living bodies outside the place where the deed was done—that is, Auschwitz itself. Expressions like "defilement," "an offence to the dead" and "inherent sacredness" found new voice. Others, including many survivors, disagreed. A Jewish religious authority offered his assurance that hair, as such, was never "alive," in that it had never contained living human cells. Ringelheim argued that a display of hair would bring needed attention to what had happened to women.

"Initially I didn't want anything taken from the site, but then I thought that if we were going to do it, we should do it right," she told me when we spoke together in her office. She recalled the committee meeting of February 13, 1990, as "volatile" and "horrific." "One of the women survivors said, 'I don't want to go in there and see my own mother's hair!' Someone else screamed at her, 'It doesn't matter what you think! This exhibition is not for you

or for me, but for the public!' There were about twenty-five or thirty people present and the room was pounding with emotion. A man said, 'Well, we wouldn't show a rape and this is like a rape.' That was when I joined in. I think I screamed something like, 'Every woman in this room knows what the difference is between getting their hair shaved and a rape!' It was just too vile. I remember saying that I didn't think the hair should have been taken out of Auschwitz or any historical site, but since it was here, no picture could substitute for the real thing. I said, 'It's not insulting, it's disgusting, but the whole Holocaust is disgusting, so if you want to portray it honestly, this will be an important part of what people remember.' "

There was a vote and the decision was to display the hair, but then, said Ringelheim, something strange happened: two female survivors went privately to the director, and the decision to exhibit the hair was quietly reversed. (The museum now displays a picture of the hair.) Almost a decade later, she still wasn't sure why the hair issue became so terribly volatile, but she did think it was an example of the moral authority of the survivors over everyone who had not shared that experience of pain, be they historians, curators or even rabbinical authorities.

After the hair incident, great care was necessary, for it had been made clear that mistakes in judgment would not be simple errors but a desecration of memory. No one put this more clearly than Menachem Rosensaft, the founding chairman of the International Network of Children of Jewish Holocaust Survivors, when he warned, "Anyone who casts aspersions on their [the victims'] memory somehow participates retroactively in their murder." Since such defamation could be unintentional, everyone involved in planning and implementation was implicitly enjoined to watch themselves carefully lest they inadvertently assassinate the dead a second time.

I don't appreciate such censoring threats, but I do understand the hostility. Listening to

Joan Ringelheim, then walking through the museum, I, too, have mixed feelings about displaying artifacts from Auschwitz. I know rationally that there would be no museums anywhere in the world if objects were not removed from their original environments, but remnants from the murder of millions cast a special shadow. I remember how angrily I reacted to two of the museums I visited in Germany: the "Jewish Section" of the museum of Rothenburg ob der Tauber, where old gravestones were exhibits and the "Holocaust" referred to a medieval pogrom; and the strange collection in the Protestant church of Jebenhausen, where neighbours had collected the religious and personal objects that lay scattered over the road after a Nazi roundup of the local Jews and made a "museum" of them, with curatorial explanations. There may be no other way to salvage memory after the fact, but some artifacts do seem more questionable than others.

In the Holocaust Museum, as in Yad Vashem, the aerial photo of the Auschwitz installations and the Allied decision not to bomb once again receive prominent billing. The last lines of the display text (in which the assistant secretary of war John J. McCloy is faulted) ground the memory firmly: "At the very least [bombing] would have demonstrated Allied concern about the fate of the Jews."

The memory to be retained is that America abandoned the Jews of Europe.

During the museum planning stages, Jewish wartime resistance was once again a touchy topic. Menachem Rosensaft thought that the idea that Jews had gone "like sheep to the slaughter" was a calumny in the ever-expanding category of defiling the dead. Heated debate was inevitable. How to define *resistance?* Conventional wisdom held it to be physical rebellion, as in the Warsaw Ghetto or among the partisans, but it was always possible to include "spiritual" resistance. Was prayer resistance? Was managing to remember the sabbath while in Auschwitz resistance? Were brave, possibly dangerous, acts of unselfishness, such as sharing a morsel of bread, resistance? Many had argued that the latter *were* acts of resistance, including the Israeli historian Yehuda Bauer, who wrote that resistance is "any *group* action consciously taken in opposition to known or surmised laws, actions, or intentions directed against the Jews by the Germans and their supporters."

The debate has not been resolved, but I note that the Holocaust Museum has downplayed unsafe subjects. "If the museum was uncontroversial when it opened, I think it was because we did not tackle most of the disputes in a contentious way," explained Ringelheim. "We could have taken a tack that would fit one community's interests over another, but we did it in a more distanced way. And I think it was the right decision."

The story of the Warsaw uprising is appropriately present (the rebellion gets an entire wall), as are other instances of resistance, but Ringelheim's "survivor voices" in the audio theatre are notably low-key. The men and women whose stories intertwine and overlap speak about brutality, fright, hunger, exhaustion, squalor and the terror of separation. Their responses are recognizably human, not unrecognizably heroic; their focus is on the everlasting need to bear witness.

The sensitive topic of collaboration is also passed over lightly. A relatively small section describes the quandary of the Nazi-installed ghetto leaders and explains their involvement. Since it would have been grossly inappropriate to use language that identified these elders with the murderous partnership of a certain number of Estonians, Ukrainians, Lithuanians and other occupied Eastern Europeans who voluntarily joined the SS in its massive killing operations, the perilous *c* word is never used in the museum displays. The Eastern Europeans are described as "accomplices," and the text and Nazi-photographed films of their contribution to the German enterprise are screened behind a low wooden barrier that offers the visitor the choice of forgoing that part of the exhibition.

A section on one wall details the suffering of the Poles. Homosexuals, until recently underresearched in Holocaust studies, are also given their due. The Armenian genocide gets a mention. No one has been entirely left out, although constituencies may well have been displeased at the wall space they managed to obtain.

Finally, since this is an American museum on the Washington Mall, the exhibition ends, as it began, with the role of U.S. liberators. With videos and testimonials. And walls upon walls covered with the names of Righteous Gentiles who took great personal risks. (By 2000, sixteen thousand such persons had been honoured by Yad Vashem.) It is proper to esteem these men and women of character, but in doing so the U.S. Holocaust Memorial Museum has, like Yad Vashem, shifted the collective memory of the "catastrophe" (*shoah*)—a plain, undoctored word—to one that favours heroism. Is this one more triumph of a "feel-good ending"? Sixteen thousand rescuers? Out of how many hundreds of million people in the countries of Nazi-occupied Europe?

The background thinking is apparent in a form letter soliciting funds for museum membership, an American institution appealing to Americans in upbeat, Hollywood-hyped language: "Finally, when breaking hearts can bear it no longer, visitors will emerge into the light—into a celebration of resistance, rebirth, and renewal for the survivors—whether they remained in Europe, or as so many did, went to Israel or America to rebuild their lives. And having witnessed the nightmare of evil, the great American monuments to democracy that surround each departing visitor will take on new meaning, as will the ideal for which they stand."

Like Yad Vashem, the U.S. Holocaust Memorial Museum directs the visitor to understand the event it portrays in an acceptably politicized manner: this is the "happy ending"

that will enable Americans to leave one of the world's most demanding exhibitions without losing faith in the future. The planners have been successful: on exiting, 90 per cent of people replying to a questionnaire have given the museum an eight- to ten-point rating on a scale of ten. Fifty per cent have ranked their visit ten out of ten.

Would an exhibit devoted to the dark night of the Holocaust have attracted such praise if it did not meet American cultural needs, I ask myself. A question to speculate on—for historical memory is shaped from just such choices.

Near the exit I see a book of visitors' comments. A teenage girl is signing in. I line up behind her and look at what she has written. In a large, childlike, loopy handwriting she wrote: "Is this planet doomed? Is everyone mean? What will happen? Is everybody evil? Can we at least stop fighting each other? Who knows all the answers to my questions? Who knows …" Her dots trail off into despair.

As I leave the building, I see her sitting on a step, bent over, with her head hanging down between her knees. I want to protect her, but something stops me from approaching. Although I am decades older and far more informed, I wonder what I can possibly say to ease this moment of her encounter with history. Her grief is not an irrational response.

The sunlight, the bracing air of this February day and every step I take back into the welcome bustle of contemporary Washington reminds me that more than fifty years have passed and that the century that witnessed the horror I have just "visited" is almost done. But the sorrow of the child on the steps stays with me. I think to myself that attributions of "holiness" and the claim that the past is "unrepresentable" and the private domain of those who survived lead away from understanding, and that understanding is the road this child, and her generation, needs to travel. I think to myself that the "lessons" of the Holocaust are, first of all, historical—having to do with the Jews—but then also universal, having to do with the impulse to genocide. What happens to human beings when they are subjected to propaganda that consistently dehumanizes an "enemy"? What happens when the highest authorities and elites of a land call for the persecution of a minority? What happens when law is "illegal" in a moral sense, as the Nuremberg Tribunal declared? What happens when good people say and do nothing?

I think that to try to understand—however tentatively, however gropingly—is a part of my own continuing quest.

QUESTIONS TO CONSIDER

1. Invoking "Never forget," during the process of constructing a museum to the memory of the Holocaust, creates a conundrum: Are the Romani and Armenians forgotten?

2. President Bill Clinton dedicated the Holocaust Museum to the consternation of Elie Wiesel. Why?

3. How did the decision to not display hair become a metaphor for sensitivity?

4. Do you agree with the author that "like Yad Vashem, the U.S. Holocaust Memorial Museum directs the visitor to understand the event it portrays in an acceptably politicized manner …"?

MAKING CONNECTIONS

1. How was Hitler's Holocaust different from the Turkish Armenian genocide?

2. Was the "Final Solution" fundamentally different from "dekulakization"?

3. How readily do American Indian reservations fit into Anne Applebaum's analysis? How similar are Hitler's concentration camps and American Indian reservations?

✔ RECOMMENDED RESOURCES

Bauer, Yehuda. *Rethinking the Holocaust.* New Haven, CT: Yale University Press, 2001.

Dwork, Deborah, and Robert Jan van Pelt. *Holocaust: A History.* New York: W. W. Norton & Company, 2002.

Hogan, David J., ed. *The Holocaust Chronicle: A History in Words and Pictures.* Lincolnwood, IL: Publications International, 2000.

Rosenbaum, Alan S., ed. *Is the Holocaust Unique? Perspectives on Comparative Genocide.* Boulder, CO: Westview Press, 1998.

Yahil, Leni. *The Holocaust: The Fate of European Jewry.* New York: Oxford University Press, 1987.

CHAPTER 6

MYTHS AND HISTORY: MANCHURIA

Many countries sanitize the teaching of less-than-glorious episodes from the past. South Africa, for example, explained past treatment of blacks in terms of white racial superiority. American texts softened the horror of slavery and the destruction of indigenous peoples. Japan refused to account for its brutal invasion and occupation of Manchuria from the early 1930s to 1945. Saburo Ienaga wrote a textbook in the 1960s that discussed some of Japan's wartime atrocities. In 1965, he sued to keep his text from censorship. He did not win his case until 1997, but Japan's Supreme Court ruled that the Education Ministry could continue to censor the text in an "appropriate" manner.

The historical amnesia for the invasion of Manchuria was not confined to Japan. After 1949, neither the People's Republic of China nor the Republic of China and Taiwan pushed Japan for acknowledgment of the atrocities because both hoped for favorable trade arrangements with Japan. Though books have documented the Nanking atrocities, it took a 1997 book, *The Rape of Nanking: The Forgotten Holocaust of World War II*, by Iris Chang, to shock historians into greater scrutiny of Japan's past. Chang wrote in her epilogue:

> Japan carries not only the legal obligation to acknowledge the evil it perpetuated at Nanking. At a minimum, the Japanese government needs to issue an official apology to the victims, pay reparations to the people whose lives were destroyed in the rampage, and, most important, educate future generations of Japanese citizens about the true facts of the massacre.

The reading that follows is a summary of her work.

The depredations by the Japanese army in Nanking do not stand alone. Andrew J. Swanger describes atrocities undertaken by another professional element of Japanese society. His article "Japanese Scientists Conducted Biological Research Experiments on Human Subjects in the Isolated Region of Manchuria," concludes this chapter.

The "Rape of Nanking"

Freelance writer

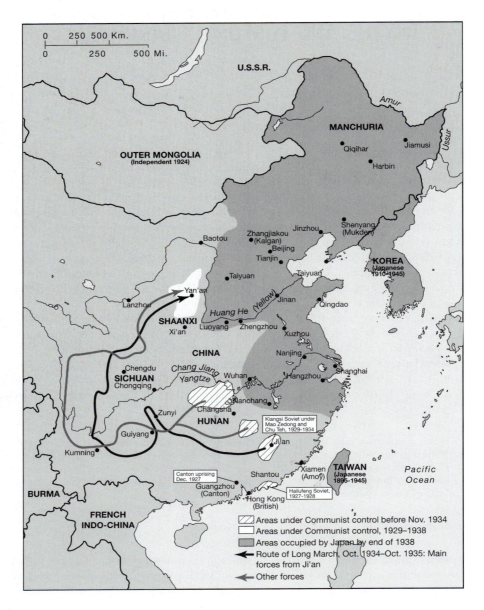

From "The 'Rape of Nanking,'" *The Bill of Rights in Action* 18(3) (Summer 2002): 5–8, by permission of the Constitutional Rights Foundation, 610 South Kingsley Drive, Los Angeles, CA 90005.

At the beginning of World War II, Japanese soldiers committed many atrocities against POWs and civilians in Nanking, China. After the war, a war crimes trial focused on who was responsible for these acts.

For much of human history, the idea of "war crimes" did not exist. Victorious armies often slaughtered defeated enemy soldiers and civilians as well. About a hundred years ago, however, most major nations in the world began to agree on certain "rules of war."

In 1899 and 1907, at a city called The Hague in the Netherlands, the world powers agreed to prohibit the killing or mistreatment of prisoners of war and civilians. In effect, these Hague Conventions made it illegal under international law for soldiers and their commanding officers to carry out acts that came to be called "war crimes."

Japan was one of the nations that signed and ratified the Hague Conventions. Japan was fast becoming a modern and industrialized country with a military force patterned after those of Europe. Following the example of European colonial powers, Japan went to war against China in 1894 to gain control of some Chinese trading ports. In 1905, Japan defeated Russia in a war over possession of ports in the Chinese territory of Manchuria. It was the first Asian nation to defeat a European power.

By the early 1930s, Japanese military and political leaders believed that it was Japan's destiny to acquire China. They thought that Japan's economic survival depended on control of Chinese agricultural lands and other resources.

Meanwhile in China, revolutionaries had overthrown the last emperor and were trying to unify the country under the leadership of Chiang Kai-shek. The Japanese viewed these events as a threat to their plans for dominating China as a colony. In response, Japan seized all of Manchuria in 1931.

In 1937, two years before Hitler started World War II in Europe, and four years before Japan attacked Pearl Harbor, the Japanese launched another invasion of Chinese territory. This time, they occupied the Chinese capital city, Peking (now spelled Beijing). In addition, they sent a major force to attack Shanghai, China's largest city (located near the mouth of the Yangtze River).

Outside Shanghai, the Japanese, under the command of General Matsui Iwane, met heavy resistance from Chiang Kai-shek's army. The battle raged on for several months, killing thousands on both sides. Finally, in early November 1937, Chiang ordered his army to retreat 250 miles inland along the Yangtze River to Nanking (now spelled Nanjing), the new Chinese capital. General Matsui's troops pursued the Chinese, who soon began to flee in panic.

Although Matsui issued orders forbidding mistreatment of the Chinese people, Japanese soldiers felt vengeful. They had endured fierce fighting in the battle for Shanghai. Japanese troops executed many Chinese soldiers who had surrendered. They also killed draft-age men, whom they suspected of being enemy soldiers disguised as civilians. Because the Japanese military high command in Tokyo had failed to establish an adequate supply system for their troops, soldiers began stealing food from the countryside. This led to further abuses of Chinese civilians.

THE FALL OF NANKING

As Japanese troops moved closer to Nanking, Chiang Kai-shek, Chinese government officials, and many civilians left the city. Chiang, however, ordered his generals and about 100,000 soldiers to remain and defend the Chinese capital.

In early December 1937, Japanese air strikes and artillery bombarded Nanking. In battles outside the city, Chinese troops proved no match for the Japanese.

The Japanese demanded that if the Chinese did not surrender Nanking, "all the horrors of war will be let loose." Chiang Kai-shek refused to permit the surrender of the capital, but finally ordered the defenders to evacuate. Panic gripped the city. Chinese soldiers and civilians desperately tried to flee Nanking before the Japanese arrived.

When the Japanese surrounded Nanking on December 12, they trapped tens of thousands of Chinese soldiers and about 200,000 civilians in the city. Although most foreigners had fled Nanking, a group of about 25 American and European businessmen, doctors, nurses, college professors, and Christian missionaries remained. In the weeks leading up to the fall of Nanking, they formed a committee to organize a two square mile "International Safety Zone" within the city.

The purpose of the Safety Zone was to shelter and protect the Chinese civilians still living in Nanking. The Safety Zone Committee elected an unlikely leader—John Rabe. He was a German businessman who also headed the Nazi Party in Nanking. Even so, Rabe worked tirelessly and put his life in danger to shelter and save the lives of many Chinese.

When Japanese troops finally marched into Nanking on December 13, 1937, thousands of civilians crowded into the Safety Zone. The Safety Zone Committee decided to also admit stranded Chinese soldiers. The Japanese never fully agreed to honor the Safety Zone, but allowed the committee of foreigners to feed and house the people seeking refuge there.

THE EXECUTION OF POWS

Thousands of Chinese soldiers had surrendered before the Japanese entered Nanking. Once in the city, Japanese troops rounded up any Chinese soldiers they found in house-to-house searches and in the Safety Zone.

Since defeated Chinese soldiers often exchanged their military uniforms for civilian clothes, the Japanese also arrested many draft-age males not in uniform. Undoubtedly, this group included many civilians—policemen, firemen, city employees, hospital workers, servants, and others.

The Japanese faced the problem of what to do with these POWs (prisoners of war). A feeling of vengeance against the Chinese ran strong among Japanese troops. The Japanese had difficulty feeding their own soldiers, let alone tens of thousands of Chinese POWs. The Japanese also saw the POWs as a security risk. They didn't have a camp to hold them. They thought the POWs threatened the safety of the Japanese soldiers as well as a planned victory parade in Nanking led by General Matsui.

The Japanese army had no clear POW policy. Division commanders in Nanking took matters into their own hands and ordered the execution of the POWs under their control. The Japanese shot some by firing squad and bayoneted others to death. In some cases, the Japanese lined up POWs in groups from 100–200 on the banks of the Yangtze and machine-gunned them. Some Japanese officers used their swords to behead POWs.

About 40,000 Chinese POWs and civilian draft-age men probably perished within a week or so. The Japanese had committed the first major war crimes of World War II. But the worst was yet to come.

"CASES OF DISORDER"

Atrocities (brutal acts) against the people of Nanking began as soon as Japanese troops entered the city. Unlike the POW executions ordered by Japanese army division commanders, most atrocities against Nanking's civilians were criminal acts done by undisciplined soldiers.

Japanese soldiers beat people, robbed them at gunpoint, and murdered them almost randomly. The soldiers stabbed people with bayonets, mutilated them with knives, and even ran over them with tanks. The soldiers vandalized, looted, and burned public buildings and private homes. They even destroyed animals for no reason.

For more than a month, Japanese soldiers roamed the city hunting for women to rape. The soldiers raped women and girls on the street, in stores, and in homes before horrified family members. The victims ranged in age from 10 to over 60. Even pregnant women were sexually assaulted. Gang rapes and kidnappings for the purpose of rape occurred. Raped women were sometimes mutilated or killed. The rapists killed children and even infants simply because they got in the way. Japanese soldiers frequently invaded the International Safety Zone in search of women. On several occasions, John Rabe, the leader of the Safety Zone Committee, stopped sexual assaults by displaying his Nazi swastika armband. The soldiers did not want to get into trouble with a country that they knew was a friend of Japan.

During the weeks of terror in Nanking, the Safety Zone Committee sent letters and eyewitness reports of the atrocities to Japanese diplomats, hoping they could stop the rampaging soldiers. Called "Cases of Disorder," these reports detailed what was happening to the people of Nanking.

The Safety Zone Committee recorded this account of a case that took place on January 15, 1938:

> Many Japanese soldiers arrived [at a Chinese temple], round[ed] up all the young women, chose 10, and raped them in a room at the temple. Later the same day a very drunken Japanese soldier came, went into one room demanding wine and women. Wine was given, but no girls. Enraged, he started to shoot wildly, killing two young boys, then left … .

WHO WAS RESPONSIBLE?

General Matsui was the overall commander of Japanese military operations in Central China. Headquartered in Shanghai, he did not personally witness the terrible events that unfolded in Nanking. A few days after Japanese forces occupied the Chinese capital, however, Matsui entered the city to lead a victory parade. Learning of the atrocities that Japanese soldiers were committing, he ordered that "Anyone who misconducts himself must be severely punished."

After General Matsui returned to Shanghai, the atrocities against the people continued in Nanking. Army division commanders did little to stop them.

In Shanghai, General Matsui issued new orders, stating that the "honor of the Japanese Army" required punishment for the illegal acts of soldiers. Again, the Japanese commanders in Nanking were unwilling or unable to control their troops. Only after Matsui returned to Nanking in early February 1938, six weeks after the fall of the city, did order and discipline improve among the occupying troops.

Even today, great controversy arises over the number of victims in the "Rape of Nanking." Official Chinese figures put the number of fatalities at 300,000. Some in Japan deny the massacre took place. But today Japanese textbooks, which for years did not mention Nanking, estimate that 200,000 were killed. The latest research indicates that Japanese troops probably killed at least 50,000 to 100,000 POWs and civilian men, women, and children. Many thousands more were rape victims and others who were injured but survived.

Who, then, was responsible for these atrocities?

As they did at Nuremberg, Germany, the victorious Allies conducted war crimes trials in several Asian nations after the war. At Nanking, a war crimes tribunal convicted and hanged three Japanese army lieutenants for beheading hundreds of Chinese POWs. The Nanking tribunal also tried and executed one Japanese general who commanded troops in Nanking.

In Tokyo, more than two dozen Japanese political and military leaders also faced a war crimes tribunal. General Matsui was indicted for "deliberately and recklessly" ignoring his legal duty "to take adequate steps to secure the observance and prevent breaches" of the laws of war (the Hague Conventions). In his defense,

General Matsui said that he never ordered the POW executions. He also argued that he had directed his army division commanders to discipline their troops for criminal acts, but was not responsible when they failed to do this.

The majority of the judges at the Tokyo tribunal ruled that General Matsui was ultimately responsible for the "orgy of crime" because, "He did nothing, or nothing effective to abate these horrors."

A dissenting judge, Radhabinod Pal from India, disagreed with the majority. He concluded that the commander-in-chief must rely on his subordinate officers to enforce soldier discipline. "The name of Justice," Pal wrote in his dissent, "should not be allowed to be invoked only for ... vindictive retaliation." American military authorities hanged General Matsui on December 27, 1948.

QUESTIONS TO CONSIDER

1. Do you agree or disagree that there should be international laws to punish persons for committing "war crimes"? Why?

2. Who do you think was responsible for the Nanking war crimes? Why?

3. Do you agree or disagree with the conviction and execution of General Matsui? Why?

Japanese Scientists Conducted Biological Research Experiments on Human Subjects in the Isolated Region of Manchuria

Andrew J. Swanger,

The history of Unit 731—a story of medical science perverted by the Japanese during World War II—has rarely been brought to the attention of the Western world. Even today, most Japanese are largely unaware of the horrible experiments performed by their own scientists during the war.

The Japanese are not alone in their reluctance to own up to the cold truth about Unit 731. The U.S. government actively, if somewhat unwillingly, helped to downplay the horror surrounding a group that once hid its darker purpose under an innocuous title—the Kwantung Army Epidemic Prevention and Water Supply Unit. Just as German scientists and Intelligence operatives with Nazi backgrounds were brought to the United States under the aegis of Operation Paperclip and the Gehlen Organization, many of the individuals involved in the bacteriological and chemical experiments conducted by the Japanese in the secluded depths of Manchuria later found sanctuary in the West.

Unit 731 was the brainchild of one man, Shiro Ishii. Born June 25, 1892, in the village of Kama in Chiba Prefecture, east of Tokyo,

From Andrew J. Swanger, "Japanese Scientists Conducted Biological Research Experiments on Human Subjects in the Isolated Region of Manchuria," *World War II* 13(2) (July 1998): 62–66. Reprinted with permission.

Shiro was the fourth son of a rich and respected land-owning family. Extremely intelligent and fiercely nationalistic, he attended Kyoto Imperial University (KIU) and graduated with a degree in medicine. Afterward, he enlisted in the Imperial Guards as an army surgeon and, in 1922, was attached to the 1st Army Hospital in Tokyo. In 1924, he resumed to KIU for postgraduate studies in bacteriology, serology, preventive medicine and pathology, and in 1927 he resumed to earn his doctorate.

In April 1928, the army sent Ishii—by then a major—on a two-year, 30-nation world study trip, with stops in Russia, the United States, France and Germany. On his return, he presented his superiors with a somewhat exaggerated account of Western interest in biological warfare research. Ishii found a receptive audience in Colonel Chikahiko Koizumi, the army's surgeon general and later Japanese health minister. Colonel Koizumi's imagination was fired by the enthusiasm Ishii displayed for biological warfare. Koizumi believed that Ishii's proposal for a vigorous program to research offensive biological weapons would give the much maligned Surgeons' Corps a military role and allow Koizumi to capitalize on the glory of war. From then on, Koizumi and a coterie of sympathetic officers gave Ishii's research top priority.

Ishii was posted as a daytime instructor at the Army Medical College. At night he pursued his true interest—secret biological warfare research. At Ishii's insistence, the Epidemic Prevention Lab was constructed on the medical college grounds, ostensibly to provide vaccines for Japanese troops.

By 1934 the prestige of the Army Medical Bureau was rising, and Ishii's main benefactor, Koizumi, had been promoted to lieutenant general and named the army's chief surgeon. Koizumi used his authority to have a facility set up in Manchuria where Ishii could continue his secret work at a more remote and secure location.

Manchuria was the perfect place for such experimentation. The Japanese had enjoyed special privileges there since the end of the 1904–1905 Russo-Japanese War, and their position was strengthened with the fall of the Manchu dynasty in 1911. On March 1, 1932, the sovereign state of Manchukuo was declared, complete with puppet emperor. The Japanese Kwantung army was the real power, however, and its officials completely ignored any weak protests from the Chinese nationalist government.

Ishii's first Manchurian efforts began at Harbin, on the eastern banks of the Sungari River. Harbin was far from any disapproving eyes. Ishii's research had reached the point where human experimentation was crucial to the continued success of his work. He needed subjects in decent health, of both sexes and all ages.

Ishii was supplied with Russian and Chinese test subjects by the Kenpeitai, the Japanese secret police. The subjects were initially held in the basement of the Harbin Japanese Consulate before being taken to the center of Ishii's research, a renovated soy sauce distillery located outside Harbin. The converted distillery was code-named "Togo Unit" in honor of the famous strategist and admiral who defeated the Russians in the celebrated naval battle at Tsushima in 1905. The Harbin facilities also began to be referred to as the Kwantung Army Epidemic Prevention and Water Supply Unit, or Unit 731.

By 1936, the Togo headquarters employed 1,000 people in a two-story building near the Harbin military hospital and the Pinchi-ang Railroad station. By that time, Ishii had built a biological bomb and tested it, but the truly grisly human experimentation that would forever blacken the record of Unit 731 did not begin for another few years.

Ishii often found people interested in helping him with the project. During the 1930s, it was prestigious for a university to have personnel involved in military research for the benefit of the nation. Drawing on the gakubatsu ("old boys' network"), Ishii contacted his college chums and masters. Many on the faculty of Kyoto Imperial University joined him in Manchuria to help pursue his diabolical goals.

The work at Harbin grew so extensive that the city could no longer house the 3,000 personnel involved in Unit 731. In collaboration with his superiors in Tokyo, Ishii had urged the construction of a brand-new, built-to-order complex 24 kilometers to the south, which became known as Pingfan.

The Manchurians living in the villages on the outskirts of the Pingfan site must have been taken aback by the enormous Japanese undertaking in their backyard. Three square kilometers of the Manchurian plain were cut off from the villagers' view behind a dry moat and a wall topped with high-voltage wires. The Pingfan Special Military Zone was a completely self-contained enterprise, employing thousands of the most talented and dedicated Japanese scientists, soldiers and technicians.

The heart of Pingfan was the Ro Block, a large building that concealed two other buildings within an expansive courtyard. Those hidden structures were Blocks 7 and 8, where prisoners were held and the most diabolical experiments were conducted.

The First Division, one of eight sections into which the Pingfan operations were divided, was concerned with the work done in the inner structures of the Ro Block where the lion's share of the ultra-secret bacteriological research on living humans was conducted. The men assigned to the First Division studied various diseases, vectors of transmission (usually rodent or insectile), methods of immunization against the diseases and blood sera research. They also were interested in frostbite, and their work eventually resulted in the production of Labanarin, a drug that increased resistance to cold, which was later dispensed to the Kwantung army.

The Fourth Division, which worked in the outer section of the Ro Block, raised and mass produced the deadly bacteria instrumental to Pingfan's operations. The personnel of the Fourth Division carefully nurtured the diseases isolated by the First Division. At full capacity, it was possible to produce 300 kilograms of plague germs in a month, an amount sufficient to kill hundreds of thousands of people.

The Fourth Division, commanded by Major Tomio Karasawa, was engaged in extremely dangerous business. The men wore hooded anti-disease suits of lightweight, rubberized silk, with heavy rubber overboots. The suit provided complete coverage and freedom of movement, but the excruciating heat produced inside the cramped confines meant that it could be worn for only a few minutes. For higher pay and longer work, some wore less protective clothing—rubber knee boots, aprons, gloves, special goggles and multilayered gauze masks.

The men of the Fourth Division retrieved handcarts loaded with deadly disease cultures from the Bacteria Store, a separate building inside the complex. They would wade through a sterilizing pool of phenol water before reaching the mass cultivators—designed by Ishii himself—on the production line.

While the Fourth Division produced the bacteria and diseases, the Second Division, under Colonel Kiyoshi Ota, used them in warfare research and field experiments. They tested various diseases at Anta, 146 kilometers away from Pingfan in the wild depths of Manchuria. The Heibo 8372 Field Aviation Unit, attached for the express purpose of carrying out the orders of Unit 731, regularly dropped bombs on the Anta sites to test the survivability of the fleas and rats used as disease-spreading agents.

At the workshops of Harbin and Pingfan, bombs 70 to 80 centimeters in diameter and weighing 25 kilograms were molded in separate halves from the native clay of Manchuria. Each bomb was hand assembled and kiln fired by expert craftsmen. Zigzag grooves were cut into each bomb, known as the Uji, in order to mount high-explosive charges for detonation. A fuse set to explode 200 to 300 meters above the ground was placed in the tail. If that failed, a 500-gram bursting tube of TNT was set into the nose to create a delayed impact detonation.

Upon detonation, the bomb was designed to disintegrate into harmless clay fragments, leaving no trace of a weapon. The bomb was loaded to its 10-liter capacity with 30,000 fleas infected with the plague. The bombs would explode in the air at the pre-set altitude, and the fleas would fall to the ground. For testing purposes, sheets of sticky paper were placed around the drop site, and technicians spent hours counting the trapped fleas. The results were very promising. Eighty percent of the fleas survived.

Uji construction progressed from clay to porcelain after a number of encouraging tests, and its great success prompted the development of deadlier weapons. The Ha was a bomb with a thin steel wall surrounding 1,500 cylindrical shot immersed in half a liter of anthrax or tetanus emulsion. Dropped on the battlefield, the Ha would explode over a 40-meter area. Later experiments involved the Ga, a glass bomb, and various other porcelain and iron bombs, all filled with deadly pathogens.

The various bombs dropped by the Heibo airplanes could not have been made without help from Ishii's brother Mitsuo, commander of the unit's Animal House. Thousands of rats were kept in the Animal House for breeding plague-carrying fleas. Sometimes the rats themselves were tested as rodent assault weapons— placed in balloons for airdrop or in floats to be introduced by sea. It was envisioned that the rats would spread their infected parasitic cargo over a far greater area than a bomb ever could.

Takeo, another Ishii sibling, controlled the Pingfan prison and provided prisoners from Blocks 7 and 8 when the Heibo squadron needed to try out Uji or Ha bombs on living targets. Gaining knowledge from the mutilated and dying bombing victims, the scientists and engineers could produce ever more efficient killing devices.

The guard ranks of the Ro Block were filled with second and third sons from Ishii's home village of Kamo. Known as the Special Squad, those men were utterly loyal to their commander. Ishii's family was so revered by Special Squad members that they always referred to him as "the Honorable Ishii" or "the War God Ishii."

The Special Squad members guarded the prisoners brought to Pingfan from Hogoin and Harbin. Hogoin, ironically named Pro section House, was a detention camp 20 kilometers from Pingfan, Hundreds of Russian civilians, servicemen and spies were held there by a Maj. Gen. Akikusa, chief of the Harbin secret service, before being sent to Pingfan. Trickling in from Harbin came an endless flow of Chinese prisoners dragooned under a long list of trumped-up charges of "anti-Manchukuoan activities." Between 500 and 600 prisoners died each year, with 3,000 losing their lives during the span of Pingfan's operation.

The Chinese and Russian prisoners— male and female, children, adults and the elderly—were injected with horrible diseases, while Japanese doctors coldly documented their symptoms. Some Pingfan prisoners were drained of their own blood and then transfused with horse plasma in an attempt to find a cheap and plentiful human blood substitute. In the operating theaters of the Ro Block, Dr. Kozo Okamoto vivisected prisoners, probing their brains and placing still-twitching organs into jars of Formalin for preservation.

The Japanese who conducted these ghastly experiments lived in a township known as Togo Village, in well-heated houses with Western-style lavatories and other luxuries. In Togo Village lived the men who daily dropped bombs contaminated with virulent diseases on prisoners chained to stakes on the Anta proving grounds. Other Togo inhabitants pushed prisoners into the open courtyard of the Ro Block in the depths of winter, dousing them with water until their limbs froze solid in obscene experiments to gather information about cold weather injuries. The village was also the home of the Special Squad, which put down at least one prisoner revolt with poison gas and used flamethrowers to conduct burn tests on prisoners at Anta.

Fortunately, the monstrous results of the Pingfan experiments were never unleashed en masse upon the Allied forces in World War II. Even as the war steadily turned against the Japanese, the fruits of Ishii's Unit 731 remained sealed away. Only a few inconclusive yet barbarous air attacks were made upon Chinese and Manchurian civilians with plague bombs of the Uji type.

Pingfan did use Allied prisoners of war for certain devastating tests. At Mukden, a Manchurian POW camp, 1,485 American, British, Australian and New Zealander POWs were tested to determine how Caucasians would react to Pingfan-developed pathogens. Hundreds of prisoners died at Mukden, though it is impossible to know how many perished from inflicted diseases and how many from a prison camp system as horrific as any found in the Pacific.

The most chilling specter raised by Pingfan was the balloon bomb. Hundreds of those devices filled with high explosives were launched into the jet stream from Japan and traversed the thousands of miles to the North American continent in only 50 to 60 hours. Although the campaign was an utter failure save for a very few tragic instances, balloon bombs did fall to earth in Hawaii; Alaska and the Aleutian Islands; the Pacific Northwest; Canada; Butte, Montana; and Grand Rapids, Michigan.

The U.S. Western Defense Command mobilized the Lightning Project to search for those balloons and to keep their presence hidden from the media. But would their efforts have been enough had the balloons carried thousands of fleas infected with bubonic plague instead of high explosives?

The war ended before Ishii was given permission to unleash such a nightmarish scenario. In mid-1945, Pingfan was destroyed on orders from the Japanese government to keep it from falling into the hands of the Nationalist Chinese or the Soviets. Those prisoners who had survived months or years of torment were killed.

And what of the Japanese who had conducted the tests? Some were captured by the Soviets and put on trial in the late 1940s. Some were condemned to death or long imprisonment for what they had done to Russians in Manchuria.

Those who fled to the West found a much different fate. It had been decided in the United States at the presidential level that Japanese Emperor Hirohito's role in the war would be soft-pedaled. Lieutenant General Shiro Ishii's case was eventually thrown out because prosecution would have revealed irrefutable links between Unit 731 and the emperor. Ishii died of throat cancer on October 9, 1959, in Japan.

Like many involved at Pingfan, Ishii was actually protected by the U.S. government so that the secrets and mostly intact research could be brought to Camp Detrick, Maryland, the United States' own burgeoning biological warfare research center. Like Ishii, most of his colleagues were never haunted by the danger of a war crimes tribunal—never called to justice for the horrific crimes they committed in distant Manchuria.

QUESTIONS TO CONSIDER

1. What was Unit 731?
2. Characterize the Fourth Division.
3. Discuss Ishii's fate.
4. Was what occurred at Unit 731 genocide?

MAKING CONNECTIONS

1. How closely did the actions of the Japanese in Manchuria reflect German imperialism in Namibia?

2. Is Japanese genocide denial different in nature from Holocaust denial?

✔ RECOMMENDED RESOURCES

Allen, Thomas B., and Norman Polmar. *Code-Name Downfall: The Invasion of Japan, November 1, 1945.* New York: Simon and Schuster, 1995.

Chang, Iris. *The Rape of Nanking, The Forgotten Holocaust of World War II.* New York: Basic Books, 1997.

Dower, John W. *War Without Mercy: Race and Power in the Pacific War.* New York: Pantheon, 1986.

Fogel, Joshua A., ed. *The Nanking Massacre in History and Historiography.* Berkeley: University of California Press, 2000.

Harris, Sheldon H. *Factories of Death: Japanese Biological Warfare, 1932–1945, and the American Cover-Up.* Rev. ed. New York: Routledge, 2002.

Lifton, Robert J., and Greg Mitchell. *Hiroshima in America: A Half Century of Denial.* New York: Grosset/Dunlap, 1996.

Yamamoto, Mashiro. *Nanking, Anatomy of an Atrocity.* Westport, CT: Praeger, 2000.

CHAPTER 7

THERE ARE BOMBS,
AND THERE ARE BOMBS: HIROSHIMA

> The unleashed power of the atom has changed everything save our modes of thinking and we drift toward unparalleled catastrophe.
>
> —Albert Einstein, Telegram 24 May 1946

During World War II, the Germans dropped 74,000 tons of bombs on Britain, killing 51,000 people. The Allies dropped nearly 2 million tons of bombs, killing 600,000 German civilians, 62,000 Italians, and more than 900,000 Japanese.

At 8:15 AM on the morning of August 6, 1945, the Japanese city of Hiroshima disappeared in an atomic blast with a yield of approximately 15 kilotons (equivalent to 15,000 tons of TNT). The bomb caused the immediate deaths of 90,000 to 100,000 persons.

By the end of 1945, approximately 140,000 people may have died from complications from the resulting burns and radiation. A second bomb, dropped at 11:02 AM on August 9, obliterated Nagasaki, killing some 35,000 to 40,000 people immediately and an additional 75,000 by the end of 1945.

The fallout from these bombs continues to make discussions of their use radioactive. Critics debate the U.S. rationales for using the bombs and the necessity of dropping the second bomb so quickly after the first.

Historian Howard Zinn flies into this debate from a unique perspective as a former bombardier in the Eighth Air Force in Europe during WW II. His description of the Allied bombing of the French town Royan, termed *liberated* as a result, leading Zinn to imply disturbing questions. He later learned of the bombing of Hiroshima while on furlough, before being transferred to the Pacific theater of the war. Yet, he questions the rationale that the use of the bombs would save a million American service men's lives. He further analyzes personal responsibility in man-made atrocities by recounting the wartime destruction of Royan, a resort on the western of France. He places human volition in such acts "against the abstractions of duty and obedience."

Hiroshima and Royan

Howard Zinn,
Boston University, Emeritus

History can remind us of what we too easily forget—that great moral crusades, whether carried on by nations or revolutionary movements, often bring atrocities committed by the crusaders.

To this fact, we might respond in several ways. Carefully considering the alternatives, we might conclude that this is unfortunate, but necessary to the success of an objective important enough to warrant the cost. Or, we might conclude that while necessary for success, it is so frightful that either the mission must be postponed or another means sought to achieve it. We might decide that it is unnecessary, but an unavoidable consequence of a useful struggle, which we regret but must accept. Or, that being unnecessary, it can be prevented without affecting the larger moral issue adversely. We might even begin to question the validity of a goal which spawns such monstrous children.

In the two-part essay which follows, I intend only two things: to remind us again of the fact of such atrocities, committed in the name of morality by our own and other nations; to propose that in present and future crusades we think hard about how to act.

Hiroshima, with which I start, has been brought to our attention often, but that episode will never be vivid enough in our minds, and we still have not shown that we understand what it suggests. Royan, with which I conclude, is virtually unknown outside of France. It is a smaller-scale atrocity (although more were killed there than in the much more publicized and condemned instances of German bombing in Coventry and Rotterdam). But it is worth recalling as an example of the countless "small"

acts of cruelty committed in situations of moral righteousness.

HIROSHIMA

With Robert Butow's research on the Japanese side, Robert Jungk's exploration of the minds of the atomic scientists concerned, Herbert Feis' study of State Department files, and the old records of the U.S. Strategic Bombing Survey—we can approach from four sides the moral question: should we have dropped the atomic bomb on Japan? More important, perhaps we can pull together the evidence, and draw some conclusions to guide us in this frightening time when hydrogen bombers are ready all over the world.

First, let me describe my four sources:

The U.S. Strategic Bombing Survey was set up in November of 1944 to study the effects of bombing on Germany. On August 15, 1945, Truman asked the Survey to do the same for Japan, and one result was its report, *Japan's Struggle to End the War*. The Survey (Paul Nitze and John Kenneth Galbraith worked on it, among others) interrogated seven hundred Japanese officials, later turned the files over to the CIA.

In 1954, an American scholar named Robert Butow, having gone through the papers of the Japanese Ministry of Foreign Affairs, the records of the International Military Tribunal of the Far East, and the interrogation files of the U.S. Army, personally interviewed many of the Japanese principals, and wrote *Japan's*

Howard Zinn, "Hiroshima and Royan," from *The Politics of History* (Urbana: University of Illinois Press, 1990) 250–274. Reprinted with permission.

Decision to Surrender. This is the most detailed study from the Japanese side.

Robert Jungk, in a book first published in German, studied the making and dropping of the bomb from the standpoint of the atomic scientists, and in 1958 the American edition was published: *Brighter Than a Thousand Suns*. This book is based largely on personal interviews with the people who played a leading part in the construction and dropping of the bombs.

In 1961, Herbert Feis, who has had unique access to the files of the State Department and to part of the Department of the Army's records on the Manhattan Project, published *Japan Subdued*, which gives us the view from Washington.

What follows now is a compressed chronology of those events which, speeding along in blind parallel on both sides of the Pacific, culminated on August 6th and August 9th of 1945 in the obliteration by blast and fire of the Japanese cities of Hiroshima and Nagasaki.

As early as the spring of 1944, top Japanese admirals anticipated ultimate defeat and began discussing ways of ending the war. In July, the Tojo government fell. In September, the Navy was ready to call a halt, while the Army stood firm. In February of 1945, the Emperor was told by a group of senior statesmen that defeat was certain and peace should be sought at once, and by March a specific peace overture was under cabinet discussion. That month, Tokyo was hit by American fire bombs, and there were eighty thousand killed.

In April of 1945, American forces landed on Okinawa, within close striking distance of Japan, and often considered the southernmost island in the Japanese chain. The Koiso government was replaced by Suzuki, who took office with the specific idea of ending the war as quickly as possible and who undertook approaches to Russian Ambassador Malik about interceding for peace. In this same month, President Roosevelt died, Truman took office, and Secretary of War Stimson told him about the Manhattan Project. In this month too, within that Project, an Interim Committee of distinguished civilians, with an advisory scientific committee of Oppenheimer, Fermi, Arthur Compton, and E. O. Lawrence, was set up to study use of the bomb.

In June of 1945, Okinawa was taken, the Emperor of Japan told a new Inner War Council to plan to end the war, and the Interim Committee advised Truman to use the bomb as quickly as possible, on a dual civilian-military target and without warning. That same month, the report drawn up by atomic scientists James Franck, Leo Szilard and Eugene Rabinowitch, urging that we not drop the bomb on Japan, was referred by Stimson to the scientific committee of four and was rejected.

On July 13, 1945, the United States intercepted Foreign Minister Togo's secret cable to Ambassador Sato in Moscow asking him to get the Soviets to end the war short of unconditional surrender. On July 16th, the test bomb exploded at Alamogordo, New Mexico, and word was sent to Truman at the Potsdam Conference, which began the next day. The Potsdam Declaration of July 26th called for unconditional surrender, not mentioning the Emperor, whose status was of primary concern to the Japanese.

The Japanese cabinet was divided on unconditional surrender, and while it continued to discuss this, the bomb was dropped August 6th on Hiroshima. While the Japanese were meeting and moving towards acceptance of the Potsdam terms, the Russians declared war August 8th, and the second bomb was dropped on Nagasaki August 9th. Washington's ambiguity about the Emperor delayed final acceptance by the Japanese, but that came August 14th.

Here are the conclusions reached by our four close students of the affair:

The U.S. Strategic Bombing Survey: "Based on a detailed investigation of all the facts and supported by the testimony of the surviving Japanese leaders involved, it is the Survey's opinion that certainly prior to 31 December 1945, and in all probability prior to 1 November 1945, Japan would have surrendered even if the atomic bombs had not been dropped, even if Russia had not entered the war, and even if no invasion had been planned or contemplated."[1]

Robert Jungk, referring to our interception of the Japanese cables: "But Truman, instead of exploiting diplomatically these significant indications of Japanese weakness, issued a proclamation on July 26 at the Potsdam Conference, which was bound to make it difficult for the Japanese to capitulate without 'losing face' in the process."

Robert Butow, referring to Prince Konoye, special emissary to Moscow who was working on Russian intercession for peace: "Had the Allies given the Prince a week of grace in which to obtain his Government's support for acceptance of the proposals, the war might have ended toward the latter part of July or the very beginning of the month of August, without the atomic bomb and without Soviet participation in the conflict."

Referring to the intercepted cables, Butow says: "The record of what occurred during the next two weeks … indicates that Washington failed to turn this newly won and unquestionably vital intelligence data to active and good account."

And: "The mere fact that the Japanese had approached the Soviet Union with a request for mediation should have suggested the possibility that Japan, for all of her talk about 'death to the last man,' might accept the Allied demand for unconditional surrender if only it were couched in more specific terms than those which Washington was already using to define its meaning." ("Specific," Butow

means, in relation to the Emperor, for former Ambassador Joseph Grew had been pounding away at the White House with the idea that this question of the Emperor was supremely important, but to no result.)

Herbert Feis: "…the curious mind lingers over the reasons why the American government waited so long before offering the Japanese those various assurances which it did extend later." These reasons, Feis says, are a complex of personal motives and national psychology. Truman was influenced by the desire of the Joint Chiefs of Staff to whip Japan further, by the desire of Secretary of State Byrnes for joint action with our allies, by the desire of Secretary of War Stimson to test the bomb, and by domestic criticism of less than unconditional surrender. Also by "the impetus of the combat effort and plans, the impulse to punish, the inclination to demonstrate how supreme was our power. …"

Feis sees two questions: was the bombing essential; and was it justified as a way of bringing early surrender. "The first of these, and by far the easiest to answer, is whether it was essential to use the bomb in order to compel the Japanese to surrender on our terms within a few months. It was not. That ought to have been obvious even at the time of decision, but … it does not seem to have been." On the second question, Feis is uncertain. He notes the tremendous desire to end the war as quickly as possible, concern that a demonstration bomb would fail. Yet he thinks it probable that such a demonstration, plus Soviet entry, would have brought victory as soon, or a few weeks later.

After rummaging through this mess of death and documents, I have some random ideas which may be worth thinking about:

1. The question of *blame* should be ignored. I can think of two ways in which blame-saying might be useful: in assessing persons

---

[1]This conclusion is supported by the statements of virtually every top military leader of that period: Eisenhower, MacArthur, Marshall, Leahy, LeMay, etc. After this essay first appeared, Gar Alperovitz published his brilliant study, *Atomic Diplomacy*. His final chapter summarizes the evidence for the argument that political considerations, not military ones, were paramount in dropping the bomb.

who are still alive and about whom a choice might need to be made in the granting of crucial responsibility (for instance if we were picking a head for the Atomic Energy Commission, we would feel safer with Leo Szilard than with Robert Oppenheimer on the basis of experience with the Manhattan Project); and in puncturing illusions about nations whose behavior has often been idealized, like our own. But in general, our concern should be to see what we can learn for the handling of our present situation, not to settle dead arguments. Also, blame-placing sets up psychological blocks to the creation of rapport with people who have made mistakes in the past.

2. One wonders about our easy generalizations as to the difference in decision-making between "democratic" and "totalitarian" countries when we learn of the incredible number of deliberations and discussions that went on in the Japanese higher councils in days when everything was quite literally crashing around their ears—and when we recall, on the other hand, Truman's quick decisions on Korea, and Kennedy's on Cuba.

3. Making sure our military-minded men do not make top political decisions seems very important after seeing how the military in Japan delayed surrender until the bombs were dropped and how military men played such a large part in our decision to drop the bomb. (General Groves, though not an official member of the crucial Interim Committee, attended all its meetings and played a leading part in its decisions. Truman, too, seemed much influenced by the military.) Yet I believe now, after reading the evidence presented by Gar Alperovitz in *Atomic Diplomacy,* that this emphasis on the special guilt of the military men is wrong. High civilian officials—Truman, Stimson, Byrnes—seem to have been the crucial decision-makers on the dropping of the bomb. It is a long chain of responsibility, and we need to concentrate on those links which we can ourselves affect.

4. While a decision-making process may seem to thunder along like a Diesel truck, a firm touch by any one of a number of people can often send it in a different direction. Truman could certainly have applied that touch. Groves could have. Stimson as head of the Interim Committee could have. James Byrnes, carrying to Potsdam a State Department memo stressing the Emperor question, might have affected the final Declaration in such a way as to bring Japanese response if only he himself had believed in the memo. Oppenheimer or Fermi or Compton (since Lawrence already seemed to have objections to the policy) might have turned the tide by a specific recommendation from the scientific advisors to the Interim Committee. Lower down in the pyramid of power, the probability of any one man changing a crucial decision decreases, but it does not disappear. Szilard and his buried petition *might* have brought results, if joined by others. The point is: no human being inside an organizational apparatus should become overwhelmed by it to the point of immobility. He needs to play the probability statistics coolly, exerting his own pressure to the utmost even in the face of complete uncertainty about what others may be doing at the same time.

5. The impulse to "win the war, and as fast as possible" seems to have dominated everyone's thinking, to the exclusion of rational and humane judgments. The most advanced thinkers in the West, its greatest liberals (and radicals), were more sold on this war than on any in history; never were the moral issues more clear in a great conflict, and the result was simplistic thinking about the war. (I recall August 6, 1945, very clearly. I had served as a bombardier in the Eighth Air Force in Europe, flew back to the States for a thirty-day furlough before a scheduled move to the Pacific, and while on furlough picked up a newspaper telling of the bomb dropped on Hiroshima. I felt only gladness that the end of the war was imminent.)

6. Oppenheimer has said that he did "not know beans about the military situation in Japan" when he and his committee decided to reject the Franck report. General Groves and the atom bomb people did not know about the messages the State Department had intercepted, while the State Department did not know the bombing was imminent. This suggests the importance of the free flow of information. But it would be naive to think that evil acts are only the result of poor communications. Some people can simply change their minds on the basis of new information; with others, a drastic revision of their sense of right and wrong is needed. If Oppenheimer and Fermi and others had only known how close Japan was to surrender, and known that an invasion was not necessary to defeat Japan, their decision would probably have been different. With others, like Groves—and probably Truman—the question would still remain: can we save *any* American lives (or gain *any* political advantage) by killing 100,000 Japanese? With them, the nationalistic morality which equates one American life with one thousand foreigners' lives seems to have obtained; or more likely, as the Stimson-Byrnes-Truman views disclosed by Alperovitz indicate, it was not even American lives, but national power that was the supreme value. Values have little to do with quantities of data; they are not necessarily changed by the mere increase of information. For some people on the verge of change this may not be true, but for most others it takes something beyond mere information: it takes direct experience, psychological convulsion, or irresistible pressure—a general assault on the emotions.

7. All this has implications for those interested in social change. It indicates, I think, that we need to distinguish, in the tactics of ideological conflict, between different kinds of human obstacles, and concentrate carefully on the type of technique needed to deal with each. For some, this means information. For others, we had better not assume that their value-system will be revolutionized in the short run. Instead, our disappointed recognition of the solidity of peoples' value-systems can urge upon us the realistic tactic of playing values against one another. A particular cherished value is not likely to be destroyed, but it can be shunted aside in favor of another which is even more desired. The supreme value of survival has often been the only bulwark against the almost supreme value of power. In the past, such value-clashes have been accidental. Perhaps men can begin to use them deliberately.

8. People must be willing to make decisions "out of their field." Oppenheimer and the other three scientists on his committee felt that the dropping of the bomb was really out of their province as scientists. We should lose our awe of the specialists and stop assuming the "expert" knows his stuff. There is a certain incompatibility between specialization and democracy.

9. The effort made to change a decision not-of-one's-own in a particular situation should match the dimensions of the peril involved. Ordinary and routine methods of protest may not be enough today, when the entire human race is at the mercy of a handful of decision-makers. More is required than calm and reasoned action. Or, to be more exact, we need to think calmly and reasonably about taking extreme measures. In C. P. Snow's novel, *The New Men*, British scientists, fearful that the United States will drop the atomic bomb on a helpless city, hold a meeting. They reject the wild and irrational plan advanced by one of them to reveal the entire secret to the public in an effort to stop the bombing. They decide instead to do the sane, sensible thing. They appoint a committee to visit the United States and to impress their ideas on top American officials. The committee departs. The other scientists wait for its return, and while waiting, they hear on the radio that the bomb has been dropped on Hiroshima. So much for their sane, sensible decision.

ROYAN

In mid-April of 1945, a combined air-ground attack completed the destruction of the French seaside resort of Royan, a town of ancient chateaux and lovely beaches (a favorite spot of Picasso), on the Atlantic coast near Bordeaux. It was ten months after D-day, the invasion of Western Europe by Allied Forces—and three weeks before the final surrender of Germany. The official history of the U.S. Army Air Forces in World War II refers briefly to the attack on Royan:

> On 14 through 16 April more than 1,200 American heavies went out each day to drop incendiaries, napalm bombs, and 2000-pound demolition bombs on stubborn German garrisons still holding out around Bordeaux. The bombing was effective, and French forces soon occupied the region.

(A note on the accuracy of bombing. According to the official history those bombs were dropped "on stubborn German garrisons." This is misleading. The bombs were dropped in the general vicinity of Royan, where there were German garrisons [mostly outside the town] and where there were also civilian occupants of the town. It was my participation in this mission, as a bombardier with the 490th Bomb Group, that prompted me, after the war, to inquire into the bombing of Royan. At the time, it seemed just another bombing mission, with a slightly different target, and a slightly different cargo of bombs. We were awakened in the early hours of morning, went to the briefing, where we were told our job was to bomb pockets of German troops remaining in and around Royan, and that in our bomb bays were thirty 100-pound bombs containing "jellied gasoline," a new substance [now known as napalm]. Our bombs were not precisely directed at German installations but were dropped by toggle switch over the Royan area, on seeing the bombs of the lead ship leave the bomb bay— a device good for saturation bombing, not pinpoint bombing [aside from the fact that the Norden bombsight, which we were trained to use, could not be

counted on to hit enemy installations and miss nearby civilians from a height of 25,000 feet]. The toggle switch was connected to an intervalometer which automatically dropped the bombs, after the first fell, in a timed sequence. I remember distinctly seeing, from our great height, the bombs explode in the town, flaring like matches struck in fog. I was completely unaware of the human chaos below.

In 1966, I spent some time in Royan, and found in the town library most of the material on which this essay is based.

In the same chapter of the official Air Force history, the sentence following the description of the Royan bombing reads:

> The last attack on an industrial target by the Eighth Air Force occurred on 25 April, when the famous Skoda works at Pilsen, Czechoslovakia, received 500 well-placed tons. Because of a warning sent out ahead of time the workers were able to escape, except for five persons.

I remember flying on that mission, too, as deputy lead bombardier, and that we did not aim specifically at the "Skoda works" [which I would have noted, because it was the one target in Czechoslovakia I had read about] but dropped our bombs, without much precision, on the city of Pilsen. Two Czech citizens who lived in Pilsen at the time told me, recently, that several hundred people were killed in that raid [that is, Czechs]—not five.

The bombing of villages by American planes in the Vietnam war has been accompanied by similar claims, in military accounts, that only military targets are aimed at. But the nature of bombing from high altitudes, saturation style, makes this a lie, whatever the intention of the spokesman. Atrocities in modern warfare need not be deliberate on the part of the fliers or their superiors; they are the inevitable result of warfare itself. This fact does not exculpate the bombardiers; it implicates the political leaders who make the wars in which bombardiers fly, and all the rest of us who tolerate those political leaders.)

A letter from Colonel H. A. Schmidt, of the Office of the Chief of Military History, Department of the Army, responding to my request for information on the bombing of Royan, stated:

> The liberation of the port of Bordeaux required the reduction of the bridgeheads of Royan, la Pointe, de Grave and Oléron. The Royan sector was the principal German garrison holding out in the Bordeaux area, and first priority in the operations. The Eighth U.S. Air Force paved the way of the Allied ground forces by massive bombing.

The quick, casual description of potentially embarrassing episodes is common in histories written by men in government. Winston Churchill, who was Prime Minister when the city of Dresden was indiscriminately saturated with firebombs in February 1945, leaving 135,000 dead, and who had approved the general strategy of bombing urban areas, confined himself to this comment in his memoirs: "We made a heavy raid in the latter month on Dresden, then a centre of communications of Germany's Eastern front."

Strenuous arguments were made for the bombing attacks on Hiroshima and Dresden on the basis of military necessity, although ultimately the evidence was overwhelmingly against such arguments. In the case of Royan, it was virtually impossible to even launch a defense of the attack on grounds of military need. It was a small town on the Atlantic coast, far from the fighting front. True, it commanded the sea entrance to Bordeaux, a great port. But this was not crucial, either for the local population, or for the general conduct of the war. At first without Bordeaux, and later without its port facilities, the Allies had invaded Normandy, taken Paris, crossed the Rhine, and were now well into Germany. Furthermore, the general air-ground assault on Royan took place three weeks before the end of the war in Europe, at a time when everyone knew it would all soon be over and all one had to do for the surrender of the German garrisons in the area was to wait.[2]

Nevertheless, on April 14, 1945, the attack on Royan began, reported as follows in a dispatch from London the next day to *The New York Times*:

> The full weight of the United States Eighth Air Force was hurled yesterday against one of Europe's forgotten fronts, the German-held pocket in the Gironde Estuary commanding the great southwestern French port of Bordeaux. The blow by 1,150 Flying Fortresses and Liberators, without fighter escort, preceded a limited land attack by French troops …
>
> Some 30,000 to 40,000 Nazi troops have been holed up in the Gironde Estuary pocket since the tides of war swept around and past them last summer … The striking force was probably the biggest heavy bombing fleet ever sent out from Britain in daylight without escorting fighters. Five of the big planes failed to return.

Was the air raid worth even the loss of only five air crews—forty-five men? That was just the tip of the tragedy, counted in lives lost, homes destroyed, persons wounded and burned. For the next day, April 15, the attack was heavier, and the airplanes had a new weapon. A front-page dispatch in *The New York Times* from Paris reported "two days of shattering aerial bombardment and savage ground attacks in the drive to open the port of Bordeaux." It went on:

> More than 1300 Flying Fortresses and Liberators of the United States Eighth Air Force prepared the way for today's successful assault by drenching the enemy's positions on both sides of the Gironde controlling the route to Bordeaux with about 460,000 gallons of liquid fire that bathed in flames the German positions and strong points …
>
> It was the first time that the Eighth Air Force had employed its new bomb. The inflammable substance is dropped in tanks that are exploded on impact by detonators that ignite the fuel, splashing the flaming contents of each tank over an area of approximately sixty square yards.

---

[2]Also, in a remark I must confine to a footnote as a gesture to the equality of all victims: there was something to distinguish Royan from both Hiroshima and Dresden; its population was, at least officially, friend, not foe.

The liquid fire was napalm, used for the first time in warfare. The following day, there was another bombing, with high explosive bombs, and further ground assaults. Altogether, it took three days of bombing and land attacks to bring the Germans in the area to surrender. The French ground forces suffered about two hundred dead; the Germans lost several hundred. There is no accurate count on the civilian dead resulting from those attacks, but *The New York Times* dispatch by a correspondent in the area reported

> French troops mopped up most of Royan, on the north side of the river's mouth … Royan, a town of 20,000, once was a vacation spot. About 350 civilians, dazed or bruised by two terrific air bombings in forty-eight hours, crawled from the ruins and said the air attacks had been "such hell as we never believed possible."

In a few weeks, the war was over in Europe. The town of Royan, "liberated," was totally in ruins.

That eve-of-victory attack in mid-April 1945 was the second disaster suffered by Royan at the hands of the Allied forces. On January 5, 1945, in the darkness before dawn, two waves of heavy British bombers, about an hour apart, flew over Royan, which was still inhabited, despite a voluntary evacuation in the preceding months, by about two thousand persons. There was no warning, there were no shelters. The bombs were dropped in the heart of the city (completely missing the German troops, who were outside) within a rectangle marked out by flares dropped by one of the planes. Over a thousand people were killed (some of the estimates are twelve hundred, others fourteen hundred). Several hundred people were wounded. Almost every building in Royan was demolished. The later attack in April, came therefore, on the ruins of buildings and the remnants of families, and made the annihilation of the city complete.

That January bombing has never been adequately explained. One phrase recurs in all the accounts— *"une tragique erreur."* The expla-

nation given by military officials at the time was that the bombers were originally scheduled to bomb in Germany, but because of bad weather there, were rerouted to Royan without a map of the German positions. French planes from nearby Cognac were supposed to mark the positions with flares but this was either not done, or done badly, or the flares were carried away by the wind.

A dispatch written by a local person soon after that bombing, entitled "La Nuit Tragique," contained this description:

> Under the German occupation. It is night, calm reigns over the sleeping town. Midnight sounds in the Royan church. Then one o'clock, then two … The Royannais sleep, muffled against the chill. Three, four o'clock. A humming is heard in the distance. Rockets light up the sky. The inhabitants are not afraid; they are tranquil, because they know that Allied airplanes, if these are such, will aim at the German fortifications, and besides, is this not the evening when German supply planes come in? The clock sounds five. Then follows the catastrophe, brutal, horrible, implacable. A deluge of steel and fire descends on Royan; a wave of 350 planes lets go 800 tons of bombs on the town. Some seconds later, the survivors are calling for aid to the wounded. Cries, death rattles … A woman appeals for help, her head appears alone, her body crushed under an enormous beam … A whole family is imprisoned in a cave, the water mounts. The rescuers lift their heads—this humming, yet, it is another wave of planes. This achieves the complete destruction of Royan and its inhabitants. Royan has gone down with the civilized world, by the error, the bestiality, the folly of man. [*Royan a sombré en même temps que le monde civilisé, par l'erreur, la bêtise et la folie des hommes.*]

Eight days after the attack, an article appeared in *La Libération* appealing for help: "American friends, you whose Florida beaches have never known such hours, take charge of the reconstruction of Royan!"

In 1948, General de Larminat, who was in charge of French forces in the West (that is, the Bordeaux region) for the last six months of the war, broke a long silence to reply to bitter criticism of both the January and April bombings by local leaders. He exonerated the French military command at Cognac, saying they were not responsible for directing the English planes to Royan. It was, rather, a "tragic error" by the Allied Command; the whole episode was one of the unfortunate consequences of war:

> Will we draw from this an excuse to attack our Allies, who gave countless lives to liberate our country? That would be profoundly unjust. All wars carry these painful errors. Where is the infantryman of 1914–18, and of this war, who has not received friendly shells, badly aimed? How many French towns, how many combat units, have suffered bombings by mistake at the hands of allied planes? This is the painful ransom, the inevitable ransom of war, against which it is vain to protest, about which it is vain to quarrel. We pay homage to those who died in the war, we help the survivors and repair the ruins; but we do not linger on the causes of these unfortunate events because, in truth, there is only a single cause: War, and the only ones truly responsible are those who wanted war.

Compare this with the explanation of the Dresden bombing given by Air Marshal Sir Robert Saundby:

> It was one of those terrible things that sometimes happen in wartime, brought about by an unfortunate combination of circumstances. Those who approved it were neither wicked nor cruel, though it may well be that they were too remote from the harsh realities of war to understand fully the appalling destructive power of air bombardment in the spring of 1945 …
>
> It is not so much this or the other means of making war that is immoral or inhumane. What is immoral is war itself. Once full-scale war has broken out it can never be humanized or civilized, and if one side attempted to do so it would be most likely to be defeated. So long as we resort to war to settle differences between nations, so long will we have to endure the horrors, the barbarities and excesses that war brings with it. That, to me, is the lesson of Dresden.

Some important evidence on the January bombing appeared in 1966 with the publication of the memoirs of Admiral Hubert Meyer, French commander in the Rochefort-La Rochelle area (the two Atlantic ports just north of Royan). Meyer, in September and October 1944, when the Germans, having fled west from the Allied invasion in northern France, were consolidating their pockets on the Atlantic coast, had begun negotiating with the German commander of La Rochelle-Rochefort, Admiral Schirlitz. In effect, they agreed that the Germans would not blow up the port installations, and in return the French would not attack the Germans. Then the Germans evacuated Rochefort, moving north into the La Rochelle area, to lines both sides agreed on.

In late December 1944, Meyer was asked to travel south along the coast from Rochefort to Royan, where the second German coastal pocket was under the command of Admiral Michahelles, to negotiate a prisoner exchange. In the course of these talks, he was told that the German admiral was disposed to sign an agreement to hold the military *status quo* around Royan, as had been done by Schirlitz at Rochefort-La Rochelle. Meyer pointed out that Royan was different, that the Allies might have to attack the Germans there because Royan commanded Bordeaux, where free passage of goods was needed to supply the Southwest. The Germans, to Meyer's surprise, replied that they might agree to open Bordeaux to all but military supplies.

Conveying this offer to the French military headquarters at Saintes and Cognac, Meyer received a cool response. The French generals could not give a sound military reason for insisting on an attack, but pointed to *"l'aspect moral."* It would be hard, said General d'Anselme, "to frustrate an ardent desire for battle—a battle where victory was certain—by the army of the Southwest, which had been champing at the bit for months." Meyer said the morale of the troops was not worth the sacrifice of a town and hundreds of lives for a limited objective, when the war was virtually won, that they did not have the right to kill a single man when the adversary had offered a truce.

Further discussion, he was told, would have to await the return of General de Larminat, who was away.

Meyer left that meeting with the distinct impression that the die was cast for the attack (*"l'impression très nette que les jeux étaient faits, que Royan serait attaquée"*). This was January 2nd. Three days later, sleeping at Rochefort, he was awakened by the sound of airplanes flying south toward Royan. Those were the British Lancasters, three hundred and fifty of them, each carrying seven tons of bombs.

Meyer adds another piece of information: that about a month before the January 5th bombing an American General, Commander of the Ninth Tactical Air Force, came to Cognac to offer the Southwest forces powerful bombing support, and suggested softening the Atlantic pockets by massive aerial bombardment. He proposed that since the Germans did not have aerial defenses for Royan, here were good targets for bomber-crew trainees in England. The French agreed, but insisted the targets be at two points which formed clear enclaves on the ocean, easily distinguishable from the city itself. No more was heard from the Americans, however, until the bombing itself. As it turned out, not trainees, but experienced pilots, did the bombing, and Meyer concludes that even the American general (sent back to the U.S. after this, as a scapegoat, Meyer suggests) was not completely responsible.

Some blame devolved, he says, on the British Bomber Command, and some on the French generals, for not insisting on a point DeGaulle had made when he visited the area in September—that aerial attacks should only be undertaken here in coordination with ground assaults. Meyer concludes, however, that the real responsibility did not rest with the local military commanders. "To wipe out such a city is beyond military decision. It is a serious political act. It is impossible that the Supreme Command [he refers to Eisenhower and his staff] had not been at least consulted." In the event, he says, that the Allies are shocked by his accusations, they should open their military dossiers and, for the first time, reveal the truth.

If by January 1945 (despite von Rundstedt's Christmas counteroffensive in the Ardennes) it seemed clear that the Allies, well into France, and the Russians, having the Germans on the run, were on the way toward victory—then by April 1945 there was little doubt that the war was near its end. The Berlin radio announced on April 15 that the Russians and Americans were about to join forces around the Elbe, and that two zones were being set up for a Germany cut in two. Nevertheless, a major land-air operation was launched April 14th against the Royan pocket, with over a thousand planes dropping bombs on a German force of 5,500 men, on a town containing at the time probably less than a thousand people.

An article written in the summer of 1946 by a local writer commented on the mid-April assault:

> These last acts left a great bitterness in the hearts of the Royannais, because the Armistice followed soon after, an Armistice foreseen by all. For the Royannais, this liberation by force was useless since Royan would have been, like La Rochelle, liberated normally some days later, without new damage, without new deaths, without new ruins. Only those who have visited Royan can give an account of the disaster. No report, no picture or drawing can convey it.

Another local person wrote:

> Surely the destruction of Royan, on January 5, 1945, was an error and a crime; but what put the finishing touches on this folly was the final air raid on the ruins, on the buildings partially damaged, and on others remarkably spared on the periphery, with that infernal cargo of incendiary bombs. Thus was accomplished a deadly work of obvious uselessness, and thus was revealed to the world the powerful destructiveness of napalm.

The evidence seems overwhelming that factors of pride, military ambition, glory, honor were powerful motives in producing an unnecessary military operation. One of the local commanders wrote later: "It would have been more logical to wait for the surrender of Germany and thus to avoid new human and material losses" but one could not "ignore important factors of morale" (*"faire abstraction de facteurs essentiels d'ordre moral"*).

In 1947, a delegation of five leaders of Royan met with General de Larminat. After the war, the citizens of Royan had barred de Larminat from the town, in anger at the military operations under his command which had destroyed it, and at the widespread looting of the Royan homes by French soldiers after "liberation." He hoped now to persuade the Royannais that they had made a mistake. The meeting is described by Dr. Veyssière Pierre, former leader of the Resistance in Royan, and a holder of the Croix de Guerre, who says he hoped to get an explanation of the "useless sacrifice" of the population of the town, but "my self-deception was total, absolute." He quotes de Larminat saying the French military did not want the enemy "to surrender of his own accord; that would give the impression the Germans were unconquered."

Another member of the French delegation, Dr. Domecq, a former Mayor and Resistance leader, responded to General de Larminat also:

Royan was destroyed by mistake, you say, my general... Those responsible have been punished, the order to attack, a few days before liberation, could not be questioned by the military... The Germans had to feel our power! Permit me, my general, to tell you, once and for all, in the name of those who paid the cost: "La Victoire de Royan" does not exist, except for you.

General de Larminat responded to the criticism in a letter addressed to Paul Métadier. Pride and military ambition, he pointed out, were not sufficient explanations for such a huge operation; one had to seek a larger source: "This pride, this ambition, did not have the power to manufacture the shells which were used, to create the units which were sent, to divert the important aerial and naval forces that participated." De Larminat said that he had prepared the necessary plans for liquidating *"les poches d'Atlantique"* but that he did not judge the date. The date was fixed for him, and he executed the plans.

He ended his reply with an appeal to patriotism: "Must we therefore, throw opprobrium on old combatants because some isolated ones committed acts, unhappily inevitable in wartime? This is how it has been in all the wars of all time. No one ever, that I know, used this as a pretext to reduce the glory and the valour of the sacrifices made by the combatants." He spoke of the "simple, brave people" who will put "glory and national independence" before "material losses" and give "the respect due to those who fell, and for which many sacrificed their lives, to a patriotic ideal that the malcontents (*"les attentistes"*) have always ignored."

Admiral Meyer, who is more sympathetic to de Larminat than most of the general's critics, had watched the attack on Royan from the heights of Medis, and described the scene:

The weather was clear, the warmth oppressive. Under a fantastic concentration of fire, the enemy positions, the woods, and the ruins of Royan flamed. The countryside and the sky were thick with powder and yellow smoke. One could with difficulty distinguish the mutilated silhouette of the clock of Saint-Pierre, which burned like a torch. I knew that the allied planes were using for the first time, a new kind of incendiary explosive, a kind of jellied gasoline, known as napalm.

Larminat, he said, had good days and bad days. And this was one of his bad days, for in the evening after Royan was taken, and Meyer went to see the General: "He was visibly satisfied with having achieved this brilliant revenge … Without saying that he was intoxicated with success, the General seemed to me however to have his appetite stimulated …"

That exultation was felt at all levels. A press correspondent on the scene described the very heavy artillery bombardment which prepared the attack on the Royan area: 27,000 shells. Then the first aerial bombing on Saturday, April 14th, with high explosives. Then the bombing all Sunday morning with napalm. By seven that evening they were in Royan. It was a blazing furnace. (*"La ville est un brasier."*) The next morning, they could still hear the clatter of machine guns in the woods nearby. Royan was still burning (*"Royan brûle encore"*). The dispatch ends: "It is a beautiful spring."

With Royan taken, they decided to attack the island of Oléron, opposite Rochefort. As Meyer says:

> The new victory had inflamed the passions of our soldiers, giving them the idea that nothing could resist them. News from the German front forecast a quick end to the war. Each one wanted a last moment to distinguish himself and get a bit of glory; moderation was scorned, prudence was seen as cowardice.

Meyer did not believe the attack on Oléron was necessary. But he participated assiduously in planning and executing it, happy to be once again involved in a naval operation, and convinced that his duty was only to carry out orders from above.

> The attack on Oléron was disputable from the point of view of general strategy. It was a costly luxury, a conquest without military value, on the eve of the war's end. But this was not for me to judge. My duty was limited to doing my best in making those military decisions which would fulfill my orders.

Meyer blames the political leaders above. Yet *blame* seems the wrong word, because Meyer believes it honorable to follow orders, whatever they are, against whatever adversary is chosen for him: *"Quant au soldat, depuis des millénaires, ce n'est plus lui qui forge ses armes et qui choisit son adversaire. Il n'a que le devoir d'obéir dans la pleine mesure de sa foi, de son courage, de sa résistance."*[3]

One can see in the destruction of Royan that infinite chain of causes, that infinite dispersion of responsibility, which can give infinite work to historical scholarship and sociological speculation, and bring an infinitely pleasurable paralysis of the will. What a complex of motives! In the Supreme Allied Command, the simple momentum of the war, the pull of prior commitments and preparations, the need to fill out the circle, to pile up the victories as high as possible. At the local military level, the ambitions, petty and large, the tug of glory, the ardent need to participate in a grand communal effort by soldiers of all ranks. On the part of the American Air Force, the urge to try out a newly developed weapon. (Paul Métadier wrote: "In effect, the operation was above all characterized by the dropping of new incendiary bombs which the Air Force had just been supplied with. According to the famous formulation of one general: 'They were marvelous!'") And among all participants, high and low, French and American, the most powerful motive of all: the habit of obedience, the universal teaching of all cultures, not to get out of line, not even to think about that which one has not been assigned to think about, the negative motive of not having either a reason or a will to intercede.

Everyone can point, rightly, to someone else as being responsible. In that remarkable

---

[3]At one point, Meyer quotes Bismarck, who made German students write: "Man was not put in the world to be happy, but to do his duty!" In another frightening glimpse of what a well-trained military man of our century can believe, Meyer talks fondly of that special bond of the sea (*"une commune maîtresse: la mer"*) which unites sailors of different nations in their patriotic duty, and points, as an example of such laudable unity in action, to the landing of European troops in China in 1900 to crush the Boxer uprising.

film *King and Country*, a simple-minded British country boy in the trenches of World War I, walks away one day from the slaughter and is condemned to death in a two-step process where no one thinks he really should be executed but the officers in each step can blame those in the other. The original court sentences him to death thinking to make a strong point and then have the appeals tribunal overturn the verdict. The appeals board, upholding the verdict, can argue that the execution was not its decision. The man is shot. That procedure, one recalls, goes back to the Inquisition, when the church only conducted the trial, and the state carried out the execution, thus confusing both God and the people about the source of the decision.

More and more in our time, the mass production of massive evil requires an enormously complicated division of labor. No one is positively responsible for the horror that ensues. But everyone is negatively responsible, because *anyone* can throw a wrench into the machinery. Not quite, of course—because only a few people have wrenches. The rest have only their hands and feet. That is, the power to interfere with the terrible progression is distributed unevenly, and therefore the sacrifice required varies, according to one's means. In that odd perversion of the natural which we call society (that is, nature seems to equip each species for its special needs) the greater one's capability for interference, the less urgent is the need to interfere.

It is the immediate victims—or tomorrow's—who have the greatest need, and the fewest wrenches. They must use their bodies (which may explain why rebellion is a rare phenomenon). This may suggest to those of us who have a bit more than our bare hands, and at least a small interest in stopping the machine, that we might play a peculiar role in breaking the social stalemate.

This may require resisting a false crusade—or refusing one or another expedition in a true one. But always, it means refusing to be transfixed by the actions of other people, the truths of other times. It means acting on what we feel and think, here, now, for human flesh and sense, against the abstractions of duty and obedience.

QUESTIONS TO CONSIDER

1. Does Howard Zinn suggest, in so many words, that the bombing of Hiroshima was genocide?

2. Does the author use the usual, credible sources on which historians commonly rely?

3. Why does Zinn avoid the question of blame?

4. According to Zinn, should Oppenheimer have been more informed about military matters?

5. Was the bombing of Royan a national act? A necessary objective?

6. What is the consequence of Zinn's observation that, "the mass production of massive evil requires an enormously complicated division of labor"?

Missing the Target

Tony Capaccio,
Editor of Defense Week

Uday Mohan,
the American University

Fifty years after the U.S. bombing missions over Hiroshima and Nagasaki, ideological fallout from the atomic bomb has settled over the Smithsonian Institution's National Air and Space Museum. Following months of text changes, charges of anti-Americanism, and the resignation of the museum's director, an exhibit originally scheduled to open in May is finally open this month, a pared down version of what was supposed to be a complex retelling of President Harry S. Truman's decision to use the atomic bomb.

Instead, the exhibit is not much more than the 60-foot fuselage of the B-29 Superfortress *Enola Gay*, the plane that dropped the bomb on Hiroshima on August 6, 1945, instantly killing at least 70,000 Japanese. Air Force historian Richard P. Hallion, a former science and technology curator at the Air and Space Museum and an exhibit adviser, ruefully calls the exhibit "a beer can with a label."

The dispute that brought about this truncated exhibit was over which version of atom bomb history would be highlighted. The controversy was largely fueled by media accounts that uncritically accepted the conventional rationale for the bomb, ignored contrary historical evidence, and reinforced the charge that the planned exhibit was a pro-Japanese, anti-American tract.

The conventional view reflects the sober accounts of Truman and his secretary of war,

Henry Stimson: The A-bombs saved as many as 1 million American soldiers who would have been killed or wounded in an invasion of the Japanese mainland—"Our Boys or the Bomb?" as one *Washington Post* op-ed headline put it. This position was defended by veterans groups, most prominently the American Legion and the Air Force Association, which campaigned vigorously against the initial plans for the exhibit.

The other version comes from historians who, since the mid-1960s, have been reassessing Truman's decision in light of documents and memoirs. They have found that:

- President Truman did not face the stark choice of either an invasion or the bomb. He had other alternatives.
- No documents back up claims made by Truman and others that an invasion of Japan would have cost as many as 1 million American casualties.
- Archival evidence reveals that a number of factors contributed to Truman's decision to drop the bomb, including bureaucratic momentum, political imperatives, psychological factors and the desire to contain an expansionist Soviet Union. Many historians have concluded the administration saw deterrence of the Soviets as a secondary benefit; they generally agree that ending the war quickly was the dominant reason.
- Some combination of the Soviet Union's August 8 entry into the Pacific war, modification of unconditional surrender terms, a blockade, and conventional bombing most likely would have forced the Japanese to surrender—without the use of the

---

From Tony Capaccio and Uday Mohan, "Missing the Target," *American Journalism Review* (July–August 1995). Reprinted with permission.

A-bomb—before the planned allied invasion of November 1, 1945. These elements in fact contributed significantly to Japan's surrender on August 15.

- The dropping of a second atomic bomb on August 9 on Nagasaki, which instantly killed at least 40,000, cannot be justified on political, military or moral grounds.

This summer, as journalists prepare for the inevitable flurry of 50th anniversary stories in August, they have a chance to test such assessments and evaluate how well they stand up against the conventional explanation for Truman's decision. The resources, both documentary and human, are readily available. However, a survey of the coverage of the *Enola Gay* exhibit flap, as well as earlier anniversary coverage, indicates there has been little willingness by major media organizations to reassess the A-bomb decision with the same energy applied to other great historical controversies, such as the Kennedy assassination or the Cuban missile crisis.

The overall coverage of the exhibit controversy "wasn't very thorough," says George Washington University history professor Ronald Spector, author of the widely acclaimed World War II Pacific theater history book, *Eagle Against the Sun*. "I don't think there was much of an attempt to really understand the issues that were involved."

A July 1993 Air and Space Museum planning document clearly describes what the Smithsonian initially intended for the exhibit scheduled to open this spring: "The primary goal of this exhibition will be to encourage visitors to undertake a thoughtful and balanced re-examination of these events in the light of political and military factors leading to the decision to drop the bomb, the human suffering experienced by the people of Hiroshima and Nagasaki and the long term implications... This exhibit can provide a crucial public service by re-examining these issues in the light of the most recent scholarship."

The museum's plan, however, was derailed by a sophisticated public relations campaign launched by the Air Force Association (AFA), a 180,000-member nonprofit organization headquartered in Arlington, Virginia.

The AFA first heard about the exhibit in August 1993 after the museum disseminated planning documents. The group believed the plans were flawed, so it contacted the museum and began what it once called a "constructive dialogue." During the next seven months AFA officials quietly lobbied the museum to change the tone of the exhibit.

Frustrated by what they felt to be only "cosmetic changes," AFA officials decided to go public in March 1994. They issued a press release, titled "Politically Correct Curating at the Air and Space Museum," stressing what they saw to be an imbalance in the script between the depictions of Japanese suffering at ground zero in Hiroshima and Nagasaki and the dearth of images depicting years of Japan's unspeakable brutality against other Asians and allied prisoners of war.

The AFA's release introduced the now infamous "war of vengeance" quote that reverberated throughout the debate: "For most Americans, it was a war of vengeance. For most Japanese, it was a war to defend their unique culture against Western imperialism."

It was those two sentences, endlessly repeated by the media outside of their original context, that did the most damage to the museum's credibility.

The AFA had other serious problems with the first draft of the exhibit script. "A recurring undertone in the plans and scripts has been suspicion about why the United States used the atomic bomb," stated one association analysis. "Museum officials have seemed reluctant to accept the explanation that it was a military action, taken to end the war and save lives."

Another AFA document suggested that the exhibit section titled "The Decision to Drop the Bomb" should be renamed "The Decision that Ended the War" and "revised to reflect widely accepted scholarship—that President Truman analyzed the… estimates of potential casualties, and made the decision to use the awesome military weapon in order to save lives… All revisionist speculation should be eliminated."

Curators did not expect the attacks. "We believed in rational discussion. We didn't want to get into a knife fight," says one shell-shocked Air and Space Museum official. But Thomas Crouch, chairman of the Air and Space Museum's aeronautics department and chief exhibit curator, concedes that "what went wrong was we didn't give enough thought to the emotional link that's still in the minds of obviously a great many Americans that binds the idea of the bomb, the memory of the bomb … to the euphoria at the end of World War II."

The controversy ignited in the summer of 1994 after the release of the first of four eventual script revisions.

First, in a widely publicized statement, *Enola Gay* pilot Paul Tibbets called the planned exhibit a "package of insults" in a speech to a military group. Then, in mid-July the AFA released internal Air and Space Museum documents, including an April 16, 1994, memo from museum director Martin Harwit acknowledging the exhibit lacked balance.

But the key story—based partly on the internal museum documents the AFA released—was a July 21 *Washington Post* "Style" section piece by Eugene L. Meyer that elevated the controversy to national status when it caught the eye of Republican Rep. Peter Blute of Massachusetts. "The critics accuse the Smithsonian of choosing political correctness over historical accuracy in the presentation," Meyer wrote. "They charge that the exhibit as planned will portray the Japanese largely as suffering, even noble victims and the Americans as racist and ruthless fighters hell-bent on revenge for Pearl Harbor."

So alerted, Blute issued a letter on August 10, co-signed by 23 other legislators, con-

demning the museum for proposing an "anti-American" and "biased" exhibit. The lawmakers wanted "an objective account of the *Enola Gay* and her mission rather than the historically narrow, revisionist view contained in the revised script."

Stanford University professor Barton Bernstein, a well-known atomic bomb historian, is amazed at how little press scrutiny the AFA received. "Any reporter who gave it four seconds of thought would conclude that the Air Force Association is a not a mainline, impartial group on this," he says. "It's a service lobby."

The AFA would keep up its media campaign for 11 months. By the group's own account, it was cited in more than 400 print and broadcast stories during the height of the controversy—from August 1994 through the end of January. Combined with the efforts of the American Legion, which began highly publicized, line by line negotiations with curators in September 1994, the AFA campaign forced the museum to kill its original exhibit concept on January 30.

After members of Congress intervened, the story, as covered by the media, degenerated into a shouting match, with the veterans' groups doing most of the shouting. But instead of covering the veterans' charges *and* the historical debate, the media focused narrowly on the allegations of imbalance and anti-Americanism.

By most accounts, the media coverage of the museum controversy itself was scrupulously fair, at least within the standard news formula of reporting charges and countercharges. Even Air and Space Museum spokesman Michael Fetters is satisfied with the way the museum was treated by the press.

"All I can ask is that before they go with a story that will really provoke a reaction is give us a call and give us an opportunity to respond," says Fetters. "Most of the reporters of the major dailies did that and I'm satisfied. They definitely made a good effort to get a response."

Fetters acknowledged a common observation made by reporters interviewed for this story: "Our own office didn't respond as strongly as we could have so we bear a lot of the responsibility" for the way the coverage turned out.

Some of the earliest accounts, which appeared in May 1994, were the most evenhanded, especially a May 9 story by *Wichita Eagle* reporter Tom Webb. It ran on the Knight-Ridder wire and was published by at least 17 newspapers, including the *Philadelphia Inquirer, Omaha World-Herald, San Diego Union-Tribune, Orlando Sentinel, Arizona Republic, Portland's Oregonian* and the *Orange County Register*. Webb gave equal weight to the veterans' charges and the Smithsonian's reponse. He also included the curators' views, which debunked the large casualty figures predicted in the event of an invasion of Japan that have been used to justify the bomb. Unfortunately those passages were often cut in the versions that ran.

The *Washington Post* first covered the debate as a federal bureaucracy story on May 31 in a "Capital Notebook" column on its "Federal" page. In contrast with the paper's later critical coverage, it concluded somewhat sympathetically: "There is something to be said for an exhibit that suggests that warplanes are not simply expensive sporting devices to be used for movie props or flyovers at presidential funerals."

But the overall tone of coverage became more strident following Rep. Blute's letter. Reporters, columnists and editorial writers often used criticism by the AFA, the American Legion and other veterans groups as a club to beat on the museum.

Former Air and Space Museum Director Harwit, who resigned in May due to the negative publicity, is more critical of the news coverage than Fetters. He believes many reporters weren't open to the curators' perspective. "I did have the feeling the stories [reporters] had in mind when they came in to see us were the stories they wrote when they left," he says. "It had nothing to do with what we were going to say because what we said would have made their stories differ so much from those that were already in the press."

But Harwit reserved his sharpest criticism for editorial writers. "Columnists took this over and these allegations were in hundreds of newspapers," he says. "One editorialist would write something and then in a day or two you'd see exactly the same wording or the same quotes" in other stories or columns.

Editorial writers in particular did land some hard punches. Perhaps the most damaging piece was written by *Washington Post* Editorial Page Editor Meg Greenfield in an August 14 op-ed column titled "Context and the *Enola Gay*." Blute spokesman Rob Gray says it was instrumental in neutralizing political support for the museum.

"What the tenor of the debate suggests," she wrote, "is a curatorial inability to perceive that political opinions are embedded in the exhibit or to identify them as such—opinions—rather than as universal objective assumptions all thinking people must necessarily share."

Meanwhile, the *Tulsa World* concluded that "a distance of 50 years makes it easy to make half-baked judgments on history." Syndicated columnist Charley Reese of the *Orlando Sentinel* repeated a favorite AFA sound bite, stating that the problem was "the intellectual arrogance of the museum director." A *Providence Journal Bulletin* editorial lamented: "Unfortunately, this latest example is all too characteristic of the way left-wing politics have smothered the Smithsonian's historical presentations." Similarly, the *Indianapolis Star*, published in the home city of the American Legion, opined that "a revisionist faction has tried to turn the planned display ... into an America-bashing enterprise." And syndicated columnist Jeff Jacoby of the *Boston Globe* called the exhibit script "tendentious and manipulative ... It portrays the United States and the Allies as militaristic and racist."

Given the emotions stirred by the controversy, one would expect strong editorial opinions. But often these columns—and many of the news stories—contained factual errors and script passages taken out of context that exacerbated an already polarized debate.

Perhaps the most glaring gap in the coverage was the failure to challenge the standard "our boys or the bomb" assumption—that the allied forces would have had to invade Japan if the atomic bombs hadn't been dropped.

"If you look at the weight of the historians who have written about this, and I'm not a historian of the era, but I've read some of the histories, it seems the evidence is very, very strong," says syndicated columnist Charles Krauthammer of the *Washington Post*. Jacoby agrees. "My best judgment is that this is by and large a settled historical conclusion," he says. "There were major preparations under way for an invasion and it was the use of the bomb that made that invasion unnecessary."

A number of historians say that the AFA, Krauthammer, Jacoby and the other journalists who accepted this "conclusion" are mistaken. "It wasn't that way," says J. Samuel Walker, the historian at the Nuclear Regulatory Commission. "Number one, there were alternatives. Number two, it wasn't at all clear that an invasion was necessary. Clearly, many high officials within the Truman White House and advisers thought the war was practically over. It's less clear Truman felt that way."

University of Southern Mississippi military history professor John Ray Skates, who has written a critical assessment of the planned invasion, says, "It's always couched in this false dichotomy of either the bomb or the invasion. The connections between the use of the bomb and the decision to invade Japan are neither direct nor close."

The view offered by historian Martin Sherwin in the 1987 edition of his book, *A World Destroyed*, was incorporated by the curators in the ill-fated exhibit. He wrote, "The choice in the summer of 1945 was not between a conventional invasion or a nuclear war. It was a choice between various forms of diplomacy and warfare. While the decision that Truman made is understandable, it was not inevitable. It was even avoidable."

University of Nebraska professor Peter Maslowski, in the Spring 1995 issue of *MHQ: The Quarterly Journal of Military History*, noted how out of the four primary options Truman faced, the bomb or invasion "remain so vivid in the national consciousness that it is as if they were always the only possibilities." At the time, however, none of the options—bomb, invasion, blockade or a negotiated settlement that modified the demands for Japan's unconditional surrender—"was self-evidently better than the others." He concluded that "strictly speaking, the bombs were not necessary ... but ... represented a way to avoid the difficulties inherent in the other three" options.

Newsweek also botched the bomb versus invasion issue. A December 12 story quoted Walker's assessment out of context to reinforce the premise that the exhibit script failed to give due consideration to the "bomb or invasion" dilemma Truman faced.

"Did the bomb prevent an invasion of Japan that would have made Normandy look like a training exercise or not?" wrote former Toyko bureau chief Bill Powell, now based in Berlin. "The subject is of fierce dispute among historians. But as J. Samuel Walker ... wrote recently, 'The historical consensus ... which held that the bomb was used primarily for military reasons [i.e., to avoid a bloody invasion of Japan] ... continues to prevail.'"

But in the same Winter 1990 issue of *Diplomatic History*, Walker also wrote: "The consensus among scholars is that the bomb was not needed to avoid an invasion of Japan and to end the war within a relatively short time. It is clear that alternatives to the bomb existed and that Truman and his advisers knew it ... [I]t bears repeating that an invasion was a remote possibility."

Powell concedes he had not seen the entire Walker article and based his story on files from other *Newsweek* reporters. "Perhaps I misinterpreted his quote," he says.

One of the most unfair and unfortunate aspects of the coverage was the consistently poor way reporters and columnists handled the infamous two-sentence "war of vengeance" quote. Although the museum removed the lines in a May 31, 1994, draft, they were repeated for more than a year by the press as representative of the museum's mindset in organizing the exhibit.

They were picked up and hammered home in stories and editorials in newspapers ranging from the *Washington Times* to the *Tulsa World*, *Rocky Mountain News* and Portland's *Oregonian*. They were uttered on the radio by Rush Limbaugh and National Public Radio newscasters, and they were turned into a graphic for the *MacNeil/Lehrer NewsHour*.

"That quote always, always came up," says museum spokesman Fetters. Despite a summer full of script changes "all the veterans groups had to do was talk about 'that *Enola Gay* exhibit that portrayed the Japanese as victims and Americans the aggressors,' and then they would use the 'war of vengeance' quote and all of the sudden we would be fighting that January 1994 script again."

Krauthammer recalled the quote in an August 19 piece with special indignation, noting that although it had been cleaned up "you can imagine the prejudices of those who would write such a thing and the kind of exhibit they would put on."

A fair comment, perhaps. Read in isolation, the quotes are inflammatory. But published in the context of what preceded it—something virtually no journalist, including Krauthammer, saw fit to do—the sentences, while clumsy and open to misinterpretation, are less offensive.

Here is the full passage:

In 1931 the Japanese Army occupied Manchuria; six years later it invaded the rest of China. From 1937 to 1945, the Japanese Empire would be constantly at war.

Japanese expansionism was marked by naked aggression and extreme brutality. The slaughter of tens of thousands of Chinese in Nanking in 1937 shocked the world. Atrocities by Japanese troops included brutal mistreatment of civilians, forced laborers and prisoners of war, and biological experiments on human victims.

In December 1941, Japan attacked U.S. bases in Pearl Harbor, Hawaii, and launched other surprise assaults against allied territories in the Pacific. Thus began a wider conflict marked by extreme bitterness. For most Americans, this war was fundamentally different than the one waged against Germany and Italy—it was a war of vengeance. For most Japanese, it was a war to defend their unique culture against Western imperialism. As the war approached its end in 1945, it appeared to both sides that it was a fight to the finish.

MHQ Editor Robert Cowley agrees the quote was portrayed inaccurately. "If you give the full thing it's not nearly so bad. But what was quoted was that last sentence," he says. "If you take that out of context it's much worse and in that sense, Krauthammer was not being entirely honest. But what we got was that last sentence. Once that was out of the bag, it was hard to stop the conflagration."

Krauthammer stands by his use of the quote. "Anybody who could write that clearly is seeing the Japanese defending their culture against Western 'imperialism.' That certainly cast them as victims."

The *Washington Times* also attacked the museum for the quote. "I couldn't believe that [passage]," says *Times* Editor in Chief Wesley Pruden. "I thought, 'My god. If that's the quality of historian they've got at the Smithsonian we ought to look into it.' ...It was almost as if they were talking about something that happened on another planet."

Pruden, like many journalists, had not seen the entire page, relying instead on previously published accounts. When he was shown the page during an interview, he conceded that "perhaps" his paper ran the quote out of context. "Maybe we should have put that text in a sidebar or graphic of some kind, it probably would have been a good idea," he said. "But I think it pretty much expresses what they had in mind."

As for what the quote intended, curator Michael Neufeld offers this explanation: The media "misread our mindset or misinterpreted our mindset. It was an attempt to interpret what was in the minds of each side at the time. It's not what we thought the Japanese were all about. We were trying to explain what *they* thought they were all about."

AFA Chief of Media Relations Jack Giese defends the association's repeated references. The passage, he says, was only one of three in the initial 500-page script of text and photos to clearly acknowledge Japanese aggression—a point conceded by the curators and subsequently corrected.

The other most common mistakes in the coverage involved the projected number of casualties from an invasion of Japan and the presumption that the exhibit called U.S. motives racist.

In his July 21, 1994, story, "Dropping the Bomb: Smithsonian Exhibit Plan Detonates Controversy," the *Washington Post*'s Meyer wrote that "military planners estimated upwards of 800,000 American casualties would result from a planned two-stage invasion." In an interview, Meyer conceded that the casualty figure was an extrapolation made by Air Force historian Richard Hallion in 1994, not a wartime planning estimate. After another historian questioned the figure, Meyer did not use it in subsequent stories.

Meyer also mischaracterized key themes in the scripts. For example, in a September 30 story, Meyer wrote that early scripts "suggested that American war planners, including President Harry S. Truman, were motivated less by concern over American casualties than by a desire to impress the Soviet Union with the new weapon, and to justify the expenditure of $2

billion in the production of the bomb." The scripts, however, clearly stated that "most scholars have rejected this argument."

"My article did not say that the early scripts made such claims," says Meyer. "It said the scripts 'suggested' conclusions. They did so through sheer repetition of the 'impress-the-Soviets' and pricetag factors, and by understating Truman's concern with lives lost in a possible invasion."

An August 1 piece by *USA Today* columnist Tony Snow was typical of the way the racism issue played. Snow wrote: "A later piece of text raises a racism charge: 'Some have argued that the atomic bomb would never have been dropped on Germans because it was much easier for Americans to bomb Asians than white people.' No serious historian takes this view, but the Smithsonian curators included it."

In fact, the issue was raised by the curators as a "historical controversy" and answered in the script: "The consensus of most, if not all, historians is that President Roosevelt would have used the bomb on Germany if such an attack would have been useful in the European war."

When asked if he unfairly pulled the quote out of context, Snow replied, "If I had to go back and look twice, I probably would have stuck in a parenthetical to say that they make note of the fact that no historian [agrees]." But the fact that the curators raised the issue, he added, "implicitly gave some sense of credence" to it.

On August 29, the *Wall Street Journal* printed one of the most damaging errors just as congressional and editorial pressure was building against the museum. In an editorial titled "War and the Smithsonian," the *Journal* stated that "it is especially curious to note the oozing romanticism with which the *Enola* show's writers describe the kamikaze pilots… These were, the script elegiacally relates, 'youths, their bodies overflowing with life.' Of the youth and life of the Americans who fought and bled in the Pacific there is no mention."

The *Journal*'s observation was picked up the next day by *Washington Post* reporter Ken Ringle, who wrote that "just yesterday, for example, an editorial in the *Wall Street Journal* found it 'especially curious to note…'" He then repeated the statement.

The quote the *Journal* attributed to elegiac curatorial prose was actually written after the war by a surviving kamikaze pilot, Ensign Yukiteru Sugiyama. This was clearly spelled out in the script text.

Journal spokesman Roger May and Ringle refuse to discuss the mistake. "We don't do postmortems on editorials," May says.

On September 26, Ringle contributed "At Ground Zero: 2 Views of History Collide Over Smithsonian A-Bomb Exhibit," a 3,780-word piece that pitted a Bataan death march survivor's perspective against the museum's. The former POW, Grayford C. Payne, told Ringle that "all of us who were prisoners in Japan—or were headed for it to probably die in the invasion—revere the *Enola Gay*. It saved our lives."

In a recent interview, Ringle argued that the Smithsonian's "perceptions are vastly different from the population at large. I can only say if the academic historians were right and all the curators were right, there would be no political pressures the other way."

A traditionally disorganized group, historians entered the debate last fall—much too late to influence public opinion. And they found getting much more than a sound bite was difficult, says a *New York Times* editorial assistant, Timothy McNulty, who wrote a "Week In Review" piece on February 5, 1995, summarizing the controversy. "It was harder for them to get their points across as easily as it was for the veterans," says McNulty. The veterans' side "was a lot more understandable because everyone was used to it. When you see people criticize or question Truman's decision, he's a legend. You knew how the vets would react."

Some reporters did attempt to weave the historical debate in with the exhibit contro-

versy, but they were exceptions. *USA Today* reporter Andrea Stone, for one, consistently incorporated the views of historians in her pieces.

And while the public was continually informed about the veterans groups' take on the exhibit plans, news organizations failed to report that a number of historians had actually praised the museum for its efforts.

Edwin Bearss, special assistant to the director of the National Park Service and a member of the exhibit's advisory board, wrote in February 1994, "As a World War II Pacific combat veteran, I commend you and your colleagues who have dared to go that extra mile to address an emotionally charged and internationally significant event in an exhibit that, besides enlightening, will challenge its viewers."

Even Hallion, one of the critics' favorite sources, had some kind words about the original script. "Overall, this is a most impressive piece of work, comprehensive and dramatic, obviously based upon a great deal of sound research, primary and secondary," he wrote in a February 1994 note.

Nor did reporters get their hands on mid-July assessments from the Joint Chiefs of Staff or the Pentagon's chief historian, Alfred Goldberg. Both judged the museum to be making progress in rewriting a flawed first script.

In a July 15 memo to museum curator Michael Neufeld on the second script, Goldberg noted, "My overall impression of the *Enola Gay* script is favorable. It shows evidence of careful research and an effort to realize a balanced presentation."

By focusing exclusively on the veterans' charges the news media failed to convey the bigger story: Whose version of the historical record is closer to explaining why the atomic bombs were dropped, the veterans groups or the Air and Space Museum curators?

The AFA and other veterans groups wanted "all revisionist speculation" removed. Many of the arguments on the other side—the view of the decision based on archival research—were ably represented by a cover story in the January/February 1995 issue of *Civilization*, a bimonthly magazine published by the Library of Congress. The article, "Why We Dropped the Bomb," was written by William Lanouette, the author of a 1993 book on Leo Szilard, one of the creators of the A-bomb.

Although Lanouette's story was available in mid-December—several weeks before the Smithsonian abandoned its original concept for the exhibit—no reporter referred to his carefully edited findings.

"[I]t still seems fair to conclude that the predominant reason for dropping the bomb was the belief that it would end the war quickly and spare American soldiers," he wrote. "But other factors clearly influenced that decision." Those factors included bureaucratic momentum, political justification, psychological factors and postwar diplomacy.

Lanouette endorsed J. Samuel Walker's conclusion that an invasion was an "unlikely possibility." Moreover, he noted that the United States' insistence on unconditional surrender when the Japanese wanted to retain their emperor "may have foreordained the use of the bomb."

The piece also pointed out that "Truman's new secretary of state, James F. Byrnes, and a number of military leaders saw the awesome weapons as a way to make the Soviets 'more manageable' …"

Indeed, Byrnes told *U.S. News & World Report* in 1960 that "of course" the bomb was dropped to finish the war before the Soviet Union entered on August 8. "We were anxious to get the war over with as soon as possible," he said. "In the days immediately preceding the dropping of that bomb his [Truman's] views were the same as mine—we wanted to get through the Japanese phase of the war before the Russians came in."

A database search found only two stories that addressed the latest historical evidence in any depth. One, a January 31 *New York Times* piece written by reporter John Kifner, wove in the views of atomic bomb historian Gar

Alperovitz—who said it could be documented that "the bomb was not only unnecessary, but known in advance not to be necessary"—with the less critical positions of Stanford's Bernstein and *MHQ*'s Cowley. Kifner also discussed the problem of inflated casualty estimates for a proposed invasion of the Japanese mainland.

Kifner's piece was nearly matched by reporter Rod Dreher of the *Washington Times*, who wrote a January 20 round-up of historians' views debunking the high preinvasion casualty estimates used by exhibit critics. Dreher's editors, however, apparently forgot about his story when they ran a piece a week later that included a chart listing estimates of between 500,000 and 1 million troops killed or wounded in an invasion. "We blew it," admits *Times* Editor in Chief Pruden.

Reflecting on the dearth of historical analysis that typified the *Enola Gay* exhibit coverage, Mark Johnson of Media General News Service summed it up this way:

"What would have been nice to do for a lot of people was to sit down in a research library and read everything they could about how the atomic bomb was created and what happened when it went off," he says. "I would have liked to have gotten more space and have written a history lesson, which you can't do."

No one expects reporters on deadline to be budding Barton Bernsteins. But the realities of time and space do not mean that the conventional wisdom on the A-bomb has to be uncritically passed along to the public. There was ample opportunity and time as the issue unfolded for reporters to incorporate the latest research into their stories.

In this case the media's shortcomings are all too obvious. Journalists did not do enough research and failed to hold the veterans' version of history to the same exacting standard they used in judging the curators' version.

The initial exhibit had flaws of context and historical perspective—but not as serious and certainly not as ill-informed as the media coverage led the public to believe.

QUESTIONS TO CONSIDER

1. Recount, briefly, the conventional account of the decision to drop the atomic bomb on Hiroshima.

2. How does the version from historians differ?

3. Why did the Air Force Association object to the exhibit?

4. How reliable were the editorials and news stories about the bombing decision and Smithsonian exhibit?

5. Should the dropping of atomic bombs on Hiroshima and Nagasaki be in any way considered genocidal acts?

MAKING CONNECTIONS

1. Does the bombing of Hiroshima meet the definition of genocide? Should the second bomb, dropped on Nagasaki, be regarded in a different context than the first bombing?

2. Does the bombing of Royan meet the definition of genocide?

3. Was the controversy over the *Enola Gay* exhibit a case of genocide denial?

4. In what ways are the *Enola Gay* and the Japanese textbook controversies basically different?

✔ RECOMMENDED RESOURCES

Adams, Michael. *The Best War Ever: America and World War II*. Baltimore: Johns Hopkins Press, 1994.

Alperovitz, Gar. *Atomic Diplomacy: Hiroshima and Potsdam: The Use of the Atomic Bomb and the American Confrontation with Soviet Power*. Rev. ed. New York: Penguin Books, 1985.

Dower, John. *War Without Mercy: Race and Power in the Pacific War*. New York: Pantheon Books, 1986.

Feis, Herbert. *The Atomic Bomb and the End of World War II*. Princeton, NJ: Princeton University Press, 1966.

Linenthal, Edward T. and Tom Engelhardt, eds. *History Wars: The Enola Gay and Other Battles for the American Past*. New York: Metropolitan Books, 1996.

CHAPTER 8

DEATH BY HUNGER REPRISE: CHINA

The Chinese famine of 1959 to 1961 caused the deaths of up to 30 million people, making it the worst famine in modern times. Simply put, the famine followed a sudden decline in the available food supply, but the policies of the Communist regime contributed to the disaster.

The central government's planned economy controlled the production and distribution of food. Policy mistakes combined with modest production of grain caused overall grain resources to drop by 15 percent in 1959 and 20 percent in 1960 and 1961. While city dwellers worked with a food-rationing system, farmers, in contrast, had to comply with compulsory grain procurement quotas reminiscent of the Ukraine thirty years earlier.

The famine resulted from the misguided policies of the Chinese Communist government, under megalomaniac Mao Tse-tung. Children, especially, suffered during the famine and the malnutrition that followed. During the famine, with rats and insects gone, peasants engaged in the ghastly practice of *yi zi er shi*—trading children—since no one could bear to eat his own child. Mao belied his propagandistic affection for the peasants, and ruthlessly eliminated all opposition to his policies as Chairman. Marshal Peng Dehusi was the only senior official to protest Mao's policies, for which he was later jailed and tortured to death.

Only after collectivization of the peasants and the Great Leap Forward had destroyed the agricultural system did the Communists begin to back away from the policies with which Mao had redirected the mass-based revolution. In an excerpt from *The Black Book of Communism: Crimes, Terror, Repression,* Jean-Louis Margolin describes "The Greatest Famine in History (1959–1961)."

The Greatest Famine in History (1959–1961)

Jean-Louis Margolin,

University of Provence

For many years one myth was common in the West: that although China was far from being a model democracy, at least Mao had managed to give a bowl of rice to every Chinese. Unfortunately, nothing could be further from the truth. The modest amount of food available per person probably did not increase significantly from the beginning to the end of his reign, despite demands made on the peasantry on a scale rarely seen in history. Mao and the system that he created were directly responsible for what was, and, one hopes, will forever remain, the most murderous famine of all time, anywhere in the world.

Undoubtedly it was not Mao's intention to kill so many of his compatriots. But the least one can say is that he seemed little concerned about the death of millions from hunger. Indeed, his main concern in those dark years seems to have been to deny a reality for which he could have been held responsible. It is always difficult to apportion blame in such situations, to know whether to attack the plan itself or its application. It is, however, indisputable that the Party leadership, and especially Mao himself, displayed economic incompetence, wholesale ignorance, and ivory-tower utopianism. The collectivization of 1955–56 had been more or less accepted by most peasants: it grouped them around their own villages, and it allowed them to pull out of the collective— 70,000 farms did so in Guangdong in 1956–57, and many of the bigger collectives were broken up. The apparent success of reform and the good harvest of 1957 pushed Mao to propose—and to impose on the more reluctant farmers—the goals of the Great Leap Forward (first announced in December 1957 and refined in May 1958) and the means of achieving it—the People's Commune (announced in August 1958).

Within a very short time ("Three years of hard work and suffering, and a thousand years of prosperity," said one slogan at the time), the Great Leap Forward caused nationwide disruption of the peasant way of life. Peasants were to form themselves into huge groups of thousands or even tens of thousands of families, with everything to become communal, including food. Agricultural production was to be developed on a massive scale through pharaonic irrigation projects and new farming methods. Finally, the difference between agricultural and industrial work was to be abolished as industrial units, in particular small furnaces, were created everywhere. The goal was quite similar to the Khrushchev ideal of the "agrotown." The aim was to ensure the self-sufficiency of local communities and to accelerate industrial takeoff by creating new rural industries and using the large agricultural surpluses that the communes were to make for the state and the industry it controlled. In this happy dream that was to bring real Communism within reach, the accumulation of capital and a rapid rise in the standard of living were to go hand in hand. All that had to be done was to achieve the simple objectives set by the Party.

For months everything seemed to be going perfectly. People worked night and day under red flags blowing in the wind. Local leaders announced the breaking of one record

---

Jean-Louis Margolin, "China: A Long March into Night," Stephane Courtois, et al., eds. Trans. by Jonathan Murphy and Mark Kramer, from *The Black Book of Communism: Crimes, Terror, Repression* (Cambridge, Massachusetts: Harvard University Press, 1999), 487–496. Reprinted with permission.

after another as people produced larger quantities "more quickly, better, and more economically." As a result, the goals were continually raised even higher: 375 million tons of grain for 1958, almost double the 195 million tons of the preceding year. In December it was announced that the goal had been met and the results verified by the staff of the Central Statistics Bureau, who had been sent out to the countryside after expressing doubts. The original plan had been to surpass Great Britain in fifteen years; now it appeared certain that it would be done in two. As production quotas continued to rise, it was decided to move more people into industrial production. In Henan, a province intended to serve as a model, 200,000 workers were generously moved to other, more needy regions where results had been poorer. "Socialist emulation" was pushed ever further: all private land and free trade was abolished along with the right to leave the collective, and there was a massive campaign to collect metal tools to transform everything into steel. At the same time, any wood, including doors, was collected to fuel the new furnaces. As compensation, all communal food reserves were eaten at memorable banquets. "Eating meat was considered revolutionary," according to one witness in Shanxi. This was no problem because the next harvest was bound to be enormous. "The human will is the master of all things," the press in Henan had already proclaimed, at the provincial hydraulic conference in October 1957.

But soon the leaders who still emerged from the Forbidden City from time to time (which Mao seldom did) were forced to face facts. They had fallen into their own trap, believing in the power of their own optimism and thinking that after the Long March, success would naturally follow because they felt themselves omnipotent and were used to commanding the workers and the economy like soldiers in a battle. It was easier for cadres to doctor the figures or to put intolerable pressure on administrators to deliver them than it was to admit that the sacrosanct objectives had not been reached. Under Mao, a move to the left (since voluntarism, dogmatism, and violence were left-wing virtues) was always less dangerous than right-wing mediocrity. In 1958–59, the bigger a lie was, the faster its author was promoted. The headlong race was under way, the barometers of success were soaring, and all potential critics were in prison or working on the irrigation projects.

The reasons for the catastrophe were fairly technical. Some agricultural methods advocated by the Soviet academic Trofim Lysenko, who rejected genetics, won great favor in China under the auspices of Mao. They were imposed on the peasants, and the results were disastrous. Mao had proclaimed his belief that "in company grain grows fast; seeds are happiest when growing together"—attempting to impose class solidarity on nature. Accordingly, seeds were sown at five to ten times the normal density, with the result that millions of young plants died. The intensity of the farming methods dried out the soil or caused the salt to rise. Wheat and maize never grow well together in the same fields, and the replacement of the traditional barley crop with wheat in the high, cold fields of Tibet was simply catastrophic. Other mistakes were made in the nationwide campaign. The extermination of the sparrows that ate the grain resulted in a massive increase in the number of parasites. A large amount of hydraulic equipment that had been hurriedly and carelessly built was found to be useless or even dangerous because of the increased erosion and the risk of flooding at the first high tide. Moreover, the cost of its construction in terms of human life had been enormous: more than 10,000 out of 60,000 workers had died on one site in Henan. Risking everything on one large cereal crop (as on steel in industry, where the slogan was "Big is beautiful") ruined all the smaller associated agricultural activities, including the raising of livestock that was often vital for balance in the ecosystem. In Fujian, for instance, the highly profitable tea plantations were all resown as rice fields.

From an economic point of view, the reallocation of resources was disastrous. Although the accumulation of capital reached a record level (43.4 percent of the gross domestic product in 1959) it was used to build ill-conceived or badly finished irrigation projects and to develop industry inside the towns. Although one famous Maoist slogan proclaimed that "China walks on two feet," all the blood from agriculture was pumped into industry. The incompetent allocation of capital was a decisive factor in the no less aberrant allocation of manpower: state industry took on 21 million new workers in 1958, which represented an 85 percent rise in a single sector in one year. In 1957–1960 the share of the population working outside agriculture increased from 15 percent to 20 percent, and all these people had to be fed by the state. Meanwhile, workers in the countryside were being exhausted by everything except agriculture. They were being drafted into large engineering projects, small steelworks whose output for the most part was worthless, the destruction of traditional villages, and the construction of new towns. After the marvelous harvest of 1958, it was decided that cereal production could be cut by 13 percent. This combination of "economic delirium and political lies" resulted in the harvests of 1960, which many of the peasants were too weak to gather. Henan, the first province to be declared "100 percent hydraulic," since the construction of dikes and irrigation work there was technically finished, was also one of the regions hardest hit by the famine; estimates of the deaths there vary from 2 million to 8 million. The state quota had reached its height, going from 48 million tons of cereal in 1957 (17 percent of all production), to 67 million in 1959 (28 percent), to 51 million in 1960. The trap closed around those who had lied, or rather, around their administrators. In the supposedly model district

of Fengyang (Anhui), 199,000 tons of grain were announced for 1959, a considerable increase over the 178,000 tons of the previous year; but real production was a mere 54,000 tons, as opposed to 89,000 in 1958. Despite the shortfall, the state took a very real part of this phantom harvest, claiming 29,000 tons. The following year, almost everyone had to eat clear rice soup, and the somewhat surreal slogan for the year 1959 in the *People's Daily* was: "Live frugally in a year of plenty." The national press began to sing the praises of a daily nap, and medical professors came out to explain the particular physiology of the Chinese, for whom fat and proteins were an unnecessary luxury.

There was perhaps still time to change direction and alter things for the better. Steps were taken in that direction in December 1958. But the inception of a serious split with the U.S.S.R., and above all the attack in July 1959 by the well-respected Marshal Peng Dehuai on the Communist Party Politburo and Mao's strategy, gave Mao purely tactical political reasons to refuse to acknowledge that the country was facing any difficulties and thus to acknowledge any blame. The overly lucid minister of defense was thus replaced by Lin Biao, who showed himself to be a servile creature of the Helmsman. Peng was sidelined but not actually arrested at the time. In 1967 he was thrown out of the Party and sentenced to life in prison, dying in 1974. Mao's hatred was long-lasting. To turn the situation to his advantage, he tried in 1959 to reinforce the Great Leap Forward by calling for people's communes to be extended into the cities (a strategy never actually implemented). China then experienced its great famine, but Mao would survive. As Lin Biao was to say later, it is geniuses who make history.

The resulting famine affected the whole country. In Beijing, playing fields and recreation areas were transformed into allotments, and 2 million chickens were to be found on people's balconies in the capital. No province was spared, despite the immense size of the country and the wide variety of climates and cultures. That fact alone shows the ridiculousness of the official explanation, which blamed the famine on some of the worst climatic conditions of the century. In fact 1954 and 1980 saw far greater climatic disturbances. In 1960, only 8 of the 120 Chinese weather stations noted a drought of any consequence, and only a third mentioned drought as a problem at all. The 1960 harvest of 143 million tons of grain was 26 percent lower than that of 1957, which was almost the same as that of 1958. The harvest had fallen to its level in 1950, while the population had grown by 100 million during the decade. The towns, which were generally privileged in terms of allocations of food stocks, partly because of the proximity of the government, were not hit as hard. In 1961, at the darkest moment, their inhabitants on average received 181 kilos of grain, whereas peasants received 153; the peasants' ration had fallen by 23 percent, that of the townspeople by 8 percent. Mao, in the tradition of Chinese leaders, but in contradiction to the legend that he encouraged to grow up around him, showed here how little he really cared for what he thought of as the clumsy and primitive peasants.

There were considerable variations among regions. The most fragile regions, in the north and northwest, the only ones that had really suffered famine over the last century, were the hardest hit. By contrast, in Heilongjiang, in the far north, which was relatively untouched and largely virgin territory, the population climbed from 14 million to 20 million as the region became a haven for the hungry. As in earlier European famines, regions that specialized in commercial agricultural products (such as oil seed, sugarcane, sugar beet, and above all cotton) saw production fall dramatically, sometimes by as much as two-thirds. Since the hungry no longer had the means to buy their products, hunger struck here with particular severity. The price of rice on the free market

(or on the black market) rose fifteen- or even thirtyfold. Maoist dogma exacerbated the disaster: because people's communes had a duty to be self-sufficient, the transfer of goods between provinces had been drastically reduced. There was also a lack of coal as hungry miners left to find food or to cultivate allotments wherever they could. The situation was compounded by the general apathy and dissolution brought on by hunger. In industrialized provinces such as Liaoning the effects were cumulative: agricultural production in 1960 fell to half of 1958 levels, and whereas an average of 1.66 million tons of foodstuffs had arrived in that region each year during the 1950s, after 1958 transfers for the whole country fell to a mere 1.5 million tons.

The fact that the famine was primarily a political phenomenon is demonstrated by the high death rates in provinces where the leaders were Maoist radicals, provinces that in previous years had actually been net exporters of grain, like Sichuan, Henan, and Anhui. This last province, in north-central China, was the worst affected of all. In 1960 the death rate soared to 68 percent from its normal level at around 15 percent, while the birth rate fell to 11 percent from its previous average of 30 percent. As a result the population fell by around 2 million people (6 percent of the total) in a single year. Like Mao himself, Party activists in Henan were convinced that all the difficulties arose from the peasants' concealment of private stocks of grain. According to the secretary of the Xinyang district (10 million inhabitants), where the first people's commune in the country had been established, "The problem is not that food is lacking. There are sufficient quantities of grain, but 90 percent of the inhabitants are suffering from ideological difficulties." In the autumn of 1959 the class war was momentarily forgotten, and a military-style offensive was launched against the peasants, using methods very similar to those used by anti-Japanese guerrilla groups. At least 10,000 peasants were imprisoned, and many died of hunger behind bars. The order was given to smash all privately owned cutlery that had not yet been turned to steel to prevent people from being able to feed themselves by pilfering the food supply of the commune. Even fires were banned, despite the approach of winter. The excesses of repression were terrifying. Thousands of detainees were systematically tortured, and children were killed and even boiled and used as fertilizer—at the very moment when a nation-wide campaign was telling people to "learn the Henan way." In Anhui, where the stated intention was to keep the red flag flying even if 99 percent of the population died, cadres returned to the traditional practices of live burials and torture with red-hot irons. Funerals were prohibited lest their number frighten survivors even more and lest they turn into protest marches. Taking in the numerous abandoned children was also banned, on the ground that "The more we take in, the more will be abandoned." Desperate villagers who tried to force their way into the towns were greeted with machine-gun fire. More than 800 people died in this manner in the Fenyang district, and 12 percent of the rural population, or 28,000 people, were punished in some manner. This campaign took on the proportions of a veritable war against the peasantry. In the words of Jean-Luc Domenach, "The intrusion of Utopia into politics coincided very closely with that of police terror in society." Deaths from hunger reached over 50 percent in certain villages, and in some cases the only survivors were cadres who abused their position. In Henan and elsewhere there were many cases of cannibalism (63 were recorded officially): children were sometimes eaten in accordance with a communal decision.

In 1968 Wei Jingsheng, an eighteen-year-old Red Guard pursued by the authorities like millions of others, took refuge with his family in a village in Anhui, where he heard many stories about the Great Leap Forward:

As soon as I arrived here, I often heard peasants talking about the Great Leap Forward as though it was some sort of apocalypse that they had by some miracle escaped. Quite fascinated, I questioned them in detail about the subject so that soon I too was convinced that the "three years of natural catastrophes" had not been as natural as all that, and had rather been the result of a series of political blunders. The peasants said, for example, that in 1959–60, during the "Communist Wind" [one of the official names for the Great Leap Forward] their hunger had been so great that they had not even been strong enough to harvest the rice crop when it was ready, and that it would otherwise have been a relatively good year for them. Many of them died of hunger watching the grains of rice fall into the fields, blown off by the wind. In some villages there was literally no one left to take in the harvest. One time I was with a relative who lived a small distance away from our village. On the way to his home, we went past a deserted village. All the houses had lost their roofs. Only the mud walls remained.

Thinking it was a village that had been abandoned during the Great Leap Forward, when all the villages were being reorganized and relocated, I asked why the walls hadn't been knocked down to make room for more fields. My relative replied: "But these houses all belong to people, and you can't knock them all down without their permission." I stared at the walls and couldn't believe that they were actually inhabited. "Of course they were inhabited! But everyone here died during the 'Communist Wind,' and no one has ever come back. The land was then shared out among the neighboring villages. But because it seemed possible that some of them might come back, the living quarters were never shared out. Still, that was so long ago, I don't think anyone will come back now."

We walked along beside the village. The rays of the sun shone on the jade-green weeds that had sprung up between the earth walls, accentuating the contrast with the rice fields all around, and adding to the desolation of the landscape. Before my eyes, among the weeds, rose up one of the scenes I had been told about, one of the banquets at which the families had swapped children in order to eat them. I could see the worried faces of the families as they chewed the flesh of other people's children. The children who were chasing butterflies in a nearby field seemed to be the reincarnation of the children devoured by their parents. I felt sorry for the children, but not as sorry as I felt for their parents. What had made them swallow that human flesh, amidst the tears and grief of other parents—flesh that they would never have imagined tasting, even in their worst nightmares? In that moment I understood what a butcher he had been, the man "whose like humanity has not seen in several centuries, and China not in several thousand years": Mao Zedong. Mao Zedong and his henchmen, with their criminal political system, had driven parents mad with hunger and led them to hand their own children over to others, and to receive the flesh of others to appease their own hunger. Mao Zedong, to wash away the crime that he had committed in assassinating democracy [an allusion to the Hundred Flowers trap], had launched the Great Leap Forward, and obliged thousands and thousands of peasants dazed by hunger to kill one another with hoes, and to save their own lives thanks to the flesh and blood of their childhood companions. They were not the real killers; the real killers were Mao Zedong and his companions. At last I understood where Peng Dehuai had found the strength to attack the Central Committee of the Party led by Mao, and at last I understood why the peasants loathed Communism so much, and why they had never allowed anyone to attack the policies of Liu Shaoqi, "three freedoms and one guarantee." For the good and simple reason that they had no intention of ever having to eat their own flesh and blood again, or of killing their companions to eat them in a moment of instinctual madness. That reason was far more important than any ideological consideration.

At the moment that Yuri Gagarin was being launched into space, a country possessing more than 30,000 miles of railway lines and an extensive radio and telephone network was being ravaged by a subsistence crisis of the sort that had plagued premodern Europe, but on a scale that in the eighteenth century would have affected the population of the entire world. Literally countless millions were trying to boil grass and bark to make soup, stripping leaves off trees in the towns, wandering the roads of the country desperate for anything to eat trying vainly to attack food convoys, and sometimes desperately banding together into gangs (as in the Xinyang and Lan Kao districts in Henan). They were sent nothing to eat, but on occasion the local cadres who were supposedly responsible for the famine were shot. There were armed raids on houses all over the country in a search for ground maize. An enormous increase in disease and infections increased the death rate further, while the birth rate fell to almost zero as women were unable to conceive because of malnutrition. Prisoners in the *laogai* were not the last to die of hunger, although their situation was no less precarious than that of the neighboring peasants who came to the camps to beg for something to eat. In August 1960, after one year of famine, three-quarters of Jean Pasqualini's work brigade were dead or dying, and the survivors were reduced to searching through horse manure for undigested grains of wheat and eating the worms they found in cowpats. People in the camps were used as guinea pigs in hunger experiments. In one case flour was mixed with 30 percent paper paste in bread to study the effects on digestion, while in another study marsh plankton were mixed with rice water. The first experiment caused atrocious constipation throughout the camp, which caused many deaths. The second also caused much illness, and many who were already weakened ended up dying.

For the entire country, the death rate rose from 11 percent in 1957 to 15 percent in 1959 and 1961, peaking at 29 percent in 1960. Birth rates fell from 33 percent in 1957 to 18 percent in 1961. Excluding the deficit in births, which was perhaps as many as 33 million (although some births were merely delayed), loss of life linked to the famine in the years 1959–1961 was somewhere between 20 million and 43 million people. The lower end of the range is the official figure used by the Chinese government since 1988. This was quite possibly the worst famine not just in the history of China but in the history of the world. The second worst had occurred in northern China in 1877–78 and had taken between 9 million and 13 million lives. The one that had struck the U.S.S.R. in a similar political and economic context in 1932–1934 had caused around 6 million deaths, a smaller proportion of the total population than in China during the Great Leap Forward. Under normal conditions, mortality in the countryside was between 30 percent and 60 percent higher than in the cities. In 1960 it doubled, climbing from 14 percent to 29 percent. Peasants managed to delay the effects of the famine slightly by consuming their own livestock, which amounted to using up their productive capital. In 1957–1961, 48 percent of pigs and 30 percent of all dairy animals were slaughtered. The surface area given over to nonfood crops such as cotton, which was the country's main industry at the time, diminished by more than one-third in 1959–1962, and this fall in production inevitably hit the manufacturing sector. Although after 1959 peasant markets were reopened to stimulate production, the prices demanded were so high and the quantities available so low that few of the starving could find enough to survive. In 1961, for example, the price of pork was fourteen times higher in the markets than in the state shops. The price of feed went up less than that of grain in the pastoral northwest, which was chronically deficient in grain. In Gansu people were still dying of hunger in 1962, and the grain ration was equivalent to only half the official limit for conditions of "semi-starvation."

Whether through unawareness of or, more likely, indifference to the several million lives that had to be sacrificed to build Communism, the state responded (if such a word can be used here) to the crisis with measures that under the circumstances were quite simply criminal. Net grain exports, principally to the U.S.S.R., rose from 2.7 million tons in 1958 to 4.2 million in 1959, and in 1960 fell only to the 1958 level. In 1961, 5.8 million tons were actually imported, up from 66,000 in 1960, but this was still too little to feed the starving. Aid from the United States was refused for political reasons. The rest of the world, which could have responded easily, remained ignorant of the scale of the catastrophe. Aid to the needy in the countryside totaled less than 450 million yuan per annum, or 0.8 yuan per person, at a time when one kilo of rice on the free market was worth 2 to 4 yuan. Chinese Communism boasted that it could move mountains and tame nature, but it left these faithful to die.

From August 1959 until 1961, the Party acted as though it was powerless to help, simply standing by and watching events unfold. Criticizing the Great Leap Forward, behind which Mao had thrown all his weight, was a dangerous business. But the situation became so bad that Liu Shaoqi, the number two leader in the regime, finally put the Chairman on the defensive and imposed a partial return to the easier form of collectivization that had been the policy before the invention of the people's communes. People were again allowed to own a small amount of land, peasant markets were reopened, small private workshops were opened, and labor teams were subdivided into labor brigades, which were equivalent to the size of the earlier village teams. As a result of these measures the country quickly emerged from the famine. But it did not emerge as fast from poverty. Agricultural production, which had grown steadily from 1952 to 1958, had lost its way, and the effects were felt for two decades. Confidence would return only "when the belly was full" (as Mao said would occur in the people's communes). Overall agricultural production doubled between 1952 and 1978, but during this time the population rose from 574 million to 959 million, and most of the per-capita increase in production had taken place in the 1950s. In most places production did not reach 1957 levels until at least 1965 (and as late as 1968–69 in Henan). Overall, agricultural productivity was severely affected; the

Great Leap Forward's astonishing waste of resources caused it to fall by about one-quarter. Not until 1983 did productivity again reach 1952 levels. Eyewitness reports from the days of the Cultural Revolution all concur that China was still a traditional village society of great poverty, functioning as a subsistence economy where luxuries were extremely rare (cooking oil, for instance, was like gold dust). The Great Leap Forward made the people extremely suspicious of the regime's propaganda. It is hardly surprising that the peasants responded most enthusiastically to Deng Xiaoping's economic reforms, and were the driving force behind the reintroduction of a market economy twenty years after the launch of the people's communes.

The disasters of 1959–1961, the regime's great secret, which many foreign visitors also managed to deny, were never recognized for what they really were. Liu went out on a limb in January 1962 when he claimed at a conference of cadres that 70 percent of the famine had been due to human error. It was impossible to say any more than that without directly incriminating Mao. Even after his death, in the Chinese Communist Party's televised final verdict on his life in 1981, there was no criticism of the Great Leap Forward.

QUESTIONS TO CONSIDER

1. Characterize Mao's response to the famine.
2. Explain how the adoption of the agricultural methods of the Soviet academic Trofim Lysenko exacerbated the famine.
3. Why does the author see the famine as "primarily a political phenomenon"?
4. Why does the author conclude that "the state responded … to the crisis with measures that under the circumstances were quite simply criminal"?

MAKING CONNECTIONS

1. How does the Chinese famine compare with the *Holodomor*?
2. Does the Chinese famine fit R. J. Rummel's definition of democide?
3. Is there something unique about communist revolutions that produces such horrific famines?

✔ RECOMMENDED RESOURCES

Becker, Joseph. *Hungry Ghosts: Mao's Secret Famine.* New York: Henry Holt and Company, 1996.

Conquest, Robert. *Reflections on a Ravaged Century.* New York: W. W. Norton & Company, 2000.

Yang, D. *Catastrophe and Reform in China.* Stanford: Stanford University Press, 1996.

CHAPTER 9

RWANDA, SUDAN, ANGOLA CASE STUDIES: POST-COLONIAL AFRICA

Rwanda and the "*g*-word,"—not saying *genocide* does not make the reality of it go away. The Rwandan genocide of 1994 exposed American reluctance to prevent genocide. After Hutu soldiers murdered ten Belgian peacekeepers on April 7, 1994, the Belgian government indicated to the U.S. that it would withdraw from Rwanda if UN forces there were not reinforced. The Clinton administration immediately backed away from involvement, and even encouraged the UN to cut the strength of the UN Assistance Mission for Rwanda (UNAMIR) from 2,500 to 500 two weeks after the genocide began. Senior administration officials decided not to act because there was no significant domestic pressure to intervene.

The combination of the lack of clarity in defining and applying the term "genocide," and the fact that genocide often occurs during war (making it hard to discern), are often used by apologists to explain government inaction toward the events in Rwanda. The leading skeptic for intervention is Alan Kuperman. He concludes in *The Limits of Humanitarian Intervention: Genocide in Rwanda*, that the Clinton administration did not know that genocide was in progress until it was too late to take action. Yet, from December 1993 onward, General Romeo Dallaire, the commander of UNAMIR, received reports anticipating mass killings. By the day after the massacres began, the U.S. Defense Intelligence Agency intercepted communications from officials in Kigoli that ordered the massacres.

Kuperman claims that the U.S. would not have marshaled the forces to make a difference quickly enough. Be that as it may, it is the lead-up to the disaster that should be scrutinized. Policy makers may have had the resources in place to make a difference if they had been disposed to act.

It could be argued that many Americans do not believe that they bear any responsibility to stop the murder of foreigners. Some may believe that the ideals on which the United States was founded—namely natural law—precludes intervention to defend it elsewhere.

Mark Huband describes how the world's governments failed to intervene to stop the slaughter, but were complicit. Francis M. Deng provides a case study of Sudan. The third reading, on Angola, requires the reader to agree or disagree with the Genocide Prevention Center's conclusion that this civil war did not constitute genocide.

Rwanda—The Genocide

Mark Huband,

Cairo Correspondent for the Financial Times *(London)*

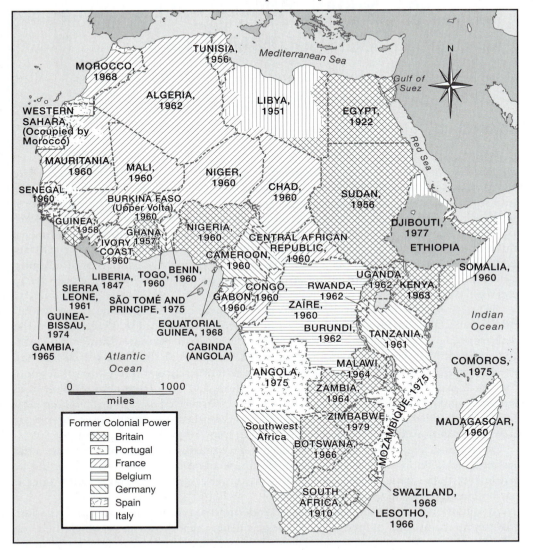

The term genocide is used widely and sometimes loosely, but what took place in Rwanda in April and May of 1994 was the third unquestionable genocide of the twentieth century. As defined by the 1948 Convention for the Prevention and Punishment of the Crime of Genocide, it consists of

Mark Huband, "Rwanda—The Genocide," Roy Gutman and David Rieff, eds. From *Crimes of War: What the Public Should Know* (New York: W.W. Norton & Company, 1999), 312–15. Reprinted with permission.

certain acts "committed with an intent to destroy, in whole or in part, a national, ethnical, racial, or religious group as such." In Rwanda, somewhere between 500,000 and 1 million Tutsis and moderate Hutus, who fit the convention's definition of a national group, were murdered.

The planning of this *genocide*, which was important legally because it established the clear intent of its architects to commit the crime, had become known to the United Nations well before it took place. The Rwandan government's effort in 1993 to carry out a census in which all Rwandans had to state their tribe had been followed by a slaughter of Tutsis in the northern part of the country. This would prove to be a macabre dress rehearsal for the genocide of 1994.

In the interim, the Rwandan president, Juvenal Habyarimana, signed a peace accord in Arusha, Tanzania, with the Tutsi-led Rwandan Patriotic Front (RPF) that was intended to end the country's four-year civil war. Whether President Habyarimana sincerely intended peace, or more likely, viewed it as a pause in which to finalize plans to exterminate the Tutsis, will probably never be answered conclusively. What is clear is that he was restructuring the Hutu-dominated national administration to put extremists in positions of authority—extremists whose main goal was to conspire to launch a final, genocidal strike against the hated Tutsi minority.

On April 6, 1994, President Habyarimana flew back from Tanzania after a meeting on the peace process. As Habyarimana's plane attempted to land in the Rwandan capital, Kigali, it was shot down by extremist members of the president's own party. They were, in any case, quite ready to sacrifice him since they believed he had conceded too much to the RPF in the peace agreement, even if only temporarily.

Habyarimana's death served as the pretext to launch the genocide. Rwanda's national radio as well as a number of private stations relayed instructions to the death squads, the so-called Interahamwe (the name, in Kinyarwanda, means "those who fight together"), and ceaselessly urged

the killers to step up their slaughter. The Rwandan armed forces backed up the Interahamwe in those areas where the killers encountered resistance from Tutsi civilians. Prepositioned transport and fuel permitted the death squads to reach even the most isolated Tutsi communities.

Other genocides—the Turkish slaughter of the Armenians, the Nazi extermination of Europe's Jews and Gypsies—took place largely in secret. Rwanda was different. There was a United Nations peacekeeping force on the ground in Rwanda. Its members stood by and watched as the killings took place. The rest of the world watched on television as Rwanda exploded.

I recall a young woman pleading silently through the terror in her eyes as she was led to her death past French UN troops. The French were guarding foreign evacuees fleeing the Rwandan capital in an open truck, and a government militia had ordered the convoy to halt on a muddy road near the city's airport. The UN troops waited obediently, saying it was "not our mandate" to intervene. Beside them in a compound, two men were kneeling in silence as the militiamen crushed their heads with clubs, then cut their throats. The woman knelt beside them. Within less than a minute her head was all but severed. Then the convoy was allowed to move on.

The world's governments not only knew what was occurring but were complicit. Article 1 of the Genocide Convention binds its signatories to act to prevent as well as to punish genocide. The fact that the UN knew the genocide was being planned and, presumably, communicated this knowledge to member-States, and the fact that once the genocide began nothing was done, makes what took place in Rwanda in 1994 more than a crime. It was an event that shamed humanity.

It is clear by now that far from having been caught unawares, the great powers were intent on obscuring the reality of what was taking place in Rwanda. When the Security Council met, it was decided that the representative of Rwanda—of the government that was committing the genocide—would be allowed to make a statement. For all practical purposes, the council's main concern appears to have been to debate for as long as possible the question of whether a genocide was taking place.

There were thousands of examples of the State's role. At the Nyarubuye Catholic Mission in eastern Rwanda, I happened upon Leoncia Mukandayambaje, a survivor, sitting outside her hut among the trees. She had fled there when the local mayor, Sylvestre Gacumbitsi, had given the local Tutsi population special passes to allow them to reach the large brick complex. After grouping them there, he arranged for two truckloads of murderers to be sent.

In school rooms, in cloisters, in corridors, and in doorways, the 2,620 victims covered the floor in a carpet of rotting death. Leoncia was saved by her baby daughter, whom she held close to her while the murderers hacked both with machetes. Her daughter's blood covered her. The murderers assumed both mother and child were dead.

By the time the UN Security Council had finally concluded what was plain from the start—that a genocide had indeed been taking place—it was too late to do anything for the people of Rwanda. To have admitted otherwise would have bound the parties to the Genocide Convention, among whom were all the permanent members of the Security Council, to intervene and bring the mass murder to a halt. The council, on May 26, did eventually find that a genocide was taking place. By that time, half a million had died. Secretary-General Boutros-Ghali's acknowledgement was too little, too late.

He was still ahead of U.S. Secretary of State Warren Christopher. From the beginning of the slaughter, the U.S. government had prohibited its officials from using the term genocide. Finally, on June 10, Christopher relented, reluctantly and with bad grace. "If there is any particular magic in calling it genocide," he conceded, "I have no hesitancy in saying that."

There was magic, all right, in the sense that using the term would have bound the United States and other governments to act. By the time Christopher made his grudging concession to reality, it was too late, which may have been the idea all along.

The complicity of the so-called world community in the Rwandan genocide should not, of course, obscure the fact that the principal responsibility for the crime lies with its Rwandan architects. Apologists for the Rwandan authorities insisted at the time that the killings were unfortunate by-products of a renewal of the civil war. Later, Hutu extremists justified the killings as acts of self-defense against Tutsi aggression. Such arguments stood reality on its head. Almost all the victims in the spring of 1994 were killed as part of a government-inspired campaign of extermination, not as casualties of the subsequent fighting between the Rwandan Army and the RPF.

According to the provisions of the Genocide Convention, the government was guilty on all counts of the Convention's Article 3: genocide, conspiracy to commit genocide, direct and public *incitement* to commit genocide, and complicity in genocide. Members of the government had used its administration to organize the slaughter and, equally grave, incited the Hutu civilian population to kill their Tutsi neighbors and even, for intermarriage was common in Rwanda, to kill Tutsi spouses and relatives.

After the slaughter was over, an international tribunal was established to bring the guilty to book, to try them under international humanitarian law and under the provisions of the Genocide Convention. Doubtless, such trials are better than nothing. At least, in the Rwandan case, there will not be total impunity. But trials are a poor substitute for prevention, and the one thing that is clear is that the Rwandan genocide could have been prevented had the outside world had the will to do so. The facts were plain. The legal basis for intervention was there. It was courage that was lacking.

QUESTIONS TO CONSIDER

1. What was the pretext for launching the Rwandan genocide?
2. In what significant way was the Rwandan genocide different from the Armenian and Nazi atrocities?
3. Explain the irony of the world's governments obscuring the genocide.
4. Describe U.S. response to the genocide.

Sudan—Civil War and Genocide

Francis M. Deng

Senior Fellow: Brookings Institution

Muslims in Total Population
- Over 50%
- 51% to 85%
- 26% to 50%
- 3% to 25%
- League of Arab States

The great challenge for Christianity in the Sudan, especially in the southern part of the country, is closely linked to the civil war between Sudan's North and South. This war has raged intermittently since 1955, making it possibly the longest civil conflict in the world.

"Sudan—Civil War and Genocide," by Francis M. Deng from *Middle East Quarterly* Winter 2001, 8(1): 13–21. Reprinted by permission.

It continues unabated, mostly outside the focus of diplomacy or the attention of international media, taking a huge and terrible human toll. Over two million people have died as a result of the war and related causes, such as war-induced famine. About five million people have been displaced, while half a million more have fled across an international border. Tens of thousands of women and children have been abducted and subjected to slavery. By all accounts, it appears to be the worst humanitarian disaster in the world today.

Religion is the pivotal factor in the conflict. The North, with roughly two-thirds of Sudan's land and population, is Muslim and Arabic-speaking; the northern identity is an inseparable amalgamation of Islam and the Arabic language. The South is more indigenously African in race, culture, and religion; its identity is indigenously African, with Christian influences and a Western orientation.

Although Christianity predated Islam in northern Sudan, it was effectively eradicated and replaced by Islam by the early sixteenth century. It was then introduced to the southern part of the country through missionary work that was associated with British colonialism. Since independence, the South has been threatened by the policies of Arabization and Islamization. Paradoxically, the religious persecution of non-Muslims has the effect of promoting Christianity; Southerners now see Christianity as the most effective means of counteracting the imposition of Islam, especially as traditional religions cannot withstand the forces of spiritual and religious globalization.

BACKGROUND: THE NORTH

The civil war culminates a long history in which the North has tried to spread its religion and language to the South, which has resisted these efforts.

The North's identification with the Middle East is an ancient one, going back several thousand years, to the time when Egyptians and Arabians expanded southward in the search for slaves, gold, ivory, and taxation revenue. Christianity entered the scene in the sixth century AD and became the religion of three kingdoms (Nubia, Magarra, and Alwa) that survived for a thousand years. The introduction of Islam a century later, primarily by traders, then led to descent groups in Sudan tracing their genealogy back to Arabia; in the case of politically or religiously prominent families, they claim to have roots going back to the Prophet Muhammad himself. Islamization set in motion a process of gradual decline for Christianity in northern Sudan, culminating in the overthrow of the Christian kingdoms in 1504 by an alliance of Arabs and the Muslim kingdom of Funj. In due course, Islam and Arabic gained hold in the North and overshadowed the indigenous and Christian cultures. Islam in northern Sudan was later reinforced by every successive regime, from the Ottoman-Egyptian administration that invaded the country in 1821 to the Mahdist Islamic revolution that overthrew it in 1885, and even to the Anglo-Egyptian Condominium that ruled the country from 1898 until Sudanese independence in 1956.

In the nineteenth century, the Turkish rulers of Egypt and the Mahdist government in Khartoum invaded the South in hopes of extending their own boundaries, as well as to gain access to more slaves. Indeed, to Southerners their actions were indistinguishable from one another; they were all slave hunters. Southern memory associates them with nothing less than the total destruction of their society. Oral history in Sudan refers to this period as the time when the world was spoiled.

While Arabs could invade the South to capture slaves, they never penetrated deeply and did not settle. Swamps, flies, mosquitoes, tropical humidity, and the fierce resistance of the people kept contact to a minimum, even as it was devastatingly violent. Arabs were interested in the material value of blacks as slaves and so had no wish to integrate with them (in contrast to their pattern of settling down with Northerners); had the southern Sudanese converted to Islam, it bears noting, Arabs could no longer have engaged in legal slave raids against them (given that Islam prohibits the enslavement of fellow Muslims).

BACKGROUND: THE SOUTH

In sharp contrast, the identity of southern Sudan has been shaped primarily by the prolonged resistance to the imposition of Arab and Islamic culture from the North. This has had the effect of unifying the Southerners as black Africans and has geared them toward Christianity and the English language as means of combating Islam and Arabism.

In contrast to the Arabs, the British were associated with the redemption of the South from the Arab slave raids. The British sought first to suppress the trade in slaves through their influence on the Turko-Egyptian administration, then, after the re-conquest of the Sudan in 1898, to abolish it; also, British occupation meant that the North's efforts to spread Islam southwards were confined to urban centers and in the end were significantly frustrated. In sharp contrast to the Muslims, Christian missionaries came to southern Sudan peacefully. They arrived with the British conquest of Sudan, encouraged by London to spread the Christian gospel through pacific means, largely by providing education, health services, and other social services. To avoid sectarian competition, the British administration allotted each sect spheres of influence for its missionaries. Over the next century, Christian missionary activity came to be associated with personal well-being and socio-economic development, positive incentives which won over many new converts.

This official favoritism toward Christian missions in the South, notwithstanding, the British authorities in Sudan sought to keep religion and state apart. Thus, the Reverend Wilson Cash, secretary of the Church Missionary Society, observed in 1930:

The government is scrupulously fair to Muslims and pagans, and in religious matters adopts a strictly neutral attitude. The task of evangelization is no part of the government's work and it falls to the mission alone to decide whether these southern pagan tribes shall be left to be captured for Islam or whether they shall be won for Jesus Christ.

Some missionaries worried that this neutrality would in the long term benefit Islam, for the latter in many ways better accommodated the African way of life and was therefore more likely to appeal to the pagans. For example, whereas the Christian proselytizer is interested in intensive religious instruction as a prerequisite to baptism, the Islamizer is more interested in the recital by the convert of the words, "There is no divinity but God, and Muhammad is His Prophet." As Charles D'Oliver Farran observed, "No other test is necessary, and it would not matter if he had never heard of Mecca or even the Koran." Among other factors which, according to northern Sudanese scholar Mahgoub Ahmed Kurdi, appear to favor Islam are the Arabic language, the equal status practiced among Muslims, the ease with which the Islamic creed was understood, the comprehensive determination by Islam of all the aspects of personal, social, and religious life, the similarities between Islam and African traditional religions, and Islam's orientation of its converts towards Islamization in southern Sudan.

In the Sudanese context, the Arabic language had special importance, for it gave the Southerners the ability to communicate with all the inhabitants of the Sudan, especially the Northerners and the government whose daily language was Arabic. Having no common language of their own, the members of various tribes took recourse to Arabic as lingua franca to understand one another. Those who mastered the language immediately found themselves in an advantaged position over those who did not. Commonly the Arabic language therefore served the religious as well as the mundane purposes.

Despite this, southern Sudanese tended to receive Christianity favorably, for they associated it with peaceful preaching and the benefits of modern education and medical services. Christianity also benefited from the sense that Europeans had come to rescue the Southerners from enslavement by Arabs. This understanding was, of course, a bit innocent, for some nineteenth-century Europeans were in fact engaged in the slave trade, but their involvement was hidden by their reliance on Egyptian or northern Sudanese middlemen whom southern Sudanese saw as the sole culprits.

CIVIL WAR SINCE INDEPENDENCE

With independence in 1956, the northern-dominated government in Khartoum sought to Arabize and Islamize the South. It had two motives: a belief that homogenizing the country would ensure national unity and a desire to spread what they considered to be a superior civilization. Some Southerners did convert, whether out of conviction or for other reasons, but most resisted.

A civil war between North and South had already begun a year before independence, in 1955, continuing until the Addis Ababa agreement of 1972 granted regional autonomy to the South. Although the issue of a constitution in conformity with Islam had been debated since independence, President Ja'far Muhammad Numayri's presidential decree of September 1983, imposing Shari'a (the sacred law of Islam) on the country placed the issue squarely on the public agenda, leading to increased tensions and eventual conflict between the government and rebels in the South. The conflict resumed in 1983 when the Khartoum government unilaterally abrogated the Addis Ababa agreement, divided the South into three regions, reduced the powers of the regional governments, and imposed Shari'a on the whole country, including the non-Muslim South.

The South fought under the leadership of the Sudan People's Liberation Movement and its military wing, the Sudan People's Liberation Army (SPLM/SPLA). The rebellion was triggered when the government attempted to transfer southern battalions to the North, thereby removing their capacity to resist. The rebels fled to Ethiopia, where they received strong support which helped them organize themselves and equipped them militarily, turning them into a strong force against the government. Although the SPLM/SPLA is composed largely of Southerners under Christian leadership, it was later joined by non-Arab ethnic groups from the North and liberal-minded Northerners who share with the movement a vision of a secular, democratic Sudan.

Then, after Numayri's ouster in 1985, the Muslim Brethren, an elite Islamist group, metamorphosed into a broader-based political party, the National Islamic Front (NIF). The NIF shot to prominence in the parliamentary elections of 1986, winning the third largest number of seats. The group's Islamic agenda was endorsed and reinforced by General 'Umar Hasan al-Bashir, who seized power on June 30, 1989, in the name of the "Revolution for National Salvation." Initially, Bashir projected himself as independent from the NIF, although he shared its Islamist agenda. In due course, however, it became clear that the *coup d'état* was in fact engineered by the NIF and that Hasan at-Turabi, the NIF's leader, wielded the real power with Bashir not much more than the executor of his will. Recently, however, a conflict over power has ensued between Bashir, supported by young hawks from Turabi's camp, and Turabi, joined by some loyal NIF members and new supporters. While the struggle continues, Bashir appears to have the upper hand while Turabi is significantly marginalized within the system. Their conflict has limited importance for the South, being internal to the Islamist agenda; both parties still agree that the South will only receive limited accommodation within an Islamic state.

Since the resumption of hostilities in 1983, the relationship between religion and the state, in particular the role of Shari'a, has emerged as the central factor in the conflict. Religion defines identity in both the Sudan's North and the South. For Northerners, Islam is not only a faith and a way of life, it is also culture and ethnic identity associated with Arabism. For Southerners, Islam is not just a religion, but also Arabism as a racial, ethnic, and cultural phenomenon that excludes them as black Africans and adherents of Christianity and indigenous religions. Race in the Sudan is not so much a function of color or features, but a state of mind, a case of self-perception; the North identifies as Arab, no matter how dark its people's skin color.

The southern backlash to Islamization and Arabization boosted its Christian identity. Southerners now combine indigenous culture, Christianity, and general elements of Western culture to combat Islam and the associated imposition of Arab identity. A northern Islamic scholar, 'Abd al-Wahhab al-Affendi, articulated the religious dilemmas for the country when he wrote:

> The close association between Islam and northern Sudanese nationalism would certainly rob Islam of an advantage [in the South] … [as] it remains beset by problems similar to those that limited the appeal of the SPLA's Africanism [in the North].

He elaborates:

> Northern Sudanese, who identify strongly with their Arab heritage, are in no danger of being seduced by Africanism. … But equally, Islamic ideology is by definition, unacceptable to non-Muslims. Its association with Arab northern self-assertion makes it even more unpalatable to Southerners.

The clash of these two antagonistic cultural outlooks has implications that go beyond the borders of Sudan, for the two identity groups have affinities within and beyond Africa along both religious and racial lines that could potentially widen the circles of conflict. The Arab-Islamic world sees in northern Sudan an identity that must be, and has been, supported. For it, the South serves as a dangerous rallying point for Christendom, the West, and

even Zionism to combat Islam. While this is largely an exaggerated conspiratorial construct, it provides a strong basis for Arab-Islamic solidarity with the North. On the other hand, black Africa sees in the plight of the South a humiliating racist oppression that must be resisted. While the commitment to African unity without racial or cultural distinctions inhibits overt support for the South, they have discreetly and clandestinely supported the SPLM/SPLA. The potential for an Arab-African clash over the Sudan remains real. There is no doubt that Sudan is as much a link as it is potentially a point of confrontation among converging diverse identities.

NORTHERN EFFORTS

From the North's perspective, the South is a legitimate domain for Arab-Islamic influence which the Christian missionaries, in alliance with British colonial rulers, wrongly usurped. Northerners believe that the roots of Christian and Western influence in the South are shallow and can easily be replaced by Islam and Arabic culture. Interestingly, just one year after independence, the government nationalized all Christian missionary schools in the South, causing them to lose their Christian character while allowing missionary schools in the North to continue to provide education to mostly Muslim students, albeit without proselytizing Christianity.

The council of ministers decided in February 1960 to change the official day of rest in the South from Sunday to Friday. When southern schools went on strike in protest against that decision, the government retaliated by prosecuting the alleged ring leaders and imposing severe prison sentences on them. A native priest, Poulino Dogali, was sentenced to twelve years' imprisonment for having printed and distributed a leaflet critical of the government's decision. Two secondary-school students received ten years each for having instigated the students' protest. On April 8, 1960, several years before the expulsion of the missionaries, the daily *Rái al-'Amm* newspaper urged northern Sudanese to join efforts with the government to proselytize Islam in the South: "There is no doubt that many in this country know how much need Islam has in the South of efforts on the part of the government. The administrative authorities and men of the Ministry of Education and of the Department of Religious Affairs continue to make gigantic efforts; but this by itself is not enough."

In 1962, the government enacted the Missionary Societies Act, regulating missionary activities. No missionary society or any member of such society should do missionary work in the Sudan except in accordance with the terms of a license granted by the council of ministers. The license could impose whatever conditions the council of ministers might think fit. The council of ministers might refuse to grant or renew a license and could revoke one at its discretion. The act imposed spatial limitations and prohibited a missionary society from doing "any missionary act towards any person or persons professing any religion or sect or belief thereof other than that specified in its license." Missionaries were not allowed to "practice any social activities except within the limits and in the manner laid down from time to time by regulations." The act also stated that: "No missionary society shall bring up in any religion or admit to any religious order, any person under the age of eighteen years without the consent of his lawful guardian." Furthermore, "No missionary society shall adopt, protect, or maintain an abandoned child without the consent of the Province Authority." The formation of clubs, establishment of societies, organization of social activities, collection of money, famine and flood relief, the holding of land, and the publication and distribution of papers, pamphlets, or books were subject to ministerial regulations.

In March 1964 the Sudan government took the final step of expelling all foreign missionaries from the South. "Foreign Missionary organizations have gone beyond the limits of their sacred mission," the government explained in a policy statement on its decision, arguing that the missionaries had

> exploited the name of religion to impart hatred and implant fear and animosity in the minds of the Southerners against their fellow countrymen in the North with the clear object of encouraging the setting up of a separate political status for the southern provinces thus endangering the integrity and unity of the country.

Since 1964, the situation has vacillated from moments of improvement to a return to confrontation and the persistent commitment of the North to the Islamic agenda. The overthrow of General Ibrahim 'Abud's dictatorship in 1965 and the assumption of power by an interim government, under Sirr al-Khatim al-Khalifa as prime minister, to coach the country back to democracy within a year seemed promising for resolving the conflict in the South. Khalifa was an educator with considerable experience in the South and sympathy for the Southern cause. His government, in which respected Southerners were members, convened a conference that laid a sound foundation for Southern autonomy. However, the return of democracy and the rule of traditional parties to government retarded the progress and plunged the country back into intensified hostilities. The military rule of Ja'far Numayri granted the South regional autonomy and ensured precarious peace for a decade. His unilateral abrogation of the peace agreement in 1983 led to the resumption of hostilities. His overthrow in 1987 brought traditional sectarian powers back to power and the war continued unabated. Indeed, with the usurpation of power by the NIF in 1989 and the intensification of the Islamic agenda, the civil war of identities reached the climax that has persisted to this day.

SOUTHERN RESISTANCE

The condescending attitude of the North toward the South has been a subject of embittered commentary by southern Sudanese politicians and intellectuals, one of whom wrote of this attitude:

> Many northern Sudanese had the notion that there were but a bunch of uncivilized tribes in the South, and very condescendingly, Northerners regarded themselves as guardians of these, their backward brethren. Finding themselves in charge of the government of an independent Sudan, northern Sudanese politicians and administrators sought to replace the colonial regime in the South with their own. Arabic was naturally to replace English and what better religion than Islam could replace Christianity?

The North promoted Arabization and Islamization to establish national cultural unity, but their effect was in fact to widen the differences between the two parts of the country, escalating the conflict between them and giving it a racial and religious dimension that eventually reached genocidal proportions. Traditionally, the North saw the South as weak and underdeveloped, making it the raw material to be molded along the Arab-Islamic lines of the North. Accordingly, the stronger the South grows, the more Northerners feel threatened and the stronger their attachment to Arab Islamic identity becomes. The National Islamic Front represents an extremist reaction to the secular challenge posed by the South in general and by the SPLM/SPLA in particular.

Even the Ngok Dinka and the Homr Arabs, who had been a model of peaceful coexistence and cooperation on the North-South border, became pitted in a zero-sum war of identities. For historical reasons the Ngok Dinka, numbering around 100,000, a segment of the estimated several million Dinka people in the Sudan, are the only Dinka group administered in northern Sudan. This is the result of a decision made by their leaders to ensure proximity to central government protection and peaceful coexistence with Arab tribes at the North-South borders. The Homr, numerically larger than the Ngok, have cooperated with the Ngok in the past, largely due to cordial ties between their ruling families. In recent years, however, the situation has dramatically changed for the worse as Ngok Dinka youth, mostly southern-educated and Christian, have taken sides with their southern kin in the war of identities. Successive governments in Khartoum have recruited the Homr Arabs, trained them, armed them, and deployed them as militias, supposedly against the southern rebel movement, but in fact unleashing them against their Dinka neighbors. They killed at random, looted cattle, razed villages to the ground, and captured children and women as slaves. A leading member of the Mahdi family (that has been in the northern ruling circles for over a century) intimated that he had received inquiries from Homr Arabs, asking whether it was permitted or forbidden by Islam to kill a Dinka; this points to the religious intolerance and identity crisis that state intervention and the politicization of Islam have meant.

Conditions of upheaval, war-related suffering, and the threat of violent death have nudged Southerners increasingly toward religion in general and Christianity in particular as a source of salvation. The southern Sudanese have always turned to God and spirits for protection at times of disaster. But as war and ensuing famine have disrupted society on a massive scale, more universalizing concepts fill the gap. The Christian church is contributing to meeting this need by offering a universal vision and also by creating broader circles of identification and unity. For example, Christian missionary groups sponsor clubs in the North for displaced Southerners, where they are allowed to operate, although with considerable scrutiny and repression, to provide religious instruction, offer literacy classes, and other social services.

As hardships in the South multiply, the Dinka increasingly identify their plight with the biblical prophecy in Isaiah 18:6-7:

> They shall be left together unto the fowls of the mountains, and to the beasts of the earth: and the fowls shall summer upon them, and all the beasts of the earth shall winter upon them. In that time shall the present be brought unto the Lord of hosts from a people vigorous and bright, from a people terrible from their beginning hitherto; a nation that meteth out and treadeth down.

In this verse, the Dinka see their tragedy and their ultimate glory, making the gospel directly relevant to their plight. Thus has the religious agenda of the National Islamic Front become a major challenge for peace and the long-term prospects of nation-building in the Sudan.

THE FUTURE OF SUDAN

Elite circles of Christian society in southern Sudan now promote the idea that Christianity should be consciously cultivated as a key element of modern southern identity to counter the Arab-Islamic model of the North. Although the educated Christians have reason to question the manner in which Christian missionary work undermined their indigenous spiritual and religious values and practices, they now tend to identify fully with Christianity. In the South, going to church is encouraged as both an act of faith and a political statement. In a mirror image of the Islamic practice, Southerners now open meetings with Christian prayers invoking divine guidance and support. For Southerners, Christianity is now both a religion and a political weapon against Islamization and Arabization.

Notwithstanding the rhetoric of the leadership in favor of a united Sudan, most southern Sudanese favor self-determination and perhaps eventual secession. There is, however, a serious difference of opinion on the means to self-determination. Some southern political figures, among them Bona Malwal and Abel Alier, believe that the South should rally around the right of self-determination, instead of pursuing the goal of a united, secular, democratic Sudan. The leadership of the SPLM/SPLA, in particular John Garang de Mabior, believes that such a focus would be self-defeating. In the view of the SPLM/SPLA leadership, northern leaders pay only lip service to self-determination but would never concede to the South the right to secede. Only military pressure and self-preservation will force them to make that concession. Meanwhile, the SPLM/SPLA needs unity with forces from the North to maintain the military pressure against the government. And this is only possible through the objective of a unified, secular, democratic Sudan, rather than by focusing on self-determination for the South. The SPLM/SPLA leadership believes that the best way to achieve self-determination for the South is to liberate the land physically, consolidate control, and move on with reconstruction and development rather than relying on the North granting the South the right to secede.

It can, however, be argued that these two positions can be bridged. Self-determination need not be synonymous with secession; it offers an opportunity for leaders on both sides to create conditions to win and sustain unity. Given Sudan's history, this may not be possible, but it is a challenge with which the Sudanese leadership in Khartoum should be confronted. The Declaration of Principles that the mediators of the InterGovernmental Authority for Development, whose members include the neighboring countries of Eritrea, Ethiopia, Kenya, and Uganda, presented to the parties in 1994, remains the principal normative basis for a resolution of the Sudanese conflict. The declaration can be combined into three main categories: self-determination as a fundamental and inalienable right, national unity as a desirable objective, and interim arrangements confirmed by referendum.

If Sudanese unity is to be maintained, the relationship of the state and Islam is the most crucial issue to resolve. Southern Christians and believers in traditional religions will continue to struggle against any Islamic order, violently if necessary, for it by definition does not permit non-Muslims equal rights. The Islamic scholar Abdullahi Ahmed An-Na`im has realistically observed that under present circumstances,

> At best, non-believers may be allowed to stay under the terms of a special compact which extremely restricts their civil and political rights. Believers who are not Muslims, mainly Jews and Christians, are allowed partial citizenship under Shari'a ... and are disqualified from holding any position of authority over Muslims.

As the South strengthens itself through education and an identity reinforced by Christianity, Western culture, and military force, its emerging parity with the North renders it less susceptible to northern disregard or manipulation. And the more seriously the South considers its grievances, the clearer it becomes that these cannot be redressed within the North's proffered Arab-Islamic framework. This means that the national framework must either be fundamentally restructured to provide for equality between North and South, or the country risks disintegration.

Sudan remains poised between these choices. One thing is, however, clear: The South has unequivocally identified itself with Christianity, which means that in a united Sudan, religious pluralism will have to be accommodated. But should the South secede, Christianity will be its dominant religion. Which way the future of the country will go remains an open question.

CONCLUSION

The challenge for Christianity in the Sudan is essentially political, and it has to do with the course and outcome of the war of visions that has afflicted the country for more than four decades and in which religion has become a pivotal factor and a symbol of a multi-faceted identity configuration. The crucial question is not only whether the Sudan is Islamic but also the related question of whether it is culturally and racially Arab. On both questions, the South asserts a contrasting identity that is culturally and racially black African and religiously traditional with Christianity as the dominant modern religion.

Assuming the South to have a religious or spiritual vacuum to be filled by introducing outside religions, as the Christian missionaries did, is no longer accurate. Christianity has become an established element of southern identity and a major factor in the war of identities raging in the Sudan. The question then is how the war will end or be resolved. Judging from the political and military dynamics, Sudan is about to revive Christianity as both a pivotal element of southern Sudanese identity and a significant factor in the legacy of Sudanese history, where Christianity, which once prevailed in the North, has a legitimate claim to a prominent place in the religious and cultural configuration of historic and modern Sudan.

QUESTIONS TO CONSIDER

1. According to Deng, what are the major divisions in Sudan?
2. Why is Islam better suited for the South than Christianity?
3. What are the "two antagonistic cultural outlooks" in Sudan?
4. What role is religion playing in Sudan's civil strife?
5. Is genocide related to religion in the Sudan?

Angola Preliminary Report

DETERMINATION: NOT GENOCIDAL IN NATURE

Genocide Prevention Center

INTRODUCTION

The Genocide Prevention Center publishes reports to highlight strong indicators and dangers of potential genocide in remote areas. The Angola report is an aberration because while there is a civil war, there are no strong indicators of genocidal activity. It is useful, however, as a tool to note how civil and human rights abuses and war crimes committed during a civil conflict may still bear no ear markings of genocide.

BACKGROUND OF THE CONFLICT

There has been a civil war raging in Angola since 1975. The origins of the conflict can be traced to the 1960s when intellectuals organized liberation movements to achieve independence from Portugal. The War of Independence began on February 4, 1961 when the MPLA (Popular Movement for the Liberation of Angola) attacked the São Paulo fortress and police headquarters in Luanda. The war spread throughout the country as two additional independence movements, the FNLA (Frente Nacianal de Libertacao de Angola) and the UNITA (Uniao Nacianal para a Independencia Total de Angola) fought in the north and south, respectively. Following a prolonged armed struggle, Portugal conceded independence to Angola on November 11, 1975.

Following the War of Independence, a civil war broke out between the MPLA and the UNITA over control of the country and its abundant resources. Angola became caught up in the Cold War as the United States and South Africa supported the UNITA while the Soviet Union and Cuba supported the MPLA. The MPLA founded the People's Republic of Angola in Luanda while the UNITA and FNLA founded the Popular Democratic Republic of Angola in Huambo.

During the 1970s and 80s, there was a low-intensity bush war. The end of the Cold War had significant effect on the conflicting parties, as the external actors stopped supporting the MPLA and the UNITA and engaged in negotiating. After a series of meetings mediated by the US, Soviet Union, and Portugal, a cease-fire was finally signed in 1991. The Estoril Peace Accord between the government and UNITA governed ceasefire, mutual disarmament and elections. Elections were held on September 29 and 30, 1992. The MPLA gained a parliamentary majority but the presidential outcome was very close between MPLA leader José Eduardo dos Santos and UNITA leader Jonas Savimbi, making a second round necessary. Despite the fact that the United Nations observed the first round of elections and declared them "basically free and fair," Savimbi declared them to be fraudulent and left Luanda before the second round of elections could take place. The fights resumed and

---

From "Angola Preliminary Report: Determination—Not Genocidal in Nature," *The Center for the Prevention of Genocide* (2002). Reprinted with permission.

between April 1991 and May 1991 an estimated 100,000 to 350,000 people died in the conflict.

Between late 1992 and 1994, the worst fighting took place in Angola. In a period of 8 months 182,000 people died. By late 1993 the UNITA gained control over 70% of the territory of Angola. On November 20, 1994, the two sides signed the internationally negotiated Lusaka Protocol. According to Human Rights Watch, the Lusaka Protocol provided for a cease-fire, the integration of UNITA generals into the government's armed forces (which were to become nonpartisan and civilian controlled), demobilization under U.N. supervision, the repatriation of mercenaries, the incorporation of UNITA troops into the Angolan National Police under the Interior Ministry, and the prohibition of any outside police or surveillance organization.

After four years of uneasy peace Savimbi abandoned the peace accord and the civil war resumed in 1998. Since 1998 localized guerrilla warfare has characterized the conflict. "Angola's war, which resumed in earnest in 1998, has claimed at least 500,000 lives and displaced some 4 million people out of the total population of 12 million." As of June 2001, "security conditions remain serious in the provinces of Benguela, Bie, Huambo, Kuando Kubango, Kwanza Norte, Malanje, Moxico, and Uige. The security situation in these provinces is characterized by ambushes, attacks, kidnappings, mine explosions, looting of civilian goods, and threats against humanitarian workers and organizations."

MAIN PARTIES

Main Actors: The civil war in Angola is fueled by a power struggle between the government MPLA and the UNITA.

1. Popular Movement for the Liberation of Angola (Movimento Popular de Libertaçao de Angola—MPLA) led by José Eduardo dos Santos, the current president of the state. The MPLA, a Marxist party, was founded by Africans and mixed-race mesticos in 1956 and had a strong following in the Angolan capital among the Creole population. This was to be crucial in the MPLA's seizure of power in 1975. The MPLA was at first led by Antonio Neto and, after his death, by Eduardo dos Santos.
2. Union for the Total Independence of Angola (Uniao Nacional para a Independencia Total de Angola—UNITA) led by Jonas Savimbi. The UNITA was formed in 1966 by Jonas Savimbi. The UNITA is supported by illiterate peasants and emphasizes ethnic (Ovimbundo) and rural rights in contrast with the urbanized Marxism of the MPLA. The UNITA was also considered to be "Maoist" in the sense that Savimbi used Mao's techniques to fight a guerrilla war.

Other Actors:

1. National Front for the Liberation of Angola (Frente Nacional de Libertaçao de Angola—FNLA)
The FNLA was formed in 1957 by Holden Roberto and a group of Bakongo nationalists. It was predominantly a northern-based party, with an ethnic base among the Bakongo people. The FNLA formed an alliance with the UNITA, announcing the formation of the Democratic Republic of Angola.
2. Unita Renovada led by Eugenio Manuvakola
3. Platform for Understanding led by Abel Chivukuvuku
4. Frente para a Libertaçao do Enclave de Cabinda (FLEC)
5. Angolan Party for Democratic Support (PADPA)

NATURE OF VIOLENCE

Frequent Civilian Casualties

The 25-year Angolan civil war has caused the death of numerous civilians. The U.S. Committee for Refugees estimates that 1 million people have been killed since the mid-1970s. Civilians have died as a result of indiscriminate shelling and both arbitrary and deliberate killings. Human Rights Watch argues that the UNITA has been primarily responsible for civilian casualties, whereas Amnesty International maintains that both the government and UNITA have carried out atrocities.

Since the resumption of fighting in 1998, the war has been reported to take "a heavy toll on the civilian population." In concert with this statement, Edwin Van Der Borght, of Medecins Sans Frontières (Doctors Without Borders) reports: "And if you speak to the people ... they will tell you that the conflict has never been so violent against them as over the past two years." Hence, the Genocide Prevention Center decided to examine the present state of the Angolan civil war and determine whether the atrocities committed against civilians are of a genocidal nature ...

ADDITIONAL HUMAN RIGHTS VIOLATIONS PRESENT IN THE CIVIL WAR

Forcible Recruitments of Adults and Children

According to the Amnesty International 2000 Report, the UNITA continued its forced recruitment of children and adults. The UNITA reportedly kidnapped 8 tribal chiefs from Quimozengou and Quichiona because they failed to recruit soldiers for the rebels. Human Rights Watch reported that the UNITA abducted 80 children from Mbanza Congo in order to train them as soldiers.

Deliberate Mutilation

Although deliberate mutilations have not been widespread, the number of incidents has increased during 2001. It is hard to confirm the identity of the perpetrators, however UNITA allegedly has been responsible for cutting off ears and hands. Amnesty International reported that in March 2000, UNITA members mutilated the ears, arms and legs of 12 independent miners in Tchinguvo, Lunda Norte province, and murdered 40 others. "Accounts of torture were not commonplace but were suf-

ficient to suggest that the rebels used torture to attempt to extract information, especially from individuals thought to have military knowledge about the government's intentions."

Landmine Victims

Although the Angolan government advocated the international landmine treaty, it has never ratified it. The BBC reported that Angola was at greater risk than ever as both the government and UNITA engaged in deploying landmines early this year. There are different estimates regarding the number of landmines and amputees. According to John Prendergast, Angola has an estimated 10 million land mines and up to 100,000 amputees. The U.N. estimated the number of landmines to be 7 million. The presence of landmine victims in Angola is very striking; as David Shukman observed "...during the next 10 minutes I saw no fewer than nine disabled people. Nearly one a minute, on an ordinary street on a typical weekday morning. No wonder the total number of landmine victims in Angola is unknown—it's beyond counting."

Refugees

As a consequence of resumed fighting, waves of refugees were fleeing Angola in 2001. UNITA rebel attacks in Uige province have driven as many as 7,400 people into the neighboring Democratic Republic of the Congo. Between 60 and 70 Angolan refugees were entering Zambia every day through the border town of Mwinilunga.

As of May 2001, the United Nations High Commissioner for Refugees (UNHCR) reported that 430,781 Angolans were refugees in other countries.

Zambia: 199,086
Democratic Republic of the Congo: 179,550
Republic of Congo: 18,515
Namibia: 28,889
South Africa: 3,902
in other countries: 839

Internally Displaced People

Continued warfare forced Angolans to flee from their homes and set up residence in IDP camps. At present, it is impossible to estimate accurately the number of IDPs. The U.S. Committee for Refugees reported that the number of internally displaced Angolans ranged from 1 million to 3.5 million people. According to Amnesty International and Human Rights Watch, the number of internally displaced persons grew to an estimated 2.5 million, approximately 20 percent of the total population of Angola.

In 2001, ongoing military activity has led to displacements from the areas of Cambandua, Chicala, Nhareia, Camacupa, and Kuninga (Belo Horizonte) into the provincial capital, Kuito. As a result, an additional 15,500 displaced families arrived from December to February in Kuito.

Targeting Humanitarian Assistance

The UNITA has been reportedly targeting humanitarian assistance in Angola. On April 30, 2000, a U.N. World Food Program convoy was attacked 85 kilometers from Lobito. On August 9, 2000, the U.N. denounced an armed attack on Catete that resulted in the deaths of a humanitarian worker and three other civilians.

Assaults against humanitarian assistance continued in 2001. In the middle of June 2001, the U.N. warned that humanitarian operation in Angola were at risk. The U.N. food agency cancelled humanitarian flights to Angola after its aircraft was attacked by UNITA missiles in early June. The spokesman for UNITA, Joffre Justino, initially maintained that "the planes were legitimate targets," but later said it "was not deliberately targeting humanitarian flights." Despite a lack of safety guarantees for its planes, the U.N. has since resumed its flights in order to avoid a humanitarian catastrophe. The U.N. food agency helps about one million people in Angola whose lives would be endangered without food aid.

Violation of the Freedom of the Press

Violation of the freedom of the press has been characteristic in Angola. The government passed a law in August 1999 that advocates harsh punishment for defamation. In consequence the government has repeatedly threatened independent journalists criticizing the MPLA. Isaias Soares, correspondent of Voice of America (VoA) and the independent Catholic radio station "Radio Ecclesia" in the northern Malange province was attacked by two men on February 22 at his home. Soares was not injured in the assault. Soares has been harassed on several occasions for his critical writings. In 1999, he was arrested after he denounced the security forces' practices. In 2000, local authorities in Malange forbade the journalist access to official buildings.

The latest reported incident occurred on July 14, when Rafael Marques was arrested by police in Luanda while visiting people who had been forcibly removed from their homes. Marques has argued that media freedom has deteriorated, citing examples of government pressure on the Catholic radio station "Radio Ecclesia" and interrogations of journalists who denounce the government.

NOT GENOCIDAL IN NATURE

This preliminary research focused on possible precursors of genocide present in the region due to the civil war in Angola. The Genocide Prevention Center has defined four standards that must be met for human rights abuses and violence to constitute genocide:

> The Center recognizes the 1948 UN Convention on the Prevention and Punishment of the Crime of Genocide definition of genocide, Article 2(a)(c):

The GPC must determine that the occurrence of massacres of unarmed civilian groups is habitual

The Center must determine that the crimes are intentional

Numerous and repeated acts of murder of a UN-recognized group must be the primary characteristic of the abuse.

In concert with the first criterion, the Genocide Prevention Center acknowledges the 1948 UN Convention on the Prevention and Punishment of the Crime of Genocide as key to identifying genocide. The UN Convention Article II classifies genocide as intentional actions aimed at destroying "in whole or in part, a national, ethnical, racial or religious group."

The civil war in Angola is a struggle for control and power between the government MPLA and the UNITA. Although both parties are supported by different ethnic groups (the MPLA by Africans and mixed race mesticos and the UNITA by the peasants and ethnic Ovimbundo population), ethnicity has never been of significance in the war. Civilians have not been targeted due to their national, ethnical, racial or religious beliefs. Hence, the Angolan civil war does not meet this portion of the UN definition of genocide and does not meet the first standard.

According to Article 2(e) of the 1948 UN Convention on Genocide, "Forcibly transferring children of the group to another group" is a genocidal act. This is taking place in Angola, as we have mentioned in the section above entitled "Forcible Recruitments of Adults and Children." Although the forced transfer of children does meet a portion of Article 2 from the UN Convention, the Genocide Prevention Center does not utilize this as a criterion for genocide as it does not share the characteristic of murder.

In order to meet the second standard for genocide, the killings in Angola must be shown to be habitual. In looking at the recent violence within the country, it is possible to make a case that the killing of civilians is in fact habitual, as there have been numerous cases in which civilians have lost their lives in the conflict. Examples include 16 killed in Calomboloca on March 16, 2001; 20 killed in Cacuso on May 15, 2001; 22

killed in Catala on July 11, 2001; and 70 killed in Chinguvu on July 17, 2001. However, a distinction must be made between the specific targeting of civilians and incidental civilian wartime casualties. In the case of incidental casualties, civilian deaths result primarily as an effect of the overall warfare and not due to the specific targeting and exterminating of the population. It is clear that in the case of Angola, the civilian victims are incidental casualties and not the primary targets of the violence. These killings do constitute war crimes, however, they are not genocidal in nature. Therefore, the violence and killing in Angola do not meet the second standard for genocide.

The third standard involves the intent behind the killings. The Genocide Prevention Center distinguishes between massive human rights abuses that have an aspect of manslaughter versus those that have an aspect of murder. In a case of murder, the action is considered to be intentional while in the case of manslaughter, the killing of civilians is a by-product of warfare and is not the intended goal. Directly related to the above analysis of the second standard, the case of Angola does not involve the intentional targeting and extermination of the civilian population. Massacres are primarily incidental civilian wartime casualties, and therefore are more closely associated with manslaughter then they are with murder. Because there is no strong indication that the killing of civilians in Angola is intentional, it therefore does not meet the third standard for genocide.

According to the fourth criterion the primary characteristic of the human rights violations must be the killing of civilians. Again, this is not the case in Angola. Angola has been suffering from two decades of civil war in which large numbers of civilians have been killed. However, the killing of civilians is not the primary characteristic of the violence. The primary characteristic of the conflict is warfare, with famine and incidental wartime casualties existing as secondary characteristics. The case of Angola is one of a civil war in which the two main sides are fighting over territory, not targeting the population for extermination. Because the killing of civilians is not the primary characteristic of the war in Angola, this case does not meet the fourth standard for genocide.

CONCLUSION

In conclusion, the Genocide Prevention Center has determined that the pattern of violence in Angola does not meet the four standards for genocide. Nevertheless, based on reports published in 2001, the UNITA is responsible for committing both war crimes and crimes against humanity. It is difficult to make a judgment on the actions of the government, as there is a lack of evidence on the nature of the violence it has committed. It is possible that the strict control the government has over the media has been responsible for this lack of information. However, as cited earlier in the report, Amnesty International has stated that both the UNITA and government MPLA have been responsible for actions against civilians.

In concert with the reported casualties, we can only conclude that it appears the atrocities committed against civilians this year have been inflicted by the UNITA. Based on the evidence, the UNITA has violated Article 3 Common to the Geneva Conventions of 12 August 1949, and Protocol Additional to the Geneva Conventions of 12 August 1949. According to Article 3, "the following acts are and shall remain prohibited at any time and in any place ... : (a) Violence to life and person, in particular murder of all kinds, mutilation, cruel treatment and torture; (b) Taking of hostages; According to Human Rights Watch, Amnesty International and numerous news articles cited in this report, the UNITA is responsible for committing murder, mutilation, and kidnapping, hence violating Article 3(a) and (b).

The UNITA has violated Part Two, Article 4, 3(c) of Protocol Additional to the Geneva Conventions of 12 August 1949 which states "children who have not attained the age of fifteen years shall neither be recruited in the armed forces or groups nor allowed to take part in hostilities."

Further, the UNITA is responsible for violating Part Four, Article 13, 2 of Protocol Additional to the Geneva Conventions of 12 August 1949 which says: "The civilian population as such, as well as individual civilians, shall not be the object of attack. Acts or threats of violence the primary purpose of which is to spread terror among the civilian population are prohibited."

Although the Genocide Prevention Center concludes that the Angolan civil war does not constitute genocide, the civil war does constitute the above mentioned war crimes. Therefore, the abuses in Angola require further attention and action to bring about an end to the violence.

QUESTIONS TO CONSIDER

1. What is the motivation for the killing in Angola?
2. Why does The Center for the Prevention of Genocide determine that this case is "not genocidal in nature"?

MAKING CONNECTIONS

1. Does the Rwandan genocide have the same elements as the Armenian genocide?

2. Despite the conclusion of the case study on the atrocities in Angola, does it meet the definition of genocide presented in this book's Introduction?

✔ RECOMMENDED RESOURCES

Berkeley, Bill. *The Graves Are Not Yet Full: Race, Tribe and Power in the Heart of Africa.* New York: Basic Books, 2001.

Destexhe, Alain. *Rwanda and Genocide in the Twentieth Century.* New York: New York University Press, 1995.

Gourevitch, Philip. *We Wish To Inform You That Tomorrow We Will Be Killed with Our Families: Stories from Rwanda.* New York: Farrar, Straus, and Giroux, 1998.

Mamdani, Mahmood. *When Victims Become Killers: Colonialism, Nativism, and the Genocide in Rwanda.* Princeton, NJ: Princeton University Press, 2001.

Neuffer, Elizabeth. *The Key To My Neighbor's House: Seeking Justice in Bosnia and Rwanda.* New York: Picador, 2001.

Peterson, Scott. *Me Against My Brother: At War in Somalia, Sudan, and Rwanda: A Journalist Reports from the Battlefield.* New York: Routledge, 2000.

Prunier, G. *The Rwanda Crisis, 1959–94: History of a Genocide.* London: Hurst & Company, 1995.

Wrong, Michela. *In the Footsetps of Mr. Kurtz: Living on the Brink of Disaster in Mobutu's Congo.* New York: HarperCollins Publishers, 2001.

CHAPTER 10

WITH FRIENDS LIKE THESE...
CASE STUDIES: ARGENTINA AND GUATEMALA

Governments in Latin American have traditionally succumbed to repressive regimes. The most repressive regimes came from the right, such as in Paraguay after the middle of the century, Nicaragua under the Samoza dynasty, and the Dominican Republic under Trujillo. Exceptions are Cuba under Castro and Nicaragua under the Sandinistas. It all mattered little to most Americans, however. A July 1984 *New York Times*–CBS opinion poll revealed that only eight percent of Americans could identify the leaders whom the U.S. administration supported in Nicaragua and El Salvador.

But even when a Latin American country elected a leftist government, the United States would inevitably regard it as a mistake, as exemplified by Secretary of State Henry Kissinger's words relating to Chile's going "Communist due to the irresponsibility of its own people." The United States government subsequently oversaw the removal of the democratically elected government of Salvador Allende to replace it with a repressive military junta under General Pinochet.

In 1954 the Eisenhower administration established the U.S. precedent for dealing with leftist governments through its actions against the new government in Guatemala under Jacobo Arbenz Guzman. The U.S. Central Intelligence Agency organized a coup that overthrew Arbenz and replaced him with a right-wing government. Subsequent U.S. support for the right-wing governments of Guatemala included sending Green Berets to "advise" the military, training future leaders in the School of the Americas, and seeing these leaders and their military terrorize, torture, and execute over 100,000 people and destroy over 400 villages. General Rios Montt's (1982–1983) policy to depopulate the indigenous areas, home to guerrilla opposition, resulted in the deaths of perhaps 1,200 of the civilians killed during the thirty-year conflict.

When the United States approached Latin American problems by supporting repressive regimes, few domestic objections were heard. The independent human rights investigators with Americas Watch provided watchdog oversight. But when an administration, such as that of George Bush, found itself in the position of having to defend its support of "unspeakable abuses" by President Cristiani's armed forces in El Salvador, it was placed in the awkward position of defending the indefensible. El Salvador showed continued support of repressive regimes that promised "stability," to be accomplished by suppression of the poor and working people by an oligarchy of the rich and powerful and their military henchmen.

According to official documents, between 1976 and 1983 the "Dirty War" in Argentina claimed at least nine thousand victims, tortured and killed by the military. Unofficial estimates of deaths during this period range as high as 30,000. Five hundred military leaders during the Dirty War were tried, convicted, and sentenced for their actions. A report by Amnesty International, "Argentina—The Military Juntas and Military Rights: Report of the Trial of the Former Junta Members 1985" is an illustration of after-the-fact indictment of atrocities. Robert Parry shows the surrogate involvement of the U.S. government in "Reagan & Guatemala's Death Files." Mireya Navarro reports that the army in Guatemala deserved censure in "Guatemalan Army Waged 'Genocide'."

Argentina: The Military Juntas and Human Rights

REPORT OF THE TRIAL OF THE FORMER JUNTA MEMBERS 1985

Amnesty International

From "Argentina: The Military Juntas and Military Rights—Report of the Trial of the Former Members 1985," *Amnesty International*, London, (1987), 2–9. Reprinted with permission of © Amnesty International.

BACKGROUND

Historical Context

In the late 1960s and early 1970s Argentina was beset by political violence which culminated in a period of severe repression—the seven years of military rule from 1976 to 1983. This period began in March 1976 when General Jorge Rafael Videla led a coup d'état against the Peronist government. In the two preceding decades, when the former President Juan Domingo Perón lived in exile, the Peronist movement, which largely controlled Argentina's industrial labour force, had been proscribed and its leaders subjected to arbitrary arrest. The clampdown, by a succession of military governments, on peaceful political expression provoked a series of public protests and, against a background of general discontent, small guerrilla groups began to emerge. But the state-authorized repression that followed failed to distinguish between legitimate dissent and unlawful violence. In May 1969 popular uprisings in Córdoba and Rosario were brutally and lethally put down by the army. On the left, armed revolutionary groups such as the Marxist *Ejército Revolucionario del Pueblo* (ERP), People's Revolutionary Army, and the avowedly Peronist *Montoneros*, engaged in a series of violent acts: bombings, kidnappings, assaults on police and military installations. In 1970 one of the first acts of violence perpetrated by the *Montoneros* was the abduction and murder of a former president, General Pedro Eugenio Aramburu, who had led the coup of 1955 which had deposed Juan Perón.

In 1972 the government of General Alejandro Agustín Lanusse moved towards the restoration of democracy by lifting the ban on Peronist parties and calling elections. These were held in March 1973 and Héctor Cámpora, the Peronist candidate, became President in May. On taking office he declared a general amnesty and revoked most of the penal laws introduced by the military. After only 49 days in office, Dr. Cámpora resigned and Juan Perón, who had finally returned to Argentina in June 1973, was elected President the following September. The advent of the Peronist government, however, failed to unite the different factions of the Peronist movement, and this period was marked by public and sometimes violent clashes between them. On his death in July 1974, Juan Perón was succeeded by his widow, María Estela Martínez de Perón. The country was facing severe economic problems and political violence was continuing. The government responded by re-introducing most of the so-called anti-subversive legislation that had been repealed in May 1973. In November 1974 a state of siege was imposed and more than 3,000 people suspected of involvement in subversive activities were placed in administrative detention.

Concurrently, from 1974 onwards, unofficial death squads and paramilitary right-wing gangs, such as the *Alianza Anti-Comunista Argentina* or Triple-A (the Argentine Anti-Communist Alliance), began to operate. These groups directed organized violence against what could broadly be called the left—students, lawyers, journalists and militant trade unionists. No one was ever charged or tried in connection with crimes attributed to these groups, and there is evidence that the authorities did more than simply tolerate them. In 1974 Argentine human rights organizations had attributed more than 300 murders to these death squads. (Even before the coup, sworn affidavits linked the Ministry of Social Welfare to the death squads. Since the return to civilian government in December 1983, more evidence about the complicity of the security services in their activities has come to light.)

In February 1975 the government called on the army to assist the police in the northern province of Tucumán in the struggle against subversion. This remote and mountainous province was the heartland of the ERP guerrillas, who hoped to use it as a rural base from which to launch a revolution. The army moved in and sealed off the region. The methods they used to combat the guerrillas were also inflicted on the general population—torture, bombing and mass arrests. But what was perhaps most significant was that, for the first time, "disappearances" began to be reported on a large scale. By October 1975, the government had extended its decree allowing the army to assist the police so that it encompassed the whole country. All branches of the armed forces were involved in the fight against subversion.

After the coup of March 1976 which brought General Videla to power, similar methods of repression were employed on a national scale. The military junta announced its intention of stamping out subversion at any cost. A purposeful reorganization of the military was put into effect straight after the coup. Anti-subversive operations were made the direct responsibility of each regional army commander. Task forces or commando units were set up, drawing men from all the services. Their job was to eliminate subversion: to capture and interrogate all known members of subversive organizations, or their sympathizers, or their associates, or anyone who might oppose the government's power. Legal guarantees were disregarded, even the rather attenuated ones that existed under the state of siege. Formal arrests were replaced by abductions: the number of "disappearance" cases expanded to enormous proportions.

Despite the climate of fear that such actions created among the general population, opposition to them was always present, eventually growing into a powerful political movement. One of the first opposition institutions to emerge was the Permanent Assembly for Human Rights, which was formed in late 1975 as a bulwark against the political violence prevalent in Argentina at that time. On the Permanent Assembly's board were many prominent figures from Argentina's political and religious life, including Dr. Raúl Alfonsín, the future president, and the Catholic Bishop of Neuquén, Monsignor Jaime de Nevares. The role of the Permanent Assembly was to collect data on "disappearance" cases and to try and influence public opinion about the human rights situation in the country (one of the first steps taken by the military government had been to prevent the press from publishing information on anti-subversive operations, killings and "disappearances").

Inevitably, much of the opposition to the ruthless methods employed by the armed forces in their "war" against subversion came from relatives of the victims. Ironically, they were first given a chance to meet and organize when the Ministry of the Interior opened an office in mid-1976 (at the height of the "disappearances") to receive complaints. The contempt with which the people presenting complaints were treated spurred a small group of women in April 1977 to make a public protest in the Plaza de Mayo, the main square of Buenos Aires, just in front of Government House (the *Casa Rosada*). These early protests gradually grew into a regular Thursday afternoon march by a large number of mothers of "disappeared" people—the "Mothers of the Plaza de Mayo." Some attempts were made by the authorities to deter them from continuing their activities. On 8 December 1977 a group of 13 relatives who had attended a mass for "disappeared" people at the Santa Cruz church in Buenos Aires were abducted by the security forces. Among them was a French nun, Sister Alice Domon. A couple of days later another French nun, Sister Léonie Duquet, and the founder of the Mothers movement, Azucena de Vicenti, were also abducted. Subsequent reports indicated that all had been taken to the navy's secret detention centre in the capital, the *Escuela Mecánica de la Armada*. None of them was ever seen again.

In May 1978 the Permanent Assembly published in the newspaper *La Prensa* a list of

2,500 "disappeared" people. In November that year it presented a collective petition on behalf of 1,542 "disappeared" people directly to the Supreme Court. The signatories stated that they were appealing to the Court because all other means of establishing the whereabouts of the "disappeared" had failed. This petition, like the thousands of individual petitions presented to the courts during the period of military rule, was dismissed, but the Supreme Court stated in December 1978 that it had no alternative, since the authorities denied that the people for whom the petitions for *habeas corpus* had been filed were registered as detained.

On 12 September 1979, in the face of mounting national and international pressure concerning the fate of the "disappeared," the military government issued a law which would have allowed all those who had been reported missing during the previous five years to be declared dead: Law 22068 on *The Presumption of Death because of Disappearance.* This law was roundly condemned both inside and outside Argentina—the Organization of American States criticized it for failing to address the fundamental question of whether these people were alive or dead—and it was never put into effect. Law 22068 was, however, one of the first attempts by the military to annul the effects of its "disappearance" policy through legislation.

By 1981 the military were facing demands from all quarters for a clarification of the fate of the "disappeared people": on the international front, foreign governments were making persistent inquiries about the fate of their nationals missing in Argentina; and the United Nations, which in January 1981 had established a Working Group on Enforced or Involuntary Disappearances, was pressing the government for details on over 7,000 cases. While the government, now under the presidency of General Leopoldo Galtieri, vacillated, officials either promised to provide information that never materialized or bluntly refused to accept any inquiry into the issue.

The continuing official silence on the fate of the "disappeared" contrasted sharply to the steady stream of evidence being published in the foreign and Argentine press. While statements appeared from released prisoners about the appalling conditions in the secret detention centres, more discoveries of unmarked graves in cemeteries throughout Argentina were reported. The government of General Galtieri was also facing greater opposition from increasingly restless trade unions and political parties, and numerous strikes and mass demonstrations were organized to press for a return to the rule of law. In the wake of military defeat in the South Atlantic War of 1982, General Galtieri was forced to resign, and General Reynaldo Bignone, heading the fourth junta, prepared the way for elections to be held. The need to resolve the question of the "disappeared" formed part of these preparations.

On 28 April 1983 the government published its *Final Document of the Military Junta on the War against Subversion and Terrorism,* which stated that all those who had "disappeared" during the previous eight years should be considered dead for administrative purposes. The government stressed that there would be no further disclosures about the consequences of the "war against subversion." Although the government admitted that there had been excesses, it stated that "the actions of the members of the Armed Forces in the conduct of the war were in the line of duty." On 23 September 1983 the junta published an amnesty law, known as the *Law of National Pacification.* This law pardoned certain crimes committed with a political motive or purpose, including kidnapping, torture and murder; it suspended criminal proceedings relating to those offences and blocked all further investigations into "disappearances."

On 29 October 1983 the state of siege was suspended, free elections took place and on 10 December 1983 the civilian government of President Raúl Alfonsín was sworn in. One of the central issues of the election campaign had been the investigation of the human rights record of the military juntas. The attempt by the military to prevent those responsible for human rights violations being brought to justice was first effectively challenged on 27 December 1983, when the Argentine Congress unanimously approved a law abrogating the Law of National Pacification (for details of the most significant laws and decrees which the Alfonsín government proposed to Congress between December 1983 and April 1984. This abrogation of the much resented Amnesty Law was the first step in a legislative process that was eventually to lead to the trial of the military commanders.

ARGENTINA'S HUMAN RIGHTS RECORD AND AMNESTY INTERNATIONAL

One of Amnesty International's earliest expressions of concern about human rights in Argentina came in August 1972 after the killing of sixteen young prisoners—all allegedly members of revolutionary organizations—in the Admiral Zar naval base. They were shot after surrendering peacefully when an escape attempt from a maximum security prison in Trelew, Patagonia, failed.

In 1974, when the Peronist government imposed a state of siege and detained a number of persons without trial, Amnesty International called for the release of prisoners of conscience among those detained. In 1975, after an increase in the incidence of killings by right-wing death squads of students and trade union leaders (most of whom were alleged to be members of Marxist organizations or of the left-wing of the Peronist movement), Amnesty International called upon the President, María Estela Martínez de Perón, to investigate crimes attributed to groups such as the Triple-A.

In 1976, following the military coup d'état, Amnesty International sent a high-level mission to Argentina to express its concern to the military authorities about a series of important questions: the numbers and whereabouts of political prisoners; allegations of torture; the alleged complicity of police and military in violent and illegal abductions; the status and security of Latin American refugees; and the nature and effects of the legislation enacted after the coup. The organization's findings and recommendations were published in the *Report of an Amnesty International Mission to Argentina*, in March 1977.

In 1978, in view of continuing evidence of widespread "disappearances" in Argentina, Amnesty International launched a world-wide publicity campaign to bring pressure on the Argentine government to end its policy of systematic abduction and to acknowledge the detention of the "disappeared." In 1980 Amnesty International published a report on secret camps in Argentina based on the testimony of former detainees. Between 1977 and 1982, the organization sent regular communications to the United Nations and the Inter-American Commission on Human Rights of the Organization of American States documenting a consistent pattern of gross violations of human rights in Argentina.

Following the inauguration of Raúl Alfonsín as President of Argentina in December 1983, Amnesty International sent two representatives to the country in April 1984 in order to improve its understanding of the measures the new government was taking to investigate past human rights abuses and to prevent a recurrence of such abuses in the future. These representatives had meetings with a number of government officials, including the president and vice president, as well as with members of the recently formed National Commission on Disappeared People (CONADEP). In February 1985, after the trial of the former military commanders had been transferred to the jurisdiction of the Buenos Aires Federal Appeals Court, Amnesty International wrote to the Chairman of the Court requesting authorization for representatives of the organization to attend the public oral proceedings. This permission was granted and in April 1985 two representatives of Amnesty International, a staff member of the International Secretariat and Edgardo Carvalho (a Uruguayan lawyer), attended the beginning of the public hearings. The organization had also written to the Argentine Ministry of Foreign Affairs, which gave assistance in arranging interviews with various government officials. These included Dr. Horacio Ravenna, Under-secretary for Human Rights at the Ministry of Foreign Affairs, and Dr. Eduardo Rabossi, Under-secretary for Human Rights at the Ministry of the Interior (the latter being also a former member of CONADEP), and Dr. Jaime Malamud Gotti, who, as one of the legal advisers to the President, was well informed on all matters relating to proposed reforms of the Penal Code and the Code of Military Justice.

The delegates also made contact with persons or institutions concerned with work on human rights within Argentina. These included Dr. Augusto Conte MacDonnell, a lawyer and deputy to the Congress, and Dr. Emilio Mignone, president of the Centre for Legal and Social Studies (CELS), which had played a vital role during the period of military rule in denouncing and investigating cases of human rights violations.

Finally, the delegates interviewed several people directly involved in the trial. These included the Public Prosecutor, Dr. Julio César Strassera, and his deputy, Dr. Luis Moreno Ocampo, and the State defence counsel for General Videla, Dr. Juan Carlos Tavares.

When the Federal Court delivered its verdict in December 1985, Edgardo Carvalho went again to Buenos Aires on behalf of Amnesty International and received from the Court Secretary a complete text of the Court's decision, as well as an explanation of the factors the Court had taken into account. He again met the Public Prosecutor and his deputy, who explained to him the grounds of the appeal that they intended to lodge against some provisions of the verdict.

DEVELOPMENTS PRIOR TO THE TRIAL

The National Commission on Disappeared People

A significant development preceding the trial of the junta members was the appointment by the government, in December 1983, of CONADEP, the *Comisión Nacional sobre la Desaparición de Personas* (National Commission on Disappeared People). Several of the human rights organizations in Argentina had asked that a congressional commission should be set up to investigate the "disappearances," but in the event CONADEP was established as an extra-parliamentary commission. Its members included representatives of religious and human rights groups and leading figures from various sections of Argentine society. Its president was the novelist, Ernesto Sábato. Requested by the government to "clarify the tragic events in which thousands of people disappeared," CONADEP presented its findings to President Alfonsín on 20 September 1984, and on 28 November 1984 a two-volume report, entitled *Nunca Más* (*Never Again*) was published.

During the course of its nine-month study, CONADEP interviewed thousands of witnesses, including former prisoners, relatives of "disappeared" prisoners and members of the army and security forces. It also carried out inspections of a number of former torture centres. The armed forces and security services were reluctant to cooperate with the commission, refusing to reply to written questions and sometimes refusing to permit inspections of military establishments. Members of CONADEP became a major target of attacks attributed by the authorities to right-wing paramilitary groups linked to the security services. In three cities—Mar del Plata, Córdoba and Rosario—the homes and offices of CONADEP delegates were bombed.

The CONADEP report catalogued 8,960 unresolved "disappearances," but warned that the true figure might be higher. It also listed 340 clandestine abduction centres in Argentina, which it said were in use at the height of the repression. The report concluded that human rights had been violated in an organized way by the armed forces using state machinery.

It rejected assertions that torture and enforced "disappearance" were exceptional excesses.

QUESTIONS TO CONSIDER

1. Should unofficial death squads and paramilitary right-wing gangs be considered genocidal organizations?
2. Were the "disappeared" victims of genocide?
3. Explain the role Amnesty International played in the events in Argentina.

Reagan & Guatemala's Death Files

Robert Parry,

Editor of American Dispatches

Ronald Reagan's election in November 1980 set off celebrations in the well-to-do communities of Central America. After four years of Jimmy Carter's human rights nagging, the region's anticommunist hard-liners were thrilled that they had someone in the White House who understood their problems. The oligarchs and the generals had good reason for optimism. For years, Reagan had been a staunch defender of right-wing regimes that engaged in bloody counter-insurgency campaigns against leftist enemies.

In the late 1970s, when Carter's human rights coordinator, Pat Derian, criticized the Argentine military for its "dirty war"—tens of thousands of "disappearances," tortures and murders—then political commentator Reagan joshed that she should "walk a mile in the moc-

casins" of the Argentine generals before criticizing them.

Despite his aw-shucks style, Reagan found virtually every anti-communist action justified, no matter how brutal. From his eight years in the White House, there is no historical indication that he was troubled by the bloodbath and even genocide that occurred in Central America during his presidency, while he was shipping hundreds of millions of dollars in military aid to the implicated forces.

The death toll was staggering—an estimated 70,000 or more political killings in El Salvador, possibly 20,000 slain from the contra war in Nicaragua, about 200 political "disappearances" in Honduras and some 100,000 people eliminated during a resurgence of political violence in Guatemala.

From Robert Parry, "Reagan & Guatemala's Death Files," *Alternative Press Review* 5(1) (Spring 2000): Reprinted with permission.

The one consistent element in these slaughters was the overarching Cold War rationalization, emanating in large part from Ronald Reagan's White House. Yet, as the world community moves to punish war crimes in the former Yugoslavia and Rwanda, no substantive discussion has occurred in the United States about facing up to this horrendous record of the 1980s.

Rather than a debate about Reagan as a potential war criminal, the ailing ex-president is honored as a conservative icon with his name attached to Washington National Airport and with an active legislative push to have his face carved into Mount Rushmore. When the national news media does briefly acknowledge the barbarities of the 1980s in Central America, it is in the context of one-day stories about the little countries bravely facing up to their violent pasts. At times, the CIA is fingered abstractly as a bad supporting actor in the violent dramas. But never does the national press lay blame on individual American officials.

The grisly reality of Central America was most recently revisited on February 25 [1999] when a Guatemalan truth commission issued a report on the staggering human rights crimes that occurred during a 34-year civil war. The Historical Clarification Commission, an independent human rights body, estimated that the conflict claimed the lives of some 200,000 people with the most savage bloodletting occurring in the 1980s. Based on a review of about 20 percent of the dead, the panel blamed the army for 93 percent of the killings and leftist guerrillas for three percent. Four percent were listed as unresolved.

The report documented that in the 1980s, the army committed 626 massacres against Mayan villages. "The massacres that eliminated entire Mayan villages … are neither perfidious allegations nor figments of the imagination, but an authentic chapter in Guatemala's history," the commission concluded. The army "completely exterminated Mayan communities, destroyed their livestock and crops," the report

said. In the north, the report termed the slaughter a "genocide."

Besides carrying out murder and "disappearances," the army routinely engaged in torture and rape. "The rape of women, during torture or before being murdered, was a common practice" by the military and paramilitary forces, the report found. The report added that the "government of the United States, through various agencies including the CIA, provided direct and indirect support for some [of these] state operations." The report concluded that the U.S. government also gave money and training to a Guatemalan military that committed "acts of genocide" against the Mayans.

"Believing that the ends justified everything, the military and the state security forces blindly pursued the anticommunist struggle, without respect for any legal principles or the most elemental ethical and religious values, and in this way, completely lost any semblance of human morals," said the commission chairman, Christian Tomuschat, a German jurist. "Within the framework of the counter-insurgency operations carried out between 1981 and 1983, in certain regions of the country agents of the Guatemalan state committed acts of genocide against groups of the Mayan people," he added. The report did not single out culpable individuals either in Guatemala or the United States. But the American official most directly responsible for renewing U.S. military aid to Guatemala and encouraging its government during the 1980s was President Reagan.

After his election, Reagan pushed aggressively to overturn an arms embargo imposed on Guatemala by President Carter because of the military's wretched human rights record. Reagan saw bolstering the Guatemalan army as part of a regional response to growing leftist insurgencies. Reagan pitched the conflicts as Moscow's machinations for surrounding and conquering the United States.

The president's chief concern about the recurring reports of human rights atrocities was to attack and discredit the information.

Sometimes personally and sometimes through surrogates, Reagan denigrated the human rights investigators and journalists who disclosed the slaughters. Typical of these attacks was an analysis prepared by Reagan's appointees at the U.S. embassy in Guatemala. The paper was among those recently released by the Clinton administration to assist the Guatemalan truth commission's investigation.

Dated Oct. 22, 1982, the analysis concluded "that a concerted disinformation campaign is being waged in the U.S. against the Guatemalan government by groups supporting the communist insurgency in Guatemala." The report claimed that "conscientious human rights and church organizations," including Amnesty International, had been duped by the communists and "may not fully appreciate that they are being utilized." "The campaign's object is simple: to deny the Guatemalan army the weapons and equipment needed from the U.S. to defeat the guerrillas," the analysis declared. "If those promoting such disinformation can convince the Congress, through the usual opinion-makers—the media, church and human rights groups—that the present GOG [government of Guatemala] is guilty of gross human rights violations they know that the Congress will refuse Guatemala the military assistance it needs.

"Those backing the communist insurgency are betting on an application, or rather misapplication, of human rights policy so as to damage the GOG and assist themselves." Reagan personally picked up this theme of a falsely accused Guatemalan military. During a swing through Latin America, Reagan discounted the mounting reports of hundreds of Maya villages being eradicated. On Dec. 4, 1982, after meeting with Guatemala's dictator, Gen. Efrain Rios Montt, Reagan hailed the general as "totally dedicated to democracy." Reagan declared that Rios Montt's government had been "getting a bum rap."

But the newly declassified U.S. government records reveal that Reagan's praise—and the embassy analysis—flew in the face of corroborated accounts from U.S. intelligence. Based on its own internal documents, the Reagan administration knew that the Guatemalan military indeed was engaged in a scorched-earth campaign against the Mayans. According to these "secret" cables, the CIA was confirming Guatemalan government massacres in 1981–82 even as Reagan was moving to loosen the military aid ban.

In April 1981, a secret CIA cable described a massacre at Cocob, near Nebaj in the Ixil Indian territory. On April 17, 1981, government troops attacked the area believed to support leftist guerrillas, the cable said. According to a CIA source, "the social population appeared to fully support the guerrillas" and "the soldiers were forced to fire at anything that moved." The CIA cable added that "the Guatemalan authorities admitted that 'many civilians' were killed in Cocob, many of whom undoubtedly were noncombatants." Despite the CIA account and other similar reports, Reagan permitted Guatemala's army to buy $3.2 million in military trucks and jeeps in June 1981. To permit the sale, Reagan removed the vehicles from a list of military equipment that was covered by the human rights embargo. Apparently confident of Reagan's sympathies, the Guatemalan government continued its political repression without apology.

According to a State Department cable on Oct. 5, 1981, Guatemalan leaders met with Reagan's roving ambassador, retired Gen. Vernon Walters, and left no doubt about their plans. Guatemala's military leader, Gen. Fernando Romeo Lucas Garcia, "made clear that his government will continue as before—that the repression will continue. He reiterated his belief that the repression is working and that the guerrilla threat will be successfully routed." Human rights groups saw the same picture. The Inter-American Human Rights Commission released a report on Oct. 15, 1981, blaming the Guatemalan government for "thousands of illegal executions."

But the Reagan administration was set on whitewashing the ugly scene. A State Department "white paper," released in December 1981, blamed the violence on leftist "extremist groups" and their "terrorist methods" prompted and supported by Cuba's Fidel Castro. Yet, even as these rationalizations were presented to the American people, U.S. agencies continued to pick up clear evidence of government-sponsored massacres. One CIA report in February 1982 described an army sweep through the so-called Ixil Triangle in central El Quiche province. "The commanding officers of the units involved have been instructed to destroy all towns and villages which are cooperating with the Guerrilla Army of the Poor [known as the EGP] and eliminate all sources of resistance," the report stated. "Since the operation began, several villages have been burned to the ground, and a large number of guerrillas and collaborators have been killed." The CIA report explained the army's modus operandi: "When an army patrol meets resistance and takes fire from a town or village, it is assumed that the entire town is hostile and it is subsequently destroyed."

When the army encountered an empty village, it was "assumed to have been supporting the EGP, and it is destroyed. There are hundreds, possibly thousands of refugees in the hills with no homes to return to. … The army high command is highly pleased with the initial results of the sweep operation, and believes that it will be successful in destroying the major EGP support area and will be able to drive the EGP out of the Ixil Triangle … The well documented belief by the army that the entire Ixil Indian population is pro-EGP has created a situation in which the army can be expected to give no quarter to combatants and non-combatants alike."

In March 1982, Gen. Rios Montt seized power. An avowed fundamentalist Christian, he immediately impressed Washington. Reagan hailed Rios Montt as "a man of great per-

sonal integrity." By July 1982, however, Rios Montt had begun a new scorched-earth campaign called his "rifles and beans" policy. The slogan meant that pacified Indians would get "beans," while all others could expect to be the target of army "rifles." In October, he secretly gave carte blanche to the feared "Archivos" intelligence unit to expand "death squad" operations. Based at the Presidential Palace, the "Archivos" masterminded many of Guatemala's most notorious assassinations. The U.S. embassy was soon hearing more accounts of the army conducting Indian massacres. On Oct. 21, 1982, one cable described how three embassy officers tried to check out some of these reports but ran into bad weather and canceled the inspection.

Still, this cable put the best possible spin on the situation. Though unable to check out the massacre reports, the embassy officials did "reach the conclusion that the army is completely up front about allowing us to check alleged massacre sites and to speak with whomever we wish." The next day, the embassy fired off its analysis that the Guatemalan government was the victim of a communist-inspired "disinformation campaign," a claim embraced by Reagan with his "bum rap" comment in December. On Jan. 7, 1983, Reagan lifted the ban on military aid to Guatemala and authorized the sale of $6 million in military hardware. Approval covered spare parts for UH-1H helicopters and A-37 aircraft used in counter-insurgency operations. Radios, batteries and battery chargers were also in the package.

State Department spokesman John Hughes said political violence in the cities had "declined dramatically" and that rural conditions had improved too. In February 1983, however, a secret CIA cable noted a rise in "suspect right-wing violence" with kidnappings of students and teachers. Bodies of victims were appearing in ditches and gullies. CIA sources traced these political murders to Rios Montt's order to the "Archivos" in October to "apprehend, hold, interrogate and dispose of suspected guerrillas as they saw fit." Despite these grisly facts on the ground, the annual State Department human rights survey praised the supposedly improved human rights situation in Guatemala. "The overall conduct of the armed forces had improved by late in the year" 1982, the report stated.

A different picture—far closer to the secret information held by the U.S. government—was coming from independent human rights investigators. On March 17, 1983, Americas Watch representatives condemned the Guatemalan army for human rights atrocities against the Indian population. New York attorney Stephen L. Kass said these findings included proof that the government carried out "virtually indiscriminate murder of men, women and children of any farm regarded by the army as possibly supportive of guerrilla insurgents." Rural women suspected of guerrilla sympathies were raped before execution, Kass said. Children were "thrown into burning homes. They are thrown in the air and speared with bayonets. We heard many, many stories of children being picked up by the ankles and swung against poles so their heads are destroyed."

Publicly, however, senior Reagan officials continued to put on a happy face. On June 12, 1983, special envoy Richard B. Stone praised "positive changes" in Rios Montt's government. But Rios Montt's vengeful Christian fundamentalism was hurtling out of control, even by Guatemalan standards. In August 1983, Gen. Oscar Mejia Victores seized power in another coup. Despite the power shift, Guatemalan security forces continued to act with impunity. When three Guatemalans working for the U.S. Agency for International Development were slain in November 1983, U.S. Ambassador Frederic Chapin suspected that "Archivos" hit squads were sending a message to the United States to back off even the mild pressure for

human rights improvements. In late November, in a brief show of displeasure, the administration postponed the sale of $2 million in helicopter spare parts. The next month, however, Reagan sent the spare parts. In 1984, Reagan succeeded, too, in pressuring Congress to approve $300,000 in military training for the Guatemalan army. By mid-1984, Chapin, who had grown bitter about the army's stubborn brutality, was gone, replaced by a far-right political appointee named Alberto Piedra, who was all for increased military assistance to Guatemala.

In January 1985, Americas Watch issued a report observing that Reagan's State Department "is apparently more concerned with improving Guatemala's image than in improving its human rights." According to the newly declassified U.S. records, the Guatemalan reality included torture out of the Middle Ages. A Defense Intelligence Agency cable reported that the Guatemalan military used an air base in Retalhuleu during the mid-1980s as a center for coordinating the counter-insurgency campaign in southwest Guatemala. At the base, pits were filled with water to hold captured suspects. "Reportedly there were cages over the pits and the water level was such that the individuals held within them were forced to hold on to the bars in order to keep their heads above water and avoid drowning," the DIA report stated. Later, the pits were filled with concrete to eliminate the evidence.

The Guatemalan military used the Pacific Ocean as another dumping spot for political victims, according to the DIA report. Bodies of insurgents tortured to death and of live prisoners marked for "disappearance" were loaded on planes that flew out over the ocean where the soldiers would shove the victims into the water. The history of the Retalhuleu death camp was uncovered by accident in the early 1990s, the DIA reported on April 11, 1994. A Guatemalan officer wanted to let soldiers cultivate their own vegetables on a corner of the base. But the officer was taken aside and told to drop the request "because the locations he had wanted to cultivate were burial sites that had been used by the D-2 [military intelligence] during the mid-eighties."

Guatemala, of course, was not the only Central American country where Reagan and his administration supported brutal counter-insurgency operations—and then sought to cover up the bloody facts. Reagan's falsification of the historical record was a hallmark of the conflicts in El Salvador and Nicaragua as well. In one case, Reagan personally lashed out at an individual human rights investigator named Reed Brody, a New York lawyer who had collected affidavits from more than 100 witnesses to atrocities carried out by the U.S.-supported contras in Nicaragua. Angered by the revelations about his pet "freedom-fighters," Reagan denounced Brody in a speech on April 15, 1985. The president called Brody "one of dictator [Daniel] Ortega's supporters, a sympathizer who has openly embraced Sandinismo."

Privately, Reagan had a far more accurate understanding of the true nature of the contras. At one point in the contra war, Reagan turned to CIA official Duane Clarridge and demanded that the contras be used to destroy some Soviet-supplied helicopters that had arrived in Nicaragua. In his memoirs, Clarridge recalled that "President Reagan pulled me aside and asked, 'Dewey, can't you get those vandals of yours to do this job.'" [See Clarridge's A Spy for All Seasons.] To conceal the truth about the war crimes of Central America, Reagan also authorized a systematic program of distorting information and intimidating American journalists. Called "public diplomacy," the project was run by a CIA propaganda veteran, Walter Raymond Jr., who was assigned to the National Security Council staff. The explicit goal of the operation was to manage U.S. "perceptions" of the wars in Central America. The project's key operatives developed propaganda "themes," selected "hot buttons" to excite the American people, cultivated pliable journalists who would cooperate and bullied reporters who wouldn't go along.

The best-known attacks were directed against New York Times correspondent Raymond Bonner for disclosing Salvadoran army massacres of civilians, including the slaughter of more than 800 men, women and children in El Mozote in December 1981. But Bonner was not alone. Reagan's operatives pressured scores of reporters and their editors in an ultimately successful campaign to minimize information about these human rights crimes reaching the American people. [For details, see Robert Parry's Lost History.] The tamed reporters, in turn, gave the administration a far freer hand to pursue its anticommunist operations throughout Central America. Despite the tens of thousands of civilian deaths and now-corroborated accounts of massacres and genocide, not a single senior military officer in Central America was held accountable for the bloodshed.

The U.S. officials who sponsored and encouraged these war crimes not only escaped any legal judgment, but remained highly respected figures in Washington. Reagan has been honored as few recent presidents have. The journalists who played along by playing down the atrocities—the likes of Fred Barnes and Charles Krauthammer—saw their careers skyrocket, while those who told the truth suffered severe consequences. Given that history, it was not surprising that the Guatemalan truth report was treated as a one-day story.

The major American newspapers did cover the findings. The New York Times made it the lead story. The Washington Post played it inside on page A19. Both cited the troubling role of the CIA and other U.S. government agencies in the Guatemalan tragedy. But no U.S. official was held accountable by name. On March 1, 1999, a strange Washington Post editorial addressed the findings, but did not confront them. One of its principal points seemed to be that President Carter's military aid cut-off to Guatemala was to blame. The editorial argued that the arms embargo removed "what minimal restraint even a feeble American presence supplied." The editorial made no reference to the 1980s and added only a mild criticism of "the CIA [because it] still bars the public from the full documentation." Then, with no apparent sense of irony, the editorial ended by stating: "We need our own truth commission."

During a visit to Central America, on March 10, President Clinton apologized for the past U.S. support of right-wing regimes in Guatemala. "For the United States, it is important that I state clearly that support for military forces and intelligence units which engaged in violence and widespread repression was wrong, and the United States must not repeat that mistake," Clinton said. But the sketchy apology appears to be all the Central Americans can expect from El Norte.

Back in Washington, Ronald Reagan remains a respected icon, not a disgraced war criminal. His name is still honored, attached to National Airport and a new federal building. A current GOP congressional initiative would chisel his face into Mount Rushmore. Meanwhile, in the Balkans and in Africa, the United States is sponsoring international tribunals to arrest and to try human rights violators—and their political patrons—for war crimes.

The modern Guatemalan tragedy traces back to 1954 and a CIA-engineered coup against the reform-minded government of Jacobo Arbenz. But other lesser-known chapters in the blood-soaked saga—spanning 40 years—also feature American officials in important supporting roles. Newly released U.S. government documents describe in chilling detail, often in cold bureaucratic language, how American advisers and their Cold War obsession spurred on the killings and hid the horrible secrets.

In the mid-1960s, for instance, the Guatemalan security forces were disorganized, suffering from internal divisions, and possibly infiltrated by leftist opponents. So, the U.S. government dispatched U.S. public safety adviser John Longon from his base in Venezuela. Arriving in late 1965, Longon sized up the problem and began reorganizing the Guatemalan security forces into a more efficient—and ultimately, more lethal—organization. In a Jan. 4, 1966, report on his activities, Longon said he recommended both overt and covert components to the military's battle against "terrorism."

One of Longon's strategies was to seal off sections of Guatemala City and begin house-to-house searches. "The idea behind this was to force some of the wanted communists out of hiding and into police hands, as well as to convince the Guatemalan public that the authorities were doing something to control the situation." Longon also arranged for U.S. advisers to begin giving "day-to-day operational advice" to Guatemalan police. On the covert side, Longon pressed for "a safe house [to] be immediately set up" for coordination of security intelligence. "A room was immediately prepared in the [Presidential] Palace for this purpose and ... Guatemalans were immediately designated to put this operation into effect." Longon's operation within the presidential compound was the starting point for the infamous "Archivos" intelligence unit that became the clearinghouse for political assassinations.

Longon's final recommendations sought assignment of special U.S. advisers to assist in the covert operations and delivery of special intelligence equipment, presumably for spying on Guatemalan citizens. With the American input, the Guatemalan security forces soon became one of the most feared counter-insurgency operations in Latin America. Just two months after Longon's report, a secret CIA cable noted the clandestine execution of several Guatemalan "communists and terrorists" on the night of March 6, 1966. By the end of the year, the Guatemalan government was bold enough to request U.S. help in establishing special kidnapping squads, according to a cable from the U.S. Southern Command that was forwarded to Washington on Dec. 3.

By 1967, the Guatemalan counter-insurgency terror had gained a fierce momentum. On Oct. 23, 1967, the State Department's Bureau of Intelligence and Research noted the "accumulating evidence that the [Guatemalan] counter-insurgency machine is out of control." The report noted that Guatemalan "counter-terror" units were carrying out abductions, bombings, torture and summary executions "of real and alleged communists." The mounting death toll in Guatemala disturbed some of the American officials assigned to the country. One official, the embassy's deputy chief of mission Viron Vaky, expressed his concerns in a remarkably candid report that he submitted on March 29, 1968, after returning to Washington.

Vaky framed his arguments in pragmatic, rather than moral, terms, but his personal anguish broke through. "The official squads are guilty of atrocities. Interrogations are brutal, torture is used and bodies are mutilated," Vaky wrote. "In the minds of many in Latin America, and, tragically, especially in the sensitive, articulate youth, we are believed to have condoned these tactics, if not actually encouraged them. Therefore our image is being tarnished and the credibility of our claims to want a better and more just world are increasingly placed in doubt. I need hardly add the aspect of domestic U.S. reactions. This leads to an aspect I personally find the most disturbing of all—that we have not been honest with ourselves. We have condoned counter-terror; we may even in effect have encouraged or blessed it. We have been so obsessed with the fear of insurgency that we have rationalized away our qualms and uneasiness."

"This is not only because we have concluded we cannot do anything about it, for we never really tried. Rather we suspected that maybe it is a good tactic, and that as long as Communists are being killed it is alright. Murder, torture and mutilation are alright if our side is doing it and the victims are Communists.

"After all, hasn't man been a savage from the beginning of time, so let us not be too queasy about terror. I have literally heard these arguments from our people. Have our values been so twisted by our adversary concept of politics in the hemisphere? Is it conceivable that we are so obsessed with insurgency that we are prepared to rationalize murder as an acceptable counter-insurgency weapon? Is it possible that a nation which so reveres the principle of due process of law has so easily acquiesced in this sort of terror tactic?"

Though kept secret from the American public for three decades, the Vaky memo obliterated any claim that Washington simply didn't know the reality in Guatemala. Still, with Vaky's memo squirreled away in State Department files, the killing went on. The repression was noted almost routinely in reports from the field. On Jan. 12, 1971, the Defense Intelligence Agency reported that Guatemalan forces had "quietly eliminated" hundreds of "terrorists and bandits" in the countryside. On Feb. 4, 1974, a State Department cable reported resumption of "death squad" activities.

On Dec. 17, 1974, a DIA biography of one U.S.-trained Guatemalan officer gave an insight into how U.S. counter-insurgency doctrine had imbued the Guatemalan strategies. According to the biography, Lt. Col. Elias Osmundo Ramirez Cervantes, chief of security section for Guatemala's president, had trained at the U.S. Army School of Intelligence at Fort Holabird in Maryland. Fort Holabird was the center for Project X, the distillation of U.S. lessons learned in conducting counter-insurgency warfare. Begun in the mid-1960s, Project X employed veterans of the Phoenix Program in Vietnam who shared their experiences on effective methods of interrogation, coercion and ambushes. [For details, see Robert Parry's Lost History.]

Back in Guatemala, Lt. Col. Ramirez Cervantes was put in charge of plotting raids on suspected subversives as well as their interrogations. As brutal as the security forces were in the 1960s and 1970s, the worst was yet to come. In the 1980s, the Guatemalan army escalated its slaughter of political dissidents and their suspected supporters to unprecedented levels.

QUESTIONS TO CONSIDER

1. Should political assassinations be classified as genocide?

2. The Historical Clarification Commission did not affix blame for atrocities in Guatemala, but Parry does. Who was directly responsible, in his opinion?

3. How did President Ronald Reagan respond to recurring reports of human rights atrocities?

4. How forthright were Guatemalan leaders when indicating their intentions in Guatemala?

5. How did the assessment of Americas Watch differ from the U.S. government's picture of what was transpiring in Guatemala?

6. Did what happened at El Mozote qualify as genocide in El Salvador?

7. Explain the importance of the Vaky memo.

Guatemalan Army Waged "Genocide," New Report Finds

Mireya Navarro,
Reporter, New York Times

[February 26, 1999.] Guatemala City. A truth commission report has concluded that the United States gave money and training to a Guatemalan military that committed "acts of genocide" against the Mayan people during the most brutal armed conflict in Latin America, Guatemala's 36-year civil war.

The report of the independent Historical Clarification Commission, which was released on Thursday, contradicts years of official denial about the torture, kidnapping and execution of thousands of civilians in a war that the commission estimated killed more than 200,000 Guatemalans.

Although the broad outlines of American support to Guatemala's military have been known, the nine-volume report confirms that the CIA aided Guatemalan military forces. The commission listed the American training of the officer corps in counter-insurgency techniques as a key factor "which had a significant bearing on human rights violations during the armed confrontation."

The commission, established as a part of a United Nations-supervised peace accord that ended the war in 1996, concluded that the government or allied paramilitary groups were to blame for more than 90 percent of the 42,000 human rights violations, 29,000 of which resulted in deaths or missing persons. That attributes a somewhat higher percentage of deaths to the government and its allies than a report last year by the Roman Catholic Church that examined human rights abuses.

The commission specifically named military intelligence as the organizer of illegal

From Mireya Navarro "Guatemalan Army Waged 'Genocide,' New Report Finds" *New York Times,* Feb. 26, 1999. Reprinted with permission.

detentions, torture, forced disappearances and executions, and it said that many massacres were a direct result of government policy. It stopped short, however, of identifying individuals responsible for various massacres.

As the conclusions of the long-awaited report were read at a solemn ceremony at the National Theater, human rights workers, relatives of victims and others among the more than 2,000 people broke into standing ovations, sobs, shouts and chants of "Justice! Justice!" The outbursts repeatedly interrupted speeches as the president and cabinet members sat silently on the theater's first row.

While the scope of the bloodshed had been generally known, the report is the first by an internationally supported panel to lay out the extent of the violence and pin it on the government and its military allies. In unexpectedly strong language, it describes the Guatemalan policy at the height of the war as a policy of genocide.

The report's estimate of more than 200,000 deaths is slightly higher than previous figures, and the number of documented massacres substantially exceeds figures used in previous examinations.

The war, which began in 1960, pitted a rightist military-controlled government against a classic Latin American left-wing insurgency. Largely a rural war carried out in the hinterlands where Mayan Indians lived, the military assumed that the Mayans sympathized with the insurgents and provided them with supplies, intelligence and shelter.

As a consequence, entire Mayan villages were attacked, burned and inhabitants were slaughtered in an effort to deny the guerrillas protection. The report said the Mayan population paid the highest price, when the military identified them as natural allies of the guerrillas. The result, the report said, was an "aggressive, racist and extremely cruel nature of violations that resulted in the massive extermination of defenseless Mayan communities."

Christian Tomuschat, the German jurist who led the commission's 18-month investigation, said, "The results of our investigation demonstrate that in general, the excuse that midlevel commanders acted with a wide margin of autonomy—an excuse used in an attempt to justify what happened as 'excesses' and 'error' not ordered by superiors—is unsubstantiated and totally lacking any basis."

The commission recommended a national reparations program for victims and exhumations of "hundreds" of clandestine cemeteries. It called on President Alvaro Arzu Irigoyen and the ex-guerrilla commanders to assume responsibility in the name of the state and ask all Guatemalans for forgiveness.

The three-member commission and an international staff of 272 workers made extensive use of declassified documents from the United States. American assistance fortified the Guatemalan armed forces with aid and training in its anti-Communist campaign. On Thursday, Tomuschat said the commission's investigation also found that until the mid-1980s, American companies and government officials "exercised pressure to maintain the country's archaic and unjust socioeconomic structure" and that the CIA supported illegal counter-insurgency operations here. Besides Tomuschat, the commission members were Edgar Balsells, a lawyer, and Otilia Lux Coti, a leading Mayan educator, both of Guatemala.

The commission did not give specific names of human rights violators, the result of military opposition during the peace negotiations to pointing fingers at specific people.

But some victims' families said no true reconciliation can be achieved in Guatemala without judicial accountability.

"There has to be an end to impunity," said Helen Mack, whose sister, Myrna, was stabbed and killed in 1990, it is believed, for her research on the refugees driven from their homes by the army. The case resulted in the only conviction yet of an army official for human rights violations, and Ms. Mack is pursuing the trial of three other officers for her sister's murder.

On Thursday, the weight of nine years of struggle with Guatemala's ineffective judicial system seem to fall on her as she broke into tears at the National Theater as the commission's conclusions were read. "We the victims feel vindicated," she later said. "No one can now tell us we're following lies or ghosts anymore."

Guatemalan officials said on Thursday that they would have a response after they have studied the report. The army leadership has remained defiant, accusing international and national "actors" for their roles in the violence and insisting the military acted under a constitutional mandate to defend the state from communism.

Asked about the accusations against the CIA by the commission, the spokesman for the intelligence agency, Bill Harlow, said, "Since we have not seen the report, it would be inappropriate for us to comment."

Donald Planty, the U.S. ambassador, said, "I believe that the report's focus is appropriate, that these were abuses committed by Guatemalans against other Guatemalans—the result of an internal conflict."

Defense Minister Hector M. Barrios, who has promised his own report on the war dead and injured, said Thursday, "I see as positive any effort that is made on behalf of peaceful co-existence in Guatemala."

Arzu left without comment after shaking hands with members of the commission and those formally receiving the report—Alvaro de Soto, a senior U.N. official, and representatives of the Guatemalan government and the ex-guerrilla group, Guatemalan National Revolutionary Unity.

Aides said protocol prevented the president from personally accepting the report, but that decision was seen by many here as intentionally distancing the government from the commission's findings. At several points on Thursday, people in the theater shouted for the president to get up on stage and receive the report.

Foreign Affairs Minister Eduardo Stein said the government was already implementing some of recommendations, including compensation for victims, judicial reform and changes in the military. Political repression has greatly been reduced in Guatemala, by most accounts, and the guerrillas have regrouped as a political party. There has also been a rise of Indigenous rights and human rights organizations—the changing times were underscored on Thursday when scores of Guatemalans openly confronted government officials in angry outbursts.

But the country is still wrestling with its transition to a full democratic state. Stark poverty and economic inequalities remain. Despite a requirement under the peace accords that the army's size and role be reduced, experts monitoring the progress say that there has been checkered compliance and that the army still has a hold on internal affairs, rather than being focused solely on the defense of the nation.

And just how fragile the peace is was shown last year when a Roman Catholic bishop and leading defender of human rights, Juan Jose Gerardi, was beaten to death with a concrete block just days after making public the results of a three-year investigation of human rights abuses during the war. That report, sponsored by the Catholic church, identified specific military officers and guerrilla groups, and church and human rights groups say they believe the killing was meant to pressure them into renewed silence.

The most heartfelt applause at the National Theater Thursday came when the bishop's name was mentioned as yet another political victim. Many here feel the truth commission's report can help the country's efforts toward change, but only if it is etched into the public consciousness.

"This is not the end of the work," said Feliciana Macario, a board member of a survivors' group called National Widows Committee, which seeks reparations for the loss of homes and land and "moral damages," such as the psychological trauma suffered by orphaned children. "To us, this is the beginning of another struggle."

QUESTIONS TO CONSIDER

1. Discuss the role of military intelligence in Guatemala's civil war.

2. Should the contents of this report be considered proof of genocide?

MAKING CONNECTIONS

1. Was the U.S. support of the Guatemalan government substantially different from Belgian involvement in the Congo?

2. Was the United States complicit in genocide in Latin America?

✔ RECOMMENDED RESOURCES

Guest, Iain. *Behind the Disappearances: Argentina's Dirty War Against Human Rights and the United Nations.* Philadelphia: University of Pennsylvania Press, 1990.

Hodges, Donald C. *Argentina's "Dirty War": An Intellectual Biography.* Austin: University of Texas Press, 1991.

Perera, Victor. *Unfinished Conquest: The Guatemalan Tragedy.* Berkeley, CA: University of California, 1993.

Rosenberg, Tina. *Children of Cain: Violence and the Violent in Latin America.* New York: Penguin Books, 1992.

Schlesinger, Stephen, and Stephen Kusir. *Bitter Fruit: The Untold Story of the American Coup in Guatemala.* Garden City, NY: Anchor Books, 1983.

CHAPTER 11

CAMBODIAN "AUTOGENOCIDE"

Pol Pot proves that the ideological progeny of Communism have the potential, on a small scale, of making a "utopia" a hell on earth. Pol Pot believed he would sit at the head of the table with Marx and Lenin, passing on the feast of praise to Stalin, Mao Tse-tung, and Fidel Castro.

Pol Pot's attempt to implement total Communism without transitional or gradual processes served to destroy a nation, people, and culture. The Khmer Rouge abolished money and achieved total collectivization in less than two years. During the same time they succeeded in obliterating social distinctions by eliminating entire classes of intelligentsia, property owners, businessmen, and urban dwellers. The Khmer Rouge emptied Phnom Phen in one week and proceeded to manage forced labor, a prolonged purge of political opponents, and a man-made famine.

In proportion to its population, Cambodia underwent a human catastrophe beyond any in the twentieth century. Almost 4 million people perished from a 1970 population of nearly 7.1 million. The mayhem the Khmer Rouge inflicted on its people led the French author Jean Lacouture to coin the word *autogenocide*, thus differentiating the horror in Cambodia from previous genocides. The Khmer Rouge targeted specific groups of people such as lawyers, teachers, engineers, and scientists because they were deemed unnecessary, subversive, or because of their Western ways. The goal of ideological purity, in a newly purified society, produced unparalleled fanaticism and rationalized the creation of a concentration-camp state.

Sydney Schanberg, a journalist who witnessed firsthand the implementation of the Khmer horror, provides an overview of the genocide. David Chandler provides a biographical sketch of Cambodia's ruthless dictator in his article "Pol Pot."

Cambodia

Sydney Schanberg,

New York Times *Journalist*

For the last three decades, without surcease, Cambodia has been consumed by war, genocide, slave labor, forced marches, starvation, disease, and now civil conflict. It is to Asia what the Holocaust was to Europe.

Roughly the size of Missouri, bordered by Thailand, Laos, and Vietnam, Cambodia had a population of perhaps 7 to 8 million in 1975 when the maniacal Khmer Rouge guerrillas swept into Phnom Penh and began the "purification" campaign that was the centerpiece of their extremist agrarian revolution. Four years later, the Khmer Rouge were pushed back into the jungle, leaving behind their legacy: 1.5 to 2 million Cambodians dead in what would become known to the world as "the Killing Fields." Twenty percent of the population erased. In America that would be 50 to 60 million people.

Some scholars say that technically what happened in Cambodia cannot be called a genocide because for the most part, it was Khmers killing other Khmers, not someone trying to destroy a different "national, racial, ethnical or religious group"—which is how international law defines genocide.

To make such semantic or legalistic distinctions, however, is sometimes to forsake common sense—after all, the Khmer Rouge set out to erase an entire culture, a major foundation stone of which was Cambodia's religion, Theravada Buddhism. And this may help explain why, over the years, the law has proved so poor a guide to the reality of human slaughter. For, whether you call the mass killing in Cambodia a *genocide* or simply a *crime against humanity*, it was the same by either name. It was a visitation of evil.

One might thus reasonably pick Cambodia as a paradigm for the law's weakness in dealing with such crimes. International law, after all, depends for its legitimacy on the willingness of the world's Nation-States to obey and enforce it. In Cambodia's case most Nation-States expressed shock and horror—and did nothing. Even after the Vietnamese Army pushed the Khmer Rouge out of power in 1979, ended the genocide, were welcomed as liberators, and installed a pro-Hanoi government in Phnom Penh, Western nations saw to it that Cambodia's seat at the United Nations continued to be occupied for several years by those very same Khmer Rouge. Washington and its allies, while denouncing the Khmer Rouge crimes, were still slaves to Cold War ideology; they decided it was better to keep the Khmer Rouge in the UN seat than to have it go to a government in the orbit of Vietnam and its mentor, the Soviet Union. Realpolitik, not the law, was the governing force.

For the human record, let us examine exactly what the Khmer Rouge did to the Cambodian population. Their first act, within hours of military victory, was to kidnap it, herding everyone out of cities and towns into work camps deep in the countryside. All villages that touched on roads were similarly emptied. Cambodia, in fact, was transformed into one giant forced-labor camp under the fist of Angka, "the organization on high." That was the mild part.

The Khmer Rouge had actively sealed off the country. The world could not look in.

Sydney Schanberg, "Cambodia," Roy Gutman and David Rieff, eds. From *Crimes of War: What the Public Should Know* (New York: W.W. Norton & Company, 1999), 58–65. Reprinted with permission.

The horror could begin. Led by Pol Pot, their Paris-educated, Maoist-influenced "Brother Number One," the new rulers proceeded to completely shatter the three underpinnings of Cambodian society—the family, the Buddhist religion, and the village. In grueling migrations, people were marched to sites as far as possible from their home villages. Children were separated from parents and placed in youth groups, where they were indoctrinated to inform on their parents and other adults for any infractions of Angka's crushing rules. Marriage was forbidden except when arranged by Angka. The schools were shuttered, currency abolished, factories abandoned. Newspapers ceased to exist. Radio sets were taken away.

As for religion, Buddhist temples were razed or closed. Of the sixty thousand Buddhist monks only three thousand were found alive after the Khmer Rouge reign; the rest had either been massacred or succumbed to hard labor, disease, or torture. The Chams, a Muslim minority, were also targets for elimination.

Religion, however, was but a starting point. Simply put, the Khmer Rouge marked for potential extinction all Cambodians they deemed not "borisot" (pure)—meaning all those with an education, those raised in population centers, those "tainted" by anything foreign (including knowledge of a foreign language), even those who wore glasses. Anyone, that is, suspected of not being in step with their pathological agrarian master plan. All suspect Cambodians were labeled "new people" and kept apart from the "pure" populations. In some instances, the "new people" were given special identifying neckerchiefs—reminiscent of the yellow Star of David—so they could always be picked out of a crowd, as they often were when taken away for execution.

The Khmer Rouge had a pet slogan: "To spare you is no profit; to destroy you, no loss." With this incantation, at least 1.5 million Cambodians were erased.

I was in Phnom Penh when the Khmer Rouge marched in victorious on April 17, 1975, their faces cold, a deadness in their eyes. They ordered the city evacuated. Everyone was to head for the countryside to join the glorious revolution. They killed those who argued against leaving. Two million frightened people started walking out of the capital. The guerrilla soldiers even ordered the wounded out of the overflowing hospitals, where the casualties had been so heavy in the final few days of the war that the floors were slick with blood. There was no time for anything but emergency surgery. When the doctors ran out of surgical gloves, they simply dipped their hands in bowls of antiseptic and moved on to the next operating table. Somewhere between five thousand and ten thousand wounded were in the city's hospitals when the order to evacuate came. Most couldn't walk so their relatives wheeled them out of the buildings on their beds, with plasma and serum bags attached, and began pushing them along the boulevards out of the city toward the "revolution."

Foreigners were allowed to take refuge in the French embassy compound. I watched many Cambodian friends being herded out of Phnom Penh. Most of them I never saw again. All of us felt like betrayers, like people who were protected and didn't do enough to save our friends. We felt shame. We still do.

Two weeks later, the Khmer Rouge expelled us from the country, shipping us out on two truck convoys to the border with Thailand. With this act, Cambodia was sealed. The world could not look in. The killing could begin.

But the story of Cambodia's misery did not start with the Khmer Rouge. It began in March 1970, when a pro-Western junta headed by Gen. Lon Nol, with Washington's blessing, deposed Prince Norodom Sihanouk, who was out of the country. Sihanouk, a neutralist, had kept Cambodia out of the Vietnam War by making concessions to appease both sides. He allowed the Americans to secretly bomb Viet Cong sanctuaries inside Cambodia while he allowed the Vietnamese Communists to use Cambodia's port city, Kompong Som (also called Sihanoukville) to ship in supplies for those sanctuaries.

With Sihanouk gone, the Lon Nol group in effect declared war on Hanoi; and President Richard Nixon, pleased to have partisans—not neutralists—in Phnom Penh, ordered American troops to push into Cambodia from Vietnam for a six-week assault on the Communist sanctuaries. However, not having real confidence in Lon Nol, the president didn't inform him of the invasion on his sovereign territory until after it had begun and after Nixon had informed the American public on national television.

This was probably the moment that marked Cambodia's transformation into a pawn of the Cold War, with the Chinese backing the Khmer Rouge, the Soviets backing Hanoi, and the Americans backing the Lon Nol regime—all of them turning the entire country into a surrogate Cold War battlefield. The great irony in this turn of events is that the Khmer Rouge were no serious threat in 1970, being a motley collection of ineffectual guerrilla bands totaling at most three thousand to five thousand men, who could never have grown into the murderous force of seventy thousand to 100,000 that swept into Phnom Penh five years later without the American intervention and the subsequent expansion of Chinese and Russian aid to the Communist side. The enlarged war gave the Khmer Rouge status and recruitment power. It also gave them tutelage and advisory help from Hanoi's forces (at least for the first two years before deep rifts drove the two apart).

This five-year war was marked by barbarism by all sides. Cambodian warriors have a battlefield custom, going back centuries, of cutting the livers from the bodies of their vanquished foes, then cooking them in a stew and eating them. The belief is that this imparts strength and also provides talismanic protection against being killed by the enemy. In this and countless other ways, the international conventions that say respect must be shown to the fallen enemy were universally disregarded.

Early in the war, in a town south of Phnom Penh, Lon Nol troops had killed two Viet Cong and recovered their badly charred bodies, which they hung upside-down in the town square to swing gruesomely in the wind—thereby sending a message to all who might consider aiding the foe. Henry Kamm, my *New York Times* colleague, tried to tell the Lon Nol commander that treating the bodies in this manner violated the Geneva Conventions. The commander found this amusing. He left the bodies twisting.

With the Vietnamese Communist units moving deeper into Cambodia, the Lon Nol government began whipping up anti-Vietnamese fervor. This visited fear and worse upon the 200,000-strong ethnic Vietnamese community in the country who, though they were citizens of Cambodia and had lived there for generations, soon became the targets of a public frenzy. Massacres began occurring. Many of the Vietnamese lived along the rivers, earning their living as fishermen; their bodies were soon floating down the Mekong by the dozens. One government general, Sosthene Fernandez, a Cambodian of Filipino ancestry who later rose to become chief of the armed forces, began using ethnic Vietnamese civilians as protective shields for his advancing troops, marching them in front into the waiting guns of the Viet Cong. This, too, is against international law. Fernandez disagreed. "It is a new form of psychological warfare," he said.

Saigon raised bitter protests against these pogroms, and Cambodia's Vietnamese population was finally interned in protective custody in schools and other public buildings. Many were eventually moved under guard to South Vietnam as a temporary measure until emotions cooled.

As the war progressed, the country—at least the part held by the Lon Nol government—progressively shrank. The energized Khmer Rouge kept grabbing more and more territory until the area under government control, aside from the capital, was reduced to a handful of transport corridors and several province towns. The Phnom Penh airport and the Mekong River were its lone links to the outside world. To preserve these lines of supply, the Americans bombed Khmer Rouge and Viet Cong targets in the countryside on a daily basis. Since most of the raids were by giant, eight-engine B-52s, each carrying about twenty-five tons of bombs and thus laying down huge carpets of destruction, the bombing was anything but surgical, and frequently hit civilian villages. The result was thousands of refugees fleeing into Phnom Penh and the province towns. The capital swelled from a population of 600,000 at the start of the war to 2 million at its end in 1975. The American embassy in Phnom Penh—and Henry Kissinger's team in Washington—insisted that the refugees were fleeing only one thing: attacks by the brutal Khmer Rouge. But in fact they were fleeing both the Khmer Rouge and the American bombs. I visited refugee camps regularly and consistently heard both accounts. Some peasants didn't flee at all; the Khmer Rouge used their anger about the bombing to recruit them as soldiers and porters.

The bombing raids illustrate what is pretty much an axiom in all wars: i.e., that so-called "conventional" weapons not forbidden by international law can produce the same horrific results as banned weapons.

In Cambodia, the B-52s carried napalm and dart cluster-bombs (since discontinued by the Pentagon). The raids were carried out by three of the mammoth planes in formation. Each plane can carry twenty-five to thirty tons of bombs, making the total load of a formation seventy-five to ninety tons. B-52s drop their bombs to form a grid, or "box," of destruction on the ground; the grid (an average one might be one kilometer wide and two kilometers long) can be altered to fit the size and shape of the troop concentration. Soldiers who manage to survive these massive explosions (which sometimes throw bodies and dirt as much as one hundred feet in the air) are often rendered unfit for further duty, having been put in permanent shock or made deaf or simply frightened to the bone of every sharp sound or movement. Such raids were what destroyed the retreating Iraqi troops on the road to Basra at the end of that war in 1991—the road that became known as the "Highway of Death."

In 1973, an accidental B-52 bombing of Neak Loeung, a government-held Mekong river town, killed and wounded some four hundred Cambodians, most of them civilians. The American embassy apologized and gave monetary gifts to victims' families on a sliding scale—a few hundred dollars for the loss of a limb, more for multiple limbs, and still more for a death. When civilians die in wars, the military calls it unintentional, even though everyone knows civilian deaths are inevitable, especially when the weapons spray their lethality over large spaces. The phrase used by the Pentagon for civilian deaths is "collateral damage"—just as napalm was called "soft ordnance"—the idea being to give war a softer, sanitized sound for the lay public.

Napalm, incidentally, was dropped by B-52s in the Vietnam and Cambodian wars, in the form of CBUs—Cluster Bomb Units. (Other planes dropped napalm in different containers and forms.) A CBU is a large bomb, say 750 pounds, that carries hundreds of smaller projectiles. A typical CBU is rigged to open, in the manner of a clamshell, a short distance above the ground, releasing its hail of explosive bomblets on the enemy troops beneath it. One variety was the CBU-3; its bomblets carried napalm, which set fire to the troops or robbed the air of oxygen, thus asphyxiating them. Another version carried special darts, which ripped through flesh or pinned the victims to trees or the ground. Sometimes it is hard for the layman to discern any great difference between these weapons and, for instance, the chemical arms banned by international law and custom. Both have a terror component. The napalm and darts have since been taken out of the American CBU inventory—because of their bad image—but conventional-bomblet CBUs are still used, as in the 1991 Gulf war with Iraq.

And what about plain old rockets? Should all of them be banned, since they are frequently used as instruments of terror against civilians? The Khmer Rouge sent rockets shrieking into Phnom Penh throughout that five-year war. These were not precisely aimed munitions by any definition. They were crudely produced Chinese projectiles with a fan-shaped tail that whistled as it cut through the air overhead; you knew when it began its downward plummet because the whistling suddenly stopped. These rockets were launched from the city's environs, set off from hand-fashioned wooden platforms; there was no aiming at specific military targets—the effort was simply to get them to land somewhere, anywhere, in the refugee-packed city. And land they did—on markets, in school rooms, in backyards—spewing jagged metal and sliced limbs. The purpose was to demoralize the civilian population, and it worked.

An artillery piece can also be used as a weapon of terror against civilians. One afternoon in the summer of 1974, the Khmer Rouge trained a captured American-made 105 mm howitzer on Phnom Penh and fanned its muzzle across the city's southern edge. At first, as the shells fell in this half-moon arc, they ex-

ploded without result, but then the arc came to a colony of houses called Psar Deum Kor, and the death began. Fires started by the shells broke out and the houses were quickly in flames, whipped by high winds. Within a half hour, nearly two hundred people were dead and another two hundred wounded, virtually all civilians. The bodies were carted off on police pickup trucks. No military target was anywhere in the vicinity.

In the end—whether in Cambodia or any other killing field—there is nothing new either about the barbarity of people destroying people or, unfortunately, about its seeming inevitability in every age. One unchanging lesson is that war or genocide or crimes against humanity are states of violence that, where they exist, remove all breath from such notions as the law and civilized behavior.

Is it hopeless, then, to try to strengthen both the international law and its enforcement? No, never hopeless, not if you believe in the possibility of improvement, no matter how slight. Journalists are by blood and tradition committed to the belief, or at least to the tenet, of trying to keep bad things from getting any worse than they already are.

QUESTIONS TO CONSIDER

1. Because Khmers killed other Khmers, does what happened in Cambodia equal genocide? Is the term "autogenocide" appropriate?
2. How did Cold War ideology influence American reaction to the Khmer Rouge?
3. What role did "Brother Number One" play in genocide?
4. Who were the "new people"?
5. What happened to the Vietnamese community in Cambodia?

Pol Pot

David Chandler,

Georgetown University

Born   May 19, 1925 in Prek Sbauv
1949   Studies left-wing politics in France
1953   Returns to Cambodia and joins Communist Party, which he leads a decade later
1975   Khmer Rouge is victor of civil war and occupies Phnom Penh; reign of terror kills 1.5 million in next four years
1979   Goes into hiding after Vietnamese invasion of Cambodia
1998   Dies April 15 in Cambodian jungle

On April 17, 1998, barely 500 meters inside Cambodia from Thailand, a frail, 73-year-old former dictator—known by his nom de guerre, Pol Pot—was cremated under a pile of rubbish and rubber tires. He had died two days earlier in a two-room hut, held prisoner by former colleagues who had accused him of betraying the revolutionary movement he had once led. It was an ignominious end for a man who inscribed a merciless agenda on the psyche of two generations of Cambodians.

Between 1975 and 1979, Pol Pot presided over a communist regime known as Democratic Kampuchea. His harsh, utopian policies, derived in part from Maoist China, drove an estimated 1.5 million Cambodians—or one in five—to their deaths from malnutrition, illness or overwork. At least 200,000 more were executed as enemies of the state. The ratio of deaths to population made the Cambodian revolution the most murderous in a century of revolutions.

There was rough justice in the closing months of Pol Pot's life, when he must have been fearful—as everyone in Democratic Kampuchea had been—that each day might be his last. Pol Pot had emerged on two recent occasions to talk to journalists. He spoke fondly of his young daughter and fretfully about his health. Pressed to acknowledge responsibility for the past, he said, "I came to carry out the struggle, not to kill people. Even now, and you can look at me, am I a savage person?" Pol Pot had either evaded the question or missed the point. No one had died because of his villainous appearance. Instead, victims had been sacrificed in a ruthless campaign to refashion Cambodian society. In the 1980s, Pol Pot had told his followers that "mistakes" had been inevitable during his rule because, using a revealing simile, "We were like babies learning to walk."

Pol Pot's own childhood was cosseted and secure. He was born in 1925, when Cambodia was still a protectorate of France. His father was a prosperous landowner, with élite connections. His sister and a female cousin were dancers in the royal ballet in the capital, Phnom Penh, living comfortably under the king's protection. Saloth Sar, as he was called in those days, went to live with them when he was six years old. He attended a series of French-language schools. Only a few hundred other Cambodians enjoyed this privilege. His academic record was lackluster; he earned no high-school diploma. He seems to have been

From David Chandler, "Pol Pot," *Time Asia* 154(7/8) (August 1999): 23–30. Reprinted with permission.

relatively popular without making much of an impression. "His manner was straightforward, pleasant and very polite," a former classmate told me. "He thought a lot but said very little."

In 1949, because of his fluency in French and his political connections, Saloth Sar was given a scholarship to study radio-electricity in France. He lived in Paris for the next three years, neglecting his studies and spending much of his time, he told an interviewer later, reading "progressive books." In 1952 he joined the French Communist Party, drawn by its anti-colonial stance. Soon afterward, because he had failed to pass any examinations, his scholarship was revoked and he went home.

After Cambodia became independent in 1954, Saloth Sar led a double life, teaching in a private school in Phnom Penh while he worked in secret in a small, beleaguered communist movement. He enjoyed the conspiratorial rituals of underground politics and dreamed of seizing power. By 1963 he was in command of Cambodia's Communist Party. Fearful of the police, he fled the capital and sought refuge with a handful of colleagues at a Vietnamese military base, "Office 100," on the Vietnam-Cambodia border. For the next two years he chafed under humiliating Vietnamese protection.

In 1965 Saloth Sar was summoned to North Vietnam for consultations. Walking north along the Ho Chi Minh Trail, he took two months to reach Hanoi, where he was taken to task for his nationalist agenda. The general secretary of the Vietnamese Communist Party, Le Duan, told him to subordinate Cambodia's interests to Vietnam's, to help Vietnam defeat the United States and to postpone armed struggle until the time was ripe.

Although bruised by these attacks, Saloth Sar said nothing to antagonize his patrons. Soon afterward, however, he travelled to China and was warmly welcomed by radical officials. Inspired by the early phases of the Cultural Revolution, Saloth Sar transferred his loyalties

to a new set of patrons and a more vibrant revolutionary model. The visit to China was a turning point in his career. Prudently, however, he said nothing to the Vietnamese about his change of heart. Back home, he established his headquarters in a remote, heavily wooded section of the country. For the next four years, with a group of like-minded colleagues, he polished his utopian ideas and nourished his hatreds.

His chance came in 1970 when Cambodia's ruler, Prince Norodom Sihanouk, was overthrown in a pro-American coup. The Vietnamese communists swiftly allied themselves with the Khmer Rouge—as Sihanouk had dismissively labeled Pol Pot's group—against the new regime in Phnom Penh. The Vietnamese provided the rag-tag Khmer Rouge with arms and training. When they withdrew in 1972, Pol Pot felt betrayed. But by then, the Phnom Penh army had been badly battered and the Khmer Rouge had become a formidable guerrilla force.

The war ended in April 1975, when the Khmer Rouge occupied Phnom Penh. Most of the city's 2 million people, exhausted by years of violence, welcomed the invaders. They saw these silent, heavily armed young men as fellow Khmers, with whom a new society might be built. Their optimism was tragically misplaced. Within days, the Khmer Rouge drove them all into the countryside to become workers in agricultural communes. They also emptied Cambodia's other towns and abolished money, markets, schools, newspapers, religious practices and private property.

The Khmer Rouge spurned anyone with money or education. The revolution derived its energy, they believed, from the empowerment of the rural poor, from their recent victory and from what they thought was the intrinsic superiority of Cambodians to the hated Vietnamese. Pol Pot assumed that the Cambodian revolution would be swifter and more authentic than anything Vietnam could carry out. His Chinese patrons, hostile to Vietnam, agreed. By mobilizing mass resentments, as Mao Zedong had done, Pol Pot inspired tens of thousands of Cambodians, especially teenagers and people in their early 20s, to join him in dismantling Cambodian society and liberating everyone from the past.

The methods he chose were naive, brutal and inept. In 1976 a hastily written Four Year Plan sought to triple the country's agricultural production within a year—without fertilizer, modern tools or material incentives. The plan paid no attention to Cambodian geography or common sense; the nation's farmers were prostrate after five years of civil war. Attempting to meet impossible quotas and frightened of reprisals, Khmer Rouge workers cut back the grain allotted for consumption. Tens of thousands of Cambodians starved to death. Thousands more collapsed from overwork and the almost total absence throughout the country of medical attention.

Pol Pot refused to accept responsibility for these disasters or to ameliorate rural conditions. Instead, he blamed "hidden enemies, burrowing from within" and set off a wholesale purge of the Communist Party. His paranoia, propping up his self-assurance, knew no bounds. In 1977 he made a state visit to China, which promised him military assistance against Vietnam and moral support for his radical agenda. Sporadic fighting between Cambodia and Vietnam flared up toward the end of the year, and full-scale war between the two countries broke out in 1978. Pol Pot declared that if every Cambodian soldier killed 30 Vietnamese, the Khmer Rouge could win the war. He also asked China to send troops to help him. The Chinese refused. Trained as guerrillas, the Khmer Rouge were outmaneuvered and outgunned.

On Christmas Day 1978, Vietnam invaded Cambodia with more than 100,000 troops. The country cracked open like an egg. Pol Pot fled by helicopter to Thailand; when the invaders entered Phnom Penh on January 7, the city was deserted. The Vietnamese established a puppet government composed largely of former cadres who had fled the Khmer Rouge reign of terror. Several of these men remain in power in Cambodia today.

Aside from brief forays to Bangkok and Beijing for medical treatment, Pol Pot spent the next 18 years in fortified encampments in the forests of Thailand and northern Cambodia, protected by Thai military forces and what remained of his guerrilla army. Throughout the 1980s, he conducted seminars for Khmer Rouge military leaders. He often mesmerized them with his sincerity, his low, melodious voice and his genteel charisma. To his disciples, there seemed to be no connection between this smooth-faced teacher and the violence of his past—except perhaps for his repeated emphasis on "enemies." In fact, Pol Pot's disconnection from reality seemed to many to be proof of his unworldliness, ardor and enlightenment.

Pol Pot remarried in the mid-'80s, after his first wife, a highly educated revolutionary he had married in 1956, succumbed to mental illness. In the mid-'90s, deprived of foreign support, the Cambodian communist movement gradually fell apart. In 1996, Pol Pot's brother-in-law, Ieng Sary, who had served as his foreign minister, defected. Thousands of Khmer Rouge followed suit. The remnants of the movement were commanded by a veteran military leader, Ta Mok, who arrested Pol Pot after the former dictator had ordered some of Ta Mok's subordinates killed.

Listening to a broadcast of the Cambodian service of the Voice of America on April 15, 1998, Pol Pot learned that Ta Mok planned to deliver him to the Americans for trial. Soon afterward, he told his wife that he felt faint. He lay down. By 10 p.m. he was dead, reportedly from heart failure, possibly from suicide. His death, like his life, left many questions unanswered.

Despite—or perhaps because of—his paranoia, ineptitude and distance from reality,

Pol Pot's place in history is assured, thanks largely to the damage he inflicted on his people. In the late 1970s, along with Mao Zedong, he enjoyed a moment of fame among those who felt, as he did, that the best way to change the world was to dismantle most of its social structure, violently and at once, regardless of the human cost. In his headlong rush toward independence and ideological perfection, Pol Pot was spurred by more experienced communist powers, eager to see if the Cambodian experiment, more radical than anything they had tried, might work.

When the extent of the disasters in Cambodia was known, Pol Pot survived in relative comfort and became a useful bit player in the cold war. When that conflict ended and Pol Pot lost his capacity for harm, his former friends began to consider bringing him to justice. He cheated their half-hearted efforts by dying in his bed, leaving history as his only judge.

QUESTIONS TO CONSIDER

1. How does David Chandler rank the Cambodian revolution in relation to others in the twentieth century?
2. What was the goal of Democratic Kampuchea?
3. Did Saloth Sar's background in any way indicate the direction his actions would take after 1970?
4. How did Pol Pot transform Cambodia?
5. What is Pol Pot's place in history, according to Chandler?
6. Can a single person commit genocide or be responsible for it?

MAKING CONNECTIONS

1. Is autogenocide fundamentally different from the Holocaust?
2. Are the Soviet, Chinese, and Cambodian genocides fundamentally different from other genocides?
3. Compare the personalities of Joseph Stalin and Pol Pot.

✔ RECOMMENDED RESOURCES

Chandler, David P. *Brother Number One: A Political Biography of Pol Pot.* Boulder, Colorado: Westview Press, 1999.

Him, Chanrithy. *When Broken Glass Floats: Growing Up under the Khmer Rouge.* New York: W. W. Norton & Company, 2000.

Kamm, Henry. *Cambodia: Report from a Stricken Land.* New York: Arcade Publishing, 1998.

Kiernan, Ben. *The Pol Pot Regime: Race, Power, and Genocide in Cambodia under the Khmer Rouge, 1975–79.* (Second ed.) New Haven and London: Yale University Press, 1996.

Ung, Loung. *First They Killed My Father: A Daughter of Cambodia Remembers.* New York: HarperCollins, 2000.

CHAPTER 12

CASE STUDIES: INDONESIA, EAST TIMOR, AND BANGLADESH

Noam Chomsky called attention to the Indonesian government's genocide against the people of East Timor and the U.S. government's complicity with the anti-Communist government of Indonesia, long before mainstream American media paid attention. Chomsky confronted administrations that projected intentional ignorance or disengagement from these matters. These cultivated public responses by the government obfuscate the dominant strategic goals of U.S. policy makers—while the fate of the civilian population was incidental. Robert Cribb places these events in the context of Indonesian political turmoil.

After strong U.S. support for Indonesian repression and killing in East Timor, Geoffrey Robinson concludes in *The New Killing Fields* that "the costs of such expediency will also be high for Americans and for the credibility of the U.S. government's war against terrorism." The story of East Timor illustrates that there is a sound basis for the skepticism with which U.S. policy is viewed in much of the world—and that perhaps there is good reason to doubt the sincerity of America's professed opposition to the use of violence against civilians.

In a general way, Bangladesh's emergence as a nation in 1971 reflects the relationship between Indonesia and East Timor. Both areas, geographically separate, had to confront forces calling for independence. Bangladesh's independence would come at the cost of three million people dead, a quarter million women and girls raped, and millions of forced refugees. Gendercide Watch describes the grim struggle for independence in Bangladesh.

In the annals of American foreign policy in the latter half of the twentieth century, American reaction to genocide is curious, if not repugnant, according to Edward S. Herman. Nine days after East Timor declared its independence, for example, and just hours after U.S. President Gerald Ford and Secretary of State Kissinger concluded a festive two-day visit with General Suharto on December 7, 1975, Indonesia invaded East Timor. U.S. support for Suharto's murderous regime continued, while reaction to Pol Pot's Khmer Rouge took a different course.

Genocide in Indonesia, 1965–1966

Robert Cribb,

The University of Queensland, Australia

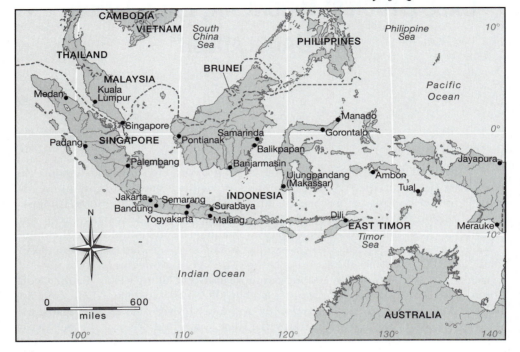

Between October, 1965 and March, 1966, approximately 500,000 people were killed in Indonesia. The killings received little international attention at the time and have seldom been studied in detail since then. The number of people killed and the precise circumstances of most deaths remain uncertain, and mistaken opinions on the identity of the victims and the motivations of their killers remain common, even in scholarly literature. One early polemical account of the killings rather implausibly described them as "the second-greatest crime of the century," but the killings received little attention in comparative literature on mass killings until the 1990s. The aim of this article is to summarize what can be said of the killings from primary and secondary literature and to suggest ways in which the Indonesian massacres can be considered within the broader discipline of genocide studies.

GENERAL CONSIDERATIONS: GENOCIDE AND THE PROBLEM OF POLITICAL KILLINGS

One of the continuing problems for scholars of genocide is to determine the boundaries of the phenomenon. Genocide is at the same time

From Robert Cribb, "Genocide in Indonesia, 1965–1966," *Journal of Genocide Research* 3(2) (2001): 219–237. Reprinted with permission of Taylor & Francis Ltd. Website http://www.tandf.co.uk/journals

both an analytical term for a complex set of political actions and consequences and a legal–moral term for what is often regarded as the worst of all human crimes, one of the few for which an appeal to state sovereignty and sovereign immunity is not an adequate defence. Although the United Nations General Assembly originally defined genocide as "the denial of the right of existence of entire human groups" and specifically mentioned racial, religious and political groups, the term has come to apply primarily to planned (and largely successful) attempts to eliminate an ethnic or ethno-religious group by violent means, whether by massacre, by promotion of epidemic disease or by creating conditions which greatly accelerate death rates from "natural" causes such as exposure.

Political murder was excluded from the 1948 United Nations Convention on Genocide on the grounds that political groups were inherently mutable and more difficult to define than ethnic and religious groups. Many scholars, too, perhaps shared a feeling that the killing of people only because of their ethnicity had a horror which transcended the crime of killing people for their political views and activities: those who chose to play politics and had lost, it seemed, were in a different category from those whose political status had been thrust upon them. Scholars and politicians may have feared that broadening the definition of genocide would risk weakening the sense of abhorrence, which the phenomenon should arouse. There was a danger that the recognition of genocidal killing might become hostage to political considerations, rather than being condemned immediately for what it was. Thus the Weberian ideal type of genocide became the elimination of an ethnic group, with the Nazi Holocaust against the Jews acknowledged as the paradigm.

Several factors, however, have worked to relax this narrow definition. Most important has been the gradual and uneven easing of Cold War tensions, especially from the 1970s, which allowed scholars to consider Stalinist repression as a genocide comparable to Hitler's without becoming immediately entangled in Cold War antagonisms. The risk that perpetrators of genocide will be exonerated because of their political affiliations still exists, but it has diminished over the last 50 years. The Stalinist repression was especially important in this respect because many of his ostensibly political victims were precisely as innocent as the victims of Nazi genocide: they were killed not for what they had done or what they believed but for who they were related to, or even just for the sake of sustaining the terror. To regard them as less innocent than the victims of Nazism or to regard Stalin's motives as less execrable than Hitler's was a difficult (though admittedly not impossible) position to hold. In addition, the supposedly tight United Nations definition has proven unequal to dealing with the problem of scale. By defining genocide to include attempts to destroy a national, ethnic, racial or religious group "in part" and by including "causing serious bodily or mental harm to members of the group" as one of the acts which characterizes genocide, the United Nations makes it difficult to distinguish between genocide and many forms of racial and religious discrimination. This weakness, it must be said, was partly intentional, because there have always been powerful reasons for seeing the Nazi genocide of Jews in Europe as a culmination of centuries of less drastic discrimination. The looseness of the United Nations definition seems to have been intended, in part at least, to allow genocidal intention to be identified well before large-scale killing actually took place.

During the 1970s, moreover, many academic disciplines, especially history and sociology, developed a strong interest in uncovering the lives of and restoring voices to the weak and powerless in history and society. Rather than focusing only on the victors, academics sought to understand the losers and those who had not made a lasting mark on the world. Even if ethnic genocide, and more specifically the Jewish experience under the Nazis, remained the main point of reference, there was a growing feeling that, if genocide is the worst of all human crimes—and one which transcends state sovereignty—then no set of victims of mass killing should be denied recognition of their victimhood and no perpetrators should escape indictment by virtue of quibbling over the precise conceptual boundaries of the phenomenon.

This relaxation, however, is still under way, and has given rise now and then to puzzling anomalies. Since the early 1990s, the Indonesian massacres of 1965–1966 and the Khmer Rouge killings in Cambodia between 1975 and 1979—both of them cases in which ethnic antagonism was a relatively marginal element—have been accepted as cases of genocide in its broad sense, whereas it appears that the 20 or 30 million deaths in China caused by the Great Leap Forward and the Cultural Revolution in the 1950s and 1960s, deaths which were inflicted in peacetime and mainly on people who were ethnically identical to their tormentors, are not. The Chinese case presents major practical problems of analysis because of the paucity of Western language sources and because the killings have not been repudiated by the Chinese authorities, but it is also likely that China has been ignored because the enormous scale of the killing there—more deaths altogether than under Nazi Germany—would change the intellectual balance of power in genocide studies if China were to be admitted, as it were, as a full member.

Nonetheless, precisely because the ethnic element in these three Asian cases is marginal, they have the potential to shed light on the phenomenon of genocide. In particular, they highlight difficulties with the concept of race and ethnicity in mainstream genocide studies. The principal reason for excluding political killing from the United Nations Genocide Convention was expressed at the time as being the fact that political groups were mutable and difficult to define. The obverse implication—that ethnic groups are fixed and easily defined—was a matter of common political and scientific wisdom at the time. The term "race" was a respectable one in academic analysis and there was a general consensus that each ethnic group was derived from its own distinct ancestral stock, although most scholars accepted that all human races had diverged from a single ancestral people, now largely lost in the mists of prehistory.

In the five decades that have passed since the promulgation of the Genocide Convention, however, research and analysis have shown how enormously malleable ethnic identity can be. Rather than seeing ethnic groups as quasi-biological entities shaped by evolution over the course of millennia, we have come to appreciate how rapidly ethnic groups can emerge, alter and disappear. This realization has two implications for genocide studies. First, it makes problematic any identification of genocide by cultural suppression where no change in the death rate is involved. Whereas the Convention on Genocide appeared to assume that culture would be lost only under hostile external pressure, we now appreciate that culture is always in flux, as a dynamic phenomenon characterized by change and exchange. The loss of a species from nature is an indubitable loss to the world, but the case for preserving all cultures as they now are is less clear. On the one hand, there can be no doubt that Japan's policy of forbidding Koreans to speak their own language during the Japanese colonial period was an attempt at cultural genocide, but it is not so clear that teaching tribal peoples of Borneo a language which will enable them to take part in the modern world is also cultural genocide or rather an act of liberation. There is a strong case to be made for preserving smaller cultures against the unequal competition of larger ones which enjoy the backing of states and access to a vast range of media, but there is a powerful counter-case that to insist on preserving people as anthropological exhibits demonstrating human diversity is an infringement of their rights of free choice. Preserving a traditional culture becomes rather more problematic when one recognizes that preservation may also involve shoring up the position of authoritarian institutions in that culture, especially the authority of men over women and of the elderly over the young.

Second, and more important in this context, recognizing that contemporary ethnic identity may have rather shallow historical roots draws our attention to the fact that ethnicity can be shaped by political and economic factors as much as by ancestry and inherited culture. Current scholarly analysis of nationalism is divided between those who see national identity as primordial and ethnic and those who see it as a construction intimately related to the rise of the state as the dominant institution in modern society. For the latter, the "constructionists," the power of the state generates a sense of national identity, sometimes unconsciously, sometimes deliberately, sometimes making the most of existing ethnic similarities, sometimes deliberately disregarding them. Sometimes of course the power of the state generates a reaction which leads to a separate sense of national identity and hence to separatist aspirations. But for constructionists, nationalism is primarily a consequence, not a cause, of the global configuration of states and for them nationalism is best understood as a political project whose aim is not just to preserve the existence of an ethnic group but rather is to shape the character of that ethnic group— always for the better in the eyes of the shapers, of course—gaining control and making use of state power.

Even if the "constructionist" analysis is only partly true, it provides a firm bridge between "classical" ethnic genocide and political genocide. Genocide, particularly in the classic cases of Nazi Germany and Stalin's Soviet Union, was intimately associated with broader plans for social and cultural engineering. We will come closer to understanding the reasons for genocide if we can understand why social and cultural engineering seemed to demand wholesale slaughter. In this context the case of Indonesia is important not because of the scale of killing—Indonesia does not make it onto Rummel's list of the fifteen most lethal governments of the twentieth century—but because the nature of Indonesian national identity shows with unusual clarity how political cleansing can also be ethnic cleansing.

NATIONALISM, ETHNICITY AND THE IDEA OF INDONESIA

More clearly than in most countries of the world, Indonesian nationalism is based on a political aspiration rather than on ethnic identity. For Indonesians, their nation has been above all an institution, which can deliver them modernity and prosperity. In this respect Indonesia resembles both the United States and the former Soviet Union, whose core national aspirations (respectively, "life, liberty and the pursuit of happiness" and the "dictatorship of the proletariat") are or were similarly devoid of specific ethnic content. This rather materialist orientation does not mean that Indonesians think of their nation only in instrumentalist terms, as a sterile tool with no symbolic meaning; on the contrary, the patriotic affection of Indonesians for their country is as striking as that of Americans. It means, however, that the political, rather than the ethnic, character of Indonesia has been at the core of nationalist politics since, the early twentieth century.

The aspiration of people in the Indonesian archipelago for prosperity and modernity long predates any sense of Indonesian identity. The archipelago has played a key role in long Asian trade routes for over 2000 years, both as a producer of spices and forest products and as a staging post on the route between China and the West. The peoples of the archipelago have a strong tradition of mobility, commercial engagement and openness to external cultural influences. The reluctance to acknowledge any kind of external cultural debt which one often finds in China and India is rare in maritime South East Asia. The cultural history of Indonesia is one of constant innovation and recombination of new elements, and most scholars emphasize the selectiveness of the peoples of the archipelago in choosing some elements of foreign cultures and rejecting others.

In the colonial era, the archipelago's access to the outside world was gradually constricted. With a combination of military force and superior shipping technology, the Dutch East Indies Company gradually excluded the indigenous trading networks of the islands and strangled the once-powerful port cities. As they established their rule across the archipelago, gradually and piecemeal, they relegated Indonesians to the role of labourers and supervisors on their plantations and in their mines. With a misplaced respect for indigenous traditions, they devoted considerable energy to recording what they saw as the pure traditions of the archipelago's many people, and they devoted political energy to preserving and strengthening the status and standing of the archipelago's many traditional elites as long as those elites were willing to put themselves at the service of Dutch colonial interests. They limited access to Dutch, and still more so to major European languages such as English, French and German, and they made little effort to introduce extensive educational facilities in their colony. Of course the archipelago could never be cut off completely from outside influences, but the people of the islands who thought about such things could see that the horizons of their world had narrowed and that

their prosperity had declined. Java in particular, once the economic and political powerhouse of the region, appeared to many in the early twentieth century to be mired in poverty and ignorance. The Dutch tended to blame this state of affairs on fecklessness and torpor in the Javanese character, but most indigenous people blamed their plight on colonialism. Nationalism therefore became a vehicle, not to recover the cultural state which had been lost when the Dutch took over—that would have been long discarded anyhow—but to reopen the possibility of change and development, to give people the chance to take what they saw as the best of Western culture, as they had previously taken what they saw as the best of Indian, Chinese and Middle Eastern culture and to create a society that was modern and prosperous.

They decided, too, almost from the start, that this society would encompass the whole of what was then the Netherlands Indies. It was an imaginative decision. The archipelago, which now comprises Indonesia, stretches 5000 kilometres from the northern tip of Sumatra to the great island of New Guinea, presently divided between the independent state of Papua New Guinea and the Indonesian province of Papua (formerly Irian Jaya). The region is ethnically enormously diverse: some 400 languages are spoken and the ancestry of the people includes both dark-skinned Melanesians, who predominate in the eastern part of the archipelago, and paler-skinned Austronesians, who dominate the west. Islam, Christianity and Hinduism all have significant followings, and there are smaller communities of Buddhists and animists. The island of Java, with its fertile volcanic soils, and the Strait of Melaka, a key choke point on the ancient trade routes between China and the spice islands on the one hand and India, the Middle East and Europe on the other, have traditionally been the two main centres of power in the region. Both regions exercised a powerful cultural influence within and beyond the area, which is now Indonesia, but neither of them was ever the centre of an empire covering more than a tiny proportion of the archipelago.

The political unification of the archipelago had been the work of Dutch colonialism. Beginning with a toehold established in the spice islands in the early seventeenth century, the Dutch established first commercial dominance, then political hegemony and finally full colonial rule over archipelago in a process which involved many wars and which was not completed until the second decade of the twentieth century. Although power in the Dutch colony centred on the governor-general in Batavia, the legal and administrative structure of the Netherlands Indies was immensely complicated. First, there were distinct administrative regimes for the densely populated islands of Java and Madura on the one hand and the so-called "outer regions" (*buitengewesten*) on the other. There was also a major distinction made between indirectly and directly ruled regions, some of them in Java, most in the outer regions. In the former, called *zelfbesturen* or self-governing territories, indigenous rulers who had signed some form of treaty with the Dutch were left in possession of at least some of their former powers, though they were extensively "guided" by Dutch officials; in the latter, the administration was more closely controlled by Dutch officials, though the European administrative corps meshed in each region with a distinct indigenous administrative corps, generally drawn from the local former ruling elite. During the first four decades of the twentieth century, the Dutch both introduced varying degrees of local democracy in "advanced" regions under their control and formally boosted the power of indigenous rulers in other regions under a so-called "detutelization" programme. The Dutch also maintained a complex and changing system of ethnic classification which in turn determined both the civil law under which people lived and the criminal procedure under which they could be prosecuted in the early twentieth century. The law distinguished primarily between Europeans, "Natives" and "Foreign Orientals," mainly Chinese and Arabs, though the latter category came under great pressure as first the Japanese and later the Siamese and Turks were reclassified as legal Europeans. For family law and various cultural purposes, indigenous subjects of the Dutch were also classified into local ethnic groups—Javanese, Balinese, Ambonese and so on.

This vast complexity meant that there were few immediately compelling borders along which the archipelago might have been divided. In addition, however, there was a positive reason for creating a single nation: within any of the regional cultures there could be found important conservative forces, old aristocracies who were likely to work to retain their power and privileges after independence. On an archipelagic scale, however, these aristocracies and the deferential traditions they relied upon were far less significant: the old elites had little experience of cooperation with each other and their standing, as local figures in a vast polity, would be marginal. The nationalist movement was convinced, almost from the start, that whatever could be made of the islands would best be made on a large scale. To represent this idea of modernization on a grand scale, they chose the name Indonesia, a nineteenth century European anthropological coinage meaning "islands of India." The point to the name, however, was not its meaning, but the fact that it represented an idea, which transcended all the complicated and interlocking regional identities of the archipelago.

In fact, not quite all the identities in the Netherlands Indies were encompassed. Many nationalists questioned whether residents of Chinese descent could be included in the Indonesia project. At first glance this suspicion is peculiar, because the idea of Indonesia did not and continues not to exclude residents of other foreign ancestries. Indonesians of part-Arab and part-European descent were prominent in the nationalist movement and for the most part have faced no formal or informal discrimination since independence. The reasons for this special suspicion were complex, but two factors seem to be especially important. First, in many parts of Indonesia, Chinese were overwhelmingly and obtrusively dominant in commerce and money-lending. Alongside the Dutch, therefore, they appeared to be agents of the colonial oppression and exploitation of Indonesians. Many Arabs occupied a similar role, but their numbers were much smaller. Eurasians tended to be concentrated in junior administrative and clerical positions; they were often part of the colonial apparatus, but they did not visibly profit from colonialism in the way of the Chinese or Dutch. Second, many Chinese retained an identification with China: they regarded Chinese civilization as superior to anything in the archipelago and they were more engaged by the Chinese nationalist movement—which emerged before its Indonesian counterpart—than by the aspirations of local politics. Whereas both the West and the Muslim world offered currents of thought which were interesting and appealing to Indonesian nationalists, there was nothing at all in the chaotic Chinese politics or the self-occupied Chinese political thought of the first half of the twentieth century to recommend itself to Indonesians. The political and cultural orientation of many Chinese towards China, therefore, tended to put all Chinese— even those who regarded Indonesia as their home and who had no significant connection with China—outside the idea of Indonesia in a way that interest in Western or Muslim thought did not.

The historian A. B. Shamsul has coined the term "nation-of-intent" to describe nations which exist more in the minds of aspiring leaders than in the hearts of the mass of the people. "Indonesia" was for many years just such a nation-of-intent: nationalist ideas took some decades to spread widely through the indigenous communities and needed the additional impetus of the Japanese occupation of 1942–1945 to become a truly national, and thus irresistible, phenomenon. More important, however, Indonesia was not so much one nation-of-intent as three. Within the nationalist movement were three streams of thought, each of them envisaging an independent, modern and prosperous Indonesia, but giving very different content to that nation. These three streams can be labelled Islamic, communist and developmentalist. In the early days of the nationalist movement they were thoroughly intertwined, but they gradually drew apart. The Islamists envisaged an Indonesia whose modernity would come from the eternal prescriptions of Islam, and the communists imagined an Indonesia whose modernity would be an expression in socialism, as the historical stage beyond capitalism and colonialism, while the developmentalists imagined simply turning the formidable apparatus of state which the Dutch had created in Indonesia to the benefit of Indonesians, rather than foreigners. All three basically envisioned a country which would enable its people to share in the prosperity and human equality which Westerners seem to arrogate to themselves. None of the three streams presented a single, coherent vision of the future. The communists were the most disciplined, but they had a sprinkling of left-wing allies who rejected the party's discipline, while the Islamists were split into a wide variety of parties on doctrinal, regional and personal grounds. The developmentalists were least united of all, because many of them drew from either Islam or Marxism or both in formulating their ideas and distinguishing themselves from the painfully slow developmentalism of the late colonial state. Each of the three streams shared, moreover, a broad consensus that ending Dutch colonialism was a necessary first step to achieving anything at all, and this tactical sense of unity remained powerful until 1948, three years into the war of independence against the Dutch which followed Japan's surrender in August 1945.

Taking advantage of the sudden Japanese surrender, nationalists declared independence on August 17, 1945, creating an Indonesian Republic which was dominated from the start by the developmentalists. The communist party was still piecing itself together after more than a decade of Dutch and Japanese repression, and the Islamists let themselves be persuaded that declaring an Islamic state, or even giving specific recognition to Islam, would drive religious minorities into the arms of the Dutch, who aimed to restore their authority after the war. The developmentalists, by contrast, had emerged relatively unscathed from Dutch and Japanese repression and they benefited from increasingly bitter antagonism between the Islamist and communist streams.

The sources of this antagonism were partly cultural, partly social, partly ideological. Although close to 90% of Indonesians were classified as Muslim, the Islam of many, especially in Java, was highly syncretic, incorporating many elements from the older Hindu, Buddhist and animist traditions of the island, as well as mystical Sufi traditions from the Middle East. Their beliefs put considerable emphasis on spirits and on magic, and they generally paid little attention to central Islamic practices such as regular prayer, fasting or attendance at the mosque. The followers of such beliefs, often called *kebatinan* or Kejawen in Java, were diverse and did not have a clear sense of common identity, but they did have a strong sense of being different from the so-called *santri*, more orthodox Muslims, who often constituted the village elite. Many *santri* despised and feared the followers of Kejawen as practitioners of black magic and followers of beliefs so heterodox that they could barely be considered Islamic. The followers of Kejawen, for their part, feared being forced into the more rigid practice of orthodox Islam. Although followers of Kejawen and its other local equivalents were most prominent amongst regional aristocracies, they were most numerous

amongst the poor and powerless, the group to which the Communist Party especially appealed. Amongst *santri* Muslims and amongst university graduates, by contrast, the communists found little following. This cultural antagonism, overlaid with class hostility, was reinforced by ideological contradictions: not all communists followed the official atheism of the party, but they all rejected religion as a source of authority over social life, and this put the Communist Party in direct and irreconcilable conflict with the Islamists.

Even if the sharp antagonism between communists and Islamists made them willing to compromise in the short term and accept the dominance of the developmentalists, both streams remained determined to come to power in the long term. In 1948, when it was clear to both Islamists and communists that their aspirations were being edged off the political agenda, they separately launched armed struggles against the developmentalist-dominated government, even though that government was still engaged in the independence struggle against the Dutch. The communists were quickly defeated, but the Islamist revolution, generally known as the Darul Islam, continued long after the Dutch capitulation in 1949 and was only suppressed in the early 1960s, after a long and brutal military campaign. Both communists and Islamists also pursued their aspirations through the democratic institutions set up after 1949: they competed in the 1955 national elections and argued their cases vigorously in the Constituent Assembly which assembled to draft the country's permanent constitution. Their bitter mutual antagonism effectively prevented either from having its way, leaving the developmentalists still more or less in charge; but throughout this period it seemed to most people that the decision over Indonesia's future had been merely postponed, not taken for good.

Indeed, despite the initial dominance of the developmentalists, both the Islamists and the communists had good reason for confidence for their futures. Development policies in the 1950s had made some progress in improving the conditions of life of the people, but those improvements fell far short of expectations, and successive governments appeared to be hobbled by continued dependence on foreign investment. The developmentalist stream had by no means proved itself. The Islamists, moreover, believed that Islam's standing as the religion of nearly 90% of the population would eventually deliver them power, and many of them were patient enough to put their primary emphasis on strengthening the Islamic character of society rather than grasping immediately for power. The communists for their part were confident that their rapport with the impoverished majority of Indonesians would in time make them an irresistible political force; this confidence, along with a realistic assessment of the meagre prospects for successful guerrilla warfare, confirmed the party in what was then the novel strategy of abjuring revolution and seeking power by parliamentary means.

In retrospect, however, we can see that there was little chance of either side coming to power on a wave of overwhelming public approval. The cultural divisions described earlier set powerful natural limits to the potential for any stream to win over wide support amongst the Indonesian people. In fact, during the 1950s, Indonesia underwent a process of political "pillarization." In other words, the relatively strong correlation between political and cultural identity was institutionalized, so that each of the identifiable cultural divisions within society was represented not only by its own political parties but by a whole range of separate social institutions. Indonesian society came increasingly to resemble what the British colonial analyst J. S. Furnivall had described as a "plural society." Furnivall coined the term in 1948 to describe societies in which different ethnic groups "mix but do not combine":

> Each group holds by its own religion, its own culture and language, its own ideas and ways. As

individuals they meet, but only in the marketplace, in buying and selling. There is a plural society, with different sections of the community living side by side, but separately, within the same political unit.

Furnivall drew a portrait sharper than any reality and even his own life contradicted his conclusion (he married a Burmese woman), but his broad analysis sums up not only the relations between ethnic groups in colonial South East Asia but the relations between political forces in independent Indonesia during the 1950s. Three nations-of-intent still contested the idea of Indonesia.

GUIDED DEMOCRACY AND THE ASCENDANCY OF THE INDONESIAN COMMUNIST PARTY

In 1957 President Sukarno stepped into an increasingly bitter political standoff between the three streams and suspended parliamentary rule. Then, in cooperation with the firmly developmentalist army, he installed a more authoritarian system which he called Guided Democracy. Sukarno believed that the three streams of aspiration in Indonesian politics were not contradictory forces bound to battle each other to the end, but were instead complementary expressions of different elements in Indonesia's make-up. He was a superb ideologist, and he was able to weave the three streams into a formulation he called NASAKOM—nationalism (which stood for developmentalism), religion (standing for Islam) and communism. His Guided Democracy was an attempt to construct a political order in which none of the streams would prevail. Not a man for administrative detail, he attempted to achieve this result by focusing politics on himself and balancing political actors in a way which led many to describe him as a master-puppeteer. His construction also involved a narrowing of the political field: the price of participation in Guided Democracy was public acceptance of NASAKOM and those who refused to accept it were excluded.

Most Indonesians, however, saw Guided Democracy as no more than a holding operation. Relatively few people truly believed in NASAKOM and all were aware by the early 1960s that Sukarno's health was in decline. The central but unspoken issue under Guided Democracy was how it would influence the relative prospects of the three streams, which competed for Indonesia's soul.

To most observers there appeared no doubt that the main beneficiary of Guided Democracy was the Indonesian Communist Party. Although regional army commanders effectively banned the party in several outlying provinces, the party was able to canvass freely for support in Java, and its numbers grew rapidly. By 1965, it claimed three million members and was said to be the largest communist party in the non-communist world. Millions more were members of peasant associations, labour unions and other organizations affiliated with the party. Until 1957 it had been excluded from government, but under Sukarno party members began to hold a range of bureaucratic and political posts. From 1957, several cities on Java had communist mayors and several provincial governors were close to the party. Communist influence was growing in the powerful armed forces, especially the air force, and in 1965 the party backed the creation of a so-called "fifth force" of workers and peasants which would operate under its influence alongside the army, navy, air force and police. In Indonesian society, moreover, the party was increasingly assertive. Through its cultural affiliates, it sought to establish the hegemony of socialist ideas of art over what it considered to be bourgeois aestheticism, while in the countryside of Java, its peasant organizations sought to implement land reform laws. In most cases, this "direct action" involved seizing land from its *santri* owners and distributing it to poorer Communist Party supporters. The party supported the in-

terests of plantation and industrial workers in North Sumatra, and of Javanese migrants in North and South Sumatra. It supported followers of Hinduism against the ascendant *santri* elite of East Java, and it backed opponents of Hindu religious authority in Bali. For the opponents of communism, these campaigns appeared to give a foretaste of the policies, which the party would follow if it were to come to power. For all its renunciation of armed struggle, neither the party's rhetoric nor its practice gave the enemies of communism hope that communist party rule would be generous or inclusive towards its antagonists.

In the countryside, the communist campaign was resisted—and with considerable success—by the *santri*, but the main obstacle to the party's success at the national level appeared to be the army, whose high command was dominated by developmentalists unsympathetic to Islamism and hostile to the Indonesian Communist Party. With its weapons and a powerful grip on important government posts, including cabinet positions, governorships and directorships of state-owned companies, the army was a formidable opponent for the communists. Other opponents of the communists, moreover, notably the Islamists, came to see the army as their best hope for halting the communist advance and then put aside their former antagonisms in a coalition of desperation. The army's strength, however, was compromised by political division. Sukarno was a master of the art of playing his subordinates off against each other, and no one in palace circles had the luxury of knowing precisely where he or she stood in the political constellation from day to day. Below the level of the high command, there was much support for Sukarno and even considerable sympathy for the communists, as well as a long-standing tradition of independent action by junior officers. The most common view of Indonesia's political prospects, therefore, was that the Communist Party had a real chance of coming to power if

Guided Democracy could be sustained long enough and if the army could somehow be prevented from seizing power itself.

The widespread feeling that Indonesia was approaching the most decisive moment in its history was exacerbated by catastrophic economic decline. Under Guided Democracy, Sukarno had pushed the developmentalists out of macro-economic management, giving rein instead to a loose vision of opposition to neo-colonialism and neo-imperialism (and thus to foreign investment). Standards of living declined, inflation took off, infrastructure decayed, government fell into disarray and even famine began to loom. The mainly developmentalist army remained the most powerful government institution, but it did not have access to the levers of economic power at the centre and in an environment of economic decay it concentrated its efforts on securing its own interests by developing its own business enterprises and maximizing its share of the limited revenue available from the state. Economic decline would have had serious political effects anywhere, but in Indonesia, where prosperity and modernity were the central political aspirations, it was deeply disturbing. In contrast with the colonial period, however, when public and intellectual opinion was virtually united in the conclusion that colonialism was the primary cause of Indonesia's malaise, under Guided Democracy the analyses of Indonesia's problems ran in sharply contrasting directions. For Sukarno, the causes of Indonesia's difficulties were external: although politically independent, Indonesia was still the victim of what he described as neo-colonialism and neo-imperialism and its plight would only improve, he argued, if Indonesia were able to join with other newly emerging countries to create a new and equitable international order. The Indonesian Communist Party accepted much of this analysis, but placed much more emphasis on internal factors: they identified the most serious obstacles to prosperity as what they called

"capitalist–bureaucrats" in the administration and "village devils" such as landlords in the countryside. For the developmentalists and the Islamists, however, the main cause of Indonesia's problems appeared to be Sukarno and the communists. Sukarno was partly to blame, in their eyes, because of his neglect of proper economic management, but they reserved their chief opprobrium for the communists, whom they saw as the ideological engine behind Sukarno's rejection of a commercially oriented economy.

Yet there was no longer any capacity for the serious public discussion of these problems. Although Guided Democracy was not cruelly repressive, Sukarno imposed an ideological orthodoxy on public discussion, which meant that political information and opinions were passed on by rumour and in half-shrouded codes. For vast numbers of Indonesians from all political streams, Guided Democracy was a time of terrible uncertainty. Daily existence was uncertain because of crumbling institutions and failing markets, but still more perplexing was the political uncertainty: no one knew for certain who would rule Indonesia in the future, and those who were not irrevocably committed to one side or the other tried as far as they could to speak and act safely, so that they could hope to survive in whatever order was to rule them. And for all Indonesians, the causes of the economic decay and the biting political tensions were so entangled in shrill rhetoric that the true causes of Indonesia's plight remained obscure.

THE 1965 "COUP" AND ITS AFTERMATH

Early in the morning of October 1, 1965, this atmosphere of enormous tension and expectation was shattered by what appeared to be a communist coup in Jakarta. Left-wing troops raided the houses of seven leading anti-communist generals, including the army commander General Ahmad Yani and the defence minister General A. H. Nasution. Three were shot on the spot and three were hauled off to an air force base south of Jakarta where they were killed. Nasution escaped under fire, but his young daughter was killed. The leader of the action was Lieutenant–Colonel Untung, commander of Sukarno's presidential guard. After a brief delay, he declared that he had acted to forestall a military coup by an alleged "Council of General" and that state power was now in the hands of a Revolutionary Council. Whether or not the plotters had originally intended to kill the generals, their actions after dawn on October 1 showed little sign of careful planning. The Revolutionary Council appeared to have been composed in haste, without any attempt to consult those named as members, and the plotters did not take serious measures to seize the important points of control in Jakarta or to neutralize potential opponents. As a result, forces from the army's Strategic Reserve, headed by Lieutenant–General Suharto, were able to take the initiative and to put an end to the "coup" within a couple of days.

The nature of the "coup" remains uncertain. It may have been the initiative of junior army officers unhappy with the lifestyles and political conservatism of the High Command and was perhaps intended to do no more than humiliate and intimidate the senior officers. If so, the action got badly out of hand. On the other hand, the junior officers may themselves have had more far-reaching intentions, or they may have been the dupes of other political forces with broader intentions. Both the Communist Party and President Sukarno had good reason to want the removal of the army High Command. Indeed, it is unlikely that the junior officers would have taken action against their superiors in the military hierarchy unless they felt sure of some political protection. Whether they assumed they would get such protection or were promised it remains uncertain. It is known that a special bureau of the Communist Party was in routine contact with some of the coup plotters as part of the party's general aim of winning support in the ranks of its most powerful opponent. Also possible is that the coup was to some extent prompted or planned by enemies of Sukarno and the communists in order to compromise them. There is inconclusive but not entirely negligible evidence implicating both Suharto and the American Central Intelligence Agency in this respect.

Whoever may have been responsible for the "coup," however, most Indonesians and most outside observers assumed at once that it was the work of the Communist Party. Indeed, many members of the party seem to have made the same assumption: if the coup were a party initiative, it could hardly have been announced in advance to the three million members scattered across the country. Still more important, most Indonesians interpreted the evident failure of the "coup" as a profound defeat for the party. In the hothouse world of Guided Democracy the communists seemed to have a chance of coming to power by dominating discourse and annexing the important instruments of government. When the killing of the generals failed to cement an immediate communist seizure of power, everyone knew that the party's chances of taking power in the short term had disappeared. The tense balance of Guided Democracy was shattered and the army would not permit the communists to come to power. The party and its three million members were suddenly helpless.

Still more seriously for the communists, their opponents were able to exploit the circumstances of the "coup" to demonize them. To begin with, murdered generals were Indonesia's first significant victims of political assassination since the chaos of the revolution against the Dutch in the 1940s. In resorting to such violence the plotters had taken the tense confrontations of Indonesian politics to another level of bitterness. The killing of Nasution's daughter, moreover, marked communists as conscienceless child-killers, even though it had clearly been accidental. The real vilification of the party, however, began with the exhumation of the bodies of the murdered generals. Wild stories began to be circulated of the events at the air force base: members of the women's organization Gerwani, generally seen as a communist affiliate, were said to have tortured and mutilated the generals sexually before abandoning themselves in a lustful orgy with senior communists and air force officers. Before long, rumours began to circulate that party members had prepared pits—cunningly disguised as rubbish pits—to receive the bodies of their slain enemies. Newspapers published accounts, sometimes graphically illustrated, of how communists had been trained to turn simple implements such as rubber-tapping implements into gruesome eye-gouging tools. This demonization of the communists in turn made it easier for people to believe that the party was the prime cause of Indonesia's economic malaise, that the communists had deliberately created hardship and suffering to serve their own political ends. In a matter of weeks, by skilful exploitation of rumour and propaganda in an environment of enormous uncertainty and tension, the opponents of the Communist Party were able to turn it from being a recognized, if somewhat feared, element in the Indonesian political system into a pariah.

THE KILLINGS

The massacre of communists began in early October in the strongly Muslim province of Aceh in northern Sumatra. The local branch of the party was small, the initiative for the killings seems to have come from local Muslim leaders, and Acehnese Muslims had a long-standing reputation for using violence against their enemies. Elsewhere, there was a longer delay, as both sides assessed the situation. In most cases,

the killings were triggered by the arrival of anti-communist special forces, especially the RPKAD para-commandos, or when local armed forces made it clear that they sanctioned the murder of communists. In some regions, military units themselves took a major role in the killing, but more commonly they used local militias. All of Indonesia's political parties had youth affiliates whose activities shaded into intimidation, protection and small-scale violence, but the army, jealous of its monopoly of armed force, had never permitted them to develop beyond a limited scale. In the aftermath of the 1965 "coup," however, the military began to provide weapons, equipment, training and encouragement to these youth organizations, especially the Muslim Ansor in Central and East Java. These organizations typically moved systematically from village to village using lists and local informants to identify party members, who were then taken away for execution. In some cases, entire villages were wiped out, but for the most part, the killers were selective, taking only those that were identified as "guilty." Teachers and other village intellectuals were especially common on the lists of victims. The killing was largely done with knives or swords, but some victims were beaten to death and some were shot. Sometimes the bodies of the victims were deliberately mutilated, an act which, for Muslims, damages the spiritual integrity of the victim's soul. In some cases, the victims were forced to dig their own shallow, mass graves in secluded places, or the bodies were dumped in rivers, or concealed in caves. There are some reports of mass graves beneath the main square in towns in central Java. In a few cases, the bodies, or body parts, of victims were put on display, sometimes laid out on rafts, which were floated down rivers.

The regions most seriously affected by the killings were Central and East Java, Bali and North Sumatra, where the party had been most active, but there were massacres in every part of the archipelago where communists could be found. No reliable figures exist for the number of people who were killed. A scholarly consensus has settled on a figure of 400–500,000, but the correct figure could be half or twice as much. Indonesia had a population at the time between 100 and 110 million, too many for even a million deaths to show up incontrovertibly in the decennial censuses. Although official figures seem to have been compiled in many regions, there are many reasons why figures might have been over- or understated by those responsible for their collection.

As in many cases of genocide, many of the victims went passively to their deaths. There are reports that victims in one place in the province of North Sumatra formed long, acquiescent lines at a river's edge while they waited to be decapitated. In Bali, party members are said to have gone placidly to their deaths wearing traditional white funeral clothes. In parts of central Java, predominantly communist villages set up palisades in a futile attempt at self-defence, but even such measures were rare. One reason for the apparent passivity of the victims may be that they simply did not expect such ferocious retaliation for events in Jakarta to which they could not possibly have contributed. It is likely, however, that the explanation is partly cultural–historical: for most of human history, Indonesia has been relatively sparsely populated, a consequence of tropical disease and, possibly, of the relatively high standing of women, whose role in society was always far more than just the production of children. Wars of conquest in early times, therefore, generally aimed at capturing people, rather than territory. Battle by proxy or champion—a way of minimizing casualties—was reasonably common and there was no tradition of wholesale massacre such as was found, for instance, in densely populated China. People, however, still had to be conquered, and conquered peoples had to be ruled; an important part of the political repertoire of conquerors and rulers, therefore, came to be

intimidation. A cultural convention arose in which the correct and safe response to fearsomeness was timidity: those who showed themselves suitably in awe of new power-holders were spared. This cultural convention probably sapped the will of the communists to resist in 1965–1966.

Remarkably little primary evidence exists concerning the detail of the killings. The military-dominated regime of President Suharto, which had presided over the killings and which ruled Indonesia for more than 30 years afterwards, strongly discouraged any investigation of the events, though it has never denied that they took place. Indeed, the nearest thing to an official estimate of the number of dead is one million. The fact that the killings took place, moreover, at the height of the Cold War meant that there was little interest in the West in investigating the past misdeeds of what was to become one of the West's most important allies in Asia. As a result, several misconceptions about the nature of the killings have become common. Some observers, for instance, have suggested that many of the killings were apolitical, that people took advantage of the turmoil to settle private grudges unrelated to politics. The reality was, however, that the Communist Party had been so successful in taking sides in social conflicts across the breadth of the archipelago that most grudges had a political dimension. All the evidence that we have indicates that the killings were precisely directed against the broad category of people whom the army identified as enemies, that is, the members and close associates of the Communist Party. Also sometimes heard is the suggestion that the killings were a form of "running amok" (*amok* being after all an Indonesian word). It was argued that traditional Indonesian (especially Javanese) peasant society was inherently peaceful, but that under conditions of extreme tension that natural patience of the Javanese suddenly shattered in a blind frenzy of killing. Apart from overstating the peacefulness of traditional Indonesian society, however, this argument has the weakness that were highly targeted. Furthermore, psycho-cultural studies of *amok* have shown that it is most commonly a response to humiliation and defeat and often works as a form of indirect suicide. Little in the detail of the 1965–1966 killings fits with this pattern.

Also surprisingly common is the perception that most of the victims were Chinese. For the reasons outlined above, Chinese Indonesians have been subject to discrimination, harassment and occasional pogroms for at least the last 250 years. In 1965–1966, however, few Chinese were targeted. This was partly because discriminatory measures a few years earlier had removed most Chinese from the countryside where the vast majority of killings took place, partly because Chinese, as outsiders, were not immediately involved in the massive resolution of issues which was taking place. "They [the Chinese] were not involved," commented a non-communist leader years later, "it was a matter between Javanese."

Perhaps the most intractable difficulty, however, lies in determining the relative importance of army initiative and local tension in accounting for the scale of the killing. At first glance, the army's role seems clearly secondary to that of the broader social and political tensions outlined above. The hatred between Islamists and communists was ancient and deep-seated and had been exacerbated by the deep political uncertainty and enormous political tension of late Guided Democracy. The army, on the other hand, had the luxury of knowing that it had won: the failure of the October, 1965 "coup" meant that the Communist Party would not come to power under Guided Democracy. Imprisonment or execution of a few thousand leading communists would have been ample to guarantee the army's victory. The commander of the RPKAD was widely reported at the time as claiming that his troops had sought to curb the killings in Bali.

Nonetheless, several factors point to a greater direct military role. As we have seen, the killings tended to take place when anti-communist army units arrived in a region, and the militias who did much of the killing received weapons, equipment, training and encouragement from the army. More significant, the militias seem to have vanished as soon as their bloody work was done. The autonomous militias which had emerged after 1945 to fight for independence against the Dutch proved to be a stubborn and persistent obstacle to the army's claim to a monopoly of armed force and one of the most important lessons which the army learnt from this period was not to allow that monopoly to be breached. Even during the early 1980s, the military had to resort to extensive violence to suppress semi-criminal gangs who had been used as paramilitary enforcers in the larger cities. The rapid and peaceful disappearance of militias who were ostensibly linked to Muslim forces suspicious of the army's developmentalism strongly suggests that they were in fact creations of the military.

If the army did indeed want a full-scale massacre of communists, three reasons seem plausible. First, although we can see in retrospect that the army's victory was sealed by the failure of the October, 1965 "coup," this fact was by no means clear at the time. In particular, the army was aware of a kind of "shadow war" with the communists which involved placing sympathizers, agents and double-agents in key positions. The army did not know just how far the communist penetration of society and of government institutions had proceeded, and it therefore made certain of delivering the party a death-blow by killing a vast number of its followers. In this atmosphere of suspicion, moreover, people who feared that they might be identified as communists often took part in killings to prove their anti-communist credentials. As mass killings, too—killings by masses as well as of them—the massacres also had the purpose of forcing all Indonesians to make an unambiguous choice for or against the Communist Party. Just in case the communists were to recover and mount a counter-offensive, the military needed to be sure that blood was on as many hands as possible. Thus there are many stories of forcible recruitment into the militias and even of family members being forced to take the first step in killing their relatives. Communists from one village were sometimes delivered to another for killing, and the whole village was thus implicated in the murders, regardless of which hands actually held the murder weapons. The hesitant fence-sitters of Guided Democracy who had done everything possible to make sure that they would survive, whoever came to power, were to have that luxury no longer. This strategy still works: when Indonesia's new president, Abdurrachman Wahid, recently suggested that an inquiry be made into the massacres of 1965–1966, an inquiry which would certainly have added to the opprobrium currently being heaped on the armed forces, Muslim leaders from his own party moved very quickly to prevent the inquiry from going ahead. Youth groups from this party had been active in the killings in many parts of Java. Third, whether or not it was intended at the time, the killings hugely reinforced the army's political position once it was in power. For those who recognized the military role in the killings, the army was a force which had shown its willingness to kill on a vast scale, and it gave no reason to doubt that it would do so again if action seemed to be needed. For those who saw the killings as a product of internecine strife between rival Indonesians, military rule, whatever its shortcomings, seemed to be a guarantee against a repetition of that terrible time. The massacres placed a curse on open politics, which was not lifted for more than three decades.

A final likely reason why the army wanted the mass killings brings the genocide in Indonesia still closer to the ethnic genocides, which dominate traditional analysis of the term. Even after the killings subsided, the army appeared to show an especial vindictiveness towards communists. During the 10 years which followed the killings, over a million and a half

people passed through a system of prisons and prison camps on the grounds of their communist connections. When they were finally released, their lives were blighted by continuing discrimination, they were banned from government jobs, they were not permitted to vote and they faced difficulties in day-to-day dealings with the authorities. In the late 1980s, the authorities introduced a new concept, *bersih lingkungan* ("environmentally clean"), under which government employees and workers in education, the media and law, as well as economically important sectors such as the oil industry and public transportation, were expected to come from a family and social environment untainted by communism. In other words, communism was treated as a permanent, semi-hereditary condition which might afflict even people born after 1965.

All these generalizations must be read, however, in the light of the enormous variation in circumstances from province to province across Indonesia and from district to district within provinces. The few local studies to have been published show a complex interaction between long-standing local political tensions, varying responses to events in Jakarta, and different personalities in local institutions. In some districts the killing was truly collective; in others the military did most of the killing; in still others local men of violence emerged to glut themselves on slaughter.

The Suharto regime was not Stalin's Soviet Union or even Hitler's Germany after 1943. The so-called New Order did not feed on a widening circle of terror, sucking innocent and guilty alike into graves and gulags for the sake of terrifying effect. It was brutal in its treatment of enemies, real and presumed, and sometimes erratic in identifying them, but the last pogroms against communists were in 1969. Thereafter the only communists to die at the hands of the state were an unfortunate handful who had been sentenced to death in show trials in the late 1960s and from whom the government occasionally picked a few victims for execution.

But the Indonesian killings of 1965–1966 were a successful exercise in national obliteration. They were a concerted attempt to transform the nature of Indonesian society by destroying one of the three ideological and social streams which had competed for domination of the idea of Indonesia since the early twentieth century. We should not suppose that the communists would necessarily have been less brutal or that they would have ruled better if they had come to power rather than the army. But the killing of half a million communists was not merely an intense political conflict, it was the impoverishment of a national ideal, the extermination of a nation as it has existed in the minds of millions of Indonesians.

QUESTIONS TO CONSIDER

1. What is the distinction between genocide and political killings?

2. At its core, is Indonesia divided ethnically or politically?

3. In the short term, why did the Communists and Islamists capitulate to the Developmentalists?

4. Characterize "Guided Democracy" under Sukarno.

5. How did Sukarno policies affect the Developmentalists, and thus the economy?

6. What happened to the Communists in the 1965 coup?

7. Why did the killings in Indonesia go largely unreported?

8. What classifies these killings as genocide?

Case Study: Genocide in Bangladesh, 1971

Adam Jones,

Center for Research and Teaching in Economics/Mexico City

SUMMARY

The mass killings in Bangladesh (then East Pakistan) in 1971 vie with the annihilation of the Soviet POWs, the Holocaust against the Jews, and the genocide in Rwanda as the most concentrated act of genocide in the twentieth century. In an attempt to crush forces seeking independence for East Pakistan, the West Pakistani military regime unleashed a systematic campaign of mass murder which aimed at killing millions of Bengalis, and likely succeeded in doing so.

THE BACKGROUND

East and West Pakistan were forged in the cauldron of independence for the Indian subcontinent, ruled for two hundred years by the British. Despite the attempts of Mahatma Gandhi and others to prevent division along religious and ethnic lines, the departing British and various Indian politicians pressed for the creation of two states, one Hindu-dominated (India), the other Muslim-dominated (Pakistan). The partition of India in 1947 was one of the great tragedies of the century. Hundreds

From Adam Jones, "Case Study: Genocide in Bangladesh, 1971," Gendercide Watch 2000. Reprinted with permission of Adam Jones/Gendercide Watch.

of thousands of people were killed in sectarian violence and military clashes, as Hindus fled to India and Muslims to Pakistan—though large minorities remained in each country.

The arrangement proved highly unstable, leading to three major wars between India and Pakistan, and very nearly a fourth fullscale conflict in 1998–99. (Kashmir, divided by a cease-fire line after the first war in 1947, became one of the world's most intractable trouble-spots.) Not the least of the difficulties was the fact that the new state of Pakistan consisted of two "wings," divided by hundreds of miles of Indian territory and a gulf of ethnic identification. Over the decades, particularly after Pakistani democracy was stifled by a military dictatorship (1958), the relationship between East and West became progressively more corrupt and neo-colonial in character, and opposition to West Pakistani domination grew among the Bengali population.

Catastrophic floods struck Bangladesh in August 1970, and the regime was widely seen as having botched (or ignored) its relief duties. The disaster gave further impetus to the Awami League, led by Sheikh Mujibur Rahman. The League demanded regional autonomy for East Pakistan, and an end to military rule. In national elections held in December, the League won an overwhelming victory across Bengali territory.

On February 22, 1971 the generals in West Pakistan took a decision to crush the Awami League and its supporters. It was recognized from the first that a campaign of genocide would be necessary to eradicate the threat: "Kill three million of them," said President Yahya Khan at the February conference, "and the rest will eat out of our hands." (Robert Payne, *Massacre* [1972], p. 50.) On March 25 the genocide was launched. The university in Dacca was attacked and students exterminated by the hundreds. Death squads roamed the streets of Dacca, killing some 7,000 people in a single night. It was only the beginning. "Within a week, half the population of Dacca had fled, and at least 30,000

people had been killed. Chittagong, too, had lost half its population. All over East Pakistan people were taking flight, and it was estimated that in April some thirty million people were wandering helplessly across East Pakistan to escape the grasp of the military." (Payne, *Massacre*, p. 48.) Ten million refugees fled to India, overwhelming that country's resources and spurring the eventual Indian military intervention. (The population of Bangladesh/East Pakistan at the outbreak of the genocide was about 75 million.)

On April 10, the surviving leadership of the Awami League declared Bangladesh independent. The Mukhta Bahini (liberation forces) were mobilized to confront the West Pakistani army. They did so with increasing skill and effectiveness, utilizing their knowledge of the terrain and ability to blend with the civilian population in classic guerrilla fashion. By the end of the war, the tide had turned, and vast areas of Bangladesh had been liberated by the popular resistance.

THE GENDERCIDE AGAINST BENGALI MEN

The war against the Bengali population proceeded in classic gendercidal fashion. According to Anthony Mascarenhas, "There is no doubt whatsoever about the targets of the genocide":

> They were: (1) The Bengali militarymen of the East Bengal Regiment, the East Pakistan Rifles, police and para-military Ansars and Mujahids. (2) The Hindus—"We are only killing the men; the women and children go free. We are soldiers not cowards to kill them …" I was to hear in Comilla [site of a major military base] [Comments R. J. Rummel: "One would think that murdering an unarmed man was a heroic act" (*Death By Government*, p. 323)] (3) The Awami Leaguers—all office bearers and volunteers down to the lowest link in the chain of command. (4) The students—college and university boys and some of the more militant girls. (5) Bengali intellectuals such as professors and teachers whenever damned by the army as "militant." (Anthony Mascarenhas, *The Rape of Bangla Desh* [Delhi: Vikas Publications, 1972(?)], pp. 116–17.)

Mascarenhas's summary makes clear the linkages between gender and social class (the "intellectuals," "professors," "teachers," "office bearers," and—obviously—"militarymen" can all be expected to be overwhelmingly if not exclusively male, although in many cases their families died or fell victim to other atrocities alongside them). In this respect, the Bangladesh events can be classed as a combined gendercide and *elitocide*, with both strategies overwhelmingly targeting males for the most annihilatory excesses.

Younger men and adolescent boys, of whatever social class, were equally targets. According to Rounaq Jahan, "All through the liberation war, able-bodied young men were suspected of being actual or potential freedom fighters. Thousands were arrested, tortured, and killed. Eventually cities and towns became bereft of young males who either took refuge in India or joined the liberation war." Especially "during the first phase" of the genocide, he writes, "young able-bodied males were the victims of indiscriminate killings." ("Genocide in Bangladesh," in Totten et al., *Century of Genocide*, p. 298.) R. J. Rummel likewise writes that "the Pakistan army [sought] out those especially likely to join the resistance—young boys. Sweeps were conducted of young men who were never seen again. Bodies of youths would be found in fields, floating down rivers, or near army camps. As can be imagined, this terrorized all young men and their families within reach of the army. Most between the ages of fifteen and twenty-five began to flee from one village to another and toward India. Many of those reluctant to leave their homes were forced to flee by mothers and sisters concerned for their safety." (*Death By Government*, p. 329.) Rummel describes (p. 323) a chilling gendercidal ritual, reminiscent of Nazi procedure towards Jewish males: "In what became province-wide acts of genocide, Hindus were sought out and killed on the spot. As a matter of course, soldiers would check males for the obligated circumcision among Moslems. If circumcised, they might live; if not, sure death."

Robert Payne describes scenes of systematic mass slaughter around Dacca that, while not explicitly "gendered" in his account, bear every hallmark of classic gender-selective roundups and gendercidal slaughters of non-combatant men:

> In the dead region surrounding Dacca, the military authorities conducted experiments in mass extermination in places unlikely to be seen by journalists. At Hariharpara, a once thriving village on the banks of the Buriganga River near Dacca, they found the three elements necessary for killing people in large numbers: a prison in which to hold the victims, a place for executing the prisoners, and a method for disposing of the bodies. The prison was a large riverside warehouse, or godown, belonging to the Pakistan National Oil Company, the place of execution was the river edge, or the shallows near the shore, and the bodies were disposed of by the simple means of permitting them to float downstream. The killing took place night after night. Usually the prisoners were roped together and made to wade out into the river. They were in batches of six or eight, and in the light of a powerful electric arc lamp, they were easy targets, black against the silvery water. The executioners stood on the pier, shooting down at the compact bunches of prisoners wading in the water. There were screams in the hot night air, and then silence. The prisoners fell on their sides and their bodies lapped against the shore. Then a new bunch of prisoners was brought out, and the process was repeated. In the morning the village boatmen hauled the bodies into midstream and the ropes binding the bodies were cut so that each body drifted separately downstream. (Payne, *Massacre* [Macmillan, 1973], p. 55.)

Strikingly similar and equally hellish scenes are described in the case-studies of genocide in Armenia and the Nanjing Massacre of 1937.

ATROCITIES AGAINST BENGALI WOMEN

As was also the case in Armenia and Nanjing, Bengali women were targeted for gender-selective atrocities and abuses, notably gang sexual assault and rape/murder, from the earliest days of the Pakistani genocide. Indeed, despite (and in part because of) the overwhelming targeting of males for mass murder, it is for the systematic brutalization of women that the "Rape of Bangladesh" is best known to Western observers.

> In her ground-breaking book, *Against Our Will: Men, Women and Rape*, Susan Brownmiller likened the 1971 events in Bangladesh to the Japanese rapes in Nanjing and German rapes in Russia during World War II. "... 200,000, 300,000 or possibly 400,000 women (three sets of statistics have been variously quoted) were raped. Eighty percent of the raped women were Moslems, reflecting the population of Bangladesh, but Hindu and Christian women were not exempt ... Hit-and-run rape of large numbers of Bengali women was brutally simple in terms of logistics as the Pakistani regulars swept through and occupied the tiny, populous land ..." (p. 81).

Typical was the description offered by reporter Aubrey Menen of one such assault, which targeted a recently-married woman:

> Two [Pakistani soldiers] went into the room that had been built for the bridal couple. The others stayed behind with the family, one of them covering them with his gun. They heard a barked order, and the bridegroom's voice protesting. Then there was silence until the bride screamed. Then there was silence again, except for some muffled cries that soon subsided. In a few minutes one of the soldiers came out, his uniform in disarray. He grinned to his companions. Another soldier took his place in the extra room. And so on, until all the six had raped the belle of the village. Then all six left, hurriedly. The father found his daughter lying on the string cot unconscious and bleeding. Her husband was crouched on the floor, kneeling over his vomit. (Quoted in Brownmiller, *Against Our Will*, p. 82.)

"Rape in Bangladesh had hardly been restricted to beauty," Brownmiller writes. "Girls of eight and grandmothers of seventy-five had been sexually assaulted ... Pakistani soldiers had not only violated Bengali women on the spot; they abducted tens of hundreds and held them by force in their military barracks for nightly use." Some women may have been raped as many as eighty times in a night. (Brownmiller, p. 83). How many died from this atrocious treatment, and how many more women were murdered as part of the generalized campaign of destruction and slaughter, can only be guessed at.

Despite government efforts at amelioration, the torment and persecution of the survivors continued long after Bangladesh had won its independence:

> Rape, abduction and forcible prostitution during the nine-month war proved to be only the first round of humiliation for the Bengali women. Prime Minister Mujibur Rahman's declaration that victims of rape were national heroines was the opening shot of an ill-starred campaign to reintegrate them into society—by smoothing the way for a return to their husbands or by finding bridegrooms for the unmarried [or widowed] ones from among his Mukti Bahini freedom fighters. Imaginative in concept for a country in which female chastity and purdah isolation are cardinal principles, the "marry them off" campaign never got off the ground. Few prospective bridegrooms stepped forward, and those who did made it plain that they expected the government, as father figure, to present them with handsome dowries. (Brownmiller, *Against Our Will*, p. 84.)

HOW MANY DIED?

The number of dead in Bangladesh in 1971 was almost certainly well into seven figures. It was one of the worst genocides of the World War II era, outstripping Rwanda (800,000 killed) and probably surpassing even Indonesia (1 million to 1.5 million killed in 1965–66). As R. J. Rummel writes,

> The human death toll over only 267 days was incredible. Just to give for five out of the eighteen districts some incomplete statistics published in Bangladesh newspapers or by an Inquiry Committee, the Pakistani army killed 100,000 Bengalis in Dacca, 150,000 in Khulna, 75,000 in Jessore, 95,000 in Comilla, and 100,000 in Chittagong. For eighteen districts the total is 1,247,000

killed. This was an incomplete toll, and to this day no one really knows the final toll. Some estimates of the democide [Rummel's "death by government"] are much lower—one is of 300,000 dead—but most range from 1 million to 3 million … The Pakistani army and allied paramilitary groups killed about one out of every sixty-one people in Pakistan overall; one out of every twenty-five Bengalis, Hindus, and others in East Pakistan. If the rate of killing for all of Pakistan is annualized over the years the Yahya martial law regime was in power (March 1969 to December 1971), then this one regime was more lethal than that of the Soviet Union, China under the communists, or Japan under the military (even through World War II). (Rummel, *Death By Government*, p. 331.)

The proportion of men versus women murdered is impossible to ascertain, but a speculation might be attempted. If we take the highest estimates for both women raped and Bengalis killed (400,000 and 3 million, respectively); if we accept that half as many women were killed as were raped; and if we double that number for murdered children of both sexes (total: 600,000), we are still left with a death-toll that is 80 percent adult male (2.4 million out of 3 million). Any such disproportion, which is almost certainly on the low side, would qualify Bangladesh as one of the worst gendercides against men in the last half-millennium.

WHO WAS RESPONSIBLE?

"For month after month in all the regions of East Pakistan the massacres went on," writes Robert Payne. "They were not the small casual killings of young officers who wanted to demonstrate their efficiency, but organized massacres conducted by sophisticated staff officers, who knew exactly what they were doing. Muslim soldiers, sent out to kill Muslim peasants, went about their work mechanically and efficiently, until killing defenseless people became a habit like smoking cigarettes or drinking wine … Not since Hitler invaded Russia had there been so vast a massacre." (Payne, *Massacre*, p. 29.)

There is no doubt that the mass killing in Bangladesh was among the most carefully and centrally planned of modern genocides. A cabal of five Pakistani generals orchestrated the events: President Yahya Khan, General Tikka Khan, chief of staff General Pirzada, security chief General Umar Khan, and intelligence chief General Akbar Khan. The U.S. government, long supportive of military rule in Pakistan, supplied some $3.8 million in military equipment to the dictatorship *after* the onset of the genocide, "and after a government spokesman told Congress that all shipments to Yahya Khan's regime had ceased." (Payne, *Massacre*, p. 102.)

The genocide and gendercidal atrocities were also perpetrated by lower-ranking officers and ordinary soldiers. These "willing executioners" were fuelled by an abiding anti-Bengali racism, especially against the Hindu minority. "Bengalis were often compared with monkeys and chickens. Said Pakistan General Niazi, 'It was a low lying land of low lying people.' The Hindus among the Bengalis were as Jews to the Nazis: scum and vermin that [should] best be exterminated. As to the Moslem Bengalis, they were to live only on the sufferance of the soldiers: any infraction, any suspicion cast on them, any need for reprisal, could mean their death. And the soldiers were free to kill at will. The journalist Dan Coggin quoted one Punjabi captain as telling him, 'We can kill anyone for anything. We are accountable to no one.' This is the arrogance of Power." (Rummel, *Death By Government*, p. 335.)

THE AFTERMATH

On December 3, India under Prime Minister Indira Gandhi, seeking to return the millions of Bengali refugees and seize an opportunity to weaken its perennial military rival, finally launched a fullscale intervention to crush West Pakistani forces and secure Bangladeshi independence. The Pakistani army, demoralized by long months of guerrilla warfare, quickly collapsed. On December 16, after a final genocidal outburst, the Pakistani regime agreed to an unconditional surrender. Awami leader Sheikh Mujib was released from detention and returned to a hero's welcome in Dacca on January 10, 1972, establishing Bangladesh's first independent parliament.

In a brutal bloodletting following the expulsion of the Pakistani army, perhaps 150,000 people were murdered by the vengeful victors. (Rummel, *Death By Government*, p. 334.) The trend is far too common in such post-genocidal circumstances. Such large-scale reprisal killings also tend to have a gendercidal character, which may have been the case in Bangladesh: Jahan writes that during the reprisal stage, "another group of Bengali *men* in the rural areas—those who were coerced or bribed to collaborate with the Pakistanis—fell victims to the attacks of Bengali freedom fighters." [emphasis added]

None of the generals involved in the genocide has ever been brought to trial, and all remain at large in Pakistan and other countries. Several movements have arisen to try to bring them before an international tribunal.

Political and military upheaval did not end with Bangladeshi independence. Rummel notes that "the massive bloodletting by all parties in Bangladesh affected its politics for the following decades. The country has experienced military coup after military coup, some of them bloody." (*Death By Government*, p. 334.)

QUESTIONS TO CONSIDER

1. What motivated the 1971 genocide?
2. Why is the attack against the Bengali population termed gendercide?
3. What was the fate of Bangali women?
4. Who was responsible?
5. What was the outcome?

Good and Bad Genocide

DOUBLE STANDARDS IN COVERAGE OF SUHARTO AND POL POT

Edward S. Herman,
University of Pennsylvania

Coverage of the fall of Suharto reveals with startling clarity the ideological biases and propaganda role of the mainstream media. Suharto was a ruthless dictator, a grand larcenist and a mass killer with as many victims as Cambodia's Pot Pot. But he served U.S. economic and geopolitical interests, was helped into power by Washington, and his dictatorial rule was warmly supported for 32 years by the U.S. economic and political establishment. The U.S. was still training the most repressive elements of Indonesia's security forces as Suharto's rule was collapsing in 1998, and the Clinton administration had established especially close

From Edward S. Herman, "Good and Bad Genocide: Double Standards in Coverage of Suharto and Pol Pot," *Extra* (September/October 1998): 15–17. Reprinted with permission.

relations with the dictator ("our kind of guy," according to a senior administration official quoted in the *New York Times*).

Suharto's overthrow of the Sukarno government in 1965–66 turned Indonesia from Cold War "neutralism" to fervent anti-Communism, and wiped out the Indonesian Communist Party—exterminating a sizable part of its mass base in the process, in widespread massacres that claimed at least 500,000 and perhaps more than a million victims. The U.S. establishment's enthusiasm for the coup–cum–mass murder was ecstatic; "almost everyone is pleased by the changes being wrought," *New York Times* columnist C. L. Sulzberger commented.

Suharto quickly transformed Indonesia into an "investors' paradise," only slightly qualified by the steep bribery charge for entry. Investors flocked in to exploit the timber, mineral and oil resources, as well as the cheap, repressed labor, often in joint ventures with Suharto family members and cronies. Investor enthusiasm for this favorable climate of investment was expressed in political support and even in public advertisements; e.g., the full page ad in the *New York Times* (9/24/92) by Chevron and Texaco entitled "Indonesia: A Model for Economic Development."

The U.S. support and investment did not slacken when Suharto's army invaded and occupied East Timor in 1975, which resulted in an estimated 200,000 deaths in a population of only 700,000. Combined with the 500,000–1,000,000+ slaughtered within Indonesia in 1965–66, the double genocide would seem to put Suharto in at least the same class of mass murderer as Pol Pot.

GOOD AND BAD GENOCIDISTS

But Suharto's killings of 1965–66 were what Noam Chomsky and I, in *The Washington Connection and Third World Fascism*, called "constructive terror," with results viewed as favorable to Western interests. His mass killings in East Timor were "benign terror," carried out by a valued client and therefore tolerable. Pol Pot's were "nefarious terror," done by an enemy, therefore appalling and to be severely condemned. Pol Pot's victims were "worthy," Suharto's "unworthy."

This politicized classification system was unfailingly employed by the media in the period of Suharto's decline and fall (1997–98). When Pol Pot died in April 1998, the media were unstinting in condemnation, calling him "wicked," "loathsome" and "monumentally evil," (*Chicago Tribune*, 4/18/98), a "lethal mass killer" and "war criminal," (*L. A. Times*, 4/17/98), "blood-soaked" and an "egregious mass murderer." (*Washington Post*, 4/17/98, 4/18/98). His rule was repeatedly described as a "reign of terror" and he was guilty of "genocide." Although he inherited a devastated country with starvation rampant, all excess deaths during his rule were attributed to him, and he was evaluated on the basis of those deaths.

Although Suharto's regime was responsible for a comparable number of deaths in Indonesia, along with more than a quarter of the population of East Timor, the word "genocide" is virtually never used in mainstream accounts of his rule. A Nexis search of major papers for the first half of 1998 turned up no news articles and only a handful of letters and opinion pieces that used the term in connection with Suharto.

Earlier, in a rare case where the word came up in a discussion of East Timor [*New York Times*], reporter Henry Kamm referred to it as "hyperbole—accusations of 'genocide' rather than mass deaths from cruel warfare and the starvation that accompanies it on this historically food short island." No such "hyperbole" was applied to the long-useful Suharto; one looks in vain for editorial descriptions of him as "blood-soaked" or a "murderer."

In the months of his exit, he was referred to as Indonesia's "soft-spoken, enigmatic president" (*USA Today*, 5/15/98), a "profoundly spiritual man," (*New York Times*, 5/17/98) a "reforming autocrat." (*New York Times*, 5/22/98). His motives were benign: "It was not simply personal ambition that led Mr. Suharto to clamp down so hard for so long; it was a fear, shared by many in this country of 210 million people, of chaos" (*New York Times*, 6/2/98); he "failed to comprehend the intensity of his people's discontent", (*New York Times*, 5/21/98); otherwise he undoubtedly would have stepped down earlier. He was sometimes described as "authoritarian," occasionally as a "dictator," but never as a mass murderer. Suharto's mass killings were referred to—if at all—in a brief and antiseptic paragraph.

It is interesting to see how the same reporters move between Pol Pot and Suharto, indignant at the former's killings, somehow unconcerned by the killings of the good genocidist. Seth Mydans, the *New York Times* principal reporter on the two leaders during the past two years, called Pol Pot "one of the century's great mass killers … who drove Cambodia to ruin, causing the deaths of more than a million people," and who "launched one of the world's most terrifying attempts at utopia." But in reference to Suharto, this same Mydans said that "more than 500,000 Indonesians are estimated to have died in a purge of leftists in 1965, the year Mr. Suharto came to power." Note that Suharto is not even the killer, let alone a "great mass killer," and this "purge"—not "murder" or "slaughter"—was not "terrifying," and was not allocated to any particular agent.

The use of the passive voice is common in dealing with Suharto's victims: They "died" instead of being killed ("the violence left a reported 500,000 people dead"— *New York Times*), or "were killed" without reference to the author of the killings (e.g., *Washington Post*). In referring to East Timor, Mydans (*New York Times*, 7/28/96) spoke of protestors shouting grievances about "the suppression of opposition in East Timor and Irian Jaya." Is "sup-

pression of opposition" the proper description of an invasion and occupation that eliminated 200,000 out of 700,000 people?

The good and bad genocidists are handled differently in other ways. For Suharto, the numbers killed always tend to the 500,000 official Indonesian estimate or below, although independent estimates run from 700,000 to well over a million. For Pol Pot, the media numbers usually range from 1 million–2 million, although the best estimates of numbers executed run from 100,000–400,000, with excess deaths from all causes (including residual effects of the prior devastation) ranging upward from 750,000. (Michael Vickery, *Cambodia*; Herman and Chomsky, *Manufacturing Consent*).

Pol Pot's killings are always attributed to him personally—the *New York Times'* Philip Shenon (4/18/98) refers to him as "the man responsible for the deaths of more than a million Cambodians." Although some analysts of the Khmer Rouge have claimed that the suffering of Cambodia under the intense U.S. bombing made them vengeful, and although the conditions they inherited were disastrous, for the media nothing mitigates Pol Pot's responsibility. The only "context" allowed explaining his, killing is his "crazed Maoist inspiration," (*New York Times*, 4/18/98), his Marxist ideological training in France and his desire to create a "utopia of equality." (*Boston Globe* editorial, 4/17/98).

With Suharto, by contrast, not only is he not responsible for the mass killings, there was a mitigating circumstance: namely, a failed leftist or Communist coup, or "leftist onslaught", (*New York Times*, 6/17/79), which "touched off a wave of violence." (*New York Times*, 8/7/96). In the *New York Times'* historical summary-(5/21/98): "General Suharto routs Communist forces who killed six senior generals in an alleged coup attempt. Estimated 500,000 people killed in backlash against Communists."

This formula is repeated in most mainstream media accounts of the 1965–66 slaughter.

Some mention that the "Communist plot" was "alleged," but none try to examine its truth or falsehood. What's interesting is that the six deaths are seen as a plausible catalyst for the Indonesian massacres, while the 450,000 killed and maimed in the U.S. bombing of Cambodia (the *Washington Post's* estimate 4/24/75), are virtually never mentioned in connection with the Khmer Rouge's violence. By suggesting a provocation, and using words like "backlash" and "touching off a wave of violence," the media justify and diffuse responsibility for the good genocide.

The good genocidist is also repeatedly allowed credit for having encouraged economic growth, which provides the regular offset for his repression and undemocratic rule as well as mass killing. In virtually every article Mydans wrote on Indonesia, the fact that Suharto brought rising incomes is featured, with the mass killings and other negatives relegated to side issues that qualify the good. Joseph Stalin also presided over a remarkable development and growth process, but the mainstream media have never been inclined to overlook his crimes on that basis. Only constructive terror deserves such contextualization.

A *New York Times* editorial declared (4/10/98): "Time cannot erase the criminal responsibility of Pol Pot, whose murderous rule of Cambodia in the late 1970s brought death to about a million people, or one out of seven Cambodians. Trying him before an international tribunal would advance justice, promote healing in Cambodia and give pause to any fanatic tempted to follow his example."

But for the *New York Times* and its media cohorts, Suharto's killings in East Timor—and the huge slaughter of 1965–66—are not crimes and do not call for retribution or any kind of justice to the victims Reporter David Sanger (*New York Times*, 3/8/98) differentiated Suharto from Iraq's Saddam Hussein, saying that "Mr. Suharto is not hoarding anthrax or threatening to invade Australia." The fact that he killed 500,000+ at home and killed another 200,000 in an invasion of East Timor has disappeared from view. This was constructive and benign terror carried out by a good genocidist.

QUESTIONS TO CONSIDER

1. Explain why Noam Chomsky and Edward S. Herman characterize Suharto's reign "constructive" and "benign terror."

2. According to Herman, why was the *g*-word not applied to Suharto?

3. How does the use of "the passive voice" soften Suharto's actions?

4. Contrast Pol Pot's portrayal in the mainstream media.

5. What is the distinction between a "good genocidist" and a "bad" one?

MAKING CONNECTIONS

1. Do you agree with the statement in the Introduction to Chapter 12 that there are similarities between East Timor and Bangladesh?

2. Does the genocide in Indonesia have significant similarities with the genocide in Rwanda?

3. Do the descriptions of events in Bangladesh seem similar to the events in Armenia?

✔ RECOMMENDED RESOURCES

Chaudhuri, Kalyan. *Genocide in Bangladesh.* Bombay, India: Orient Longman, 1972.

Cribb, Robert. "Genocide in Indonesia, 1965–1966," *Journal of Genocide Research* 3(2) (2001): 219–237. Reprinted with permission of Taylor & Francis Ltd. Website http://www.tandf.co.uk/journals

Crouch, Harold. *The Army and Politics in Indonesia.* Ithaca, NY: Cornell University Press, 1978.

Griswold, Deirdre. *The Bloodbath That Was.* New York: World View Publishers, 1975.

Herman, Edward S. "Good and Bad Genocide: Double Standards in Coverage of Suharto and Pol Pot," *Extra* (September/October 1998): 15–17. Reprinted with permission.

Jardine, Matthew. *East Timor: Genocide in Paradise,* 2nd ed. Chicago: Common Courage Press, 1999.

Jones, Adam. "Case Study: Genocide in Bangladesh, 1971," Genocide Watch 2000. Reprinted with permission of Adam Jones/Gendercide Watch.

CHAPTER 13

ETHNIC CLEANSING: BOSNIA

In Bosnia, Serbs sought "ethnic cleansing" of Muslims—driving them into concentration camps, systematically gang-raping women and girls, and murdering civilians. This genocide followed a long civil war reminiscent of the strife in the Spanish civil war when Spanish Loyalists engaged in a bloodbath with Fascists. Serbian military commander Ratko Mladic issued specific orders to his subordinates to shell one village instead of another because the village to be bombed had more Muslims than Serbs.

Florence Hartmann surveys the details of the conflict in "Bosnia." In the reading "Middle Managers of Genocide," by Ed Vulliamy, we are offered insights into the chain of command and implementation of genocide at the local level. Kathleen Knox describes the first verdict of a perpetrator in the article "Bosnia: First Genocide Verdict May Bolster Other Cases." Social critic Michael Parenti analyzes the response of the United States to the Bosnian genocide in "The Rational Destruction of Yugoslavia." He suggests that U.S. media demonized Serbs, thus directing public opinion and government policy.

Bosnia

Florence Hartmann,

*Spokeswoman for Chief Prosecutor Carla Del Ponte
International War Crimes Tribunal*

The conflict in Bosnia-Herzegovina, which began in April 1992 and ended in November 1995, has come to be seen as the model for wars of ethnic cleansing throughout the world. This was the most violent event Europe experienced since World War II, and the devastation of the small multiethnic state recalled the ruins of Germany after the Allied bombing. The methods of ethnic cleansing, used for conquest of territory, were a repudiation of the lessons of World War II as codified in the Geneva Conventions. Practically

the only saving grace in Western policy making during the three-and-a-half-year war was the decision to launch an international war crimes tribunal to indict and try some of those responsible.

Everyone knows by now that the war was both the result of Yugoslavia's collapse and the event that ensured it could never be reconstituted. Long before the war began, Slobodan Milosevic in Serbia and, following his example, Franjo Tudjman in Croatia, had turned their backs on the Yugoslav ideal of an ethnically

Florence Hartmann, "Bosnia," Roy Gutman and David Rieff, eds. From *Crimes of War: What the Public Should Know* (New York: W.W. Norton & Company, 1999), 50–56. Reprinted with permission.

mixed federal State and set about carving out their own ethnically homogeneous States. With Milosevic's failure, in 1991, to take control of all of Yugoslavia, the die was cast for war.

Flatly rejecting proposals for a loosely based federation, refusing to adopt the democratic and Western market reforms that had swept the former Soviet bloc, and facing challenges in the streets from students, Milosevic opted for a military contest. He had effective control of the federal army and police, an aroused Serbian diaspora in the republics heading for independence, with ultranationalists at the fore, and the ability to manipulate all the key institutions in Serbia—the academics, the media, the Serbian Orthodox Church. Thus the wars over the succession to multinational Yugoslavia illustrated perfectly Clausewitz's idea that war is a continuation of politics by other means.

To strengthen his hold on the domestic power base, Milosevic made it his mission to set Yugoslavia's ethnic and national groups against one another. In the end, he succeeded in chasing out of what remained of Yugoslavia all those national groups that refused to submit to the hegemony of the Serb people and of Milosevic's Socialist Party (the successor to the League of Communists).

The Serbian political project, first in Croatia, then in Bosnia-Herzegovina, envisioned the creation of ethnically homogeneous States, fashioned by seizing territory from other States. *Ethnic cleansing* meant using violence and deportations to remove any trace of the other ethnic communities who had previously cohabited with Serbs in the coveted territories. This "cleansing" was the goal of the war, not the unintended consequence. It was not the inability of the different ethnic groups to live together that brought on the conflict, but rather the political aim of separating them.

The violence unleashed grew directly out of the artificiality of the political agenda, which stood in total contradiction to the centuries-old multiethnic history of the Balkans. Simply put, achieving ethnically homogeneous States in a region of historic mixing could not be achieved except through extreme violence. In Bosnia, cleansing clearly took the form of *genocide*, for it was aimed to eliminate enough of the population, starting with the annihilation of its elite, so it could no longer form a plurality. For the Serbs, war crimes served as a force multiplier—a means to achieve greater effect from other resources. They did not have enough military assets to achieve their ambitions otherwise.

Western governments, starting with the United States, chose not to intervene for three and a half years. In response to the atrocities reported by the media, relief organizations, and even their own diplomats, and to quell the public outcry over the haunting images of starved *concentration camp* inmates behind barbed wire, the Security Council passed resolutions its members then failed to implement and, in conjunction with the European Community, set up a diplomatic process which neither would back up by force. To evade their obligations under the 1948 Genocide Convention, which requires parties to prevent and punish genocide, Western leaders took frequent recourse to the term used by Serbian officials, ethnic cleansing, and then stated that all parties had committed the practice. They did not use the term genocide until the war had ended. The major powers recognized Bosnia-Herzegovina as a sovereign State, admitted it as a full member of the United Nations, and established diplomatic relations, meanwhile suspending the UN membership of the rump Yugoslavia and imposing sanctions on it for supporting the war. But they refused to identify the conflict as an international armed *aggression* and instead characterized it as a *civil war* and an ancient ethnic feud, a posture that permitted them to avoid their collective security obligations under the United Nations Charter. They also refused to document from their intelligence sources the links between the Serbian and Bosnian Serb Armies—an integrated command structure, a single logistical infrastructure, and a common paymaster. A top American diplomat called the international failure to respond the worst crisis in European collective security since the 1930s.

The evidence of concentration camps, systematic rape, massacres, torture, and mass deportation of civilians was undeniable, and in February 1993, largely at American behest, the Security Council set up "an International Tribunal for the Prosecution of Persons Responsible for Serious Violations of International Humanitarian Law Committed in the Territory of the Former Yugoslavia Since 1991" (ICTY) in The Hague. But the major powers did not get around to naming a chief prosecutor until July 1994, and they gave no support to the Bosnian government when it brought a case for genocide against Serbia at the International Court of Justice in The Hague, and Western governments instead have repeatedly urged Bosnia to drop that case.

Prosecuting primarily lower-level officials, the ICTY was unable to unmask the silence of the West on the real nature of the enterprise. It was not until July 1995, when NATO intervention in Bosnia-Herzegovina was at hand, that the tribunal indicted political leader Radovan Karadzic and military commander Ratko Mladic for genocide. And when Dusko Tadic was put on trial in 1996 for crimes committed at the Omarska detention camp and elsewhere in Prijedor County, the tribunal, working with such evidence it was able to obtain from open sources, victims, and ever-balking major powers, analyzed the atrocities as if they had occurred during a military campaign and a civil war rather than in an international conflict. The tribunal had ample jurisdiction to indict him for an internal conflict, but the tight focus of its charges effectively shielded Serbia, which had organized

the genocide in which Dusko Tadic took part, from direct accountability.

A key factor in *incitement* of ethnic hatreds, first in Serbia, and later in Croatia, was a media under the thumb of the political leaders. This psychological conditioning disguised the conflict in civil and ethnic terms by using the supreme alibi, namely the impossibility of the people of the former Yugoslavia to live together on the same territory. But it also awakened that barbarity which sleeps in all of us, and pushed the people to commit these massive atrocities.

Historically, in conventional conflicts, defeating the enemy's army on the battlefield and seizing territory are usually each side's principal war aims. The killing and wounding of civilians, the destruction of property, and the creation of refugees or displaced people are often by-products of these aims. While much of this devastation is legal under international law, since the codes of war offer no complete guarantees for the safety of civilians caught in zones of combat, the essence of the laws of war is that suffering must be minimized. This makes it imperative that the civilian population should not be made the object of attack. Soldiers from proper armies who contravene these laws are subject to trial for war crimes. In Bosnia-Herzegovina, the killing of civilians was not a by-product of war, for the goal of ethnic cleansing was the annihilation of civilians.

By the time Yugoslavia collapsed, the reputation of the Yugoslav Federal Army was irreparably stained, for under Milosevic's guidance the army coordinated and supported many of the militias who did the dirty work.

These were not the isolated, sporadic acts committed by militia factions running amok. To the contrary, the manner in which they were perpetrated, their ritualization, duration, and the pattern of commission across the territory under army control all testify that they were the product of a systematic policy, planned and coordinated at the highest political and military levels of the Yugoslav government.

To accomplish the war aim, there was probably no other way. In a multiethnic society like the former Yugoslavia before 1991, the annexation of territories while necessary could not be sufficient. Too many members of rival ethnic communities would have remained, and the more territories were conquered, the more difficult, paradoxically, it would become to occupy and administer. Only ethnic cleansing, that is, the elimination of the other ethnic communities present in the coveted territories, could bring to fruition the war aims of the Serbs, and, later, of the Croats as well. Both Milosevic and Tudjman realized this from the start. The horrors and the goals of the war were one, or, more precisely, the success of the war depended on its horrors.

The war began on April 6, 1992, with the assault on key cities such as Bijeljina and Zvornik on the Bosnian-Serbian border by the Yugoslav Army and its allied paramilitary groups, followed by the siege of Sarajevo. Though planned over a long period, the order to activate the impressive military might secretly put in place around the Bosnian capital was held until the recognition of Bosnia-Herzegovina's independence by the Europeans and Americans.

From the very beginning of the conflict, *terror* was the method used to separate the communities. The violations of international humanitarian law testify to the determination to reach this goal. Bombardments of the civilian population, first of Sarajevo, then of besieged villages; massacres during the conquest, then the forced evacuation of civilians to modify the ethnic structure of the particular area; illegal internment of the civilian population in concentration camps; torture; systematic rape; summary executions; appropriation and pillage of civilian property; systematic destruction of the cultural and religious heritage with the sole aim of eliminating any trace of non-Serbs in the conquered territories; using detainees as human shields on front lines and in minefields; and starvation of civilians who resisted—these were only some of the violations of international humanitarian law and the laws of war of which the Serbs were guilty.

Violence breeds violence. In 1993, emboldened by Milosevic's campaign of terror against the Muslims and the Western powers' consistent denial that genocide had taken place, the Croats entered the war against their former Muslim allies, using many of the same methods as the Serbs—terror, deportations, concentration camps, indiscriminate bombardments of civilians, massacres, the blocking of humanitarian aid, destruction of religious shrines, and appropriation of property.

They were encouraged by Slobodan Milosevic's support for a Greater Croatia (which would include western Herzegovina and a part of central Bosnia, where a majority of 800,000 Bosnian Croats lived). These grave breaches of the laws of armed conflict were always on a smaller scale than those of the Serbs.

Victims of a double aggression, the Muslims certainly committed violations of international humanitarian law. But the Sarajevo government never made ethnic cleansing their cardinal policy, as had their enemies. This does not excuse the acts of certain special units of the Bosnian Army, the summary executions of some Serbs in Sarajevo, and the establishment of several concentration camps in which sexual assaults, assassinations, and torture were reportedly regularly practiced.

In an exhaustive report to the United Nations, a special Commission of Experts, chaired by Cherif Bassiouni of DePaul University in Chicago, concluded that globally 90 percent of the crimes committed in Bosnia-Herzegovina were the responsibility of Serb extremists, 6 percent by Croat extremists, and 4 percent by Muslim extremists. These conform roughly to an assessment drafted by the American CIA.

Whatever the apportionment of blame, what is tragically clear is that the ethnic cleansers were all too successful in their work. Whether bringing the architects and perpetrators of these crimes to justice can reverse any of this remains to be seen.

QUESTIONS TO CONSIDER

1. Why did Milosevic make it his mission to set one Yugoslav group against another?
2. Did "ethnic cleansing" equal genocide?
3. Why were Muslims targeted?

Middle Managers of Genocide

Ed Vulliamy,

The Guardian, *London, Correspondent*

Almost four years ago, a television reporter and I stumbled into a place that bewildered and outraged the world. Omarska was a concentration camp in northwestern Bosnia run by Bosnian Serbs and dedicated to the humiliation and murder of Muslims and Croats. It seemed unbelievable that a network of such camps—with their echo of the Third Reich—could have existed in the heart of Europe, hidden from view for three months while thousands were slaughtered and those who remained were kept skeletal, bloodied by torture and living in abject, desolate terror.

Now, with Bosnia's guns at least temporarily silenced, comes the bitter reckoning. On May 7, one of Omarska's most notorious alleged torturers and killers, Dusko Tadic, took his place in the dock at the war crimes tribunal in The Hague, standing where no man has stood since Göring and Hess, charged with crimes against humanity. (I am obliged to testify at the trial as a witness for the prosecution.) But the reckoning is more than a judicial matter. It is an attempt to try to understand the most ferocious carnage to blight Europe in fifty years. To understand the war, I had to return to the iron-ore mine that had housed the accursed concentration camp.

In 1992 it took five putrid summer days to argue our way into the camp. But now the road is empty at the turnoff for Omarska. Flakes of snow, which mute all sound and drape the mine in virgin white, have overlaid what happened here. It is seven below zero, but our shivers are not from the cold. Children play with sleds in the yard behind the gate. A couple of stray mongrels now frolic in and out of the jaw of a hydraulic door.

In 1992, this tarmac was a killing yard, the bodies loaded onto trucks by bulldozer. Omarska was a place where cruelty and mass murder had become a form of recreation. The guards were often drunk and singing while they tortured. A prisoner called Fikret Harambasic was castrated by one of his fellow inmates before being beaten to death. One inmate was made to bark like a dog and lap at a puddle of motor oil while a guard and his mates from the

From Ed Vulliamy, "Middle Managers of Genocide," *The Nation* (June 10, 1996): 11–15. Reprinted with permission.

village jumped up and down on his back until he was dead. The guards would make videos of this butchery for their home entertainment. But the most extraordinary hallmark of the carnage was its grotesque intimacy. People knew their torturers, and had often grown up alongside them.

The mine installations have become emblems of evil: Rusty boxcars sit along the railway tracks leading out of the complex. In 1992, this rolling stock was loaded with Muslim deportees. Spidery iron tentacles, conveyor belts and limbs of machinery link one shed to another, silent and skeletal like the inmates that were packed inside.

Now, three sentries stop us. Two of these lads are from the village of Omarska itself, and had worked at the mine. "Nothing happened here," asserts a bright-eyed 28-year-old who was employed as a mine technician and has stayed on with the security staff, now in military uniform. Iron ore was processed here, he says, up until the end of 1992. "So how can it have been any kind of camp in August that year? We are from Omarska, we would have known." He elaborates: "They came here recently, the Americans, looking for mass graves, but they didn't find any. There are no mass graves here. There was no camp—ever." The technician's friend and co-sentry is only 24, from the village but "too young to have worked at the mine." He says: "I blame the journalists. The Muslims paid the media, and the television pictures were forged." There is a fascination with deception. "Anyone could do that," says the 28-year-old.

We ask them their names. The answer from the technician, suddenly harsh, is unexpected. "We had a nice chat, but names are a secret. The Muslims know me, and I know them. But they have to produce evidence of what I did. These days, they can just come up to you in the street and take you to The Hague. That's how they work."

"Did you know Dusko Tadic?" I ask. They shrug and mumble. "Not well. He had a nice cafe in Kozarac... There was no camp here..."

At the briefing in August 1992 at the Prijedor town hall, from where Omarska was administered, the authorities insisted that there was no camp, only an "investigation center." (It was in the town hall that I briefly met Tadic that year.) The figure responsible for day-to-day administration of the camp was Milan Kovacevic, a man with a swashbuckling mustache and a "US Marines" T-shirt. He decreed then that there was nothing the world could teach the Serbs about concentration camps, since he had been raised in one—Jasenovac, where the Croatian Nazi-puppet regime imprisoned and killed thousands of Serbs, Jews and Croatian dissidents between 1941 and 1945. After our discovery of Omarska, the media circus descended and the camp was hastily closed. Kovacevic was assigned the task of explaining to the world's cameras what an "investigation center" is.

In 1992, Kovacevic's eyes were fiery with enthusiasm for what he called "a great moment in the history of the Serbs." They are still fiery now, but from some other emotion. He has a taste for homemade plum brandy, and he extracts some from his cupboard at 9 AM. It's been a good year for plums, he explains, but the jam factories are all shut. Shame to let the fruit go to waste.

Kovacevic is also a medical man, now director of the town hospital of Prijedor. Despite growing up "to learn that all Germans were killers," he elected to go to Germany to study anesthesiology. He is still a proud nationalist who "wanted to make this a Serb land, without Muslims." But his certainty about the ends conceals doubt about the means. What about burning the Muslim houses along the road? Was that necessary, or a moment of madness? Kovacevic proceeds cautiously, accompanied by a second glass of brandy: "Both things. A necessary fight and a moment of madness. The

11

houses were burned at the beginning, when people were losing control. People weren't behaving normally." This comes as a surprise. Was it all a terrible mistake? "To be sure, it was a terrible mistake." A third glass, and suddenly, unprompted: "We knew very well what happened at Auschwitz and Dachau, and we knew very well how it started and how it was done. What we did was not the same as Auschwitz or Dachau, but it was a mistake. It was planned to have a camp, but not a concentration camp."

Usually it is only "enemies of the Serbian people" who invoke Auschwitz when talking about Omarska. But the anesthetist plows boldly on. He has never had this conversation before, he says. In fact, no one in Bosnia has had this conversation before. "Omarska," he continues, "was planned as a camp, but was turned into something else because of this loss of control. I cannot explain the loss of control. You could call it collective madness."

Another glass of brandy to steel the spirit, and for reasons not hard to guess, his childhood in Jasenovac comes to mind. "Six hundred thousand were killed in Jasenovac," he muses. "I was taken there as a baby, by my aunt. My mother was in the mountains, hiding. We remember everything. History is made that way." But Jasenovac was run by Croats; why did the Serbs turn on the Muslims? Kovacevic straightens himself. "There is a direct connection between what happened to the Muslims in our camps and the fact that there had been some Muslim soldiers in the [pro-Nazi] Greater Croatia. They committed war crimes, and now it is the other way round."

In Omarska, he says, "there were not more than 100 killed, whereas Jasenovac was a killing factory." Only 100 killed at Omarska? He blushes. "I said there were 100 *killed*, not died." Then Kovacevic loses his way and throws off caution: "Oh, I don't know how many were killed in there; God knows. It's a wind tunnel,

this part of the world, a hurricane blowing to and fro…"

By now the cheaply paneled room is steaming with the exhaled fumes of fast-disappearing cigarettes, a fifth glass and talk of death. So, Doctor, who planned this madness? "It all looks very well planned if your view is from New York," he says. He edges forward on his low chair, as if to whisper some personal advice. "But here, when everything is burning, and breaking apart inside people's heads—this was something for the psychiatrists. These people should all have been taken to the psychiatrist, but there wasn't enough time."

In 1992, Kovacevic did not hide his role in operating the camp, but now The Hague is becoming serious. Were you part of this insanity, Doctor? "If someone acquitted me, saying that I was not part of that collective madness, then I would admit that this was not true … If things go wrong in the hospital, then I am guilty. If you have to do things by killing people, well—that is my personal secret. Now my hair is white. I don't sleep so well."

Kovacevic's boss was the mayor of Prijedor, Milomir Stakic. I remember him barking in 1992 about an armed Islamic conspiracy against the Serbs, coordinated by the United States. At the time he was the man with the authority to grant or refuse access to Omarska. When I meet Stakic again, I find out he is also a medical man, director of the daycare health center in Prijedor, not too far from Omarska. His specialization in neuropsychiatry was interrupted by war and political office. Dr. Stakic introduces a fellow with a menacing air, Viktor Kondic, whom he calls his deputy at the health center.

Stakic swivels back and forth in his chair as he speaks. "As a doctor," he says, "I saw many wounded and mutilated people. The question was: Do the Serbs stay on their knees, or go back to Jasenovac a second time?" If there was a threat to the Serbs, was the reaction perhaps a little too much? "No," he snaps. What about Omarska? Kondic intervenes quickly and disagreeably. "Omarska was a mine. An iron-ore mine. That is all." The reports, the television pictures? Dr. Stakic clarifies: "They were pictures of Serbs in Muslim camps. There were no prisoners there."

Then comes an immediate negation: "Omarska was for Muslims with illegal weapons. Omarska was not a hotel"—he manages his only smile, and it is not an agreeable one—"but Omarska was not a concentration camp."

"The Serbs go to extremes only when their freedom is threatened," says Stakic, suddenly and oddly. "Unfortunately," chimes in Kondic, who now describes himself as "a lawyer" (we later find out he is a secret policeman) and whose eyes roll skyward, "we learned to defend our freedom in concentration camps." There ensues a long, torturous conversation not about Omarska but about Jasenovac. The wintry night has fallen, the streets outside are still, Prijedor is wrapped in fog. Within there is a leaden silence, until Stakic volunteers a strange remark: "It is very brave of you to be sitting here like this, with us so late in the evening."

The journey to Omarska in 1992 began and ended in the Serbian capital of Belgrade. Upon arrival, we were welcomed by a senior middle manager of the proclaimed Serbian Republic of Bosnia-Herzegovina, Professor Nikola Koljevic. He was to supervise our access to Omarska.

An expert on Shakespeare, the impish Koljevic has seduced many Westerners with his ample quoting of the Bard and command of English. The day after we finally found the camps, his invitation to tea and cakes at a smart hotel back in Belgrade was irresistible. "So you found them," he said sardonically, "congratulations!" And then, in a piquant voice that evoked his favorite Shakespearean character,

Iago, he embarked on a double-edged reproach: "It took you a long time to find them, didn't it? Three months! And so near *Venice*! All you people could think about was poor, sophisticated Sarajevo. Ha-ha!" And then, with a chill in his voice: "None of you ever had your holidays at Omarska, did you? No Olympic games in Prijedor!"

I find him again, in wintry Banja Luka, in 1996. Koljevic walks over to the window and stares down at the people trudging through the slush. This miserable place has achieved what it wanted; it has "won" its war: every Muslim gone, every mosque disappeared without a trace. Koljevic, transfixed, loses his flow and begins to talk to himself: "Bones," he mutters. "Bones, we were digging up the bones." His eyes widen unpleasantly; he appears hypnotized, his imagination ambushed. "The bones of our dead from 1941. We dug them up to give them proper burial on Serbian land... We found shoes. Children's shoes. How much more alive a shoe is than bones..." (This was a macabre prologue to the war, in the late eighties: a Serbian cult of exhuming their World War II dead.) Then the professor suddenly comes to his senses. "Er... I'm just trying to illustrate the psychology." Finally, I feel, we are approaching an answer to the question: How did Omarska happen?

What the Serbs have done is to project their own obsessive and disastrous "racial memory" (Koljevic's term) onto their perceived enemies. The Serbs' inimitable cult of the victim demanded that they create victims. Their experience of concentration camps demanded that they create concentration camps. They lie and manipulate, but insist on a conspiracy of lies and manipulation against them. When they look into the mirror they see someone they must call their enemy, so as not to see themselves. When they look at history they must contort it, lest they see what they do. They must rewrite the history they defile.

And then there is the psychodrama of the restless dead, of Professor Koljevic's bones. The Serbs exhumed the bones of their own dead from World War II, only to bury their enemies in mass graves. Now they exhume those victims and move them away from the glare of the Hague investigations, meanwhile disinterring their own relatives for reburial on "Serbian" soil. The joke is that the only people enjoying freedom of movement under the Dayton plan are the dead.

Professor Koljevic is fascinated by victims and masters. "The basic problem with Muslims," he says, "is their problem with equality. Psychologically, historically, they are either masters or servants. Now they want to be masters again." It is a description not of the Muslims but of the Serbs. By way of farewell, the professor produces his current reading, Daniel Boorstin's *The Image*. He reads aloud from the foreword: "This book is about our art of self-deception. How we hide reality from ourselves." For the perpetrators of Bosnia's carnage, the reckoning is an opportunity to confront what they have done and exorcise it—much as the Germans did out of the ashes of the Third Reich. But, undefeated, the Serbs choose to "hide reality from themselves." They think they were right, and they can think it again.

Thousands of miles away this spring, a book is published—Daniel Goldhagen's *Hitler's Willing Executioners*—positing the terrifying notion that it was a whole society that unleashed the Nazi Holocaust, not an elite that poisoned the minds of an otherwise innocent people. We had the same argument here, over and over again: Can such a whirlwind of violence be dictated by an elite that dupes an otherwise kindly, boozy folk?

Here at the village of Omarska, in the shadow of the accursed mine, everyone knew and nobody objected. There are soldiers and pretty girls sipping coffee at the Wiski Bar where the main street meets the railway sid-

ings that run into the mine. For four months, as they freebooted around the scrappy streets, these people were yards away from the screaming and the mutilation. They would have watched the "ethnic cleansing" convoys pass, out on the road to nowhere. I was part of such a convoy of 1,600 wretched Muslim deportees myself; we were herded over the mountains at gunpoint, through a terrifying gantlet of hatred and spitting, or else cold nonchalance, by the Serbs who beheld us from the roadside.

These people in Omarska's Wiski Bar, listening to Madonna on the jukebox, would have watched the trucks enter Camp Omarska full of people, only to come out empty. Perhaps they spat then, too. But now, in the frozen village, we are told, "There was no camp here—ever."

Meanwhile, the outside world, as Professor Koljevic rightly mocked, failed to uncover Omarska, "so near Venice." The media and the politicians cared for a few days once Omarska was forced into the spotlight, but then the world did as little as possible about it. Now, a few bloody years later, NATO's commanding admiral, Leighton Smith, is breaking through Omarska, leading platoons of writers from glossy magazines and experts from the human rights industry in a search for buried bones. When there was everything to be done, we pretended to know nothing. Today, when there is so little left to do, we want to know everything. Such is the dark triumph of the middle managers of genocide.

QUESTIONS TO CONSIDER

1. Describe Omarska.
2. What role did Kovacevic play at Omarska?
3. What did Professor Koljevic do in relation to Omarska?
4. The author compares what happened at Omarska with Goldhagen's thesis. Is this comparison appropriate?

Bosnia: First Genocide Verdict May Bolster Other Cases

Kathleen Knox,

Radio Free Europe, Correspondent

The international war crimes tribunal's guilty verdict for Bosnian Serb General Radislav Krstic yesterday was the Hague court's first conviction on a charge of genocide in the wars that broke up Yugoslavia. The case sets a precedent for the tribunal and is likely to have ramifications for Krstic's superiors.

Prague, 3 August 2001 [Radio Free Europe/Radio Liberty (RFE/RL)]—"In July 1995, General Krstic, individually, you agreed to evil, and this is why today, this trial chamber convicts you and sentences you to 46 years in prison." That was the verdict pronounced by Presiding Judge Almiro Rodrigues yesterday as he sentenced former Bosnian Serb General Radislav Krstic for the 1995 massacre of up to 8,000 unarmed Bosnian Muslim men in the UN "safe haven" of Srebrenica—the most notorious atrocity in Europe since World War II.

The verdict by the International Criminal Tribunal for the former Yugoslavia (ICTY) in The Hague was the court's first conviction on a charge of genocide relating to the Yugoslav wars. ICTY spokesman Jim Landale told RFE/RL the judgment was a triumph for the 8-year-old tribunal:

Well, this is a landmark judgement today at the tribunal. While we have had other people charged with genocide, and, in fact, two people acquitted of genocide, this is the first time any individual has been convicted of genocide. So, it is an extremely significant development for the tribunal.

The verdict is likely to have an impact beyond Krstic himself. Observers say it will have far-reaching ramifications for other suspects from the former Yugoslavia. Those include former Bosnian Serb leader Radovan Karadzic and his top general Ratko Mladic—both of whom have been indicted for genocide—and former Yugoslav President Slobodan Milosevic, who is awaiting trial in The Hague on lesser charges of crimes against humanity that are limited to his actions in Kosovo.

Richard Goldstone, the former chief prosecutor for both the Rwanda and former Yugoslavia tribunals, welcomed the verdict as a victory for international justice:

The Prosecutor Carla del Ponte has indicated that [further] charges [against Milosevic] will be coming, and I think that's very important, but the significance of [yesterday's ruling is] only going to be relevant if and when Milosevic will be indicted for crimes which are directly related to what happened in Bosnia.

Avril McDonald, a lawyer working at the Asser Institute in The Hague, was in the courtroom to hear the verdict. She notes that while Krstic's conviction doesn't mark the first international genocide verdict—the Rwanda tribunal in Tanzania has already handed down nine such convictions—the ruling is a harbinger of how future Yugoslav cases will be handled:

Krstic was merely executing a plan which had been cooked up by [his superiors]. Krstic was the second-most senior military person in Bosnia at the most relevant time, under Mladic he was the most senior person. Responsibility for planning the genocide—as the courts said, the ethnic cleansing became a genocide—laid with highers-up. Who could that be? Probably Karadzic, Mladic, and Milosevic. So it's only going to help any case against them. Milosevic hasn't yet been charged for Bosnia but this is definitely going to make it easier.

McDonald says another significant aspect to the Krstic case is that it contributes to determining what constitutes genocide, especially as the judges said they had been influenced by earlier verdicts:

> What that appeals chamber found was that a single person could actually commit genocide. It's not necessary to be part of a group to commit genocide. It all turns on the intent the person has, and one person acting alone could conceivably commit genocide. So that was something new. The Rwandan tribunal has already found genocide has been committed there, and has analyzed it pretty exhaustively. [This] is the first attempt to analyze [genocide] within the Yugoslav context.

She said if the tribunal had been unable to get a conviction against Krstic for the Srebrenica massacre—which had been painstakingly investigated—it would not be able to get one in any other case. But she believes that despite the conviction, the sentence was very lenient:

> Given that I felt the case against Krstic was pretty strong, I was quietly optimistic that they would get a conviction. So I'm very satisfied with that result, with the conviction, though not with the sentence. I believe it doesn't really reflect the gravity of the crime.

This is a view shared by many, not least the women whose husbands and sons were killed. Critics point to the 45-year sentence given to General Tihomir Blaskic, a Bosnian Croat who was convicted on lesser charges of crimes against humanity and war crimes.

The Croatian daily "Vecernji list" said Krstic's sentence makes a mockery of the victims of Srebrenica. It said: "For every person in Srebrenica he ordered to be killed, Krstic got two days of prison." But Mary Greer, the Hague representative of the non-governmental Coalition for International Justice, says it's always tricky to compare sentences.

> You could tell with the 46 years they were trying to get barely over the 45 years, which was the sentence that General Blaskic got. Obviously they are saving life sentences—life in the legal definition—for other individuals that would likely be Mladic, Karadzic, Milosevic.

Balkan Stability Pact coordinator Bodo Hombach said today he expected Karadzic and Mladic to be arrested and transferred to The Hague tribunal this year. Until that happens, Krstic's conviction will mark just the first step in bringing to justice those responsible for what happened in the fields around Srebrenica in July 1995.

(RFE/RL's Bruce Jacobs and Oleh Zwadiuk contributed to this report.)

QUESTIONS TO CONSIDER

1. Why was this verdict seen as a landmark?

2. Is it possible for a single person to commit genocide, as suggested in the reading?

The Rational Destruction of Yugoslavia

Michael Parenti,

Writer and Lecturer

In 1999, the U.S. national security state—which has been involved throughout the world in subversion, sabotage, terrorism, torture, drug trafficking, and death squads—launched round-the-clock aerial attacks against Yugoslavia for 78 days, dropping 20,000 tons of bombs and killing thousands of women, children, and men. All this was done out of humanitarian concern for Albanians in Kosovo. Or so we were asked to believe. In the span of a few months, President Clinton bombed four countries: Sudan, Afghanistan, Iraq repeatedly, and Yugoslavia massively. At the same time, the United States was involved in proxy wars in Angola, Mexico (Chiapas), Colombia, East Timor, and various other places. And U.S. forces are deployed on every continent and ocean, with some 300 major overseas support bases—all in the name of peace, democracy, national security, and humanitarianism.

While showing themselves ready and willing to bomb Yugoslavia on behalf of an ostensibly oppressed minority in Kosovo, U.S. leaders have made no moves against the Czech Republic for its mistreatment of the Romany people (gypsies), or Britain for oppressing the Catholic minority in Northern Ireland, or the Hutu for the mass murder of a half million Tutsi in Rwanda—not to mention the French who were complicit in that massacre. Nor have U.S. leaders considered launching "humanitarian bombings" against the Turkish people for what their leaders have done to the Kurds, or the Indonesian people because their generals killed over 200,000 East Timorese and were continuing such slaughter through the summer of 1999, or the Guatemalans for the Guatemalan military's systematic extermination of tens of thousands of Mayan villagers. In such cases, U.S. leaders not only tolerated such atrocities but were actively complicit with the perpetrators—who usually happened to be faithful client-state allies dedicated to helping Washington make the world safe for the Fortune 500.

Why then did U.S. leaders wage an unrestrainedly murderous assault upon Yugoslavia?

THE THIRD WORLDIZATION OF YUGOSLAVIA

Yugoslavia was built on an idea, namely that the Southern Slavs would not remain weak and divided peoples, squabbling among themselves and easy prey to outside imperial interests. Together they could form a substantial territory capable of its own economic development. Indeed, after World War II, socialist Yugoslavia became a viable nation and an economic success. Between 1960 and 1980 it had one of the most vigorous growth rates: a decent standard of living, free medical care and education, a guaranteed right to a job, one-month vacation with pay, a literacy rate of over 90 percent, and a life expectancy of 72 years. Yugoslavia also offered its multi-ethnic citizenry affordable public transportation, housing, and utilities, with a not-for-profit economy that was mostly publicly owned. This was not the kind of country global capitalism would normally tolerate. Still, socialistic Yugoslavia was allowed to exist for 45 years because it was seen as a nonaligned buffer to the Warsaw Pact nations.

The dismemberment and mutilation of Yugoslavia was part of a concerted policy initiated by the United States and the other Western powers in 1989. Yugoslavia was the one

From Michael Parenti, *The Rational Destruction of Yugoslavia* (2002). Reprinted with permission.

country in Eastern Europe that would not voluntarily overthrow what remained of its socialist system and install a free-market economic order. In fact, Yugoslavs were proud of their postwar economic development and of their independence from both the Warsaw Pact and NATO. The U.S. goal has been to transform the Yugoslav nation into a Third-World region, a cluster of weak right-wing principalities with the following characteristics:

- incapable of charting an independent course of self-development;
- a shattered economy and natural resources completely accessible to multinational corporate exploitation, including the enormous mineral wealth in Kosovo;
- an impoverished, but literate and skilled population forced to work at subsistence wages, constituting a cheap labor pool that will help depress wages in western Europe and elsewhere;
- dismantled petroleum, engineering, mining, fertilizer, and automobile industries, and various light industries, that offer no further competition with existing Western producers.

U.S. policymakers also want to abolish Yugoslavia's public sector services and social programs—for the same reason they want to abolish our public sector services and social programs. The ultimate goal is the privatization and Third Worldization of Yugoslavia, as it is the Third Worldization of the United States and every other nation. In some respects, the fury of the West's destruction of Yugoslavia is a backhanded tribute to that nation's success as an alternative form of development, and to the pull it exerted on neighboring populations both East and West.

In the late 1960s and 1970s, Belgrade's leaders, not unlike the Communist leadership in Poland, sought simultaneously to expand the country's industrial base and increase consumer goods, a feat they intended to accomplish by borrowing heavily from the West. But with an enormous IMF debt came the inevitable demand for "restructuring," a harsh austerity program that brought wage freezes, cutbacks in public spending, increased unemployment,

and the abolition of worker-managed enterprises. Still, much of the economy remained in the not-for-profit public sector, including the Trepca mining complex in Kosovo, described in the *New York Times* as "war's glittering prize ... the most valuable piece of real estate in the Balkans ... worth at least $5 billion" in rich deposits of coal, lead, zinc, cadmium, gold, and silver.

That U.S. leaders have consciously sought to dismember Yugoslavia is not a matter of speculation but of public record. In November 1990, the Bush administration pressured Congress into passing the 1991 Foreign Operations Appropriations Act, which provided that any part of Yugoslavia failing to declare independence within six months would lose U.S. financial support. The law demanded separate elections in each of the six Yugoslav republics, and mandated U.S. State Department approval of both election procedures and results as a condition for any future aid. Aid would go only to the separate republics, not to the Yugoslav government, and only to those forces whom Washington defined as "democratic," meaning right-wing, free-market, separatist parties.

Another goal of U.S. policy has been media monopoly and ideological control. In 1997, in what remained of Serbian Bosnia, the last radio station critical of NATO policy was forcibly shut down by NATO "peacekeepers." The story in the *New York Times* took elaborate pains to explain why silencing the only existing dissident Serbian station was necessary for advancing democratic pluralism. The Times used the term "hardline" eleven times to describe Bosnian Serb leaders who opposed the shutdown and who failed to see it as "a step toward bringing about responsible news coverage in Bosnia."

Likewise, a portion of Yugoslav television remained in the hands of people who refused to view the world as do the U.S. State Department, the White House, and the corporate-owned U.S. news media, and this was not to be tolerated. The NATO bombings destroyed the two government TV channels and dozens of local radio and television stations, so that by the summer of 1999 the only TV one could see in Belgrade, when I visited that city, were the private channels along with CNN, German television, and various U.S. programs. Yugoslavia's sin was not that it had a media monopoly but that the publicly owned portion of its media deviated from the western media monopoly that blankets most of the world, including Yugoslavia itself.

In 1992, another blow was delivered against Belgrade: international sanctions. Led by the United States, a freeze was imposed on all trade to and from Yugoslavia, with disastrous results for the economy: hyperinflation, mass unemployment of up to 70 percent, malnourishment, and the collapse of the health care system.

DIVIDE AND CONQUER

One of the great deceptions, notes Joan Phillips, is that "those who are mainly responsible for the bloodshed in Yugoslavia—not the Serbs, Croats or Muslims, but the Western powers—are depicted as saviors." While pretending to work for harmony, U.S. leaders supported the most divisive, reactionary forces from Croatia to Kosovo.

In Croatia, the West's man-of-the-hour was Franjo Tudjman, who claimed in a book he authored in 1989, that "the establishment of Hitler's new European order can be justified by the need to be rid of the Jews," and that only 900,000 Jews, not six million, were killed in the Holocaust. Tudjman's government adopted the fascist Ustasha checkered flag and anthem. Tudjman presided over the forced evacuation of over half a million Serbs from Croatia between 1991 and 1995, replete with rapes and summary executions. This included the 200,000 from Krajina in 1995, whose expulsion was facilitated by attacks from NATO war planes and missiles. Needless to say, U.S. leaders did noth-

ing to stop and much to assist these atrocities, while the U.S. media looked the other way. Tudjman and his cronies now reside in obscene wealth while the people of Croatia are suffering the afflictions of the free market paradise. Tight controls have been imposed on Croatian media, and anyone who criticizes President Tudjman's government risks incarceration. Yet the White House hails Croatia as a new democracy.

In Bosnia, U.S. leaders supported the Muslim fundamentalist, Alija Izetbegovic, an active Nazi in his youth, who has called for strict religious control over the media and now wants to establish an Islamic Bosnian republic. Izetbegovic himself does not have the support of most Bosnian Muslims. He was decisively outpolled in his bid for the presidency yet managed to take over that office by cutting a mysterious deal with frontrunner Fikret Abdic. Bosnia is now under IMF and NATO regency. It is not permitted to develop its own internal resources, nor allowed to extend credit or self-finance through an independent monetary system. Its state-owned assets, including energy, water, telecommunications, media, and transportation, have been sold off to private firms at garage sale prices.

In the former Yugoslavia, NATO powers have put aside neoimperialism and have opted for out-and-out colonial occupation. In early 1999, the democratically elected president of Republika Srpska, the Serb ministate in Bosnia, who had defeated NATO's chosen candidate, was removed by NATO troops because he proved less than fully cooperative with NATO's "high representative" in Bosnia. The latter retains authority to impose his own solutions and remove elected officials who prove in any way obstructive. This too was represented in the western press as a necessary measure to advance democracy.

In Kosovo, we see the same dreary pattern. The U.S. gave aid and encouragement to violently right-wing separatist forces such as the self-styled Kosovo Liberation Army, previously considered a terrorist organization by Washington. The KLA has been a longtime player in the enormous heroin trade that reaches to Switzerland, Austria, Belgium, Germany, Hungary, the Czech Republic, Norway, and Sweden. KLA leaders had no social program other than the stated goal of cleansing Kosovo of all non-Albanians, a campaign that had been going on for decades. Between 1945 and 1998, the non-Albanian Kosovar population of Serbs, Roma, Turks, Gorani (Muslim Slavs), Montenegrins, and several other ethnic groups shrank from some 60 percent to about 20 percent. Meanwhile, the Albanian population grew from 40 to 80 percent (not the 90 percent repeatedly reported in the press), benefiting from a higher birth rate, a heavy influx of immigrants from Albania, and the systematic intimidation and expulsion of Serbs.

In 1987, in an early untutored moment of truth, the *New York Times* reported: "Ethnic Albanians in the Government have manipulated public funds and regulations to take over land belonging to Serbs ... Slavic Orthodox churches have been attacked, and flags have been torn down. Wells have been poisoned and crops burned. Slavic boys have been knifed, and some young ethnic Albanians have been told by their elders to rape Serbian girls ... As the Slavs flee the protracted violence, Kosovo is becoming what ethnic Albanian nationalists have been demanding for years ... an 'ethnically pure' Albanian region ..." Ironically, while the Serbs were repeatedly charged with ethnic cleansing, Serbia itself is now the only multi-ethnic society left in the former Yugoslavia, with some twenty-six nationality groups including thousands of Albanians who live in and around Belgrade.

DEMONIZING THE SERBS

The propaganda campaign to demonize the Serbs fits the larger policy of the Western powers. The Serbs were targeted for demonization because they were the largest nationality and the one most opposed to the breakup of Yugoslavia. None other than Charles Boyd, former deputy commander of the U.S. European command, commented on it in 1994: "The popular image of this war in Bosnia is one of unrelenting Serb expansionism. Much of what the Croatians call 'the occupied territories' is land that has been held by Serbs for more that three centuries. The same is true of most Serb land in Bosnia ... In short the Serbs were not trying to conquer new territory, but merely to hold onto what was already theirs." While U.S. leaders claim they want peace, Boyd concludes, they have encouraged a deepening of the war.

But what of the atrocities they committed? All sides committed atrocities, but the reporting was consistently one-sided. Grisly incidents of Croat and Muslim atrocities against the Serbs rarely made it into the U.S. press, and when they did they were accorded only passing mention. Meanwhile Serb atrocities were played up and sometimes even fabricated, as we shall see. Recently, three Croatian generals were indicted by the Hague War Crimes Tribunal for the bombardment and deaths of Serbs in Krajina and elsewhere. Where were U.S. leaders and U.S. television crews when these war crimes were being committed? John Ranz, chair of Survivors of the Buchenwald Concentration Camp, USA, asks: Where were the TV cameras when hundreds of Serbs were slaughtered by Muslims near Srebrenica? The official line, faithfully parroted in the U.S. media, is that the Serbs committed all the atrocities at Srebrenica.

Before uncritically ingesting the atrocity stories dished out by U.S. leaders and the corporate-owned news media, we might recall the five hundred premature babies whom Iraqi soldiers laughingly ripped from incubators in Kuwait, a story repeated and believed until exposed as a total fabrication years later. During the Bosnian war in 1993, the Serbs were accused of having an official policy of rape. "Go forth and rape" a Bosnian Serb commander supposedly publicly instructed his troops. The source of that story never could be traced. The commander's name was never produced. As far as we know, no such utterance was ever made. Even the *New York Times* belatedly ran a tiny retraction, coyly allowing that "the existence of 'a systematic rape policy' by the Serbs remains to be proved."

Bosnian Serb forces supposedly raped anywhere from 25,000 to 100,000 Muslim women. The Bosnian Serb army numbered not more than 30,000 or so, many of whom were engaged in desperate military engagements. A representative from Helsinki Watch noted that stories of massive Serbian rapes originated with the Bosnian Muslim and Croatian governments and had no credible supporting evidence. Common sense would dictate that these stories be treated with the utmost skepticism—and not be used as an excuse for an aggressive and punitive policy against Yugoslavia.

The mass rape propaganda theme was resuscitated in 1999 to justify NATO's renewed attacks on Yugoslavia. A headline in the *San Francisco Examiner* tells us: "Serb Tactic Is Organized Rape, Kosovo Refugees Say." Only at the bottom of the story, in the nineteenth paragraph, do we read that reports gathered by the Kosovo mission of the Organization for Security and Cooperation in Europe found no such organized rape policy. The actual number of rapes were in the dozens "and not many dozens," according to the OSCE spokesperson. This same story did note that the U.N. War Crimes Tribunal sentenced a Bosnian Croat military commander to ten years in prison for failing to stop his troops from raping Muslim women in 1993—an atrocity we heard little about when it was happening.

The Serbs were blamed for the infamous Sarajevo market massacre of 1992. But according to the report leaked out on French TV, Western intelligence knew that it was Muslim operatives who had bombed Bosnian civilians in the marketplace in order to induce NATO involvement. Even international negotiator David Owen, who worked with Cyrus Vance, admitted in his memoir that the NATO powers knew all along that it was a Muslim bomb. However, the well-timed fabrication served its purpose of inducing the United Nations to go along with the U.S.-sponsored sanctions.

On one occasion, notes Barry Lituchy, the *New York Times* ran a photo purporting to be of Croats grieving over Serbian atrocities when in fact the murders had been committed by Bosnian Muslims. The *Times* printed an obscure retraction the following week.

We repeatedly have seen how "rogue nations" are designated and demonized. The process is predictably transparent. First, the leaders are targeted. Qaddafi of Libya was a "Hitlerite megalomaniac" and a "madman." Noriega of Panama was a "a swamp rat," one of the world's worst "drug thieves and scums," and "a Hitler admirer." Saddam Hussein of Iraq was "the Butcher of Baghdad," a "madman," and "worse than Hitler." Each of these leaders then had their countries attacked by U.S. forces and U.S.-led sanctions. What they really had in common was that each was charting a somewhat independent course of self-development or somehow was not complying with the dictates of the global free market and the U.S. national security state.

Yugoslav president Slobodan Milosevic has been described by Bill Clinton as "a new Hitler." Yet he was not always considered so. At first, the Western press, viewing the ex-banker as a bourgeois Serbian nationalist who might hasten the break-up of the federation, hailed him as a "charismatic personality." Only later, when they saw him as an obstacle rather than a tool, did they begin to depict him as the demon who "started all four wars." This was too much even for the managing editor of the U.S. establishment journal *Foreign Affairs*, Fareed Zakaria. He noted in the *New York Times* that Milosevic who rules "an impoverished country that has not attacked its neighbors—is no Adolf Hitler. He is not even Saddam Hussein."

Some opposition radio stations and newspapers were reportedly shut down during the NATO bombing. But, during my trip to Belgrade in August 1999, I observed nongovernmental media and opposition party newspapers going strong. There are more opposition parties in the Yugoslav parliament than in any other European parliament. Yet the government is repeatedly labeled a dictatorship. Milosevic was elected as president of Yugoslavia in a contest that foreign observers said had relatively few violations. As of the end of 1999, he presided over a coalition government that included four parties. Opposition groups openly criticized and demonstrated against his government. Yet he was called a dictator.

The propaganda campaign against Belgrade has been so relentless that prominent personages on the Left—who oppose the NATO policy against Yugoslavia—have felt compelled to genuflect before this demonization orthodoxy. Thus do they reveal themselves as having been influenced by the very media propaganda machine they criticize on so many other issues. To reject the demonized image of Milosevic and of the Serbian people is not to idealize them or claim they are faultless or free of crimes. It is merely to challenge the one-sided propaganda that laid the grounds for NATO's destruction of Yugoslavia.

MORE ATROCITY STORIES

Atrocities (murders and rapes) occur in every war, which is not to condone them. Indeed, murders and rapes occur in many peacetime communities. What the media propaganda campaign against Yugoslavia charged was that atrocities were conducted on a mass genocidal scale. Such charges were used to justify the murderous aerial assault by NATO forces.

Up until the bombings began in March 1999, the conflict in Kosovo had taken 2000 lives altogether from both sides, according to Kosovo Albanian sources. Yugoslavian sources had put the figure at 800. In either case, such casualties reveal a limited insurgency, not genocide. The forced expulsion policy began after the NATO bombings, with thousands being uprooted by Serb forces mostly in areas where the KLA was operating or was suspected of operating. In addition, if the unconfirmed reports by the ethnic Albanian refugees can be believed, there was much plundering and instances of summary execution by Serbian paramilitary forces—who were unleashed after the NATO bombing started.

We should keep in mind that tens of thousands fled Kosovo because of the bombings, or because the province was the scene of sustained ground fighting between Yugoslav forces and the KLA, or because they were just afraid and hungry. An Albanian woman crossing into Macedonia was eagerly asked by a news crew if she had been forced out by Serb police. She responded: "There were no Serbs. We were frightened of the [NATO] bombs." During the bombings, an estimated 70,000 to 100,000 Serbian residents of Kosovo took flight (mostly north but some to the south), as did thousands of Roma and other non-Albanian ethnic groups. Were these people ethnically cleansing themselves? Or were they not fleeing the bombing and the ground war?

The *New York Times* reported that "a major purpose of the NATO effort is to end the Serb atrocities that drove more than one million Albanians from their homes." So, we are told to believe, the refugee tide was caused not by the ground war against the KLA and not by the massive NATO bombing but by unspecified atrocities. The bombing, which was the major cause of the refugee problem was now seen as the solution. The refugee problem created in part by the massive aerial attacks was now treated as justification for such attacks, a way of putting pressure on Milosevic to allow "the safe return of ethnic Albanian refugees."

While Kosovo Albanians were leaving in great numbers—usually well-clothed and in good health, some riding their tractors, trucks, or cars, many of them young men of recruitment age—they were described as being "slaughtered." Serbian attacks on KLA strongholds and the forced expulsion of Albanian villagers were described as "genocide." But experts in surveillance photography and wartime propaganda charged NATO with running a "propaganda campaign" on Kosovo that lacked any supporting evidence. State Department reports of mass graves and of 100,000 to 500,000 missing Albanian men "are just ludicrous," according to these independent critics.

As with the Croatian and Bosnian conflicts, the image of mass killings was hyped once again. The *Washington Post* reported that 350 ethnic Albanians "might be buried in mass graves" around a mountain village in western Kosovo. Such speculations were based on sources that NATO officials refused to identify. Getting down to specifics, the article mentions "four decomposing bodies" discovered near a large ash heap, with no details as to who they might be or how they died.

An ABC "Nightline" program made dramatic and repeated references to the "Serbian atrocities in Kosovo" while offering no specifics. Ted Kopple asked angry Albanian refugees what they had witnessed? They pointed to an old man in their group who wore a wool hat. The Serbs had thrown the man's hat to the ground and stepped on it, "because the Serbs knew that his hat was the most important thing to him," they told Kopple, who was appropriately appalled by this one example of a "war crime" offered in the hour-long program.

A widely circulated story in the *New York Times*, headlined "U.S. Report Outlines Serb Attacks in Kosovo," tells us that the State Department issued "the most comprehensive documentary record to date on atrocities." The report concludes that there had been organized rapes and systematic executions. But

reading further into the article, one finds that stories of such crimes "depend almost entirely on information from refugee accounts. There was no suggestion that American intelligence agencies had been able to verify, most, or even many, of the accounts ... and the word 'reportedly' and 'allegedly' appear throughout the document."

British journalist Audrey Gillan interviewed Kosovo refugees about atrocities and found an impressive lack of evidence. One woman caught him glancing at the watch on her wrist, while her husband told him how all the women had been robbed of their jewelry and other possessions. A spokesperson for the U.N. High Commissioner for Refugees talked of mass rapes and what sounded like hundreds of killings in three villages. When Gillan pressed him for more precise information, he reduced it drastically to five or six teenage rape victims. But he admitted that he had not spoken to any witnesses and that "we have no way of verifying these reports."

Gillan noted that some refugees had seen killings and other atrocities, but there was little to suggest that they had seen it on the scale that was being reported. Officials told him of refugees who talked of sixty or more being killed in one village and fifty in another, but Gillan "could not find one eye-witness who actually saw these things happening." It was always in some other village that the mass atrocities seem to have occurred. Yet every day western journalists reported "hundreds" of rapes and murders. Sometimes they noted in passing that the reports had yet to be substantiated, but then why were such stories being so eagerly publicized?

In contrast to its public assertions, the German Foreign Office privately denied there was any evidence that genocide or ethnic cleansing was a component of Yugoslav policy: "Even in Kosovo, an explicit political persecution linked to Albanian ethnicity is not verifiable ... The actions of the [Yugoslav] security forces [were] not directed against the Kosovo-Albanians as an ethnically defined group, but against the military opponent and its actual or alleged supporters."

Still, Milosevic was indicted as a war criminal, charged with the forced expulsion of Albanian Kosovars, and with summary executions of a hundred or so individuals. Again, alleged crimes that occurred after the NATO bombing had started were used as justification for the bombing. The biggest war criminals of all were the NATO political leaders who orchestrated the aerial campaign of death and destruction.

As the White House saw it, since the stated aim of the aerial attacks was not to kill civilians; there was no liability, only regrettable mistakes. In other words, only the professed intent of an action counted and not its ineluctable effects. But a perpetrator can be judged guilty of willful murder without explicitly intending the death of a particular victim—as with an unlawful act that the perpetrator knew would likely cause death. As George Kenney, a former State Department official under the Bush Administration, put it: "Dropping cluster bombs on highly populated urban areas doesn't result in accidental fatalities. It is purposeful terror bombing."

In the first weeks of the NATO occupation of Kosovo, tens of thousands of Serbs were driven from the province and hundreds were killed by KLA gunmen in what was described in the western press as acts of "revenge" and "retaliation," as if the victims were deserving of such a fate. Also numbering among the victims of "retribution" were the Roma, Gorani, Turks, Montenegrins, and Albanians who had "collaborated" with the Serbs by speaking Serbian, opposing separatism, and otherwise identifying themselves as Yugoslavs. Others continued to be killed or maimed by the mines planted by the KLA and the Serb military, and by the large number of NATO cluster bombs sprinkled over the land.

It was repeatedly announced in the first days of the NATO occupation that 10,000 Al-banians had been killed by the Serbs (down from the 100,000 and even 500,000 Albanian men supposedly executed during the war). No evidence was ever offered to support the 10,000 figure, nor even to explain how it was so swiftly determined—even before NATO forces had moved into most of Kosovo.

Repeatedly unsubstantiated references to "mass graves," each purportedly filled with hundreds or even thousands of Albanian victims also failed to materialize. Through the summer of 1999, the media hype about mass graves devolved into an occasional unspecified reference. The few sites actually unearthed offered up as many as a dozen bodies or sometimes twice that number, but with no certain evidence regarding causes of death or even the nationality of victims. In some cases there was reason to believe the victims were Serbs.

Lacking evidence of mass graves, by late August 1999 the *Los Angeles Times* focused on wells "as mass graves in their own right … Serbian forces apparently stuffed … many bodies of ethnic Albanians into wells during their campaign of terror." Apparently? The story itself dwelled on only one village in which the body of a 39-year-old male was found in a well, along with three dead cows and a dog. No cause was given for his death and "no other human remains were discovered." The well's owner was not identified. Again when getting down to specifics, the atrocities seem not endemic but sporadic.

ETHNIC ENMITY AND U.S. "DIPLOMACY"

Some people argue that nationalism, not class, is the real motor force behind the Yugoslav conflict. This presumes that class and ethnicity are mutually exclusive forces. In fact, ethnic enmity can be enlisted to serve class interests, as the CIA tried to do with indigenous peoples in Indochina and Nicaragua—and more recently in Bosnia.

When different national groups are living together with some measure of social and material security, they tend to get along. There is intermingling and even intermarriage. But when the economy goes into a tailspin, thanks to sanctions and IMF destabilization, then it becomes easier to induce internecine conflicts and social discombobulation. In order to hasten that process in Yugoslavia, the Western powers provided the most retrograde separatist elements with every advantage in money, organization, propaganda, arms, hired thugs, and the full might of the U.S. national security state at their backs. Once more the Balkans are to be balkanized.

NATO's attacks on Yugoslavia have been in violation of its own charter, which says it can take military action only in response to aggression committed against one of its members. Yugoslavia attacked no NATO member. U.S. leaders discarded international law and diplomacy. Traditional diplomacy is a process of negotiating disputes through give and take, proposal and counterproposal, a way of pressing one's interests only so far, arriving eventually at a solution that may leave one side more dissatisfied than the other but not to the point of forcing either party to war.

U.S. diplomacy is something else, as evidenced in its dealings with Vietnam, Nicaragua, Panama, Iraq, and now Yugoslavia. It consists of laying down a set of demands that are treated as nonnegotiable, though called "accords" or "agreements," as in the Dayton Accords or Rambouillet Agreements. The other side's reluctance to surrender completely to every condition is labeled "stonewalling," and is publicly misrepresented as an unwillingness to negotiate in good faith. U.S. leaders, we hear, run out of patience as their "offers" are "snubbed." Ultimatums are issued, then aerial destruction is delivered upon the recalcitrant nation so that it might learn to see things the way Washington does.

Milosevic balked because the Rambouillet plan, drawn up by the U.S. State Department, demanded that he hand over a large, rich region of Serbia, that is, Kosovo, to foreign occupation. The plan further stipulated that these foreign troops shall have complete occupational power over all of Yugoslavia, with immunity from arrest and with supremacy over Yugoslav police and authorities. Even more revealing of the U.S. agenda, the Rambouillet plan stated: "The economy of Kosovo shall function in accordance with free market principles."

RATIONAL DESTRUCTION

While professing to having been discomforted by the aerial destruction of Yugoslavia, many liberals and progressives were convinced that "this time" the U.S. national security state was really fighting the good fight. "Yes, the bombings don't work. The bombings are stupid!" they said at the time, "but we have to do something." In fact, the bombings were other than stupid: they were profoundly immoral. And in fact they did work; they destroyed much of what was left of Yugoslavia, turning it into a privatized, deindustrialized, recolonized, beggar-poor country of cheap labor, defenseless against capital penetration, so battered that it will never rise again, so shattered that it will never reunite, not even as a viable bourgeois country.

When the productive social capital of any part of the world is obliterated, the potential value of private capital elsewhere is enhanced—especially when the crisis faced today by western capitalism is one of overcapacity. Every agricultural base destroyed by western aerial attacks (as in Iraq) or by NAFTA and GATT (as in Mexico and elsewhere), diminishes the potential competition and increases the market opportunities for multinational corporate agribusiness. To destroy publicly-run Yugoslav factories that produced auto parts, appliances, or fertilizer—or a publicly financed Sudanese plant that produced pharmaceuticals at prices substantially below their western competitors—is to enhance the investment value of western producers. And every television or radio station closed down by NATO troops or blown up by NATO bombs extends the monopolizing dominance of the western media cartels. The aerial destruction of Yugoslavia's social capital served that purpose.

We have yet to understand the full effect of NATO's aggression. Serbia is one of the greatest sources of underground waters in Europe, and the contamination from U.S. depleted uranium and other explosives is being felt in the whole surrounding area all the way to the Black Sea. In Pancevo alone, huge amounts of ammonia were released into the air when NATO bombed the fertilizer factory. In that same city, a petrochemical plant was bombed seven times. After 20,000 tons of crude oil were burnt up in only one bombardment of an oil refinery, a massive cloud of smoke hung in the air for ten days. Some 1,400 tons of ethylene dichloride spilled into the Danube, the source of drinking water for ten million people. Meanwhile, concentrations of vinyl chloride were released into the atmosphere at more than 10,000 times the permitted level. In some areas, people have broken out in red blotches and blisters, and health officials predict sharp increases in cancer rates in the years ahead.

National parks and reservations that make Yugoslavia among thirteen of the world's richest bio-diversity countries were bombed. The depleted uranium missiles that NATO used through many parts of the country have a half-life of 4.5 billion years. It is the same depleted uranium that now delivers cancer, birth defects, and premature death upon the people of Iraq. In Novi Sad, I was told that crops were dying because of the contamination. And power transformers could not be repaired because U.N. sanctions prohibited the importation of replacement parts. The people I spoke to were facing famine and cold in the winter ahead.

With words that might make us question his humanity, the NATO commander, U.S. General Wesley Clark, boasted that the aim of the air war was to "demolish, destroy, devastate, degrade, and ultimately eliminate the essential infrastructure" of Yugoslavia. Even if Serbian atrocities had been committed, and I have no doubt that some were, where is the sense of proportionality? Paramilitary killings in Kosovo (which occurred mostly after the aerial war began) are no justification for bombing fifteen cities in hundreds of around-the-clock raids for over two months, spewing hundreds of thousands of tons of highly toxic and carcinogenic chemicals into the water, air, and soil, killing thousands of Serbs, Albanians, Roma, Turks, and others, and destroying bridges, residential areas, and over two hundred hospitals, clinics, schools, and churches, along with the productive capital of an entire nation.

A report released in London in August 1999 by the Economist Intelligence Unit concluded that the enormous damage NATO's aerial war inflicted on Yugoslavia's infrastructure will cause the economy to shrink dramatically in the next few years. Gross domestic product will drop by 40 percent this year and remain at levels far below those of a decade ago. Yugoslavia, the report predicted, will become the poorest country in Europe. Mission accomplished.

POSTSCRIPT

In mid-September 1999, the investigative journalist Diana Johnstone emailed associates in the U.S. that former U.S. ambassador to Croatia, Peter Galbraith, who had backed Tudjman's "operation storm" that drove 200,000 Serbians (mostly farming families) out of the Krajina region of Croatia four years ago, was recently in Montenegro, chiding Serbian opposition politicians for their reluctance to plunge Yugoslavia into civil war. Such a war would be brief, he assured them, and would "solve all your problems." Another strategy under consideration by U.S. leaders, heard recently in Yugoslavia, is to turn over the northern Serbian province of Vojvodina to Hungary. Vojvodina has some twenty-six nationalities including several hundred thousand persons of Hungarian descent who, on the whole, show no signs of wanting to secede, and who certainly are better treated than the larger Hungarian minorities in Rumania and Slovakia. Still, a recent $100 million appropriation from the U.S. Congress fuels separatist activity in what remains of Yugoslavia—at least until Serbia gets a government sufficiently pleasing to the free-market globalists in the West. Johnstone concludes: "With their electric power stations ruined and factories destroyed by NATO bombing, isolated, sanctioned and treated as pariahs by the West, Serbs have the choice between freezing honorably in a homeland plunged into destitution, or following the 'friendly advice' of the same people who have methodically destroyed their country. As the choice is unlikely to be unanimous one way or the other, civil war and further destruction of the country are probable."

QUESTIONS TO CONSIDER

1. Describe U.S. foreign policy goals for Yugoslavia before 1989.
2. Is Parenti justified in saying that, "NATO powers have put aside neoimperialism and have opted for out-and-out colonial occupation"?
3. What conclusion do you draw from Parenti's analysis of rape stories?
4. What role did the U.S. media play in shaping the U.S. reaction to events in Yugoslavia?
5. Describe how Parenti sees Western producers benefiting from the destruction of Yugoslavia.

MAKING CONNECTIONS

1. Is the parallel between Bosnia and the Spanish civil war appropriate?

2. Are the events in Bosnia comparable to Rwanda?

✔ RECOMMENDED RESOURCES

Mousavizadeh, Nader, ed. *The Black Book of Bosnia: The Consequences of Appeasement.* New York: Basic Books, 1996.

Neier, Aryeh. *War Crimes: Brutality, Genocide, Terror, and the Struggle for Justice.* New York: Times Books, 1998.

Silber, Laura, and Allan Little. *Yugoslavia: Death of a Nation.* New York: Penguin Books, 1997.

CHAPTER 14

A TOUGH NEIGHBORHOOD: THE MIDDLE EAST

IRAQ

Before Iraq's attack on Kmall in 1990, the U.S. shared intelligence with Iraq, supplied the dictator Saddam Hussein with cluster bombs through a Chilean front company, and facilitated Iraq's acquisition of the chemical and biological precursors to weapons of mass destruction. It was Donald H. Rumsfeld, as special presidential envoy in fact, who met with Hussein in 1983 and paved the way for normalization of relations between the United States and Iraq.

American assistance to Iraq helped it prevent Iraqi collapse at the hands of advancing Iranian troops. The Reagan administration preferred a weaker Iran; U.S. valuable intelligence was provided, which enabled Iraq to respond decisively to Iranian troop buildups. Concurrently, the Reagan administration removed Iraq from the State Department terrorism list, despite congressional objections. First drawn up in 1979, it listed South Yemen, Syria, and Libya in addition to Iraq as potential terrorist threats. The Reagan administration actively aided Iraq's weapons buildup. When UN weapons inspectors surveyed Iraq after the 1991 Gulf War, they compiled long lists of chemicals, missile components, and computers from American suppliers such as Union Carbide and Honeywell.

Dozens of biological agents were shipped to Iraq during the 1980s under license from the U.S. Commerce Department—supplying the Iraqi biological warfare program. In 1987 the Iraqi airpower used these chemical agents against Kurds in the north, as part of a "scorched earth" policy to eliminate rebel-controlled villages. United States policy supporting Hussein continued until the Iraqi invasion of Kuwait in 1990.

On the morning of September 11, 2001, terrorists crashed two airliners into the twin towers of New York's World Trade Center and another into the Pentagon, the home offices of the U.S. Department of Defense, for an estimated loss of some 3000 lives. President George W. Bush announced his "war on terrorism," which later became a justification for a preventive war on Iraq, neutralizing one third of the "axis of evil," including Iran and North Korea.

With the fall of the Ba'athist regime of Saddam Hussein in Iraq, the first difficulty facing U.S. and British forces is to deal with the social and political vacuum. If not handled deftly promises to be the beginning of an allied guagmire with liberation supplanted by occupation. Some may even believe that 30 years of repression has erased political contention in Iraq, an illusion eclipsed only by selective memory of thte relationship between Iraq's internal political affairs and the U.S.

As Adam Jones of Gendercide Watch points out, for example, while the U.S. supported Saddam Hussein in his war against Iran, Hussein conducted a genocidal anti-Kurdish campaign between February and September 1988.

Through overuse the administration devalued the label "axis of evil" to little more than a sound bite following its tepid response to North Korean nuclear saber rattling and the elusive evidence of Osama bin Laden's demise. However, all of the hyperbole in the debate about security and terrorism failed to deconstruct the flawed American policies that aided a genocidal regime.

Case Study: The Anfal Campaign (Iraqi Kurdistan), 1988

Adam Jones,
Gendercide Watch

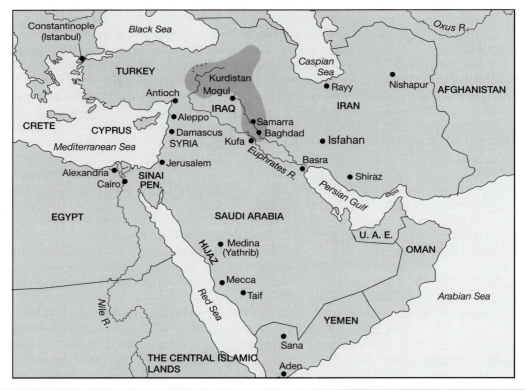

From Adam Jones, "Case Study: The Anfal Campaign (Iraqi Kurdistan), 1988," Gendercide Watch (2002). Reprinted with permission of Adam Jones/Gendercide Watch.

SUMMARY

The anti-Kurdish "Anfal" campaign, mounted between February and September 1988 by the Iraqi regime of Saddam Hussein, was both genocidal and gendercidal in nature. "Battle-age" men were the primary targets of Anfal, according to Human Rights Watch/Middle East (hereafter, HRW/ME). The organization writes in its book *Iraq's Crime of Genocide*: "Throughout Iraqi Kurdistan, although women and children vanished in certain clearly defined areas, adult males who were captured disappeared en masse... It is apparent that a principal purpose of Anfal was to exterminate all adult males of military service age captured in rural Iraqi Kurdistan." (pp. 96, 170). Only a handful survived the execution squads.

THE BACKGROUND

The Kurds are considered the world's largest nation without a state of their own. Numbering approximately 20–25 million people, their traditional territory is divided among the modern states of Turkey, Iraq, Iran, and Syria, with a small number in the states of the former Soviet Union. Just over four million of these Kurds live in Iraq, constituting about 23 percent of the population.

In the wake of World War I, with U.S. President Woodrow Wilson's call for "self-determination" echoing loudly, the Kurds were promised a homeland—Kurdistan—in the Treaty of Sèvres (1920). However, the victorious allies backed away from their pledge in an attempt to court the new Turkish regime of Kemal Ataturk, and in fear of destabilizing Iraq and Syria, which were granted to Britain and France, respectively, as mandated territories. The 1923 Treaty of Lausanne thus reneged on Kurdish independence and divided the Kurds among Turkey, Iraq, and Syria. Ataturk's discrimination against Turkey's Kurdish population began almost immediately, with Kurdish

political groups and manifestations of cultural identity banned outright. In the immediate aftermath of the Second World War, the Kurds of Iran, with Soviet support, succeeded in establishing the first independent Kurdish state (the Kurdish Republic of Mahabad). But this was quickly crushed by Iranian troops.

In 1946, an Iraqi Kurd, Mustafa Barzani, founded the Kurdistan Democratic Party—Iraq (KDP). Barzani died in 1979, but the KDP remains one of the most prominent Kurdish resistance organizations. Its more radical rival, the Patriotic Union of Kurdistan (PUK), was founded in 1975 by Jalal Talabani. It was the PUK that would bear the brunt of the Anfal campaign in 1988.

The ascent to power of Iraqi leader Saddam Hussein in 1968 (though he did not become president until 1979) at first seemed to augur well for the Iraqi Kurds. In 1970, Saddam's Ba'ath Party reached a wide-ranging agreement with the Kurdish rebel groups, granting the Kurds the right to use and broadcast their language, as well as a considerable degree of political autonomy. But the agreement broke down when the Ba'ath Party "embarked on the Arabization of the oil-producing areas in Kurdistan, evicting Kurdish farmers and replacing them with poor Arab tribesmen [and women] from the south, guarded by government troops." In March 1974, the KDP rose up against Saddam, sparking a full-scale war the following year, when some 130,000 Kurds fled to Iran. "In March 1975," writes Khaled Salih, "tens of thousands of villagers from the Barzani tribes were forcibly removed from their homes and relocated to barren sites in the desert south of Iraq, where they had to rebuild their lives by themselves, without any form of assistance." (Khaled "Anfal: The Kurdish Genocide in Iraq".)

It was these displaced populations of Barzani tribespeople who, after the onset of the Iran-Iraq war in 1980, would fall prey to one of the largest gendercidal massacres of modern times. Martin van Bruinessen writes:

In [July-]August 1983, Iraqi security troops rounded up the men of the Barzani tribe from four re-settlement camps near Arbil. These people were not engaged in any antigovernment activities … Two of Barzani's sons at that time led the Kurdistan Democratic Party and were engaged in guerrilla activities against the Baghdad government, but only a part of the tribe was with them … *All eight thousand men of this group*, then, were taken from their families and transported to southern Iraq. Thereafter they disappeared. All efforts to find out what happened to them or where they had gone, including diplomatic inquiries by several European countries, failed. It is feared that they are dead. The KDP [Kurdish Democratic Party] has received consistent reports from sources within the military that at least part of this group has been used as guinea pigs to test the effects of various chemical agents. (van Bruinessen, "Genocide in Kurdistan?," in George J. Andreopoulos, ed., Genocide: *Conceptual and Historical Dimensions* (pp. 156–57, emphasis added.)

One Barzani woman described the roundup of the menfolk: "Before dawn, as people were getting dressed and ready to go to work, all the soldiers charged through the camp [Qushtapa]. They captured the men walking on the street and even took an old man who was mentally deranged and was usually left tied up. They took the preacher who went to the mosque to call for prayers. They were breaking down doors and entering the houses searching for our men. They looked inside the chicken coops, water tanks, refrigerators, everywhere, and took all the men over the age of thirteen. The women cried and clutched the Qur`an [Koran] and begged the soldiers not to take their men away." In 1993, Saddam Hussein strongly hinted at the final fate of the Barzani men: "They betrayed the country and they betrayed the covenant, and we meted out a stern punishment to them, and they went to hell." As Human Rights Watch noted, "In many respects, the 1983 Barzani operation foreshadowed the techniques that would be used on a much larger scale during the Anfal campaign." (Human Rights Watch, *Iraq's Crime of Genocide*, pp. 4, 26–27.) Khaled Salih notes that "No doubt, the absence of any international outcry encouraged Baghdad to believe that it could get away with an even larger operation without any

hostile reaction. In this respect the Ba'ath Party seems to have been correct in its calculations and judgement of the international inaction." (Khaled, "Anfal: The Kurdish Genocide in Iraq"; see also "Who was responsible?," below.)

Among the most horrific features of the Iraqi campaigns against the Kurds in the 1980s was the regime's resort to chemical weapons strikes against civilian populations. On April 16, 1987, a chemical raid on the Balisan valley killed dozens of civilians; in its wake, "some seventy men were taken away in buses and, like the Barzanis, never seen again. The surviving women and children were dumped on the plain outside Erbil and left to fend for themselves." (Jonathan C. Randal, *After Such Knowledge, What Forgiveness?*, p. 230.) Less than a year later, on March 16, 1988, a far more concentrated chemical attack was launched on the town of Halabji, near the Iranian border, which had briefly been held by a combined force of Kurdish rebels and Iranian troops. Thousands of civilians died, and with the town still under Iranian occupation after the raid, journalists and photographers were able to reach the scene. "Their photographs, mainly of women, children, and elderly people huddled inertly in the streets or lying on their backs with mouths agape, circulated widely, demonstrating eloquently that the great mass of the dead had been Kurdish civilian noncombatants." (*Iraq's Crime of Genocide*, p. 72.) Although it took place during the Anfal campaign, however, the attack on Halabji is not normally considered part of that campaign.

THE GENDERCIDE

> The male is born to be slaughtered.
> —Kurdish proverb
> Your men have gone to hell.
> —Iraqi soldier to a survivor of the attack on
> Qaranaw village, Fourth Anfal, May 1988

In March 1987, Saddam Hussein's cousin from his hometown of Tikrit, Ali Hassan al-Majid, was appointed secretary-general of the Ba'ath Party's Northern Region, which included Iraqi Kurdistan. Under al-Majid, who "even by the standards of the Ba'ath security apparatus ... had a particular reputation for brutality," control of policies against the Kurdish insurgents passed from the Iraqi army to the Ba'ath Party itself. This was the prelude to the intended "final solution" to the Kurdish problem undertaken within months of al-Majid's arrival in his post. It would be known as "al-Anfai" ("The Spoils"), a reference to the eighth sura of the Qur`an, which details revelations that the Prophet Muhammad received after the first great victory of Islamic forces in AD 624. "I shall cast into the unbelievers' hearts terror," reads one of the verses; "so smite above the necks, and smite every finger of them ... the chastisement of the Fire is for the unbelievers." Anfal, officially conducted between February 23 and September 6, 1988, would have eight stages altogether, seven of them targeting areas controlled by the PUK. For these assaults, the Iraqis mustered up to 200,000 soldiers with air support—matched against Kurdish guerrilla forces that numbered no more than a few thousand.

On June 20, 1987, a crucial directive for the Anfal campaign, SF/4008, was issued under al-Majid's signature. Of greatest significance is clause 5. Referring to those areas designated "prohibited zones," al-Majid ordered that "all persons captured in those villages shall be detained and interrogated by the security services and those between the ages of 15 and 70 shall be executed after any useful information has been obtained from them, of which we should be duly notified." However, it seems clear from the application of this policy that "those between the ages of 15 and 70" meant "those *males*" in the designated age range. HRW/ME, for example, takes this as given, writing that clause 5's "order [was] to kill all adult males," and later: "Under the terms of al-Majid's June 1987 directives, death was the automatic penalty for any male of an age to bear arms who was found in an Anfal area." (*Iraq's Crime of Geno-*

cide, pp. 11, 14.) A subsequent directive on September 6, 1987, supports this conclusion: it calls for "the deportation of ... families to the areas where their saboteur relatives are ... , except for the male [members], between the ages of 12 inclusive and 50 inclusive, who must be detained." (Cited in *Iraq's Crime of Genocide*, p. 298.)

Accordingly, when captured Kurdish populations were transported to detention centres (notably the concentration camp of Topzawa near the city of Kirkuk), they were subjected to the classic process of gendercidal selection: separating adult and teenage males from the remainder of the community. According to HRW/ME,

> With only minor variations ... the standard pattern for sorting new arrivals [at Topzawa was as follows]. Men and women were segregated on the spot as soon as the trucks had rolled to a halt in the base's large central courtyard or parade ground. The process was brutal ... A little later, the men were further divided by age, small children were kept with their mothers, and the elderly and infirm were shunted off to separate quarters. Men and teenage boys considered to be of an age to use a weapon were herded together. Roughly speaking, this meant males of between fifteen and fifty, but there was no rigorous check of identity documents, and strict chronological age seems to have been less of a criterion than size and appearance. A strapping twelve-year-old might fail to make the cut; an undersized sixteen-year-old might be told to remain with his female relatives ... It was then time to process the younger males. They were split into smaller groups ... Once duly registered, the prisoners were hustled into large rooms, or halls, each filled with the residents of a single area ... Although the conditions at Topzawa were appalling for everyone, the most grossly overcrowded quarter seem to have been those where the male detainees were held ... For the men, beatings were routine. (*Iraq's Crime of Genocide*, pp. 143–45.)

After a few days of such treatment, *without a single known exception*, the men thus "processed" were trucked off to be killed in mass executions. According to HRW/ME, the "standard operating procedures" of the gendercidal killings (extended, in some cases, to other segments of the population) were "uncannily reminiscent of … the activities of the *Einsatzkommandos*, or mobile killing units, in the Nazi-occupied lands of Eastern Europe":

> Some groups of prisoners were lined up, shot from the front, and dragged into predug mass graves; others were made to lie down in pairs, sardine-style, next to mounds of fresh corpses, before being killed; still others were tied together, made to stand on the lip of the pit, and shot in the back so that they would fall forward into it—a method that was presumably more efficient from the point of view of the killers. Bulldozers then pushed earth or sand loosely over the heaps of corpses. Some of the grave sites contained dozens of separate pits and obviously contained the bodies of thousands of victims. (*Iraq's Crime of Genocide*, p. 12.)

The genocidal and gendercidal focus of the Iraqi killing campaign varied from one stage of Anfal to another. No mass killings of civilians appear to have taken place during first Anfal (February 23–March 19, 1988). The most exclusive targeting of the male population, meanwhile, occurred during the final Anfal (August 25–September 6, 1988). This was launched immediately after the signing of a ceasefire with Iran, which allowed the transfer of large amounts of men and matériel from the southern battlefronts. It focused on "the steep, narrow valleys of Badinan, a four-thousand-square mile chunk of the Zagros Mountains bounded on the east by the Greater Zab River and on the north by Turkey." Here, uniquely in the Anfal campaigns, lists of the "disappeared" provided to HRW/ME by survivors "invariably included only adult and teenage males, with the single exception of Assyrian and Caldean Christians and Yezidi Kurds," who were subsidiary targets of the slaughter. Many of the men of Badinan did not even make it as far as "processing" stations, being simply "lined up and murdered at their point of capture, executed by firing squads on the authority of a local army officer." (*Iraq's Crime of Genocide*, pp. 178, 190, 192; on the fate of the Christians

and Yezidi Kurds, see pp. 209–13.) The best-known case is the assault on the village of Koreme, where a forensic investigation conducted by Middle East Watch and Physicians for Human Rights in May–June 1992 uncovered the bodies of 27 men and adolescent boys executed on August 28. (See Middle East Watch/Physicians for Human Rights, *The Anfal Campaign in Iraqi Kurdistan: The Destruction of Koreme*.)

Even amidst this most systematic slaughter of adult men and boys, however, "hundreds of women and young children perished, too," though "the causes of their deaths were different—gassing, starvation, exposure, and willful neglect—rather than bullets fired from a Kalashnikov [rifle]." (*Iraq's Crime of Genocide*, p. 191.) The fate of other segments of the Kurdish community throughout Anfal receives attention in the following section.

GENOCIDE AGAINST WOMEN, THE ELDERLY, AND CHILDREN

In its landmark study of the Iraqi genocide in Kurdistan, HRW/ME calls the decisions surrounding the deaths of thousands of women, children, and elderly Kurds "one of the great enigmas of the Anfal campaign." "Many thousands of women and children perished," the organization notes, "but their deaths were subject to extreme regional variations, with most being residents of two distinct 'clusters' that were affected by the third and fourth Anfals." One factor apparently was "whether the [Iraqi] troops encountered armed resistance in a given area," something which characterized "most, but not all, the areas marked by the killing of women and children." (*Iraq's Crime of Genocide*, pp. 13, 96.)

The hardest-hit area of all appears to have been the region of southern Germian, abutting the Arab heartland of Iraq, which was targeted during the third Anfal (April 7–20, 1988). Southern Germian was apparently a special focus for "root-and-branch" genocide because it was the heartland of the PUK resistance and strongly supportive of the Kurdish PUK rebels. "Although males aged fifteen to fifty routinely vanished from all parts of Germian," writes HRW/ME, "only in the south did the disappeared include significant numbers of women and children. Most were from the Daoudi and Jaff-Roghyazi tribes," and they accounted for more than half the "disappeared" in the affected regions. Mass executions involving "an estimated two thousand women and children" took place at a site on Hamrin Mountain, between the cities of Tikrit and Kirkuk. (*Iraq's Crime of Genocide*, pp. 115, 171.)

One such execution left a survivor, a young boy named Taimour Abdullah Ahmad, "the only eyewitness to the mass killing of women and children" (*Iraq's Crime of Genocide*, p. 171). His account received extensive attention in the western press, and describes scenes virtually identical to the *Einsatzgruppen*-style massacres of "battle-aged" males which preceded the killing of women, children, and the elderly from southern Germian.

Most members of the Kurdish community who remained after "battle-age" men had been "disappeared" were trucked off to resettlement camps to the south. To the extent that women, children, and the elderly were killed in mass executions, these were usually perpetrated after a period of detention in such camps. Those not slaughtered in this fashion were usually transported to relocation camps where conditions were squalid and unsanitary; thousands—especially children—died from deprivation and neglect.

The infrastructure of life in Iraqi Kurdistan, meanwhile, was left almost totally destroyed by the Anfal campaign and its predecessors. "By the time the genocidal frenzy ended, 90% of Kurdish villages, and over twenty small towns and cities, had been wiped off the map. The countryside was riddled with 15 million landmines, intended to make agriculture and hus-

bandry impossible. A million and a half Kurdish peasants had been interned in camps … About 10% of the total Kurdish population of Iraq had perished [since 1974]." (Kendal Nezan, "When our 'friend' Saddam was gassing the Kurds", *Le Monde diplomatique*, March 1998.)

HOW MANY DIED?

According to HRW/ME, "at least fifty thousand rural Kurds … died in Anfal alone, and very possibly the real figure was twice that number … All told, the total number of Kurds killed over the decade since the Barzani men were taken from their homes is well into six figures." "On the basis of extensive interviews in Kurdistan and perusal of extant Iraqi documents, Shoresh Resoul, a meticulous Kurdish researcher … conservatively estimated that 'between 60,000 and 110,000' died during [al-]Majid's Kurdish mandate," i.e., beginning shortly before Anfal and ending shortly afterwards. (Randal, *After Such Knowledge …*, p. 214.) Other Kurdish estimates are even higher. "When Kurdish leaders met with Iraqi government officials in the wake of the spring 1991 uprising, they raised the question of the Anfal dead and mentioned a figure of 182,000—a rough extrapolation based on the number of destroyed villages. Ali Hassan al-Majid reportedly jumped to his feet in a rage when the discussion took this turn. 'What is this exaggerated figure of 182,000?' he is said to have asked. 'It couldn't have been more than 100,000'—as if this somehow mitigated the catastrophe that he and his subordinates had visited on the Iraqi Kurds." (*Iraq's Crime of Genocide*, pp. 14, 230.)

It is impossible to state with certainty what proportion of the victims of Anfal were adult men and adolescent boys. The most detailed investigation, conducted by HRW/ME, tabulated the number of "disappeared" from the various stages of Anfal, based on field interviews with some 350 survivors. The organization gathered the names of 1,255 men, 184 women, and 359 children—"only a fraction of the numbers lost during Anfal." This would suggest that some 87 percent of the adults "disappeared," all of whom were apparently executed, were male; and that about 70 percent of all those who "disappeared" were "battle-age" males. (See *Iraq's Crime of Genocide*, pp. 266–88.) These calculations do not, however, include the large number of Kurdish civilians killed indiscriminately in chemical attacks and other generalized assaults.

WHO WAS RESPONSIBLE?

The tens of thousands of Anfal deaths, according to HRW/ME,

> did not come in the heat of battle—as "collateral damage," in the military euphemism. Nor were they the result of acts of aberration by individual commanders whose excesses passed unnoticed or unpunished by their superiors. Rather, these Kurds were systematically put to death in large numbers by order of the central Iraqi government in Baghdad days or weeks after being rounded up in villages marked for destruction or while fleeing army assaults in "prohibited areas." ... Documentary materials captured from the Iraqi intelligence agencies demonstrate with great clarity that the mass killings, disappearances, and forced relocations associated with Anfal and the other anti-Kurdish campaigns of 1987–89 were planned in a coherent fashion. Although power over these campaigns was highly centralized, their success depended on the orchestration of the efforts of a large number of agencies and institutions at the local, regional, and national level, from the office of the president of the republic down to the lowliest jahsh [pro-Iraqi Kurdish] unit. (*Iraq's Crime of Genocide*, pp. xvii, 9–10. For more on the role of the pro-regime Kurdish forces, which were crucial in the Anfal roundups, see pp. 109–12, and Kanan Makiya, *Cruelty and Silence*, pp. 143–45.)

Noam Chomsky has called Iraq "perhaps the most violent and repressive state in the world." (Quoted in Makiya, *Cruelty and Silence*, p. 273.)

Atop the state structure stands the murderous dictator Saddam Hussein. In classic "patrimonial" fashion, Saddam has constructed a brutal one-party regime consisting largely of his relatives from Tikrit and surrounding areas. (For a powerful description of Saddam's rule-by-terror, see Kanan Makiya, *Republic of Fear: The Politics of Modem Iraq.*) The Ba'ath Party's "point man" during the worst of the atrocities in Iraqi Kurdistan was, as noted, Ali Hassan al-Majid. After Anfal, he was transferred from his post, to become—in August 1990—the governor of Iraqi-occupied Kuwait.

Saddam's dictatorship reaches to the grassroots of Iraqi society through the intertwined institutions of the Ba'ath Party and the Iraqi army and security forces. At every level, its violence exhibits strong patriarchal overtones. Jonathan Randal describes the "perverted form of male bonding" evident in an internal purge that Saddam carried out in 1979, in which "surviving ministers and senior party officials [were obliged] to join the firing squad which executed the condemned men." The "pattern [was] repeated throughout the chain of command: from the lowliest secret-police operative on up they shared responsibility in the executions, thus enforcing loyalty and subservience to Saddam Hussein." Such practices "were also useful in intimidating anyone less inclined to terror and cruelty." (Randal, *After Such Knowledge* ... , p. 208.)

The international community must accept a share of the blame for Saddam's genocide against the Iraqi Kurds. For the duration of the Iran-Iraq war—which also witnessed most of the horrors against the Kurds—Saddam was considered an important bulwark against the spread of Iranian-style Islamic fundamentalism to the strategic and oil-rich countries of the Middle East. Accordingly, the West supplied and armed him throughout his campaigns against both the Iranians and the Kurds, eventually providing the critical intelligence information that allowed Iraq to emerge victorious in the war against Iran. In August 1988—with the Anfal campaign nearly over, and in the wake of a year-and-a-half of vicious chemical attacks on civilian populations—"the United Nations Sub-Committee on Human Rights voted by 11 votes to 8 not to condemn Iraq for human rights violations. Only the Scandinavian countries, Australia and Canada, together with bodies like the European Parliament and the Socialist International, saved their honour by clearly condemning Iraq." (Nezan, "When our 'friend' Saddam was gassing the Kurds".)

THE AFTERMATH

In August 1990, the Iraqi regime finally overreached with its invasion of neighbouring Kuwait, sparking the Gulf War, in which a U.S.-led coalition succeeded in expelling the Iraqi occupying forces. At the tail end of the war, in March 1991, the Kurdish population of northern Iraq launched a general uprising against the Iraqi regime, and briefly managed to expel it from the region. When the Iraqis counterattacked, nearly half a million Kurds fled to Turkey and Iran; the resultant humanitarian crisis led the members of the Allied coalition to declare a "safe haven" in the northern part of Iraqi Kurdistan. A coalition of seven Kurdish parties then established authority over the enclave, which exists to the present day—despite the outbreak of serious fighting between the PUK and KDP in May 1994, which killed an estimated 1,000 people. In September 1998, the two rebel groups forged a new power-sharing agreement brokered by the United States. Meanwhile, in the Iraqi capital of Baghdad, Saddam Hussein remained in power, despite his devastating defeat in the Gulf War.

During the March 1991 uprising, Kurdish forces managed to seize some four million documents from Iraqi archives in the region, and transported these to safe areas.

These documents, combined with the investigative missions undertaken in the Kurdish zone by HRW/ME and other organizations, allowed a definitive reconstruction of the events of Anfal. As HRW/ME noted, "To have the opportunity to speak to survivors of human rights violations, to dig up the bones of those who had not survived, and then to read the official account of what had taken place—all while the regime that had carried out the outrages was still in power—was unique in the annals of human rights research." (*Iraq's Crime of Genocide*, p. xx.) In light of this mountain of documentation, eyewitness testimony, and forensic data, the organization announced its "confidence" that "concerning the crucial 1987–1989 period… the evidence is sufficiently strong to prove a case of genocidal intent on the part of the Iraqi Government," and has called for the creation of a war-crimes tribunal at the Hague such as those established for Bosnia-Herzegovina, Rwanda, and Kosovo. (HRW/ME, *Bureaucracy of Repression: The Iraqi Government in Its Own Words*, p. x.)

A number of observers have noted the still-visible evidence of gendercide among the Kurdish population of northern Iraq. In September 1988, as Anfal was officially winding down, U.S. ambassador to Iraq, April Glaspie, "recalled travelling westward from Sulaimaniyah… and coming across large groups of disconsolate women and children standing next to their meager bundled belongings on the roadside. 'They were obviously without menfolk. I suspected the authorities meant me to see them.'" (Randal, *After Such Knowledge…*, p. 223.) In 1999, the Christian Aid organization noted that "Many Kurdish households are headed by widows—their husbands have disappeared." ("Working in Iraq: Christian Aid's Experience 1990-98".) Retired U.S. Brigadier-General Jeffrey Pilkington, who commanded the relief campaign "Operation Provide Comfort" in 1993–94, reported from a trip to the Kurdish zone that

The signs of almost total economic stagnation were everywhere. Fields were mostly bare—for lack of fertilizer or insecticide or because there was no market for the wheat grown or no-one who could afford to buy it. Factories which had employed hundreds of workers were now deserted … Many villages were populated by only women and children, the majority of men having been detained or killed. (Pilkington, "Beyond Humanitarian Relief: Economic Development Efforts in Northern Iraq", in *Forced Migration Review*.)

Likewise, the Iraq Assessment undertaken by the Country Information and Policy Unit of the British Home Office (April 2000) stated that "there is an unusually high percentage of women in the Kurdish areas, purportedly caused by the disappearances of tens of thousands of Kurdish men during the Anfal Campaign. The Special Rapporteur reported that the widows, daughters, and mothers of the

Anfal Campaign victims are economically dependent on their relatives or villages because they may not inherit the property or assets of their missing family members." (On the plight of the widows of the Anfal victims, see also Teresa Thornhill, "Anfal Widows: Saddam's Genocide," *New Internationalist*, no. 247 [September 1993].)

QUESTIONS TO CONSIDER

1. Who were the targets of the Anfal campaign?
2. What role did chemical weapons play in the Anfal?
3. What is gendercide and how was it implemented in Iraq?
4. Describe the gendercide "against women."
5. Who is responsible for the genocide?
6. What are the long-term consequences of gendercide?

Anfal: The Kurdish Genocide in Iraq

IRAQ AND THE KURDS: A BIBLIOGRAPHIC ESSAY

Khaled Salih,

University of Southern Denmark

In October 1988, while the destruction of Kurdistan and the mass killing of the Kurds by the Iraqi regime was a well-known fact, though understandably not documented, at least in the West, Milton Viorst published a peculiar article in the *International Hearald Tribune* under the title: "Iraq and the Kurds: Where Is the Proof of Poison Gas?"

Viorst felt that it was unjust to punish the Iraqi government "for a particular crime that, according to some authorities, may never have taken place." To do the Iraqi government some good he then spent a week in Iraq "looking into the question." Since those who alleged that Iraq had used chemical weapons against the Kurds were not

From Khaled Salih, "Anfal: The Kurdish Genocide in Iraq," *Digest of Middle East Studies*, 4(2) (Spring 1995): 24–29. Reprinted with permission.

able to proove it, Viorst's visit to Iraq was presented in the article as a proof of the opposite.

After confirming that Iraq sent its army "to crush a rebellion of the Kurds who fought at Iran's side," as Iraq aimed "to stamp out the insurgency," Viorst tells his readers what he saw from an Iraqi helicopter: "the ruins of hundreds of Kurdish mountain villages that the Iraqi army destroyed to deny the rebels sanctuary." From what he saw, he could though conclude that "if lethal gas was used, it was not used genocidally—that is, for mass killing." Since the Kurdish population in Iraq constitute a tightly knit community, "If there had been large-scale killing, it is likely they would know and tell the world. But neither I nor any Westerner I encountered heard such allegations."

During his visit, Viorst could not see that the Kurdish society showed "discernible signs of tension." In his eyes, everything seemed to take its normal course. "The northern cities, where the men wear Kurdish turbans and baggy pants, were as bustling as I had ever seen them." To convince his readers about the "normality" of life in the Kurdish areas, he tells us that he talked to armed Kurds, members of Iraqi military units mobilised against the rebels.

Even if Iraq used chemical weapons, Viorst says doubtfully, it "probably used gas of some kind in air attacks on rebel positions," but not against the civilians, since the symptoms the refugees showed to doctors sent by France, the UN and the Red Cross to the Turkish camps, "could have been produced by a powerful, but nonlethal, tear gas." Stop then annoying Iraq and harm the relationship between Iraq and the United States, was Mr Viorst's clear message.

Less than two years later we came to realise how prophetically Viorst spoke in October 1988, when he self-confidently reminded the U.S. officials and decision-makers that, "Iraq, having put down the Kurdish rebellion, has no wars on its agenda, and it has pledged to abide by the Geneva convention on chemi-

cal warfare." In August 1990 Iraq invaded Kuwait, an event that led to the Gulf War.

A SECOND VOICE

During the war over Kuwait, the Iraqi regime's repression of "its own" people, in particular the use of chemical weapons against the Kurds, became an important part of the ideological justification in the "just war" to restore Kuwait. The anti-war camp was no doubt irritated and upset by this rather cynical strategy. They pointed out many inconsistencies in the Allies' policies, being in the Middle East, worldwide, historically or contemporary.

One person who could not leave this major event uncommented was of course Edward Said. Several aspects of the event could encourage him to get involved, such as the question of imperialism, Arab nationalism, and human rights violation, to name but a few. On 7 March 1991, Said wrote:

> The claim that Iraq gassed its own citizens has often been repeated. At best, this is uncertain. There is at least one War College report, done while Iraq was a U.S. ally claims that the gassing of the Kurds in Halabja was done by Iran. Few people mention such reports in the media today.

Given his public image of being among the critical intellectuals, Said's attempt to cast doubt on Iraq's use of chemical weapons against the Kurds was not only surprising but shocking, since it came from a "secular oppositional intellectual" who belonged to a "class of informed," who did not allow himself "the luxury of playing the identity game," who desired to "more compassionately press the interests of the unheard, the unrepresented, the unconnected people of our world," and who wanted to do that "with the accents of personal restraint, historical scepticism and committed intellect."

DETAILED DOCUMENTS

Although, at that time, no one would have been able to quote an Iraqi document to help Edward Said to overcome his uncertainty, the events after the war had at least one unimaginable dimension: it provided an unprecedented opportunity to give sufficient proofs that the Iraqi regime was using chemical weapons against the Kurds, and to do so by using the regime's own detailed documents.

In her introduction to a documentary book, *Saddam Speaks on the Gulf Crisis: A Collection of Documents*, an Israeli specialist on modern Iraq, Ofra Bengio, indicated that the invasion of Kuwait could best be understood against the background of Iraq's internal political development since July 1979, i.e., after Saddam Hussein's rise to power. By August 1990, Saddam Hussein's "megalomania led him to apply his domestic style of rule to foreign policy." But what do we exactly know about the characteristics of this "domestic style of rule?" Is it possible to understand and comprehend the scale of violence inflicted upon the Kuwaitis, without having a proper picture of this domestic style of rule applied to foreign policy?

During the unsuccessful Kurdish uprising of March 1991, huge quantities of Iraqi government records were captured by the Kurds in the secret police buildings in the major towns and cities. Although much of the documents ware burned or destroyed during the confusing days of the uprising, more than 18 tons of documents, contained in 847 boxes with a total number of pages estimated as over four million, are now in the USA for safe-keeping, under the auspices of the Middle East Watch (MEW). Genocide in Iraq and Bureaucracy of Repression are the latest to be published by Middle East Watch in order to reconstruct, document, and demonstrate the Iraqi regime's policy against the Kurds, particularly during the years of 1987 through 1989. Their conclusion is that the organisation "believes it can demonstrate convincingly a deliberate intent on the part of the government of President Saddam Hussein to destroy, through mass murder, part of Iraq's Kurdish minority. [The Kurds] were targeted during the Anfal as Kurds. [And that] Saddam Hussein's regime committed a panoply of war crimes, together with crimes against humanity and genocide." This is not a hasty conclusion; but rather one based on a unique combination of three painstaking research projects lasting over eighteen months:

1. oral testimony from over 350 eyewitnesses or survivors;
2. forensic evidence from areas of mass graves; and
3. huge amount of captured Iraqi documents.

Bureaucracy of Repression is published in order to give a general picture about the Iraqi documents currently being analysed by Middle East Watch. It is "a Holy Grail for researchers: to have opportunity to speak to survivors of human rights violations, dig up bones of those who did not survive, and then read the official account of what took place—all while the regime that carried out these outrages was still in power—was unique in the annals of human rights research." The sample of 38 Arabic documents with English translation that the book contains serves as a very good introduction to that huge amount of documents.

The samples are organised around several important categories, such as Arabization of the Kurdish areas, a policy with many roots in the 1960s; policy towards prohibited areas created prior to the major operations of 1987–1989; destruction of thousands of Kurdish villages and dozens of towns; chemical attacks against the Kurdish civilians; the administrative framework of the most important campaign called Anfal by the regime itself, from March 1987 to April 1989; the Anfal campaign, lasting officially from 23 February to 6 September, 1988; the war over Kuwait and the subsequent domestic uprisings; and last category as other documents of interests.

PROCEDURAL LANGUAGE

All together, the documents "display a remarkable consistency in style. The language is dry and formal, indicating rigid bureaucratic procedures. [They] highlight, as well as show the methodology and routine character of a bureaucracy of repression in action. [They] offer a unique vista on the inner workings of a sophisticated one-party police state. [The completeness and sophistication of the Iraqi archive] emphasize that the documents constitute a credible, authentic expression of the state's action against the Kurds." This report offers a clear introduction to the unique discourse of repression the Ba'thi regime developed in an enclosed, isolated and concealed Iraq from which little was escaping the machinery of state censorship, prior to March 1991.

Scholars writing on authoritarian and totalitarian regimes admit the diffculties of obtaining reliable documentary information on most of the subjects, but more so when it comes to the question of "sensitive" issues such as violation of human rights, ideology-related projects of relocation, displacing part of the country's inhabitants and re-shaping the social composition of the entire population, often referred to as "modernisation." This is also true in the case of Iraq.

SCHOLARLY CIRCUMSPECTION

Two kinds of scholarly publications on the Ba'thi rule in Iraq are dominant. One of them is at its best exemplified by Frederick Axelgard's book published in 1988. His main theme is that, during the Iraq-Iran war in Iraq, a "coherent national identity" emerged, thanks duly to the leadership of Saddam Hussein and the Ba'th Party. The war and the "modernisation" policies embarked on by the regime of Saddam Hussein, although it appeared to be harsh in outsiders' eyes, created a "new nation" charac-

terised by loyalty to the Iraqi state and the leadership of Saddam Hussein. The main evidence of this successful enterprise is that the Shi'is in the South, despite all the Iranian attempts, never attempted to rise against the Ba'thi regime. The Kurds were also brought under control, and were in 1988 mainly loyal to the regime.

Characteristic of this kind of literature is the absence of any discussion regarding the conditions of "stability" and "cohesion" they praise the Ba'th regime has brought about in such a highly "unstable," "unruly" and "fragmented" society like that in Iraq. There is no account of the kind and extent of the suffering inflicted on the population by such policies.

The other kind of literature, which is highly critical, is of course best exemplified by Marion Farouk-Sluglett and Peter Sluglett's publications and by Samir al-Khalil's book. Despite their critical account of the events and their distaste for the Ba'thist methods of conducting politics, their attempts to document the political events were limited by the politics of secrecy and the suppression of information, characteristic of the Ba'th in Iraq since 1968.

Iraq's invasion of Kuwait, the subsequent war and the March 1991 uprisings of the Shi'is in the South and the Kurds in the North radically changed that. The vicious circle of fear and apathy was broken by the new conditions emerged gradually during the Gulf War and the Iraqi army's final defeat by the Allied forces. The uprisings did not only show how superficial the image of stability and cohesion was; they suddenly made it possible to report on its internal conditions, the methods and the procedures used, and the level of the suffering of the entire population, particularly that of the Kurdish civilians in northern Iraq.

In this sense *Genocide in Iraq* is most welcome to fill this gap. It demonstrates with cold precision, though forcefully and above all honestly, how the crime of genocide was committed by the present Ba'thi regime in Iraq against the Kurdish population. It does not give an account of the events from an Iraqi helicopter, nor does it quote a War College source to denounce allegations. Rather, it is based on the experience and testimony of those who were affected by the horror of chemical weapons, brutal army attacks, terror of security services and collaboration of Kurdish militia men rounding up villagers. To substantiate the testimonies *Genocide in Iraq* quotes instead Iraqi documents never meant to see daylight, in written forms, on recorded audio tapes and on video tapes, as well as forensic evidence from identified sites of mass graves.

ANFAL OPERATIONS

Despite all public denial of using chemical weapons against the Kurdish civilians in 1988, the Iraqi regime did not deny a campaign it called Anfal. In a reply to a petition by a former Kurdish POW, Chief of the Bureau of the Presidency informed the man that his "wife and children were lost during the Anfal Operations that took place in the Northern Region in 1988." Anfal, a name of a sura in the Koran, is thus the official military codename used by the Iraqi government in its public pronouncements and internal memoranda. It was a name given to a concerted series of military offensives, eight in all, conducted in six distinct Kurdish geographic areas between late February and early September 1988.

It is important to note that in reality Anfal corresponded to something more than military offensives against the Kurdish villages and Kurdish resistance. Anfal meant co-ordination of many measures starting with destruction of thousands of villages; gathering rural population after multiple chemical attacks; transporting them to the camps; processing the captives through isolating them and determining who should be sent to death; transporting different groups to different destinies—women and chil-

dren to particular camps, elderly people to southern Iraq and the men aged between 15 and 50 to gravesites—under extreme secrecy; using fire squads to kill large groups of men near pre-dug mass graves and then covering the mass graves as well as denying to know anything about their fates.

Iraqi authorities did nothing to hide the Anfal campaign from public view. "On the contrary, as each phase of the operation triumphed, its successes were trumpeted with the same propaganda fanfare that attended the victorious battles in the Iran-Iraq War."

As such, Anfal was a logical extension of nearly two decades of government Arabization of the Kurdish areas. For all its horror, Anfal was not entirely unprecedented, because terrible atrocities had been visited on the Kurds by the Ba'th Party on many occasions, particularly since 1968. In the wake of an official autonomy granted to the Kurds in the first half of the 70's, the Ba'th Party embarked on the Arabization of the oil-producing areas in Kurdistan, evicting Kurdish farmers and replacing them with poor Arab tribesmen from the south, guarded by government troops. After the Kurdistan Democratic Party (KDP) fled into Iran after the collapse of the Kurdish revolt in March 1975, tens of thousands of villagers from the Barzani tribes forcibly removed from their homes and relocated to barren sites in the desert south of Iraq, where they had to rebuild their lives by themselves, without any form of assistance.

EVACUATION, PUNISHMENT, AND WASTE

In the mid- and late 1970s, the regime again moved against the Kurds, forcibly evacuating at least a quarter of a million people from Iraq's borders with Iraq and Turkey, destroying their villages to create a cordon sanitaire along these sensitive frontiers. Most of the displaced Kurds were relocated into mujamma'at, crude new settlements located on the main highways in army-controlled areas of Iraqi Kurdistan.

KDP revived its alliance with Tehran after the Iranian revolution of 1978; in 1983 they had a joint action to capture a border town, an event that led immediately to retribution by the regime in Baghdad: in an operation against the complexes where the Barzanis Kurds were relocated, Iraqi troops abducted five to eight thousand males aged twelve or over. None of them have ever been seen again. In September 1983, Saddam Hussein gave the clearest indication regarding the fate of the Barzanis: "They betrayed the country and they betrayed the convenant," he said, "and we meted out a stern punishment to them and they went to hell." In many respects, the 1983 Barzani operation anticipated the techniques that would be used on a much larger scale during the Anfal campaign. No doubt, the absence of any international outcry encouraged Baghdad to believe that it could get away with an even larger operation without any hostile reaction. In this respect the Ba'th Party seems to have been correct in its calculations and judgement of the international inaction.

Since 1975, over 4,000 Kurdish villages had been destroyed; by a conservative estimate more than 100,000 rural Kurds had died in Anfal alone; half of Iraq's productive farmland is believed to have been laid waste.

The destruction campaigns of April 1987–April 1989, which MEW rightly calls the Kurdish genocide, had the Anfal campaign as its centrepiece. The Anfal campaign should by no means be regarded as a function or by-product of the Iraq-Iran war, since it was a rational, pre-planned enterprise in which modern techniques of management and expertise were effectively co-ordinated. The Iran-Iraq war provided the crucial element with which Baghdad could cover-up its opportunity to bring to a climax its long-standing efforts to bring the Kurds to heel. The Iraqi regime's anti-Kurdish drive dates back to more than fifteen years, well before the outbreak of that war.

ANOTHER HOLOCAUST

Theoretically, *Genocide in Iraq* attempts to locate the Kurdish genocide of 1987–1989 within a paradigm presented by Raul Hilberg in his book on the history of Holocaust. The reasoning presented in *Genocide in Iraq* is both complex and subtle, a fact that does not allow for a short synopsis to do the book and the victims of Anfal justice. Despite that, the basic argument can be summarised fairly briefly. The Kurdish genocide "fits Hilberg's paradigm to perfection," which is summarised in the following key concepts: "definition - concentration (or seizure) - annihilation."

The process of defining those who would be targeted by Anfal began shortly after Ali Hassan al-Majid, one of Saddam Hussein's cousins, was granted "special powers" as the secretary general of the Northern Bureau of Iraq's ruling Bath Arab Socialist Party, in March 1987. At the first stage, al-Majid decreed that "saboteurs" would lose their property rights, suspended the legal rights of all the residents of prohibited villages, to be followed by the execution of first-degree relatives of "saboteurs" and of wounded civilians whose hostility to the regime had been determined by the intelligence services.

In June 1987, the process of drawing irreversible boundaries—the red line between "us" and "them"—was legalised by issuing two sets of standing orders, which were based on a simple axiom with a result few, if any, of the Kurds could comprehend: in the "prohibited" rural areas, all Kurdish residents were coterminous with the peshmerga insurgents (Kurdish guerrilla), and they would be dealt with accordingly.

Through a policy of shoot-to-kill, the first of al-Majid's directives was to ban all human existence in the "prohibited areas." The second constitutes an unmistakable inducement to mass murder, spelled out in the a chilling clear language. In clause 4, army commanders are ordered *"to carry out random bombardments, using* *artillery, helicopters and aircraft, at all times of the day or night, in order to **kill the largest number of persons** present in these prohibited zones."*

In clause 5, al-Majid ordered that, *"All persons captured in those villages shall be detained and interrogated by the security services and **those between the ages of 15 to 70** shall be executed after any useful information has been obtained from them, of which we should be duly notified."*

While still engaged in this phase of definition, the Iraqi authorities did not hesitate to test their chemical capacity. Within the range of at least forty documented chemical attacks on Kurdish targets over a period of eighteen months, Iraqi aircraft dropped its first poison gas on the undefended civilian villagers in mid-April 1987, killing more than a hundred people, most of them women and children. These attacks were the first signs of the degree to which the regime was prepared in killing large numbers of Kurdish civilians without discrimination.

In order to create a buffer zone between "us" and "them," between the government and the peshmerge-controlled areas, a three-stage programme of village clearances or "collectivisation" was embarked on in mid-April 1987. During this programme's first two phases, between 21 April–20 May and 21 May–20 June, more than 700 villages were burned and bull-dozed, most of them along the main highways in government-controlled areas. Due to the war efforts on the Iranian frontiers, the third phase was to be postponed, but accomplished by Anfal.

In terms of defining the target group for annihilation, the national census of 17 October 1987 was the most important single administrative step of the Iraqi regime in the desired direction. Having created a virtual buffer strip between the government and the peshmerge-controlled zones by the village clearances, the Ba'th Party offered the inhabitants of the prohibited areas an ultimatum: either you "return to the national ranks"—that is, abandon your home and livelihood and accept compulsory relocation in a sordid camp under the eye of the security forces; or you lose your Iraqi citizenship and be regarded as military deserter. This second option was subject to an August 1987 decree of the ruling Revolutionary Command Council, imposing the death penalty on deserters. Not choosing the "national ranks" was, in effect, tantamount to a death sentence, to be carried out by Party organisations. Prior to the census date, proper measures were taken by security and intelligence agencies to prevent any contact or movement between the two sides, other than on the regime's terms.

DEFINITION

In the period leading up to the census, al-Majid encircled the target group further. He ordered intelligence officials to prepare detailed case-by-case dossiers of "saboteurs" families who were still living in the government-controlled areas, on which countless women, children and elderly people were forcibly transferred to the rural areas to share the fate of their peshmerge relatives. This technique of sieving of the population was also crucial to the decisions made during the Anfal on the question of who should live and who should die.

Concomitant with this phase of definition was also the military operations to destroy the habitat of the rural population that roughly followed the same pattern. These operations started characteristically with chemical attacks from the air on both civilian and peshmerge targets, accompanied by a military blitz against the Kurdish military bases. After this initial assault, ground troops and jash (pro-government Kurdish militias) enveloped the target areas from all sides, destroying all human habitation in their path, looting household possessions and farm animals and setting fire to homes, before calling in demolition crews.

In areas of greater peshmerga resistance brutal government harassment in all the forms familiar in the rest of Iraqi Kurdistan was followed—punitive jash incursions, burning and looting, shelling from artillery, rocketing and occasional bombing from the air.

As the definition processes proceeded, so did the phase of the concentration or seizure of the target group. By now, convoys of army trucks stood by to transport the villagers to holding centres and transit camps. To prevent anyone from escaping, the jash had to comb the hillsides at the first stage, while the secret police had to search the towns, cities and complexes to hunt fugitives at a later stage. In several cases those who still managed to hide had to be lured out with false offers of amnesty and "return to the national ranks."

The processing of the detainees took place in a network of camps and prisons that followed a standard pattern. Men and women were segregated on the spot. The process was brutal and did not spare the elderly. A little later, the men were further divided by age—small children kept with their mothers, the elderly and weak sidelined to separate quarters, and men and teenage boys considered to be able to carry a weapon herded together, without rigorous check of identity documents.

The women and children were also suffering grievously in their own ways. After a short time the guards dragged the older women away violently from their daughters and grandchildren and bundled them away to yet another unknown destination. In at least two cases, soldiers and guards burst into the women's quarters during their first night at a camp and removed their small children, even infants at the breast. All night long the women could hear the cries and screams of their children in another room. But above all the women and children in one camp endured the torment of seeing their husbands, brothers and fathers suffer, beaten routinely in front of their female relatives, and, in the end, disappear.

CONCENTRATION

The first temporary holding centres were in operation, under the control of military intelligence as early as mid-March 1988; peaking in mid-April and early May, the mass disappearances had begun in earnest shortly thereafter. At this stage most of the detainees were transferred to a place called Topzawa, a Popular Army camp on the outskirts of Kirkuk; others were trucked to another Popular Army barracks in Tikrit. Women and children were trucked on from Topzawa to a separate camp in the town of Dibs; between 6,000 and 8,000 elderly detainees were taken to an abandoned prison called Nugra Salman in the southern desert, where hundreds of them died as a result of neglect, starvation and disease.

During the last stage of Anfal villagers from Badinan were detained in a huge army fort at Dohuk. The women and children were transferred later from Dohuk to a prison camp in Salamiyeh close to Mosul. Although the majority of the women, children and elderly released after an official amnesty to mark the end of Anfal on 6 September 1988, none of the Anfal men were never released. Only six people, all from the Third and the bloodiest Anfal—aged between 12 and 38, have managed to escape in order to tell the true story of what happened to tens of thousands of Kurds who were driven away in convoys of sealed vehicles from the camps to southern Iraq.

The process of defining those who were actually to be killed, if they managed to survive indiscriminate chemical attacks, harsh conditions of the transit camps and occasionally torture, was under way long before the actual killing by the firing squads. Two days before the national census, that is to say 15 October, 1987, army and intelligence agencies were ordered to compile lists of the Kurds from the "prohibited areas" and the case-by-case of "saboteurs" families. During Anfal, the captives were registered by name, sex, age, place of birth and place of residence. Accordingly, men between ages 15 and 50 years old from the "prohibited areas" and families of "saboteurs," were sent to death in the south.

ANNIHILATION

The method of executing the Kurdish men by firing squads is, according to the MEW, "uncannily reminiscent of another," that of the Einsatzkommandos, or mobile killing units, in Eastern Europe occupied by the Nazis.

> Some groups of prisoners were lined up, shot from the front and dragged into pre-dug mass graves; others were shoved roughly into trenches and machine gunned where they stood; others were made to lie down in pairs, sardine-style next to mouths of fresh corpses, before being killed; others were tied together, made to stand on the lip of the pit, and shot in the back so that they would fall forward into it - a method that was presumably more efficient from the point of view of the killers. Bulldozers then pushed earth or sand loosely over the heaps of corpses. Some of the gravesites contained dozens of separate pits, and obviously contained the bodies of thousands of victims. Circumstantial evidence suggests that the executioners were uniformed members of the Ba'th Party, or perhaps of Iraq's General Security Directorate (Amn).

Rigid bureaucratic norms were governing this annihilation process. Those who were executed were not murdered because they were condemned for committing a specific crime; rather their only crime was to be born in a place declared by a central government as "prohibited," that is to say, Kurds in areas outside government control.

The locations of at least three mass gravesites have been pinpointed through the testimony of survivors at Ramadi, al-Hadar and Samawah.

Genocide in Iraq quotes Raul Hilberg saying, "There are not so many ways in which a modern society can, in short order, kill a large number of people living in its midst. This is an efficiency problem of the greatest dimensions…" The captured Iraqi documents demonstrate "in astonishing breadth and detail how the Iraqi state bureaucracy organised the Kurdish genocide."

MODERN GENOCIDE

The book demonstrates convincingly that the Kurdish genocide of 1987–1989 had a distinct modern flavour, to paraphrase Zygmunt Bauman. Although mass murder is not a modern invention, contemporary mass murder within the perimeters of the modern territorial state is. It is "distinguished by a virtual absence of all spontaneity on the one hand, and the prominence of rational, carefully calculated design on the other. It is marked by an almost complete elimination of contingency and chance, and independence from group emotions and personal motives." Modern genocide is thus a genocide with a purpose. It has initiators and the managers with a particular view of the society.

The purpose of the modern genocide is "a grand vision of a better, and radically different, society." Here a "gardener's vision," projected upon a society, is involved. As in the case of the gardeners, the designers of the perfect society hate the weeds that spoil their design. The weeds surrounding the desired society must be exterminated, it is a problem that has to be solved; the "weeds must die not so much because of what they are, as because of that the beautiful, orderly garden ought to be."

The Ba'thist rulers in Iraq have always desired to create a harmonious, conflict-free society, orderly, controlled and docile in their hands. The Kurds have constituted the main challenge to this vision based on the rhetoric of pan-Arabism. The Kurds have been viewed as the weeds disturbing the Ba'thist vision of the Arab Iraq. But the Ba'thists have been patient in materialising their vision. They have advanced their position by consolidating their power step by step, under more than twenty years. They have never given up their dream. "When the modernist dream is embraced by an absolute power able to monopolise modern vehicle of rational action, and when that power attains freedom from effective social control, genocide follows."

That is exactly what happened in the case of Iraq under the Bath Party. Five factors identified by Sarah Gordon are important in producing a modern genocide, which is also true in the case of Kurdish genocide of 1987–1989.

1. There was a radical anti-Kurdish drive.
2. The drive was transformed into the policy of a powerful, centralised state.
3. The state was in command of a huge, efficient bureaucratic apparatus.
4. A "state of emergency" was called—an extraordinary, wartime condition, which allowed government and bureaucracy it controlled to get away with things which could, possibly, face more serious obstacles in time of peace.
5. The population and the international community at large reacted with non-interference and passive acceptance of those things.

Given the circumstances, the mass killing of the Kurds was presented as a bureaucratic task to be implemented by different state organisations. The violence was turned into a technique of solving this bureaucratic mission. The bureaucrats within the Party, the army, numerous intelligence agencies, and civilian administration were presented with meticulous functional division of labour without any moral responsibility. Having been presented with a definition of the task, the bureaucracy in Iraq carried out the task to its end with a remarkable degree of rationality and efficiency. At the end of its task, only the bureaucracy's ability to refine its methods and efficiency could sufficiently explain why not even a single soul managed to escape from the Final Anfal's firing squads.

Once set in motion, refined and honoured and glorified, the machinery of murder developed its own impetus: after accomplishing its task faithfully in Kurdistan, it sought new territories where it could exercise its newly acquired skills. Is it not possible to view the invasion of Kuwait, and the killing of the civilians there as the externalisation of the Iraqi bureaucracy's "domestic style of rule to foreign policy," a modern skill, efficiency and capacity seeking by now territories outside Iraq? A close examination of the language, symbols and circumlocutions used in Iraq's propaganda war to justify the occupation of Kuwait might reveal that the Kuwaits were presented as yet another kind of weed to be removed from the Ba'thist vision of a united Arab world under that particular leadership.

QUESTIONS TO CONSIDER

1. How did the assessment of what was happening in Iraq by Edward Said reflect the lack of information about events in Iraq?

2. What evidence has been amassed to support the allegation of genocidal acts by Saddam Hussein? Do you agree with the definition of genocide Salih uses?

3. What did the Iraqi defeat in 1991 reveal about Saddam Hussein's Iraq?

4. How does the author say that what happened in Iraq fits Raul Hilberg's description of the Holocaust?

5. Why does the author classify the killings in Iraq as "modern genocide?"

Sanctions Against Iraq Are Genocide

George Bisharat,

Hastings College of Law

A serious legal argument can be made that sanctions imposed against Iraq in 1990 by the United Nations have come to constitute genocide.

Sanctions—which will come up for renewal in Congress this month—were originally instituted to compel Iraq's withdrawal from Kuwait. Iraq refused, and was forced out militarily in early 1991 through Operation Desert Storm. Sanctions against Iraq—a country devastated by war, dependent on oil exports for 90 percent of its foreign revenue and one which imports 70 percent of its food—were nonetheless re-imposed after the Gulf War.

The vanquished country was faced with a long list of demands, chief among them that it submit to extensive inspections and surrender its weapons of mass destruction. The Iraqi government's overall failure to satisfy the demands of the United Nations are a matter of record and are not in dispute here. The same is true of the autocratic, even murderous character of the regime of Saddam Hussein.

What is less recognized, however, is that the main reason for Iraq's recalcitrance is the United States insistence on "regime change" as a condition for the lifting of sanctions. Ousting Saddam Hussein, however desirable that may be from the perspective of U.S. policymakers, has never been endorsed by the international community. Nor is it a condition that the Iraqi government will ever willingly meet.

Unilateral action by the United States to overthrow the government of another sovereign nation, moreover, would constitute a grave breach of international law.

The real problem with the sanctions is that they target the wrong people: the poor, young, elderly and otherwise infirm members of Iraqi society. In the past 12 years, as many as 1 million to 2 million Iraqis may have died as a result of the sanctions, many of them children under the age of 5. This is more than were massacred in Rwanda in 1994, and on a par with the Armenian Holocaust of 1915–1919. UNICEF officials estimated in 2000 that 5,000 to 6,000 Iraqi children were dying each month primarily due to sanctions. That is equivalent to a World Trade Towers–scale calamity—in a nation of only 18 million—every month for the past decade or more.

Yet these Iraqi victims of sanctions have no more control over their government's behavior than we do. U.S. officials have clearly known the lethal impact of sanctions for years and have actively campaigned to maintain them regardless.

Knowing pursuit of a policy that kills members of a group, causes serious bodily or mental harm to them or inflicts on them conditions of life calculated to bring about their physical destruction in whole or in part constitutes genocide under international law. The crime of genocide is defined in the U.N. Convention on the Prevention and Punishment of the Crime of Genocide, a treaty we ratified in 1988.

It is not enough to say that Saddam is responsible for the plight of his people. That claim is legally and factually inaccurate. We are not free of all constraints in the way we respond to illegal acts by others. Police, for example, do not have the right to slaughter innocents on the way to apprehending criminals, even serious ones. Neither has Saddam's government misspent funds meant to alleviate the suffering of the Iraqi people, at least not in any degree likely to have altered their terrible fate.

From George Bisharat, "Sanctions Against Iraq Are Genocide," *Seattle Post-Intelligencer* (May 3, 2002). Reprinted with permission.

Our officials have simply made a conscious calculation that the cost of Iraqi lives destroyed by sanctions are, to quote former Secretary of State Madeleine Albright when questioned about the issue, "worth it."

Meanwhile, the American public, spared graphic images of more conventional warfare by a policy that operates by more insidious means, has been lulled into complacency. It is hard to imagine that Americans would tolerate a conventional military campaign that caused almost exclusively civilian deaths numbering a million or more, many of them children under the age of 5, no matter how worthy the ends sought. But 12 years of sanctions have accomplished just that, while evoking scarcely a ripple of public protest.

No benefit attained by sanctions can justify genocide. Sanctions themselves are indefensible. They also engender cynicism, even hatred, toward the United States among Muslims and peoples of the Middle East and elsewhere. They represent a failed, bankrupt policy. Sanctions should be finally abandoned, not just "smartened."

Past efforts to tailor sanctions to avoid humanitarian repercussions have never succeeded, and are not likely to succeed now. Alternatives to sanctions—other than war—do exist. They require patience, building consensus within the international community, a consistent plan for regional disarmament and, above all, respect for international law. There is always an alternative to genocide: no genocide.

QUESTIONS TO CONSIDER

1. Do you agree with the author that the UN sanctions imposed against Iraq in 1990 constituted genocide?
2. Describe the consequences of the sanctions.
3. Were these conditions caused by sanctions, or the Iraqi regime's policies?
4. Why is it "not enough to say that Saddam is responsible for the plight of his people"?
5. What is the reason for the American public's seeming complacency toward the effect of the sanctions on Iraqi civilians?

ISRAELIS AND PALESTINIANS

The Middle East is always in the news. Arguably, no conflict garners more intense, polarized debate than the broader Arab–Israeli or the narrower Israeli–Palestinian dispute. Certainly since Ben-Gurion's proclamation in May 1948 of "the establishment of the Jewish State in Palestine" and the Arab–Israeli war that followed, the Jewish state remains the focus of conflict in region.

At the heart of the confrontation is Zionism. Is Zionism racist? Can one be anti-Zionist and not be anti-Semitic? In a similar vein, superficial mainstream media portrayals homogenize Palestinians as "terrorists" intent on killing all Jews. Can Palestinian resistance be classified as racist?

Complicating the conflict is the integral role of the United States Noam Chomsky calls the conflict in the Middle East a "fateful triangle" with the United States sanctioning Israel's Palestinian solutions. To what extent is the United States complicit in the violence in the Middle East?

Edward Said looks at the conflict in the Middle East from a Palestinian perspective, while Caroline Glick offers an Israeli point of view.

Palestinians Under Siege

Edward Said,

Columbia University

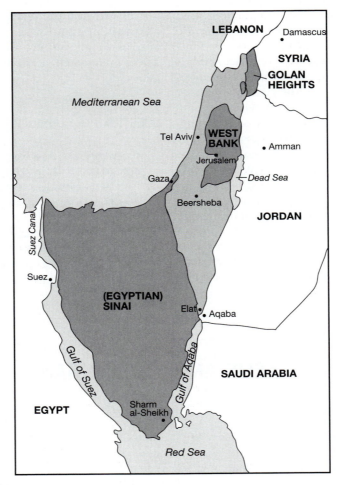

On 29 September, the day after Ariel Sharon, guarded by about a thousand Israeli police and soldiers strode into Jerusalem's Haram al-Sharif (the "Noble Sanctuary") in a gesture designed to assert his right as an Israeli to visit the Muslim holy place, a conflagration started which continues as I write in late November. Sharon himself is unrepentant, blaming the Palestinian Authority for "deliberate incitement" against Israel "as a strong democracy" whose "Jewish and democratic character" the Palestinians wish to change. He went to Haram al-Sharif, he wrote in the *Wall Street Journal* a few days later, "to inspect and ascertain that freedom of wor-

From Edward Said, "Palestinians Under Siege," *London Review of Books* (December 14, 2000). Reprinted with permission.

ship and free access to the Temple Mount is granted to everyone," but he didn't mention his huge armed entourage or the fact that the area was sealed off before, during and after his visit, which scarcely ensures freedom of access. He also neglected to say anything about the consequence of his visit: on the 29th, the Israeli Army shot eight Palestinians dead. What everyone ignored, moreover, is that the natives of a place under military occupation—which East Jerusalem has been since it was annexed by Israel in 1967—are entitled by international law to resist by any means possible. Besides, two of the oldest and greatest Muslim shrines in the world, dating back a millennium and a half, are supposed by archaeologists to have been built on the site of the Temple Mount— a convergence of religious topoi that a provocative visit by an extremist Israeli general was never going to help to sort out. A general, it's as well to recall, who had played a role in a number of atrocities dating back to the 1950s, and including Sabra, Shatila, Qibya and Gaza.

According to the Union of Palestinian Medical Relief Committees, as of early November, 170 people had been killed, 6000 wounded: these figures do not include 14 Israeli deaths (eight of them soldiers) and a slightly larger number of wounded. The Palestinian deaths include at least 22 boys under the age of 15 and, says the Israeli organisation B'tselem, 13 Palestinian citizens of Israel, killed by the Israeli police in demonstrations inside Israel. Both Amnesty International and Human Rights Watch have issued stern condemnations of Israel for the disproportionate use of force against civilians; Amnesty has published a report detailing the harassment, torture and illegal arrest of Arab children in Israel and Jerusalem. Parts of the Israeli press have been considerably more forthcoming and straightforward in their reporting and commentary on what has been taking place than the U.S. and European media. Writing in *Ha'aretz* on 12 November, Gideon Levy noted with alarm that most of the handful of Arab members of the

Knesset have been punished for objecting to Israel's policy towards Palestinians: some have been relieved of committee work, others are facing trial, still others are undergoing police interrogation. All this, he concludes, is part of "the process of demonisation and delegitimisation being conducted against the Palestinians" inside Israel as well as those in the Occupied Territories

"Normal life," such as it was, for Palestinians living in the occupied West Bank and the Gaza Strip is now impossible. Even the three hundred or so Palestinians allowed freedom of movement and other VIP privileges under the terms of the peace process have now lost these advantages, and like the rest of the three million or so people who endure the double burden of life under the Palestinian Authority and the Israeli occupation regime—to say nothing of the brutality of thousands of Israeli settlers, some of whom act as vigilantes terrorising Palestinian villages and large towns like Hebron—they are subject to the closures, encirclements and barricaded roads that have made movement impossible. Even Yasser Arafat has to ask permission to leave or enter the West Bank or Gaza, where his airport is opened and closed at will by the Israelis, and his headquarters have been bombed punitively by missiles fired from helicopter gunships. As for the flow of goods into and out of the territories, it has come to a standstill. According to the UN Special Co-ordinator's Office in the Occupied Territories, trade with Israel accounts for 79.8 per cent of Palestinian commercial transactions; trade with Jordan, which comes next, accounts for 2.39 per cent. That this figure is so low is directly ascribable to Israel's control of the Palestine-Jordan frontier (in addition to the Syrian, Lebanese and Egyptian borders). With Israel closed off, therefore, the Palestinian economy is losing $19.5 million a day on average—this already amounts to three times the total aid received from donor sources during the first six months of this year. For a population which continues to depend on the Israeli economy—thanks to the economic agreements signed by the PLO under Oslo—this is a severe hardship.

What hasn't slowed down is the rate of Israeli settlement building. On the contrary, according to the authoritative Report on Israeli Settlement in the Occupied Territories (RISOT), it has almost doubled over the past few years. The Report adds that "1924 settlement units have been started" since the start of the "pro-peace" regime of Ehud Barak in July 1999—and there is in addition the continuing programme of road-building and the expropriation of property for that purpose, as well as the degradation of Palestinian agricultural land both by the Army and the settlers. The Gaza-based Palestinian Centre for Human Rights has documented the "sweepings" of olive groves and vegetable farms by the Israeli Army (or, as it prefers to be known, Israeli Defence Force) near the Rafah border, for example, and on either side of the Gush Katif settlement block. Gush Katif is an area of Gaza—about 40 per cent—occupied by a few thousand settlers, who can water their lawns and fill their swimming pools, while the one million Palestinian inhabitants of the Strip (800,000 of them refugees from former Palestine) live in a parched, water-free zone. In fact, Israel controls the whole water supply of the Occupied Territories and assigns 80 per cent of it for the personal use of its Jewish citizens, rationing the rest for the Palestinian population: this issue was never seriously discussed during the Oslo peace process.

What of this vaunted peace process? What has it achieved and why, if indeed it was a peace process, has the miserable condition of the Palestinians and the loss of life become so much worse than before the Oslo Accords were signed in September 1993? And why is it, as the *New York Times* noted on 5 November, that "the Palestinian landscape is now decorated with the ruins of projects that were predicated on peaceful integration"? And what does it mean to speak of peace if Israeli troops and settle-

ments are still present in such large numbers? Again, according to RISOT, 110,000 Jews lived in illegal settlements in Gaza and the West Bank before Oslo; the number has since increased to 195,000, a figure that doesn't include those Jews—more than 150,000—who have taken up residence in Arab East Jerusalem. Has the world been deluded or has the rhetoric of "peace" been in essence a gigantic fraud?

Some of the answers to these questions lie buried in reams of documents signed by the two parties under American auspices, unread except by the small handful of people who negotiated them. Others are simply ignored by the media and the governments whose job, it now appears, was to press on with disastrous information, investment and enforcement policies, regardless of the horrors taking place on the ground. A few people, myself included, have tried to chronicle what has been going on, from the initial Palestinian surrender at Oslo until the present, but in comparison with the mainstream media and governments, not to mention the status reports and recommendations circulated by huge funding agencies like the World Bank, the European Union and many private foundations—notably the Ford Foundation—who have played along with the deception, our voices have had a negligible effect except, sadly, as prophecy.

The disturbances of the past few weeks have not been confined to Palestine and Israel. The displays of anti-American and anti-Israeli sentiment in the Arab and Islamic worlds are comparable to those of 1967. Angry street demonstrations are a daily occurrence in Cairo, Damascus, Casablanca, Tunis, Beirut, Baghdad and Kuwait. Millions of people have expressed their support for the al-Aqsa Intifada, as it has become known, as well as their outrage at the submissiveness of their governments. The Arab Summit in Cairo in October produced the usual ringing denunciations of Israel and a few more dollars for Arafat's Authority, but even the minimum diplomatic protest—the recall of ambassadors—was not made by any of the participants. On the day after the Summit, the American-educated Abdullah of Jordan, whose knowledge of Arabic is reported to have progressed to secondary school level, flew off to Washington to sign a trade agreement with the US, Israel's chief supporter. After six weeks of turbulence, Mubarak reluctantly withdrew his ambassador from Tel Aviv, but he depends greatly on the two billion dollars Egypt receives in annual U.S. aid and is unlikely to go any further. Like other leaders in the Arab world, he also needs the U.S. to protect him from his people. Meanwhile Arab anger, humiliation and frustration continue to build up, whether because their regimes are so undemocratic and unpopular or because the basics—employment, income, nutrition, health, education, infrastructure—have fallen below tolerable levels. Appeals to Islam and generalised expressions of outrage stand in for a sense of citizenship and participatory democracy. This bodes ill for the future, of the Arabs as well as of Israel. In foreign affairs circles during the last 25 years, the word has been that the cause of Palestine is dead, that pan-Arabism is a mirage, and that Arab leaders, mostly discredited, have accepted Israel and the U.S. as partners, and in the process of shedding their nationalism have settled for the panacea of deregulation in a global economy, whose early prophet in the Arab world was Anwar al-Sadat and whose influential drummer-boy has been the *New York Times* columnist and Middle East expert Thomas Friedman. Last October, after seven years of writing columns in praise of the Oslo peace process, Friedman found himself in Ramallah, under siege by the Israeli Army (and under fire). "Israeli propaganda that the Palestinians mostly rule themselves in the West Bank is fatuous nonsense," he announced. "Sure, the Palestinians control their own towns, but the Israelis control all the roads connecting these towns and therefore all their movements. Israeli confiscation of Palestinian land for more settle-

ments is going on to this day—seven years into Oslo." He concludes that only "a Palestinian state in Gaza and the West Bank" can bring peace, but says nothing about what kind of state it would be. Nor does he say anything about ending military occupation, but neither do the Oslo documents. Why Friedman never discussed this in the thousands of column inches he has published since September 1993, and why even now he doesn't say that today's events are the logical outcome of Oslo defies common sense, but it is typical of the disingenuousness that surrounds the subject.

The optimism of those who took it on themselves to ensure that the misery of the Palestinians was kept out of the news seems to have disappeared in a cloud of dust along with the "peace" which the U.S. and Israel have worked so hard to consolidate in their own narrow interests. At the same time, the old framework that survived the Cold War is slowly crumbling as the Arab leaderships age, without viable successors in sight. Mubarak has refused even to appoint a vice-president, Arafat has no clear successor; in Iraq and Syria's "democratic socialist" Ba'ath republics, as in the Kingdom of Jordan, the sons have taken over—or will take over—from the fathers, covering the process of dynastic autocracy with the merest fig-leaf of legitimacy

A turning point has been reached, however, and for this the Palestinian Intifada is a significant marker. For not only is it an anti-colonial rebellion of the kind that has been seen periodically in Setif, Sharpeville, Soweto and elsewhere, it is another example of the general discontent with the post-Cold War order (economic and political) displayed in the events of Seattle and Prague. Most of the world's Muslims see the uprising as part of a broader picture that includes Sarajevo, Mogadishu, Baghdad under U.S.-led sanctions and Chechnya. What must be clear to every ruler, including Clinton and Barak, is that the period of stability guaranteed by the tripartite dominance of Israel, the U.S. and local Arab regimes is now threatened by popular forces of uncertain magnitude, unknown direction, unclear vision. Whatever shape they eventually take, theirs will be an unofficial culture of the dispossessed, the silenced and the scorned. Very likely, too, it will bear in itself the distortions of years of past official policy.

Meanwhile, it is correct to say that most people hearing phrases like "the parties are negotiating," or "let's get back to the negotiating table," or "you are my peace partner," have assumed that there is parity between Palestinians and Israelis and that, thanks to the brave souls from each side who met secretly in Oslo, the two parties have at last been settling the questions that "divide" them, as if each had a piece of land, a territory from which to face the other. This is seriously, indeed mischievously misleading. In fact, the disproportion between the two antagonists is immense, in terms of the territory they control and the weapons at their disposal. Biased reporting disguises the extent of the disparity. Consider the following: citing an Anti-Defamation League survey of editorials published in the mainstream U.S. press, *Ha'aretz* on 25 October found "a pattern of support" for Israel, with 19 newspapers expressing sympathy for Israel in 67 editorials, 17 giving "balanced analysis," and only nine "voicing criticism against Israeli leaders (particularly Ariel Sharon), whom they accused of responsibility for the conflagration." In November, FAIR (Fairness and Accuracy in Reporting) noted that of the 99 Intifada stories broadcast by the three major U.S. networks between 28 September and 2 November, only four made reference to the "Occupied Territories." The same report drew attention to phrases such as "Israel ... again feeling isolated and under siege," "Israeli soldiers under daily attack," and, in a confrontation where its soldiers were forced back, "Israelis have surrendered territory to Palestinian violence." Highly partial formulations of this kind are threaded through

network news commentary, obscuring the facts of occupation and military imbalance: the Israeli Defence Forces have been using tanks, American and British-supplied Cobra and Apache attack helicopters, missiles, mortars and heavy machine-guns; the Palestinians have none of these things.

The *New York Times* has run only one op-ed piece by a Palestinian or an Arab (and he happens to be a supporter of Oslo) in a blizzard of editorial comment that favours the U.S. and Israeli positions; the *Wall Street Journal* has not run any such articles; nor has the *Washington Post*. On 12 November one of the most popular U.S. television programmes, CBS's *Sixty Minutes*, broadcast a sequence which seemed to be designed to let the Israeli Army "prove" that the killing of the 12-year-old Mohammad al-Dura, the icon of Palestinian suffering, was stage-managed by the Palestinian Authority. The Authority, it was said, had planted the boy's father in front of Israeli gun positions and moved the French TV crew that recorded the killing into position nearby—all to prove an ideological point.

Misrepresentation has made it almost impossible for the American public to understand the geographical basis of the events, in this, the most geographical of contests. No one can be expected to follow and, more important, retain a cumulatively accurate picture of the arcane provisions that obtain on the ground, the result of mostly secret negotiations between Israel and a disorganised, pre-modern and tragically incompetent Palestinian team, under Arafat's thumb. Crucially, the relevant UN Security Council Resolutions—242 and 338—are now forgotten, having been marginalised by Israel and the U.S. Both resolutions stipulate unequivocally that the land acquired by Israel as a result of the war of 1967 must be given back in return for peace. The Oslo process began by effectively consigning those resolutions to the rubbish bin—and so it was a great deal easier, after the failure of the Camp David summit last

July, to claim, as Clinton and Barak have done, that the Palestinians were to blame for the impasse, rather than the Israelis, whose position remains that the 1967 territories are not to be returned. The U.S. press referred again and again to Israel's "generous" offer and Barak's willingness to concede part of East Jerusalem plus anything between 90 and 94 per cent of the West Bank to the Palestinians. Yet no one writing in the U.S. or European press has established precisely what was to be "conceded" or quite what territory on the West Bank he was "offering" 90 per cent of. The whole thing was chimerical nonsense, as Tanya Reinhart showed in *Yediot Aharanot*, Israel's largest daily. In "The Camp David Fraud" (13 July), she writes that the Palestinians were offered 50 per cent of the West Bank in separated cantons; 10 per cent was to be annexed by Israel and no less than 40 per cent was to be left "under debate," to use the euphemism for continued Israeli control. If you annex 10 per cent, decline (as Barak did) to dismantle or stop settlements, refuse over and over again to return to the 1967 lines or give back East Jerusalem, deciding at the same time to hold onto whole areas like the Jordan Valley, and so completely encircle the Palestinian territories as to let them have no borders with any state except Israel, in addition to retaining the notorious "bypass" roads and their adjacent areas, the famous "90 per cent" is rapidly reduced to something like 50–60 per cent, the greater part of which is only up for discussion some time in the very distant future. After all, even the last Israeli redeployment agreed at the Wye River Plantation meetings of 1998 and reconfirmed at Sharm el Sheikh in 1999, has still not occurred. It bears repeating, of course, that Israel is still the only state in the world with no officially declared borders. And when we look at that 50–60 per cent in terms of the former Palestine, it amounts to about 12 per cent of the land from which the Palestinians were driven in 1948. The Israelis talk of "conceding" these territories. But they were taken by con-

quest and, in a strict sense, Barak's offer would only mean that they were being returned, by no means in their entirety.

To begin with, some facts. In 1948 Israel took over most of what was historical or Mandatory Palestine, destroying and depopulating 531 Arab villages in the process. Two thirds of the population were driven out: they are the four million refugees of today. The West Bank and Gaza, however, went to Jordan and Egypt respectively. Both were subsequently lost to Israel in 1967 and remain under its control to this day, except for a few areas that operate under a highly circumscribed Palestinian "autonomy"—the size and contours of these areas was decided unilaterally by Israel, as the Oslo process specifies. Few people realise that even under the terms of Oslo, the Palestinian areas that have this autonomy or self-rule do not enjoy sovereignty: that can only be decided as part of the Final Status Negotiations. In other words, Israel took 78 per cent of Palestine in 1948 and the remaining 22 per cent in 1967. Only that 22 per cent is in question now, and it excludes West Jerusalem (of 19,000 dunams there, Jews owned 4830 and Arabs 11,190, the rest was state land), all of which Arafat conceded in advance to Israel at Camp David.

What land, then, has Israel returned so far? It is impossible to detail in any straightforward way—impossible by design. It is part of Oslo's malign genius that even Israel's "concessions" were so heavily encumbered with conditions, qualifications and entailments—like one of the endlessly deferred and physically unobtainable estates in a Jane Austen novel—that the Palestinians could not feel that they enjoyed any semblance of self-determination. On the other hand, they could be described as concessions, making it possible for everyone (including the Palestinian leadership) to say that certain areas of land were now (mostly) under Palestinian control. It is the geographical map of the peace process that most dramatically shows the distortions which have been building up and have been systematically disguised by the measured discourse of peace and bilateral negotiations. Ironically, in none of the many dozens of news reports published or broadcast since the present crisis began has a map been provided to help explain why the conflict has reached such a pitch.

The Oslo strategy was to redivide and subdivide an already divided Palestinian territory into three subzones, A, B and C, in ways entirely devised and controlled by the Israeli side since, as I have been pointing out for several years, the Palestinians themselves have until recently been mapless. They had no detailed maps of their own at Oslo; nor, unbelievably, were there any individuals on the negotiating team familiar enough with the geography of the Occupied Territories to contest decisions or to provide alternative plans. Whence the bizarre arrangements for subdividing Hebron after the 1994 massacre of 29 Palestinians at the Horahimi mosque by Baruch Goldstein— measures undertaken to "protect" the settlers, not the Palestinians. [...]

In other words, the closures and encirclements that have turned the Palestinian areas into besieged spots on the map have been long in the making and, worse still, the Palestinian Authority has conspired in this: it has approved all the relevant documents since 1994. In October Amira Hass, the *Ha'aretz* correspondent in the Palestinian territories, wrote that in 1993 the two sides agreed on a period of five years for completion of the new deployment and the negotiations on a final agreement. The Palestinian leadership agreed again and again to extend its trial period, in the shadow of Hamas terrorist attacks and the Israeli elections. The "peace strategy" and the tactic of gradualism adopted by the leadership were at first supported by most of the Palestinian public, which craves normalcy—and, I would have thought, a real ending of the occupation which, to repeat, was nowhere mentioned in any of the Oslo documents. She goes on: "Fatah (the main

faction of the PLO) was the backbone of support for the concept of gradual release from the yoke of military occupation. Its members were the ones who kept track of the Palestinian opposition, arrested suspects whose names were given to them by Israel, imprisoned those who signed manifestos claiming that Israel did not intend to rescind its domination over the Palestinian nation. The personal advantage gained by some of these Fatah members is not enough to explain their support of the process: for a long time they really and truly believed that this was the way to independence."

By "advantage" Hass means the VIP privileges I mentioned earlier. But then, as she points out, these men, too, were members of "the Palestinian nation," with wives, children and siblings who suffered the consequences of Israeli occupation, and were bound, at some point, to ask whether support for the peace process did not also mean support for the occupation. She concludes: "More than seven years have gone by, and Israel has security and administrative control of 61.2 per cent of the West Bank and about 20 per cent of the Gaza Strip, and security control over another 26.8 per cent of the West Bank."

This control is what has enabled Israel to double the number of settlers in ten years, to enlarge the settlements, to continue its discriminatory policy of cutting back water quotas for three million Palestinians, to prevent Palestinian development in most of the area of the West Bank, and to seal an entire nation into restricted areas, imprisoned in a network of bypass roads meant for Jews only. During these days of strict internal restriction of movement in the West Bank, one can see how carefully each road was planned: so that 200,000 Jews have freedom of movement and about three million Palestinians are locked into their Bantustans until they submit to Israeli demands. To which one should add, by way of clarification, that the main aquifers for Israel's water supply are on the West Bank; that the "entire nation" excludes the four million refugees who are categorically denied the right of return, even though any Jew anywhere still enjoys an absolute right of "return" at any time; that restriction of movement is as severe in Gaza as it is on the West Bank; and that Hass's figure of 200,000 Jews in Gaza and on the West Bank enjoying freedom of movement does not include the 150,000 new Israeli-Jewish inhabitants who have been brought in to "Judaise" East Jerusalem.

The Palestinian Authority is locked into this astonishingly ingenious, if in the long run fruitless, arrangement via security committees made up of Mossad, the CIA and the Palestinian security services. At the same time, Israel and high-ranking members of the Authority operate lucrative monopolies on building materials, tobacco, oil, etc. (profits are deposited in Israeli banks). Not only are Palestinians subject to harassment from Israeli troops, but their own men participate in this abuse of their rights, alongside hated non-Palestinian agencies. These largely secret security committees also have a mandate to censor anything that might be construed as "incitement" against Israel. Palestinians, of course, have no such right against American or Israeli incitements.

The slow pace of this unfolding process is justified by the U.S. and Israel in terms of safeguarding the latter's security; one hears nothing about Palestinian security. Clearly we must conclude, as Zionist discourse has always stipulated, that the very existence of Palestinians, no matter how confined or disempowered, constitutes a racial and religious threat to Israel's security. All the more remarkable that in the midst of such amazing unanimity, at the height of the present crisis, Danny Rabinowitz, an Israeli anthropologist, spoke bravely in *Ha'aretz* (17 October) of Israel's "original sin" in destroying Palestine in 1948, which with few exceptions Israelis have chosen either to deny or to forget completely.

If the geography of the West Bank has been altered to Israel's advantage, Jerusalem's has been changed entirely. The annexation of East Jerusalem in 1967 added 70 square kilometres to the state of Israel; another 54 square kilometres were filched from the West Bank and added to the metropolitan area ruled for so long by Mayor Teddy Kollek, the darling of Western liberals, who with his deputy, Meron Benvenisti, was responsible for the demolition of several hundred Palestinian homes in Haret al-Maghariba to make way for the immense plaza in front of the Wailing Wall. Since 1967 East Jerusalem has been systematically Judaised, its borders inflated, enormous housing projects built, new roads and bypasses constructed so as to make it unmistakably and virtually unreturnable and, for the dwindling, harassed Arab population of the city, all but uninhabitable. As Deputy Mayor Abraham Kehiia said in July 1993, "I want to make the Palestinians open their eyes to reality and understand that the unification of Jerusalem under Israeli sovereignty is irreversible."

The Camp David summit in July broke down because Israel and the U.S. presented all the territorial arrangements I have been discussing here—only slightly modified to give Palestinians back two "nature areas," a euphemism for desert land, so as to increase their portion of the total land area—as the basis for the final settlement of the Palestinian-Israeli conflict. Reparations were, in effect, dismissed by the Israelis, although they are not an entirely alien idea to many Jews. I have seen no mention in the Western media of a long report on Camp David written by Akram Haniyeh, editor of the Ramallah daily *Al-Ayyam*, and a Fatah loyalist who, since his deportation by the Israelis in 1987, has been close to Arafat. Haniyeh makes it clear that from the Palestinian point of view Clinton simply reinforced the Israeli position, and that, in order to save his career, Barak wanted a quick conclusion to critical issues such as the refugee problem and

Jerusalem, as well as a formal declaration from Arafat ending the conflict definitively. (Barak has since called for early elections as a way of staving off a total Parliamentary defeat.) Haniyeh's gripping account of what took place is soon to appear in English translation in the Washington-based *Journal of Palestine Studies*. It shows that the "unprecedented" Israeli position on Jerusalem was in fact tailored to that of the Israeli right-wing—in other words, that Israel would retain conclusive sovereignty over even the al-Aqsa mosque. "The Israeli position," Haniyeh says, "was to reap everything"—and to give almost nothing in return. Israel would have got the "golden signature" from Arafat, final recognition and "the precious end of conflict promise." All this without a complete return of occupied territory, an acknowledgment of full sovereignty or a recognition of the refugee issue.

Since 1967 the U.S. has disbursed more than $200 billion dollars in unconditional financial and military aid to Israel, while offering blanket political support that allows Israel to do as it pleases. Britain, whose foreign policy is a carbon copy of Washington's, also supplies military hardware that goes directly to the West Bank and Gaza to facilitate the killing of Palestinians. No state has received anywhere near as much foreign aid as Israel and no state (aside from the U.S. itself) has defied the international community on so many issues for so long. Were Al Gore to become President this policy would remain unchanged. Gore is uncompromisingly pro-Israeli, and a close associate of Martin Peretz, Israel's leading pro-rejectionist and anti-Arab rhetorician in the U.S., and owner of the *New Republic*. At least George W. Bush made an effort during the campaign to address Arab American concerns, but like most past Republican Presidents, he would be only sightly less pro-Israeli than Gore.

For seven years, Arafat had been signing peace process agreements with Israel. Camp David was obviously meant to be the last. He balked, no doubt, because he had woken up to the enormity of what he had already signed away; no doubt, too, because he was aware how much popularity he had lost. Never mind the corruption, the despotism, the spiralling unemployment, now up to 25 per cent, the sheer poverty of most of his people: he finally understood that, having been kept alive by Israel and the U.S., he would be thrown back to his people without the Haram al-Sharif and without a real state, or even the prospect of viable statehood. Young Palestinians have had enough and, despite Arafat's feeble efforts to control them, have taken to the streets to throw stones and fire slingshots at Israeli Merkavas and Cobras.

What Israel has depended on in the past, the ignorance, complicity or laziness of journalists outside Israel, is now countered by the fantastic amount of alternative information available on the Internet. Cyber activists and hackers have opened a vast new reservoir of material which anyone with a minimum of literacy can tap into. There are reports not only by journalists from the British press (there aren't any equivalents in the U.S. establishment media) but also from the Israeli and Europe-based Arab press; there is research by individual scholars and information gleaned from archives, international organisations and UN agencies, as well as from NGO collectives in Palestine, Israel, Europe, Australia and North America. Here, as in many other instances, reliable information is the greatest enemy of oppression and injustice. The most demoralising aspect of the Zionist-Palestinian conflict is the almost total opposition between mainstream Israeli and Palestinian points of view. We were dispossessed and uprooted in 1948, they think they won independence and that the means were just. We recall that the land we left and the territories we are trying to liberate from military occupation are all part of our national patrimony; they think it is theirs by Biblical fiat and diasporic affiliation. Today, by any conceivable standards, we are the victims of the violence; they think they are. There is simply no common ground, no common narrative, no possible area for genuine reconciliation. Our claims are mutually exclusive. Even the notion of a common life shared in the same small piece of land is unthinkable. Each of us thinks of separation, perhaps even of isolating and forgetting the other.

The greater moral pressure to change is on the Israelis, whose military actions and unwise peace strategy derive from a preponderance of power on their side, and an unwillingness to see that they are laying up years of resentment and hatred on the part of Muslims and Arabs. Ten years from now there will be demographic parity between Arabs and Jews in historical Palestine: what then? Can the tank deployments, road blocks and house demolitions continue as before? Might it not make sense for a group of respected historians and intellectuals, composed equally of Palestinians and Israelis, to hold a series of meetings to try to agree a modicum of truth about this conflict, to see whether the known sources can guide the two sides to agree on a body of facts— who took what from whom, who did what to whom, and so on—which in turn might reveal a way out of the present impasse? It is too early, perhaps, for a Truth and Reconciliation Commission, but something like a Historical Truth and Political Justice Committee would be appropriate.

It is clear to everyone on the ground that the old Oslo framework which has done so much damage is no longer workable (a recent poll conducted by Bir Zeit University shows that only 3 per cent of the Palestinian population want to return to the old negotiations) and that the Palestinian negotiating team led by Arafat can no longer hold the centre, much less the nation. Everyone feels that enough is enough: the occupation has gone on too long, the peace talks have dragged on with too little to show for them, the goal, if it was to have been independence, seems no closer (thank Rabin, Peres and their Palestinian counterparts for that particular failure), and the suffering of ordinary people has gone further than can be endured. Hence the stone-throwing in the streets, yet another futile activity with its own tragic consequences. The only hope is to keep trying to rely on an idea of coexistence between two peoples in one land. For now, though, the Palestinians are in desperate need of guidance and, above all, physical protection. Barak's plan to punish, contain and stifle them has already had calamitous results, but it cannot, as he and his American mentors suppose, bring them to heel. Why is it that more Israelis do not realise—as some already have—that a policy of brutality against Arabs in a part of the world containing three hundred million Arabs and 1.2 billion Muslims, will not make the Jewish state more secure?

QUESTIONS TO CONSIDER

1. According to Said, what are Palestinians justified in doing by international law?
2. Do you think it would be necessary for Said to include figures for Israeli deaths?
3. Why is continued Israeli settlement building an important issue?
4. Why is calling for equal parties to negotiate not appropriate in this instance?
5. What were the disadvantages for the Palestinians at the Oslo peace talks?
6. Why did the July Camp David summit collapse?
7. Even though Said does not use the word, is Israel engaged in genocidal policies against the Palestinians?

No Tolerance for Genocide

Caroline B. Glick

The television camera lens moves with seeming effortlessness from the pictures of suffering and death at the Hebrew University to the carnival in Gaza City, where thousands take to the streets in celebration of the pictures from Jerusalem. Gazing at the revelers on the screen, one strains one's eyes to find an expression of shame, guilt, or remorse on the faces in the crowd. One unconsciously prays to discern anything that would show that those in front of the camera are there by accident or because they were forced to be there. But no, the faces on the screen are uninhibited, joyful ones.

Far from being forced to participate in the festivities, each and every one of the people at the parade in Gaza makes a personal decision to leave his or her home and join the crowd in applauding the mass murder of Jews. They are there because they support the murders. They are there because such murders make them happy.

These Gazans, and their counterparts at Balata refugee camp near Nablus, were not celebrating a military victory. There was no battle at the cafeteria in the Frank Sinatra International Student Center. These Palestinians—men, women, teenagers, and small children—came together to celebrate another massacre in their genocidal campaign against the Jewish people. Yes, genocide. The Palestinians have reached a point in this war where it has now become clear that their goal in this struggle is not the end of the so-called "occupation," but rather the organized, premeditated mass murder of Jews because they are Jewish. That is, the Palestinian goal today is genocide.

In a seminal article in *Commentary* magazine this past February on the recent rise of anti-Semitism, Hillel Halkin argued, counterintuitively, that the Holocaust is the main reason why it is so difficult for Jews today to accept the fact of anti-Semitism. In his words, "The Holocaust has made some Jews less, rather than more, able to see anti-Semitism around them. This is because if the Nazis demonized the Jew, they also demonized the anti-Semite." In short, if an anti-Semite is not a Nazi, then it is hard for Jews to perceive him as a threat.

Just so, even as generations of Jews adopted "Never Again" as their rallying cry, the Holocaust made it difficult for us to notice when genocide is adopted as a policy against the Jewish people, without gas chambers present. The fact that the Palestinians currently lack the means used by the Germans to perpetrate their genocidal policy against the Jews blinds us from the fact that their desire to do so is the same as that of the Germans in the 1930s and 1940s.

The absence of the trappings of the Nazi Holocaust also prevents us from properly identifying repeated massacres of Israelis by Palestinians. Contrary to what we tell ourselves, these attacks are not expressions of rage or reactions to specific actions by the IDF. They are acts of genocide perpetrated against Jews as Jews because the Palestinians have descended to the level of depravity where they do not view the Jews as human beings whose murder is an inherently immoral act.

The fact that the Palestinians don ski masks and keffiyehs rather than brown shirts and swastikas also makes us undervalue the fact

From Caroline B. Glick, "No Tolerance for Genocide," The *Jerusalem Post* (August 2, 2002). Reprinted with permission.

that, like the Nazis, the Palestinians are utilizing all their technological know-how and military resources to kill Jews and are making their best efforts to constantly improve and enhance these resources to increase their kill rate.

Daniel Goldhagen showed in his masterful book, *Hitler's Willing Executioners—Ordinary Germans and the Holocaust,* that contrary to popular belief, the Holocaust was not a Nazi-specific affair, but rather a German affair. While Hitler and his Nazi Party dominated Germany, the Germans allowed themselves to be dominated. While the Nazis were the architects of the Holocaust, they perpetrated it with the active support and participation of many rank-and-file Germans from all walks of life, in all sectors of German society regardless of membership in the Nazi Party.

Such is also the case in Palestinian society today. It is not just Hamas or Tanzim or Islamic Jihad that we must fight, but Palestinian society itself must be transformed for there to be peaceful coexistence. All major indicators point to the conclusion that the overwhelming majority of Palestinians is complicit in the aim of committing genocide against the Israelis. Poll after poll shows that a solid majority of Palestinians from all socio-economic levels supports suicide bombers and other forms of terrorism against Israel. In fact the polls show that the higher the socio-economic level of the respondents, the stronger their support for terrorism.

Virulent, Nazi-style Jew hatred and dehumanization has become for the Palestinians, as for the Germans before them, the central unifying theme of society. The best-seller lists in the PA for years have included such works as *Mein Kampf* and the *Protocols of the Elders of Zion.* Being a relative of a suicide bomber is a status symbol.

From the schoolrooms to the mosques to the daily papers to the art studios, Palestinians teach, preach, write, and paint in praise of genocide. Even Yasser Arafat's purportedly democratic and pro-Western opposition has no moral qualms about massacring Israelis. Leaders like the much-feted Sari Nusseibeh argue against suicide bombings not because they are morally reprehensible, but because of their tactical inconvenience.

In an interview on Al-Jazeera television on July 14, translated by Palestinian Media Watch, Nusseibeh praised everyone involved in jihad against Israel. Explaining that he did not want to pass moral judgment on the murderers when he signed a petition a month earlier calling for an end to suicide bombers, Nusseibeh said that terrorism presents no moral dilemma, it is only a question of whether or not "political benefit" accrues from killing Israeli civilians.

Nusseibeh's explanation echoes the official PA condemnations of every attack. There is never a moral judgment made, only a cost-benefit analysis. That killing Jews is acceptable is quite simply taken for granted.

Once we understand that this is the situation in Palestinian society, we reconcile ourselves with the fact that we are not in a struggle against a political movement for national sovereignty. We are being victimized by a genocidal campaign for our violent elimination supported by the overwhelming majority of Palestinians.

To defuse the danger presented to Israel by the genocidal Palestinians, we must also look to the German experience and take our cue from the Allied policy for the de-Nazification of postwar Germany. In World War II it was clear to the Allies that Germany would have to undergo along process of social and political transformation before the Germans could again be trusted with sovereignty. The first step on the road was an unconditional surrender of the German army to Allied forces. As part of their military surrender, German nationals were forcibly deported from the strategically vital Danzig corridor and East Prussia, which were handed over to Poland. The Germans ceded all claims to the territory and deported nationals were banished with no right of return.

Furthermore, the surrender terms for Germany involved the stationing of a permanent occupation force on German soil, which still exists today, 58 years later, and forced limitations on German military capabilities and troop levels.

The transformation of German politics involved permanently banning anyone involved in the Nazi regime or supportive of that regime from participation in German political life.

There is no longer any room to doubt that the Palestinians, to become a nation that will live at peace with Israel, must undergo a similar transformation. Whether Israel can force such a process onto the Palestinians by itself or whether such a transformation will necessarily take place as part of a reshuffling of the Arab world that supports its genocidal program remains to be seen. But what is clear enough is that there can be no negotiations, no legitimacy, and no tolerance for a society whose central organizing principle is the physical elimination of the Jewish people.

QUESTIONS TO CONSIDER

1. Why does the author term Palestinian actions as "genocide"?
2. Does the author offer any evidence to support the claim that a majority of Palestinians support genocide?
3. What is the precondition advocated by the author before Palestine could become a nation?
4. Does calling the Palestinian-Israeli conflict genocide make it so?

MAKING CONNECTIONS

1. Does the Anfal have elements of the Armenian genocide?
2. Does Zionism in some ways reflect Manifest Destiny?
3. Is the relationship of the United States to Israel similar in nature to the relationship between Guatemala and the United States?

✔ RECOMMENDED RESOURCES

Butler, Richard. *The Greatest Threat: Iraq, Weapons of Mass Destruction, and the Crisis of Global Security.* New York: PublicAffairs, 2000.

Byman, Daniel, and Matthew C. Waxman. *Confronting Iraq: U.S. Policy and the Use of Force Since the Gulf War.* Santa Monica, CA: RAND, 2000.

Francona, Rick. *Ally to Adversary: An Eyewitness Account of Iraq's Fall From Grace.* Annapolis, MD: Naval Institute Press.

Khalil, Samir. *Republic of Fear: The Politics of Modern Iraq.* Berkeley: University of California Press, 1990.

Lewis, Bernard. *The Middle East: A Brief History of the Last 2,000 Years.* New York: Touchstone Books, 1997.

Morris, Benny. *Righteous Victims: A History of the Zionist—Arab Conflict, 1881–1999.* New York: Knopf, 2000.

Shalaim, Avi. *The Iron Wall: Israel and the Arab World.* New York: W. W. Norton & Company, 1999.

CHAPTER 15

BASTARD CHILD OF THE COLD WAR: NORTH KOREA

At the end of World War II, North Korea came under Communist domination while the southern portion of Korea became Western oriented. Kim Il Sung ruled North Korea until his death in 1994, when his son Kim Jong Il, the "Great Leader," succeeded him. His rule commenced as agricultural supports from the former USSR and China ceased.

From 1994 to 1998, two to three million North Koreans died of starvation and hunger-related illnesses. Similar to Stalin's man-made famine, Kim Jong Il targeted the northeast region of the country by terminating the public food distribution system. The severity of the food shortage reached Pyongyang, where party cadres supplied themselves and workers in critical industries, letting the rest of the population fend for themselves. North Korean refugees poured into China, especially from the hardest hit area around the city of Hamhŭng.

Early explanations for what happened in North Korea suggested that the famine resulted from natural disaster. Devastating floods in August 1995 and successive droughts and floods over the next three years accounted for about 15 to 20 percent of the food deficit, but the rest of the shortage has been attributed to collectivist agricultural policies. At the same time, Kim Jong Il thwarted a reported military coup in the Northeast. Andrew Natsios describes the politics of famine explaining how famine devastated one part of North Korea and not another. Pierre Rigoulot and Aidan Foster-Carter explain the consequences of the famine in the context of the Stalinist precedent.

The Politics of Famine in North Korea

Andrew Natsios,

*Secretary of Administration and Finance
for the Commonwealth of Massachusetts*

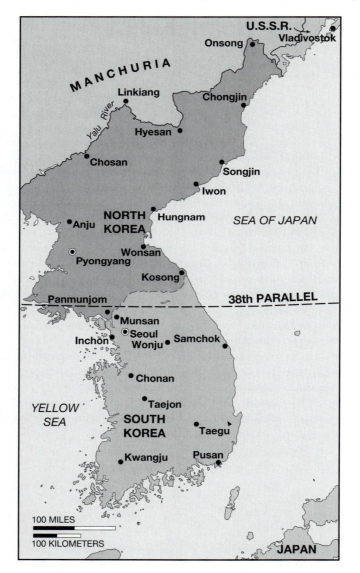

From Andrew Natsios, "The Politics of Famine in North Korea," *United States Institute of Peace Special Report* (August 2, 1999). Reprinted with permission.

BRIEFLY …

- Because of the withdrawal of USSR and Chinese food subsidies in the early 1990s and the cumulative effect of collective farming, food availability in North Korea declined steadily and then plummeted between 1995 and 1997 when flooding followed by drought struck the country.
- From 1994 to 1998, 2–3 million people died of starvation and hunger-related illnesses, and the famine has generated a range of social and political effects.
- Beginning in 1994, the central authorities appear to have triaged the northeast region of the country by shutting down the public distribution system. In 1996, they appear to have begun selective food distributions to people in the capital city, workers in critical industries, and party cadres, leaving the rest of the population to fend for itself in the private markets.
- Refugees report that the famine has undermined popular support for the current political leadership. In 1995, a planned coup by military officers was uncovered by secret police in Hamhung, the city most devastated by the famine. Public anger is more typically reflected in growing corruption, black market activities, and other anti-system behavior.
- International food aid has stimulated private markets, reduced the price of food in the markets 25–35 percent, and undermined central government propaganda concerning South Korea and the United States.
- Those who have died or suffered most during the famine have been those unable to adjust to the economic reality of these new markets either by growing their own food or by producing some other marketable product, labor, or service to exchange for food.
- Reduced purchases of Chinese maize in 1999 will force higher prices in the private markets. Given the fragility of the private food system, and absent international aid, this situation may plunge the mountainous regions of the country into a new round of famine-related deaths.

INTRODUCTION

While it is widely acknowledged that the collapse of the North Korean economy has caused a severe food crisis, the severity and political implications of the crisis have been a source of considerable dispute. A substantial body of new evidence indicates that the country has been experiencing a major famine with abnormally high mortality rates since 1994.

The food crisis did not begin with the floods in August 1995, as has been commonly understood, but with the sharp reduction in heavily subsidized food, equipment, and crude oil from the Soviet Union and China in the early 1990s. This reduction precipitated an agricultural and industrial decline of enormous magnitude. As output fell, the central government initiated a "Let's eat two meals a day" campaign to ration diminishing food supplies. A family of defectors to South Korea in 1994 reported that elderly people were going out to the fields to die to relieve their families of the burden of feeding them (Samuel Kim, *The Foreign Policy of North Korea*, 1998). In their study of North Korea's demographics, Nicholas Eberstadt and Judith Bannister speculate that the underreporting of elderly female deaths in official population figures may have been a function of families wishing to continue to receive their relatives' rations even after they had died (*The Population of North Korea*, 1992).

The massive floods during August 1995 led to a central government appeal to the World Food Program (WFP) for food aid. This natural disaster and a series of successive droughts and floods over the next three years are responsible for about 15–20 percent of the food deficit facing the country, the rest being attributable to collectivist agricultural policies [WFP/Food and Agriculture Organization (FAO) crop assessment, 1995].

Most of the food production estimates of the North Korean harvest fail to include postharvest losses attributable to poor storage, rot, rodents, and insect infestation. WFP/FAO reports have gradually increased this estimate from 0 percent in 1995 to 6 percent in 1996 and 15 percent in 1998. Russian scholar Marina Yi Tribuyenko estimates the North Korean loss rate to be comparable to the annual Soviet loss rate of 30 percent ("Economic Characteristics and Prospects for Development" in *North Korea: Ideology, Politics and Economy*, edited by S. Han Park, 1995).

An acrimonious policy debate has been taking place within humanitarian organizations about the severity of the famine—indeed, its very existence—and the role of international food assistance in ending it. The questions being raised in the debate are not new; they reflect legitimate concerns about the effect of food aid to a country where those with political authority may have objectives very different from those of humanitarian agencies trying to reduce death rates.

North Korea is notable, even among its former eastern bloc allies, for being the most controlled and reclusive society on earth. Discerning what is actually happening in such a society is no easy matter. Much of the reporting on the famine has been based on visual observation by humanitarian aid workers who have visited or worked in the country. While these visits do provide some information, neither field visits nor the data provided by the North Korean government about the food situation are conclusive evidence of anything because they present conditions as the central authorities wish them to appear to the outside world.

In addition to field reports, seven other sources provide valuable anecdotal and empirical evidence about North Korea's food crisis: United States Institute of Peace Special Reports by Scott Snyder ("A Coming Crisis on the Korean Peninsula?" and "North Korea's Decline and China's Strategic Dilemmas"); defector interviews; a book by the preeminent defector Hwang Jong Yop (*North Korea: Truth or Lies?* 1998); research by scholars of North Korea; the collected reports of Jasper Becker, reporter for the *South China Morning Post*, and of Hilary Mackenzie, a Canadian journalist with unusual internal access; four studies based on refugee interviews (two very large surveys of more than 2,000 interviews and two smaller nongovernmental organization surveys); and the speeches of Kim Jong Il, particularly his speech of December 1996, which provides exceptional insight into the dynamics of the famine. I visited North Korea in June 1997 and the Chinese border with North Korea in September 1998 to interview 20 food refugees

through meetings arranged with the assistance of a South Korean nongovernmental organization (NGO). I have attempted to cross-check information with at least three independent sources before concluding that it is accurate.

CAUSES OF THE CRISIS

The Economics of the Famine

Traditionally, famines have been principally economic phenomena with political and public health consequences, not vice versa. In totalitarian regimes in which economics is subordinated to ideology, famines can be politically driven. Despite manipulation and control, who lives and who dies is ultimately determined by microeconomic forces affecting specific regions, ages, incomes, and job groups differently, complicated by local food market prices. Macroeconomic perspectives offer less insight.

As food becomes scarcer in a famine, its marginal value increases exponentially. Beginning in 1995, North Korea's central authorities reduced the grain ration for farm families from 167 kilograms per person per year to 107 kilograms, which was insufficient to live on. Reducing farm family rations proved disastrous to the food distribution system because it instantly changed the economic incentive for farmers. This reduction had three pathological consequences for the North Korean food system:

- It broke the social contract between farmers and the rest of society that farmers would grow food in exchange for industrial production from the urban and mining areas. Under the traditional arrangement, the state and collective farms took control of the harvest each year and then gave an allotted ration back to the farmer and his family. Because of the economic downturn after the withdrawal of Soviet oil and food subsidies, the system could not produce the pesticides, fertilizer, and herbicides needed to supply the farms, further reducing agricultural production. With the farmers' rations reduced, any incentive to provide food to industrial areas disappeared.

- It encouraged farmers to divert production from the agricultural system before the harvest. The sudden drastic reduction in the food ration meant that farmers were given the choice of letting their families starve or secretly preharvesting and saving food to build up family stocks before the harvest was actually taken. Kim Jong Il complained bitterly about this secret preharvesting in a speech (December 1996). One defector said that he had seen reports of the roofs of many farmers' homes collapsing under the weight of hidden grain. The fall 1996 WFP/FAO agricultural assessment acknowledges that half the corn harvest was missing—nearly 1.3 million metric tons (MT). This hoarding began an undeclared war between the central authorities and the individual farmers. According to defector and refugee interviews, soldiers—called corn guards—were dispatched to protect the fields as the harvest matured in an effort to prevent this enormous diversion. However, this command and control tactic failed when farmers simply bribed the soldiers, hungry themselves because of a breakdown in the military distribution system, to join them in the diversion.

- It encouraged farmers in mountainous maize-growing areas to spend their time, expertise, and energy cultivating the private plots of land the government gave them decades ago to grow vegetables for household use, and on cultivating secret plots of land in the mountains outside the control of the collective agricultural system. Though technically illegal, these secret plots, called fire fields, can be seen across the country on mountaintops so steep and infertile that it is difficult to imagine that crops can grow there. Soldiers have traditionally helped plant and harvest crops. In the maize-growing areas, soldiers now appear to have taken the place of farmers, because farmers are spending so much time on their private plots (refugee interviews, September 1998; Natsios interview with Democratic People's Republic of Korea official, June 1997).

The rise of farmer's markets and the shutdown of the public distribution system for the non-farm population made food inaccessible to families that had no way of paying higher prices, particularly when the economic downturn reduced the purchasing power of families. As industrial production plummeted, salaries of urban and mining workers were either reduced or stopped entirely, as was the heavily subsidized food from the public distribution system on which these workers had relied for 50 years. The public distribution system was not a social service system, but a means of workforce compensation. The nonsubsidized price in the farmer's markets for a kilogram of maize (not enough to feed a family for a day) equaled an average industrial worker's monthly salary, while under the subsidized rate a month's industrial salary easily bought the maximum ration allowed through the public distribution system. Thus, these urban families sustained a major reduction in family purchasing power at the same time the price of food increased exponentially.

According to a Johns Hopkins University study of 440 refugees, 39 percent of the people in the far northern region of North Hamgyong province rely on farmer's markets as their principal source of food (through either barter or cash purchases), while only 5.7 percent rely on the public distribution system ("Rising Mortality in North Korean Households Reported by Migrants to China" by W. Courtland Robinson, Myung Ken Lee, Kenneth Hill, and Gilbert Burnham, *Lancet,* July 1999). Surveys by the Korean Buddhist Sharing Movement (KBSM), a South Korean NGO working in the North Korean-Chinese border area, show a similar shift from the public distribution system to markets in other provinces. A Republic of Korea (ROK) Unification Ministry study using defector information indicates that there are 300–350 farmer's markets in North Korea and that people get approximately 60–70 percent of their food from them.

The phenomenal increase in the frequency, selection of products, and size of these markets over the past four years has been noted by United Nations (UN) and NGO workers. Kim Jong Il has publicly attacked these markets as unsocialist (December 1996). He tried to shut these markets down after his father's death but was forced to rescind the order because of urban unrest (defector interview, September 1998). He tolerates them now because they are essential to the survival of the cities.

His father, Kim Il Sung, had wisely sanctioned the farmer's markets, saying that they would exist one way or the other and that it was better to have them out in the open so they could be regulated, though it is clear even Kim Il Sung never envisioned that these markets would become this large and essential (Kim Il Sung, "On Some Theoretical Problems of the Socialist Economy," March 1969). Without these markets, the urban areas would be even more depopulated than they are now. The rise of these farmer's markets amounts to a de facto privatization of an important part of what remains of the North Korean economy. The regime's embarrassment may be one reason why officials have prohibited any expatriate visits to observe these markets or to study food prices in them.

The people who have died in the famine or who have suffered the most deprivation are those who were unable to adjust to the economic reality of these new markets either by growing their own food or by producing some marketable product, labor, or service that they could exchange for food.

Famines usually evolve in phases along a timeline that affects different socioeconomic groups and geographic regions at different points depending on access to harvest surplus and the strength of coping mechanisms. Food distributions from the public system in the northeast became intermittent in 1992–1994, effectively stopping during the summer of 1994, though two to three days' worth of rations are still distributed six times a year on national holidays (Jasper Becker, *Hungry Ghosts*, 1998; KBSM, "Survey of North Korean Refugees," 1997; and Robinson, Lee, Hill, and Burnham, July 1999). In 1994, the central authorities coped with the sharp decline in food availability by triaging the four eastern provinces (North Hamgyong, South Hamgyong, Rangang, and Kangwon), which are politically and militarily less important to the survival of the central government than the western provinces, and by shutting down any food shipments there from other regions (defector interviews, Sept. 1998; merchant and refugee interviews, Sept. 1998; UN staff interviews, Jan. 1999). This triaging also occurred as the regional economic system, under which the northeastern industrial cities and mines had sent their products to the rice-growing areas of the west in exchange for food, fell apart. Thus, the famine began in the northeastern provinces two years earlier than in the western provinces.

In 1996, the central authorities made a momentous decision to deal with the famine by decentralizing authority for feeding the population from national bureaucracies in Pyongyang to county administrators. If county administrators were particularly skillful and energetic, fewer people died; if bureaucratic and lethargic, the effect of the famine was acute (Sue Lautze, "Independent Food Observer to the PRC & DPRK Final Report," June 1996). In January 1998 a decision was announced through the government apparatus that each individual family was henceforth responsible for feeding itself, rather than relying on the traditional public distribution as before the famine or on the county administrators since 1996 (defector interview, September 1998). This decision may have simply recognized the evolving reality rather than deliberately decentralizing decision making. Earlier, Kim Jong Il deplored decentralization and the idea of individual responsibility, which he said would make people less dependent on the state and party, endangering socialism in North Korea (December 1996). Despite his misgivings, he seems to have decided in favor of this new system by 1998, probably out of administrative necessity.

The economics of the famine may be entering a new phase in 1999. The Chinese maize crop in provinces north of the border was quite poor because of exceedingly wet and overcast weather, with reductions in harvest of 70–90 percent (Korean-Chinese merchant and agronomist interviews, September 1998). Extensive flooding damaged the general harvest in other regions of China. These developments have already begun to affect barter exchange rates on the border. In September 1998, North Korean timber was trading for reduced amounts of Chinese corn. The remaining timber is less accessible for cutting and scrap metal from cannibalized industrial machinery which could be bartered for corn by the North Koreans is exhausted. Thus, in 1999, commercial purchases of Chinese maize will decline, increasing the price of grain in the farmer's markets in the northern provinces. Without international aid, this situation, combined with the fragility of the new private food system, may plunge the mountainous regions of the country into a new round of deaths.

Death Rates

The outside world will likely not have access to conclusive mortality rate data until the regime falls or internal changes cause embarrassing information to be released to the public. However, we do have enough information now from very different sources to make some rough estimates of the severity of the crisis.

Hwang Jong Yop, former party ideologue and philosopher of juche, published *North Korea: Truth or Lies* in June 1998 following his defection to South Korea in February 1997. In it he writes the following:

> In November 1996, I was very concerned about the economy and asked a top official in charge of agricultural statistics and food how many people had starved to death. He replied, "In 1995, about 500,000 people starved to death including 50,000 party cadres. In 1996, about one million people are estimated to have starved to death." He continued, "In 1997, about 2 million people would starve to death if no international aid were provided."

In interviews with the South Korean media, Hwang has subsequently estimated that the death toll has reached 2.5 million people since 1995. (He suggests that one million died in 1997.)

A second source of information on death rates comes from the KBSM, which between September 30, 1997, and November 1, 1998, interviewed 1,679 food refugees who moved to China to escape the famine. The survey employed the same interview techniques used by international human rights organizations to gather information from refugees escaping abuse. The study found that the mortality rates among the family and ban members who had not moved to China (the ban is the lowest level of North Korean society and is composed of 30–50 families) were 26–28 percent. These rates cannot be applied against the entire population because everyone is not equally at risk (indeed, many are not at risk at all because their political power allows them to accumulate resources to ensure their survival) and because this is not a random sampling of the population. However, because of the very large number of interviews, their depth, and the collection of data over time, the KBSM survey does offer telling insights.

The refugees interviewed in the KBSM survey are overwhelmingly urban workers from factories, the transportation sector, or the mines. Farmers are poorly represented in the population of refugees crossing the border, though they represent 25–35 percent of the population. These data confirm the reports of Pyongyang officials, NGO and UN reports, and defector interviews that the famine is centered in urban and mining areas (other than the capital city of Pyongyang, where a minimum food ration has been maintained). Some maize-growing mountainous areas suffering localized crop failures from flooding (1995 and 1996) or drought (1997) have also experienced high death rates. Hwang's report that 10 percent of the deaths in 1995 were of party cadres [who, according to Eberstadt and Bannister (1992), make up 15 percent of the total population], indicates that middle and lower-level cadres are also suffering.

A team from the Johns Hopkins University School of Public Health has completed a second study of famine death and birth rates in North Korea based on interviews in China with 440 food refugees from North Hamgyong province (Robinson, Lee, Hill, and Burnham, July 1999). The study shows that from 1995–1997 death rates rose eightfold over what they had been in pre-famine North Korea, rising from 0.55 percent in the 1993 census to an annual average of 4.3 percent during each of the three years of the study. During this same period, the number of people reporting the public distribution system as their principal source of food declined from 61 percent in 1994 to 6 percent in 1997, confirming earlier findings by KBSM, Jasper Becker, and my own interviews. Births declined by 50 percent from 21.8 per thousand in 1995 to 11 per thousand in 1997-another famine indicator. Even though the authors are reluctant to extrapolate their figures to the general population of North Hamgyong, they do estimate that 245,000 out of a population of 2 million people may have starved to death in that province alone.

How severe has the famine been in North Hamgyong province compared with other provinces? North Hamgyong has three advantages not enjoyed by other provinces. First, travel and trade restrictions across the North Korean border with the ethnic Korean region of China are markedly weaker than in other regions, allowing hungry North Koreans to migrate in order to work and to beg and borrow food from relatives in China. Second, barter for food between North Hamgyong and China is extensive. Third, the province traditionally produces larger agricultural surpluses on the farmlands along the Tumen River than do the rest of the mountainous eastern provinces, according to a United States Agency for International Development/Office of Foreign Disaster Assistance (USAID/OFDA) map of agricultural production. As a result, North Hamgyong province likely experienced lower, not higher, death rates than other mountainous provinces without these coping mechanisms.

The death rates in North Hamgyong may be conservative on another count as well. The Hopkins study, like the KBSM study, considers only family members of interviewees who died at home in North Korea. The study did not account for deaths of family members who left home before the interviewees themselves fled to China, because the interviewees could not know the fate of relatives who left home before them. This likely means that mortality rates have been underestimated, because experience from other famines shows that the death rates for people displaced by a famine rise precipitously compared to the death rates for famine victims who remain at home, if those displaced cannot find work or humanitarian assistance. In these cases, the food refugees are more vulnerable because they lose the protection of their home, family, and neighbors. In North Korea, economic collapse and the highly centralized distribution of humanitarian assistance have left most food refugees with few options except fleeing the country. No one can be certain how many food refugees have died along the way. Thus, a large number of deaths of hungry migrating people are not recorded in either the Hopkins or KBSM surveys.

Other studies show that the famine is not limited to North Hamgyong. The WFP and UNICEF nutritional surveys show malnutrition rates similar to those of the Hopkins study across the country. The first nutritional study of children under five years old, done in September–October 1998 by UN agencies, the European Union (ECHO), and Save the Children Fund/UK, shows acute malnutrition and wasting (of body mass) of 18 percent and stunting of 62 percent. These are alarmingly high rates, particularly considering four other factors: (1) for the past year WFP has been concentrating its feeding program on children under age 7; thus, their condition should have improved; (2) the survey did not include abandoned, internally displaced, or refugee children who are much more vulnerable to malnutrition; (3) central authorities excluded 30 percent of the population from access by the survey teams (in what I surmise are militarily sensitive areas); and (4) the peak of the famine took place during the last half of 1996 and the first half of 1997 (a year before the children were measured), at which time many of the most vulnerable children died. This study appears to have underestimated the severity of the crisis again.

The KBSM study plotted the home villages of the 1,679 refugees interviewed on a map of the 211 counties and then averaged the death rates by county, which were once again similar. The only exception is Pyongyang, which in the KBSM study showed a death rate one-third lower than the other counties—the lowest in the country. In both the Hopkins and KBSM surveys, death rates varied by age, gender, and profession rather than by geography.

The Hopkins death rates, therefore, are a consistent, though conservative, estimate of the severity of the famine across the country. If anything, extrapolating the Hopkins death rates to the country as a whole understates rather than exaggerates the famine's severity. By deducting the 2 million people living in Pyongyang (the senior party cadre who have suffered least in the famine are heavily concentrated in the capital) and the 1.2 million soldiers, and then applying the 12 percent Hopkins rate of mortality to the 20 million people remaining, the total number of famine deaths would approach 2.5 million, the same number of deaths claimed by Hwang Jong Yop. Thus, we have several independent studies that give credence to Hwang Jong Yop's estimate.

International Food Aid and the Famine

Sizable amounts of food have been imported into North Korea either as food aid, subsidized commercial sales, or cross-border barter trade between 1995 and 1999 primarily from China, Japan, South Korea, United States, and the European Union. As reported by WFP, food imports from all sources totaled the following amounts:

1995–1996:	903,374 Metric Tons
1996–1997:	1,171,665 Metric Tons
1997–1998:	1,321,528 Metric Tons

Why have so many people died after so much food has been delivered? While it is true that major contributions or sales were made by the Chinese, donor governments, and private organizations, the timing of the pledges and deliveries did not match the peak period of the famine. Second, the central authorities seem to have panicked at the poor crop in the fall of 1996 and the lack of donor governments' pledges or delivery of food until late spring and early summer 1997, which resulted in a shutdown of the public distribution system. Third, the central government saw to it that triaged populations did not have access to imported food because they were not seen as critical to the survival of the state. The drop in death rates appears to have taken place because the vulnerable urban and mining population had either died down to a sustainable level or moved to agricultural areas or to China. Some people found new income sources to purchase higher-priced grain in farmer's markets.

The international food aid provided privately through NGOs, the Red Cross, bilaterally from the European Union, and through WFP seems to have had several unintended but ameliorative outcomes.

- **Privatization of markets.** In some areas, food aid, diverted from the aid program by corrupt officials who sold it on the urban markets, has stimulated the size and robustness of the urban markets, a form of unplanned and unintended privatization. People are no longer dependent on the state for their food supply, thus undermining a principal means of control. Donor food aid has appeared for sale in many of the markets in South Hamgyong provincial cities. (The maize for sale in the northern border city markets is Chinese, while the rice in the southwestern urban markets appears to be locally grown, according to refugee interviews.) Refugees who have seen the food in South

Hamgyong markets remark that the maize and rice for sale are in donor government bags (from the United States, European Union, and ROK) and that the grain in them is not grown in China or North Korea (refugee interviews, September 1998; Medicins Sans Frontières interviews, 1998).

- **Food price stabilization and reduction.** The volume of international food aid and Chinese imports is such that according to refugee interviews, the price of food in the private markets diminished by 25–35 percent between March and September 1998—the last half of the harvest year—just when it should have been increasing. The volume of food on the markets has reduced the price sufficiently so that families with limited assets can purchase or barter for food; they can get one-third more food for the same price.

- **Diversions undermine regime support.** Refugees from South Hamgyong know that countries they have been taught are their enemies are giving food aid. As one refugee from Hamhung City told me, "We were taught all these years that the South Koreans and Americans were our enemies. Now we see they are trying to feed us. We are wondering who our real enemies are." When asked why they had not received the food aid free through the public distribution system, refugees repeatedly replied, "The corrupt cadres [or bureaucracy] are stealing the food and selling it on the markets for their own profit while we starve. We see it there for sale." Medicins Sans Frontières refugee interviews provide similar testimony as does the *Washington Post* investigation based on refugee interviews (February 11, 1999). Thus, the inability of the regime to feed its population and the presence of food aid in the markets are undermining popular support among those without political power. Given the nature of the regime, this public dissatisfaction is not reflected in overt opposition but in growing corruption, black market activities, sabotage, and other antisystem behavior that reflects public cynicism and anger.

Food aid has reduced the malnutrition rates among some of the population under seven years old in school settings, the more recent focus of WFP distributions along with a food-for-work program.

The larger question is whether this food program has kept the North Korean government in power. Kim Jong Il clearly does not like the aid program and has attacked it publicly in an official speech, "On Preserving the *Juche* Character and National Character of the Revolution and Construction" (June 19, 1997): "The imperialist's aid is a noose of plunder and subjugation aimed at robbing ten and even a hundred things for one thing that is given." The food aid program is visible evidence of the failure of *juche*, the governing state ideology; it has undermined state propaganda about the outside capitalist world; and it has accelerated the privatization of the economy. Perhaps this is one reason the military opposed the initial food program in 1995 and forced the temporary shutdown of the program in 1996. Thus, the food aid program is undermining state ideology rather than propping the system up, just as Paul Bracken suggested outside aid would do in his "poisoned carrot" article ("Nuclear Weapons and State Survival in North Korea," *Survival*, Vol. 35 No. 3, Autumn 1993).

CONSEQUENCES OF THE FAMINE

Political and Security Consequences

North Korea has sustained more destabilizing change over the past five years than it has over the previous 40 years combined. The arrival of 100 expatriate humanitarian relief workers at a high point from mid-1997 to mid-1998 and, with them, the exposure of the internal problems of the country to the international news media, have made the central authorities very uncomfortable. For the most part, these changes cannot be revoked by the central authorities, and they have shaken an already teetering system.

If the death rates are as substantial as suggested, a significant portion of urban families have seen members die. Nearly 40 percent of the 16–24-year-olds in the country (or 6 percent of the total population of the country) are in the military (Eberstadt and Bannister, 1992). These are exceptionally high percentages, comparable only to a general mobilization during all-out war. Under other circumstances, this percentage of people under arms would mean a strong base of popular support for the military and a high level of political mobilization in the society. Under famine conditions, the reverse would appear to be true. A popularly based military of such enormous size means that a large proportion of the military will have seen their parents, brothers, and sisters die. Thus, the regime has a large number of young men with weapons, albeit in a highly controlled and disciplined organizational structure, who are likely to be unhappy about deaths in their families. Such anger in the ranks in China in 1963 contributed to the end of the disastrous Great Leap Forward famine (Becker, 1998).

Coup Plot

In *The Two Koreas*, Don Oberdorfer reports that in early fall 1995 in the northeastern region of the country, "the Sixth Corps of the North Korean Army ... was disbanded, its officers purged, and units submerged into others." A defector confirmed this incident as a coup plot (planned but never attempted) by a corps-level army unit in Hamhung City in fall 1995. Hwang Jong Yop reports that 500,000 people died from the famine in 1995, most of whom would have died in early fall at the end of the agricultural harvest year as food stocks ran out. According to refugee accounts, the worst famine-affected city in North Korea was Hamhung City, the country's largest industrialized city with the highest proportion of factory workers, and coincidentally the headquarters of the corps-level unit that planned the coup at the peak of the famine. The coup plot thus appears to have been driven by the famine sweeping across the northeast.

During the peak of the famine in late 1996 and early 1997, Kim Jong Il began purging general officers who had dominated the military establishment for decades and replacing them with younger officers who presumably were more loyal. Unconfirmable media reports claim that martial law was imposed in

early 1997, again as the famine was peaking. Perhaps Kim Jong Il realized that he was at risk because of the coup plot in late 1995, which in turn was a result of the chaos and death caused by the famine.

The purges and the coup plot suggest that the famine has already had a convulsive effect on the political system. While the newly promoted general officer corps may be loyal to Kim Jong Il, it is not clear that field and company grade officers share the same loyalty. The KBSM survey, though clearly of a disaffected population, shows that refugees attribute the famine far more to poor political leadership than to natural disasters.

Beginning in September 1998, the regime began to reimpose order in the country beginning with the transportation system (refugee interviews, September 1998). Internally displaced people were no longer allowed onto trains without travel permits and paid tickets, which had not been the case since 1995. One refugee who had been across the border five times said that security was "six times more severe" than what he had experienced since the start of the crisis. In addition, authorities imposed new fines on unauthorized population movements, issued new internal identification cards in June, and instituted new measures to increase security in the "927" detention centers for displaced people.

Critics argue that the United States and other donor nations should starve the North Korean regime into collapse. Yet the famine has already taken a large number of lives, and the regime, though shaken, is still in power. It is important to remember that no Communist government has been overturned during or after a famine, though coups or popular revolts have frequently replaced authoritarian governments after famines. However, the Communist record in this century may not be applicable in the case of North Korea, because other Communist regimes experienced famine early in their histories when revolutionary fervor was at its peak, and they maintained control of the food distribution system so that dissenters would starve if they were not put down by internal security forces. The North Korean regime has de facto privatized the food distribution system; its revolutionary fervor has diminished over time and by the famine itself; and it has no allies left to save it in the event of a military coup, which is the only serious threat to the survival of the regime. Given the likely anger in the military over famine deaths, Kim Jong Il must now fear the military as his greatest threat, which is perhaps why he avoids visiting military units that are engaged in exercises using live ammunition (U.S. government sources).

Population Movements

Famines are accompanied by widespread population movements as people attempt to cope with their hunger; these generally occur in the latter stages of the crisis. North Korea is no exception to this pattern of behavior, though the population control system appears to have constrained some of these movements (unlike Africa where the population is more nomadic and national boundaries do not constrain movement). Estimates of the aggregated migration to China from North Korea over the past several years ranges from 100,000 to 400,000, though not all of these people are in China at the same time. The figure refugees quote most often from party cadre sources is 200,000 people (refugee interviews, September 1998; Becker, 1998, p. 330). People move back and forth many times. Given the extraordinary measures taken by the North Korean and Chinese authorities to prevent this refugee migration (they are building a string of detention centers to house captured North Korean refugees before returning them to North Korean authorities) and given the difficulty of moving through the mountain ranges of the northeast to get to the border area, the size of the migration is impressive evidence of the severity of the deprivation in North Korea. Traditionally, anyone caught escaping was executed. The more usual penalty now is a beating, the confiscation of all belongings and money earned in China, and confinement for several months before being sent to more permanent local prisons for former displaced people.

The figure of 200,000 comes from party cadre members, probably based on data collected in the population census in the summer of 1998. The mass population movements, coupled with the national elections held in 1998, caused the government to issue new identification cards for all North Koreans, which meant that anyone in China who harbored any intention of returning home needed to get this new identification card or face the possibility of permanent exile. So the refugees came home and were counted and carded, and in the process the authorities likely could identify who had moved and who had not.

Next to the starvation itself, the most politically insidious consequence of the famine is population movement. Party propaganda has claimed that, despite their problems, people in North Korea were better off than in China, where civil war, epidemic, and famine rage (a credible claim during the Great Leap Forward and the Cultural Revolution). The refugee movements across the border into China have given lie to this propaganda as the prosperous reality is evident. One refugee from Harnhung City put it well: "Our first border crossing is a grammar school degree, the second time you visit China is a high school diploma, and the third and fourth trips are college and graduate degrees in reality. They have been lying to us all these years." The decision to encourage population reentry from China for registration and voting in the national elections damaged the regime. It contributed to the further erosion of its base of popular support as these refugees with graduate degrees in economic reality returned to their home villages to tell their families and friends what they had seen. Refugees confirmed this transfer of information.

Two KBSM refugee interviews provide fascinating data on the voter turnout for the summer

1998 elections, which were depressed by the devastation of the famine. In one county, part urban and part rural (rural areas have far less migration, as people are eating relatively well), the number of people who voted (and everyone must vote) was 68 percent of what it had been in the elections before the famine. In another mining city, the vote was 54 percent of what it had been previously. These disparities likely represent both population movements and famine deaths.

On September 27, 1997, Kim Jong Il ordered all of the county administrators in each of the 210 counties to set up facilities, appropriately called "927 camps" (the date the order was made) to forcibly confine those who were caught outside their village or city without a travel permit. The Stalinist permit system had kept most people in their home villages most of their lives. However, it effectively controlled the population movements: people did not receive their food ration unless they were in their home village. As the public distribution system collapsed, these regulations became far less effective at controlling population movements as people no longer relied on the state for food.

Many refugees in China were captured by police and spent time in these squalid 927 camps (usually located in the county hotel) and then escaped back to China. The camps cram 40–50 people into a room. There is no heat in the Arctic winters, sanitation is terrible, food is sparse, and infectious disease and death rates are high. Refugees report that each camp holds between 300 and 1,500 people, so at any one time between 63,000 and 315,000 people countrywide are housed in these camps before they are forcibly returned to their home villages. Although no comprehensive study has been done of turnover rates in the camps, they are intentionally high. Anecdotal information suggests that average stays range from several weeks to two months. Extrapolating these population figures at a turnover rate of six times a year translates to a minimum of 378,000 and a maximum of 1.9 million people per year passing through them. Given that many internally

displaced people avoid capture while others die as they move to areas that may have no more food than where they left, the people in these camps do not reflect all internal population movements. The very existence of the camps is testimony to official concern about displaced people wandering around the country. In his December 1996 speech, Kim Jong Il complained of chaos and anarchy in the countryside, which may be a veiled reference to these population movements.

Communicable Disease

The health of the general population is poor and worsening. All famines are accompanied by epidemics of communicable diseases because the immune system deteriorates as malnutrition becomes more severe. People regularly die of disease well before they die of actual starvation. In North Korea the problem has been complicated by a sharp downturn in the health care, water, and sanitation systems. Hospitals for the general population have no western pharmaceuticals, relying instead on traditional herbal drugs, and have no food to feed patients. According to a provincial survey by Oxfam, much of the public water system, when it functions at all, is of such poor quality that it causes health problems.

CONCLUSIONS AND RECOMMENDATIONS

North Korean military incidents against Japan, the United States, and South Korea may be an effort by Kim Jong Il to focus the attention of his military, whose loyalty he doubts, on an external threat that he himself regularly provokes. Kim Jong Il opposes economic and agricultural reforms needed to end the famine because he sees the threat these reforms pose to his control and the threat he feels from his own military as greater than the consequences of the famine.

Donor governments, UN agencies, and humanitarian organizations have been too willing to accept the geographic distribution plans of the central government, even though it is increasingly clear that they have been based on political, not humanitarian, objectives. Donor governments should insist that their food be distributed where it is most needed, particularly to the mountainous regions of the country. Given the lack of reliable information coming from inside the country, donor governments should provide support for more studies of the famine based on refugee and defector interviews.

The central questions for U.S. policymakers are these:

- Will Kim Jong Il exercise power in a ruthless enough manner to restore his control over the population, the military, and the cadres to ensure his own survival following the chaos of the famine? The regime is attempting to reimpose order and control after a period of chaos. Political indoctrination campaigns will yield fewer and fewer results because growing numbers of families have watched loved ones die and the continued suffering of survivors has embittered the population. Public cynicism toward the regime is irreversible and is reflected in growing corruption, sabotage, an expanded black market, and other antisystem activities. Central authorities will be forced to rule exclusively by terror and repression, a fear expressed by Kim Jong Il (December 1996).
- Has the famine peaked and is now receding, having killed off the most vulnerable population, or is it migrating to other areas of the country? The famine may be migrating from the northeastern mountainous provinces to the rice-growing regions to the southwest (merchant and refugee interviews, September 1998). The fragile new food security system may be easily disrupted by price fluctuations, market failure, or the inability to barter or purchase food in these new private markets.

International food aid, however distorted its distribution has been, has had several beneficial consequences that would be lost if it were terminated. Donor governments should consider expanding the food program by initiating a food monetization program in port cities,

particularly on the east coast. WFP would sell food aid on the informal markets to reduce prices to an affordable level, but not so low that they would discourage increased production by farmers. The local currency generated could be used for mass employment programs in industrial cities and mining areas to increase urban worker income.

Expatriate monitoring of food sales in urban markets, assisted by expatriate translators, should be a required part of the program. Donor governments should avoid using the public distribution system because it is no longer functional in most of the country and serves purposes other than simply feeding the population.

- Even if reducing or terminating international food aid caused the regime to collapse, would the resulting chaos from such a collapse improve or diminish the prospects for a peaceful transition to a unified Korea? The chaos resulting from a collapse of the regime would threaten far more lives than those the famine has thus far claimed and could create an unpredictable military situation as well. Population movement to South Korea or China could prove explosive as both countries simultaneously take military measures to restore order, increasing the risk of conflict between them. The collapse of the regime may be superficially attractive, but it is a dangerous risk.

QUESTIONS TO CONSIDER

1. Explain why giving food aid to starving North Korea is debated by relief agencies.
2. Why did the rise of farmer's markets make it more difficult for the non-farm population to obtain food?
3. Has American and South Korean aid affected North Koreans in any way?
4. Is food aid the primary reason Kim Jong I is still in power?
5. If the United States opted to withhold food aid to topple Kim Jong II, would it be complicit in genocide?
6. Is the famine refugee problem genocidal in nature?

Control of the Population

Pierre Rigoulot,
Cashiers d'histoire sociale, *Editor-in-Chief*

Repression and terror affect the mind and spirit as well as the body. The effects of deliberate total isolation on the inhabitants of the country, together with the permanent ideological barrage to which they are subjected on a scale unknown elsewhere, must also be counted among the crimes of Communism. The reports of the few who have managed to slip through the net and leave the country are a remarkable testimony to the resilience of the human spirit.

There are two main forms of propaganda in North Korea. One is the classic Marxist-Leninist axis, which claims that the socialist and revolutionary state offers the best of all possible worlds to its citizens. People are to be constantly alert, on the lookout for the imperialist enemy, all the more so today since so many erstwhile friends on the outside have now "surrendered." The second type of propaganda is peculiarly national and almost mystical. Instead of relying on the arguments of dialectical materialism, the government has created a whole mythology around the idea that the Kim dynasty represents the will of both heaven and earth. A few examples from among the thousands that could be cited may clarify this type of propaganda. On 24 November 1996 in Panmunjon—the village where the armistice was negotiated, and the only place where the armies of North and South Korea and the United States are in immediate contact—during an inspection of the North Korean army by Kim Jong Il, a thick fog suddenly covered the area. The leader could thus come

and go in the mist, examining the positions while remaining more or less hidden. Equally mysteriously, the fog lifted at the moment he was to be photographed with a group of soldiers … A similar thing happened on an island in the Yellow Sea. He came to an observation post and began to study a map of the operations. The wind and rain suddenly stopped, the clouds cleared, and the sun came out and shone radiantly. Dispatches from the same official agency also mention "a series of mysterious phenomena that have been noted all over Korea as the third anniversary of the death of the Great Leader [Kim Il Sung] approaches... The dark sky was suddenly filled with light in the Kumchon canton... Three groups of red clouds were seen to be heading toward Pyongyang... At 8:10 PM on 4 July the rain that had been falling since early morning suddenly stopped, and a double rainbow unfolded over the statue of the President... then a bright star shone in the sky right above the statue."

A STRICT HIERARCHY

In a state claiming to base itself on socialism, the population is not only carefully monitored and controlled; it is also subject to disparate treatment depending on social origin, geographic origin (that is, whether the family originates in North or South Korea), political affiliation, and recent signs of loyalty toward the regime. In the 1950s the whole society was

Pierre Rigoulot, "Control of the Population," Stephane Courtois, et al., eds. From *The Black Book of Communism, Crimes, Terror, Repression*. Trans. by Jonathan Murphy and Mark Kramer (Cambridge, Massachusetts: Harvard University Press, 1999), 559, 563. Reprinted with permission.

carefully subdivided into fifty-one social categories that powerfully determined people's social, political, and material future. This extremely cumbersome system was streamlined in the 1980s; now there are only three social categories. Even so, the system of classification remains very complex. In addition to these three basic classes, the secret services are particularly vigilant in regard to certain categories within the classes, particularly people who have come from abroad, who have traveled overseas, or who have received visitors.

The country is divided into a "central" class, which forms the core of society, an "undecided" class, and a "hostile" class, which includes approximately one-quarter of the North Korean population. The North Korean Communist system uses these divisions to create what is in effect a sort of apartheid: "a young man of 'good origin,' who might have relatives who fought against the Japanese, cannot marry a girl of 'bad origin,' such as a family that originated in the South." One former North Korean diplomat, Koh Young Hwan, notes that "North Korea has what is in effect an extremely inflexible caste system."

Although this system in its early days may have had some basis in Marxist-Leninist theory, biological discrimination is much harder to justify. Yet the facts are there: anyone who is handicapped in North Korea suffers terrible social exclusion. The handicapped are not allowed to live in Pyongyang. Until recently they were all kept in special locations in the suburbs so that family members could visit them. Today they are exiled to remote mountainous regions or to islands in the Yellow Sea. Two such locations have been identified with certainty: Boujun and Euijo, in the north of the country, close to the Chinese border. This policy of discrimination has recently spread beyond Pyongyang to Nampo, Kaesong, and Chongjin.

Similar treatment applies to anyone out of the ordinary. Dwarves, for instance, are now arrested and sent to camps; they are not only forced to live in isolation but also prevented from having children. Kim Jong Il himself has said that "the race of dwarves must disappear."

FINAL FIGURES

In North Korea, perhaps more than anywhere else, the effects of Communism are difficult to translate into numbers. Some of the reasons are insufficient statistical data, the impossibility of carrying out any field research, and the inaccessibility of all the relevant archives. But there are also other reasons. How can one calculate the soul-destroying effects of constant, mindless propaganda? How can one put a figure on the absence of freedom of expression, freedom of association, and freedom of movement; on the ways in which a child's life is destroyed simply because his grandfather received a prison sentence; on the consequences for a woman who is forced to have an abortion in atrocious conditions? How could statistics show what life is really like when people are obsessed by the possibility of starvation, by lack of heating, and by other acute shortages and privations? How can one compare the admittedly imperfect democracy in the South with the nightmarish situation in North Korea?

Some have argued that North Korean Communism is a caricature, a throwback to Stalinism. But this museum of Communism, the Asian Madame Tussaud's, is all too alive.

To the 100,000 who have died in Party purges and the 1.5 million deaths in concentration camps must be added at least 1.3 million deaths stemming from the war, which was organized and instigated by the Communists, a war that continues in small but murderous actions, including commando attacks on the South and acts of terrorism; and the uncertain but growing number of direct and indirect victims of malnutrition. Even if we content ourselves with a figure of 500,000 victims of the primary or even secondary effects of malnutrition (including the usual, unverifiable reports of cannibalism), we end up with an overall figure of more than 3 million victims in a country of 23 million inhabitants that has lived under Communism for fifty years.

The Koreas

IS NORTH KOREA STALINIST?

Aidan Foster-Carter

Some people find Stalinism offensive. Not the reality, which would be understandable considering the body-count—but the word, as applied to North Korea.

Sometimes this is what the late Nobel economics prize winner Gunnar Myrdal called "diplomacy by terminology"—as in the phrase "developing countries," many of which aren't.

True, it can be irritating when the Seoul press lazily uses "the Stalinist state" as a homonym for North Korea or the DPRK: either to put the boot in, or just avoid repetition. They do this less now, under the "Sunshine" policy. But it still crops up—even sometimes in quotes from sources who couldn't possibly have used that particular turn of phrase. This of course is just sloppy journalism.

A more interesting objection is analytical. Here, two of the academics whose books I recommended in an earlier column take different views. For the American historian Bruce Cumings, the DPRK reflects mainly indigenous Korean traditions—but if generalizing, he'd file it under "corporatist," not Stalinist.

Adrian Buzo begs to differ. In his book *The Guerilla Dynasty*, this Australian analyst and ex-diplomat makes the most cogent case I've seen for why the word Stalinist can rightly be applied to North Korea. In fact, he lists no fewer than 24 separate points, under four headings: party organization and political style, ideology, economic policy and personal style. Here I try to summarize and illustrate his case.

Politics first. Buzo's rigorous argument is about more than mere Marxism-Leninism. If anything, he stresses the points where Stalin and Kim Il Sung alike departed from the M-L model—such as breaking their own rules on how often party congresses should be held. Other traits include exalting violence and debasing political debate with both military imagery and grossly abusive language (stooges, etc).

From Aidan Foster-Carter, "Is North Korea Stalinist?" *Asia Times* (September 5, 2001). Reprinted with permission. Asia Times Online: http://www.atimes.com

In ideology, Buzo notes several traits which those ignorant of wider history wrongly think are peculiar to North Korea. One is the theme of remaking human nature, which is straight from the New Soviet Man. Another is voluntarism, meaning an emphasis on sheer human will (man is master) as against Marx's materialism.

Just as un-Marxist is the use of kinship metaphors: Kim Il Sung was not the first Fatherly Leader. The cult of personality has wider consequences. The leader wipes out his rivals, both literally and from the history books. Stalin did it to Trotsky—with an ice pick, and touching up photos—just as Kim did it to a whole raft of Korean communists. Conversely, the leader is responsible for everything good—so all policies have to be buttressed by quasi-religious quotations from what becomes holy writ.

On economic policy, I don't wholly follow Buzo. Some of his themes—a highly centralized planned economy, over-emphasis on heavy industry, "grand nature-remaking projects"—strike me as harking back to Lenin or even Marx, rather than as Stalinist aberrations. On the other hand, Stalin's utterly un-Marxist "socialism in one country" was clearly the model for *juche* or *jarip* (economic self-sufficiency, so-called). And North Korea's endless "speed battles" to boost output are straight from Stakhanov, the Soviet model worker whose alleged feats were trumpeted under Stalin to make everyone work harder.

Personal style, Buzo's final category, has some striking similarities: from the dreary list of compulsory honorifics (respected and beloved leader, iron-willed commander, etc) right down to using a special bold typeface for the thoughts and name of the leader, and no other. Omniscient and infallible, the leader pronounces on every topic under the sun—often in written answers to easy questions from so-called news agencies. Even the Myohyangsan museum of gifts to the Great Leader—and now

also the Dear Leader—has a precedent; Stalin had one too, in his birthplace in Georgia. (Bet it wasn't as big.)

But I'm less sure of "highly interventionist working style"—true in spades of Kim Il Sung's on-the-spot guidance—but Stalin rarely went out, and formidable grasp of detail isn't quite the same thing. Again, Stalin's suspicions of science and mathematics don't really jibe with the DPRK's praise of these.

Yet overall, Buzo's case seems to me unanswerable. As he says, "It is hard to imagine the DPRK as we know it without a Stalinist blueprint." Nor is this surprising. The young Kim Il Sung spent four years (1941–45) in Stalin's USSR, before coming home as a Red Army major. Thereafter, both for his project (rapid development) and himself as the boss, Stalin was his abiding role model. And now Kim Jong Il is continuing with the same system. (But even Stalin didn't go as far as hereditary monarchy.)

This is not to deny that there were other influences too, such as Mao Zedong. Nor is Stalinism the only possible comparison. Read North Korean propaganda in German, and the emphasis on der Fuhrer and the triumph of the will suggest a very different (or is it?) totalitarian comparison.

Bruce Cumings's idea of corporatism is helpful too. And let no one down play Kim Il Sung's own contribution in taking what was already extreme just that bit further.

But at the end of the day, anyone familiar with North Korea who encounters Soviet materials from the Stalin era—books, magazines, pictures, films—cannot fail to have a powerful sense of déjà vu. Stalinism with Korean characteristics, to be sure. But it is Stalinism.

QUESTIONS TO CONSIDER

1. What are the parallels between Joseph Stalin's and Kim Il Sung's "cult of personality"?
2. Did both leaders have similar "personal styles"?

MAKING CONNECTIONS

1. What are the similarities between the famines in the Ukraine, China, and North Korea?

2. Are genocides from the Left—Ukraine, China, Cambodia, North Korea—different from those on the Right—Armenia, The Holocaust, Rwanda, Guatemala?

✔ RECOMMENDED RESOURCES

Clifford, Mark. *Troubled Tiger: Businessmen, Bureaucrats, and Generals in South Korea.* Armonk, NY: M.E. Sharpe, 1994.

Cumings, Bruce. *Korea's Place in the Sun: A Modern History.* New York: W.W. Norton & Company, 1997.

Hastings, Max. *The Korean War.* New York: Simon & Schuster, 1987.

MacDonald, Callum. *Korea: The War Before Vietnam.* New York: Free Press, 1987.

Khil, Young W., ed. *Korea and the World: Beyond the Cold War.* Boulder, CO: Westview Press, 1994.

Oberdorfer, Don. *The Two Koreas—A Contemporary History.* Rev. ed. Boulder, CO: Basic Books, 2002.

CHAPTER 16

EPILOGUE

COMMISSION BY OMISSION

As a rule, Americans do not address genocide. The resulting ignorance is not simply a void, but a direction without options, where other perspectives and viewpoints do not exist.

Ignoring genocides by simply mentioning them in passing, or weighing them in a kind of numbers game of ranking, sends implicit messages that these historical events and their victims are unimportant, or simply the "collateral damage" of a larger of more complex confict. Failure to debate the basic issues involved, allows no vocabulary of understanding to develop. A comparative investigation of the issues will render a broader insight into the why, what, and how of genocide.

Genocide is not inevitable. Human actions lead to it, perpetrate it, and cover it up. Studying these aspects of genocide offers insights into prevention, intervention, and ideally, punishment for genocidal acts.

The question "How can genocide be prevented?" suggests that a formula, once devised, will provide *the* solution. But the answer, which for some readers will be wholly unsatisfying, is that there may be no *one* answer. For example, the Euro-American near-extermination of indigenous peoples is not the same as Pol Pot's war on his own people. Thus steps that could have been taken to prevent one may not have been successful in stopping the other.

Another question, essential to a better understanding of genocide, is "Why do other countries react to, or refuse to acknowledge genocide?" The frequent reference to the inaction of the United States in these events undermines some of the sophistries about the American Century.

Never Again

THE WORLD'S MOST UNFULFILLED PROMISE

Samantha Power,
Harvard University

Fifty years ago a state-centric universe allowed governments to treat their own citizens virtually as they chose within national borders. Today the concept of human rights is flourishing, and the rights of individuals are prized (if not always protected). Across the contemporary legal, political and social landscape, we see abundant evidence of the legitimation of the movement: we see global conventions that outlaw discrimination on the basis of gender and race and outline the rights of refugees and children; a planet-wide ban on land-mines that was sparked by the outrage of a Vermonter; a pair of ad hoc international war crimes tribunals that take certain mass murderers to task; and an abundance of human rights lawyers who have acquired a respected presence at the policy-making table. In short, when it comes to human rights as a whole, states and citizens have traveled vast distances.

But one ugly, deadly and recurrent reality check persists: genocide. Genocide has occurred so often and so uncontested in the last fifty years that an epithet more apt in describing recent events than the oft-chanted "Never Again" is in fact "Again and Again." The gap between the promise and the practice of the last fifty years is dispiriting indeed. How can this be?

In 1948 the member states of the United Nations General Assembly—repulsed and emboldened by the sinister scale and intent of the crimes they had just witnessed—unanimously passed the Genocide Convention. Signatories agreed to suppress and punish perpetrators who slaughtered victims simply because they belonged to an "undesirable" national, ethnic, or religious group.

The wrongfulness of such mindful killings was manifest. Though genocide has been practiced by colonizers, crusaders and ideologues from time immemorial, the word "genocide," which means the "killing:" (Latin, cide) of a "people" (Greek, genos), had only been added to the English language in 1944 so as to capture this special kind of evil. In the words of Champetier de Ribes, the French Prosecutor at the Nuremberg trials, "This [was] a crime so monstrous, so undreamt of in history throughout the Christian era up to the birth of Hitlerism, that the term 'genocide' has had to be coined to define it." Genocide differed from ordinary conflict because, while surrender in war normally stopped the killing, surrender in the face of genocide only expedited it. It was—and remains—agreed that the systematic, large-scale massacre of innocents, stands atop any "hierarchy of horribles."

The United States led the movement to build on the precedents of the Nuremberg war crimes trials, enshrine the "lessons" of the Holocaust, and ban genocide. Though slow to enter the Second World War, this country emerged from the armistice as a global spokesperson against crimes against humanity, taking charge of the Nuremberg proceedings and helping draft the 1948 Genocide Convention, which embodied the moral and popular consensus in the United States and the rest of the world that genocide should "never again" be perpetrated while outsiders stand idly by. President Harry Truman called on U.S. Senators to endorse the Convention on the gounds that America had "long been a symbol of freedom and democratic progress to peoples less favored," and because it was time to outlaw the "world-shocking crime of genocide."

The American people appeared to embrace these abstract principles. And though one wing of the American establishment still downplayed the importance of human rights and resisted "meddling" in the internal affairs of fellow nations, even its spokesmen appeared to make an exception for human rights abuses that rose to the level of genocide. Though Americans disagreed fervently over whether their foreign policy should be driven by realism or idealism, interests or values, pragmatism or principle, they united over the cause of combating genocide. A whole range of improbable bed fellows placed genocide, perhaps the lone universal, in a category unto itself.

In recent years this consensus has gained indirect support from the popular growth of a veritable cult of "Never Again" in the United States. The creation of a Holocaust industry of sorts has seen the establishment of a slew of Holocaust memorials and museums—the Holocaust Museum in Washington, D.C. is the most heavily frequented museum on the Mall—and an unprecedented burst of Holocaust-related news stories (be they about *Schindler's List*, Daniel Goldhagen's account of the role of ordinary Germans, the contemporary war crimes trials against aging Nazis like Papon, or Switzerland's fall-from-grace). There have in fact been more stories on Holocaust-related themes in the major American newspapers in the 1990s than in the preceding forty-five years combined. Though interest in the Holocaust does not translate into a popular outrage over the commission of contemporary genocides, it has

caused many of us to question the war-time passivity of great powers and individual citizens. And American presidents have responded to these lamentations: ever since the Holocaust first entered mainstream discourse two decades ago, U.S. leaders have gone out of their way to pledge never again to let genocide happen. Jimmy Carter said it, Ronald Reagan said it, George Bush said it, and, most recently, Bill Clinton said it.

But in the half century since, something has gone badly wrong. In Bosnia the men, women and children of Stupni Do, Srebrenica, Ahmici, Zvornik, Prijedor, etc., all learned in recent years that the promise of "never again" counted for little. And they were not alone. Notwithstanding a promising beginning, and a half-century of rhetorical ballast, the American consensus that genocide is wrong has not been accompanied by a willingness to stop or even condemn the crime itself.

Since the Holocaust, the United States has intervened militarily for a panoply of purposes—securing foreign ports, removing unpalatable dictators, combating evil ideology, protecting American oil interests, etc.—all of which provoke extreme moral and legal controversy. Yet, despite an impressive postwar surge in moral resolve, the United States has never intervened to stop the one overseas occurrence that all agree is wrong, and that most agree demands forceful measures. Irrespective of the political affiliation of the President at the time, the major genocides of the post-war era—Cambodia (Carter), northern Iraq (Reagan, Bush), Bosnia (Bush, Clinton) and Rwanda (Clinton)—have yielded virtually no American action and few stern words. American leaders have not merely refrained from sending GIs to combat genocide; when it came to atrocities in Cambodia, Iraq and Rwanda, the United States also refrained from condemning the crimes or imposing economic sanctions; and, again in Rwanda, the United States refused to authorize the deployment of a multinational U.N. force, and also squabbled over who would foot the bill for American transport vehicles.

What are the causes of this gap between American principle and American practice?

During the Cold War, one might be tempted to chalk up America's tepid responses to real-world geopolitical circumstance. With the nuclear shadow looming, and the world an ideological playground, every American intervention in the internal affairs of another country carried with it the risk of counter-intervention by its rival, and the commensurate danger of escalation. In the same vein, while the United States was embroiled in its war with the Soviet Union, it was said, humanitarian concerns could not be permitted to distract American leaders, soldiers and resources from the life-or-death struggle that mattered most. Henry Kissinger was one of many who believed it was best not to ask questions about the domestic behavior of states but to focus on how they behave outside their borders. Countries that didn't satisfy vital security needs, or serve some economic or ideological end, were of little concern. And since staging a multilateral intervention would have required Security Council clearance, the superpower veto effectively ruled out such operations.

But the end of communism eliminated many of the Cold War concerns regarding intervention. The superpower rivalry withered, leaving the United States free to engage abroad with few fears of nuclear escalation and often with the backing (and even troops) of its former nemesis. Free of the shadow of the veto, the U.N. Security Council claimed some of its intended function—as a dispatcher of troops and a proliferator of resolutions. The war against Saddam Hussein—himself a packageable panacea for the American Vietnam syndrome—seemed to usher in an era in which American-led U.N. coalitions would tackle intolerable acts of aggression and patrol the "new world order."

Yet, despite the propitiousness of circumstance, mass atrocity was rarely met with reprisal. The reasons for this are numerous—some familiar but many surprising. The most common justification for non-intervention is that, while leaving genocide alone threatens no vital American interests, suppressing it can threaten the lives of American soldiers.

But this does not explain the American failure to condemn genocide or employ non-military sanction. Moreover, if it was so very obvious that the story ended there and that, by definition, "mere genocide" could not pass a Pentagon cost-benefit analysis, it is unlikely that Americans would be so vocal and persistent in their legal and moral commitments to prevent "another genocide."

American leaders say they are simply respecting the wishes of the American people, who have elected them, first and foremost, to fulfill the American dream of equality and freedom for all at home. Though this claim conforms with our intuitions and with the mounting data that the American public is becoming ever more isolationist, it may be misleading. Polls taken during the Bosnian war indicated that, while most Americans opposed unilateral American intervention or the deployment of U.S. ground troops, two-thirds supported American participation in multilateral efforts—flying in humanitarian air-drops or bombing Bosnian Serb positions. In the Iraqi case, likewise, a Gallup poll reported that 59 percent of Americans thought the coalition should have continued fighting until Hussein was overthrown and 57 percent supported shooting down Iraqi gun ships targeting the Kurds.

If American leaders ever used the word "genocide" to describe atrocities, it is likely that this public support would have grown. A July 1994 Program on International Policy Attitudes (PIPA) poll found that when citizens were asked, "If genocidal situations occur, do you think that the U.N., including the U.S., should intervene with whatever force is necessary to stop the acts of genocide"—65 percent said "always" or "in most cases," while 23 percent said "only when American interests are also involved" and just 6 percent said "never." When asked how they would react if a U.N. commission decided that events in Bosnia and Rwanda constituted genocide, 80 percent said they would favor intervention in both places.

It is possible that such support is superficial and would fade once U.S. forces incurred casualties, but it also arose without prompting from American leaders. In no postwar case of genocide has an American president attempted to argue that mass atrocity makes military or political intervention morally necessary. Yet it is notable that when the United States has intervened for other reasons, its leaders have garnered popular support by appealing to American sensibilities regarding mass killing. In the lead-up to the Gulf War, for example. Saddam Hussein was transformed into American "Enemy #1" not so much because he seized Kuwaiti oil fields but because he was "another Hitler" who "killed Kuwaiti babies." The advancement of humanitarian values in fact appears to "sell" in a way that "protecting American oil interests" in Kuwait or "saving the NATO alliance" in Bosnia do not. When it came time to deploy American soldiers as part of a postwar NATO peacekeeping mission in Bosnia, for instance, two-thirds of Americans polled found "stopping the killing" a persuasive reason for deploying troops (64 percent, CBS/NYT 12/9/95), while only 29 percent agreed with Clinton that deployment was necessary so as to maintain a stable Europe and preserve American leadership.

Contrary to conventional wisdom, the modern media is probably not making intervention more likely. For starters, unlike in cases of famine or natural disaster, genocide can be exceedingly difficult to cover. Despite all the "globaloney" about reporters being "everywhere," stories about the early stages of genocide are often unattainable because the price of accessing such terrain may be the life of the reporter. And even if technological advances—such as Internet television images or flying, unmanned rescue cameras—succeed in bringing viewers live genocide, the "CNN effect" will not necessarily translate into louder or wider calls for humanitarian intervention, as television images both attract and repel concern.

On the one hand, as we saw in Bosnia and Rwanda, the publicity given to mass atrocity can attract public interest and pull foreign governments toward intervention. On the other hand, the seeming intractability of the hatreds, the sight of the carnage, the visible danger to anyone who sets foot in the region, and the apparent remoteness of events from American homes can repel American voters and leaders and keep American troops out. In effect, this very tension may explain the United States' tendency to deliver a hearty humanitarian response but nonexistent military response to genocide.

Part of the problem in galvanizing a firm response lies in the instruments that were intended to serve as the solution. The Genocide Convention, which will celebrate its fifty-year anniversary in December, never received either the commitment of the United States or the teeth for enforcement that it needed to become "law" in any meaningful sense.

Despite the indispensability of the United States in drafting the 1948 Convention—and some 3,000 speeches by Senator William Proxmire on the Senate floor on behalf of it—the Senate did not pass the Act until 1988—a full forty years after President Truman signed it. American law-makers were petrified that African- or Native Americans would haul the United States before the International Court of Justice (ICJ) on genocide charges, or that other states would infringe upon American national sovereignty. By the time the Convention had finally become U.S. law, the Congress had attached so many reservations that ratification was rendered largely meaningless. For instance, by requiring that the United States would never be brought before the ICJ on a genocide count, the Congress barred the United States (under the legal rule of reciprocity) from filing charges against other nations—such as Hussein's Iraq or Pol Pot's Cambodia. The United States has tended to further international law, only so long as it does not find its sovereignty impinged or its practices or officials called before international judiciary bodies.

When it came to enforcing the convention's provisions, the drafters envisioned that a standing International Criminal Court would come into existence almost immediately. Ironically, that court may very well *be established this year*—the very same year that the Convention celebrates its fifty-year anniversary. And, already Washington's insistence that the United States (via the UN Security Council) retain prosecutorial authority, indicates that, as with the Convention itself, Washington's reluctance to have its own citizens and soldiers held accountable under international law may well impair the legitimacy and effectiveness of the new body.

The Convention's half century of impotence highlights the importance of retaining an independent arbiter of which cases should appear before the new International Criminal Court. Thanks to international and national politics, and the demands of individual member states over the last fifty years, the word "genocide" itself lost salience—misused, overused and generally abused. To begin with, the Convention, which defined the crime as "a systematic attempt to destroy, in whole or in part, a national, ethnic, or religious group as such," was both under-inclusive (excluding Pol Pot's attempted extermination of a political class) and over-inclusive (potentially capturing a white racist's attempt to cause bodily injury to a carload of

African-Americans). But, because it was drafted in order to satisfy all the major powers, it also ended up with wording so imprecise that the genocide label quickly became a political tool. For instance, President Truman labeled the North Koreans as genocidal perpetrators; France was charged with genocide in 1956 for its bloody involvement in Algeria; and the potent Asia-Africa block within the UN frequently charged Israel with orchestrating genocidal killing. American leaders in the fifties and sixties both levied the charge (usually against the Soviets), and found itself accused of such acts. In 1951 the Civil Rights Congress, an activist organization, published a book called *We Charge Genocide*, which asserted that "the oppressed Negro citizens of the United States, segregated, discriminated against, and long the target of violence, suffer from genocide …" And, two decades later, philosophers Bertrand Russell and Jean Paul Sartre established their own war crimes tribunal to try the United States for committing genocide against Vietnam. Tribunal President Sartre compared American intervention in Southeast Asia with Hitler's chosen means of conquest of Europe. In Hitler's Europe, "A Jew had to be put to death, whoever he was, not for having been caught carrying a weapon or for having joined a resistance movement, but simply because he was a Jew"; likewise, in his day, Americans were "killing Vietnamese in Vietnam for the simple reason that they are Vietnamese." Far from representing the ultimate "stain" on a nation, galvanizing swift and stern retribution, the genocide label has been applied to everything from desegregation in the United States to birth control and abortions in the developing world. And no impartial body exists to restore the word's intended meaning and use.

In the last fifty years, nothing has gone quite as planned. The Universal Declaration of Human Rights, which will also celebrate its fiftieth birthday in December, has become a bedrock document in international law, outlining the basic rights that individuals all over the world are entitled to claim. The Genocide Convention initially succeeded in articulating a post-war international consensus that genocide was a monstrous evil. But, as Pol Pot, Hussein, Karadzic and the Rwandan Interahamwe discovered, neither it nor the rhetorical commitments of the American leaders have translated into a willingness to halt the masterminds of genocide.

QUESTIONS TO CONSIDER

1. Why is the epithet "Never again" inappropriate for addressing genocide in the past fifty years?
2. What does Power mean by "growth of a veritable cult of 'Never again' in the United States"?
3. What is the "gap between American principle and American practice?"
4. Bertrand Russell and Jean Paul Sartre established a war crimes mock-tribunal to try the United States for genocide in Southeast Asia. Was this "tribunal" justifiable?

Murder Most Foul

FOR GENOCIDE TO RETAIN ITS UNIQUE LEGAL STANDING, WE MUST USE THE LABEL WITH CARE

Bruce Fein,

Attorney

A Review of "A Problem From Hell": America and the Age of Genocide, by Samantha Power

GENOCIDE!

The crime of crimes.

Evocative of the tear-stained displays of the Holocaust Museum and the chilling Nazi artifacts of Auschwitz, Dachau, and Bergen-Belsen.

If genocide is to retain its unique legal and moral horror and stigmatization carrying unforgiving punishments by governments, it must stand apart from lesser

abominations in public discourse, just as hate crime homicides are distinguished from second-degree murder or manslaughter. All wisdom, whether about genocide or otherwise, is a matter of degree, even if chiaroscuro rather than prime colors demarcates dividing lines. If just any massacre or atrocity becomes a genocide, then its searing moral repugnance is sapped. Victims of the Holocaust and authentic genocides will be slighted. And moral suasion prodding governments to respond will wither. Genocide is thus too important to be left to the amateur, the sophist, or the dogmatist. On that score, Samantha Power disappoints in *A Problem*

From Hell. Her credentials are reputable: a former Balkan war correspondent, a Harvard Law School graduate, and now executive director of the Carr Center for Human Rights at the John F. Kennedy School of Government. The trouble is with her thin and facile genocide observations unworthy of the difficulty of the subject.

Power's reportorial and readable genocide treatise pronounces the mass killings of the Armenians during World War I, the Holocaust, and the carnage of Bosnian Muslims, Cambodians, Iraqi Kurds, and Rwandan Tutus as authentic genocides. Such pronouncements startle because the author neglects a satisfactory attempt to define the crime of crimes, although Power addresses the sticky problem in Chapter 5, "A Most Lethal Pair of Foes."

The 1948 Genocide Convention confines genocide to actions intended to "destroy in whole or in part" by killings or otherwise a group because of nationality, ethnicity, race, or religion. But ambiguities abound. The term in part is generally understood to mean "substantial part" to avoid the absurdity of conflating one hate-inspired murder by a Ku Klux Klan member hoping to exterminate blacks with genocide. But that still leaves oceans unnavigated.

Does substantial imply a gross numerical count—for example, 5,000, 10,000, 100,000, or a million—or a benchmark percentage of the victimized group, such as 25 to 30 percent? Further, what is the relevant geographic area for calculating the group denominator? One nation, a group of nations, the entire planet? Mathematical precision cannot be expected. But the law should warn before it strikes, and the Genocide Convention is completely clueless in defining substantial part. Vagueness would be more tolerable if culprits might otherwise escape with impunity. That is not the case with genocide. Malevolence falling short of the benchmark is typically punishable as a war crime, a crime against humanity, or a war of aggression, as with most of the Nazi and Japanese criminals tried at Nuremberg and Tokyo.

The problem of defining genocide is far from academic; it recurs chronically on the world stage. Power glibly insists that "when the Khmer Rouge, the Iraqi government, and the Bosnian Serbs began eradicating minority groups, those who opposed a U.S. response often ignored the genocide convention's terms and denied genocide was under way, claiming the number of dead or the percentage of the group was too small." Power purports to find clarity in the convention from the gloss of its intellectual father, Raphael Lempkin, that partial destruction meant "of such substantial nature that it affects the existence of the group as a group," or, metaphorically, "by cutting the brains of a nation the entire body becomes paralyzed."

But on Lempkin's own terms, did the Khmer Rouge, Bosnian Serbs in cahoots with Yugoslavia's Slobodan Milosevic, or Saddam Hussein commit genocide? Neither Cambodians, Bosnian Muslims, nor Kurds were seriously threatened with extinction. Millions in the groups were left unattacked by the malefactors despite their opportunity to kill all. None of the groups became culturally or socially paralyzed; indeed, at present, Kurds operate a semistate in northern Iraq, Bosnian Muslims in collaboration with Croats preside over a national government in Bosnia, and Cambodians have culturally triumphed over Pol Pot and his gruesome Khmer Rouge survivors. Pol Pot, Saddam Hussein, and Milosevic seem incontestably guilty of war crimes or crimes against humanity. But a genocide charge seems doubtful pivoting on numbers or percentages alone. And the doubts multiply because the concept excludes mass killings or atrocities turning on political beliefs or sympathies, which seemingly fueled the charnel houses of the three. The Khmer Rouge despised all civilized non-Communists, Hussein implacably opposed an independent Kurdistan craved by Kurdish leaders Barzani and Talabani, and Milosevic oppressed and killed Bosnian Muslims for refusing to bow to a Greater Serbian state.

Power's historical scholarship is also unsettling. She writes ex cathedra that an Ottoman triumvirate during World War I was guilty of an Armenian genocide, although the term had not yet been coined. The anemic American and international response is tacitly deplored as a bow to Realpolitik.

A historical consensus concedes that Ottoman Armenians and Ottoman Muslims suffered horribly from a cycle of massacre and countermassacre during World War I and its aftermath. But the Armenian genocide claim stands on a different plane. Power declares that 1.5 million Armenians died. But the most reliable demographic studies show a fewer number lived in the entire empire. The most authoritative casualty study by University of Louisville professor Justin McCarthy estimates Armenian deaths at 300,000 to 600,000.

Power also fails to inform the reader that Armenians at the Paris Peace Conference boasted of defecting en masse to fight for the enemies of the Ottoman Empire, and acted as de facto belligerents under international law seeking an independent state; established a temporary government at Van in collaboration with Russia; were generally left undisturbed outside militarily sensitive zones, such as Istanbul and Izmir; and had occupied the commanding heights of the Ottoman bureaucracy and economy for long years antedating World War I. She further fails to mention that approximately 1,400 Ottoman soldiers were punished for killing or abusing Armenians, and some were executed. No Ottoman official was ever found guilty of anything approaching mass murder or atrocities against Armenians because of race, religion, or nationality. And the British dropped all thought of prosecuting 144 Ot-

toman detainees on Malta for Armenian massacres on the advice of legal counsel. After more than two years of investigation, and a dry hole at the U.S. State Department, the British attorney general responded to the British Foreign Office, which was urging a trial of the detainees for "cruelty practiced against native Christians," as follows: "The Attorney-General feels he cannot do better than refer Mr. Ruxton's minute of 11th August, 1920, in which attention is called to the inherent difficulties with which the prosecution will be faced, if the military Tribunals, before which these persons are to be arraigned, require the production of evidence of a character which alone would be admissible before an English Court of Justice. Up to the present no statements have been taken from witnesses who can depose to the truth of the charges made against the prisoners. It is indeed uncertain whether any witnesses can be found."

Power, on the other hand, performs yeoman's service in collating for the non-expert the evidence of human rights atrocities (whether or not genocides) in Cambodia, Iraq, Bosnia, and Rwanda. They were known by the United States and occasioned pianissimo rather than fortissimo American government protests or sanctions. But her conclusions seem much less acute or helpful.

She maintains the United States underestimates its ability to stop horror stories abroad at reasonable cost. Bosnia, Kosovo, and northern and southern safe haven zones in Iraq are cited as exemplary. But the United States also intervened militarily in Somalia and Haiti without result while incurring serious casualties and costs. Should we be intervening militarily today in Liberia, Sierra Leone, the Democratic Republic of the Congo, Burundi, Kashmir, or Nepal to deter gruesome and widespread human rights violations? How many casualties could we expect? Would our opponents surrender or fight implacably like the North Vietnamese? In other words, contrary to Power's insinuation, America in the modern age may be reasonably calculating the costs and humanitarian benefits for both its citizens and mankind generally in selectively risking the lives of its soldiers abroad.

The author preaches that the "first and most compelling reason [for the United States to stop genocide]" is that when "innocent life is being taken on such a scale and the United States has the power to stop the killing at reasonable risk, it has a duty to act." That may be magnificent sermonizing, but it assuredly is not edifying. When does the United States know it holds the power of prevention? Could we have stopped Stalin's massacres of the Kulaks, Ukrainian starvation, and mass purges that killed tens of millions? What about stopping Mao Tse-tung's lethal Great Leap Forward and Cultural Revolution, which brought deaths to a ghastly 80 million? Had the United States fought with the courage and devotion in these countries as it had in World War II and the Civil War, the unspeakable atrocities in the Soviet Union and communist China might have been interrupted and punished. But at what risk? Suffering the fate of Napoleon and Hitler's Operation Barbarossa? Would such a risk be reasonable? Power is tabula rasa on these questions, although they are central to her critique of U.S. foreign policy.

Power additionally maintains that enlightened self-interest dictates U.S. interventions against genocides. She inaccurately maintains that perpetrators of genocide inevitably next seek conquest of foreign lands. But Mao did not launch aggression after the Great Leap Forward or the Cultural Revolution. Pol Pot did not seek conquest of Thai-

land or Laos after his mass killings of one million to two million. And Hitler's aggression against Poland began before he had decided on the Final Solution. In other words, sensible foreign policy gambits must be fact-driven and case-specific, not mesmerized by mellifluous sound bites.

Power finally fails to explain why genocide should be treated differently from other human rights horrors in the American national security equation. North Korea, for example, is known to have starved to death approximately two million citizens in recent years, a toll far exceeding genocide carnage that Power believes dictates intervention. Should the United States thus invade, overthrow the government, and architect a new dispensation as in post–World War II Japan? Would the potential payoff be worth the gamble? If we invaded, would North Korea launch nuclear warheads against South Korea and Japan with its advanced missiles? Does it enjoy such an arsenal? Should the United States decide differently if the North Korean government killed its own because of religious or ethnic hatreds as opposed to sheer barbarism?

Power implies that answers to these types of imponderables, which are staples of foreign policy, are readily discernable by the people of the United States and its government. Do you?

QUESTIONS TO CONSIDER

1. Why does Fein caution against using the word "genocide" for any and all atrocities?
2. What does Fein say is Power's mistake regarding genocidal regimes and expansion?
3. In Fein's estimation, why is North Korea such a problem?

Universal Social Theory and the Denial of Genocide: Norman Itzkowitz Revisited

Hank Theriault,

Worcester State University

As we enter the twenty-first century, denial is becoming the inevitable future of genocide. This is true for numerous particular genocides, including the Holocaust. It is also true of genocide as a general phenomenon, as instance after instance of genocide is swept under the rug by biased politicians, journalists, academics, and others. The intensity, organization, and sophistication of some denials—for example, the Turkish denial of the Armenian genocide and the Japanese denial of various genocidal atrocities in Asia during the 1931–1945 period—is steadily, even exponentially, increasing—as are the institutional support and financial resources backing them.

Denials operate through a broad range of strategies, tactics, and methods. What follows is an analysis and critique of a novel strategy, adopted by Princeton University Near Eastern Studies Professor Norman Itzkowitz to deny the Armenian genocide and its concrete links to and serious implications for denials or dismissals of other genocides, including the Holocaust.

From 1915 to 1923 the Ottoman Turkish government run by the Young Turk Committee of Union and Progress (CUP) (1915–1918) and subsequently by the forces under the direction of Kemal Ataturk (1919–23) perpetrated a genocide against the Armenian population of Asia Minor. Of between two and two and a half million Armenians in Ottoman Turkish territory before 1915, the Ottoman and later Kemalist forces, officially sanctioned "irregular"

forces, and "bystanders" killed at least one million and probably as many as one and a half million. The CUP leadership, especially Talaat Bey, directed every aspect of the main segment of the genocide (1915–1916), through a hierarchical network of Young Turk party members extending from the central government and military into the local governments and general Turkish populations in Armenian-inhabited areas of the Ottoman Empire. After Armenian men in the Ottoman Turkish army and national and local political, religious, and intellectual leaders were killed en masse, the large number of killers practiced almost unimaginable cruelties and barbarities on the remaining women, elderly, and children as part of a systematic extermination plan. They forced victims to walk naked with little or no food and water for weeks through the intense heat of the Syrian desert until their burnt bodies finally collapsed from exhaustion, starvation, disease, or thirst; they raped (often repeatedly) most women and girls; they burned masses of victims alive in caves, churches, and village centers; nailed victims to wooden planks; preyed upon caravans in every imaginable way; engaged in favorite games, such as throwing little children in the water and stoning them to death as they tried to swim ashore, smashing the heads of babies against walls, throwing babies up in the air and catching them on bayonets, and cutting open pregnant women's abdomens to see if perpetrators had guessed the sex of the fetus correctly; and on and on. Some Turkish torturers

Hank Theriault, "Universal Social Theory and the Denial of Genocide: Norman Itzkowitz Revisited," *Journal of Genocide Research* 3(2) (2001): 242–256. Reprinted with permission of Taylor & Francis, Ltd. Website: http://www.tandf.co.uk/journals

admitted to nightly discussions to develop new methods of increasing the pain and torment of their victims, while others did historical research on such things as the Spanish Inquisition to learn of different torture techniques (Morgenthau, 2000, pp. 204–205). As Hilmar Kaiser has noted, during the course of the genocide, virtually every harm that could possibly be inflicted on the human body was.

The horrors of the genocide have been redoubled by a comprehensive denial of the veracity of the genocide by successive Turkish governments. In the past three decades, the denial has become increasingly systematic, at first comprised of the efforts of Turkish government officials, diplomats, and foreign service staffs; later supplemented by Turkish "scholars" producing denial propaganda and falsifications; and, finally, in the United States and elsewhere, including paid lobbyists, defense contractors and oil companies, and accredited non-Turkish academics. As the exposé by Roger Smith, Eric Markusen and Robert Jay Lifton (1995) shows, this denial is a centrally directed governmental endeavor.

Denials have taken two main forms: simple omission from Turkish history books and attacks on claims of and evidence of the genocide. The latter have ranged from complete rejections that anything happened to Armenians in the Empire and claims that both Armenians and Turks killed each other due to an unfortunate ethnic-based civil war, to claims that Armenians were in general revolt and the government had to defend itself against them, resulting in some deaths—and even to the patently absurd and logistically impossible assertion that, far short of being victims themselves, Armenians actually perpetrated a genocide on 2.5 million "Muslims." Denial texts have ignored extensive evidence; manipulated, altered, and falsified source documents and demographic data; and employed logically flawed argumentation and shoddy social science. Deniers have routinely manipulated the sense of fairness inherent in the principles of "freedom of speech" and "academic freedom," in order to legitimize dissemination of denials.

Though not as well known as deniers such as Bernard Lewis, Heath Lowry, Stanford Shaw, or Justin McCarthy, Norman Itzkowitz has a long history of denying the Armenian genocide, dating at least from a review of Ulrich Trumpener's *Germany and the Ottoman Empire* that appeared in the Autumn, 1968 issue of the *Middle East Journal*. In that review, Itzkowitz presents a clear line, against Trumpener's discussion of the genocide, that Armenians caused whatever befell them, which was not genocide anyway, but mob violence in reaction to Armenian insurgency. This is a very standard Turkish denial view, and already 30 years ago was derivative of Turkish governmental policy.

Even given this history, however, the comments Itzkowitz made about Armenians during a November, 1997 Princeton University conference on the Nanjing Massacre of 1937 were shocking. In a November 22 session entitled (ironically enough) "Healing past wounds: from conflict to cooperation," Itzkowitz began his presentation with the following statements:

> When I was the Master at Wilson College here [at Princeton] I had a student, an Armenian, who followed me almost every day and had at least one meal a day with me and asked me over many, many times how could I teach the history that I teach. I teach the history of the Turks. How could I give the students the things to read. Didn't I know what the Turks had done to his people?
>
> I'm very slow to anger. After two years I asked him to come to my office and he came to my office and I asked him, "where do you get this from? What have you read?"
>
> And he stopped and he said, "I haven't read anything."
>
> I said, "Where did you get it from?"
>
> He said, "I get it from my grandmother."
>
> I said, "Well that's typical. Your mother and father are out working to make enough money to send you to Princeton and *granny's* got nothing to do but sit at home and fill you full of this stuff." [my emphasis]
>
> [laughter from the audience]
>
> And I gave him a long list of books. I said "read them and come back." Well he never came back.

And the reason is that all of this ethnic conflict business, I think we have to understand, at the bottom is irrational. It has nothing to do with rationality. They don't want to know anything and they will not take the time to inform themselves about what's going on.

Itzkowitz has indicated that the student was at Princeton roughly 20 years ago, and so it is highly probable that the grandmother is a survivor. Itzkowitz' comments thus denigrate her as a survivor of the Armenian genocide—belittling the tremendous suffering she presumably endured—and her grandson for being sympathetic to her and indignant about Itzkowitz' long-term denial of the genocide that caused her so much suffering. His reference to her as "granny" is especially condescending. As this anecdote is meant as a general criticism of all Armenians who discuss the genocide, by his direct and clear implication his words also denigrate all survivors who offer testimony to family members and others about their suffering, as well as descendants who express sympathy for them and press the issue publicly. For Itzkowitz, the former are deluded and the latter irrational.

What is particularly noticeable about these remarks as a denial of the genocide is the anti-Armenian prejudice made explicit in them. Israel Charny has analyzed the "meta-messages" of genocide denial to include a mockery of members of the victim group and a renewed opportunity to discharge the same hatred at them as motivated the original genocide (Charny, 1991, 1992) but usually these meta-messages are buried within apparently dispassionate and unbiased scholarly language. In this instance, however, Itzkowitz does not hide his contempt for Armenians, including genocide survivors, but rather mocks them openly. His remarks thus offer a rare direct look at the psychology of genocide denial.

Scholars, anti-genocide activists, and concerned political leaders and other individuals have called Itzkowitz to account for these re-

marks. Criticism of Itzkowitz has rightly focused on the insulting nature of his remarks, the anti-Armenian racism manifested by them, and his unethical public denial of the Armenian genocide. For instance, in a September 16, 1998 letter copied to Princeton President Harold T. Shapiro, New Jersey Governor and *ex officio* member of the Princeton Board of Trustees, Christine Todd Whitman indicated that she was "deeply concerned about the insensitivity to horrific human suffering [Itzkowitz'] remarks seemed to convey."

Itzkowitz, however, has repeatedly responded that critics have misunderstood his remarks. He meant no insult, and did not try to falsify anything. Rather, he used the story of the Armenians to illustrate his general theory of the psychology of ethnic conflict.

This defense is revealing and significant. In typical cases of active denial of the Armenian genocide, deniers attack its veracity directly. They offer false or manipulated evidence or faulty argumentation to create the impression that it is not a historical fact. Itzkowitz, on the contrary, backs his denial by appeal to an apparently credible general account of ethnic conflict. He represents his rejection of the veracity of the Armenian genocide as a function of this theory of ethnic conflict. Within that theory, an intent to deny the Armenian genocide is not explicit or visible; on the contrary, Itzkowitz represents the theory as an attempt to mitigate ethnic conflict and thus as opposed to genocide. The rejection of the veracity of the genocide appears consistent with and supported by an independently produced and verified general theory of ethnic conflict. In this way, Itzkowitz legitimizes these remarks *as something other than a denial of genocide*. This allows him the full "deniability of denial" of the genocide that he has exercised in the above-referenced comments.

Though direct criticism of Itzkowitz' anti-Armenian racism and denial of the veracity of the genocide *can* stimulate critical reflection about and rejection of the denial, the innocuous and progressive appearance of his theory tends to pre-empt them—and even to render apparently innocent his November, 1997 comments. Just as importantly, the theory's generality together with these features allows the theory to gain credibility in circles where "Armenian issues" and the relevant history are not well known or taken to be important. In this context, even recognition of Itzkowitz' anti-Armenian prejudice might not occasion a rejection of the theory—with this failure leaving the theory intact as apparently strong support for denial of the Armenian genocide in contexts where the issue is central. Thus, criticisms focused on the racism and falsification are not sufficient to defeat this subtle form of denial. In order to increase the likelihood of critical reflection by third parties on the extremely harmful implications of his general theory—even to make it a moral imperative for them—it is necessary to expose (1) the relationship between Itzkowitz' general theory and his intent to deny a genocide and (2) the flaws in the theory that allow it to obscure the historical facts of a genocide and that support its use in oppression of an ethnic group despite its presentation to the contrary. The general theory itself must be engaged to counter adequately Itzkowitz' denial of the Armenian genocide.

The following will analyze Itzkowitz' theory of ethnic conflict and its relationship to denial of the Armenian genocide. In describing the theory, the main source is Itzkowitz (in Itzkowitz and Volkan, 1994). In the introduction to this work, the authors lay out the theory in detail, before applying it to the specific case of the "conflict" between Turkey and Greece. The intergenerational transmission issue, an important part of this theory, Itzkowitz also elaborated in his Nanjing conference remarks. Itzkowitz confirmed my understanding of the basic tenets of his theory in our October 23, 1998, telephone conversation.

For Itzkowitz, ethnic identity is a "second layer of clothing," which is shared by all individual members and serves a protective function, like a mother. A healthy ethnic identity provides important psychological security for members of the group (Itzkowitz and Volkan, 1994, pp. 11–12). Ethnic violence and conflict are driven by the insecurity of the ethnic identity on one or both sides.

This insecurity generally derives from the inability to "mourn" past "losses." In the shifting whirlwind of historical change, ethnic groups rise and fall, gain and lose empires, wealth, security, etc. When they fall, this threatens their ethnic self-image. If they cannot properly mourn their loss (of empire, status, etc., but also of autonomy, killed community members, etc.), they will become fixated on the historical loss, even long after the series of events comprising it have concluded. Fundamental to a healthy reaction is their *acceptance of the new state of affairs* that they perceive as traumatic. Change itself is loss, and human groups have difficulty adjusting to change. Psychological health depends on group development through a positive response to loss—that is, overcoming it in a creative, progressive manner, and thereby improving as a result of it. If a group refuses to make such a positive, progressive response, it will stagnate at the point of a loss (Itzkowitz and Volkan, 1994, pp. 7–8).

The losing group has a choice in the matter—it can fixate or not. Thus, fixation is *chosen*. Though a group cannot always choose what happens to it, it can choose whether or not to continue a focus on a real or perceived trauma after the traumatic events conclude (Itzkowitz and Volkan, 1994, p. 7).

Ethnic hatred and conflict derive from "chosen trauma" (Itzkowitz and Volkan, 1994, p. 7). As the group that has lost focuses on the trauma, it attaches culpability to the real or perceived cause of the loss. Since this is an unhealthy reaction, whether or not the loss (1) is actual and (2) actually caused by another ethnic group becomes irrelevant. Indeed, the chosen trauma as a mental representation becomes detached from reality and real history, and takes on a life of its own. (Itzkowitz and Volkan, 1994, p. 6ff.) It becomes the psychical force behind an irrational fear or hatred of the "other"—the other ethnic group recognized or perceived to have caused the trauma. The first group becomes a "perpetual mourner," which cannot get over its loss, but instead focuses its anger and frustration at the loss on the "other."

This fuels stereotyping and denigration of the "other" and involves "projection" onto the "other." The projection far outstrips any historical cause—the "other" becomes the object of all manner of the first group's frustration and anger. Criticism of the "other" is really self-hatred projected onto an innocent "other": the projecting—that is, angry or critical—group projects negative aspects of itself onto the "other," in order to consolidate a viable self-respecting ethnic self-image in the face of traumatic loss and change. Its psychical response to trauma or loss that threatens its cohesive, positive self-image is to create a myth about itself as purely good and so undeserving of such threats or losses. It also creates a corresponding negative image of the perceived agent of its loss (see especially Itzkowitz and Volkan, 1994, pp. 2–3).

The perpetually mourning group often develops a "victim mentality," in which it sees itself as a perpetual victim—justified in any aggression against its supposed victimizer—even when its fortunes improve (Itzkowitz and Volkan, 1994, p. 10). Itzkowitz specifically refers to Armenians as a clear example of a group with a victim mentality (Itzkowitz and Volkan, 1994, p. 198, note 26).

The fixation on a chosen trauma and the resultant hatred or fear and projection "are passed on from generation to generation," through such things as ceremonies, but also presumably through the mechanisms of political propaganda, formal education, and the news media (Itzkowitz and Volkan, 1994, pp. 2, 9–10).

Transmission also occurs within families. Itzkowitz' Nanjing conference remarks about Armenians focused on the familial intergenerational transmission of what he represents as an "ethnic conflict." Children are indoctrinated into perpetual mourning and ethnic hatred through the stories told by parents and grandparents. Intergenerational transmission completes separation from reality—over generations, mourning and hatred become rooted in the very family life of an ethnic group. As part of this hatred, it separates itself from the contemporary reality of the "other," maintaining a false and negative image based on an idealization of the "other." Thus Itzkowitz' frustration— if "grannies" did not fill their grandchildren's heads full of "this stuff," then the children could perceive the "others" without the negative projection and resentment. There could be hope for a lessening or end to the relevant "ethnic conflict."

At an initial glance, this appears to be a plausible account of some "ethnic conflicts" and hatreds. One can see in it some of the mechanisms that contribute/have contributed to ethnic violence. Adding to its plausibility is the theory's resonance with concepts of negative stereotyping of victim groups and credible psychoanalytic and post-structural accounts of self- and group cohesiveness through hatred or fear of a constructed "other."

Itzkowitz' theory, however, grounds a two-tiered denial of the Armenian genocide. First, as suggested above, Itzkowitz relies on his theory to make appealing his misrepresentation of Armenian concerns about a Turkish genocide of Armenians as "irrational" and historically inaccurate. His general model displaces a particular engagement with the specific issue of the genocide. Rather, it becomes a basic conceptual frame through which an accepting reader or listener approaches all issues that can be construed as ethnic tensions, that is, all situations in which two national groups have tensions between them, including those in actuality caused by a genocide. Once an individual has assimilated the framework, he/she will attribute Armenian indignation at a claimed genocide *and its claimed denial* (by Itzkowitz and others) to the resentment Armenians have built up because they were never able to accept their status as subjects of the Turks and could not deal with the consequences of their "disloyalty." Itzkowitz thereby relativizes the assertions of the truth about the genocide and criticisms of Turkish denial positions into one side of an "ethnic conflict."

An individual who accepts the theory is led to accept the specific account of the historical period in question that most accords with Itzkowitz' theory, which is precisely what Itzkowitz offers. In this way, Itzkowitz' very standard denial position—which reiterates the rationalization for the genocide used even by its perpetrators as they were committing it—comes to appear to be the superior explanation:

> With the Russians advancing against the Ottoman Army [in World War I], Armenians in eastern Anatolia saw supporting the Russians as a means toward the realization of their national ambitions. For a long time, the Armenian *millet* had been considered the most loyal *millet*. The Ottoman response to what they perceived as a strategic military threat was to relocate Armenians from eastern Anatolia to Syria and Lebanon. Tragically, the central government lost control of the situation on the ground, where in war time it took very little to ignite the passions of communal strife. Hundreds of thousands of Armenians lost their lives. Those events have embittered relationships between those two peoples ever since. (Itzkowitz and Volkan, 1994, p. 67)

He adds in the footnote at the end of this section that, of course, about twice as many "Muslims" died, citing another well-known denier: "according to McCarthy, Justin (1983), 584,268 Armenians and 1,040,376 Muslims died in the six provinces where these events took place." Thus, Armenians claiming a genocide have allowed their resentment at civil strife that their forebears were at least half responsible for and that had harsh consequences for them to transform the events in their memories into a terrible crime that justifies their current anger toward Turks.

The potential effectiveness of this denial technique is greater than that of typical techniques. Countering typical denials (falsifications and omissions) usually at worst produces a stalemate, in which outside parties take both sides equally seriously and cannot or do not reach a conclusion about the veracity of the genocide. As described above, Itzkowitz' denial strategy, however, actually tips the balance in favor of a Turkish denial position. Within Itzkowitz' theoretical framework, when denial is countered by a "civil strife" argument claiming mutual ethnic conflict between Armenian and Turks, the latter is the *more* tenable position; the claim of genocide is reduced to the less likely position, rather than being even one of two equally likely positions. To the extent that outside parties are aware of the specific claims of Armenians and deniers, the choice of which set of facts to believe becomes a function of Itzkowitz' theoretical framework, and not actual evidence or "material logic" (for instance, Armenians in the provinces did not as a rule have guns and most able-bodied Armenian men of military age were conscripted into the Ottoman army and soon murdered, so it is extremely unlikely if not impossible that the remaining Armenians killed roughly one million Muslims, especially in a short period of time). Affected individuals actually come to *perceive* history and the world in such a way as to organize it in line with Itzkowitz' framework and, hence, his denial of the Armenian genocide.

Even if a reader or listener has knowledge of the genocide that belies its outright denial, Itzkowitz' model *still* implies the irrationality of contemporary Armenian concerns about it. For Itzkowitz, whatever happened to Armenians—whether the genocide is real or imagined—should long ago have been accepted and overcome. Armenians have chosen this trauma, and must let it go if they are going to stop fomenting ethnic hatred between themselves and Turks. They must stop passing it on to subsequent generations.

Though this second tier or back-up denial is not explicitly directed at Armenians in *Turks and Greeks*, the text does make it explicit in reference to another instance of genocide:

> An incident that occurred in 1864 demonstrates how a chosen trauma may evolve. Approximately eight thousand Navajo Indians in New Mexico were left homeless when US soldiers, under the direction of Kit Carson, burned and destroyed their property. The Indians were forced on a three-hundred-mile march to Fort Sumner, New Mexico, where they were cruelly imprisoned for four years; during the march and after, two thousand five hundred of them died. The march became known as the "Long Walk." David A. Maurer, a Charlottesville [Virginia] newspaper reporter, interviewed two local pastors, Neal Knight and Harold L. Bare, Sr., who were involved in a project with Navajo Indians. The pastors relayed to Maurer their perception that for many Navajo, time had stopped in 1864 when Kit Carson and his men destroyed their way of life. Pastor Bare remarked: "The Indians were telling me about the 'Long Walk,' and at first I thought they were talking about something that had happened the day before. I was really taken aback when I realized they were talking about something that had happened more than 125 years ago … to the Indians, the 'Long Walk' is as real as the morning sunlight." (Itzkowitz and Volkan, 1994, p. 8)

For Itzkowitz, the concern of the Navajo is irrational. What is especially significant here is that *Itzkowitz acknowledges that these atrocities against the Navajo did take place and destroyed their way of life; yet, after a proper (short) period for "mourning," it is* still *irrational to focus on them*. After all, for Itzkowitz, the reason that Navajo are concerned is because the event represents a political and military "humiliation." Navajos are upset because they lost status and control of territory in a "defeat," and their self-esteem suffered.

Itzkowitz' general theory supports such indifference to the suffering of genocide victims—and even blames them for their own continued suffering—because it ignores the *context* of the attitudes groups have toward other groups. For him, the attitudes—in the Armenian and Navajo cases, concern, outrage, deep sadness, etc.—are facts in themselves, which he analyzes and presents without reference to the material factors that have produced them and that make their reasonableness clear. As mentioned above, Itzkowitz is quite explicit that, according to his theory, evaluation of attitudes does not depend on the facts of a situation: "We [Volkan and Itzkowitz] do not mean to belittle the influence of … real world issues … but it is becoming increasingly evident that psychological issues may dominate in episodes of ethnic conflict" (Itzkowitz and Volkan, 1994, p. 6). Even more explicitly, "once a trauma becomes a chosen trauma, the historical truth about it does not really matter" (Itzkowitz and Volkan, 1994, p. 7).

This relativizes situations of one-sided violence along ethnic lines. By taking only the attitudes—and not the material facts—into consideration, Itzkowitz transforms cases of oppression along ethnic lines into cases of "ethnic conflict," in which any anger or criticism by one group directed toward the other cannot be recognized as a legitimate reaction to oppression or having been wronged, but rather must be viewed *itself* as a full or partial causal factor for the tensions between the groups. Armenian outrage at the genocide is represented not as a reasonable and understandable reaction to a horrific act of violence, but rather itself as a primary cause of contemporary tensions between Turks and Armenians.

But when one recognizes the reality and importance of the genocide, these reactions are perfectly understandable and reasonable: they require no claims of an exceptional psychological mechanism. A similar objection to Itzkowitz holds in the case of the "Long Walk."

It is enough to recognize the intense suffering inflicted with impunity by agents of the United States government to recognize the reasonableness of present-day Navajo concerns. They become all the more reasonable and even expected when one recognizes that U.S. oppression of Native Americans has continued to the present day. Indeed, the very fact that the United States, without recognition or apology, continues to occupy the lands taken from the Navajo through a genocidal deportation—enjoying the fruit of its violence—makes the issue extremely relevant, whether members of the dominant group such as Itzkowitz choose to ignore the history or not. Itzkowitz' solution is that the Navajo should just forget the "losses" of the past, but especially when the past has materially and directly produced the suffering of the present (poverty, racism, and so forth), it is reasonable to be indignant about it. The "Long Walk" was not a discrete event, but rather a defining moment in an ongoing tradition of oppression of Navajo. Forgetting about or ignoring it would seem only to reinforce and support intensification of this oppression. If it is not "irrational" to deny this important history as Itzkowitz does, then it is certainly unjust and immoral.

Characterizing the Navajo response to the "Long Walk" as resentment at a humiliation also ignores another aspect of that response. Presumably, alongside indignation at injustice is empathy and compassion for the victims. Even non-Navajos in the contemporary era are often moved by the accounts of this atrocity—just as many of my non-Armenian or non-Tutsi contemporary American students have been moved to tears upon reading survivor accounts of or viewing a documentary on the Armenian or Rwandan genocide. We can expect members of a victim group to feel empathy even more strongly—this would seem very normal. But Itzkowitz claims it to be irrational. Itzkowitz' theory forces the same reduction in the case of the Armenian genocide. This is well illustrated

in the Nanjing conference anecdote: it seems a natural response for a grandchild to feel great compassion for a grandparent who survived the genocide, and to take offense at any individual denying the well-proven purposeful origins of her intense suffering. But Itzkowitz' theory asserts the opposite.

At stake is not just the accuracy of representations of apparent "ethnic tensions" or the reasonableness of victim-group responses to oppression, but the ethical dimensions of "ethnic conflict" as well. Unconcerned with the facts of a situation, Itzkowitz utterly ignores the question "Was a past event an injustice, that is, the unfair use of power by one group against another?" Indeed, Itzkowitz' manipulative de-emphasis of the *causes* of attitudes marking tensions between groups allows him to equate natural events or catastrophes with intentional infliction of mass harm.

What results is an *amoral* or *anti-moral* theory. By focusing attention on the victims, Itzkowitz removes perpetrators of mass violence from scrutiny. They escape responsibility entirely. Whereas a morally tenable analysis would demand action *from the perpetrators* to overcome the tensions they have caused, Itzkowitz' theory does not. Itzkowitz does not recognize that a genocide perpetrator group—particularly an unrepentant one that has devoted itself to an ongoing effort to cover up a genocide and attack the victim group politically—is responsible for the resulting tension between the groups. Instead, through a perverse logic, the *victim group becomes culpable even for the "pain" that unrepentant members of the perpetrator group feel at the charges of genocide that on Itzkowitz' mistaken account drive the "tensions" between the groups.*

Underlying Itzkowitz' theory and its lack of concern about the effects of oppression and violence on victim groups is what I will term a "macho ethics," which is most fully evident in his celebratory account of the conquests, military victories, massacres, and political intrigues that produced and maintained the Ottoman

Empire, in Itzkowitz (1972, especially pp. 1–38)—much of which is included or summarized in Itzkowitz and Volkan (1994). For Itzkowitz, history is a struggle among groups, and at times this or that group will come up short (see, for instance, Itzkowitz and Volkan, 1994, p. 140). There is no point to resenting this—a group must acclimate itself to the new realities of reduced status, power, land—and even partial annihilation. A dominator's exercise of power through violence and conquest is, in fact, a healthy discharge of energy (see, for example, Itzkowitz, 1972, p. 11). In this world, the weak are allowed only two options: irrationally resent their position or stoically accept their inferiority and the harms that come with it.

This "ethics" recalls two problematic strains of social theory. First, it echoes and perhaps derives from Friedrich Nietzsche's condemnation of "resentment" as a force in group relations (Nietzsche, 1989). Nietzsche argues that "resentment" at a subservient status is characteristic of weak or slavish groups. Psychological health depends on "having done with," that is, forgetting, one's suffering at the hands of others—which is precisely what the weak and ignoble groups (especially the Jews) cannot do. Instead, the latter infect the strong and noble with their resentment, which registers as guilt. This weakens the strong and makes their culture more and more banal and stagnant. Nietzsche's perspective was entirely aristocratic, and he had nothing but contempt for so-called "slavish" ethnic groups (especially the Jews) and even the general masses of Germans, French, etc. For him, violence against and domination of the weak by the strong was inherently moral, because "good" is (or should be) defined only and precisely by the desires and acts of the powerful. To be powerful is automatically to be or do "good."

Second, the idea that history is an evolution in which powerful groups rightfully rise to the top of a hierarchy of nations recalls disturbing forms of social Darwinism and racist nationalism, including strains in Germany that grounded Hitler's ideology of a struggle among national races that pitted naturally superior Aryans against the inferior, subhuman Jews, Roma (Gypsies), Slavs, and others.

This aspect of Itzkowitz' theory, in fact, is in tension with and ultimately undermines his pretensions to mitigating and providing a framework for solving "ethnic conflicts." By choosing to ignore the material causes and moral dimensions of ethnic tensions in cases of one-sided violence, Itzkowitz legitimizes the violence by dominators and genocide perpetrators. But a genuine overcoming of "ethnic conflict" in such situations would seem to have to begin with a proper assessment of responsibility for the tensions, and include acceptance of an appropriate punishment and atonement as a restorative measure and show of good faith. This is true not only for an abstractly just political solution, but for a solution that will lessen psychological tensions. As Dan Bar-On (1999, p. 148), a psychologist concerned with the long-term effects of the Holocaust on survivors and on the relationship between the children of victims and perpetrators, puts it, reconciliation between a perpetrator and victim group appears greatly hindered when no or insufficient "legal measures have been undertaken against the perpetrators of inhuman atrocities committed within the conflict."

There is also an additional problem with Itzkowitz' reduction of one-sided mass violence to "ethnic conflict." Itzkowitz' theory implies that claims of genocide are made only by victim groups and concern only that group and its "other": claims of genocide are manifestations of and in fact causes of "ethnic tensions." As Hilmar Kaiser has emphasized, however, that in its aftermath a genocide should not be reduced to an ethnic relations problem, but must be conceived of as a universal human rights issue. It appears never to be true that *only* members of a victim group are concerned about a genocide perpetrated against them; in their concerns about and condemnation of the genocide, they are inevitably joined by "outside" scholars, political leaders, political and human rights activists, and simply decent "average" people. This has become particularly true in the past three decades with the rise of (1) a global human rights movement and (2) a committed study of genocide as a general phenomenon, by the growing ranks of comparative genocide scholars and by specialists on this or that particular genocide who recognize and research analogical and historical connections to other genocides.

Itzkowitz is not constrained by his central focus on Turkish history and his related long-term denial of the Armenian genocide. If the universal, abstract nature of Itzkowitz' general theory markedly increases the apparent credibility of Itzkowitz' Armenian genocide denial, the universality also makes the theory readily applicable to other instances of genocide and one-sided mass violence. What is especially interesting is that Itzkowitz does not leave such applications to be worked out by readers of *Turks and Greeks*, but in fact makes a number of them explicit. His analysis of the Navajo "Long Walk" is, of course, not just important in its implications for Itzkowitz' denial of the Armenian genocide, but represents a denial—or, more accurately, "dismissal"—of an episode in another genocide.

Itzkowitz actualizes his theory's potential for denial or dismissal of other genocides as well. In a footnote to a line quoted above ("...once a trauma becomes a chosen trauma, the historical truth about it does not really matter ..."), for which the Navajo story is an illustration, Itzkowitz includes the Holocaust and other Native American genocides in this category of chosen trauma that should be gotten over: "Jews remember the Holocaust, the Navajo remember 'The Long Walk' of 1864, Mexicans and Guatemalans remember the conquest of their territory by the Spanish nearly 500 years ago, and Serbian Slavs remember the 'betray-

al' of Bosnian Slavs who converted to Islam under Ottoman rule." Assuming that he accepts the veracity of the events listed here, Itzkowitz dismisses remembrance of and concern about the genocides as psychological failings and irrational.

Certain subtle features of this statement are particularly manipulative. Itzkowitz suggests that present-day Guatemalans—presumably he means the indigenous Mayans who were conquered by the Spanish—are concerned about a 500-year-past event. This ignores the fact that the Guatemalan government—a legacy of the Spanish conquest—has committed a genocide against the Mayans over the past three decades that has resulted in 100,000–140,000 dead (Totten, 1999, pp. 281–284). Itzkowitz' statement obscures completely this contemporary reality and suggests that present-day Mayan concerns about genocide and injustice are hold-overs from centuries-past events, rather than direct references to a present attempt at eradication. In this way, denial of the contemporary genocide of Mayans is served by dismissal of a past genocide.

The inclusion of Serbian remembrance is manipulative as well. On the one hand, this extends Itzkowitz' trivialization of the mass violence perpetrated by the Ottoman Turks, by covering over their brutal, long-term subjugation of the Serbs, which included mass killings, rapes, forced conversions, and material and cultural destruction. On the other hand, when viewed in the context of the early 1990s (*Turks and Greeks* was published in 1994), it also suggests a deeply inaccurate and inappropriate analogy between (1) legitimate and reasonable concern about the Holocaust and Native American genocides and (2) the historically focused propaganda that contemporary Serbian leaders had employed in the early 1990s to motivate Serbian mass violence against Bosnian Muslims.

Beyond these numerous applications to different genocides is the fact that genocide in general is quite difficult to discern through Itzkowitz' conceptual lens. The framework filters out the one-sided nature of many "ethnic tensions" that might otherwise jar third parties into rejecting Itzkowitz' cavalier attitude toward mass human suffering. In the murky history that results, there are no clear victims or perpetrators, just ongoing conflicts.

In this way, Itzkowitz is in effect responding to the development of comparative genocide studies by establishing himself as the first universal denier of genocide. If he starts with the Armenian genocide, it is clear that no genocide is safe from the implications of his theory, and he begins the process of extending its application himself. His universal theory does not justify denial or dismissal only of one particular genocide, but of *all* genocides. He becomes a concrete example supporting the frequently made assertion that a denier of one genocide in fact holds the victims of all genocides in contempt and is a threat to victims of all genocides.

Ironically enough, despite Itzkowitz' claim to have employed the anecdote about Armenians only as an illustration of a thesis meant to help understand the Nanjing Massacre, an obvious step in the expanding use of Itzkowitz' theory is *application to the Nanjing Massacre itself.* Prominent Japanese governmental, media, and academic personages and institutions, in addition to or overlapping with right- and ultra-right-wing political groups, have long engaged in a denial of the Japanese military's centrally authorized genocide of Nanjing's inhabitants in 1937. Even Tokyo's popular current mayor, Shintaro Ichihara, is an active denier. On Itzkowitz' model, Chinese survivor testimony regarding, documentation of, and continuing concern about the genocide must be viewed as the product and partial cause of a mutual conflict between Chinese and Japanese that can only be resolved when the former end their irrational fixation on Nanjing. Such

a false, relativized account is especially appealing in this case, given the political, economic, and military ascendance of China in recent years, as well as its own extensive human rights violations that suggest that it must be an active party to any apparent "conflict" with a neighboring group.

Itzkowitz' model also flips a compelling critique of genocide denial back on itself. Israel Charny has led efforts to excavate and analyze the psychological mechanisms and motivations behind denial of a known genocide (Charny, 1991, 1992; Charny and Fromer, 1998). The results have become a powerful tool for understanding genocide denials and exposing the oppressive and genocidal drives behind them. Itzkowitz' theory applies psychoanalytic theory to the victims, asserting a manipulative and flawed pseudo-psychological analysis that pretends to expose irrational and deluded mechanisms and hateful motivations behind victim groups' quests for acknowledgment and justice.

Perhaps the ultimate irony of Itzkowitz' model of "ethnic conflict" is that, in cases of one-sided violence, it "otherizes" the victim group in much the same way that he claims he is criticizing. For example, Itzkowitz generalizes about all Armenians who reference the genocide—that is, most Armenians in the world: they share a single psychological structure that accounts for their delusional claims and anger, and renders them worthy of insult and dismissal. He ignores the diversity of Armenian responses to the genocide, and denies that Armenians possess the capacity to take up the issue critically and with self-reflection. He denies, in fact, Armenians' capacity for critical ethical perspectives on issues of deep concern to them. What is more, his condescending dismissal of the serious and legitimate concerns of Armenians, Navajos, Jews, and others actually instigates ethnic-based indignation, and would seem to *foment* tensions rather than alleviate them.

QUESTIONS TO CONSIDER

1. Describe the two main forms of denial of genocide.
2. What are the "meta-messages" of genocide denial according to Israel Charny?
3. What does a fixation on a chosen trauma produce?
4. Describe how deniers use the issue of responsibility to plead their case.

5. What does Itzkowitz leave out of his use of the Armenian and Navajo cases?
6. Using Itzkowitz as an example, why is it wrong to focus only on the victims of genocide?
7. Why does Theriault claim that Itzkowitz has established "himself as the first universal denier of genocide"?

MAKING CONNECTIONS

1. Should the twentieth century be studied as "The American Century," or "The Century of Genocide"?

2. How much space should the author of a history-survey text of the twentieth century devote to genocide?

✔ RECOMMENDED RESOURCES

Belgrade Circle, eds. *The Politics of Human Rights.* London and New York: Verso, 1999.

Davies, John L., and Ted Robert Gurr, eds. *Preventive Measures: Building Risk Assessment and Crisis Early Warning Systems.* Lanham, MD: Rowman & Littlefield Publishers, Inc., 1998.

Glover, Jonathan. *Humanity: A Moral History of the Twentieth Century.* New Haven and London: Yale University Press, 1999.